N. T. Mirov, Ph.D., University of California, Berkeley, holds a life appointment as Research Associate in Geography at the University of California, Berkeley. For some thirty years, he served as Plant Physiologist with the Pacific Southwest Forest and Range Experiment Station, U.S. Forest Service. From 1961 to 1964, Dr. Mirov was a Research Fellow in Forest Botany with the Maria Moors Cabot Foundation for Botanical Research. He has also received grants for research from the Rockefeller Foundation and Resources for the Future, Inc. Dr. Mirov is the recipient of a gold medal for research in forestry from the United States Department of Agriculture, and he also holds an award for Achievement in Biological Research from the Society of American Foresters. He has written over one hundred technical papers, chiefly on different aspects of pines, that have appeared in many journals in several languages and is the author of a book on Russian geography.

# The Genus
# *PINUS*

**N. T. MIROV**

University of California, Berkeley

*Prepared under the auspices of the*
*Maria Moors Cabot Foundation*

**THE RONALD PRESS COMPANY • NEW YORK**

Library of Congress Catalog Card Number: 67–14783
PRINTED IN THE UNITED STATES OF AMERICA

# Preface

Working for many years with pines, I have been asked many questions I could not answer. Often I have thought how useful it would be for both the curious layman and the busy scholar to have assembled together as much information as possible on pines.

Being a biologist, I am primarily interested in the biology of pines—their origin and development, their chemical composition, and their physiological processes. These considerations have naturally led me to the past and present distribution of pines.

Difficulties of presenting these aspects of the subject are many. The literature on pines is enormous; it is scattered through scientific, trade, and popular journals. What should be included and what omitted were not easy decisions. For instance, chemical components of pine wood are considered; but physical properties of pine lumber are not, although there is a wealth of published information in that field.

Keeping in mind the traditional remoteness of chemistry from plant taxonomy, I have perhaps oversimplified, in a conciliatory mood, the presentation of the chemical aspects of pines. On the other hand, I have attempted to make the presentation of taxonomy palatable to chemists, who are not always concerned with the ways and rules of classifying plants and are apt either to disregard accepted nomenclature entirely or to accept it in an amazingly uncritical manner.

Our knowledge of the genus *Pinus* is rather uneven. Certain groups of chemical substances (polyphenols, terpenes) have been studied extensively; others, such as fats, are still known only sporadically. Alkaloids have been discovered in some pines only recently. Some physiological processes, such as mineral nutrition, have been investigated more thoroughly than others, for example, transpiration. Such unevenness will be noticed throughout the book.

I have attempted to give answers to many questions about pines; many have remained unanswered, and new ones have arisen. I have even attempted to offer some generalizations and speculations, hoping that their presentation would not be condemned as heresy but, rather, would be accepted as a stimulus to more research along controversial lines. I have always been encouraged by Darwin's remark, in one of his letters to Wallace, that without speculation there would be no progress.

N. T. Mɪʀᴏᴠ

Berkeley, California
January, 1967

# Acknowledgments

Many people have assisted me in the preparation of this book. Chapters of the manuscript were commented on or read by: Rimo Bacigalupi, University of California at Berkeley; Irving W. Bailey, Harvard University; Elso S. Barghoorn, Harvard University; Ralph W. Chaney, University of California at Berkeley; Duncan Clement, National Science Foundation; William B. Dauben, University of California at Berkeley; John W. Duffield, North Carolina State of the University of North Carolina; Wayne L. Fry, University of California at Berkeley; Jane Gray, University of Oregon; Hugh H. Iltis, University of Wisconsin; Gene Kritchevsky, Department of Biochemistry, City of Hope Medical Center, Duarte, California; Stanley Krugman, U.S. Forest Service; William J. Libby, University of California at Berkeley; Jack Major, University of California at Davis; Paul C. Mangelsdorf, Harvard University; Elliott T. Merrick, U.S. Forest Service; Robert Ornduff, University of California at Berkeley; Thomas R. Pray, University of California at Los Angeles; Franklin Raney, University of California at Davis; Hugh M. Raup, Harvard University; John W. Rowe, U.S. Forest Service; Jonathan D. Sauer, University of Wisconsin; Howard H. Schorn, University of California at Berkeley; Arthur R. Spurr, University of California at Davis; Robert G. Stanley, U.S. Forest Service; G. Ledyard Stebbins, University of California at Davis; William S. Ting, University of California at Los Angeles; Arthur Westing, Purdue University; Louis E. Wise, The Institute of Paper Chemistry, Appleton, Wisconsin; Eugene Zavarin, University of California at Berkeley; and Martin H. Zimmermann, Harvard University.

They helped me greatly and gave me so many valuable suggestions that I am tempted to say that the book is more theirs than mine. I have to admit, however, that the idea of writing it was mine and that I am wholly responsible for selection and presentation of the material as well as for all conclusions. Thus the book's shortcomings are totally mine.

v

To Dr. Shigeru Miki, Professor of Paleontology, Osaka City University, Japan, I wish to express appreciation for his hospitality and for his views on paleogeography of East Asiatic pines. The memory of my numerous visits to the late Dr. Maximino Martínez, of the Universidad Nacional Autónoma de Mexico, Mexico City, I always will cherish.

Many others throughout the world contributed to my knowledge of pines. To all of them I extend my appreciation.

Photographs to illustrate the text came from widely scattered sources. My thanks are extended to the persons who sent them to me.

To the Department of Geography, University of California at Berkeley, I am obliged for advice and for a peaceful and friendly atmosphere, so important when one is writing a book.

To the Pacific Southwest Forest and Range Experiment Station of the U.S. Forest Service, for which I did all my lifelong research on pines, I express my gratitude; the idea of writing this book was conceived there; my thanks extend to the whole U.S. Forest Service.

To the Rockefeller Foundation I am indebted for generous support of my chemical research on pines and for a grant that enabled me to visit pine regions of several countries of eastern Asia.

To Resources for the Future, Inc., I am thankful for equally generous support of my physiological research on pines.

The writing of this book was partially supported by Grant No. NSF–G19403 from the National Science Foundation.

I deeply appreciate the generous assistance the Maria Moors Cabot Foundation for Botanical Research, Harvard University, rendered me during the preparation of the book. To the former Chairman of the Foundation, Dr. Kenneth V. Thimann, and to the present Chairman, Dr. Martin H. Zimmermann, I extend my thanks for their patience and understanding.

N. T. M.

# Contents

# The Genus
## *PINUS*

# 1

# History—from Theophrastus to the End of the Nineteenth Century

The genus *Pinus* consists of over one hundred species, the exact number being a matter of individual judgment of botanists. Many systems of classification have been proposed since the time of the discovery and earliest description of pines; in the Englerian system (Pilger, 1926), widely used at the present time, the genus *Pinus* occupies a place in the plant kingdom in the division IV Embryophyta-Siphonogama, more commonly known as Spermatophyta. In this division, *Pinus* is found (in descending order) in subdivision Gymnospermae, order Coniferae, family Pinaceae. According to Lawrence (1955, p. 359), certain changes are to be expected in the above system of plant classification, but these changes will not affect the genus as a group of plants except for some minor readjustments (see Chapter 9, p. 540, on *P. krempfii*).

It has been a long way between the first acquaintance of man with pines and the establishment of a more or less permanent place for them in the system of plant classification. Pines are conspicuous trees (rarely shrubs), either forming extensive forests or contrastingly admixed with broadleaf trees; they are easily noticeable to explorers and travelers.

Pines are useful; man has known them from time immemorial. He cut them for fuel, and he extracted resin from them. He burned them to clear the land for agriculture, and he planted them where needed (Plate 6–13). Pines are beautiful; their decorative value is seen in old Chinese paintings; their branches were used in festivals of ancient peoples (Carrière, 1867). Burning pinewood yields fragrant smoke (Mirov, 1959); pine incense was

3

used in religious ceremonies by the Aztecs, the Mayas, and the Romans. Pines were mentioned in Greek mythology. Pitys, a nymph, was transformed into a pine tree by Boreas. Greek scholars knew a great deal about pines, for these trees occupied, and still occupy, a prominent place in the landscape of the classical world.

Theophrastus (370–285 B.C.), in his *Enquiry into Plants* (Theophrastus, 1916), wrote at length on the morphology of pines, their reproduction, and their usefulness to man. He described pines as evergreen plants with a woody core and linear leaves and said that they are best propagated by seeds (rather than by vegetative means; see Chapter 5, p. 367). Opinions differ, said Theophrastus, as to whether pines have true flowers, but they definitely have a "flowering tuft." In those days, pitch was made from *Pinus halepensis* No. 77 * and *P. nigra* No. 74, and charcoal was manufactured from pines in much the same way as it is manufactured in many places in the world at the present time. Occasional information is given on the time of bud opening, which, for *P. halepensis,* was "at the time of the setting of the Pleiades."

It is remarkable that Theophrastus considered all known pines together as a group and yet differentiated them into two distinct kinds and believed them to be closely related to firs. The world of the ancient Greeks was limited to the Mediterranean region (see Chapter 3, pp. 237–61) and the pines they knew were Mediterranean pines. Often they applied the names *"peuke"* (Πεύκη) and *"pitys"* (Πίτυς) to the same species. In translations of the classics by European scholars of Greek, names of pines and related conifers are often hopelessly confused. In Hort's translation of Theophrastus' text, for example, the *peuke* of Theophrastus is not a fir but a pine. Similar errors are quite common in our non-technical literature: Douglas-fir is not a fir (*Abies*), and Mountain ash is not an ash (*Fraxinus*).

When one reads Theophrastus' text carefully, one forms an impression (perhaps erroneous) that when a pine was scrubby and resinous, used chiefly for pitch production, it was referred to as *"pitys,"* while the same pine in the mountains, where it often forms magnificent forests, was apt to be called *"peuke."* In mountainous regions, *P. nigra* No. 74 was called *"peuke."* *Pinus pinea* No. 73 was a notable exception. It had been and still is planted so much for its edible nuts that it became a "domestic" pine. It was (and still is) a stately tree, and it was not a *pitys* but a *peuke.* *Pinus pinaster* No. 80 also sometimes was called *"peuke."*

The genus *Pinus* is called today in Greek *"peuke,"* which includes also the *pitys* of Theophrastus. No distinction is made today in Greece between the two.

* Numbers after species refer to Tables 1–1 and 1–2, pp. 18–22.

The original Greek designations of pines are commemorated in the names of *P. pityusa* No. 79, a spreading coastal *"pitys"* pine, and *P. peuce* No. 71, a stately mountain pine that often looks like a fir (Plate 1–1) (see Chapter 3, on species No. 71).

Theophrastus recognized the following species of pines: (1) *P. halepensis* No. 77 (*pitys* or sometimes *pitys agria*); (2) *P. brutia* No. 78 (*pitys ftheiropoios*); (3) *P. nigra* No. 74, an extremely variable pine (see Chapter 3, under this number), which was mentioned under several names such as *"peuke e acarpos," "peuke theleia," "peuke idaia,"* and *"peuke peteris"*; (4) *P. sylvestris* (*pitys agria*); (5) *P. pinea* No. 73 (*peuke emeros, peuke conoforos*). *Pinus cembra* No. 70 was possibly not known to him. The names were not descriptive as were those of later herbalists (such as *"Pinus sempervirens foliis quinis, nucleis edibilus"*), but, rather, they resembled Linnaean binomials.

The identity of the genus *Pinus* having been established by Theophrastus, it was only natural that classical geographers often mentioned pines in their writings. Strabo (reference in "Literature Citations," Chapter 2), who lived at the beginning of our era (he died in A.D. 21), mentioned pines in many parts of the Mediterranean region. He called the Balearics (see Chapter 2, p. 74) the "Pine Islands" and described a certain region on the Black Sea coast of the Caucasus as "Great Pityum." No doubt, in classical times the Mediterranean pines were planted in places where they had not been growing spontaneously earlier. This is possibly the reason for the unexpected occurrence of *P. brutia* No. 78, an eastern Mediterranean species, in southern Italy (ancient Brutium, hence the name), and the cause of controversy regarding the original natural habitat of *P. pinea* (see Chapter 3, under Nos. 78 and 73, respectively).

Pliny the Elder, a native of northern Italy, lived also in the first century of our era. He did not contribute much to the knowledge of pines; what he wrote he mostly borrowed from the Greeks. He did not differentiate between *"peuke"* and *"pitys"*; he listed three kinds of pines, identified by translators as *P. cembra, P. sylvestris,* and *P. pinea,* and he also mentioned *"pinaster,"* which, he said, is nothing but *P. sylvestris* (*"Pinaster nihil aliud est quam Pinus silvestris"*) and the mysterious *"taeda,"* which apparently was introduced to literature by Ovid in his *Metamorphoses* (I:658) as follows: *"At tibi ego ignarus thalamos taedasque parabam."* Pliny explained that the *"Sextum genus* [of pines] *est taeda propie dicta."* The wood of this tree is employed for kindling fires and giving torch light in religious ceremonies. Pliny's enigmatic remark that *"Laricis morbus est ut taeda fiat"* caused a great deal of confusion among the later students of the genus *Pinus*.

Columella, a native of Cádiz, who lived at about the same time as Pliny, contributed even less to our knowledge of pines, mentioning only

**Plate 1-1.** *Left: P. peuce* Griseb No. 71 in Macedonia, Yugoslavia. (Photo by Branislav Pejoski.) *Right: P. pityusa* Steven No. 79—a pine from Great Pithyum of Strabo, now known as Pitsunda, on the Black Sea Coast of the Caucasus. (Photo from Kolesnikov, 1963.)

different kinds of pitch used in purifying wine or in treating the containers (Columella, 1941).

Apparently through the Middle Ages, up to Albertus Magnus' time (1193–1280), only two kinds of pines were commonly known to Europeans: a "cultivated," or "domestic," pine (*P. domestica,* or *P. sativa,* now known as *P. pinea* No. 73) and a "savage," or "wild," pine, *P. silvestris* (at that time always spelled in the Latin way, with "i" in the first syllable) (Albertus Magnus, 1867).

In *Novi Herbarii* by Brunfels (1536), the "*Rhapsodia* CLII" is devoted to pines. Six genera are listed: *Pinus, Pinaster, Abies, Picea, Larix,* and *Taeda,* obviously after Pliny, also with repetition of his statement that when the larch is diseased it turns into a *taeda.*

Andrea Cesalpino (1519–1603), in his *De Plantis* (1583), Book III, Chapter 52 (pp. 129–32), gives a general description of the "genus *Pinus*" (i.e., *P. sylvestris*): its habitat (in sunny places in the mountains), the appearance of its bark and branches, the quality of its wood, the existence of male and female trees. He repeats after his predecessors that *Pinaster* is a variety of *P. sylvestris. Pinus cembra* in all aspects is *Picea,* but it has pine foliage and thin-shelled nuts. In the Alps, spruce is called "*taeda.*" He also repeats the old story of conversion of any "Pinaceae genus" into "*taeda*" because of disease. Cesalpino, following Theophrastus, recognized "two genera of pines: *urbanum* and *sylvestrem,*" i.e., cultivated and wild pines.

The Bauhin brothers contributed a great deal to the elucidation of the genus *Pinus.* Jean (or Johann) Bauhin (1541–1631) wrote a *Historia Plantarum Universalis Liber Nonus* (1650, posthumously published). His account of pines (pp. 245–64, comprising *Capita* IV through VII) is by far more complete than all previous treatises. At the beginning, he defines what really is the "*Peuce veterum*" of Greeks. Both "*peuce*" and "*pitys*" are discussed. As to "*taeda,*" Bauhin explains that in old age a pine changes gradually into *taeda* and that after death the whole of it becomes *taeda. Taeda* is not a different species, it is merely a final stage in the life of a conifer. It is, or is caused by, a disease ("*Teda morbus est non arbor*"), which is a paraphrase of Theophrastus' statement (translated into Latin) that "*Pini interitus est ut taeda fiat.*" *Taeda* is torchwood used for domestic and for ceremonial purposes.

Discussion of *Pini aeqvivoca* is concerned chiefly with difficulties of distinguishing among pines. Truly, pines may be "*urbana*" or "*montana,*" or, again, they may be "*maritima.*" "*Pinus urbanum,*" Bauhin said, "I will call *sativum.*" He listed among wild pines (*P. sylvestris*), also called "*Pinaster,*" that do not yield to cultivation *Genenensis, Taeda, Pinaster hispanicus major, Mugo.* He complained about confusing terminology: Larch is called now "*Pinus,*" now "*Picea.*" He mentioned the mythological

story of the nymph "Pitys," who, according to Theophrastus, was transformed into a pine tree. Bauhin further stated that, to Theophrastus,
*piton* was always *Picea,* but it is difficult to say what the Greek really did
call *"pitys." "Hinc illa autorum confusis, hinc de Pity grave chaos."* Real
chaos did, however, start when Roezl (1857, 1858) described over one
hundred species of pines from Mexico, more about which later. Bauhin,
describing *P. cembra* as *"pinus ossiculis duris, foliis longis,"* remarked that,
in his opinion, ancient Greeks called this pine *"peuke,"* which is at variance with John Ray's pronouncement that *P. cembra* was not known to
the Greeks. It appears that Bauhin's statement was more nearly correct
than that of Ray (q.v.).

Finally, Bauhin analyzed his *Pinus silvestris vulgaris*—the common
wild pine. Under this name are grouped *Pinus silvestris* proper; *Pinaster,*
or *Pinus sylvestris hispanicus major; Pinaster austriacus major, albus*
(*Pinus heldreichii* No. 75 var. *leucodermis*), and *niger* (*P. nigra* No. 74);
*Pinus silvestris mugo* (i.e., *Pinus montana* No. 76); *Pinus tertius hispanicus pumilus* (found only in Murcia); and three different forms of *Pinus
maritima* (or *Pinus pinaster* No. 80).

The other Bauhin brother, Caspar (or Kaspar or Gaspard) (1560–
1624), published in 1623 his *Pinax* (i.e., catalog of pines). As Lawrence
(1955) pointed out, Gaspard Bauhin was "one of the first to distinguish
nomenclaturally between species and genera." As regards pines, he gave
generic and specific names to some, while to others he applied a ternary
nomenclature. Still others were described according to the customs of
herbalists, such as *"Pinus indica nucleo purgante,"* which was not a pine.
Names of authors were often given after the names of pines. All told,
twenty-five pines were listed but two or three of them were of genera not
included now in the genus *Pinus.*

It can be seen from the foregoing that in Gaspard Bauhin's time the
ground was already prepared for a binary nomenclature for pines. The
medieval method of a descriptive nomenclature for pines was, however,
still much in use.

John Ray (1628–1705) published, in 1688, the second volume of
*Historia Plantarum,* which gave a penetrating analysis of pines. In his
Chapter 2, entitled *"De Pinu Arbore,"* he tried to untangle semantics in
the Greek and Latin nomenclature of pines. After the names of pines,
John Ray appended the names of authorities, chiefly those of the Bauhin
brothers. Ray described a pine that grows in Rhaetia (present eastern
Switzerland and Tyrol) as *"P. cembra* J.[ean] B.[auhin]" and remarked
that *"Pini folliis breviora sunt Cembri folia."* According to Bellonius (Ray
said), this pine was not known to Theophrastus.

John Ray also mentioned *P. sativa* C.B. (i.e., Caspar Bauhin), *"sive
domestica."* Under *P. sylvestris* C.B. were considered *P. nigra, P. mari-*

*tima* (i.e., *P. pinaster*), and *P. montana*. Concerning *taeda*, he wrote that *"transeunt in taedam quandoque Picea & Larix"*; that is, spruce and larch sometimes turn into *taeda*. Pine resin, which was used as a stomach medicine and as a diuretic, was also prescribed for expelling gallstones, for relieving arthritis, and for alleviating coughs and pulmonary disorders. The rest of *De Pino Arbore* was devoted to other genera (Ray, 1688).

It is apparent from the writings of the herbalists that the concept of the genus *Pinus* was not too definite. It remained for Tournefort (1658–1708), in his *Institutiones Rei Herbarii*, to introduce it formally into botanical literature. In the 1719 edition of this work, under the class XIX, Section 3, were described seven genera: *Abies, Pinus, Larix, Thuya, Cupressus, Alnus,* and *Betula*. The genus II *Pinus* was defined in the following words: *"Pinus est plantae genus . . . ,"* and then followed a description of the genus, illustrated with engravings (Tournefort, 1719).

In the subsequent description of different pines, Tournefort listed the American *P. strobus* as *"Larix canadensis longissimo folio."* The Mediterranean pines were those recognized by previous herbalists.

Duhamel wrote a treatise on trees and shrubs in 1755—during the lifetime, be it noted, of Linnaeus. Among other genera, there was included the genus *"Pinus* Tournef.[ort] & Linn.[aeus]."* Duhamel listed pines, but these were not species but "kinds" of pines described in the manner of the herbalists. Duhamel arranged his twenty pines into three sections: *Bifoliis,* having two needles in each short shoot; *Trifoliis,* with three needles; and *Quinquefoliis,* with five needles. He also added eight American species to the list of known pines. Among the two-needle pines he described were 8. *P. canadensis bifolia* Gault. (after a Canadian physician and botanist, Dr. Gaultier), *"Pin rouge"* (i.e., *P. resinosa* No. 21); 9. *P. canadensis bifolia* Gault., with shorter and finer needles; and 10. *P. canadensis bifolia, foliis curtis et falcatis, conis mediis, incurvis* Gault. (apparently *P. banksiana* No. 32). In the three-needle group are found 15. *P. virginiana, praelongis foliis tenurioribus, cone echinate* Pluck. and 16. *P. canadensis trifolia cones aculeatis* Gault. He questioned the validity of this last species and suggested that perhaps it was the same as his No. 17 *P. americana . . . foliis ternis,* called *"Pin-à-trochet"* (*P. echinata* No. 25). The 18 *P. americana palustris trifolia foliis longissimis* of Duhamel is easy to recognize as *P. palustris* No. 22.

In the section, *Quinquefoliis* was listed as 19. *P. canadensis quinque-folia* Gault., which was commonly called "white pine" or *"Pin de* Lord Wimouth." Thus Duhamel advanced our knowledge of the genus *Pinus* by enriching it with American pines; he used epithets of genus and species, accompanied by the names of authors, and arranged the known species into three sections, using number of needles in a bundle as a criterion.

This was the first attempt to subdivide the genus into taxonomically signifi-cant groups. Duhamel lived and worked during the transition period when new ideas of classification of plants were developing, but when also the old ways of the herbalists with their longer descriptive phrases still were widely used. Even in Lambert's *Description of the Genus Pinus* (1828), the influence of herbalists was much in evidence.

The *Species Plantarum* of Linnaeus appeared in 1753 (two years before Duhamel's treatise). There, under "Monoecia Monadelphia," he listed the genus *Pinus.* It included not only pines but also *Cedrus, Larix, Picea,* and *Abies.* Under the genus *Pinus* are described only five species of pines: 1. *Pinus sylvestris* L., which formerly also included "*P. maritima altera, Pinaster latifolius,*" and other pines; 2. *P. pinea* L., formerly known as "*P. sativa* or *P. ossiculis duris, foliis longis*"; 3. *P. taeda* L., which used to be known as *P. virginiana tenuifolia tripilis*" (for this species Linnaeus used the Latin name for the pitchy wood of any conifer); 4. *P. cembra* L.; and 5. *Pinus strobus* L. It is strange that Linnaeus included so few species of pines; many more already had been described by Theophrastus and by some herbalists. Surely, such pines as *P. halepensis, P. pinaster* (in its present sense), or *P. nigra* should have been sufficiently known to plant collectors of Linnaean times. It is possible that the species listed in Linnaeus' *Species Plantarum* were intended merely to illustrate the scope of the genus *Pinus* as was done frequently later by other taxonomists (cf. Eichler, 1889). Moreover, at the time of Linnaeus, the identity of some Mediterranean pines was still controversial, and the species of eastern Asia and Mexico and western America were hardly known to European botanists.

During the ensuing century, botanists have acquired a great deal more information about the genus *Pinus.* The New World became better explored, and eastern Asia, more known. In 1803, Roxburgh described *P. longifolia* (Shaw, 1914). *Pinus excelsa* Wallich ex Lambert was incom-pletely described in Lambert's 1824 edition of the *Genus Pinus.* A valid description of this pine, as *P. griffithii,* was given by McClelland in 1854 (Shaw, 1914).

Link (1841) relied, in his classification of pines, on the number of leaves in the short shoots, and thus did not advance the taxonomy of the genus. Link's genus *Pinus* contained twenty-nine species arranged into five sections: I, *Folia gemina;* II, *Folia bina ternaque* (containing only one species, *P. variabilis,* i.e., *P. echinata*); III, *Folia terna;* IV, *Folia terna et quaterna* (including *P. sabiniana* and *P. cembroides*); and V, *Folia quina.* The inadequacy of such a classification is obvious, but it lingered on in the taxonomy of pines for a long time (see Chapter 9, p. 526).

Spach (1842) recognized the family Abietinae; he divided it into two sections: I, Auracariaceae Reichb. and II, Abieteae Reichb. In this latter section, he placed the genus *Pinus* Tourn. and subdivided it into four sections: I, *Eupitys* Spach; II, *Taeda* Spach; III, *Strobus* Sweet (ex Spach); and IV, *Cembra* Spach.

In Endlicher's *Synopsis Coniferarum* (1847), as many as 114 species of pines were included, of which *P. arabica* (*P. halepensis*) and *P. finlaysoniana* (*P. merkusii* No. 101) are marked as dubious. In the family Abietineae, and under it in the Abietineae verae, is the genus *Pinus* divided into sections: I, *Tsuga;* II, *Abies;* III, *Picea;* IV, *Larix;* V, *Cedrus;* VI, *Cembra;* VII, *Strobus;* VIII, *Pseudo-Strobus;* IX, *Taeda;* X, *Pinaster;* and XI, *Pinea.* Therefore, the genus *Pinus,* as accepted now, embraces sections VI through XI.

Endlicher was the first to recognize the importance of cone-scale morphology for taxonomic purposes.

In 1857 and 1858, Roezl published his catalogs of seeds of Mexican plants in which he listed over one hundred species of pines, some described by others (Lindley, Endlicher, Gordon, Schiede), but most by Roezl himself. Of these, only one species, *P. lawsoniana* Roezl, is recognized today. This fantastic number of pine "species" had a confusing effect on the classification of pines. Its rather embarrassing impact on paleogeography of European Tertiary pines is noted on page 75.

In the 1858 edition of Gordon's *Pinetum,* Roezl's pines increased the number of species in the genus to 152. In the 1880 edition, however, many of these were deleted.

Carrière (1867) published the very useful *Traité général des Conifères.* In its first part, he listed 94 species of pines, which he divided, according to Endlicher's system (Section B, *Pinées*) of *Abiétinées,* into 6 tribes: *Cembra* Spach, *Strobus* Spach, *Pseudostrobus* Endl., *Taeda* Spach, *Pinea* Endl., and *Pinaster* Endl. For each species (some are not in use any more), Carrière gave synonymy, description, and habitat, and also supplied his own observations.

In the second part of Carrière's chapter on pines are described seventy-nine of Roezl's species of pines, which Carrière found "tentative" and "faulty." Each species is accompanied by critical remarks based chiefly on Gordon's (1858) opinions.

Both Gordon's and Carrière's analyses of Roezl's pines are indispensable for untangling the nomenclature of the Mexican pines. Neither Gordon nor Carrière, however, commented on the causes of such an abundance of different kinds or forms of pines in the Mexican highlands. As we now know, Roezl unintentionally made, in this connection, an extremely important discovery; in the Mexican highlands is located a secondary center of evolution and speciation in the genus *Pinus*: hence the never ending and utterly confusing variability of Mexican–Central American pines (see Chapter 4, p. 341).

In De Candolle's *Prodromus,* Parlatore (Parlatore, 1868) placed pines in the *tribus* I, Abietineae, *subtribus* Pineae, genus *Pinus* Linn., subgenus *Pinus* Endlicher. Parlatore followed Endlicher in recognizing the morphology of the cone scales as an important taxonomic character. The subgenus was divided into two sections. Section I, *Pinea,* was subdivided into the following subsections: A. *Pinaster* (*Eupitys* Spach), B. *Taeda* Spach, and C. *Pseudo-Strobus* Endl. Section II, *Cembra,* consisted of the sections *Cembra* and *Strobus* of Spach and of Endlicher). The total number of species was sixty-six; some of Parlatore's names are no longer used. Many Asiatic and Mexican species were included. Taxonomic annotations make this work valuable in studies of the genus *Pinus.*

Bentham and Hooker (1880) placed the genus *Pinus* in the order Coniferae, tribe VI, Abietinae. They did not consider division of the genus into sections, nor did they list any species.

In Engler and Prantl's *Natürlichen Pflanzenfamilien* (Vol. II published in 1889), the Coniferae were prepared by Eichler (Eichler, 1889). There, the genus *Pinus,* with eight other genera, was in the family Pinoideae, subfamily (tribe) Abietinae. The genus was divided into two sections: I, *Pinaster,* which contained the groups *Pinea* and *Taeda,* and II, *Strobus,* which was subdivided into two groups: *Eustrobus* and *Cembra* (Eichler, 1889). Seven species of pines were listed (see Table 1–2, Nos. 3, 4, 12, 68, 69, 73, and 70). A revised classification of the genus *Pinus* in the second edition of Engler and Prantl's *Pflanzenfamilien,* written thirty-seven years later, is mentioned in Chapter 9.

Toward the end of the nineteenth century, it became apparent that, with enlarged knowledge of the genus *Pinus* and with the difficulties of identifying pines, a closer analysis of the genus *Pinus* was urgent. It was evident that herbarium studies of external morphology alone often were not sufficient to differentiate among species of pines.

In 1880, Engelmann published his important *Revision of the Genus Pinus.* In the introductory remarks, he clearly indicated a need for intensive studies toward a better understanding of pines. Said Engelmann,

No difficulty exists in the circumscription of the genus *Pinus;* floral characters unite with vegetative to establish it so firmly and so plainly that nobody fails to recognize the species belonging to it [but see *Pinus krempfii,* Chapter 9, pages 540–43]. But when we come to analyze and to group 60 or 70 species of pines [over one hundred are known now], which are known to us, we find that they appear so similar that all attempts to arrange them satisfactorily have failed.

Engelmann approached his revision of the genus *Pinus* in a thorough manner. He described the appearance of pine trees, their age and size, their bark, their width, and the color of their sapwood and heartwood. He examined different types of leaves (cotyledons, primary and secondary leaves) and observed the position of stomata and differences in needle-bundle sheaths (deciduous vs. persistent). He also inquired into the internal structure of the needles and found it to be "of the greatest importance for the classification of pines." Of particular value was the observed difference in the position of the resin ducts (peripheral, parenchymatous, internal) and the structure of the "strengthening cells" in the needles. He studied differences in male and female flowers, measured the size of the pollen, and described the size and shape of the cones. He did not consider phylotaxis of cone scales important for diagnostic purposes. On the other hand, "cone-scales furnish us the most valuable characters for classification of the species."

Morphology of seeds also attracted his attention. He found that a wing is always present (cf. Spach, 1842) but that sometimes it is reduced to a narrow rim. The size of the seed and the proportion of the wing to it were also found to be useful. His data on the number of cotyledons are accurate, showing that he examined large numbers of seedlings.

On the whole, Engelmann had undertaken an enormous amount of work before he proposed his arrangement of species of *Pinus*. Working as an American botanist, he had a better opportunity to study *in situ* the pines of the New World. The nomenclature of Parlatore (1868) was generally adopted by Engelmann in his revision of the genus *Pinus*.

In Engelmann's system, the genus *Pinus* was divided into two sections: I, *Strobus* and II, *Pinaster*. The section *Strobus* consisted of Endlicher's sections *Strobus* and *Cembra*, renamed subsections 1, *Eustrobi* and 2, *Cembrae*. The section *Pinaster*, Endlicher, was divided into six subsections: 3, *Integrifoliae* (which included groups *Cembroides* and *Balfouriana*); 4, *Sylvestres* (including groups *Indicae, Eusylvestres,* and *Pinea*); 5, *Halepensis* (groups *Gerardianae* and *Euhalepensis*); 6, *Ponderosae* (groups *Pseudostrobi, Euponderosae, Lariciones*); 7, *Taedae* (groups *Eutaedae, Pungentes, Mitis*); and 8, *Australes* (consisting of two groups: *Euaustrales* and *Elliottii*). Engelmann's system has considerably influenced the classification of pines of later investigators.

At the end of the nineteenth century and into the twentieth, there appeared important publications on comparative morphology and experimental taxonomy of *Pinus* by Masters (1891, 1895), culminating in his presentation in 1903 before the Linnaean Society of "A General Review of the Genus *Pinus*" (Masters, 1904). He paid particular attention to the internal morphology of needles, and his conclusions were based on researches by Van Tieghem (1891) and Penhallow (1896), as well as on his own studies.

Masters was aware of Koehne's (1893) having divided the genus *Pinus* into two sections: *Haploxylon*, in which the fibrovascular bundle of the needles is simple, and *Diploxylon*, in which it is double. He hesitated to accept the significance of juvenile characters in the structure of leaves, as proposed by Casimir de Candolle (1903). To quote Masters, "In what way we are to distinguish between what is peculiar to the individual, and what is of genealogical significance is not apparent [from De Candolle's reasoning]."

In his proposed classification of pines, Masters divided the genus into two divisions: division I, *Tenuisquammae* (subdivided into two sections: 1, *Strobus* and 2, *Cembra*, all species with single vascular bundle) and Division II, *Crassisquamae*, containing the rest of the pines. The divisions were based on the nature of cone scales—either leathery and thin or woody and thick. The significance of the structure of the vascular bundle was not strictly observed. Thus ten species (our Nos. 1, 2, 5, 6, 7, 8, 9, 36, 87, and 92; see Table 1–2) possessing a single vascular bundle formed section 3 and a part of section 4. These are included in division II, which mostly consisted of species having double vascular bundles. These latter species were grouped into sections: 5. *Indicae*, 6. *Ponderosae*, 7. *Filifoliae*, 8. *Cubenses*, 9. *Sylvestres*, and 10. *Pinaster*. All told, seventy-three species were listed; their description and their occurrence were given in an appendix entitled "Incidental Remarks on the Species of *Pinus*," in which were listed seven little-known pines. A valuable "Chronological List of Specific Names" of pines from 1753 (Linnaeus, 1753) to 1903 (Rowlee, 1903), with synonyms, is useful for tracing our knowledge of the genus *Pinus*.

With the studies of Engelmann and those of Masters, the old era of inquiries into the nature of the genus *Pinus* ended and ground was prepared for a further revision of the genus. This subject will be considered in Chapter 9.

The above historical review does not include all treatises on pines. There were, for instance, excellent horticultural books on this subject, such as Loudon's *Arboretum and Fruticetum Britannicum* (Loudon, 1838) or Beissner's *Handbuch der Nadelholzkunde*, in which a prominent place is devoted to pines (Beissner, 1891, third edition published in 1930). It is thought, however, that the material presented here gives a sufficiently clear picture of the development of our knowledge of pines from ancient times to the beginning of the present century.

In the course of the taxonomic history of the genus *Pinus*, several attempts have been made by botanists to split the genus *Pinus*. Necker (1790) divided it into two genera, *Pinus* and *Apinus*. Opiz (1852, 1854) considered *Cembra* and *Strobus* as different genera. Small (1903) introduced a new genus, *Caryopitys*, to accommodate *P. edulis* and presumably to include all other piñon pines (our Nos. 7, 9, 36, 37, 38, and 39, see Table 1-2). None of these subdivisions, however, have been generally accepted, and pines entered the new era of their classification at the beginning of the twentieth century as a single well-defined genus, *Pinus*. The problem ahead was how to classify species within the genus.

In the following chapters, 2 through 8, will be considered various aspects of the pines: paleobotanical, geographic, genetic, morphological, physiological, ecological, and chemical. Familiarity with all these aspects is important for understanding of the nature of the genus *Pinus*.

Tables 1-1 and 1-2 list all the pine species considered in this book, each accompanied by its identification number. Table 1-1 contains pine species listed in alphabetical order. In Table 1-2, the species are arranged in numerical order and at the same time grouped into geographical regions. In Chapter 3, each species is preceded by the same number as in Tables 1-1 and 1-2. In the other chapters, each species is usually followed by its identification number. Pines of uncertain taxonomic status mentioned in the text have no reference numbers.

On the map in Fig. 1-1 is shown the distribution of the species of the genus *Pinus*. The numbers are again the same as in Tables 1-1 and 1-2. This arrangement is made to facilitate cross-reference.

## LITERATURE CITATIONS

ALBERTUS MAGNUS. 1867. De vegetabilibus Libri VII. Historiae Naturalis. Pars XVIII. Editionem criticam ab ERNESTO MEYERS coeptam, absolvit CAROLUS JESSEN. George Reimeri, Berlin.

BAUHIN, JOHANN. 1650. Historia Plantarum Universalis. Auctoribus . . . prepared partially by Dr. JOHN HENRY CHERLERUS and revised by DOMINICUS CHABRAEUS. Tome I. Ebrod-vni.

BAUHIN, KASPAR (GASPARD). 1623. Pinax Theatri botanici Caspari Bavhini. Ludovici Regis, Basel.

BEISSNER, LUDWIG. 1891. Handbuch der Nadelholzkunde. Paul Parey, Berlin.

———. 1930. Handbuch der Nadelholzkunde. Herausgegeben von J. FITSCHEN (3d ed.). Paul Parey, Berlin.

BENTHAM, GEORGE, and J. D. HOOKER. 1880. Genera Plantarum. Reeve & Co., London.

BRUNFELS, OTTO. 1536. Novi Herbarii Tomus III per Othonem Brunfels. Brunfelsii. . . . 1536. Argentorati, Apud I. Schottū.

CANDOLLE, C(ASIMIR) DE. 1903. Questions de Morphologie et de biologie végétales. Bibliothèque Universelle, Archives des Sciences Physiques et Naturelles 16:50-70.

CARRIÈRE, É. A. 1867. Traité Général des Conifères, ou description de toutes les espèces et variétés de ce genre aujourd'hui connues avec leur synonymie. Nouvelle édition. Première partie. Privately printed, Paris.

CESALPINO, ANDREA. 1583. De Plantis. Libri XVI. Andreae Caesalpini Aretini. (For Coniferae see Liber III, Cap. 52 [pp. 129-32]: "Pinus, Picea, Abies, Cupressus, et altera. . . .) Apud Georgium Marescottum, Florence.

COLUMELLA, LUCIUS JUNIUS MODERATUS. 1941. On agriculture, with a recension of

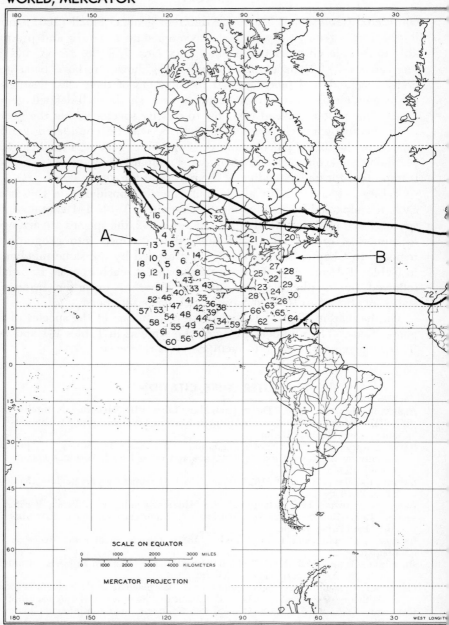

**Fig. 1—1.**

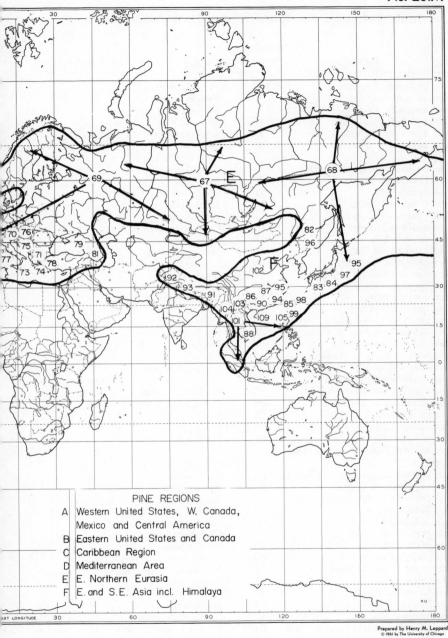

PINE REGIONS

A  Western United States, W. Canada, Mexico and Central America
B  Eastern United States and Canada
C  Caribbean Region
D  Mediterranean Area
E  E. Northern Eurasia
F  E. and S.E. Asia incl. Himalaya

Prepared by Henry M. Leppard
© 1961 by The University of Chicago

**Distribution of *Pinus* species.**

17

**Table 1–1.** List of Pine Species Arranged in Alphabetical Order *

| Name | Reference Number | American-English Name † |
|---|---|---|
| *Pinus albicaulis* Engelm. | 1 | Whitebark pine |
| *Pinus aristata* Engelm. | 6 | Bristlecone pine |
| *Pinus arizonica* Engelm. | 43 | Arizona pine |
| *Pinus armandi* Franchet | 86 | Armand pine |
| *Pinus attenuata* Lemmon | 17 | Knobcone pine |
| *Pinus ayacahuite* Ehrenberg | 33 | Mexican white pine (*Pinabete, Pino de azucar*) |
| *Pinus balfouriana* Grev. & Balf. | 5 | Foxtail pine |
| *Pinus banksiana* Lamb. | 32 | Jack pine |
| *Pinus brutia* Ten. | 78 | Calabrian pine |
| *Pinus bungeana* Zucc. | 87 | Lace-bark pine |
| *Pinus canariensis* Smith | 72 | Canary pine |
| *Pinus caribaea* Morelet | 62 | Caribbean pine |
| *Pinus cembra* L. | 70 | Swiss stone pine |
| *Pinus cembroides* Zucc. | 36 | Mexican piñon |
| *Pinus chihuahuana* Engelm. | 40 | Chihuahua pine |
| *Pinus clausa* (Chapm.) Vasey | 28 | Sand pine |
| *Pinus contorta* Dougl. | 16 | Lodgepole pine |
| *Pinus cooperi* Blanco | 51 | Cooper pine |
| *Pinus coulteri* D. Don | 12 | Coulter pine |
| *Pinus cubensis* Grisebach | 65 | Cuba pine |
| *Pinus culminicola* And. & Beam. | 39 | No English name |
| *Pinus dalatensis* de Ferré | 88 | No English name |
| *Pinus densata* Mast. (hybrid between 102 and 103) | | No English name |
| *Pinus densiflora* Sieb. & Zucc. | 95 | Japanese red pine (*Akamatsu*) |
| *Pinus douglasiana* Martínez | 56 | No English name |
| *Pinus durangensis* Martínez | 48 | Durango pine |
| *Pinus echinata* Mill. | 25 | Shortleaf pine |
| *Pinus edulis* Engelm. | 8 | Colorado piñon |
| *Pinus eldarica* Medw. | 81 | No English name |
| *Pinus elliottii* Engelm. var. *densa* Little & Dor. | 63 | So. Fla. var. of slash pine |
| *Pinus elliottii* Engelm. var. *elliottii* | 23 | Slash pine |
| *Pinus engelmannii* Carr. | 53 | Apache pine |
| *Pinus fenzeliana* Hand.-Maz. | 89 | No English name |
| *Pinus flexilis* James | 2 | Limber pine |
| *Pinus funebris* Komarov | 96 | No English name |
| *Pinus gerardiana* Wall. | 92 | Ghilghoza pine |
| *Pinus glabra* Walt | 26 | Spruce pine |
| *Pinus greggii* Engelm. | 60 | Gregg pine |
| *Pinus griffithii* McClelland | 91 | Himalayan white pine |
| *Pinus halepensis* Mill. | 77 | Aleppo pine |
| *Pinus hartwegii* Lindl. | 49 | Hartweg pine |
| *Pinus heldreichii* Chr. | 75 | Heldreich pine |
| *Pinus herrerai* Mart. | 46 | No English name |
| *Pinus himekomatsu* Miyabe & Kudo | 84 | Japanese white pine (*Himekomatsu*) |
| *Pinus hwangshanensis* Hsia | 100 | No English name |
| *Pinus insularis* Endl. | 105 | Benguet or Luzon pine |
| *Pinus jeffreyi* Grev. & Balf. | 13 | Jeffrey pine |
| *Pinus khasya* Royle | 104 | Khasia pine |
| *Pinus koraiensis* Sieb. & Zucc. | 82 | Korean pine |

**Table 1–1.** (Continued)

| Name | Reference Number | American-English Name † |
|------|------------------|-------------------------|
| *Pinus kwangtungensis* Chun | 90 | No English name |
| *Pinus lambertiana* Dougl. | 3 | Sugar pine |
| *Pinus lawsonii* Roezl | 44 | Lawson pine |
| *Pinus leiophylla* Sch. & Deppe | 41 | Smooth-leaved pine |
| *Pinus luchuensis* Mayr | 98 | Luchu or Okinawa pine |
| *Pinus lumholtzii* Rob & Fern. | 42 | Lumholtz pine |
| *Pinus massoniana* Lamb. | 94 | Masson pine |
| *Pinus merkusii* De Vriese | 101 | Merkus pine or Tenasserim pine |
| *Pinus michoacana* Martínez | 52 | No English name |
| *Pinus monophylla* Torrey | 7 | Singleleaf piñon |
| *Pinus montana* Mill. | 76 | Mountain pine |
| *Pinus montezumae* Lamb. | 47 | Montezuma pine |
| *Pinus monticola* Dougl. | 4 | Western white pine |
| *Pinus morrisonicola* Hayata | 85 | No English name |
| *Pinus muricata* D. Don | 18 | Bishop pine |
| *Pinus nelsonii* Shaw | 38 | Nelson piñon pine |
| *Pinus nigra* Arn. | 74 | Austrian pine |
| *Pinus oaxacana* Mirov | 57 | No English name |
| *Pinus occidentalis* Swartz | 64 | Cuban pine |
| *Pinus oocarpa* Schiede | 59 | No English name |
| *Pinus palustris* Mill. | 22 | Longleaf pine |
| *Pinus patula* Schl. & Cham. | 61 | Jelecote pine |
| *Pinus pentaphylla* Mayr | 83 | Japanese white pine |
| *Pinus peuce* Grisebach | 71 | Balkan pine |
| *Pinus pinaster* Ait. | 80 | French maritime pine or cluster pine |
| *Pinus pinceana* Gord. | 37 | Pince's pine |
| *Pinus pinea* L. | 73 | Italian stone pine |
| *Pinus pityusa* Steven | 79 | Pitzunda pine |
| *Pinus ponderosa* Laws. | 14 | Ponderosa pine |
| *Pinus pringlei* Shaw | 58 | Pringle pine |
| *Pinus pseudostrobus* Lindl. | 54 | False Weimouth pine |
| *Pinus pumila* Regel | 68 | Dwarf Siberian pine or Japanese stone pine |
| *Pinus pungens* Lamb. | 31 | Table mountain pine |
| *Pinus quadrifolia* Sud. | 9 | Parry piñon |
| *Pinus radiata* D. Don | 19 | Monterey pine |
| *Pinus resinosa* Ait. | 21 | Norway pine or red pine |
| *Pinus rigida* Mill. | 29 | Pitch pine |
| *Pinus roxburghii* Sarg. | 93 | Chir pine |
| *Pinus rudis* Endl. | 50 | No English name |
| *Pinus sabiniana* Dougl. | 10 | Digger pine |
| *Pinus serotina* Michx. | 30 | Pond pine |
| *Pinus sibirica* Mayr | 67 | Siberian pine (in Siberia it is called "Kedr," i.e., cedar) |
| *Pinus strobiformis* Engelm. | 35 | No English name |
| *Pinus strobus* L. | 20 | Eastern white pine (in England and in Europe in general it is called Weimouth pine) |
| *Pinus strobus* L. var. *chiapensis*, Martínez | 34 | Chiapas pine |
| *Pinus sylvestris* L. | 69 | Scots pine (German *Gemeine Kiefer*) |
| *Pinus tabulaeformis* Carr. | 102 | Chinese pine |

**Table 1–1.** (Continued)

| Name | Reference Number | American-English Name † |
|------|------------------|-------------------------|
| *Pinus taeda* L. | 24 | Loblolly pine |
| *Pinus taiwanensis* Hayata | 99 | Formosa pine |
| *Pinus tenuifolia* Benth. | 55 | No English name |
| *Pinus teocote* Schl. & Cham. | 45 | Aztec pine |
| *Pinus thunbergii* Parl. | 97 | Japanese black pine (*Kuramatsu*) |
| *Pinus torreyana* Parry | 11 | Torrey pine |
| *Pinus tropicalis* Morelet | 66 | No English name |
| *Pinus virginiana* Mill. | 27 | Virginia pine |
| *Pinus washoensis* Mason & Stockwell | 15 | Washoe pine |
| *Pinus yunnanensis* Franchet | 103 | Yunnan pine |

NOTE: English names were taken chiefly (but not always) from Kelsey and Dayton's *Standardized Plant Names* (2d ed.). 1942. J. Horace McFarland Co., Harrisburg, Pa.

* Description of each will be found under its reference (identification) number in Chapter 3.

† Local names given in parenthesis.

**Table 1–2.** List of Pine Species Arranged in Numerical Order

WESTERN AMERICA
(north of Mexico)

*Haploxylon pines*

1. *Pinus albicaulis* Engelm.
2. *Pinus flexilis* James
3. *Pinus lambertiana* Dougl.[a]
4. *Pinus monticola* Dougl.
5. *Pinus balfouriana* Balf.
6. *Pinus aristata* Engelm.
7. *Pinus monophylla* Torr.[a]
8. *Pinus edulis* Engelm.[a]
9. *Pinus quadrifolia* Sud.[a]

*Diploxylon pines*

10. *Pinus sabiniana* Dougl.
11. *Pinus torreyana* Parry
12. *Pinus coulteri* D. Don [a]
13. *Pinus jeffreyi* Grev. & Balf.[a]
14. *Pinus ponderosa* Laws.
15. *Pinus washoensis* Mason & Stockwell
16. *Pinus contorta* Dougl.[a]
17. *Pinus attenuata* Lemmon [a]
18. *Pinus muricata* D. Don [a]
19. *Pinus radiata* D. Don [a]

EASTERN AMERICA
(north of Mexico)

*Haploxylon pines*

20. *Pinus strobus* L.

*Diploxylon pines*

21. *Pinus resinosa* Ait.
22. *Pinus palustris* Mill.
23. *Pinus elliottii* Engelm. var. *elliottii*
24. *Pinus taeda* L.
25. *Pinus echinata* Mill.
26. *Pinus glabra* Walt.
27. *Pinus virginiana* Mill.
28. *Pinus clausa* (Chapm.) Vasey
29. *Pinus rigida* Mill.
30. *Pinus serotina* Michx.
31. *Pinus pungens* Lamb.
32. *Pinus banksiana* Lamb.

**Table 1–2.** (Continued)

MEXICO AND MOST OF CENTRAL AMERICA

*Haploxylon pines*

33. *Pinus ayacahuite* Ehrenberg
34. *Pinus strobus* L. var. *chiapensis* Martínez
35. *Pinus strobiformis* Engelm.[b]
36. *Pinus cembroides* Zucc.[b]
37. *Pinus pinceana* Gord.
38. *Pinus nelsonii* Shaw
39. *Pinus culminicola* And. & Beam.

*Diploxylon pines*

40. *Pinus chihauhuana* Engelm.[b]
41. *Pinus leiophylla* Sch. & Deppe
42. *Pinus lumholtzii* Rob & Fern.
43. *Pinus arizonica* Engelm.[b]
44. *Pinus lawsonii* Roezl
45. *Pinus teocote* Schl. & Cham.
46. *Pinus herrerai* Martínez
47. *Pinus montezumae* Lamb.
48. *Pinus durangensis* Martínez
49. *Pinus hartwegii* Lindl.
50. *Pinus rudis* Endl.
51. *Pinus cooperi* Blanco
52. *Pinus michoacana* Martínez
53. *Pinus engelmannii* Carr.[b]
54. *Pinus pseudostrobus* Lindl.
55. *Pinus tenuifolia* Benth.
56. *Pinus douglasiana* Martínez
57. *Pinus oaxacana* Mirov
58. *Pinus pringlei* Shaw
59. *Pinus oocarpa* Schiede
60. *Pinus greggii* Engelm.
61. *Pinus patula* Schl. & Cham.

CARIBBEAN AREA including southernmost part of Florida and Gulf Coast of Central America

*Haploxylon pines*

None

*Diploxylon pines*

62. *Pinus caribaea* Morelet
63. *Pinus elliottii* var. *densa*, Little & Dor.
64. *Pinus occidentalis* Swartz
65. *Pinus cubensis* Grisebach
66. *Pinus tropicalis* Morelet

NORTHERN EURASIA

*Haploxylon pines*

67. *Pinus sibirica* Mayr
68. *Pinus pumila* Regel[c]

*Diploxylon pines*

69. *Pinus sylvestris* L.[d]

MEDITERRANEAN REGION

*Haploxylon pines*

70. *Pinus cembra* L.[e]
71. *Pinus peuce* Grisebach

*Diploxylon pines*

72. *Pinus canariensis* Smith
73. *Pinus pinea* L.
74. *Pinus nigra* Arn.
75. *Pinus heldreichii* Christ.
76. *Pinus montana* Mill.[e]
77. *Pinus halepensis* Mill.
78. *Pinus brutia* Ten.
79. *Pinus pityusa* Steven
80. *Pinus pinaster* Ait.
81. *Pinus eldarica* Medw.

# 2

# Paleobotanical Record and Paleogeography

## INTRODUCTION

Since their incipience in the Mesozoic era, pines have spread all over the Northern Hemisphere; one species even crossed the Equator. Apparently, until the end of the Tertiary, pines never had been the chief components of major floras, but they were found as an admixture to many fossil floras from many places in the Northern Hemisphere. Accordingly, enormous amounts of material on fossil pines have been accumulated. Merely to prepare a complete bibliography on fossil pines would take a long time; to review critically the available information would be a very difficult task. Some of the material presented in literature is interesting and instructive; some is hardly usable.

A serious difficulty in identifying fossil pines is caused by the tendency of some paleobotanists to describe a new pine without careful comparison with previous findings, often from the same general area. This tendency apparently had disturbed Chaney and Axelrod (1959) when they wrote,

In our study of the fossil pines represented in the Miocene floras of the far West we have found eight described species of white pine that are sufficiently alike so that they can be grouped together at least into a generalized species. These include the species . . . from the Florissant, Tulameen, Republic, Latah, Upper Cedarville, Lower Idaho, and Thorn Creek floras. Since they all show relationship to such living species as *Pinus monticola* Douglas and *P. strobus* Linnaeus, it seems best to consider them, at least tentatively, as one biologic entity rather than as eight different species of white pine.

Still another difficulty, experienced probably by all paleobotanists working with pines, was commented upon in the same publication by Chaney and Axelrod (1959):

24

Among American fossil conifers, members of the genus *Pinus* are probably the most difficult to evaluate. This is due largely to the fragmentary nature of much of the material  Fascicles, for example, often have missing needles, so that the number per bundle cannot easily be determined. In the case of seeds, allocation to species is hampered by the fact that modern specimens in many cases represent immature seeds which are difficult to determine. For these and other reasons, it is only natural that fossil species of pines have been greatly overmultiplied; also a large amount of material has been referred only to the genus, because of the incomplete nature of the fossils. It is obvious that until someone can assemble all fossil pine material and completely revise the described species, further duplication of species will occur.

Obviously, a complete revision of the several hundred fossil pines would be a time-consuming and costly proposition.

The situation has been aggravated since introduction of the palynological method for identification of pines. Recently, Kremp remarked that there has been, during the last ten years, a tremendous expansion in this area. "The number of descriptions of new species is mounting with such speed that all signs indicate that palynology is drifting very rapidly in the direction of taxonomic chaos" (Kremp, 1959). Nevertheless, the palynological method is very useful in paleobotanical studies of pines. Pine pollen can be relatively readily identified as to genus; a distinction between haploxylon and diploxylon pines can be easily made. When used with other evidence, the palynological method might prove that the origin of the genus *Pinus* was much more ancient than previously supposed.

In the study of the paleobotany of the genus *Pinus*, it is often futile to assign fossil pines to different sections into which the living species of the genus are grouped. This is because the sections themselves are not yet definitely established. As to assigning a specific name to a fossil pine, it should be kept in mind that, even for identification of living species of *Pinus*, one has to have at one's disposal a complete living plant, observed in its native habitat. Herbarium material alone often is not adequate for taxonomic studies. Difficulties are much greater when one attempts to give a specific name to a fossil pine. It is dangerous to assume that a fossil pine, no matter how closely resembling a living pine, is of the same species. I shall illustrate taxonomic complications of this kind when I discuss fossil pines of North America on page 31. It is interesting to note Berry's (1916) remark that "For the purpose of correlation of distant geological formations, fossils are theoretically as useful unnamed as named, or at least they would be if there is some medium for intellectual exchange that did not require names." In a study of the evolution of the genus *Pinus* through geological ages, the most important thing is not to give names to the fossil pines but to find out where these pines grew, when and under what ecological and climatic conditions, to find whether or not the pine under investigation was a haploxylon or diploxylon pine, which is relatively easy to ascertain, but not to give them specific names at a first glance.

As a whole, the paleobotanical record of the genus *Pinus* is satisfactory and sufficient to enable one to understand its history. The chief difficulty in outlining the paleobotany of the genus is that one has to consider its development against the background of development of many Mesozoic and Cenozoic floras of the whole Northern Hemisphere, and not study the genus *Pinus* as a separate group of plants.

In the following description of paleobotany of pines, the author was guided by the general plan of Wulff's history of the floras of the earth (Wulff, 1944). Available literature has been reviewed, and in this chapter the author has attempted, by using *the paleobotanical approach alone,* to arrive at certain conclusions regarding the origin and development of the genus *Pinus*. Other approaches will be considered in the following chapters.

## NORTH AMERICA

In the region of North America are included Canada, the United States, Mexico, Central America, and the islands of the Caribbean.

Although the physiography of the whole North American continent has certain common features, it is expedient to consider its northern part (Canada and the United States) separately from its southern part (Mexico, Central America, and the Caribbean islands).

## Canada and the United States

**Physiography.** Continental North America can be divided into two parts: the western and the eastern. In the western part, a series of mountain chains extends all the way from the Bering Strait to the Isthmus of Tehuantepec, in southern Mexico. These chains are known as the "North American Cordillera"; the eastern chain is the Rocky Mountains. Along the coast, there are several mountain ranges: Cascades, Sierra Nevada, and Mexican Sierras. East of the northern Rocky Mountains extend lowlands of the Canadian Shield (with considerable elevations in Labrador). To the southeast are located interior plains, which in the United States lie between the Rocky Mountains and the Appalachian Mountains, of the East. In the south, the interior plains merge into the southeastern coastal plain, which extends north to the mouth of the Hudson River and south to the tip of Florida. The coastal plain also extends east and southeast along the Gulf of Mexico to Texas and farther south as far as, and including, the peninsula of Yucatán (Atwood, 1940). The Appalachian

Mountains are located between the Interior Plains and the Atlantic Coast Plain.

In British Columbia, the western chain of the Cordillera, known as the "Cascades," is close to the coast, but farther south, in the United States, it is located farther inland. Near the ocean, it is replaced by the Coast Range. The Cascades end in northern California, and the mountain range located farther south is known as the "Sierra Nevada." It extends to central California, approximately to the thirty-fifth parallel. The Coast Range, however, continues almost to the southern tip of Baja California.

The Yukon Basin, Fraser Plateau, Columbia Plateau, and Colorado Plateau (see map, Fig. 2–1) are located between the western chain and the Rocky Mountains. The Basin and Range geomorphological province lies between the Sierra Nevada and the Colorado Plateau; latitudinally, it extends from the Columbia Plateau deep into western and, especially, eastern Mexico.

Geologically, the eastern part of North America is older than its western part. The Appalachian Mountains are of Paleozoic origin. In the Lower Upper Cretaceous, sea connected the Arctic Ocean and the Gulf of Mexico, dividing the continent in two (see Fig. 2–2 and Schuchert, 1955). During the Tertiary, when the sea regressed, considerable lowland area along the coast became a part of the continent.

The western part of America was formed much later. The Cordillera appeared above water only at the end of the Mesozoic and assumed its present appearance only at the middle of the Tertiary.

From the Middle Triassic, North America and northeastern Asia had a broad land connection in the place now occupied by the Bering Sea (Schuchert, 1955, Maps 61–63; Krishtofovich, 1959). The configuration of this land connection underwent many changes. During the Upper Triassic, the northwestern part of America was actually part of Asia, for the sea connected the Pacific and the Arctic between the thirty-eighth and forty-fourth meridians. Throughout the Jurassic, and until the end of the Tertiary, the land connections between America and Asia were frequent, and only recently (in the middle of the Pleistocene) did the two continents finally become separated.

During the Lower Jurassic, there was apparently land connection also between the western and eastern parts of North America, but later this connection became disrupted. It was restored again only after the Lower Upper Cretaceous.

At the end of the Tertiary and in the Quaternary, the ice sheet covered the northern part of the continent, although there remained some unglaciated areas in Alaska, in the Yukon Valley, and possibly in other places.

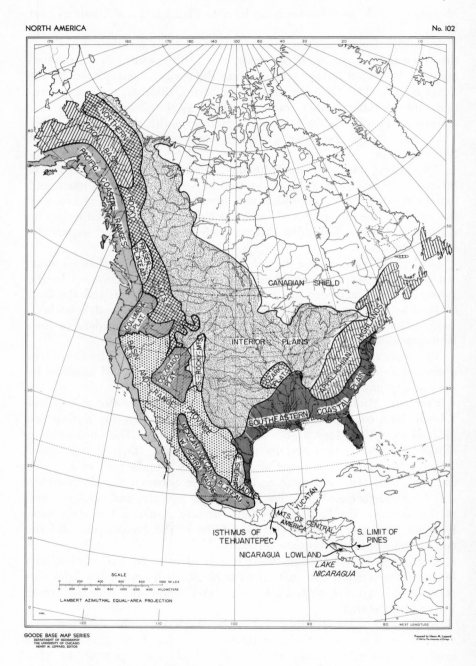

**Fig. 2–1.** Geomorphological provinces of North America.

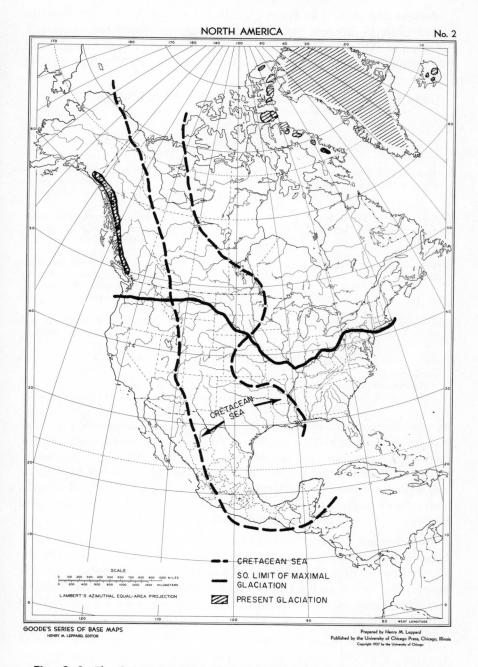

**Fig. 2–2.** The Cretacean sea and Quaternary glaciation in North America.

**Present Distribution of Pines.** Table 2–1 shows the present distribution of pines in different parts of North America. Thirty-two species of pines are found in the United States and in adjacent parts of Canada, and thirty-four species are found south of the border, i.e., in Mexico, including

**Table 2–1.** Present Distribution of Pines in Several Parts of North America

| Locality | Number of Species | | Remarks |
| --- | --- | --- | --- |
| | Haploxylon | Diploxylon | |
| Eastern United States and adjacent parts of Canada | 1 | 12 | Only four species in Canada. *P. rigida* just crosses the Canadian border. |
| Western United States and adjacent parts of Canada | 9 | 10 | Five species occur in western Canada (also *P. banksiana*). |
| Mexico, including Central America | 7 | 22 | Only two pines in Nicaragua; nine or ten in Guatemala. *P. caribaea* not included. |
| Caribbean area | 0 | 5 | Including *P. caribaea* and *P. elliottii* var. *densa*. |
| Total | 17 | 49 | |
| Grand total for the New World | | 66 | |

five species on the Caribbean islands. The highest concentration of pines is in California and Mexico combined. In this part of North America grow forty-eight known species, i.e., about half the total number of species in the genus *Pinus*. Interesting are the almost equal numbers of haploxylon and diploxylon pines in California. There is also a similar distribution in eastern and southeastern Asia (see pages 59 and 65). The geography of pines of North America is considered more fully in Chapter 3.

**Paleobotany.** Nobody has yet found Triassic pines in America. Newberry (as quoted by Daugherty, 1941) did not mention any pines in the Upper Triassic flora in Los Broncos, Sonora, Mexico. Daugherty (1941) himself discovered, in the Upper Triassic of Arizona, many fossil conifers including "Araucariaceae and Abietaceae," but no pines were mentioned in his report.

JURASSIC. The earliest known pines of North America were those of the Jurassic period. The presence of pine remains in the Jurassic deposits in Douglas County, Oregon (Fontaine, 1905), has been questioned by some paleobotanists, although Fontaine's material reproduced on Plate 35 of Ward's (1905) monograph looks like pine needles. Fontaine remarked, "The leaves are pretty surely those of a *Pinus*. They never appear . . . in large numbers, but are . . . scattered. The leaves measured up to 115 mm in length and to 5 mm in width." Generally, however, they were much narrower.

CRETACEOUS. Leaves and cones of *P. quenstedti* Heer from the Cretaceous of Kansas were described by Lesquereux (1883). The leaves of this pine are in fives, and the cone is elongated and asymmetrical. Lesquereux noticed the resemblance of this pine to the living Mexican pines, and Chaney (1954) commented that the pine from Kansas has cones most similar to those of *P. michoacana* var. *cornuta*, i.e., to a pine of the *P. montezumae* complex.*

Lesquereux (1895) also reported a pine from near New Ulm, Minnesota, and thought that it was the same pine as that he described from the Cretaceous of Kansas, but Chaney showed that this was an entirely different species. In 1954, Chaney described a pine from Dakota Cretaceous sandstone of Minnesota, about 40 km west of New Ulm. He named this pine "*Pinus clementsii*." The following is my diagnosis of this pine, prepared at Dr. Chaney's request and reproduced in his paper (Chaney, 1954):

The fossil cone you sent me apparently belongs to the subgenus *Diploxylon* (hard pines). Within the subgenus, the cone falls into the group *Lariciones* "which represents the first stage in the evolution of the hard pines" (Shaw, 1914, p. 51). This group consists of 12 living species; seven are Asiatic, three European and two American, *P. resinosa* and *P. tropicalis*. The cone in question differs a great deal from the cones of the European and Asiatic *Lariciones* either in shape or in the appearance of the apophysis. A difference in shape and size is also apparent when it is compared with *P. tropicalis*. The fossil cone is indistinguishable from the cone of *P. resinosa* in its shape and especially in the appearance of the apophysis, characterized by an unarmed, delicately outlined umbo.

The close resemblance of *P. clementsii* to *P. resinosa* does not mean, of course, that both belong to the same species. This was strongly emphasized by Dr. Chaney in his description of the pine.

Pierce (1957) made an important contribution to the paleobotany of pines in reporting a species from the Upper Cretaceous (Dakota Series) deposits near New Ulm, only 40 km east of Springfield, Minnesota, which Chaney described as the site of *P. clementsii*. Pierce's pollen grains were indistinguishable from those of *P. resinosa*. Incidentally, the Tertiary

---

* Generally, five-needle pines are haploxylon pines, but in Mexico are several diploxylon pines having five needles to a bundle. This has caused a great deal of confusion. For instance, a five-needle diploxylon pine, *P. pseudostrobus*, often has been described as a haploxylon pine.

record of *P. resinosa* is unknown, so for the time being we should assume that, although the pollen was not necessarily from *P. resinosa,* it probably came from a closely related pine. These discoveries comprise the most important contributions to the early paleobotany of pines of North America. The occurrence of a pine resembling *P. resinosa* in the Cretaceous deposits of Minnesota is of utmost significance to understanding of the migration of pines. Fontaine (Ward, 1905, p. 262) reported *P. shastensis* from the Lower Cretaceous near Horsetown, Shasta County, California.

On the Atlantic Coast of the United States, in New York and New Jersey and along the Potomac River, Hollick and Jeffrey (1909) found abundant remains of pines in the Cretaceous strata. Although cones and even cone scales were poorly represented, there was enough evidence in needle and wood structure to differentiate the collected material and to describe three distinct pines: *P. triphylla* Jeff., possessing three needles to a bundle; *P. tetraphylla* Jeff., with four needles; * and *P. quinquifolia* Jeff., with five needles to a bundle.

In 1947, Penny described some fossil pines from the Magothy formation of the Upper Cretaceous along the Chesapeake and Delaware Canal, west of Summit Bridge, Delaware. The remains of cones of a haploxylon pine had previously been reported by Berry (1905) from the Magothy at Cliffwood, New Jersey, and this pine was thought to be similar to the Belgian Cretaceous *P. andraei* Coem. (Coemans, 1867). However, it was found to be different and was given the name *P. magothensis* Penny. Two more haploxylon pines were found in the Magothy Flora: *P. quinquefolia* Jeff. and *P. quadrifolia* Jeff.

Among other Mesozoic findings should be mentioned *P. protoscleropitys* Holden (1913), described as being from the Upper Cretaceous (Magothy) Flora, Cliffwood, New Jersey. Holden believed that this species "probably [was] the earliest form with all the characters of modern hard pine, yet retaining certain ancestral features as the association of primary and fasciscular leaves, the latter borne on brachyblasts, subtended by a foliar trace." *Pinus delicatulus,* another Upper Cretaceous pine from the Magothy formation, was described by Berry (1905) from the same locality in New Jersey.

*Pinus raritanensis* Berry (1910) was reported from several Upper Cretaceous floras: Raritan of South Amboy, New Jersey; Tuscaloosa of Cottondale, Alabama; Black Creek of Cape Fear River, North Carolina; and Black Creek of Middendorf, South Carolina. Pine pollen was discovered in the Raritan and the Magothy of Long Island by Steeves (1959).

One more reference should be given on the occurrence of Cretaceous pines in America. In 1893, Fontaine described a pine, identified as to the

---

* Four-needle pines are unusual. Might this have been a five-needle pine with the fifth needle lost?

genus only, from Lower Cretaceous deposits near Glen Rose, Texas. The available material consisted of several broken pieces of narrow leaves 1½ mm wide and up to 3 cm in length. As Glen Rose is not far from the place in Kansas where Lesquereux discovered *P. quenstedti*, perhaps one should accept Fontaine's material as true pine needles, although the evidence submitted is rather meager.

More Cretaceous pines have been found in the East than in the West. In the western parts of the continent, Cretaceous deposits are rare, hence there is a scarcity of pine material from that period.

The above are just examples of the occurrence of Cretaceous pines in North America. The list is far from complete. All reports agree that pines have been growing on the American continent at least since the Cretaceous period. Although they did not form extensive forests, they were much more widely distributed than they are now.

TERTIARY. On the North American continent, in the early Tertiary period, pines were widely distributed. The paleobotanical record of pines is, however, somewhat confusing. There have been so many changes in designation of age of the pine fossils and in their synonymy that the paleobotanical status of pines during that period of time should be considered critically (see Becker, 1961, and Chaney and Axelrod, 1959).

Knowlton (1919) described *P. iddingsii*, belonging to what he called, erroneously, the "Fort Union formation," from the Eocene strata, Yellowstone Park, Wyoming. Brown (1934) found, in the Green River formation in northwestern Colorado, a Middle Eocene three-needle pine. From the excellent photograph in Brown's paper, it appears that the pine was a piñon pine. Brown also mentioned three pines from the same locality (*P. scopulipites*, *P. strobipites*, and *P. tuberculipites*) that were described by Wodehouse on the basis of their pollen grains (Wodehouse, 1933).

From the eastern United States, we have a report on an Eocene pine from Brandon, Vermont (Berry, 1937). Traverse (1955), however, is of the opinion that the Brandon Flora is not of Upper Eocene age but that "an Upper Oligocene, to Lower Miocene is strongly indicated." The Brandon, Vermont, *Pinus* described by Jeffrey and cited by Berry (1937) as an Eocene pine was, in fact, poorly preserved wood of *Gordonia* erroneously identified as *Pinus* (Dr. E. S. Barghoorn, personal communication). A very recent and very important report by Jane Gray (1960) deals with finding pines of "Haploxylon and *sylvestris* type" in a Clairborne (Middle Eocene) formation, Alabama. The identification was made from analysis of pollen.

Berry could not find any pines in the Eocene floras from the Trans-Pecos region of Texas (Berry, 1919), from several localities of the Wilcox Flora of the American Southeast (Berry, 1916a), or from the Clairborne of Alabama (Berry, 1924). But Gray's findings give us hope that more pine fossils will be found in the future in the Southeast of the United States and even perhaps in northeastern Mexico. Farther north, however, Berry (1934) found an Eocene pine in the Potomac River area. He called it *"Pinus linni."*

*Pinus premurriana* Knowlton was growing during the Eocene in the present area of Yellowstone Park. *Pinus murrayana* is abundant there now. Knowlton (1919, p. 455) erroneously referred this pine to the Miocene, but his decision to indicate that the pine in question was not *P. murrayana*, but rather its predecessor, was a wise one.

Reports of occurrence of pines in the Oligocene are satisfactorily numerous. *Pinus steenstrupiana* Heer (Penhallow, 1908) was indicated as dating from the Oligocene (or Upper Eocene) of Quilchena, British Columbia. *Pinus columbiensis* Penhallow (1908) comes from Oligocene strata, Kettle River, above Midway, British Columbia. *Pinus tulameenensis* Penhallow (1908) was described as being from the Oligocene strata of Tulameen River, British Columbia. Apparently, it is the same species as the Oligocene *P. wheeleri* Cockerell. (Dr. H. D. MacGinitie, personal communication).

Mason (1927) found *P. torreyana* in the Bridge Creek (Oligocene) Flora, eastern Oregon. At present, this pine is a very restricted California endemic. Mason also mentioned that *P. trunculus* Dawson, from the Oligocene and Miocene of British Columbia, is possibly related to *P. torreyana*.

In this connection, a quotation from Cockerell (1934) is pertinent, for it deals with identification of fossil pines.

In common with other writers I have assumed [the fossil] species to be distinct from their modern relatives, even when visible differences were slight, and such as might indicate only a variety or form in the modern flora. Considering the millions of years intervening it has seemed reasonable to assume that the species would be different and to suppose that if we had the complete plants, other differences than those recorded would be apparent. What shall we do, however, when there are no visible differences? In such cases it appears premature to offer a new specific name, though an argument can be made that in all probability the plants are not identical, and only appear so owing to the lack of adequate fossil material.

From a general biological point of view it is relatively immaterial whether a fossil pine is exactly the same as the modern one. The significant thing is that it is substantially the same and that this type of pine has existed.

Cockerell proposed the use of trinomials such as *Pinus aristata crossi* (now known to be a Pliocene species) to indicate that a pine was described as a fossil (LaMotte, 1944, p. 231).

*Pinus knowltoni* Chaney has been found in the Oligocene and in the Miocene in several localities of eastern Oregon (LaMotte, 1944). Both haploxylon and diploxylon pines were found by Becker (1961) in Oligocene strata of the Upper Ruby River Basin, southwestern Montana. His four-leaved pine *P. tetrafolia* Berry most likely was also a haploxylon species.

There is also an interesting report by MacGinitie (1953) on Oligocene pines in Florissant beds not far from Colorado Springs, Colorado. The three pine species were *P. florissanti* Lesquereux (the same pine as *P. storgisi* Cockerell), taxonomically about the same as *P. macrophylla* Berry; *P. hambachi* Kirchner (Cockerell, 1908), which resembled southeastern living pines *P. clausa* No. 28, *P. echinata* No. 25, and *P. virginiana* No. 27; and *P. wheeleri* Cockerell (1908). This last pine is apparently the same as *P. pseudostrobus* Lesq. (not Heer), *P. latahensis* Berry, *P. monticolensis* Berry, and *P. tulameenensis* Penhallow. It is a haploxylon pine with five needles to a bundle. Traverse (1955) described three kinds of pine pollen from the Brandon Flora of Vermont and presented evidence that both haploxylon and diploxylon pines were found in the Brandon Flora. If we assume that the Brandon Flora is Upper Oligocene, as, according to Traverse, had been postulated in 1949 by Spackman, Brandon is the only place where Oligocene pines have been found so far in the eastern United States.

In the Miocene, pines grew in many places in the western United States. *Pinus florissanti* Lesquereux (1883), which may be considered as related to living *P. ponderosa*, was first described as coming from Florissant, Colorado, and later was found in many other localities such as near Fallon, Nevada, by Axelrod (1956). *Pinus knowltoni* Chaney, which is closely related to *P. attenuata*, was reported by Mason (1927) to be in Mascall formation near Tipton, eastern Oregon. Axelrod (1939) found piñon pines in Pinole, in middle California; in Tehachapi, in the southern part of the state (Middle Pliocene?); and in southwestern Idaho (Uppermost Miocene). He also discovered *P. wheeleri* (resembling living *P. monticola*) in Miocene-Pliocene strata near Carson City, Nevada, and, as already mentioned, *P. florissanti* of the same Miocene-Pliocene age near Fallon, Nevada.

Templeton (1953) described an Upper Miocene pine from Point Germin, Los Angeles County, California. The pine was named "*Pinus paucisquamosa.*" The author thought that it showed certain similarities to *P. remorata* (see page 170), *P. contorta,* and *P. muricata* of Shaw's group *Insignes,* but perhaps more closely resembled *P. chihauhuana,* of the group *Australes.* After having studied Templeton's excellent photographs,* I am inclined to think that the relationship of this fossil pine is with Shaw's *Insignes* pines rather than with *P. chihuahuana.*

---

* Photographs of fossil pines are much more reliable than (often exquisite) engravings so common in older works. It appears that sometimes in the past the artist exaggerated morphological characters, possibly to please the scientist.

Chaney and Axelrod (1959) studied thoroughly the Miocene pines of the West. Many investigators reported occurrence of haploxylon pines under different names at several places. Apparently, all these pines (*P. tulameenensis* Penhallow; *P. trunculus* Daws.; *P. tetrafolia* Berry, perhaps a five-needle pine with one needle lost; *P. monticolensis* Berry; *P. latahensis* Berry; *P. knowltoni* Chaney; *P. russelli* LaMotte; *P. sp.* of Brown) belong to the same species, most likely a predecessor of *P. monticola*. *Pinus tiptoniana*, apparently related to *P. resinosa*, was found in a Miocene flora of the Columbia Plateau. Possibly, it is related to the previously mentioned Cretaceous *P. clementsii* (page 31).

There are very few reports on occurrence of Miocene pine in the eastern United States. Perkins (1904) described *P. conoides* Perk. and *P. cuneatus* Perk. from Brandon, Vermont, possibly of Upper Oligocene–Lower Miocene age (cf. Traverse, 1955).* Berry (1916b) found a pine (*P. sp.*) in the Calvert formation, Virginia. It closely resembled living *P. taeda* of the same region.

Berry (1936), describing *P. collinsi* sp. n. from the Calvert formation of the Miocene (near Plum Point, Calvert County, Maryland), remarked that "this is the only trace of *Pinus* known from eastern North America in the interval between the Eocene and the Pleistocene." It appears that the pines, although they had already established themselves on the East Coast during the Cretaceous, moved north (Berry, 1930) very early in the Tertiary, when the climate was warm. Contemporary pines of the East Coast are, therefore, relatively recent migrants.

There are more reports on occurrence of Tertiary fossil pines in North America, but perhaps those mentioned above will suffice to indicate the extent of their distribution during this period.

TERTIARY PINES OF THE GREAT BASIN AND CALIFORNIA. Of utmost interest to us are these events in the paleobotany of western American pines: (1) almost complete disappearance, or at least drastic rearrangements, of pines in the area between the coastal ranges and the Rocky Mountains—generally designated as the Great Basin—and (2) behavior of Tertiary pines in California. Axelrod (1939, 1940) contributed a great deal to the understanding of the behavior of pines in the Great Basin during the Tertiary period. When, in the late Miocene and the early Pliocene, the Sierra Nevada and Cascade ranges were formed, climatic conditions of the Great Basin were changed because the newly formed mountains intercepted the moist air from the Pacific; temperatures soared and precipitation drastically decreased. Later studies (Axelrod, 1962) suggest that the Sierra Nevada as a major topographical barrier originated

---

* The age of the Brandon deposit has been variously interpreted over the years it has been studied.

in the post-Pliocene time. The Rocky Mountains east of the Great Basin already constituted a formidable obstacle to migration of plants eastward during Miocene time.

During the earlier Tertiary (until the Miocene and early Pliocene), the Great Basin mountain slopes and uplands were sparsely covered with the same pines that grew on the western slopes of the Cascades and the Sierra Nevada. The climatic conditions of the Great Basin, after the uplift in the late Miocene and early Pliocene, were not favorable for the widespread forest of the North. Many species and genera of forest trees perished, but pines, being xerophytes and light-enduring trees (see Chapter 6), survived.

Chaney and Sanborn (1933) suggested that a general resemblance existed between Miocene vegetation of the Columbian Plateau and the upland forests of southern Mexico and Central America. This statement also may be applied to pines.

It has been indicated (Chaney and Sanborn, 1933) that pines also migrated with angiosperm genera to the uplands of Mexico and farther down to Nicaragua. Some angiosperm genera perished during this migration; others such as *Liquidambar* survived. I may add that the genus *Pinus* not only survived but, in southern Mexico, it formed the most important secondary center of speciation (see Chapter 4).

Axelrod (1937), discussing a Pliocene flora from the Mount Eden formation, near Beaumont, southern California, on the northern slopes of the San Jacinto Mountains, west of San Gorgonio Pass, mentioned three species of pines: *P. hazeni* sp. n., whose modern equivalent is *P. coulteri; P. pieperi* Dorf., akin to the present Digger pine, *P. sabiniana;* and *P. pretuberculata* sp. n., which was an apparent predecessor of *P. attenuata.* Both *P. coulteri* and *P. attenuata* grow in the San Jacinto Mountains now, while *P. sabiniana* does not. Occurrence of a pre-*sabiniana* pine in the Mount Eden Flora seemed to indicate that in the Pliocene this pine grew farther south than it does now. The northward movement of Digger pine from southern California was attributed to rising winter temperatures in that area since the Pleistocene. Margot Forde (1962), who reviewed very carefully the paleobotany of the western American closed-cone pines, thinks that Axelrod's cones of *P. pretuberculata* are much closer to those of the present-day *P. radiata* than to those of *P. attenuata.*

A possible physiological explanation of the disappearance of *P. sabiniana* from southern California is that its seeds require for their germination a prolonged chilling period of temperatures between 0° and 5° C. with adequate soil moisture. Apparently, a change in these conditions was detrimental to Digger pine at the southern part of its range. Perhaps, disappearance of *P. sabiniana* from the south should not be called a "northward movement." Such a movement, or migration, of this pine would presuppose also its advance in the extreme northern parts of its distribution. No such advance has been recorded.

Axelrod (1958) summed up the Tertiary situation in North America, stating that

. . . occupying the southern half of the continent was the broadleaf evergreen Neotropical-Tertiary Geoflora; in the north was the temperate mixed deciduous Arcto-Tertiary Geoflora and between them, centered in the southern Rocky Mountains and adjacent Mexico the sclerophyllous and microphyllous Madro-Tertiary Geoflora[*] was making its initial appearance.

The Green River Middle Eocene Flora in the Rockies contained in its upland temperate genera of a "Miocene aspect" (Axelrod, 1939). Many of the upland Green River plants may have extended southward into Mexico along the Cordilleran axis during the Eocene. The genus *Pinus* was possibly among other genera, and the Cordilleran route of migration of pines from the north to Mexico was apparently of more importance than the tortuous route from the Appalachian uplands around the Gulf of Mexico.

Axelrod's statement that Madro-Tertiary plants were evolving in these areas of scattered dry sites from Middle Cretaceous (or earlier) through Pliocene time, a span of fully 60 million years, most likely holds for the evolution of piñon pines from the more northern species of temperate climates. The present relict high mountain pines, *P. albicaulis* No. 1, *P. aristata* No. 6, and *P. balfouriana* No. 5, probably are of the same origin in area and in time. It appears that piñon pines evolved from ancient haploxylon pines akin to *P. aristata crossi* Knowlton, in the late Oligocene, i.e., about the time when the Eocene deciduous forest of the present desert region was replaced by xeric species (Clements, 1936).

Axelrod (1939) found in Miocene deposits of the western Mojave Desert a pine nut that he identified as a seed of a fossil piñon pine— *Pinus lindgreni* Knowlton. This finding caused him to discuss the piñon pines in general, and the discussion is very valuable and useful to us. Piñon pines have been recorded in the Middle Miocene Tehachapi Flora, in the uppermost Miocene Idaho Flora, and in the Middle Pliocene Pinole formation in west-central California. These findings suggest the northward migration of piñons in later Tertiary time. But it was a secondary migration of a local character. The main path of migration of pines in North America always has been southward and eastward.

At the end of the Tertiary period in the Great Basin, *Sequoia* disappeared, but some pines (piñons, *P. sabiniana*) survived (Axelrod,

---

[*] The prefix "Madro-" is used to connect this flora with the floras of the Sierra Madre ranges of Mexico.

1940). Later *P. sabiniana* also disappeared because of lowered winter temperatures, and piñons retreated somewhat south, although one of them (*P. monophylla*) is still found in southern Idaho and in northern Utah. Generally, piñon pines occupied areas where montane pines had been growing previously. Some of these montane pines such as *Pinus pre-lambertiana* perished because of insufficient rainfall; others such as *P. ponderosa* and *P. aristata* survived in higher altitudes. It should be noted that even now the conditions in some places of the Great Basin are favorable for growth of mixed conifer forest with *P. ponderosa* and occasional *P. flexilis* and *P. aristata*. I observed such a forest in southwestern Utah at an elevation of about 2440 m. Axelrod (1956) found in the Miocene-Pliocene deposits of west central Nevada *P. florissanti*, which is akin to *P. ponderosa,* and *P. wheeleri*, resembling *P. monticola*. No *P. lambertiana* was found. This Tertiary forest apparently resembled the contemporary forest I saw in Utah.

We also owe to Axelrod (1958) interpretation of pine paleobotany of the off-shore California islands. He mentioned *P. remorata* and *P. torreyana*, but his interpretations also hold for *P. radiata* and *P. muricata*. The original suggestion of LeConte (1887) that the islands were colonized by pines from the mainland during the Pliocene, when the islands were largely connected with the mainland, still holds in the light of recent paleobotanical data.

As winters grew colder in central California in the late Pliocene, the California pines (which now are found only in the islands) disappeared from the mainland, but some persisted in the southern part of the state into the Pleistocene, as is shown by the occurrence of *P. remorata* (see page 170) in Plio-Pleistocene strata at Santa Monica (Potrero Canyon) and in Pleistocene strata at Carpinteria (Chaney and Mason, 1934).

The most recent contribution to our knowledge of Tertiary pines is Axelrod and Ting's (1960) *Late Pliocene Floras of the Sierra Nevada*. The reported results are based on identification of pollen. The report was offered essentially to show some errors involved in earlier versions of the sequence of events in tectonic changes of the Sierra Nevada. For us the report is valuable because it lists ten species of west-slope pines that migrated in late Pliocene to the western part of the Great Basin.

Axelrod and Ting found that, at Wichman, in western Nevada (see map, Fig. 2–3, location 1), where now there are desert flats and low ranges with scattered *P. monophylla* No. 7, during the late Pliocene there were growing *P. attenuata* No. 17, *P. jeffreyi* No. 13, *P. lambertiana* No. 3, and, in the uplands, *P. monticola* No. 4 and *P. flexilis* No. 2 (or *P. aristata?*). In view of difficulties in identifying species by their pollen (Wilson and Webster, 1943), it is not certain that all identifications were accurate.

In the Owens Gorge (Fig. 2–3, location 2), among other pines was also listed *P. murrayana* No. 16. Farther south, west of Panamint Springs (Fig. 2–3, location 3), the following pines were growing during the late Pliocene: *P. attenuata* No. 17, *P. coulteri* No. 12, *P. jeffreyi* No. 13, *P. ponderosa* No. 14, and *P.* cf. *monophylla* No. 7. At present, the area is a desert. Attention is called to excellent photographs in Axelrod and Ting's

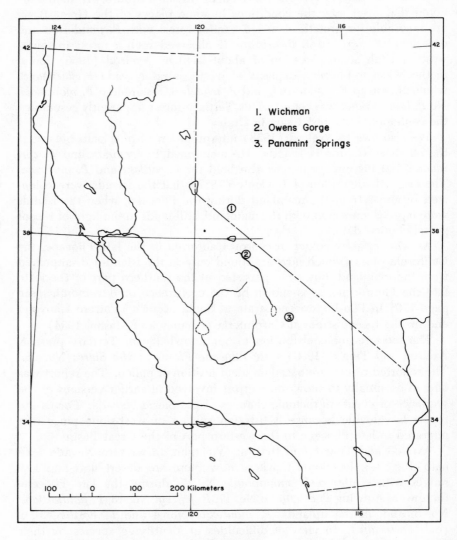

1. Wichman
2. Owens Gorge
3. Panamint Springs

**Fig. 2–3.** Late Pliocene floras east of the Sierra Nevada, California. (After Axelrod and Ting, 1960.)

paper showing the present aspect of the sites where pine pollen was found and of forests that probably existed there in the late Pliocene.

Mason contributed a very important study to the paleobotany of pines. It deals with the evolution of California closed-cone pines during the Tertiary. His papers were abstracted and discussed so well by Cain (1944) that it is not necessary to do it again. I note only that Mason's studies were unique in that they did not follow a general pattern of paleobotanical researches by merely describing fossil floras; he employed all available methods (as Cain already noted) for understanding evolution of pines. I do not know of any comparable study of pine evolution. Mason's studies are concerned with five "closed-cone" (group *Insignes*) pines: *Pinus attenuata* No. 17, *P. muricata* No. 18, *P. remorata* No. 18, *P. radiata* No. 19, and *P. radiata* var. *binata*. Duffield (1951) suggested that *P. remorata* be considered a variety of *P. muricata*, but this taxonomic readjustment does not change the picture presented by Mason.

Summing up the paleogeography of pines, we see that, at the end of the Tertiary, pines had occupied in America essentially the same areas they occupy now, only the northern boundary was much farther north. It is possible that, from the Mesozoic all the way into the Pleistocene, pines occurred in the Northern Hemisphere generally only as small and scattered groves rather than as extensive forests (Krishtofovich, 1959, pp. 197–98). During the Tertiary period, pines gradually advanced southward. The Tertiary period was the time of origin of piñon pines (Nos. 7, 8, and 9, and Mexican piñons in southwestern North America).

QUATERNARY. Then came the great glaciation, "when through many thousands of years ice sheets and glaciers devastated not less than 8,000,000 square miles of country in North America and in Europe" (Seward, 1941, p. 481). In America, the ice sheet descended as far south as Seattle, Washington, and the city of New York, with a pronounced dip approximately at the ninetieth meridian as far south as the thirty-eighth parallel in Illinois (see map, Fig. 2–2, page 29).

At the advent of glaciation in the northern part of the continent, there were growing chiefly, as now, only two pines: *P. contorta* No. 16, in the west, and *P. banksiana* No. 32, in the east.

During the Wisconsin glaciation, *P. banksiana* forests of Canada were completely destroyed. When forest trees reinvaded Canada, *P. banksiana* came from refugia located on the Appalachian land mass, that is, it came from the southeast. *Pinus contorta* No. 16 migrated southward, probably from refugia in the Upper Yukon Valley (Hulten, 1937), even before the Wisconsin glaciation and may have persisted in ice-free areas close to the ice front during at least the late Wisconsin glaciation, when the land located both eastward and westward was still covered with ice.

The region about the Bering Sea, including central Alaska, was also unglaciated. *Pinus contorta* possibly persisted in these areas during the late Wisconsin glaciation, from where it migrated after the retreat of the ice. But, most likely, *P. contorta* migrated northward from the unglaciated areas of the Pacific Coast, i.e., from the south.

Hansen (1949) studied the presence of pollen in the postglacial peat deposits around Edmonton, Alberta (probably late Wisconsin). He found that, while in the Great Lakes region and in New England there was a predominance of spruce-fir in the earliest postglacial sediments, in Alberta, i.e., to the west, *P. contorta* No. 16 was predominant. Wilson and Webster (1943), however, pointed out that, in Ontario, the earliest recorded postglacial spruce and fir forests included also *P. banksiana*, which became dominant as the climate became warmer and drier. Later, when the climate became cooler and moister, spruce became dominant, but, with the advent of man, fire and cultivation interrupted spruce expansion, and *P. contorta* expanded again in the Cordilleran forest. At present, *P. contorta* occurs as far east as the Black Hills of South Dakota, probably as a survivor from a more or less continuous range that was disrupted by the relatively recent formation of the Great Plains grassland.

Hansen (1943), studying postglacial pollen deposits on the southern Oregon coast, found that, relatively recently (4000–7000 years ago), *P. contorta* was usually the "pioneer arboreal invader of stabilized dunes," to be replaced later by other conifers as conditions changed. This was, in fact, a statement that *P. contorta* behaved 7000 years ago as it behaves now; it is the first to invade unoccupied areas.

It should be noted, however, that succession and establishment of pines in the post-Pleistocene were sometimes determined not by direct or indirect effects of glaciation but by edaphic factors or by the influence of fire (see Chapter 6).

Hansen (1943) described an interesting succession of forest trees on the newly exposed eastern slope of the Cascades in Oregon. Initially, after repeated fires, the area was occupied by larch. Later, *P. contorta* invaded the site. As the climate became drier and warmer, *P. ponderosa* No. 14 replaced *P. contorta*.

Pumice, falling from nearby volcanoes and forming a layer from 2 to 4.5 m thick, caused *P. ponderosa* to decline and to be replaced once more by *P. contorta*. Throughout the rest of the post-Pleistocene, ponderosa pine gained, but then another pumice fall, from 5000 to 10,000 years ago, again destroyed this pine either by burying the seedlings or "because of further fire" and once again made the ground available to *P. contorta* (Hansen, 1942). At present, the site is occupied by *P. ponderosa*.

During the Pleistocene, pines also grew in the northern Great Basin. Hansen (1947) found that, in late Pleistocene and early postglacial times, because of moister climate, pine forests occupied, in the northern part of the Great Basin, a larger area than at present. When later the climate became drier and warmer, forests including pines retreated upward on the slopes and were reduced in their areal extent. *Pinus contorta,* in the northern Great Basin, was not the pioneer invader as in the glaciated areas farther north. On the contrary, because of the absence of edaphic disturbances, *P. monticola* No. 4 and *P. ponderosa* persisted in the northern Great Basin during the late Pleistocene and into the postglacial times. *Pinus contorta* was abundant only locally, where fire occurred or where the ground was covered with volcanic ashes and pumice.

*Pinus monticola* No. 4 was abundant early in postglacial times, "reflecting the cool, moist climate" (Hansen, 1942). Later, because the climate became warmer and drier, this pine declined and never regained its former importance. Only in a few places did it increase and maintain itself because of local favorable conditions.

*Pinus ponderosa* No. 14 was predominant in the northern Great Basin during the postglacial period, except in the early part, when *P. monticola* was most abundant. Apparently, *P. ponderosa* occupied slopes of the mountains. As the postglacial period progressed and the climate became warmer and drier, this pine rapidly expanded. There were also minor fluctuations throughout the postglacial period in response to warming or cooling of the climate. Of course, we should realize that what was described by Hansen had taken place in the northern outskirts of the Great Basin. In the rest of it, pines most likely never had formed dense forests but occurred in parklike groves. With the uplift of the Sierra Nevada, as described previously, pines almost completely disappeared. Some such as *P. lambertiana* No. 3 perished. Others such as *P. aristata* No. 6 were preserved only in a few high places where they could find less heat and slightly more moisture. Still other pines originated somewhere in the south (as Axelrod suggested) and became piñons; these pines, having been already equipped to withstand drought, slowly reoccupied slopes of the Great Basin ranges.

In an article on postglacial forests in British Columbia, Hansen (1950) came to the conclusion that there *P. contorta* has maintained its own or even expanded, not so much because of climatic changes after glaciation as because of frequent and extensive fires.

That pines were not too numerous in North America before the glacial age was indicated by Beals (1957), who studied the preglacial forests buried in Indiana during the Pleistocene. These were not pine forests but mostly conifers of spruce-larch type. Perhaps, pines were not too abundant even in Alaska before and during the Pleistocene. Chaney and Mason (1936) failed to find pines in the Pleistocene frozen muck near Fairbanks, Alaska.

Clisby, Foreman, and Sears (1959) found pine pollen in Pliocene-Pleistocene sediments in Playa Lake, San Augustin, New Mexico. At the end of the Tertiary and into the Quaternary pine was there, and apparently abundant, and it was mixed with *Pterocarya* and other broadleaf temperate-climate trees. As a whole, the pine was ecologically a component of a woodland type. During the Pleistocene (Wisconsin) time in the uplands of the coastal plains of southwestern North Carolina, where *P. palustris* No. 22 and *P. taeda* No. 24 now grow, *P. banksiana* No. 32 and possibly *P. glabra* No. 26 were to be found. Buell (1945) suggested that, in the Pleistocene, pines invaded the area after fires had destroyed the broadleaf forest (see Chapter 6).

Raup (1946) suggested that there are no indications of the presence of extensive forests including *P. banksiana* No. 32 and *P. contorta* No. 16 in the Peace River and the Athabaska River basins until the postglacial warm and dry period, which occurred from 4000 to 8000 years ago. It appears possible, then, that absence of extensive pine forests before the Ice Age was a rather widespread and common feature of the landscape in the north of the continent.

In the eastern United States, where glaciation reached New York and northwestern New Jersey, pines—*P. banksiana* No. 32 and *P. resinosa* No. 21, for sure, and possibly *P. strobus* No. 20—migrated south as far as North Carolina and Texas, and with the retreat of the ice the three pines were among the pioneers that occupied the newly available area. Dr. Hugh Iltis, of the University of Wisconsin (personal communication), believes that such a migration through a dense eastern deciduous forest was not possible. In the northern and northwestern glaciated parts of New Jersey, the initial pine-spruce association was gradually replaced by pine (Potzger and Otto, 1943).

Potzger (1946) showed very well that pines were dominant in eastern North America during the postglacial period. In 1956, a paper by Potzger and Courtemanche (1956) was published (shortly after Potzger's death, in 1955), dealing with behavior of pines in the northeastern part of America during late glacial and postglacial times. The authors postulated five major climatic changes in Quebec during the period studied. The initial warm period was marked by the prominence of *P. banksiana*. During the subsequent major xerothermic period, this pine, or perhaps its immediate ancestor, was replaced partially by *P. resinosa* No. 21 and *P. strobus* No. 20. During the warm, dry period, these two pines extended their range northward to the latitude of 51½° N. In some places, *P. banksiana* replaced the two other pines. In other areas, it formed, with *Picea mariana*, a forest type that exists north of 48° even today.

Cain and Cain (1948) found that, in southeastern Michigan, *P. banksiana* had its period of greatest abundance immediately after the spruce-fir period. *Pinus resinosa* was also there, but it never became very important. *Pinus strobus* came later.

In another locality (Oakland County, Michigan), as shown by Cain and his co-workers (Cain, Cain, and Thomson, 1951), behavior of the three pines varied somewhat, but essentially the picture of pine succession was about the same as in other localities.

Although the direct "killing" effect on pines of the great Pleistocene glaciation was restricted only to the northern part of the continent, its influence was felt far beyond the southern limits of ice.

Potzger and Tharp (1947) studied pollen deposits in Lee County, Texas. During the glacial age, the climate there was cooler than now. When the glaciers advanced to the Ohio Valley of Indiana, the climate was suitable for pines to migrate southward to Texas. Present-day southern pines were already growing there during the Pleistocene.

In the Piedmont of South Carolina, Cain (1944, p. 135) found an "abundance of pine pollen," which was identified as that of *P. banksiana*. This pine does not grow now south of northeastern New York and the southern end of Lake Michigan. Dr. Hugh Iltis (personal letter) believes that claims of occurrence of *P. banksiana* pollen in South Carolina are errors caused by mistaken identity of the pollen. Moreover, disturbing reports are found in the literature, indicating that too much significance is given to the results of pollen analysis. Deevey (1939) and also Potzger and Richards (1942) think that *P. banksiana* pollen cannot be distinguished from the pollen of other fossil pines. One of Cain's students (Grayson, 1954) also complained about the difficulty of differentiation of pine pollen.

There has been a great deal of interpretation of pollen analyses by Potzger and his associates, by Deevey, and by others. It seems that some investigators assigned to pines a certain climatic niche in the past when the climate was assumed to be favorable to them. But in the past, as at present, the same species might have been growing under very different environmental conditions. One should be careful in assigning a particular environmental position to any pine species of the past.

Dansereau (1953) has shown clearly how dangerous it is to assume that, if a pine species is growing under such and such climatic conditions now, it must have been growing under the same climatic conditions during previous geological ages. Moreover, some species have shown great stability, while others differentiated continuously. Processes determining stability and others determining variability are at work, and very little is known about them. Mason's study of evolution of closed-cone pines during the Pleistocene showed well how some ancient pines perished or merely held their own while others were developing rapidly (Mason, 1932).

Physiological changes are not necessarily accompanied by morphological changes. This has been suggested by Dansereau, and it previously
had been amply shown by Penfold and his associates, working with
Myrtaceae of Australia (Penfold, 1935). Pines, however, have possessed
two characteristics since the Mesozoic origin of the genus: their xeromorphy and their ability to endure direct sunlight. These characteristics
may be considered as generally the same throughout the whole paleobotanical history of the pines. (See Chapter 6.)

In reviewing the history of Cenozoic plants bordering the northern
basin of the Pacific, Chaney (1936a) suggested that the major movements
of the plants in this region have been southward, because of a progressive
trend toward cooling and drying since the early Tertiary. Secondary
movements in the opposite direction have occurred and have played a
part in establishing the modern vegetation. Pines constituted a part of
the Cenozoic forest on both sides of the North Pacific, and they also
followed the migration pattern outlined by Chaney for the major forms of
vegetation. To quote from Chaney's essay: "The gradual shifting southward of the northern limits of most of the Eocene species . . . has resulted in their shifting to the lower latitudes of Asia and America . . . in
the forests of which there is a remarkable correspondence of genera on
both sides of the Pacific."

Under changing conditions of climate, the temperate Miocene flora
moved from the northern regions and "became widely established in the
middle latitudes of both continents" (Chaney, 1936a). Later in the
Tertiary, many genera disappeared from the middle latitudes; some such
as *Sequoia* became restricted to a relatively small area; pines, however,
survived. After the late Tertiary uplift of the Cascades and the Sierra
Nevada, the relatively uniform floras of the middle Tertiary became
diversified. A modified type of Miocene flora has migrated from the West
Coast of North America as far as Guatemala (Chaney, 1936a), where the
genus *Pinus*, together with other western genera, now occupies the highlands above the subtropical vegetation of the lower slopes.

## Mexico, Central America, and the Caribbean Islands

Engler's (1882) neotropical floristic region largely occupies the tropical parts of South America from Colombia to southern Brazil. But it also
includes most of Mexico, Central America, the Caribbean islands, and
the southern part of Florida. In these parts of the neotropical region—
from the United States–Mexico border and southern Florida to Nicaragua
—pine forests commonly occupy extensive areas.

**Physiography.** The historical geology of Mexico and Central America
is, briefly, as follows: Folded mountains of Mexico were formed at the

end of the Cretaceous period. During the Miocene, almost the entire Central Mexican Plateau (Mesa Central) was covered with lava.

The mountain chains of Mexico are made up the the Sierra Madre Occidental in the west, a broad and rugged extension of the North American Cordillera, rising to about 3000 m, and the much narrower Sierra Madre Oriental in the east. Between these lies the Mexican volcanic plateau.

These two Sierras of northern Mexico are connected with numerous pine-clad mountain ranges extending across the country approximately from southeastern Jalisco on the Pacific side, through the state of Puebla, to the state of Veracruz. Here are located the mighty volcanoes of Mexico—Citlaltepetl, or Orizaba, 5500 m; Popocatepetl, 5450 m; and Iztaccihuatl, 5300 m. Along the Pacific Coast, in the states of Guerrero and Oaxaca, lies the Sierra Madre del Sur. Mexico City is located on the Central Mexican Plateau at an elevation of about 2400 m. From Mexico City the North American continent trends eastward. The Central Mexican Plateau descends to the lowland of Tehuantepec. According to Schuchert (1955), Tehuantepec was above water in the Lower and Middle Eocene. In the Upper Eocene, it was submerged, and it remained under water through the Oligocene and Miocene. During the Pliocene, the land contact between Mexico and Central America was re-established. As it appears now, the Tehuantepec Lowland is a difficult terrain for pines to cross. Farther east lies the Yucatán peninsula, which is essentially a flat plain, and the mountains of Chiapas and of Central America. Yucatán remained submerged throughout the Tertiary period (only partly appearing above water during the Upper Eocene). Along the Gulf of Mexico coast and the coast of the Pacific, between the sea and the Sierras bordering the plateau, lie narrow strips of lowland—the Mexican Tierra Caliente.

Connections between Central America and Caribbean islands were intermittent; a connection existed during the Middle Eocene, but in the Upper Eocene the connection was lost.* During the Miocene, Central America was connected with Hispaniola; apparently, there have been no land connections with any Caribbean islands since that time.

Southern Florida, which we have to consider in context with the geomorphology of the Caribbean area, appeared above water only in the Pleistocene.

I should also mention another geomorphological feature of Central America—the Nicaragua lowland. South of it, mountains again rise high, forming the Cordilleras of Costa Rica.

---

* Earlier maps by Schuchert (1935) showed land connections during the Upper Miocene between Central America and western Cuba.

Present occurrence of pines in Mexico and the Caribbean area was mentioned on page 30 and in Table 2–1. It may be added that, in Mexico, pines are restricted to the mountains, while, in Central America, one species (*P. caribaea*) grows at sea level along the Caribbean coast of British Honduras, Guatemala, Honduras, and Nicaragua. *Pinus caribaea* and four other pine species are found in the Caribbean area.

**Paleobotany.** Apparently, no fossil pines were ever found in the floras south of the United States–Mexico border. Berry (1923) failed to find pines or any other conifers in Miocene strata in Tehuantepec. Neither have there been any findings of fossil pines in the Caribbean area (Berry, 1921, 1922, 1939; Hollick, 1924).

**Migration of Pines.** From before the Upper Cretaceous, Central America was separated from South America by the sea. Therefore, any possibility of migration of the genus *Pinus* from South America has to be ruled out. During the Jurassic, pines already could have been found in northern Eurasia and, apparently, in western North America (cf. page 30), and, during the Cretaceous, they were flourishing and differentiated considerably in many parts of the Northern Hemisphere. Moreover, fossil pines have never been found in South America—a fact, according to Florin (1940), of utmost significance.* Therefore, we may conclude that pines migrated to Mexico from the north.

Since the Central Mexican Plateau became available to invasion by pines only after the Miocene volcanic activity ceased, Wulff (1944) concluded that the existence of the pine forests of Mexico (and thus Central America and the Caribbean islands) does not go farther back than the second half of the Tertiary, possibly the end of that period. But, as Chaney once remarked, there is a great difference between the existence of forests in the past and the occurrence of species of which the forest was composed. It is not improbable that pine species penetrated to Mexico much earlier, probably at the very beginning of the Tertiary, and not later than the Miocene. The pine forests were developed later.

Two migration routes were available: one along the West Coast ranges, and the other around the Gulf of Mexico. The latter route is well known to botanists. It appears that pines penetrated to Mexico via both routes.

Berry, as early as 1930, remarked that the present flora of eastern Mexico shares many genera with the Eocene Wilcox Flora of the Mississippi embayment (Berry, 1930). When Sharp (1951) compared the Eocene Wilcox Flora with the present vegetation of eastern Mexico, he remarked that pines were lacking in the Wilcox Flora but suggested that perhaps they were poorly preserved there. "Perhaps pollen analysis of

---

* On page 93 of Florin's book, we read, "A negative feature of great importance is . . . the total absence in the southern hemisphere [of fossils] of all Pinaceae."

the Wilcox Clays would change the picture," as, may I add, Penny's pollen analyses have changed the picture of the Magothy Flora (Penny, 1947). Thus far, however, as Sharp (1951) said, there was still no evidence that any pine was a part of the flora in the region adjoining the basin of Wilcox deposition.

Miranda and Sharp (1950), in describing forests of the temperate regions of eastern Mexico, listed several species of essentially north-temperate genera, common to Mexico and the eastern part of the United States. To quote Miranda and Sharp,

. . . the floristic dissimilarities which exist between eastern and western United States appear to extend into Mexico but with diminished intensity. There are species of *Alnus, Quercus* and *Pinus,* whose relationships are with the flora of western United States, growing in the communities of eastern Mexico along with the species of *Liquidambar, Nyssa, Carpinus, Ostrya* and other genera whose affinities distinctly lie with plants in the vegetation of the eastern United States.

Pine forests of the eastern escarpment of the Central Mexican Plateau, as described by Miranda and Sharp (1950), consist in the northern part, from San Luis Potosí to Veracruz, of *P. patula* No. 61 and a variety of *P. pseudostrobus* No. 54, both sometimes forming pure forests.

Steyermark (1950), describing the origin of the flora of Guatemala, mentioned that some plants of that country resemble those of the eastern United States, while others are related to the species of the southwestern United States or of the Rocky Mountains. Pine forests of Guatemala are not only a continuation of Mexican pine forests, but they have a close resemblance to the forests of the southwestern Rocky Mountains, especially those of New Mexico.

Steyermark is of the opinion that, since the Appalachian and Ozark uplands have been unglaciated and have remained above the sea since the end of the Paleozoic, the flora confined to the uplands is likely to be of ancient origin. Many plants migrated from the Appalachian and Ozark uplands into the coastal plains and farther south around the Gulf of Mexico and eventually reached Central America. Probably, they represent some of the oldest elements of the Guatemalan flora.

Steyermark further stated that

. . . during the *early part* of the Tertiary period, following widespread submergence by Cretaceous seas in Guatemala and the West Central part of the United States, the area of the eastern United States (especially the Appalachian and Ozark regions), most of Mexico and part of Central America was opened to continuous plant migration. Then, following later Tertiary uplifts, many of the land connections were disrupted and much of the flora failed to survive.

Many species of plants (and among them, of course, pines) now occur in remote places, hundreds of miles from their stations in Mexico or the

United States. These are early Tertiary migrants from the Appalachian or Ozark uplands. Generally, however, western American pines played a larger part in the development of the Mexican pines. Steyermark (1950) fully recognized the importance of both the eastern and the western United States in shaping the Mexican and Central American flora.

The Cretaceous sea (see map, Fig. 2–2, page 29) divided the continent into two parts; subsequent development of the eastern and western floras was different. The elements of the flora of the eastern United States reached Mexico and Central America rather early, possibly in the early Tertiary, when the country all the way to Guatemala was low-lying and "peneplained, and previous to the later uplifts" (Braun, 1955). Western United States pines may have migrated to Mexico and Central America either before or coincidentally with the last Oligocene uplift, i.e., either when the eastern migration took place or as late as the Pliocene. This was the conclusion reached by Steyermark (1950) in regard to many components of the Mexican–Central American flora, and this conclusion is equally valid for pines. Braun (1955) reviewed the subject thoroughly. It appeared that, from the eastern United States, pines came to Mexico not later than the middle of the Tertiary period. There is no evidence of opportunity for free interchange between the southeastern United States and the highlands of Mexico since Pliocene times.

Pines penetrated to Mexico from the western United States, apparently, not later than the middle of the Tertiary period. Martin and Harrell (1957), after a careful consideration of the problem, suggested that Tertiary migration of plants from the north to Mexico took place at the latest by the mid-Cenozoic.

The conclusions of Steyermark, and of Martin and Harrell, are important not only for a better understanding of migration of pines to Mexico but also for explaining how pines reached the Bahamas and the Antilles. Of course, expansion of pines in the Caribbean region, such as the post-Tertiary penetration of pines from Yucatán to western Cuba, or the appearance of pines in the Bahamas, probably cannot be explained without accepting the possibility of over-water migration (Asprey and Robbins, 1953).

Perhaps the easiest way to resolve the problem of migration of pines to the Caribbean area would be to say that when the pines reached Florida from the north they somehow established themselves in several Caribbean islands. But Florida never had Tertiary land connections with the Caribbean islands. Moreover, there was little chance of seeds being carried by air currents from the continent to the islands, for the high-velocity winds in the Caribbean are toward Florida and not from it.

On the other hand, there were land connections between Central America and the Antilles during the early Tertiary, in the Eocene and in the

Miocene (Schuchert, 1935). Pines might have penetrated to the Caribbean islands via these Tertiary land bridges.

The southern, neotropical part of Florida offers an interesting problem in the distribution of pines. Florida was under water from the Upper Jurassic to the Miocene, and its southern half even through the Pleistocene (Schuchert, 1935, Maps 67 to 84). Uphof (1938) said that many plants migrated to southern Florida from the Antilles during postglacial times. Most likely, *P. elliottii* var. *densa* No. 63 penetrated there by the same route. It arrived in southern Florida rather recently, since the mid-Wisconsin recession (Davis, 1943). *Pinus elliottii* var. *elliottii* and *P. palustris* came to Florida from the north, but they have not reached the southern part of the state.

The Bahamas emerged only during or after the Pleistocene and have never been connected with the other islands of the Caribbean. Migration of pines to the Bahamas was apparently airborne and recent.

The whole problem of pines of the Caribbean area including southern Florida was discussed in a complete and scholarly fashion by Little and Dorman (1954). Apparently, *P. caribaea* No. 62 already existed on the islands before the Pliocene and over a larger and more or less connected area. According to Florin (1933), it became disjoined late in the Tertiary. Its present large and disjunct distribution suggests a relatively old age.

*Pinus caribaea* No. 62 occurs on at least six of the Bahama Islands, but the other three Caribbean pines do not grow there. Little and Dorman (1954) suggested that this type of distribution might be caused by different factors such as a rapid rate of migration of *P. caribaea*, or its greater age, and the irregularities in distribution could have been caused also by the uncertainties and slowness of migration of pines across the water. Little and Dorman also noted that the flora of the West Indies, in general, is related to that of Central America and, to a much lesser degree, to that of southern Florida. They reviewed Seifriz' (1943) work on migration of plants in the Caribbean and suggested that strong winds, especially hurricanes from the southeast, and migrating birds may have aided dispersal of pine seeds to the United States (chiefly to Florida). Seifriz suggested that there were lesser, but still very strong, ties of the Caribbean islands with southern North America through Mexico and Florida. The Mexican route, in a broad sense, i.e., including the route from the United States, was the more probable path for penetration of pines to the Caribbean area than the across-the-water route from Florida.

## Summary

Throughout the Mesozoic and Cenozoic eras, up to the middle of the Pleistocene, North America was intermittently connected with north-

eastern Asia. Since the Upper Cretaceous, there have been land connections extending from the area of the present Bering Sea to eastern North
America. In the northeast, the land extended, until the middle of the
Cenozoic era, to Greenland, Iceland, and northern Europe. Thus, land
routes for migration of pines in the northern part of the continent had
been open for a long time.

In the Lower Upper Cretaceous and the first part of the Tertiary, the
North American Cordillera was much lower than it is now, and there
was not much difference in the general composition of North American
forests. Pines were found all over present-day Canada and the United
States, except perhaps the extreme south of the latter (Texas). The pines
did not occupy extensive areas but, rather, occurred as admixtures to the
prevailing subtropical or temperate forests in places where competition
was not too pressing, such as in the marginal areas, in the dry uplands,
or on the exposed mineral soil of the mountain slopes.

General migration of pines in America was from the northwest to the
south down the coast of the Pacific (Chaney, 1936a), east to the eastern
United States, and northeast to Greenland and Europe. With the rising
of the Cordillera in the middle of the Miocene, with the decrease of
precipitation in the west, and with the general cooling of the climate,
eastern and western forests became different. Most of the broadleaf trees
disappeared from the west. Among the conifers, *Sequoia* disappeared
from the east and *Taxodium* disappeared from the west. Pines, however,
possibly because of their ancestral xeromorphism, have survived both in
the west and in the east, disappearing gradually from the southern parts
of the Great Plains but maintaining a continuous belt in the north. *Pinus
ponderosa* No. 14 in northeastern Nebraska and in the eastern panhandle
of Oklahoma, apparently, is a relic of the old Tertiary western pines that
survived east of the Rocky Mountains.

In the West, drastic readjustments took place among the pines. With
the rise of the Sierra Nevada and the Cascades, pines of the Great Basin
either perished or moved to higher elevations in search of more moisture.
Apparently, at that time, piñon pines were evolved from the haploxylon
pines. Secondary migrations occurred in this group in a direction opposite
to the southward migration routes of pines. The general migration, however, continued south until pines reached Nicaragua; from Central America, they migrated northeast to the Caribbean area.

General cooling, toward the end of the Tertiary and, especially, the
Quaternary glaciation, destroyed the pine forests of the north. Species
such as *P. monticola*, and several other pines that had grown in the Arctic
before the Ice Age, became extinct there. *Pinus contorta* survived in
places not covered with ice, and, after the ice retreated, it became a
pioneer in re-establishing the pine forests in the northwest of Canada.

Other pines—*P. flexilis* No. 2, *P. albicaulis* No. 1, *P. ponderosa* No. 14— appeared later and only in the southern part of the previously glaciated area.

From the Northeast, the glaciation caused the Pleistocene pines— *P. banksiana* No. 32, *P. resinosa* No. 21, and possibly *P. strobus* No. 20—to migrate south. Possibly, there existed in the Northeast some refugia for pines, within the glaciated area itself.

## THE ARCTIC REGION

## Physiography

North of the present forest zones of both America and Eurasia lies the Arctic Zone, with its barrens and tundra. It also includes several archipelagoes and very large islands. Many islands are covered with ice.

Greenland, the largest island in the world, is about 2400 km long and about 1200 km wide. It is located northeast of the North American continent, between 11° 40′ and 73° 8′ west. From north to south, it lies between 59° 45′ and 83° 39′ north. Geologically, it is a part of the Pre-Cambrian Canadian Shield (Laurentian Plateau).

Geomorphologically, Greenland is a basin with mountains on the periphery. The highest peak is about 3650 m. Most of Greenland is covered with an ice cap from about 2000 to over 2400 m thick. Only some of the coastal land is free of ice at the present time.

Greenland is separated from the arctic islands of North America by Robson Strait and Smith Strait in the north and by Baffin Sea and Davis Strait in the south. Greenland was connected with the American continent even before the Mesozoic era and until the Pliocene (Schuchert, 1955), and perhaps much later, until the beginning of the Quaternary (Wulff, 1944).

Iceland lies east of southern Greenland and about 800 km from Scotland. Its location is approximately between 63½° and 66½° north and between 13½° and 24½° west. Its central plateau is about 600 to 760 m above sea level, and its highest mountain is over 3100 m. There are active volcanoes on the island, and, in its southwestern parts, glaciers. At present, there are no natural pine forests on the island.

Spitzbergen is located east of northern Greenland. It is an archipelago of several large islands. The total area of the archipelago is about 62,000 sq. km, and its boundaries are near 74° and 81° north and 10° and 35° east. The islands are remains of a dissected plateau whose elevations run up to about 1700 m. The archipelago is located about 650 km from Norway and about the same distance from Greenland.

## Paleobotany

During the Mesozoic (Jurassic and Cretaceous) and early in the Tertiary, the flora of the Arctic region was of a temperate character. Pines occurred in the Arctic region during the Mesozoic era. Two Jurassic pines from Spitzbergen were described by Heer (1876): *P. prodromus* Heer and *P. nordenskiöldi* Heer. The latter was also found in the Lena River area at 70° to 71° north (Krishtofovich, 1941). From the material collected in the southern part of the island Novaia Sibir, in the New Siberian Archipelago in the Arctic, Schmalhausen (Krishtofovich, 1941) described a pine that he thought was of the Miocene age. Baikovskaia (1956), however, came to the conclusion that this flora was of the Upper Cretaceous age. Cretaceous species *P. vaginalis* Heer, *P. quenstedti*, and *P. staratchini* Heer were reported from Greenland (Heer, 1875), and *P. peterseni, P. quenstedti,* and *P. staratchini* were reported from Spitzbergen (Heer, 1876).

Although some other conifers (firs, hemlocks) were reported by Heer under *Pinus,* there were several real pines, both haploxylon and diploxylon. *Pinus quenstedti* later was found in several more southerly places on the North American continent. Recently, Langenheim, Smiley, and Gray (1960) found that winged pollen grains of the *Picea* and *Pinus* types were abundant in Cretaceous deposits throughout the area near Wainwright, Alaska, southwest of Point Barrow.

In the Eocene, pines were growing in many places in the American Arctic. *Pinus armstrongi* Heer was described from Banksland; *P. bathursti,* from Bathurstland; *P. maclurii* Heer, from Banksland and from Yukon Territory; and *P. nordenskiöldi,* also from Yukon (Heer, 1868). Heer found remains of a pine, *Pinus* sp., from the Eocene, in the Mackenzie River area, Northwest Territory, Canada; another pine (also without a specific name) was found by Heer (1869) in the Kenai formation of the Eocene at Port Graham, in southern Alaska.

Heer (1868) described several Miocene pines from the arctic islands lying north and northwest of Canada. These are listed in Table 2–2.

From Greenland came *P. crameri, P. hyperborea,* and *P. peterseni.* From the Miocene of Spitzbergen, Heer described *P. polaris,* which is the same as *P. wheeleri* Cockerell. A Tertiary *P. arctica* Schmalhausen was reported from the New Siberian Islands. Possibly it was not *Pinus* but *Larix.* Another pine from these islands was identified only as to the genus (Krishtofovich, 1941).

Even before the Quaternary glaciation—during the second half of the Tertiary—pines disappeared from Greenland, Spitzbergen, and other islands of the Arctic.

**Table 2–2.** Miocene Pines of the Arctic Region

| Species | Locality |
|---------|----------|
| P. aemula | Iceland |
| P. armstrongi | Banksland |
| P. bathursti | Bathurstland |
| P. brachyptera | Iceland |
| P. ingulfiana | Steenstrup Island |
| P. maccluri | Banksland |
| P. martinsi | Steenstrup Island and Iceland |
| P. microsperma | Steenstrup Island |
| P. pannonica Ung. | Kenai, Alaska |
| P. steenstrupiana | Steenstrup Island |
| P. thulensis | Iceland |
| P. sp. | Mackenzie River |

## Migration of Pines

Greenland was once connected with North America. On the other hand, it was also connected with Spitzbergen. Pines penetrated to Greenland from America; from Greenland, they migrated to western Europe.

Migration of pines from America to Europe could have been accomplished along the same routes used by most plants, i.e., one via southern Greenland and Iceland and the other via northern Greenland and Spitzbergen (Steffen, 1937).

Pines of the Arctic Coast of eastern Siberia are apparently of a different origin. Discovery of a pre-Pleistocene *P. monticola* near the mouth of the Omoloi (approximately 71° north and 135° east) suggests this possibility (Sukachev, 1910). It is doubtful that pines advanced from northeastern Siberia as far west as Spitzbergen; there are no reports of the occurrence of pines in the Russian arctic islands, i.e., on Severnaia Zemlia, Novaia Zemlia, or any of the numerous islands of Franz Joseph Land. Pines, however, have been found on the New Siberian Islands.

Wulff (1944, p. 350) suggested that the arctic flora had its origin in northeastern Asia (east of the Taimyr Peninsula) and also in Alaska, i.e., on both sides of the present Bering Strait. This suggestion is of utmost importance, for it suggests that the same general, possibly more southerly, location was the place where pines originated.

## Summary

Pines were to be found in the Arctic in the Mesozoic era and until the middle of the Tertiary period. Having begun to disappear from the arctic islands during the latter part of the Tertiary, when the climate deteriorated, they migrated from America to the western arctic islands via Greenland. Not much is known regarding fossil pines of the eastern Arctic region, but, judging from findings on the New Siberian Islands, and especially on the Arctic Coast of Siberia, pines arrived there from the opposite direction, i.e., from the east.

## EASTERN ASIA

### Physiography

The pine region of eastern Asia includes Japan, the Ryukyus, Korea, adjacent parts of the Soviet Union (Maritime Province, located between the Ussuri River in the west and the coast in the east), the Lower Amur, Sakhalin, the peninsula of Kamchatka, the Kurile Islands, and most of China (except its southwestern part, which will be considered as a part of southeastern Asia). Formosa also is included in the eastern Asiatic region.

In the northeast, the region is well defined. It is distinctly separated by the Bureia Mountains from the pine region of northern Eurasia, although *P. pumila* No. 68, whose area lies chiefly in eastern Siberia, also occurs in Korea and on the Island of Sakhalin, the Kuriles, and the islands Hokkaido and Honshu, of Japan.

In the north, and as far east as approximately the one hundred and twenty-fourth meridian, the pine region of eastern Asia is separated by deserts from the Siberian pine forests. In the south, pines of the eastern-Asia region gradually merge into the pine region of southeastern Asia.

Wulff (1944) suggested that, in the Tertiary period, the floristic province of eastern Asia extended farther north, reaching the present Arctic Zone of Asia. Occurrence of *P. monticola* in northeastern Siberia during the late Tertiary (Sukachev, 1910) lends good support to this statement.

**China.** In China, the region essentially occupies a country gradually descending from the northwestern mountain ranges toward the Pacific. Mighty rivers flow from the mountains, cutting deep valleys on their way toward the ocean. The mountain system of Tsin-Ling-Shan divides the whole of China into northern (plains) * and southern (mountains) parts.

The coastal area between the Yangtze and Hwan Ho and farther north to Tientsin is a lowland, and pines do not grow there. *Pinus densiflora* No. 95, however, occurs on the Shantung peninsula.

**Korea.** The peninsula of Korea extends from the mainland approximately between 124° and 128° east and from 34° to 40° north. It is separated from the Japanese archipelago by Tsushima Strait. Pines occur sparsely in Korea.

* There are also high mountains in the north (in the province of Kansu).

**Sakhalin.** The island of Sakhalin lies north of Japan. It is located between 46° and 54° north. Two mountain ranges extend along the whole island, with a depression between. This type of geomorphology is observed in several places of northeastern Siberia and also along the West Coast of North America (Mirov, 1951). Sakhalin is separated from the mainland by a strait, which, at its narrowest part, is less than 10 km wide. Cretaceous, Tertiary, and post-Pliocene rocks are widely distributed on the island.

The main mountain-forming processes occurred on the island between the Pliocene and the time of the advance of the post-Pliocene sea. Before that time, Sakhalin had been connected with the mainland. At present, only one species of pine grows there—*P. pumila,* which forms thickets below the alpine zone.

**Kamchatka.** The peninsula of Kamchatka is located between 51° and 60° north. Its northeastern part is connected with the mainland by a stretch of tundra that has acted as an efficient barrier preventing penetration of plants and animals from the continent (Mirov, 1951).

The peninsula is about 1200 km long, and its greatest width is about 480 km. Topographically, Kamchatka consists essentially of two parallel mountain ranges with a depression between, and lowland areas along the coasts. A spectacular volcanic region of Kamchatka is located on a high, hilly plain between the eastern range and the Bering Sea. Of seventy-four volcanoes on the east coast, thirteen are active. Kliuchevskaia Sopka (a volcano) is 4850 meters high.

Kamchatka is situated on the outskirts of a monsoon-climate region, which in that part of the world entails a great deal of cold drizzle and fog in summer. The only pine of Kamchatka is *P. pumila,* which grows at altitudes between 500 and 2000 m, forming thickets on the rocky southern slopes (Suslov, 1947). Below this belt is located the spruce-larch-birch forest zone; above it are alpine meadows and highland tundra.

**The Kuriles.** The Kurile Islands extend from the tip of Kamchatka to the Japanese island of Hokkaido. They form a chain of thirty-five large and twenty smaller islands, which are essentially volcanic cones of lava that broke through the Paleozoic and Mesozoic sediments of an ancient geosyncline (Mirov, 1951).

The northern islands are covered with arctic-alpine vegetation; on the slopes of the mountains grows trailing *P. pumila* No. 68. On the southern islands there are fir-spruce forests; above these are birch groves; and still higher are impenetrable thickets of *P. pumila.* No fossil pines have been reported from the Kuriles.

**Japan.** During the Cretaceous and also early in the Tertiary, the Japanese archipelago was a part of the continent. The islands of Japan

were formed during the Tertiary, as a result of mountain-folding processes. In the Eocene and Oligocene, the sea covered the southern island,
Kyushu, and possibly the southwestern part of Honshu.

Japan became separated from the mainland during the Miocene; at the
beginning of that epoch, the northern part of the archipelago was under
water. During the Pliocene, the sea receded, and, early in this epoch, the
southern part of Japan again became connected with the continent. The
connection was disrupted toward the end of the Pliocene, and Japan has
maintained its insular position to the present time (Wulff, 1944).

**The Ryukyus.** The Ryukyu Islands form a 1000 km chain between
Japan and Formosa, separating the East China Sea from the Philippine
Sea. The larger islands are volcanic and mountainous; the smaller ones
are low and flat.

On the largest island, Okinawa, and on some lesser islands of the
Ryukyus grows the endemic pine, *P. luchuensis* No. 98. It is morphologically closely related to *P. hwangshanensis* No. 100 of the mainland.
No fossil pines have been reported from the Ryukyus. The general
location of the Ryukyu chain seems to indicate that the islands were
separated from the mainland at about the same time as Japan, i.e., at
the beginning of the Pliocene. Later, the archipelago was reunited with
the mainland. At the end of the Pliocene, the Ryukyus were again separated and assumed their present appearance.

**Formosa.** Formosa, or Taiwan, is located some 120 km from the
coast of China. The Tropic of Cancer crosses the island somewhat below
its middle. Formosa is 380 km long and 141 km wide. It has an extremely
rugged topography. The central mountain range runs from north to south;
to the east it drops sharply to the coast; in the west, the terrain slopes
into broad alluvial plains extending along most of the coast. The mountains are high and steep, with the two highest peaks, the Tz'u Kao Shan
to the north and Mount Morrison in the central part, both reaching altitudes of slightly under 4000 m. Formosa has been separated from Japan
and the Philippines since before the Pliocene, but it was still connected
with the mainland at the beginning of the Quaternary.

Apparently no fossil pines have been found in Formosa. Hayata
(1905) pointed out the close relationship between Japan and Formosa,
based on his study of the coniferous trees. However, Kanehira (1933)
suggested that this statement was based on erroneous identifications.
More recent studies indicate that relationship of the flora of Japan and
Formosa and also of Formosa and the Ryukyus is very weak. Pines of
Japan, of Formosa, and the only pine of the Ryukyus came, in each case,
directly from the mainland and did not migrate from one island to another.

## Present Distribution of Pines

The present distribution of pines (see Table 2–3) in eastern Asia is, broadly speaking, as follows: There is a complex of haploxylon pines represented in Japan by *P. pentaphylla* No. 83 and *P. himekomatsu* No. 84, in Formosa by *P. morrisonicola* No. 85. This complex extends to southeastern Asia.

*Pinus pumila* No. 68 occurs chiefly in northeastern Siberia, but it also is found in Manchuria, Korea, and Japan. *Pinus koraiensis* No. 82 grows in the Amur and Maritime provinces of Russia, in Korea, and in a few spots on the Japanese island of Honshu. The largest area of another haploxylon pine, *P. armandi* No. 86, is in the Tsing-Lin Mountains, but its outlying areas extend from Upper Burma, Yunnan, Kweichow, and the island of Hainan (all in the region of southeastern Asia) to the southern tip of Japan, to Formosa, and to Hupeh. The last three stations are in the region of eastern Asia. *Pinus bungeana* No. 87 grows in central China.

Of the diploxylon pines there are two in Japan and also in southern Korea: *P. thunbergii* No. 97 and *P. densiflora* Sieb. & Zucc. No. 95, which also occurs on the Shantung peninsula of China. *Pinus funebris* No. 96,

#### Table 2–3. Pines of Eastern Asia

| Subgenus *Haploxylon* | Subgenus *Diploxylon* |
|---|---|
| *P. pumila* No. 68 [a] | *P. massoniana* No. 94 [b] |
| *P. koraiensis* No. 82 | *P. densiflora* No. 95 |
| *P. pentaphylla* No. 83 | *P. funebris* No. 96 |
| *P. himekomatsu* No. 84 | *P. thunbergii* No. 97 |
| *P. morrisonicola* No. 85 | *P. luchuensis* No. 98 |
| *P. armandi* No. 86 [b] | *P. taiwanensis* No. 99 |
| *P. bungeana* No. 87 | *P. hwangshanensis* No. 100 |
| | *P. tabulaeformis* No. 102 and its numerous varieties |

Note: This tabulation shows an almost equal number of haploxylon (7) and diploxylon (8) pines in the region of eastern Asia.

[a] Also in the region of northeastern Eurasia (in eastern Siberia).
[b] Also in the region of southeastern Asia.

closely related to *P. densiflora*, is found in an isolated location on the sand hills in the Maritime Province of Russia and in adjacent parts of Korea.

The northern part of China is occupied by scattered *P. tabulaeformis* No. 102. The southern part of China, approximately between 32° and 19° north, and from the coast of the South China Sea to approximately the one hundred and fifth meridian, is the area of *P. massoniana* No. 94, which also ocurs in southwestern China, on Hainan, and on Formosa. *Pinus hwangshanensis* No. 100 is found occasionally within the *P. massoniana* area. *Pinus luchuensis* No. 98, as has been already mentioned, is an endemic of the Ryukyu Islands; *P. taiwanensis* No. 99 is native only in Formosa.

## Paleobotany

Krishtofovich (1941) found a Jurassic pine in the far eastern Martime Province of Russia and identified it as *P. nordenskiöldi* Heer. Kawasaki (1926) reported a Cretaceous pine (apparently, Albian) from southern Korea. Depape (1932) described a pine from Tertiary deposits of Weichang, Jehol (latitude 44° north; longitude 117° east), apparently closely related to *P. koraiensis* No. 82. Florin (1920) found pine seeds of the Middle(?) Tertiary in Mongolia, north of Kalgan; no closer identification was made.

During the Tertiary, pines grew on Sakhalin. Schenk (1888) found, in Tertiary deposits of the island, a diploxylon pine that he identified as *P. longifolia* Roxb. (now known as *P. roxburghii* No. 93). Krishtofovich (1941, page 407) lists two pines (*Pinus* spp.) from the early Tertiary of the Maritime Province. Heer described a Tertiary *P. podosperma* from near Lake Khanka, also in the Maritime Province.

Not much information is available on occurrence of fossil pines from continental China. Chaney and Hu (1940), who studied Miocene Flora from Shantung Province, could not find any pines there. They thought that lack of pines might have been caused by their occurrence on slopes so far above the sites of deposition that their foliage and seeds could not readily enter the sedimentary record.

Endo and Okutsu (1939) described, from Eocene marine shell beds of Sunakawa, Hokkaido, a pine that they named "*Pinus hokkaidoensis.*" Isizima (1936) discovered a fossil cone of a Tertiary pine also in Hokkaido. Its cone appeared to be similar to the cones of *P. parviflora* (i.e., *P. pentaphylla* No. 83). In his review of "Pinaceae of Japan," Miki (1957) listed nine fossil Tertiary pines; these were "especially rich in the Lower Pliocene." The following four were diploxylon pines:

1. *Pinus fujiii* Miki is strictly fossil pine. Its cones looked like those of *P. thunbergii* No. 97 but differed "in hooklike recurved umbo of cone scale. . . . Fossils which have the same characters were collected from Miocene bed of Noto by Isida and from tuff bed in Prefecture Giho by Hoigawa, also belonging to the Miocene."

2. *Pinus densiflora,* which is widespread in Japan now, was found in many places in the Pleistocene interglacial deposits.

3. *Pinus oligolepis* Miki, also an extinct pine, was found in a few localities in Japan, together with *Metasequoia, Glyptostrobus,* etc., in Pliocene beds.

4. *Pinus thunbergii* No. 97 is a living pine, growing on the seacoast of central and southern Japan. Abundant remains of this pine—cones, twigs, and leaves—were found in five localities of the Pliocene age and nineteen Pleistocene localities of the southern half of Japan.

Two Tertiary haploxylon pines described by Miki were *P. amamiana* Koidz (a variety of *P. armandi*) and *P. koraiensis* Sieb. & Zucc. Up to the date of Miki's publication of "Pinaceae of Japan," in 1957, this latter pine was collected from twenty-five localities. Usually, it was associated with *Picea jezonensis* and *Abies veitchii* in the Pleistocene glacials, except for a single (Pliocene) locality. It is still living in Japan. The remains of this pine occurred chiefly as seeds; cones (which are soft and perishable) were encountered very rarely. In addition, Miki described three other such pines: Remains of *P. parviflora* Sieb. & Zucc. (cones and seeds) were found in numerous localities in Pliocene and Pleistocene deposits. This pine, now split into two species—Nos. 83 and 84—still grows in Japan. *Pinus protodiphylla* Miki is a two-leaf haploxylon pine from two Pliocene floras and from one Pleistocene flora. According to Miki, a Miocene pine of similar characteristics was collected "by Y. Ooga at Sirakawa in Kobe City." It was named "*Pinus trifolia* Miki" (1939). The morphological characters of this pine were intermediate between those of haploxylon and diploxylon pines. Large cones of this three- or four-leaf pine, 9 to 14 cm long and 8 to 9 cm wide, are strikingly similar to the cones of *P. sabiniana* of California. The cones were in a perfect state of preservation. It has so far been found in the Seto and Tazinii districts in central Honshu, in Pliocene deposits.

Miki (1956) believes that *P. koraiensis* No. 82 came to Japan from the north during the Miocene. It grew in mountains and descended to lower elevations in the Pleistocene. Interesting are his reports that, whereas some Pleistocene pines—*P. fujiii, P. trifolia, P. protodiphylla,* and *P. oligolepsis*—became extinct, *P. densiflora* No. 95 not only survived but is still expanding. On the other hand, *P. koraiensis* No. 82, which covered extensive areas relatively recently, "during the cold ages of Pleistocene," has been on the decrease and now is found only in a few places.

Kolesnikov (1935) found *P. koraiensis* in an isolated area in the southern part of the Okhotsk region (in the drainage of the river Gorin). This finding indicated that, in Tertiary times, the pine was growing farther northeast than it does now (cf. Wulff, 1944, p. 449). But Neishtadt (1957) maintained there are no indications that *P. koraiensis* is a Tertiary relic in the Far Eastern region of Russia, i.e., in the Middle Amur and in the Maritime Province, between the seacoast and the Ussuri River, as well as in adjacent parts of Manchuria. This pine came to the Far Eastern region from the south and as late as Postglacial times (the Holocene). Previously, during the Pleistocene, *P. koraiensis* grew only south of the present border of Russia.

On the peninsula of Kamchatka, *P. pumila* No. 68 was growing during the Tertiary. During the Ice Age, only the mountains were glaciated in Kamchatka. There was no continuous ice cover, and pines could have survived there in the refugia of the lower elevations, as *P. ajanensis* did. *Pinus pumila* returned to the higher elevations only after the end of the Ice Age. The postglacial history of this pine, according to Neishtadt (1957), was as follows: It grew in Kamchatka during the beginning of the Holocene. In the early Holocene, it reached more or less its present limits of distribution (near Lake Baikal).

## Summary

The pine region of eastern Asia contains fifteen species of pines—seven haploxylon and eight diploxylon. *Pinus pumila* No. 68, extends deeply into the pine region of eastern Eurasia; *P. tabulaeformis* comes in contact with *P. yunnanensis* of the region of southeastern Asia. Pines generally do not form extensive forests in this region, occurring in groves or mixed as individual trees with other conifer and broadleaf species.

Sargent, in his introduction to Wilson's *A Naturalist in Western China* (Wilson, 1913), remarked that, in Korea and in adjacent parts of Manchuria and Russia, pines are scattered over a restricted area. His remarks hold also with respect to other pines of eastern Asia. As climatic conditions have not changed drastically in eastern Asia since the end of the Mesozoic and as the vegetation has retained its Tertiary character, it appears that, during that period, pines also did not form extensive forests but, rather, were scattered as they are now, mostly on the mountain slopes.

The fossil record of the region as a whole is good. Reports on occurrence of a Jurassic pine in Sakhalin and a Cretaceous pine in Korea are highly significant. Together with Miki's findings in Japan and considering absence of fossil pines farther south, they seem to indicate that migration of pines in eastern Asia has been from the north.

Scarcity of fossil records on pines in continental China does not mean that they were absent there during the Tertiary period; their habitat in the mountain slopes far above the sites of deposition was not favorable for preservation of their remains in sedimentary records. During Postglacial times, reversed migrations of some pines took place, but there, as in other regions, they were of a local and secondary character.

## SOUTHEASTERN ASIA

## Physiography

The pine region of southeastern Asia embraces southern China (chiefly the province of Yunnan and adjacent parts of Sikang and Szechwan) and the whole peninsula of Indochina, Burma, and Thailand. Westward it extends to the Khasi Hills of northeastern India, and in northern Burma it reaches the high mountains of the Himalaya. Along the Himalaya, a narrow pine zone extends farther west to eastern Afghanistan. The pine belt along the Himalaya is not exactly a part of southeastern Asia, although it begins there.

To the region of southeastern Asia belongs the pine-wooded northern part of the Philippines (northern Luzon and Mindoro). In Indonesia, on the island of Sumatra, the region extends somewhat south of the Equator. In the north, the region of southeastern Asia merges imperceptibly into the region of eastern Asia. The main range of *P. massoniana* Lamb. is in eastern Asia, but this pine also is found in the southwestern part of Szechwan and in northwestern Indochina. *Pinus armandi* grows on the mainland in the Tsin-Ling-Shan range, i.e., between the thirty-fourth and thirty-fifth parallels and also below the thirtieth parallel in Kweichow, and in Szechwan (including the former Sikang), extending to northeastern Burma. It is also found in Yunnan and on the island of Hainan. The boundary between eastern and southeastern Asia is roughly a line extending from the point where the Tropic of Cancer crosses the coast of China (i.e., at Swatow) northwest to the intersection of the one hundredth meridian and the thirtieth parallel.

The highland of Yunnan is a plateau reaching altitudes of 1800 to 2400 m, with occasional mountain ranges. At the latitude of 30° north in Szechwan, mountains may reach 7500 m, while valley floors may be located at 2500 m. Farther north lie high, dry grasslands merging into deserts.

East of Yunnan lies Upper Burma, with its Shan, Kachin, and Chin states; still farther east is Assam, of India, with the Naga Hills and the Khasi Hills, which gave the name to *P. khasya*.

The countries located south of Yunnan are Thailand, Laos, Cambodia, North Viet Nam, and South Viet Nam. Several big rivers—Irrawaddy, Salween, Mekong—flow from the high mountains of the north. Between the broad river valleys extend mountain ranges gradually decreasing in height. In Upper Burma, the mountain peaks may reach over 3000 m, but, in the pine region of South Shan State (near Taunggyi), the highest mountain is only a little over 2500 m. Generally elevations are much lower. Only in the Tenessarim range (which extends south to the Malay Peninsula), just south of Kanchanaburi, there may be higher summits (up to 2000 m). Farther south, down the Malay Peninsula, the terrain is moderately mountainous.

Thailand is mountainous only in its northern part (highest peak, 2576 m). The rest of the country is moderately hilly or is flat; so is Cambodia, where only in the southwest do the mountains reach over 1700 m.

Laos is, in places, a mountainous country. Viet Nam, except in its southern part, is rather mountainous—up to 3142 m near the Red River, 2598 m along the fifteenth parallel. Some summits rise to 2287 m. Near Dalat, at 12° north, however, the country is much lower.

Hainan island is located, roughly, between the eighteenth and twentieth parallels and between the one hundred and ninth and one hundred and eleventh meridians. Its northern, and especially northeastern, part is low. The more elevated portions are in the southeastern and central parts. Mountains do not reach great heights. The highest peak, Wuchih Shan, is only 1879 m high. The island is separated from the low-lying Luichow peninsula by a narrow strait—no wider than 30 km. The nearest mountains on the continent are those of Viet Nam, across the shallow part (not deeper than 50 m) of the Gulf of Tonkin. Hainan's connection with the mainland still existed at the beginning of the Quaternary period.

Connections between the Philippines and Formosa were broken in the early Tertiary. During the Eocene and Oligocene, most of the Philippine archipelago was already above water. During the Miocene, after a widespread submergence, intensive folding and faulting occurred. Then much of the Philippines submerged and Pliocene deposits were formed. Pliocene floras contained no pines. During the Pleistocene, much uplifting occurred, and through this period and well into the Holocene there occurred frequent and great depressions and elevations of the terrain.

The highlands of northern Luzon—higher than 1500 m—are covered with vegetation that is not tropical as in the lowlands. There are no bamboos, palms, or bananas; there are pine forests and shrubs and grasses typical of the temperate regions. These plants, and we are particularly concerned with pines, now found geographically in the very center of surrounding tropical vegetation, came from the mountain regions of the continent.

Sumatra, the only island of Indonesia where pines occur naturally, is about 1200 km long and about 400 km wide. It extends from northwest to southeast, alongside and south of the Malay Peninsula, from which it is separated by the narrow and not too deep Strait of Malacca. To the northwest lie the Nicobar and Andaman islands, and, in the southeast,

Sumatra is separated from Java by a 40-km strait (Selat Sunda). The northwestern part of Sumatra is hilly, with mountain peaks reaching over 3000 m. Farther southeast, the mountains press closer to the coast while the larger part of the island, facing northeast, is flat, occasionally swampy and intensively cultivated. One can see, on the crests of the mountains, conspicuous high peaks, of which magnificent Mount Korintji (or Kerintji), in the northwestern part of the Barisan range, about 1° 40′ south latitude, is the highest—about 3800 m.

## Present Distribution of Pines

The living pines of southeastern Asia are listed in Table 2–4.

*Pinus yunnanensis* is the pine of the province of Yunnan. It merges in the southwest with *P. khasya*. This latter grows from the Khasi Hills of India, intermittently in the South Shan Hills of Burma, southeast through northern Thailand, Laos, and Cambodia, to Viet Nam. *Pinus merkusii* grows in spots from South Shan State to Viet Nam. It reappears on Sumatra, where it crosses the Equator. It extends to the vicinity of the Korintji-peak area, some 2° south latitude. This is the southernmost locality of distribution of pines in the Old World. Pines do not occur naturally farther south, although on several islands of Indonesia they have been planted. There are no native pines on Java, on Borneo, or on Timor * as occasionally reported.

In the vicinity of Dalat, besides *P. khasya* and *P. merkusii*, there also grows a strange conifer described as *P. krempfii* (Lecomte, 1924). *Pinus dalatensis* of the same locality belongs, according to Ferré (1960), to the *P. griffithii* group. Farther north, between Hué and the Bolovens, there occurs a *"pin du moyen Annam"* (Ferré, 1960), a haploxylon pine whose

**Table 2–4.** Species of Genus *Pinus* in Southeastern Asia

| Subgenus *Haploxylon* | Subgenus *Diploxylon* |
|---|---|
| P. armandi No. 86 [a] | P. roxburghii No. 93 [b] |
| P. dalatensis No. 88 | P. massoniana No. 94 |
| P. fenzeliana No. 89 | P. merkusii No. 101 |
| P. kwangtungensis No. 90 | P. yunnanensis No. 103 |
| P. griffithii No. 91 [b] | P. khasya No. 104 |
| P. gerardiana No. 92 [b] | P. insularis No. 105 |

Note: A controversial conifer, *P. krempfii* Lecomte (*Ducampopinus krempfii* Chevalier), is not listed in this table.

[a] Listed in eastern Asia.

[b] *P. griffithii*—chiefly in the Himalaya; *P. roxburghii*—entirely of the Himalaya; *P. gerardiana*—of the western Himalaya.

* *Pinus timoriensis* Loudon, described as being from the island of Timor, is planted *P. insularis* No. 105.

status is uncertain. In the province of Kwangtung grows *P. kwangtung-ensis,* another haploxylon pine.

Pine groves of all these countries are scattered and not very large. Only occasionally do they assume an aspect of real forests. *Pinus armandi* and *P. griffithii* are found only in the extreme north of Burma. Certain areas of southeastern Asia, such as Viet Nam between 12° and 16° north latitude, have not yet been explored botanically.

On Hainan island there are two haploxylon pines: *P. fenzeliana* (of the *P. parviflora* complex) and *P. armandi,* which is found on the continent north of Hainan in several places and which also occurs in Formosa and in southern Japan. The only diploxylon pine growing on Hainan is *P. massoniana,* whose extensive range is on the continent.

It appears that pines migrated to Hainan from northern Indochina recently, most likely during the cool period of the Quaternary.

Only two pines (both diploxylon species) grow in the Philippines: *P. merkusii,* on the island of Mindoro and in the Zambales Mountains on the west coast of central Luzon, and *P. insularis,* in the northern part of Luzon.

One of the three pines of the Himalaya, *P. griffithii* (*P. excelsa,* a haploxylon pine), is still a component of the southeast-Asian pine community. Farther west, *P. longifolia* (*P. roxburghii,* a diploxylon pine) appears at lower elevations, and, finally, a haploxylon, *P. gerardiana,* is found in a few places in the western Himalaya. These pines represent an extension of the pine region of southeastern Asia. A more detailed description of the distribution of pine species in southeastern Asia can be found in Chapter 3.

## Paleobotany

Generally, the paleobotany of the region of southeastern Asia is known well. Kräusel (1929) reported on fossil Tertiary plants in Sumatra, and Posthumus (1931) has done a great deal of paleobotanical work in southeastern Asia; both failed to find any fossil pines. There are no reports on fossil pines from Yunnan or other parts of China lying within the boundaries of this region.

Sitholey (1954), who reviewed thoroughly the Mesozoic and Tertiary floras of India, listed many Coniferales, but pines were not among them. There is no doubt that pines grew in the locality of the present Himalaya during the Tertiary, but apparently they were not very numerous.

Vidal (1934–60), in his "La Végétation du Laos," made a brief but complete review of paleobotanical findings in the region of southeastern Asia. Paleozoic remains of *Lepidodendron* from Yunnan were reported by Colani. In Laos, Hoffett found, in the Stephanian (Upper Carboniferous) strata, several plants such as *Calamites, Sigillaria,* and others. Some Paleozoic plants were also found north and east of Vientiane. Mesozoic plants were studied by Boreau, who described Aruacariaceous remains from the Lower Jurassic of central Viet Nam and some species of the family Moraceae from Lias, Cambodia. *Aruacarioxylon* trunks were described by Colani from the Rhaetic stage of several regions of Viet Nam and from Louang Prabang, Laos. Zeiller described many species of ferns and cycadophytes from Tonkin. A Ginkgoales-group tree and one species of Taxodiaceae were found in Annam. No pines were reported.

The Tertiary flora of the region contained *Dipterocarpoxylon* and *Dipterocarpophyllum* (described from Burma, Indonesia, Assam). In Tonkin grew trees of many tropical- and temperate-climate families— Lauraceae, Fagaceae, Betulaceae; conifers such as *Taxus, Libocedrus, Glyptostrobus* were admixed, but the genus *Pinus* was not found. The Tertiary flora of Indochina was about the same as it is now, consisting of a mixture of temperate-climate trees and trees of tropical regions.

During my travels in southeastern Asia in 1960, I inquired in all countries about fossil pines, but the answers were always negative. Dr. K. N. Kaul, director of the National Botanical Gardens, Lucknow, India (a paleobotanist himself), informed me in a letter that he did not remember anything published on fossil pines in the region. Dr. Kaul further said that "it seems pines appeared in the Himalaya at a later date and therefore are of recent [Tertiary] introduction on the Himalaya." Apparently, pines migrated during the Tertiary period via the mountain ranges north of the present extent of the Himalaya. By this route pines reached the Mediterranean area.

While in the Philippines, I visited Dr. Eduardo Quisumbing, a paleobotanist and the director of the National Museum in Manila. He told me that nobody had yet found fossil pines in the Philippines.

While traveling on the mainland of southeastern Asia—in Burma, Singapore, and Thailand—I also inquired about the possible occurrence of fossil pines there, but without hearing of any. Mr. Clive R. Jones, a geologist of the Malay Geological Survey, Kuala Kangsar, Malaya, informed me that "very few fossil plants have been recorded from the Malayan sedimentary formations due, no doubt, to their marine character. Some specimens of *Pecopteris* and *Cordaites* from the Stephanian of Kelantan and *Dadoxylon* from the Trias of the same state are the only records we have of fossil flora in the older sediments."

Lack of information regarding possible occurrence of fossil pines in southeastern Asia is not a result of scarcity of paleobotanical researches. Far from it! A great many fossil plants have been reported from the region by well-known scholars. Pines simply were not among the fossils. Apparently pines are recent (Tertiary) migrants to southeastern China.

Their part in the floras described from this region was insignificant; their occurrence on the mountain slopes and plateaus far from the valleys, the usual sites of deposition, accounts for their absence from the sediments.

## Migration of Pines

According to Merrill (1926), Malaysia including the Philippines was, during the Cretaceous, a component of the Asiatic-Australian continent. At the end of the Cretaceous, or during the Eocene, Australia was separated from Asia and the Philippines became a group of islands.

Land connection between the Philippines and Formosa was terminated in the early Tertiary; therefore, pines that grow on Luzon and on Mindoro could not have migrated from Formosa; they came directly from the mainland. As has been already mentioned, pines of Formosa reached that island via southern China.

The Asiatic-Philippine migration route generally, according to Merrill, was less important than the Malay Peninsula–Sumatra–Borneo route. Apparently this was the migration route for pines; with interruptions it persisted through the Pleistocene and probably into the Holocene. According to Merrill (1926),

The Asiatic elements in the archipelago, especially those of northern Luzon, are probably to be explained on the basis of previous land connections with southeastern Asia and Formosa, but those connections were ancient. The Formosan rift extending through the Bashi Channel between Formosa and the Batan Islands was apparently established in the early Tertiary and since that time there has been no land connection between the Philippines and Formosa or direct connection between the Philippines and southern Asia.

On the other hand, the route via the Malay Peninsula and Sumatra remained open until the close of the Pleistocene.

Merrill emphasized the fact that pines came to the Philippines from Asia. They migrated from the continent either at the end of the Tertiary or, more likely, much later—in the Quaternary from Malay northward (while the main migration was from eastern Asia southward). It appears that this happened during cool periods at the time of the Ice Age. Similar reversed migrations of pines during the Quaternary also occurred in northern Eurasia and in North America. These were of a local character.

Vidal (1934–60) concluded that migration of plants to Indonesia (i.e., southward) from the continent took place during the Upper Pliocene and (mostly) during the Quaternary, when the climate became cooler.

From the above review it appears that *P. merkusii* No. 101, a low-elevation pine, and *P. insularis* No. 105, related to *P. khasya* No. 104, a higher-elevation species, established themselves in Mindoro and as far north as the Zambales Mountains, south of the Lingayen Gulf on the South China Sea coast of Luzon. Later, with warming up of climate, *P. insularis* disappeared from Mindoro, became almost extinct in Zambales, and migrated to the higher elevation of northern Luzon, where it now forms extensive forests.

*Pinus merkusii*, being more tolerant to the warmer climate of low altitudes, survived in the lower altitudes in Zambales and Mindoro. Northern Luzon was too high for this pine.

All available information indicates that pines migrated relatively recently to the Philippines—from Indochina (vicinity of Dalat in Viet Nam) via North Borneo and the Palawan-Calamian group to Mindoro, Zambales (*P. merkusii*), and finally northern Luzon (*P. insularis*). Figure 2–4 illustrates the possibility of existence of this migration route.

Of course, it is possible that pines penetrated to Indonesia via the Malay Peninsula, reaching southern Sumatra, and that Philippine pines somehow crossed the South China Sea directly from the continent. It should be remembered, however, that, in the Quaternary cool period, the South China Sea still was a formidable stretch of water for pines to cross.

## Summary

The pine region of southeastern Asia has no sharp boundaries to separate it from the region of eastern Asia. The change from north to south is gradual. There is a certain overlap of species in the two regions. If one recognizes pines Nos. 88, 89, and 90 (see Table 1–2) as valid species, one has, in the region of southeastern Asia, equal numbers of haploxylon and diploxylon species—six in each subgenus. In this region and the region of eastern Asia together, there are twelve haploxylon and thirteen diploxylon pines.

The most conspicuous feature of the pine region of southeastern Asia is a total absence of fossil pines there. Now pines occur in the region in small groves or as single trees admixed with other conifers and with broadleaf species. Only in the Himalaya, Yunnan, and Luzon do they form more extensive forests; these forests are of recent origin. Pines migrated to southeastern Asia from the north not earlier than the Tertiary, and they penetrated to Indonesia and the Philippines even later, possibly during the cooler times of the Quaternary, when, in the north, there was a period of widespread glaciation. Migration of pines to the Philippines was of a reversed nature—from south to north.

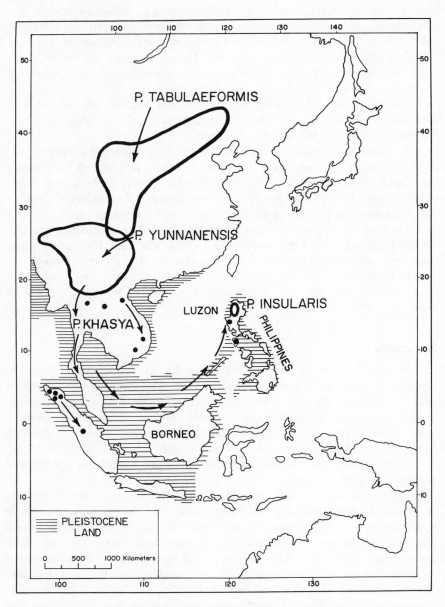

**Fig. 2—4.** Pleistocene migration of pines to the Philippines.

## THE MEDITERRANEAN REGION

### Physiography

Under the Mediterranean pine region will be considered not only the coastal areas of southern Europe, northern Africa, the Lebanon, and Asia Minor that surround the Mediterranean Sea but also the high mountains of southern Europe—the Pyrenees, the Alps, the Carpathians, the mountains of the Balkan Peninsula, the Crimean Mountains, and the Caucasus. The pine area of the Canary Islands also will be included here. In the Tertiary period, these mountains were connected in the east (with some interruptions), via ranges lying north of the Himalaya, with the mountains of eastern Asia. That was a route of migration of many plants and, among them, of some pines. The geological history and geomorphology of the region have been taken chiefly from Wulff's *Historical Plant Geography* (Wulff, 1944).

The Mediterranean Sea is the remains of the ancient Tethys Sea, which divided the Old World into northern and southern parts. Along its northern shores extended mountain ranges, and pines were growing there (Suslov, 1947).

During the second half of the Tertiary, once continuous east-west mountain ranges were broken by violent faulting processes, and considerable areas sank, forming the present Mediterranean Sea.

During the Miocene, the Mediterranean Sea was connected with the Atlantic along the valley of Guadalquivir. Italy consisted of a series of mountain islands. Corsica and Sardinia were united. Western Greece, southern Asia Minor, Lower Egypt, and the northern fringe of Libya were under water. Most of Greece was connected with Asia Minor. After regression at the end of the Miocene, and in the early Pliocene, the sea advanced again, and, in the Middle Pliocene, it penetrated far up the Rhone Valley and flooded the Po Valley and both slopes of the Apennines.

At the end of the Pliocene and the beginning of the Quaternary, the terrain was uplifted, and the sea receded once again.

During the Pliocene, the Black Sea acquired its present form and became connected with the Mediterranean. As a whole, the Mediterranean region experienced many tectonic changes throughout the Tertiary. In the Quaternary, there occurred intensive faulting and sinking of considerable areas, resulting in the formation of separate mountain ranges and many islands. In consequence, the present distribution of pines in the Mediterranean region is sporadic and irregular.

## Present Distribution of Pines

Living pines of the Mediterranean region are listed in Table 2–5. These will be discussed separately in terms of different parts of the region. It suffices to say here only that some of the Mediterranean pines are distributed widely—such are *P. nigra* No. 74, with its several varieties; *P. halepensis* No. 77; and *P. pinea* No. 73.

Other pines, on the contrary, are extremely local. These are *P. peuce* No. 71, of the Balkans; *P. eldarica* No. 81, of Transcaucasia; and *P. pityusa* No. 79, of the Black Sea coast of the Caucasus.

**Table 2–5.** Pines of the Mediterranean Region

| Species | Distribution |
|---|---|
| SUBGENUS HAPLOXYLON | |
| P. cembra No. 70 | Alps, Carpathians |
| P. peuce No. 71 | Balkans |
| SUBGENUS DIPLOXYLON | |
| P. sylvestris No. 69 | From Spain to Turkey; also Caucasus |
| P. canariensis No. 72 | Canary Islands |
| P. pinea No. 73 | The whole region |
| P. nigra No. 74 | The whole region |
| P. heldreichii No. 75 | Chiefly Balkans |
| P. montana No. 76 | Mountains (Alps, etc.) |
| P. halepensis No. 77 | The whole region |
| P. brutia No. 78 | E. Mediterranean |
| P. pityusa No. 79 | Caucasus |
| P. pinaster No. 80 | Western part |
| P. eldarica No. 81 | Transcaucasia |

*Pinus sylvestris* No. 69, whose main area is in northern Eurasia, occurs in several Mediterranean countries. *Pinus canariensis* No. 72 grows far from the Mediterranean, but historically it belongs to this region.

## Paleobotany

At the beginning of the Tertiary, the Mediterranean flora was of a tropical character, but there already had begun to appear deciduous trees, predecessors of the future vegetation of a more temperate flora. Toward the end of the Tertiary, the Mediterranean flora essentially acquired its present aspect. The Quaternary climate impoverished the Mediterranean flora and made it more xerophytic. Because of the complexity of the Mediterranean region, paleobotany of pines and physiography of the country will be described together for different parts of the region.

**The Iberian Peninsula.** The central part of the Peninsula is occupied by the Meseta—a combination of Paleozoic mountain ranges and the Tertiary plateaus. The most ancient land of the Peninsula that appeared above the water in the lower Carboniferous is the southern part of Portugal. During the Upper Carboniferous, the whole region of the present Peninsula, and farther south to Morocco, was subject to violent mountain-forming processes.

In the Upper Jurassic, the Mediterranean became connected with the Atlantic through the valley of Guadalquivir. During the Upper Cretaceous, most of the Peninsula submerged, and the submergence continued well into the Tertiary. During the Miocene, the Guadalquivir Strait disappeared.

During the Lower Pliocene, the Mediterranean Sea receded considerably, but, in the Upper Pliocene and in the Pleistocene, it expanded again, having separated the Balearic Islands from Spain. At that time, the Gibraltar Strait was formed. Thus, the Iberian Peninsula was in contact with Africa until relatively recently. From the European continent, the Peninsula was separated by the mountain ranges of Cretaceous and early Tertiary origin.

Tertiary pines in Portugal, have been mentioned by several authors. Teixeira (1944) described a pine (*P. praepinaster*) from the Pliocene deposits of Rio Major. This pine was related to *P. pinaster* No. 80.

Montenegro de Andrade (1945) described pollen of several pines from the Upper Pliocene of Portugal.

More recently, Rodriguez (1950) reported the presence of *P. pinaster* and *P. sylvestris* pollen in the Sierra de Geres and concluded that the former was a comparatively recent arrival in Portugal and the latter was a Tertiary relic.

Turning to Spain, we also find good evidence of the occurrence of pines there during the Tertiary and the Quaternary. Wulff (1944, p. 119) mentioned that a three-needle pine resembling *P. canariensis* No. 72 was discovered in Tertiary deposits in Murcia, on the coast of southeastern Spain.

Menendez Amor (1951) found a pine cone in Pliocene deposits near Málaga and called it "*Pinus pseudopinea.*" Apparently, it was a predecessor of the present *P. pinea* No. 73, or even the same species, which grows now in the Mediterranean region.

Menendez Amor and Florschütz (1959) discovered pine pollen in the late glacial ("*tardiglaciaire*") sediments of northern Spain, in the provinces of Zamora and Barcelona. In the most ancient Dryas time, pine grew in parklike formation and was predominant.

During the next, or Bölling, time, pine, together with birch, formed open forests; later, in the Alleröd period, pine predominated again. And it appears that, throughout the late glacial period, pine was often inter-mixed with broadleaf trees. It, nevertheless, always dominated the land-scape that was more or less of a savanna type (*"paysage steppique à arbres dispersés"* Menendez Amor and Florschütz [1959]).

**The Canary Islands.** The Canary Islands are located near Africa, approximately between 28° and 29° north and between 15° and 18° west. The archipelago consists of two groups: The eastern (lesser) group is composed of two low islands covered with xerophytic vegetation; the western group consists of eleven mountainous islands. Their peaks are ancient volcanoes.

The Canaries are the home of living *P. canariensis* No. 72. It occurs on the five main islands of the archipelago: Tenerife, La Palma, Gomera, Hierro, and Gran Canaria.

The nearest pine forests are found in Spain, Portugal, and North Africa. As the Mediterranean Straits connecting the sea with the ocean were either narrow at the time or nonexistent, they presented no obstacle for pines to penetrate in migrating from southern Europe to northern Africa. It seems probable that *P. canariensis* came to the Islands via the Tertiary land connection of the Iberian Peninsula with northwestern Africa. The Atlas Mountains already existed during the Tertiary, and they might have provided the way of migration of pines to the Islands, while most of the northern coast of Africa was under water.

Wulff (1944) gave as an example of an early connection of the Iberian Peninsula with the Canaries occurrence of *Myrica faya,* which also occurs in Portugal and is less closely related to *Myrica gale* of northern Europe than to *Myrica sapida* of tropical Asia and the Himalaya. It is possible that Canary Island pine also came from eastern Asia in the early Tertiary via the mountain ranges situated along the northeastern shores of the Tethys Sea. The nearest relative of *P. canariensis* closely resembling it is *P. roxburghii* No. 93, of the Himalaya.

**The Balearic Islands.** The Balearic Islands lie near the coast of the Iberian Peninsula, south of Barcelona and east of Valencia. The Balearics appeared above water at the end of the Cretaceous. During the Eocene and Oligocene, they were connected with Catalonia and with Corsica-Sardinia, forming an extensive land area.

The Balearics became separated from the other components of this land area either in the Miocene or in the Pliocene. Thus, pine apparently migrated to the Islands early in the Tertiary; this was *P. halepensis* Mill. At present, this pine still grows on the western Balearic Islands—Ibisa and Formentera. These two islands were known in classical times as *pityusae insulae,* i.e., pine islands (Strabo, 1917–32).

**Southern France.**   The Mediterranean region of France is limited in the west by the Pyrenees, and in the east it extends to the Maritime Alps. Palms, laurel, camphor, and other warm-climate trees grew in that region during the Eocene. With the beginning of the Upper Oligocene, tropical species began to decrease and the more temperate trees became more prominent. The Alps and the Pyrenees were uplifed already in the Oligocene, and since that time they formed a barrier against migration of pines from the north. During glaciation, most of the Tertiary pines of France perished rather than migrated south to the Mediterranean region. At present, only four species of pines are found in this area: *P. sylvestris* and *P. montana* in the mountains, *P. pinaster* near the Bay of Biscay, and *P. nigra* near the Mediterranean Coast.

The pine fossil record of southern France is voluminous. The old and numerous publications of Saporta are full of references to fossil Tertiary pines. In one of his articles, for instance, Saporta (1865) described twenty-eight species of Tertiary pines from the southeast of France. Some of those pines resembled Mexican living pines: One looked like *P. sabiniana* of California; another, like *P. longifolia* of the Himalaya. "*L'abondance des Pinus est un des traits caractéristiques de la Flore d'Armissan*," said Saporta. Many different sections were recognized. There were some haploxylon pines. His *P. echinostrobus* had recurved scales and resembled *P. ayacahuite* No. 33. Other five-needle pines were definitely diploxylon pines.

In an earlier article, Saporta (1864) described several pines from the Marseille Basin: *P. paleostrobus* Etting., *P. pseudopinea,* and *P. megalophylla* (a two-needle pine whose cone was lacking).

In Provence (Vaucluse), Saporta (1867) found also several Tertiary pines—*P. debilis,* similar to *P. leiophylla* No. 41; *P. parvinucula; P. manuescense;* and *P. copidopterum,* previously reported by him from Armissan.

Such an abundance of pine material from a single locality is unique in the paleobotany of pines. There is no doubt that numerous pines grew on the Mediterranean Coast of France between the Pyrenees and the Alps. Some of those pines were compared by Saporta with Mexican pines listed in the seed catalogs of Roezl (1857, 1858). Most of Roezl's species however are not recognized by botanists. Some of Saporta's identifications describing many exotics and using nonexistent characters, with impossible analogies, appear fantastic (Krishtofovich, 1959).

Boulay (1887) reported in a Tertiary flora near Privas, the Ardèche, southern France, four pines—*P. junonis* Kov., similar to *P. nigra; P. echinostrobus* Sap., which, according to Saporta, resembles *P. ayacahuite* (a Mexican haploxylon pine); *P. goethana* Al. Br., which looked like the present *P. montana* No. 76; and *P. consimilis* Sap., whose seeds, according to Saporta, were comparable to those of *P. canariensis* No. 72. It seems that comparison of these fossil pines with living species was rather hastily made; nevertheless, it is important to know that both haploxylon and diploxylon pines were growing during the Tertiary on the Rhone slopes of the Cévennes.

Florschütz (1959) analyzed sediments of an ancient lake near Lourdes in the central Pyrenees. The deposits, dated by $C^{14}$, proved to be about 16,000 years old; i.e., they date to the beginning of the late glacial stage. At the earliest times, i.e., before the Bölling, the landscape was a grassland with pines either rare or totally absent. During the second part of the Bölling, there developed open forests of pine and birch. Later, after a small recession during the Alleröd, pines became more dense, and, at the beginning of the Holocene, they became a component of pine-birch-oak forests. Therefore, the history of pines during the glacial period was about the same on both sides of the Pyrenees (cf. Menendéz Amor and Florschütz, 1959).

It appears from the above paleobotanical records of southern France that, during the Tertiary, both haploxylon and diploxylon pines flourished in that region. In northern France, the history of pines has been different. It will be considered later, in discussing the pine region of western Europe.

**Italy.** The Apennine peninsula is separated from continental Europe by the Alps. In the east, it is separated from the Balkans by the Adriatic Sea. In the southwest, with its continuation, Sicily, it comes close to Africa. In the west are located the islands of the Tyrrhenian Sea—Sardinia (Italian), Corsica (French), and the Balearic Islands (Spanish).

Italy is mountainous. In the north are the Alps, and along the whole length of the peninsula extend the Apennine Mountains, which have been connected once with the Balkans and also with the Pyrenees and with the mountains of northern Africa. The pines listed in Table 2–6 grow now in Italy. Of these species, *P. cembra* occurs sparingly in northern Italy, in high elevations of the Alps. *Pinus sylvestris* also occurs only in the north, occupying lower slopes of the mountains. *Pinus nigra* No. 74 is represented by two distinct races: var. *austriaca* in the northeastern part of Italy and var. *calabrica* in the southwestern part of the country and in the northeastern part of Sicily. There are also groves of *P. nigra* in the middle part of Italy, but its subspecific position is uncertain. Possibly it is intermediate between var. *austriaca* and var. *calabrica*.

*Pinus heldreichii* var. *leucodermis* No. 75 occurs sparingly in southern Italy. *Pinus halepensis* No. 77, which is a typical Mediterranean pine, grows only in the southeastern part of Italy. It is not certain if the closely related *P. brutia* No. 78, which occurs in two spots in Calabria (i.e., in

**Table 2–6.** Living Pines of Italy

| Species | Remarks |
| --- | --- |
| P. sylvestris No. 69 | In the north |
| P. cembra No. 70 | A haploxylon pine of the Alps |
| P. pinea No. 73 | |
| P. nigra No. 74 | |
| P. heldreichii var. leucodermis Ant. No. 75 | |
| P. montana Mill. No. 76 | In the Alps, Pyrenees, Carpathians |
| P. halepensis No. 77 | |
| P. brutia No. 78 | Not certain if native to Italy |
| P. pinaster No. 80 | |

ancient Brutium, hence the name) is native there. Possibly it represents an early introduction from the eastern Mediterranean.

*Pinus pinea* No. 73, also a typical Mediterranean pine, was probably introduced from other parts of the region. It Italy it grows chiefly along the Mediterranean Coast between Villareggia and Livorno and less frequently farther south and on the Adriatic Coast and on Sardinia and Sicily.

As regards the paleobotany of pines, there is ample evidence of pines growing in Italy during the Tertiary period. Omboni (1892) reported that a Tertiary pine was found in northeastern Italy (Veneto). He named it *"Pinus priabonensis."*

In Romagna, Tongiorgi (1946) found a Tertiary haploxylon pine, which he called *"Pinus strobus* forma *zagherii."* But from his description it appears that this pine resembles *P. peuce* No. 71 from the Balkans more than *P. strobus* No. 20 of America.

*Pinus santiana* Gaud. of the section *Australes* was described from Pliocene strata of Siena (Studt, 1926).

While the late-Tertiary–early-Quaternary floras of Italy are relatively well studied, those that developed toward the end of the Quaternary are not so. Information is particularly lacking on Günz-Mindel and Mindel-Riss interglacial stages (Lona, 1954). Of utmost interest for us is Lona's report on occurrence of *P. peuce* No. 71 in Pianico Sellere (Riss-Würm) sediments; this pine was reported also by Bianotti from Riss-Würm deposits of Val Vigezzo.

Emberger (1944, p. 388) mentioned that, during the glacial period, *P. cembra* No. 70 was growing in northern Italy, which shows that this now rare alpine species was more widespread in former times.

*Pinus nigra* No. 74 was a very important tree in the forest of the Umbro-Marchigiano Apennines during the postglacial time. In the early stages following glaciation, it was decidedly dominant. It lost its dominance only at the end of the oak period (Marchesoni, 1958). This pine was a pioneer invader after the retreat of the ice, as were pines in all other parts of the Northern Hemisphere.

**The Islands of the Tyrrhenian Sea.** The major islands lying southwest of Italy—French Corsica and Italian Sardinia—during the first half of the Tertiary formed a land mass connected with Spain by means of the Balearics and also with Tunisia, France, and Middle Italy. The breaking up of this large land mass into several islands occurred before the advent of the Quaternary. Corsica and Sardinia were separated from the continent either at the end of the Miocene or at the beginning of the Pliocene, although land connections between Corsica and the Apennine peninsula might have been maintained in the Quaternary.

In Corsica, *P. pinaster* No. 80 and *P. nigra* No. 74 grow above the scrub (maquis) belt, at an elevation of 1000 to 1600 m. *Pinus halepensis* No. 77 also occurs on the island. These pines are Tertiary relics there.

*Pinus pinaster* is found as a Tertiary relic in the northeastern part of the island of Sardinia.

Early in the Tertiary, in the Eocene and the Oligocene, only the northeastern part of Sicily was above water. At the end of the Miocene the island became connected to Italy. At the beginning of the Pliocene, the sea covered the island almost completely, except the small northeastern part of it. Most of the vegetation perished. It was only at the end of the Pliocene that Sicily emerged again and became connected once more with the Apennine peninsula and also with North Africa. These connections lasted until the Quaternary; the Messina Strait was formed at the end of the glacial period.

At present there is only one native pine in Sicily—*P. nigra* No. 74 var. *calabrica,* which also is found in the southern part of Italy. This pine is most probably a relic that survived on the elevated northeastern parts of the island since the early Tertiary.

The other pine found in Sicily is *P. pinea* No. 73, but it is not certain whether this pine is a Tertiary relic on the island (Zodda, 1903) or was introduced there by man (Francini, 1958).

**The Islands of the Eastern Mediterranean.** Pines are found on some of the islands of the eastern Mediterranean. *Pinus brutia* No. 78 grows on the islands of Chios, Rhodes, Crete, and Cyprus. To understand the existence of pines on these islands it would be sufficient to review briefly, as an example, the geological history of the largest of them, Cyprus, located in the northeastern corner of the Mediterranean about 100 km from Syria and about the same distance from Turkey. The most elevated parts of the island appeared above water probably toward the end of the Miocene. At the middle of the Pliocene, Cyprus was connected with Syria and Asia Minor, which, in turn, were connected with the Balkans. At the end of the Pliocene, sea separated the island from the mainland and also flooded its low part, Messaria, dividing Cyprus into two islands. Only during the Quaternary did Messaria emerge again and the island assume its present configuration. The Taurus Mountains of Asia Minor have their continuation on Cyprus. According to Strabo (1917–32), Cyprus once was covered with magnificent forests. At present, there are just remains of forests. The only naturally growing pines are *P. brutia* No. 78 and *P. nigra* No. 74.

Other islands of the eastern Mediterranean have a similar history; they were previously part of a larger land mass; they were connected with Asia Minor and the Balkans, and their pines, *P. brutia* No. 78, *P. pityusa* No. 79, and *P. halepensis* No. 77, are closely related.

**The Alps.** The Alps extend from Marseilles, France, in the west, to Vienna, Austria, in the east. Along the meridian of Verona, the Alps are about 250 km wide.

Essentially the Alps were formed during the Teritary; the dislocations that elevated the mountains to their present height took place at the beginning of the Miocene. Quaternary glaciation was extensive.

No fossil pines of the Tertiary period have been found in the high elevations of the Alps, although ecological conditions suitable for their growth existed there. In contrast, Quaternary remains of pines (*P. cembra* No. 70) are quite common and very numerous in the alpine zone of the mountains. Apparently these semifossilized pine remains are of the time when the glaciers retreated from this part of southern Europe. Rikli (1909) suggested that during that time *P. cembra* occupied an almost continuous belt in the higher elevations of the Alps. At present this pine occurs there only sporadically.

Several Tertiary pines have been described from Switzerland: *P. hampeana* Unger, *P. langiana* Heer, *P. taedaeformis* Heer (Kräusel in Engler and Prantl, 1926, p. 342).

In the subalpine zone, after the retreat of the ice, the pioneer invaders were birch and pine. Other broadleaf trees appeared later. Pines also were to be found in the forests of the Alps during interglacial times.

Diels (1910), analyzing the elements of the flora of the Alps, came to the conclusion that the center of their origin was apparently in eastern Asia. This reasoning can be equally well applied to explain the migration of pines westward in general and to the Alps in particular.

Kulczynski's (1923) suggestion that the migration of plants along the mountain ranges of Eurasia already had been completed during the

Tertiary period appears to be plausible. His conclusions explain satisfactorily the migration of pines, not only to the Alps but also to the whole
of southern Europe and particurarly to the Mediterranean region.

During the Ice Age, the high mountain pines of the Alps either perished
or were preserved in the lower areas not covered with ice. *Pinus cembra*
No. 70, found occasionally in northern Italy (Emberger, 1944), is the
relic preserved in one of such refugia; with subsequent warming up, it
penetrated again to the high elevation of the central Alps. There is, of
course, a possibility of the existence of non-glaciated refugia even in the
central parts of the Alps. *Pinus cembra* might have survived in some of
these not too numerous areas that remained free from the ice.

**The Balkans.** The Balkan Peninsula is a mountainous region. Its
chief ranges are (1) the Dinaric Alps, which extend from Slovenia along
the coast of the Adriatic Sea, with the Pindus Mountains farther to the
south; (2) the Rhodope system, located in the central part of the Peninsula, roughly between Bulgaria and the Aegean Sea; (3) the Balkan
range, which lies chiefly in the northern part of Bulgaria; and (4) Istranca
Dagh, extending along the Black Sea coast from southeastern Bulgaria
to eastern Thrace. Northwest of the Balkans lie the Austrian Alps; to
the north are the Carpathian Mountains, which form an arc extending east
and then south from northern Czechoslovakia through Romania. The
Carpathians separate the Balkans from Poland in the north and eastern
Europe (U.S.S.R.) in the northeast.

There are lowlands only along the forty-sixth parallel between the
twenty-seventh and thirtieth meridians, i.e., between the Carpathians and
the Black Sea. There is also a gap between the Sudeten and western
Beskids, known as the Moravian Gate, which might have served as a
migration route for pines between northern Europe and the Balkans.

During the Cretaceous, the Balkans were almost entirely covered with
water. Only the Rhodope highland appeared as a chain of islands.
Whereas in the Eocene the submergence increased, after the Miocene
the Balkans became a rather extensive land, forming a peninsula of
western Asia and not of Europe as now.

At the end of the Miocene, the Aegean Sea and the Sea of Marmora
were still land and the Balkan Peninsula was a mountain land connecting
Europe and Asia. However, besides this chain of mountains, most of the
Peninsula was separated from Europe by the sea. The Aegean land
submerged only in the Pliocene, and the Hellespont and the Bosporus
Straits were formed and the Black Sea became connected with the
Mediterranean only in the Quaternary.

During the Tertiary, the warm and humid climate extended farther
north in the whole Mediterranean region and particularly in its eastern

parts. Quaternary glaciation was restricted to the mountain summits; the rest of the Balkan Peninsula remained unglaciated.

Present distribution of pines over the Balkan Peninsula is as follows: In Greece, *P. nigra* No. 74 is scattered over a considerable area, *P. halepensis* No. 77 grows in the southern part, and *P. brutia* No. 78 occurs in the south and on some nearby islands. *Pinus pinea* No. 73 is found along the coast in the southern parts of the Balkan Peninsula. It is difficult to say whether it is native or introduced. *Pinus heldreichii* No. 75 occurs in scattered localities in the mountains of the region, and its variety *leucodermis* is also found in a few places. Endemic *P. peuce* No. 71 is very local in Bulgaria, Albania, and Yugoslavia. It is a haploxylon pine, closely related to *P. griffithii* No. 91 (*P. excelsa*) of the Himalaya. Turrill (1929) considered it to be a Balkan endemic; it has been isolated from other haploxylon pines since the Tertiary. Although isolated for a long time, *P. peuce* has been crossed with other haploxylon pines. Judging by the chemical composition of its turpentine (Iloff and Mirov, 1956), it has a close affinity to eastern Asiatic and western American pines.

Hayek (1928), who studied the flora of Thessalian Olympus found there at lower elevations *P. nigra* No. 74 var. *pallasiana* and *P. heldreichii*. He came to the conclusion that most of the vegetation of that area was not of northern origin. As applied to pines, his conclusion means that the pines found in Greece developed from the Tertiary, Mediterranean ancestors.

During the Pliocene, *P. nigra* No. 74 grew in the Balkans in the same places where it grows now. *Pinus halepensis* No. 77 also was found there, and in places much farther north than its present habitat. Both these pines were considered by Stojanoff and Stefanoff (1929) as typically Mediterranean (i.e., Tertiary) trees. These authors also indicated that the Tertiary flora of the Balkan Peninsula was similar to that of southern France, and thus to the whole Tertiary flora of southern Europe. They found the same vegetation zones in the Tertiary forests as in Mediterranean France. In the lowest belt grew *P. halepensis* in association with other trees such as *Cedrus, Cupressus,* and *Arbutus*. Above were forests of oak and pine (*P. nigra*), together with maple, ash, and some shrubs. On the higher slopes grew conifer forests of *Picea* and *Abies*, and among them *Pinus* sp. of Shaw's group *Strobi* (probably *P. peuce* No. 71) and minor trees such as aspen and birch.

The relict character of Balkan pines, *P. peuce* and *P. heldreichii* var. *leucodermis*, is fully discussed by Stojanoff in his analysis of the "Relict Elements of the Flora of the Balkan Peninsula" (Stojanoff, 1930). Stojanoff and Stefanoff (1929) found the following Pliocene pines on the plains of Sofia: *P.* aff. *halepensis* Mill., *P.* aff. *laricio* Poir., *P. foliis ternis* (Pilger's Sec. *Taeda*) and *P.* sp. (Pilger's sec. *Strobus*). (See Table 9–2.) This last pine possessed needles that looked like those of *P. strobus* No. 20, but its cones resembled more closely the cones of *P. peuce* No. 71.

Studt (1926) listed Tertiary *P. hampeana* Ung. for Greece. Apparently (Gaussen, 1960) this name is a synonym of *P. thomasiana* Geop. and *P. kotschyana* Ung. from Tertiary deposits of Romania.

Czeczott (1954), who studied past and present distribution of the two Mediterranean pines *P. halepensis* No. 77 and *P. brutia* No. 78, reported "ten authentic occurrences" of these pines in the Tertiary period (Table 2–7). It can be seen from this table that fossil material of pines similar to the two living pines mentioned was found in the Tertiary floras of Czechoslovakia. The Tertiary range of pines that were related to *P. brutia* and *P. halepensis* extended, during the first half of the Tertiary, farther north. Czeczott suggested that the much greater Tertiary range of the two pines was a consequence of the much greater extension of the Tethys Sea.

In the Austrian Alps and the Carpathian Mountains grow *P. montana* No. 76 and *P. cembra* No. 70.

**Table 2–7.** The Paleobotanical Record of *P. halepensis* and *P. brutia* (Czeczott, 1954)

| Species | Tertiary Epoch | Locality | Remarks |
|---|---|---|---|
| *P. halepensis* var. *atavorum* Marion | Plio-Pleistocene | La Valentine, France | |
| *P. ferreri* Massal | Middle Miocene | Near Ancona, Italy | Related to *P. brutia* No. 78 |
| *P. saturni* Unger. | Middle Miocene | Redojob, Croatia | Predecessor of *P. brutia* No. 78 |
| *P. halepensis* (?) | Middle Miocene | Leoben, Austria | Cones resemble those of *P. halepensis* No. 77 |
| *P. sarmatica* Palib. | Miocene | Crimea, U.S.S.R. | Related to *P. brutia* No. 78 |
| *P. prepityusa* Palib. | Oligocene | Chiaturi, W. Trans-caucasia | |
| *P. wassoewiczi* Palib. | Miocene | Transcaucasia | Related to *P. pityusa,* No. 79 var. *stankewiczii,* of Crimea |
| *P. pityusa fossili* Palib. | Upper Pliocene | Kila Kupra, Caucasus | Akin to *P. pityusa* No. 79 |
| *P. salinarum* Part. | Lower Miocene | Wielichka, Poland | Resembles *P. halepensis* No. 77 and *P. brutia* No. 78 |
| Pine cones | Upper Oligocene | N. Bohemia | Intermediate between *P. halepensis* No. 77 and *P. brutia* No. 78 |
| *P. hageni* Heer | Lower Miocene | Baltic region | Similar to *P. halepensis* No. 77 |

**The Mountains of the Crimean Peninsula.** The Crimean peninsula extends into the northern part of the Black Sea, being connected with the mainland by an 8-km-wide neck of land. Most of the peninsula is flat or gently rolling grassland, a continuation of the steppes of eastern Europe (Mirov, 1951). Three mountain ranges, of which the southernmost is the highest (a little over 900 m above sea level; the highest peak 1543 m), are located in its southern part. These mountains are remains of a once large land mass that connected the Balkans with Asia Minor. Most of this land has sunk, and the area is still in the process of sinking. According to Wulff (1944), there was no direct Tertiary connection between Crimea and the Caucasus.

On the mountains of the Crimean peninsula are found *P. nigra* No. 74, *P. sylvestris* No. 69, and *P. pityusa* No. 79 var. *stankewiczii*. *Pinus nigra* is represented in Crimea by the variety *pallasiana* Lamb. On the north slope of the main chain of the flat-topped grassy mountains, this pine has been completely destroyed by man. On the south slope, it still may be found in the western part at lower elevations. Above it grows *P. sylvestris* var. *hamata*, D. Sosn.

*Pinus pityusa* Steven var. *stankewiczii* Suk. is found only in two places on the south slope of the mountains facing the Black Sea. This pine is very closely related to *P. pityusa* of the Black Sea coast of the Caucasus.

The three Crimean pines are Tertiary relics. It is possible that *P. sylvestris* No. 69 migrated to Crimea from eastern Asia via the Tertiary ranges of the northern shores of the Tethys. *Pinus pityusa* No. 79 reminds us of the early land connection of the peninsula with the eastern Mediterranean (see page 79), and *P. nigra* No. 74 reminds us of the connection with the Balkans, and thus with central Europe.

The fossil record shows that, during the Tertiary, pines did grow in Crimea. *Pinus sarmatica* Palibin, a Miocene pine, described from the northeastern (Kerch) region of the peninsula, is very similar to living *P. pityusa* (Malejeff, 1929). It is doubtful that the three Crimean pines migrated to the peninsula from the north after the end of the Ice Age, because the arid climate and saline soils of the northern part of the peninsula and of the adjacent lowlands of eastern Europe precluded migration of any pines from the continent.

**The Caucasus.** The Caucasus is located between the Black Sea and the Caspian Sea. Geographically it belongs to western Asia. It is a complicated mountain region. The Greater Caucasus is a system of mountain ranges extending from northwest to southeast from the Black Sea to the Caspian Sea for about 1500 km. The elevations of the crest of the main range run about 3400 m. The highest peaks of the system (Elbrus 5633 m and Kazbek 5043 m), however, are not located on the watershed divide of the main range but somewhat north of it. South of the Greater Caucasus are the ranges of the Lesser Caucasus, bordering on the north the Armenian Volcanic Plateau. The Greater Caucasus and the Lesser Caucasus are connected by the Suram Range which serves as a watershed divide between the Rion, flowing to the Black Sea, and the Kura, flowing to the Caspian Sea (Mirov, 1951).

The system of the Lesser Caucasus is independent of that of the Greater Caucasus; geologically it belongs to the mountains of Asia Minor. Up to the middle of the Miocene, it was separated by a sea strait from the Greater Caucasus. The Lesser Caucasus became connected with the Greater Caucasus only at the end of the Miocene.

At the end of the Cretaceous, the Greater Caucasus appeared as a long island. The mountains underwent a continuous change during the whole Tertiary period and assumed their present aspect only toward the beginning of the Quaternary. The Greater Caucasus had been connected once with the land situated east of the Mediterranean.

In the north, from the end of the Cretaceous and all the way until the first half of the Pliocene, there existed a broad sea strait separating the Caucasus from the southern part of eastern Europe. During the Kimmerian age (i.e., the Middle Pliocene), the strait disappeared, but later the sea transgressed again, connecting the Black and Caspian seas. Only at the very end of the Tertiary was the land connection, as it now exists, established between southern European Russia and the Caucasus, thus forming the link between Europe and Asia Minor.

The present glaciation of the Greater Caucasus is extensive, especially in the central part of the main range. It covers 1965 sq. km, but it is only about half as extensive as the glaciation of the Alps. During the Ice Age, glaciation of the Caucasus was much more widespread. The snow line, which in the main range is now between about 3000 and 3500 m, was much lower. It is doubtful though if the whole range was covered with ice.

The geological history of the Caucasus clearly indicates that during the Tertiary its forest flora was part of the larger Mediterranean flora (Kuznetsov, 1909). Accordingly, Caucasian pines are all Tertiary relics and not postglacial migrants from the north. Wulff (1944, p. 210) summarized his discussion of Caucasian flora in general in these words: "It is a result of evolution of a Tertiary floristic nucleus enriched by migration from the south of the Mediterranean and East-Asiatic elements with only a small addition of recent migrations from the north." Pines of the Caucasus, therefore, cannot be considered as recent postglacial migrants.

The following pines are found at the present time in the Caucasus: *P. sylvestris* var. *hamata* D. Sosn., *P. kochiana* Klotzsch, *P. armena* Koch.

(all three generally considered varieties of *P. sylvestris* No. 69), *P. pityusa* Steven., *P. eldarica* Medw., and *P. nigra* No. 74 var. *pallasiana*.

The area occupied at present by *P. sylvestris* var. *hamata* coincides with the boundaries of Pleistocene glaciation. Apparently, postglacial invasion by this pine began immediately after retreat of the ice in much the same manner as the invasion of pines after retreat of ice in North America or in western Europe.

The oldest pine from the Caucasian region apparently was one found by Palibin (1937) in Cretaceous deposits of southern Armenia. The material consisted only of needles 4 to 5 cm long. Palibin thought that the needles resembled the pine needles collected by Krishtofovich in western Kazakstan along the river Kulenden-Temir south of Aktiubinsk in the Upper Cretaceous (Senonian) deposits and identified by him as *P. quenstedti* Heer. Unfortunately, the evidence presented by Palibin is not strong enough to prove specificity of his pine. Nevertheless, presence of pine needles in Cretaceous rocks of Transcaucasia is extremely interesting.

Palibin (1935) also described *P. maikopiae* (of Engler and Prantl's section *Banksia*) from the Oligocene in the Apsheron peninsula (near Baku). From southwestern Transcaucasia (near Dushet in the Lesser Caucasus), he described a Miocene (Sarmatian) pine, *P. rjabinini,* and in southern Kakhetia, also in Transcaucasia, a pine closely related to the living Caucasian endemics *P. pityusa* No. 79 and *P. eldarica* No. 81, which have existed in the Caucasus since the Oligocene. In Palibin's opinion, these pines, both living and fossil, came to the Caucasian region from the south.

Grossheim (Wulff, 1944) reported an Oligocene pine from the Caucasus. It was related to *P. pityusa,* which at present grows as a Tertiary relic in Crimea, the Caucasus, and Asia Minor. Grossheim considers *P. eldarica* as a Tertiary relic of a xerophytic Mediterranean type. Toward the end of the Tertiary, when the climate became colder and drier, some pines such as *P. sylvestris* var. *hamata* expanded; others such as *P. eldarica* and *P. pityusa* became almost extinct.

Maleev (1940) mentioned that *P. prepityusa* and *P. paradoxa* were described by Palibin as appearing in the Oligocene strata of Chiatura in the southwestern part of Transcaucasia.

I. A. Shilkina (1958) recently reviewed thoroughly the flora of the Goderdzi Pass, in western Transcaucasia, a classical location studied previously by several prominent Russian paleobotanists. This pass is located in the Adjarian Mountains, on a highway connecting the port of Batumi, on the Black Sea coast, and the town of Akhaltsikhe. The exact age of the Goderdzi Flora is not yet known. Palibin considers it Pliocene, but Krishtofovich was inclined to think the flora of Goderdzi was older; most likely it is a Miocene flora.

During the Miocene-Pliocene, the climate of the western Trans-caucasus was humid and warm and the low elevations were covered with subtropical forests. Oddly enough, in these humid places there grew a haploxylon pine of the section *Paracembra* (see Table 9–2), whose annual rings were not distinct. Shilkina believes that this unique Tertiary pine adapted itself to the humid subtropical zone. In the higher elevations, closer to the Goderdzi Pass, where climate was temperate, pines of the section *Cembrae* with distinct annual growth layers predominated. (See Chapter 5, page 354.)

From the above considerations of living and fossil pines of the Caucasus, as well as from its geological history, we are justified in making the following conclusions: (1) Pines in the Caucasus are Tertiary relics. (2) They could not have come from the north. (3) They are part of the major Tertiary Mediterranean flora. (4) Apparently their ancestors arrived from southeastern Asia.

**Asia Minor.** Asia Minor (Turkey) is a land lying between the Black and Mediterranean seas. It extends eastward approximately to the forty-fourth meridian. It is separated from the Balkan Peninsula by a narrow strait—the Bosporus and the Dardanelles—and by the Aegean Sea with its numerous islands.

The central part of Asia Minor is occupied by an arid plateau reaching elevations of 900 m in the west and 1400 m in the east. Annual precipitation in Ankara is 236 mm. In the north, along the Black Sea coast, extend the mountain chains of the Pontic Range. The Taurus Mountains are located along the southern coast of Asia Minor. Both mountain ranges intercept a great deal of the precipitation (Trebizond has an annual precipitation of over 800 mm). Wulff (1944) considers these mountain ranges very important from the historical plant geography point of view, for they served as Tertiary refugia for plants.

During the Upper Carboniferous, the northern and eastern parts of the peninsula appeared above the water, while its western part remained under the sea until the Permian.

During the Mesozoic era, there occurred intermittent sea transgressions. At the end of the Eocene and during the Oligocene, intensive folding processes extended to Iran and Syria. During the Miocene, the sea covered the southern part of Asia Minor and penetrated, via Armenia, to its central part. The northern and eastern parts went under water in the Upper Miocene.

After the Miocene, most of Asia Minor became dry land; more folding took place, and it continued during the Pliocene. At the end of this epoch, the mountains reached their present height. Sinking of the Aegean area, formation of the Dardanelles, and separation of Crete from the mainland took place only in the Quaternary.

At the present time, pines are scattered all over Asia Minor except in the more arid central and east-central parts. Five species of the genus *Pinus* are found now on the peninsula: *P. brutia* No. 78, *P. halepensis* No. 77, *P. nigra* No. 74, *P. sylvestris* No. 69 var. *hamata* D. Sosn., and *P. pinea* No. 73. Besides these, *P. kochiana* Klotzsch and *P. armena* Koch occur near the Russian border. These are generally considered as varieties of *P. sylvestris*. There is some doubt whether *P. pinea* is native in the vicinity of Artvin and Trebizond (Francini, 1958).

*Pinus nigra* No. 74 var. *pallasiana* is the most widely distributed pine in Asia Minor. *Pinus halepensis* No. 77 grows in a relatively small area north of the Gulf of Alexandretta, in the very northeast corner of the Mediterranean, on the slopes of the Taurus Mountains. By contrast, *P. brutia* No. 78 is widespread, occurring from somewhat farther northeast than Adana and along the Mediterranean Coast all the way to the Aegean Sea coast and to Zonguldak, on the Black Sea.

Asia Minor had been a connecting link between the western Mediterranean region and eastern Asia via the Caucasus, the mountains of Iran and Afghanistan, and the ranges that extended along the north shore of the Tertiary Tethys Sea.

There exists a report of occurrence of a diploxylon pine (presumably related to *P. brutia*) between Herat, Afghanistan, and Tebes, Iran. This pine is known only by one herbarium specimen, without cones (Maléjeff, 1929). Unfortunately, nothing more is known about this interesting finding (Mirov, 1955). Possibly it was a cultivated pine.

Apparently no fossil pines have been found from Asia Minor. Engelhardt (1903), who reported on Tertiary plants of the peninsula, did not mention any pines there; but, judging by the relative abundance of oak species listed in his work, there is little doubt that pines also were growing on the peninsula during the Tertiary.

A pine-oak association is common in many parts of the world—California and southeastern Asia, for instance.

**The Near East.** The countries bordering the Mediterranean on the east, and lying between Asia Minor and Africa, constitute the Near East. This area includes Syria, Lebanon, Iraq, Jordan, and Israel. The coastal countries are also known as the "Levant."

Only near the sea is there a strip of land that can be included in the Mediterranean pine region. Jordan and Iraq lie farther inland. The mountains of the area have never submerged since the Eocene. The coastal zone often was covered with water in its low parts. The last of these transgressions occurred in the Middle Pliocene. The mountains remained continuously above the water after the Oligocene.

*Pinus halepensis* No. 77, or Aleppo pine, grows in this region naturally. It occurs sparingly in Syria and in Lebanon and only in a few spots in Israel. In Jordan, it covers a small area, being associated with oak, *Cistus, Arbutus, Pistacea. Pinus brutia* occurs in northwestern Syria (Nahal, 1960) and in northern Iraq, near Turkey. *Pinus pinea,* which is encountered near the coast of the Levant, generally is considered to have been introduced there by man (Francini, 1958). However, Feinbrun (1959) recently showed that it is native in Lebanon.

*Pinus halepensis* No. 77 is the most common Mediterranean pine. As to its former distribution, Czeczott listed ten "authentic" reports of the occurrence of Tertiary *P. halepensis* and *P. brutia,* or rather their predecessors, from western and middle Europe—much farther north than the Mediterranean region. How authentic these reports are is difficult to say. Czeczott's findings have been mentioned already in discussion of the Balkan pines (see Table 2–7). No fossil pines have been reported from the Near East.

**Africa.**  Pines do not grow in Egypt, but they do grow farther west along the Mediterranean Coast of Africa. Cyrenaica (Libya) is generally a semidesert and desert country, but in the Barce Peninsula the vegetation is a maquis type that includes some typical Mediterranean trees such as *Arbutus, Seratonia, Quercus ilex, Cupressus sempervirens,* and also *P. halepensis* No. 77, which sometimes occupies rather large areas. In Tunisia, *P. halepensis* and *Quercus ilex* (and *Q. lusitanica* in the west) are the only trees in the Mediterranean maquis near the coast. *Pinus pinaster* No. 80 was found in one spot there.

The coastal part of Algeria is covered with Mediterranean vegetation. Farther southwest, the country is mountainous and grassy. *Pinus halepensis* grows in Algeria in the coastal maquis scrub and is absent from the higher elevations. *Pinus pinaster* was reported from one locality.

The northwestern part of Africa was relatively recently connected with southern Spain. In the west and in the north of Morocco, there stretches a narrow strip of land gradually ascending toward the Atlas Mountains. The area between the Atlantic and the Atlas Mountains is known as the "Meseta" of Morocco. It is a continuation of the Central Meseta of Spain. The Atlas Mountains system is composed of three chains extending from northeast to southwest, toward the Canary Islands (see page 74).

*Pinus halepensis* No. 77, together with *P. pinaster* No. 80, penetrates rather deeply southwest in Morocco along the Atlas Mountains (to about 30–31° north latitude between, say, 6° and 7° west longitude). *Pinus nigra* No. 74 is found in only a few spots in Africa southeast of Tangier.

Apparently pines grew in North Africa (Atlas Mountains) throughout the Tertiary period, at least since the Oligocene, but no pine fossils have been reported from this part of the Mediterranean region.

## Summary

In the above description, the Mediterranean pine region is understood broadly. It includes not only the coastal areas of the Mediterranean Sea but the surrounding mountains and the Canaries as well.

Thirteen pine species grow in the Mediterranean region: eleven diploxylon pines and only two haploxylon pines. Some pine species are widely distributed throughout the region; others are extremely local. Pines seldom form extensive forests, mostly growing in small groups or mixed with other Mediterranean xerophytic shrubs and trees. Pine forests are found only some distance from the seashore. One pine, *P. sylvestris,* is unique in that most of its area is located in northern Eurasia. The Mediterranean and northern areas of this pine are disjunct. In the Mediterranean region, *P. sylvestris* is a Tertiary relic; in the north, it is chiefly of Quaternary age.

As the region has been inhabited by man for a long time, often it is difficult to decide where a certain species is native and where it has been introduced. There are no authentic reports on occurrence of Mesozoic pines in the region. The Tertiary fossil record is good for most parts of the region. Most striking is the diversity of Tertiary pines in southern France.

There are indications that Mediterranean pines migrated to the region from eastern Asia along the mountain ranges that once extended north of, and parallel to, the Himalayas.

### WESTERN EUROPE

## Physiography

Under the term *western Europe* will be described the countries lying west of the present border of the Soviet Union and north of the Mediterranean region, i.e., north of the Pyrenees, the Alps, and the Carpathian Mountains. Western Europe, then, will include the following: France, Germany, Belgium, Holland, part of Austria, the northern part of Yugoslavia, Poland, Scandinavia, and Great Britain. Czechoslovakia, part of Austria, and Hungary, are intermediate between the Mediterranean and western European pine regions. The Austrian Alps and the Carpathian Mountains have already been mentioned briefly in describing their position separating the Balkans from the rest of Europe (see page 80).

**France, Germany, and Austria.** This area is limited in the south by the Tertiary ranges of the Pyrenees and the Alps. The southern part of France is connected with the Mediterranean region by means of two corridors—one along the Rhone, which flows to the Mediterranean Sea, and the other between the Pyrenees and the Cévennes. The Cévennes themselves represent the elevated and upturned edge of the ancient Massif Central. Southern France was included in the Mediterranean region.

In the northeastern part of France, and chiefly in Belgium, lie the old, worn-out Ardennes; farther south along the Rhine are located the low, mature Vosges. Still farther south, near Switzerland, are the Mesozoic Jura Mountains. The rest of the country, besides some remains of the old Armorican Massif of Normandy and Brittany, is lowlands where elevations generally are below 200 meters. The Paris Basin lies in the north-central part of France where marine deposits accumulated in shallow seas of the Tertiary period. Some remains of pines have been found there.

The lowlands of northern France extend to Belgium (except the Ardennes in the southern part of that country), to the Netherlands, and to Denmark; they occupy the whole of northern Germany and the area near the border of Czechoslovakia. The more southerly part of Germany (below the fifty-second parallel) is, in places, moderately mountainous. The southern part of Bavaria is more elevated; it is known as the "Alpine Foreland." During the Eocene and Oligocene the alpine ranges were formed.

During the Oligocene, the sea, which in the Eocene only encroached on Europe near Kaliningrad, broadened through the whole of northern Germany and Poland and joined the sea that extended to the Ukraine. Farther northeast, it joined the Arctic along the east side of the Ural Mountains. This sea, in places, was connected with the Mediterranean Sea.

At the end of the Oligocene, the sea retreated north from Germany and the Ukraine to the present location of the North Sea.

At the beginning of the Miocene, the Mediterranean Sea opened to the ocean and most of the alpine ranges became elevated. These ranges were surrounded by water. At that time, in the vicinity of Lausanne, for instance, the climate was as mild as it is in Louisiana now, and there grew in abundance different palms with laurel, camphor, and numerous broadleaf trees, but, toward the upper Miocene, palms disappeared while broadleaf deciduous species began to dominate.

Toward the end of the Miocene, the lowlands that surrounded the mountain ranges became filled with alluvial sediments. But in the eastern part of Europe, near Vienna, and in Transylvania, Romania, there were found great brackish lakes. The sea encroached on western Europe in only a few places.

The Alps, after their Miocene uprising, were subjected to intensive erosion. At the end of the Pliocene, the climate became much colder, and its effects were felt even in the Mediterranean region (Gagnebin in Engel, 1943).

During the first half of the Tertiary period, the climate in western Europe was tropical, merging into subtropical and temperate in the north. Between the Pliocene and the Quaternary period, the flora of the German lowland was approximately the same as that now in the north of the Mediterranean region. In the second half of the Tertiary, the climate of western Europe deteriorated.

With the advent of the Ice Age, the great Scandinavian glacier descended upon Europe (Fig. 2–5). There were four glaciations—Günz, Mindel, Riss, and Würm. The Mindel glaciation was the most extensive; its ice sheet covered almost the whole of the British Isles and the north of continental Europe approximately from Antwerp to Prague, to Krakow, and farther east to the Soviet Union. South of this limit of the ice mantle, glaciation of Europe was generally spotty, being confined to the high mountains. In the Alpine Foreland, however, glaciation was rather extensive, descending north to the adjacent plains of western Europe.

Between the four glaciations there were three interglacial periods. The duration of the first interglacial (Günz-Mindel) period is estimated at 60,000 years (Seward, 1941).

Pines had begun to disappear from western Europe even during the second half of the Tertiary, and especially toward the end of the period. Some of them were killed by ice, but most disappeared even before the Ice Age, because of low temperature. Moreover, at the end of the Tertiary, in the Mediterranean region there was already developed a specialized xerophytic flora. The two corridors connecting western Europe with the Mediterranean region apparently did not serve as southward migration routes for northern pines.

In the Quaternary, the Alps began to rise again and glaciers increased in their size. During the interglacial times, which extended for 50,000 to 100,000 years, the climate of Europe probably was about the same as at the present time. In the period between the second and third glaciations, however, it was warmer and drier than now.

## Present Distribution of Pines

Western Europe is the poorest pine region in the whole Northern Hemisphere. *Pinus cembra* No. 67 occurs sporadically in southernmost Germany and in adjacent parts of Austria. It may be encountered occa-

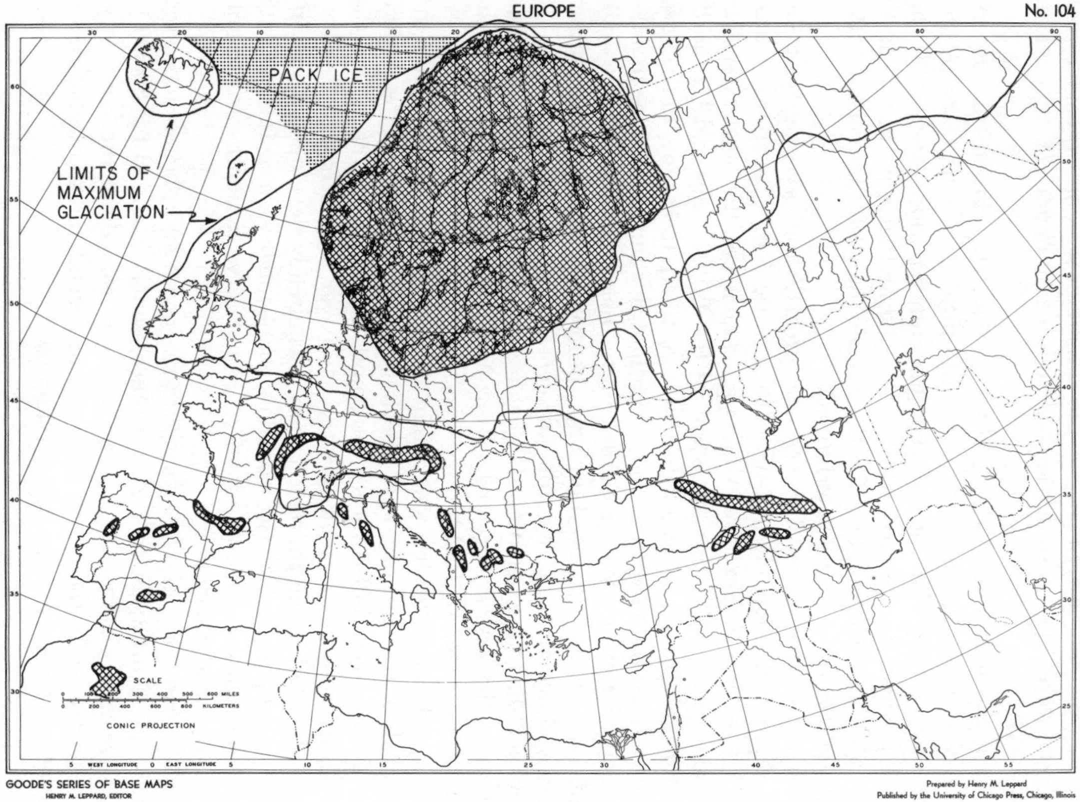
EUROPE
No. 104
PACK ICE
LIMITS OF
MAXIMUM
GLACIATION
SCALE
CONIC PROJECTION
WEST LONGITUDE
EAST LONGITUDE
GOODE'S SERIES OF BASE MAPS
HENRY M. LEPPARD, EDITOR
Prepared by Henry M. Leppard
Published by the University of Chicago Press, Chicago, Illinois

**Fig. 2–5.** Glaciation in Europe.

sionally in the mountains of Czechoslovakia and even in the High Tatra of southern Poland. More of this pine is found in Switzerland. *Pinus montana* No. 76 forms subalpine scrub forests in southern Germany, Austria, Czechoslovakia, the Carpathian Ukraine, and southern Poland. It occurs rarely in the mountains of France (Jura, Vosges, Massif Central).

Besides these two now essentially Mediterranean species, only one pine grows in western Europe; it is *P. sylvestris* No. 69. In Denmark, Ireland, and southern England, *P. sylvestris* is extinct now, but apparently it was still there when man first inhabited those countries.

## Paleobotany

The earliest pines of western Europe are represented by Jurassic fragments from the region of Nancy-Frouard in northeastern France. Studt (1926) listed two pinelike fossils from the Upper Jurassic in France from near Boulogne-sur-Mer, on the English Channel. These fossils were named *Pitystrobus* (Pinites) *strobiformis* Fliche et Zeill. and *Pinus sauvagii* Fliche et Zeill. Several Cretaceous pines were listed by Studt. These are given in Table 2–8.

Perhaps we should not go as far as assigning Cretaceous pines to definite groups or sections as shown in Studt's publication. It would suffice to say that, for the whole Cretaceous period in western Europe, both diploxylon and haploxylon pines already have been found in several places.

In the Tertiary, pines in Europe were numerous. Remains of *P. langiana* Heer and *P. taedaformis* Heer were found in Miocene strata in Switzerland. *Pinus hampeana* was found in Tertiary deposits of Switzerland and in Austria. Berger (1951) reported *P. stellwagi* Kink. from a pre-Pliocene deposit (Pannon) near Vienna. Previously this diploxylon pine was reported only from the Lower Pliocene of western Germany.

Weyland and Schönfeld (1958) described *P. marcoduriae*, from Tertiary brown-coal (apparently Pliocene) deposits of Ville in the East Vosges, France. Theirs was a very thorough investigation, and there is no doubt that it was a haploxylon pine from Engler and Prantl's *Strobus* group.

In the Paris Basin in early Eocene (Lutecian) deposits a pine was found which, according to Combes (1908), should be known as "*P.* (*Pseudostrobus*) *defrancei.*" Thomson (1954) investigated Miocene brown-coal deposits in the northwestern Rhineland. Several species of pines were found there among the dominating angiosperms of the families Myricaceae, Betulaceae, and Ericaceae. As a whole, the Miocene forest of the northwestern Rhineland appears to have been predominantly temperate, although some subtropical elements were also present.

**Table 2–8.** Cretaceous Pines of Belgium, France, and Moravia (after Studt, 1926)

| Species | Place |
| --- | --- |
| P. andraei Coem. | Belgium |
| P. coemansi Heer | Belgium |
| P. rhombifera Corn. | Paris Basin, France |
| P. gracilis Carr. | Paris Basin, France |
| P. saportana Fliche | Argonne, France |
| P. argonensis Fliche | Argonne, France |
| P. quenstedti Heer | Moravia |

For the parts of Germany facing the Baltic Sea, Studt (1926) mentions an Oligocene pine from Prussia, *P. succinifera* (in part Goep.) Conw. (which resembled pines of the group *Gerardianae* and also those of the group *Cembroides*). *Pinus banksianoides* Goep. and Menge came from the early Tertiary of the same region.

Farther west in northwestern Europe, Tertiary pines (*P. cembrifolia* Casp.) were reported in Holland (Studt, 1926).

Remains of pines were found with other vegetation in the late Tertiary peat near Bremen, Germany (Weber, 1905). Weber suggested that forests of northwestern Germany were then about the same as they are now.

Studt (1926) listed the following Tertiary pines from the Lower Main Valley in central Germany: *P. laricio* Eng. and Kink. (it resembled living *P. nigra*); *P. hepios* Ung. (akin to *P. halepensis*); *P. montana* Mill.; and *P. cortesii* A. Brong. (which was also thought to be related to *P. halepensis*).

*Pinus silvatica* Goep. and Menge, *P. uncinoides* Gaudin, *P. baltica* Conw., and *P. banksianoides* Goep. and Menge were found in early Tertiary deposits of the Baltic region. *Pinus uncinoides* Gaudin grew there also in the Miocene. *Pinus cembrifolia* Casp. was reported from the early Tertiary of Holland.

Budantsev and Sveshnikova (1958) presented excellent photographs of Tertiary fossil pine cones from the Kaliningrad area (Samland). According to these authors, Heer long ago described *P. hageni* from Samland, and Goeppert listed, from the Baltic region, *P. thomasiana* (Goep.) E. Reich, *P. brachylepis* Sap., *P. sylvestris* L., and *P. pumilio* (i.e., *P. montana*). As regards *P. thomasiana*, Budantsev and Sveshnikova held that it was widely distributed in western Europe from the Lower Oligocene to the Pliocene; it has been reported from Germany, from Austria (Graz, Lower Lausitz), and from as far east as the Ukraine. *Pinus thomasiana* is related to living *P. halepensis* and *P. nigra*. Budantsev and Sveshnikova found, in the same area, remains of one more pine but were unable to identify its specific status.

During the Tertiary as a whole, many different species of pines were growing in western Europe. They were both haploxylon and diploxylon pines.

In the Pliocene, western European pines suffered extinction.

At the beginning of the Ice Age, the vegetation of western Europe was already of an alpine or tundra type, consisting of sphagnum, northern *Vaccinium*, dwarf birch, and *P. montana* No. 76. Then the ice mantle covered the whole northern part of western Europe.

What happened after the retreat of the ice in western Europe was outlined by Bertsch (1951), who analyzed pollen samples from peat near Lake Boden, in the southern part of Germany. In the lowest horizons, pollen grains of *P. montana* were found together with pollen of arctic willows and dwarf birch showing that the pine, as in North America, was the first pioneer tree to reoccupy the newly available area after the ice retreated. Later, to *P. montana* was added *P. sylvestris*. It came from the refugia of the Carpathian Mountains. After the retreat of ice in Germany, the tree succession was as follows: birch-pine, pine-hazel-oak forests, beech, spruce (Bertsch, 1951).

During all these stages, *P. sylvestris* was migrating north and northeast, and already, during early postglacial "pine time" (Bertsch's "*Kieferzeit*"), it advanced beyond the northeastern border of Germany. During the "beech time," *P. sylvestris* greatly expanded in northeastern Germany and farther east toward Siberia.

According to Bertsch, *P. sylvestris* was a common Tertiary pine in Germany. It was growing in the Main Valley during the Pliocene, together with seven other pine species; these were cold-tender and they disappeared when the climate became colder later in the Tertiary. *Pinus sylvestris* was, even at that time, as cold-resistant as it is now.

The present much restricted distribution of *P. sylvestris*, in western Germany, depends, according to Bertsch, partly on the competition with beech and spruce and partly on the change of climate, which became more oceanic and in which *P. sylvestris* did not thrive. Bertsch asserted that, where it does grow near the sea now, it has developed special climatic races.

*Pinus cembra* was found in Germany during the hazelnut time. Now it occurs in the alpine zone. *Pinus cembra* was growing during the last glaciation in the land adjacent to the Carpathians, and during the last interglacial it was to be found in the Inn Valley in Upper Austria. Its refugium, during the last glaciation, was probably in Hungary. Because *P. montana* and *P. cembra* were (and are) frost-hardy pines, they were not damaged much during the Ice Age.

Bertsch (1951) presented the following picture of distribution of vegetation in Germany during the last glaciation: South of the Scandinavian glacier lay a stretch of tundra, and farther south lay a scrub zone. A similar situation also existed in the south, where the ice sheet of the Alps descended north to the lowlands of Germany. In between was located a forest zone; the northern fringe of this forest was composed of birch and pine (*P. sylvestris*).

Similar forests, with an admixture of fir, alder, and hazelnut, also were found south of the Alps all the way to Pisa and the Pontine marshes of Italy.

The forests of the Cévennes, of central Italy, and of the northern reaches of the Balkans, contained a great number of broadleaf deciduous species; still farther south were found the evergreen Mediterranean forests.

The decrease of pine dominance in the southern part of Germany (Federsee, near Lake Boden) coincided with the hazelnut period and the Stone Age. During the Neolithic Age pine mostly was replaced by oak. Beech became dominant during the Bronze Age.

Ludi (1953) gave about the same picture of the occurrence of pine in the Foreland of the Swiss Alps. *Pinus sylvestris* was present there from the earliest time, just after the Dryas period, and it reached its maximum later, when the climate became drier and warmer. *Pinus cembra* was more restricted; it reached prominence earlier than *P. sylvestris*.

Siegfried (1961) studied remains of European bison (*Bison bonasus*) in Westphalia, Germany, and found that the animal lived there during the Pre-Boreal time. In this connection, Siegfried analyzed fossil pollen of nearby bogs and reported that, in the postglacial period (Dryas time), *P. sylvestris* was growing in abundance in that part of Germany.

Dubois and Dubois (1945), in their study of the forests of French Flanders during the last glacial and postglacial times, concluded that the succession of forests before the Sub-Boreal was this: After retreat of the ice, the first trees to appear were willow, birch, and pine; then pines became dominant. Before the Sub-Boreal time, there was not much difference in succession in the mountains, on one hand, and the hills, plains, and plateaus, on the other. The difference became evident only after the Sub-Boreal and through the Sub-Atlantic and until the present time.

**Hungary and Yugoslavia.** The plains of Hungary were once a large lake, which gradually filled with sediments. A subsequent, gentle uplift of the terrain drained the waters out. Several fossil pines have been reported from Hungary, but these were not from the central plains but from the slopes of surrounding mountains.

Andreanszky (1959) found remains of several pines in the Sarmatian (i.e., Miocene) deposits in the Zemplen Mountains of northeastern Hungary—*P. paleostrobus* Ett.; *P. goethana* Al. Br.; *P. hungarica* Kov.; a pine resembling *P. brutia; P. rigios* Ung., resembling living *P. taeda; P. aequimontana* (Ung.) Goep.; a pine resembling *P. halepensis* Mill.; and *P. kotschyana* Ung. (*P. junonis* Kov.), also resembling living *P. halepensis.*

That *P. sylvestris* was already growing during the Lower Pliocene in northern Croatia, Yugoslavia, was shown by Spoljaríc (1952).

**Czechoslovakia.** Czechoslovakia is a well-defined geographical region located between the Mediterranean region (in a broad sense) and the region of western Europe. The country is surrounded by mountains. In the north are the Sudeten; farther east are the Carpathian Mountains (West Beskids; rugged Tatra Mountains, with the highest peak over 2650 m; East Beskids; and Carpathians proper). In the northwest are the Erz Gebirge (Ore Mountains), and in the southwest is the Bohemian Forest Range. Between the Sudeten and the Carpathians is a broad, low gap—the Moravian Gate—that connects the country with the northern European lowlands. The northwestern part of the country—Bohemia— is a rolling lowland north of Prague and a plateau south of the capital. The eastern part—Slovakia—is a mountainous region, gradually descending in the south to the plains of Hungary and northern Yugoslavia.

At present, three pines are found in Czechoslovakia—*P. sylvestris* No. 69 in lower elevations, *P. montana* No. 76 in the subalpine zone of the mountains of Bohemia and in Slovakia, and *P. cembra* No. 70 of scattered occurrence above *P. montana* groves. *Pinus montana* and *P. cembra* occur also in the Carpathian Mountains, in Ruthenia—the easternmost part of the country, which, after World War II, was ceded to Russia.

Pines were growing in Czechoslovakia during the Cretaceous period. *Pinus macrostrobilina* Menz and *P. sulcata* Velen were described from Bohemia, and *P. quenstedti* from Moravia (Studt, 1926). Kräusel (Engler and Prantl, 1926) mentioned a Cretaceous pine from Bohemia, *P. longissima* Velen.

As regards Tertiary pines, Studt (1926) mentioned *P. uncinoides* Gaudin from the Pliocene of northern Bohemia; he placed this pine close to *P. montana* var. *uncinata.* Also, for northern Bohemia, Studt listed the following Tertiary pines: *P. ornata* Stern (near *P. pinaster*); *P. oviformis* Engl. (near *P. pinaster*); *P. saturni* Ung. (resembling such distant species as *P. sabiniana, P. patula,* and *P. serotina,* which is difficult to believe); *P. engelhardti* Menzel, which he placed near *P. longifolia* and *P. gerardiana; P. laricio* Engel.; *P. laricioides* Menzel; and *P. hepios* Ung. (akin to the Mediterranean *P. halepensis*). Although attempts to correlate these Bohemian Tertiary pines to living species are often hastily made and thus misleading, this list is important because it shows that several species of the genus *Pinus*, all apparently of the subgenus *Diploxylon*, were growing in the northern parts of Czechoslovakia.

Pollen analyses have shown that, during the Ancient Holocene, i.e., the period that immediately followed the last glaciation, *P. montana* No. 76 was much more common in the Carpathians (Neishtadt, 1957). It grows there now in a shrub form and is known as variety *mughus*, or Mugo pine; *P. cembra* No. 70 also occurs sporadically. The lower elevations are now occupied with broadleaf forests, with an admixture of *P. sylvestris* No. 69. In the Ancient Holocene, *P. montana* No. 76 occupied a much larger area, descending the lower slopes at that time covered with alpine and sub-alpine vegetation. Later in the Holocene, when the climate became warmer, Mugo pine retreated to its present alpine and subalpine environment.

**Poland.** Poland is a glaciated, rolling country of broadleaf forests. It forms a transition between western Europe and eastern Europe. At present only one species of pine grows there—*P. sylvestris*, except a few occurrences of *P. cembra* and *P. montana* in the southern (Tatra) mountains. During the Tertiary, the pine flora of Poland was more diversified, for several pines have been described from that country. Studt (1926) mentioned a Tertiary pine—*P. tarnocziensis* from Galicia. It is dubious though that it is closely related to *P. longifolia. Pinus salinarum* Part. of the Lower Miocene comes from the Wieliczka salt mines of Poland. From Silesia was reported Tertiary *P. spinosa* Herbst, which looked like *P. taeda* No. 24 or *P. pinaster* No. 80. *Pinus geanthradis* E. Reich appeared to be near *P. strobus* No. 20. Occurrence of *P. cembra* No. 70 in Poland during the Tertiary was reported by Holmboe (Charlesworth, 1957). According to Budantsev and Sveshnikova (1958), *P. thomasiana* was found in Tertiary deposits near Tarnovitz and at Gdansk (Danzig).

**Scandinavia and Denmark.** The Scandinavian Peninsula is a mountainous country. Its backbone is an old range of Pre-Cambrian age. Only in the southern part of Sweden is the country a lowland. The central part of Finland is a low granitic plateau. The same Pre-Cambrian rocks and structures appear in Scotland and in Ireland.

There is no doubt that pines were growing on the Scandinavian Peninsula even during the Mesozoic era. *Pinus narhorsti* Conw. was described from the Upper Cretaceous of southern Sweden, and also remains of a pine were found there that resembled *P. montana* No. 76 (Conwentz, 1892). *Pinus herningensis* Koch., a haploxylon pine of the group *Cembrae*, was described from Miocene or Lower Pliocene strata in western Jutland, Denmark (Koch, 1959). During the Tertiary period, pines were growing on the Scandinavian Peninsula and in Jutland, as well as in other places in the Baltic Sea region.

During the glaciation, all pines of the Baltic Sea region were destroyed and *P. sylvestris* No. 69 reinvaded the area, not immediately after the retreat of the ice but only when the Dryas Flora had occupied the newly available areas.

The postglacial history of pines in the northwestern heath region of Jutland, in Denmark, was studied by Jonassen (1950). He came to the important conclusions that pine exceeded all other tree species in pollen production and that diffusion of its pollen was widespread. This capacity of pines to produce abundant pollen often caused erroneous conclusions of the part played by pines in postglacial succession.

Essentially, plant succession in Jutland was about the same as in all glaciated parts of western Europe, only it was simpler. After the retreat of the ice and a tundra period, the pioneer invaders were birch and pine (*P. sylvestris*); these were followed by hazel and by oak mixed forest. Eventually *Calluna* appeared and gradually encroached on the forest.

The appearance of man was detrimental to pines, when in the Stone Age he repeatedly cleared patches of forest and abandoned the old clearings, practicing a shifting cultivation similar to that still being practiced in southeastern Asia now. Changes in the climate of Jutland have also contributed to the disappearance of pines. The retreat of the ice coincided with the rise of the land; the Scandinavian Peninsula became connected with western Europe via Denmark, and through this land bridge the birch came to Scandinavia. *Pinus sylvestris* migrated somewhat later. It is entirely possible that *P. sylvestris* also survived the Ice Age in the not too numerous unglaciated refugia (Nordhagen, 1935).

For thousands of years after that, *P. sylvestris* was a dominant conifer on the Scandinavian Peninsula. Gradually pine was replaced by spruce, and later, in the southern part of Sweden, by oak. From Denmark, pine disappeared completely, and, in southern Sweden, it was pushed somewhat north, and it ceased to be a dominant conifer of Scandinavia. The end of the "pine time," i.e., of the dominance of *P. sylvestris*, occurred about 12,000 years ago. Man contributed much to the destruction of pine forests in southern Sweden, either by cutting pines and leaving them to be replaced by spruce and oak or by clearing the land for agriculture.

**Great Britain.** The British Isles were once a part of the continent, and their physiography is the same as that of western Europe. The Scandinavian Pre-Cambrian structure is evident in Scotland and in parts of Ireland. Much of Wales, southern Ireland, and Cornwall originated in the same age as the Vosges Mountains of France (Hubbard, 1937).

A strait separated Great Britain from continental Europe at the end of the Jurassic and the beginning of the Cretaceous. From then until the beginning of the Tertiary, the islands were connected partly with northern Atlantis and partly with Europe. During the Eocene and Oligocene, there was no land connection between Great Britain and northwestern Europe, although there was a land bridge to Normandy. In the beginning of the Miocene, there was a connection, but it was disrupted later in that epoch.

During the Pliocene, contacts and disruptions occurred again.

During the Upper Pleistocene, the Scandinavian ice shield reached the British Isles. Ice covered almost all of Great Britain except the southern parts of Ireland and England. During the Ice Age also, there were intermittent land connections between England and the continent. The present English Channel was formed after the Ice Age.

There is a reference to the presence in the early Cretaceous (Walden) Flora of fossil remains of pine "with clusters of long needles and long pendulous cones recalling the Himalayan *Pinus excelsa*" (Seward, 1941), i.e., *P. griffithii* No. 91. Couper (1958) described pollen grains of *Abietieneaepollenites* from the Jurassic and Lower Cretaceous of England. The morphology of pollen was similar to that of *Pinus* (*P. cembra* No. 70 and *P. peuce* No. 71). The Lower Cretaceous specimens were judged to belong to plants closely related to *Pinus*. They appeared to be distinct from pollen grains of other genera of the Abietaceae: *Abies, Picea,* and *Cedrus*. Couper commented on the close similarity of pine pollen grains of the Lower Cretaceous and the Jurassic.

The early Tertiary flora of southern England was of a tropical character. Reid and Chandler (1933), describing the Middle Eocene London Flora, mentioned that it came from southeastern Asia along the north shores of the ancient Tethys Sea.

During the Tertiary, pines were growing in the British Isles. Chandler (1961) included two pines in her London Clay Eocene Flora: *P. macrocephalus* (Lindley and Hutton) Gardner (formerly described by Gardner as *Sequoia*), and *P. bowerbanki* (Carruthers) Gardner. Commenting on the former, Chandler said,

. . . the occurrence of *Pinus* in a flora as tropical as that of London Clay is curious, for the genus is essentially temperate. Very few species extend into the tropical latitudes even at considerable altitudes, and none lives at the present day at low altitudes strictly within the tropics. Perhaps the cones were transported a considerable distance from some upland area. But it seems more probable that this is a tropical species and that the range of the genus has contracted since early Eocene times. Moreover, as stated [previously] pine forests now occur behind the mangroves in Florida.

Chandler was in error when she said that very few species extend into tropical latitudes (see Chapter 3), but she was right in saying that the genus *Pinus* is historically a genus of temperate climates and that few pines are found in low altitudes in the tropics. Some pines adapted themselves to the tropical lowlands, but this was a rare and local phenomenon. Compare Chandler's report with the findings of Shilkina (p. 86), and see the discussion of *P. strobus* var. *chiapensis* No. 34 in Chapter 3.

The cold climate of the late Tertiary and the subsequent glaciation that covered most of the British Isles exterminated all pines except one, as these phenomena exterminated all pines in northern Europe. The only pine species that survived the Ice Age in the non-glaciated areas of southern England, and possibly also in refugia within the glaciated parts of the islands, was *P. sylvestris*.

As a result of his studies based on pollen analysis of forest-tree succession in North Yorkshire and west of Manchester, Erdtman (1926, 1929) concluded that, after the retreat of the ice, birch and pine (*P. sylvestris* No. 69) were the first trees to reach middle England from the south. Hazel and other hardwoods came later. Generally, the postglacial history of pines in England—represented by only one species, *P. sylvestris*—was the same as on the continent. Godwin (1940) arrived at essentially the same conclusions.

In a later paper, Godwin (1956) mentioned that pine pollen has been found in every British interglacial deposit examined by pollen analysts. It was exclusively *P. sylvestris* pollen. *Pinus sylvestris* was dominant during the period of increasing warmth in the middle of the Holocene (Godwin, 1940). The almost complete extermination of *P. sylvestris* in the British Isles happened recently, after man arrived there. Pine stumps have been found in peat bogs of Ireland and southern England. At present, *P. sylvestris* is found only in Scotland, from where it has acquired its "common" English name, "Scots Pine."

## Summary

Strictly speaking, only one pine (*P. sylvestris* No. 69) grows in the region of western Europe. *Pinus cembra* No. 70 and *P. montana* No. 76 are found in the mountains separating western Europe from the Mediterranean pine region. In rare instances, *P. montana* penetrates rather deeply into western Europe.

The oldest European fossil pines appear to be from the Jurassic. Reports on occurrence of Cretaceous pines are frequent.

During the Tertiary, many different species of pines were growing in western Europe. The Tertiary flora of western Europe generally was similar to the living floras of North America and eastern Asia (Reid, 1920). The pines were both haploxylon and diploxylon, and they were similar to the North American and eastern Asiatic pines.

After the Miocene, the climate became colder and pines began to disappear. In the Pliocene, all but two of the remaining western European pine species suffered extinction. While in North America and eastern Asia the way to the south was open to the pines retreating before the advancing ice, in western Europe escape south during the Pliocene was blocked by the high ranges of the already formed Alps and their eastern extensions. After the end of glaciation, *P. sylvestris* No. 69 (and rarely *P. montana* No. 76) returned north from the unglaciated refugia.

## EASTERN EUROPE AND NORTHERN ASIA

### Physiography *

The pine region of eastern Europe and northern Asia occupies an enormous expanse of land located between western Europe and the North Pacific Ocean. In the north, it borders the Arctic region and in the south the dry grasslands of eastern Europe and of central Asia and Mongolia. In the southeast, it merges into the pine region of eastern Asia.

Eastern Europe is generally either gently rolling or a flat plain. Only on the Kola Peninsula of the northwest are there plateau-like mountains, elevated to 1200 m and higher above the plain. In the midst of eastern Europe, the elevations are slightly higher than the surrounding plains, not exceeding 350 m. This is the so-called Central Russian Upland.

Two tectonic depressions are located in the south of eastern Europe corresponding to the Caspian and Black Sea lowlands. Considerable readjustments of the earth's crust took place in this part of eastern Europe during the Cenozoic era. These were accompanied by sea transgressions and regressions. The Caspian tectonic depression was formed between Miocene and Pliocene times, or perhaps in the Upper Pliocene. The Black Sea Lowland is smaller than the Caspian Lowland. It is formed with strata of Miocene and Pliocene age, deposited by the shallow seas that repeatedly covered the area.

During the Quaternary glaciations of the north, most of the Caspian Lowland was covered with water. The Caspian Sea itself is even now 28 m below sea level. As to the Black Sea, its Quaternary history was rather complicated; the Sea advanced and retreated, now connected with the Mediterranean, now separated from it. Apparently the Black

---

* Physiographic description of this region is taken chiefly from the author's *Geography of Russia* (Mirov, 1951).

Sea assumed its present shape and established its present contact with the Mediterranean only about 50,000 years ago (Dobrynin, 1948).

Farther east, in Asia, are the stretches of the Turan Lowland with its deserts. The country between the Aral Sea and western Siberia is known as the "Turgai Tableland." The central part of the Tableland (so-called Turgai Gate) is depressed to absolute elevations of about 100 to 125 m. During the Tertiary this depression was under water, connecting the western Siberian Lower Tertiary sea with the Turan Sea. The whole area of the Turgai Tableland is composed of Oligocene marine sediments and Miocene continental deposits. Its name has a paleobotanical significance, for it gave the name to the Turgaian Floristic Province (see page 111). Western Siberia is an enormous lowland where thick layers of Tertiary and, especially, Quaternary sediments lie upon the Hercynian folds.

East of the Yenisei, the Western Siberian Lowland changes abruptly to the Central Siberian Plateau formed on the Pre-Cambrian platform. It is the primeval continent of Asia known as "Angara Land," or "Angaride." The country there is rather flat, crossed by broad and deep river valleys. Mountains are flat topped and not too high.

Northeastern Siberia, except the stretches of arctic, low-lying tundra near the ocean, is a mountainous country. The Cherski Range reaches from about 2000 to 2500 m in height. During the Paleozoic and Mesozoic eras, this region was a huge geosynclinal basin extending from the mouth of the Lena to the Bering Sea. It was covered with an ancient sea in which marine sediments accumulated to a depth of about 9000 to 15,000 m.

The geomorphology of northeastern Siberia is chiefly a product of Mesozoic foldings. Farther south, in the southern Transbaikal, and in the Maritime Province of Russia, mountains are also of Mesozoic origin. The extreme northeast of Siberia near the Bering and Okhotsk seas is the region of Tertiary foldings.

Eastern Europe is separated from Siberia by the low, much worked out Upper Paleozoic (Hercynian) Ural Mountains. Their continuation in the north is evident in the islands of Novaia Zemlia; in the south, the Ural Mountains merge into a plateau-like arid range of the Mugodjars.

The Altai Mountains in the south of western Siberia lying partly in Mongolia-Dzhungaria, and the mountains of central Asia (except older, northern ranges of the Tien Shan), were also formed by the Hercynian foldings. Northern arcs of the Tien Shan system were formed in the Lower Paleozoic, and the Kopet-Dagh system is of Tertiary origin. The Sayan Mountains are located east of the Altai; both the Altai and the Sayans are essentially an ancient peneplain uplifted during the Tertiary.

The ancient mountain ranges of the southern part of northern Asia (along the north shore of the ancient Tethys Sea) were to be of utmost importance for the present study, for they apparently formed a route of migration of pines from eastern Asia to the Mediterranean region.

During the Ice Age, the Scandinavian glacier moved south on both sides of the Central Russian Upland. Eastern Europe bears unmistakable evidence of the Riss and Würm glaciations. The southern limits of glaciation extended from Lvov (Lwow, Lemberg) in the western Ukraine (about 50° north latitude) to the northern Urals and beyond. The ice mantle was over 2000 m thick.

In Belorussia, i.e., in the area located between Poland and the Ukraine, the history of the Ice Age was about the same as in western Europe. However, the glaciation of its southern part was not as extensive as farther north. There was no Würm glaciation in southern Belorussia. (See map, Fig. 2–5.)

Western Siberia apparently has had only one glaciation; it was contemporary with the Riss glaciation of Europe. Because of the drier climate of western Siberia, glaciation did not extend as far south as the European glaciation, nor was the thickness of the ice mantle as great as in Europe. It measured only about 700 m. The western Siberian glaciers centered in the northern Urals and on the Taimyr Peninsula.

The Würm glaciation in western Siberia was of a local character, having been restricted to the Ural Mountains and to the Altai system.

In eastern Siberia, because of insufficient moisture, there was no extensive glaciation; it occurred only locally and for the most part was restricted to mountains such as the Sayans. The climate of eastern Siberia during the Ice Age was even more severe than it is now. Extensive areas of the land were cooled to temperatures much below freezing even before the advent of the Ice Age, and they have remained frozen until the present time. Some late Tertiary remains of pines have been well preserved in the frozen soils of northeastern Siberia (Sukachev, 1910).

In the mountains of central Asia, glaciation was confined to the high mountains, and extensive glaciers exist even at present in the Tien Shan system.

## Present Distribution of Pines

Only three species are found over the vast expanse of land from the borders of western Europe to the Pacific Coast of northern Asia. *Pinus sylvestris* No. 69 almost reaches the coast of the Okhotsk Sea in the far east of Asia. *Pinus sibirica* No. 67 forms extensive forests in northeastern Europe and western and eastern Siberia. Although previously (Shaw, 1914) this pine was considered identical to *P. cembra* No. 70, there are sufficient grounds to describe it as an independent species.

*Pinus pumila* No. 68, a timber-line species often forming dense thickets, is found from Lake Baikal to Korea, the Japanese island of Honshu, the coast of the Bering Sea, nearby islands, Kamchatka, and the Kurile archipelago. Thus, its area extends to the region of eastern Asia (Tikhomirov, 1949).

On the Central Russian Upland, *P. sylvestris* grows either in low-lying sandy places or, rarely, on limestone hills or exposed chalk cliffs. It is generally assumed (Wulff, 1944) that *P. sylvestris* of the limestone hills, which were not covered with ice during the Quaternary glaciation, is a Tertiary relic, while the lowland pine is a secondary, postglacial invader. Usually the pine growing on limestone is accompanied by other Tertiary relics such as *Daphne sophia, D. juliae,* or *Androsace villosa.* Therefore, *P. sylvestris* was growing in central eastern Europe during the Tertiary. Possibly it had migrated there from eastern Asia by way of the northern shores of the Tethys Sea.

## Paleobotany

**The Mesozoic Era.** Many fossil pines are listed for eastern Europe and Siberia by Krishtofovich in his *Prodromus Florae Fossilis* (1941). These, mostly early, findings are assembled in Table 2–9.

Heer's findings from eastern Siberia, also listed in Table 2–9, were critically reviewed and verified by Krishtofovich.

Zauer, Kara-Murza, and Sedova (1954), all three well-known palynologists, published a brief review based on pollen studies on the main stages of development of vegetation in the U.S.S.R. during the Mesozoic time. During the Lower Triassic, when Cordaitales began to disappear and Bennettitales just began to appear, Ginkgoales, cycads, and conifers also became prominent. Among the last, the family Pinaceae attained considerable importance. Pollen analyses of Middle Triassic sediments showed still a great deal of the Paleozoic relics, but the gradual change in composition of forest was already evident, as, for instance, more and more prominence was gained by the gymnosperms. The genus *Pinus* appeared in the Upper Triassic, already represented by both subgenera, *Haploxylon* and *Diploxylon.* At the same time, in northern Siberia, Bennettitales, Ginkgoales, and cycads had reached their maximum development. This rather casual mention of the presence of pine pollen in the Upper Triassic is quite startling. No reference was made in the review to the original source. Neishtadt (1960), in his historical sketch of palynology in the U.S.S.R., was more cautious. He remarked that "the spore-pollen complexes of the Triassic are not yet sufficiently known, in comparison to other periods of the Mesozoic era." However, as pollen of the genus *Pinus* can be easily distinguished from the pollen of other conifer genera, and also remembering other supporting evidence (see

**Table 2–9.** Fossil Pines of Eastern Europe and Northern Asia (Compiled from Krishtofovich [1941])

| Species | Locality |
| --- | --- |
| JURASSIC | |
| P. maakiana Heer | Ust Balei, eastern Siberia |
| P. nordenskiöldi Heer | Ust Balei; also Far East, Yakut Republic, Amur Region |
| P. nordenskiöldi Heer (?) | Chita Province, River Zeia |
| P. prodromus Heer | Ust Balei, eastern Siberia |
| P. vitimi Reiss | River Vitim, Transbaikal (Upper Jurassic) |
| CRETACEOUS | |
| P. elliptica Trautsch. | Klin, Moscow Province |
| P. (cedrus) lopatini Heer | Simonova, Krasnoyask Territory, Eastern Siberia |
| P. sp. (Heer-Krisht.) | Simonova, Krasnoyask Territory, Eastern Siberia |
| P. tanaica Kutorga | River Don area |
| P. viatkensis Prinada | Kirov Province, northeastern Europe |
| Pinus sp. | River Bureia, tributary to the Amur |
| Pinus sp. | River Bureia, tributary to the Amur |
| Pinus sp. ind. of P. exogyra Corda | Kuibyshev Province, Middle Volga |
| TERTIARY | |
| P. monticola D. Don | Post-Pliocene (Preglacial) |
| P. paleostrobus Heer | Oligocene-Miocene; Kursk Province, eastern Europe |
| P. sarmatica Palibin | Northeast Crimea |
| P. sylvestris | Kiev, Ukraine |
| Pinus sp. (Sukachev) | Arctic northeastern Siberia |
| Pinus sp. (Pacht) | Kuibyshev Province, Middle Volga |
| Pinus sp. (Schmal.) | Miocene or Pliocene; East Kazakhstan Province |
| Pinus sp. (Krisht.) | Sarmatian (Lower Miocene); Lower Dnieper, Ukraine |
| Pinus sp. (Palibin) | Miocene; Kerch, northeast Crimea |
| Pinus sp. (Neuburg) | River Kara-Irtysh, East Kazakhstan Province |
| Pinus sp. (Nikitin) | Pliocene; Voronezh Province, eastern Europe |
| Pinus sp. (Nikitin) | Upper Pliocene; Voronezh Province |
| Pinus sp. (Ianishevsky) | Miocene; Tomsk, western Siberia |
| Pinus sp. (Vosinsky) | Post-Pliocene; Moscow Province, central part of eastern Europe |
| Pinus sp. (Nikitin) | Post-Pliocene; Voronezh Province, eastern Europe |
| Pinus sp. (Nikitin) | Riss-Würm Interglacial; Voronezh Province |
| Pinus sp. (Nikitin) | Mindel-Riss Interglacial; Voronezh Province |
| Pinus sp. (Nesterov) | Post-Pliocene; Middle Urals, Sverdlovsk Province |

NOTE: Names in parentheses after *Pinus* sp. are names of those who described material as to genus only.

Names of about thirty-four wood remains, presumably of pines, are given in Krishtofovich's *Prodromus*. Some probably belong to the genus *Pinus*; others (for instance, those described as from the Permian) obviously are not pines.

Mason, 1927, p. 146), it is possible that the genus *Pinus* appeared during the Triassic.

Neiburg (1959) listed many gymnosperms of Triassic Age in the Pechora Basin of northeastern Europe, but the genus *Pinus* was not among them; if pines originated during the Triassic, they may not have reached northeastern Europe during that period.

Jurassic pines listed by Krishtofovich (1941) were all from eastern Siberia. Baikovskaia (1956) published an excellent and scholarly review of the Upper Cretaceous flora of northern Asia. The Upper Cretaceous flora of Asia is the foundation for establishing the two large floristic provinces of Krishtofovich—the Turgaian (see pages 111–112), with its deciduous forests, and the Poltavian (after the city of Poltava, Ukraine), characterized by tropical and subtropical evergreen trees.

In the Chulym-Yenisei region of the southern part of eastern Siberia, in the Upper Cretaceous strata (Cenomanian-Turonian), Baikovskaia found abundant pine material. Wisely, she made no attempts to run the material down to the species level. Another location, which has been well known since Heer's days, where Upper Cretaceous pines were found in 1878 by Lopatin in western Siberia, is at the village Simonova near the town of Achinsk. From there, Heer (1878) described *P.* (*Cedrus*) *Lopatini* and also another pine (*P.* sp.). Baikovskaia believes that the Simonova Flora was of the Turonian stage of the Cretaceous. She commented that conifers were poorly represented in that flora and this means that pines also comprised not too prominent components of the forest; rather, they were sparsely admixed. Scarcity of pines during the Cretaceous in Siberia was made obvious by the review.

In the southern Urals, from Cenomanian-Turonian deposits, Palibin described *P. uralensis*. Some pines of the same age have been described from other parts of the southern Urals. Farther south, in western Kazakhstan (River Temir), south of the town of Aktubinsk, Krishtofovich found *P. quenstedti* Heer (but with a question mark after its specific name). On the River Lemva in the western Urals (i.e., in the European part of Russia), a Turonian pine was found.

Bolkhovitina (1953) summarized many reports on occurrence of pine pollen in Cretaceous deposits of western Siberia, Kazakhstan, and the southern half of eastern Europe. She mentioned difficulties of differentiation between pollen grains of different species of the genus. Partly, these difficulties exist because some pine species have been extinct for a long time and thus could not be compared with any living pines, and, partly, they exist because pollen grains were compressed and distorted. Nevertheless, these were pine pollen grains of both of the subgenera—*Haploxylon* and *Diploxylon*. Her findings are presented in Table 2–10.

**Table 2-10. Cretaceous Pines Identified by Bolkhovitina by Their Pollen**

| Species | Suggested Taxonomic Position Within Genus | Locality | Remarks |
|---|---|---|---|
| *P. incrassata* Naum. | Uncertain. | Eastern slope, Middle Urals, north shore of Aral Sea. Aaghiz, River Emba; Jurassic? | Possibly a Jurassic relic, disappeared toward the Tertiary. |
| *P. kulandyensis* sp. n. | Uncertain. | North shore of Aral Sea. | |
| *P. trivialis* Naum. | A haploxylon pine. | North shore of Aral; also from Apt epoch. Moscow Province, European Russia. | Probable distribution: Middle Jurassic of Transcaucasus; southern Urals. |
| *P. aequalis* Naum. | A haploxylon pine. | Crimea, western Kazakhstan. | |
| *P. subconcinua* Naum. | Close to *P. banksiana* No. 32 of the section *Insignes*. | Eastern slope, Middle Urals, Crimea, western Kazakhstan. | |
| *P. aralica*, sp. n. | Section *Strobus*. Similar to *P. excelsa* Wall. | North shore of Aral Sea. | |
| *P. strobiformis* sp. n. | Section *Strobus*. | Moscow Province, European Russia. | Not to be confused with living *P. strobiformis* Engelm. or *P. strobiformis* Sarg. |
| *P. vulgaris* Naum. | Haploxylon pine of section *Paracembra*. | Eastern slope of northern Urals, Crimea, north shore of Aral Sea, eastern slope of southern Urals. | Also found in Lower Cretaceous in western Siberia. |
| *P. concessa* Naum. | Section *Paracembra*. Pollen looked like that of *P. edulis* No. 8, but it is highly improbable that a piñon pine would have grown there. | Kaluga Province, European Russia. | Also found in Cretaceous in western Siberia. |
| *P. insignis* Naum. | Pollen is similar to that of *P. montana* No. 76 of Shaw's group *Lariciones*. | Eastern slope of Middle Urals, north shore of Aral Sea, western Kazakhstan. Also occurred in western Siberia. | Not to be confused with living *P. insignis Douglas* (No. 19). |
| *P. nigraeformis* sp. n. | Appeared to be close to *P. nigra* No. 74 of Shaw's group *Lariciones*. | Moscow Province, European Russia. | |

In the Russian manual *Fundamentals of Paleontology of the U.S.S.R.,* recent volumes of which are devoted to paleobotany and have been edited by A. L. Takhtajan, the following information on pines is given:

In the fossil state are known pine cones, foliage, seeds, pollen. The genus *Pinus* is known since the Jurassic from Transbaikal region, Irkutsk province, Amur area. Cretaceous pines are known from Caucasus, the Kuban Area (north of the Caucasus), the lower Don River, northern Ural, Moscow, Kirov and Kuibyshev provinces (i.e., central and northeastern parts of European Russia), western Kazakhstan, western Siberia, New Siberian Islands. Pollen in Jurassic and Cretaceous deposits has been found in many localities of U.S.S.R.[*]

All these findings apparently have been carefully checked and edited. Reports on occurrence of pines older than those of Jurassic times were not included in the manual.

**The Tertiary Period.** The records of Tertiary pines from eastern Europe and northern Asia are abundant. The early findings have been listed in Table 2–9. More recent information is available from all parts of the region.

Forests of the Ukraine during the Tertiary period were of tropical or subtropical character. The paleobotanical record shows that pines were admixed in these forests. They were not too numerous, apparently being located on the fringes of the more elevated places.

In the southern part of eastern Europe—on the territory of the Ukraine —during the Eocene, pines occurred only occasionally, whereas tropical and subtropical plants predominated (Schekina, 1953). Pine pollen also was found in Eocene flora of the west bank of the Don (Chiguriaeva, 1952), in the southeastern part of eastern Europe. Tertiary fossil pines have been reported also from Belorussia.

An Eocene pine resembling *P. sabiniana* No. 10 was described from near Kiev; judging from the drawing of the cone scale, it did not belong necessarily to a pine close to living *P. sabiniana,* but it was a diploxylon pine, and that is sufficiently important. A Tertiary *P. sylvestris* was reported also from the vicinity of Kiev. *Pinus sarmatica* Palib. from the Miocene of the Crimean Lowland was a "pre-*brutia*" pine, indicating that the Tertiary flora of the south of eastern Europe also contained some Mediterranean species.

Dorofeev (1955) described *P. palibini* from the Sarmatian (Lower Miocene) sediments of the Taman Peninsula, of the Azov Sea, i.e., between the Ukraine and the Caucasus.

Gradually, when the climate became colder—and the Tertiary flora of the Ukraine became much impoverished—almost all pines perished. *Pinus nigra, P. sylvestris,* and *P. pityusa* survived only in the mountain

[*] Takhtajan, 1963.

ranges of Crimea, i.e., in the Mediterranean region adjacent to the Ukraine.

In the Asiatic part of Russia, Gorbunov (1958) described several Tertiary pines from Middle Oligocene, or possibly Miocene, times, from near Tomsk, western Siberia (56° 30′ north, 85° east). These pines were *P. paleostrobus* (Ett.) Heer; *P. spinosa* Herbst, which possibly was related to *P. taeda; P. petri-nikitinii* sp. n. ("like *P. rigida*"); *P. thomasiana* (Goep.) P. Reich, represented by three varieties: *kasparanica, kompassica,* and *tomskiana.* The report is accompanied by excellent photographs of well-preserved cones.

Dorofeev (1957) reported on a Tertiary flora near Tara, in the southern part of western Siberia, which can be broadly determined as dating from a period from the Upper Oligocene to the Sarmatian (i.e. Lower Miocene). There he found well-preserved cones of a pine that he identified as *P. spinosa* Herbst, formerly reported from the Tertiary of Silesia and of Czechoslovakia. It was different from *P. spinosa* from Poland. There were some discrepancies in the description of this pine, but suffice it to say that the pine looked like *P. taeda* or perhaps like *P. rigida.* Besides finding this pine, Dorofeev found some remains of two more diploxylon pines, but he could not identify them more precisely.

Abuziarova (1953), as did many others, found pine pollen from the middle of the Oligocene in the Turgai country (Kazakhstan). Pines were also growing near Pavlodar in northern Kazakhstan (Zaklinskaia, 1953). An Eocene *P. nikitinii* was described from the same locality (Budantsev, 1957).

Kornilova (1960) found both haploxylon and diploxylon pines in the Lower Miocene deposits of Kustanai Province, northwestern Kazakhstan. Climate during the Lower Miocene was drier than in the northern parts of Asia.

Karavaev (1960) described a diploxylon pine from Miocene-Pliocene strata in central Yakut country (the Middle Lena River). He commented on the unusual shape of the cone scales of this pine; the scales were elongated parallel to the axis of the cone rather than in a crosswise direction as was common with most other diploxylon pines of that period. He named this pine *"Pinus sukaczewi."*

During the Pleistocene, *P. sylvestris* was growing in northern Kazakhstan; there it still occurs occasionally. Apparently there were no reports of fossil pines from the countries lying farther south, i.e., from the deserts and mountains of central Asia.

The area of the present Altai Mountains in the Tertiary period was a plain bordered with sea basins. Higher mountains of an alpine character were formed in the Altai system only at the end of the Tertiary. The climate there was humid and warm. Temperate-climate forests developed on the shores of these Tertiary basins. Suslov (1947) mentions *Taxodium, Sequoia, Ginkgo, Pterocarya,* and *Liriodendron;* no doubt, pines also were admixed there, perhaps on more elevated places. Farther east, in the region of the present Sayan Mountains, Tertiary forests of the swampy lowlands were of a mixed type similar to that in the Altai; *Carpinus, Ulmus,* and *Tilia* predominated. There were also conifers— *Tsuga, Taxodium,* and *Picea* (resembling *Picea sitchensis* of western North America)—and there was an admixture of pines "similar to the pines of the United States" (Suslov, 1947).

In the discussion of the Arctic region on page 55, a reference was made to a discovery of *P. monticola* No. 4 in preglacial deposits of the Lower Lena region, northeastern Siberia. This was an outstanding discovery. The material (cones and branches) was, no doubt, of the Tertiary age, preserved so well in frozen strata that it was identified without any difficulty as *P. monticola.* Occurrence of this western American haploxylon pine, or its immediate ancestor, in northeastern Siberia shows not only that a great similarity existed between pines of northeastern Asia and northwestern America but also that a North American pine had grown in the late Tertiary period on the continent of Asia.

Krishtofovich outlined in numerous publications the general development of the flora of northern Eurasia. During the Eocene and Oligocene, the vegetation of the middle Ural Mountains (at 61° north latitude), which now divide Siberia from Europe, was about the same as that of Greenland. It was of a warm-temperate character, and it included *Magnolia, Ficus, Populus, Ilex, Macclintockia trinervis* Heer, and *Sequoia langsdorfii* Brong. Pines also were growing at that time both in Greenland and in the middle Urals. As a whole, this flora was similar to that of the present eastern United States. On the other hand, it had no similarity to the subtropical and tropical Paleogene floras of the Ukraine (i.e., the south of eastern Europe) and of western Europe.

At the same time, in the whole of Siberia, from the Ural Mountains to Kamchatka, in the Pacific northeast, the vegetation was strikingly monotonous. It was composed of *Alnus, Castanea, Platanus, Fagus, Carpinus, Populus, Macclintockia,* and *Liquidambar.* It was a temperate-climate flora that contained conifers including pines. A similar monotonous flora existed on the other side of the Pacific; it did not contain any southern (tropical) elements (Krishtofovich, 1930, 1956).

As a result of his researches, Krishtofovich divided Eurasia into two large Tertiary floristic regions: (1) the evergreen tropical or subtropical flora of the south of east Europe including the Ukraine, Belorussia, and the southern part of Russia proper and (2) the temperate Arcto-Tertiary flora of northeastern Europe and northern Asia. He called the former the "Poltavian Flora." In the latter, he distinguished three provinces:

(1) The Greenland province occupied the northern Urals and adjacent parts of northeastern Europe. It was limited in the east by the Turgai Sea (i.e., the body of water that cut longitudinally across western Siberia). (2) The enormous area of the middle zone of Siberia, northern Turkestan, Manchuria, Korea, and northern parts of Japan, as well as Alaska, was occupied by extensive deciduous forests at least until the lower Miocene. Krishtofovich considered these forests as belonging to the Turgaian Flora (after the Turgai region of central Kazakhstan), where Abich, in 1858 (Krishtofovich, 1941), discovered the components of this flora (with several species of *Comptonia*). Although the terms *Poltavian Flora* and *Turgaian Flora* apparently are seldom used outside of Russia, the Soviet paleobotanists always refer to these floristic regions. Possibly, among the early Tertiary pines of the Ukraine there were some tropical species similar to a pine described by Shilkina (1958) for Transcaucasia. (3) The third Tertiary floristic province of Eurasia was designated by Krishtofovich as the "North Siberian" province, which, being perhaps older than the Turgaian province, was characterized by the large-size leaves of *Populus richardsonii* Heer (*Cercidiphyllum arcticum* [Heer] Brown), described from the New Siberian Islands and from Anadyr (Krishtofovich, 1941). Possibly this flora was the most ancient Tertiary flora. It was still very close to Upper Cretaceous floras, and it was related to the ancient floras of Greenland and those of North America, such as the Fort Union Flora.

**Postglacial Northern Eurasia.** Toward the end of the Tertiary, and especially during the Ice Age, all but three pines of eastern Europe and Siberia perished. *Pinus sylvestris* No. 69 survived in the refugia of western Europe, in the south of western Siberia, and even possibly in the nonglaciated areas of the Central Russian Upland. *Pinus sibirica* No. 67 survived in the refugia of the Altai Mountains, and *P. pumila* No. 68 in the eastern and southern parts of its present range, probably somewhere in Japan (see page 59).

The pattern of postglacial migration was different for each of these three pines. *Pinus sylvestris* was the pioneer invader of areas available after the retreat of ice. The postglaciation history of this pine in Belorussia was similar to that in western Europe. At present, it is the only pine naturally growing in Belorussia. Its path of migration has been from southwest to northeast (Bertsch, 1951).

According to Neishtadt (1957), at the advent of the Ice Age, *P. sylvestris* was widely distributed in eastern Europe. Apparently, at the time of glaciation, this pine, together with birch and aspen, formed groves that had advanced and retreated repeatedly following the arctic flora. Near Moscow, Sukachev *et al.* (1960) found in the interglacial

Pleistocene deposits an abundance of *P. sylvestris* pollen. At the beginning of the Holocene (i.e., postglacial), not more than half of the present area of *P. sylvestris* was occupied by this species. It was absent from the northern part of eastern Europe. It was also absent from the northern and middle Ural Mountains. The center of its distribution in eastern Europe was in the basin of the Middle and Upper Dnieper and along the coast of the Gulf of Finland.

Another center of distribution of *P. sylvestris* was on the Ob-Irtysh low watershed divide in western Siberia. During the Ancient Holocene, *P. sylvestris* was expanding eastward, but it did not reach farther than Lake Baikal and the River Angara.

The northern boundary of *P. sylvestris* was determined in the Ancient Holocene by the southern limit of permanently frozen ground. In the next period, the Early Holocené, when the climate became warmer and northern limits of frozen ground retreated somewhat, the area of *P. sylvestris* expanded almost to the limits of its present distribution. In the north of eastern Europe, it reached the Kola Peninsula and the coast of the Barents Sea. It occupied the whole Ural range, and in eastern Siberia it reached the meridian of the Zeia (on the Amur). In the south of eastern Europe, *P. sylvestris* grew near the mouths of the Dnieper and other rivers, thus reaching the Black Sea coast.

In the Middle Holocene, the northern boundary of *P. sylvestris* in eastern Europe was somewhat farther north than it is now. In western Siberia, it reached its present limits both in the north and in the south. In eastern Siberia, it still was expanding eastward.

During the Late Holocene, *P. sylvestris* became more abundant within its area. At present, it is still expanding in the east.

*Pinus sibirica* No. 67 was widely distributed in the Pleistocene in Siberia. Analyses of pollen from the Altai Mountains support the general contention of existence of the southwestern center of postglacial distribution of this pine in the Altai. Neishtadt is of the opinion that *P. sibirica* has grown in the Altai Mountains since the Pleistocene and "perhaps even earlier." During glaciation, it found a refugium in the foothills of the Altai Mountains. In the postglacial, it spread from these mountains to the east and to the west, reaching the Ob-Irtysh mesopotamic area during the Ancient Holocene. Apparently, this pine also grew in the Early Holocene in the lower reaches of the Yenisei. In the Middle Holocene, *P. sibirica* expanded across the Urals to the northeastern part of European Russia.

Pollen of *P. sibirica* was found north of the Arctic Circle, on the River Ob, in deposits of the Middle and Upper Pleistocene; less in the latter deposits. *Pinus sylvestris* was more abundant and more uniformly distributed throughout the Middle and Upper Pleistocene than *P. sibirica*

(Golubeva, 1958). During the Late Holocene, *P. sibirica* reached the western limits of its distribution. At present, it is continuing to expand westward.

After the warm postglacial period was over, general deterioration of climate ensued. This cool period, which corresponded to the sub-Atlantic period of western Europe, had its effect on pine forests of northwestern Siberia; the northern limit of distribution was pushed south. Kats and Kats (1958) presented the following account of succession of forests in that part of Siberia:

| Forests of Northern Western Siberia as Indicated by Pollen Zones | Corresponding Glacial and Postglacial Periods | Duration, Years |
|---|---|---|
| *Present* | *Contemporary* | |
| 1st spruce minimum ⎫<br>1st spruce maximum ⎭ | Sub-Atlantic | 0–2500 |
| 2nd spruce minimum ⎫<br>2nd spruce maximum ⎭ | Sub-Boreal | 2500–4500 |
| 3rd spruce minimum ⎫<br>3rd spruce maximum ⎭ | Atlantic | 4500–7500 |
| Spruce and *P. cembra* | Boreal | 7500–8000 |
| *P. cembra* | Pre-Boreal, Sub-Arctic | 8000–13,000 |
| No pollen found | Ice Age | – |
| *P. cembra* | Last Interglacial | – |

The pine in question was, of course, not *P. cembra* No. 70 but *P. sibirica* No. 67. The two have been considered as one species (Shaw, 1914), but they are significantly different. It is questionable if the western European *P. cembra* area was ever in contact with the eastern European area of *P. sibirica*, essentially an Asiatic pine. The above tabulation shows that *P. sibirica* was growing in the north of Siberia in the Tertiary, pushed south during the glaciation, and was the first to occupy the area during interglacial stages and also after the Ice Age. When the glacier had retreated, *P. sibirica* was a pioneer invader of the ice-free area much as *P. contorta* No. 16 was the pioneer invader in western North America.

Tikhomirov (1941) found pollen of *P. sylvestris* and *P. sibirica* in a peat bog on the arctic Lesser Yamal peninsula (located between the estuaries of the Ob and the Taz rivers, western Siberia). The sediments were of "the thermal maximum period of Postglacial time." Present occurrence of *P. sylvestris* is 300 to 350 km south of the location of the peat bog; living *P. sibirica* is found also about 300 km south of the Yamal peat bog.

*Pinus pumila* No. 68 was growing on the Kamchatka peninsula (i.e., in the region of eastern Asia) during the beginning of the Holocene. In the Early Holocene, this pine already had about reached the limits of its present area. While in eastern Asia this pine occurred in mountains, in northern Asia it occupied lower elevations.

## Summary

The enormous region of northern Eurasia has only three pines: *P. sibirica* No. 67, *P. pumila* No. 68, and *P. sylvestris* No. 69. Of these three, pine No. 69 occurs also in the regions of western Europe and of the Mediterranean, pine No. 68 also is found in the region of eastern Asia, and *P. sibirica* alone is found solely in the region of northern Eurasia.

There are unconfirmed reports of finding pine pollen in deposits of the Triassic period.

In the Jurassic and the Cretaceous, pines grew in many places in the northern part of the continent.

During the Tertiary, pines were widespread in the region. The Pleistocene glaciation and intense cold in the non-glaciated parts destroyed most pines in the north; some such as *P. sylvestris*, however, survived in the more southerly parts of the continent.

During the Ancient Holocene, the northern parts of western Siberia and the whole of eastern Siberia including the present Far Eastern region of Russia (except perhaps the southernmost areas) were devoid of pines. The consequent history has been one of expansion of pines—since the Early Holocene, *P. sylvestris* to the north and to the east, and *P. pumila* to the west and northwest; the postglacial expansion of *P. sibirica* has been to the northwest.

## CONCLUSIONS

The paleobotanical records show that conifers originated in the Permian period of the Paleozoic era (Seward, 1941). The place of origin of the family Pinaceae was in the Northern Hemisphere, possibly Asia. Fossil Pinaceae have never been found south of the Equator (Florin, 1940).

## Fossils

The fossil record of the genus *Pinus* is abundant but spotty. Reports of occurrence of pine pollen in the Upper Triassic sediments (Zauer *et al.*, 1954) are yet to be verified. Jurassic remains of pines have been found in several places: eastern Siberia, the Maritime Province of Asiatic Russia, Spitzbergen, and possibly Oregon (Fontaine, 1905). There are no reports on occurrence of Jurassic pines in the eastern United States. Jurassic pine remains have been reported from the Channel Coast of France and also from the northeastern part of that country.

During the Cretaceous, the genus *Pinus* was already differentiated into the two subgenera, *Haploxylon* and *Diploxylon,* and pines were widely distributed throughout the Northern Hemisphere. They apparently were growing near Point Barrow, in the northwestern Arctic part of North America (Langenheim *et al.,* 1960), and they were reported from Greenland, Spitzbergen, and the New Siberian Islands. In more southerly latitudes, Cretaceous pines have been found in Minnesota, Kansas, New Jersey, South Carolina, Alabama, England, Belgium, southern France, southern Sweden, the Ukraine, eastern Siberia, and Korea.

On the whole, no Mesozoic pines have been found in Asia south of approximately 35° north latitude; in Europe, none south of approximately 40° north latitude. In America, the most southerly occurrence of fossil Mesozoic pines was apparently at Glen Rose, Texas, at 32° north latitude. The Mesozoic fossil record indicates that the genus *Pinus* developed in the north.

The Tertiary period was a time of further development of pines. Tertiary pines have been discovered in many places both in the Old World and the New World, but, again, all findings were from the northern part of the Northern Hemisphere. No remains of Tertiary pine have been reported south of Japan in Asia (i.e., south of approximately 32° north latitude).

In America, the southernmost location of Tertiary pines is Claiborne, Alabama (about 32° north). Pines, however, did grow farther south during the Tertiary period than the fossil findings indicate, but they apparently did not form forests.

The Quaternary glaciation destroyed all pine species in the northern part of the Hemisphere. Quaternary remains, especially pollen, of pines found in peat bogs, or in lake sediments, present an interesting picture of the return of pines to the areas where they had been killed by the advancing ice.

## Migration

During the Mesozoic era and well into the Tertiary, pines occurred only sparsely, as a minor component of the dominant floras; they were growing on uplands and mountain slopes and chiefly on the fringes of the forests.

During the Jurassic and Cretaceous periods, pines were already migrating from the North American–northern Asian area southward on both sides of the Pacific, and also eastward in North America and westward (and to the north) in Siberia. Expansion also took place to the northwest and northeast from the above-mentioned area.

In North America, pines reached the eastern United States and migrated, during the Jurassic, to western Europe via Greenland and Spitzbergen. In northern Asia, pines reached the Arctic Coast of Siberia and the New Siberian Islands, apparently from the southeast.

The Tertiary period was a period of accelerated advance of pines. The general southward trend of migration on both sides of the Pacific continued. Berry (1930) recorded a reversed migration in the eastern United States in which the pines that had been established there during the Cretaceous moved northward very early in the Tertiary. Some reversed migration (i.e., northward from the South) also took place in southeastern Asia, probably at the end of the Tertiary or even later.

During the Tertiary, there was a spectacular development of pines in western Europe where climate during the first half of the period was mild and the vegetation was subtropical in the north and tropical in the south. In the northern part of western Europe, pines perished in the second half of the Tertiary because the climate became colder; in southern France, disappearance of pines toward the end of the Tertiary was caused by the increasing aridity of the Mediterranean region.

Pines migrated from the north to Mexico and Central America and to some Caribbean islands during the Tertiary period.

Adaptation of pines to humid tropical climate, as in the southern part of western Europe in the first half of the Tertiary, was a local phenomenon. Similar adaptations to humid tropical climate also occurred in several other places in the Northern Hemisphere. These tropical pines did not possess drought-resistance. Generally, however, the genus *Pinus* has retained its original tolerance to drought and sunshine throughout the geological ages.

There are reports that *P. halepensis* and *P. brutia* grew in the Tertiary in northwestern Europe, but, no doubt, these were Mediterranean pines that advanced north from the Balkans during the Tertiary and never returned to their home; those that remained in the Mediterranean region are still there.

Mediterranean Tertiary pines were not refugees from the north; they originated *in situ* during the Tertiary period from the ancestral stock that apparently migrated along the mountain ranges that once extended from eastern Asia to the Caucasus and farther west. By this route, for instance, *P. roxburghii*, which was reported by Schenk (1888) as a Tertiary fossil from the island of Sakhalin, migrated to the Himalaya, and closely related *P. canariensis* reached the Canary Islands. At the same time, *P. peuce*, which is closely related to the Himalayan *P. griffithii*, migrated to the Balkans from eastern Asia.

Development of pines in eastern Asia from the Cretaceous through the Tertiary was gradual. Climate there has been uniform—temperate in the north and gradually merging into tropical in the south. There was some cooling after the Miocene, especially at the time of the Quaternary glaciation of the north, but there never have been such drastic changes in climate as in western Europe. Habitat of the pines in eastern and southeastern Asia did not change much from the end of the Cretaceous through the Tertiary. Pines do not form extensive forests there, but generally are rather scattered in small groups throughout the eastern Asiatic broadleaf-conifer forests—a strange mixture of tropical- and temperate-climate species. Where pines do occasionally form more or less extensive forests, as in northern Luzon or the Himalaya, they are of recent, Quaternary origin.

When, after the Quaternary glaciation, the ice shield retreated and vast areas of mineral ground were exposed, pines were among the first trees to invade the available area. In America, the pioneers were almost always *P. banksiana* No. 32 (and to a lesser degree *P. strobus* No. 20 and *P. resinosa* No. 21) in the east and *P. contorta* No. 16 in the west. In the Old World, the postglacial pioneer invader was *P. sylvestris* No. 69 (and occasionally *P. sibirica* No. 67).

After the Ice Age, the pines reoccupied the available land, but neither in America nor in Eurasia have they reached the latitudes where they grew during the Tertiary period.

This tendency of pines to occupy newly exposed ground can be observed even now in abandoned fields ("old field pine" is the common name for *P. taeda* No. 25), on banks and fills of newly constructed roads, and on burned-over areas (see Chapter 6).

In the Mediterranean area and southeastern Asia, Tertiary pines survived the general deterioration of climate of the second half of the period. Moreover, during the Ice Age, the climate in these two regions was benign enough to permit continuation of pines there.

In their Quaternary advance south, pines of most of Eurasia and North Africa, from Gibraltar to Afghanistan, were blocked by the aridity of the climate; farther east, the obstacle was the excessive humidity of India.

Two routes have been open to the southward advance of pines, in southeastern Asia and in America. While in Central America they have reached 12° north latitude, in Asia they advanced farther south. At present only one pine, *P. merkusii* No. 101, occurs somewhat south of the Equator (on Sumatra), but, during the Pleistocene, when the Ice Age occurred in the north, apparently at least two pine species crossed the Equator, and in a reversed migration they both reached the Philippines. One of them, *P. merkusii* No. 101, is local and scanty in Mindoro and in the Zambales Mountains of Luzon, and another, *P. insularis* No. 105, has formed larger forests in the northern part of Luzon.

## LITERATURE CITATIONS

ABUZIAROVA, R. I. 1953. Iskopaemaia flora chinka Nausha (Turgai) po dannym pyl'tsevogo analiza (Fossil flora of the cliff [chink] Nausha [Turgai] as based on pollen analysis). Univ. of Kazakhstan. Sci. Proc. Vol. XIV. Biologia No. 4, 66–79.

ANDREÁNSZKY, GÁBOR. 1959. Die Flora der sarmatischen Stufe in Ungarn. Akadémiai Kiadó, Budapest.

ASPREY, G. F., and R. G. ROBBINS. 1953. Vegetation of Jamaica. Ecolog. Monog., 23:359–412.

ATWOOD, WALLACE W. 1940. The physiographic provinces of North America. Ginn & Co., Boston.

AXELROD, DANIEL I. 1937. A Pliocene flora from the Mt. Eden beds, southern California. Carnegie Inst. Wash. Pub. No. 476, pp. 125–83, issued 1937, published 1938.

———. 1939. A Miocene flora from the western border of the Mohave Desert. Carnegie Inst. Wash. Pub. No. 516.

———. 1940. Late Tertiary floras of the Great Basin and border areas. Bull. Torrey Bot. Club, 67:477–87.

———. 1956. Mio-Pliocene floras from west-central Nevada. Calif. Univ. Pub., Geol. Sci., 33:1–322.

———. 1958. Evolution of the Madro-Tertiary geoflora. Bot. Rev., 24:433–509.

———. 1962. Post-Pliocene uplift of the Sierra Nevada, California. Geol. Soc. Amer. Bul., 73:183–98.

———, and WILLIAM S. TING. 1960. Late Pliocene floras east of the Sierra Nevada. Calif. Univ. Pub., Geol. Sci., 39(1):1–118.

BAIKOVSKAIA, T. N. 1956. Verkhnemelovye flory severnoi Asii (Upper Cretaceous floras of northern Asia). Paleobotanika II, 47–194. Akad. Nauk S.S.S.R. Bot. Inst. im. V. L. Komarova Trudy. Seriia 8.

BEALS, H. O. 1957. Buried forests of Indiana. Abstracted in Ind. Acad. Sci. Proc., 67:103.

BECKER, HERMAN F. 1961. Oligocene plants from the Upper Ruby River Basin, southwestern Montana. Geol. Soc. Amer. Memoir 82.

BERGER, WALTER. 1951. *Pinus stellwagi* Kink. aus dem Unterpliozän (Pannon) von Wien. Österr. Bot. Ztschr., 98 (1–2):138–41.

BERRY, EDWARD W. 1905. The flora of the Cliffwood Clays, New Jersey. Geol. Survey Ann. Rpt. Pp. 135–72.

———. 1910. Contribution to the Mesozoic flora of the Atlantic coastal plain. V. North Carolina. Bull. Torrey Bot. Club, 37:181–200.

———. 1916a. The Lower Eocene floras of southeastern North America. U.S. Geol. Survey Prof. Paper 91. Government Printing Office, Washington, D.C.

———. 1916b. The physical conditions indicated by the flora of the Calvert formation. U.S. Geol. Survey Prof. Paper 98:61–73.

———. 1919. An Eocene flora from Trans-Pecos, Texas. U.S. Geol. Survey Prof. Paper 125: 1–9.

———. 1921. Tertiary fossil plants from the Dominican Republic. U.S. Natl. Mus. Proc., 59:117–27.

———. 1922. Tertiary fossil plants from the Republic of Haiti. U.S. Natl. Mus. Proc Article 14, 62:1–10.

———. 1923. Miocene plants from southern Mexico. U.S. Natl. Mus. Proc. Article 19, 62:1–27.

———. 1924. The Middle and Upper Eocene floras of southeastern North America. U.S. Geol. Survey Prof. Paper 92. Government Printing Office, Washington, D.C.

————. 1930. Revision of the Lower Eocene Wilcox Flora of the southeastern states. U.S. Geol. Survey Prof. Paper 156. Government Printing Office, Washington, D.C.

————. 1934. A pine from the Potomac Eocene. Wash. Acad. Sci. Jour., **24**:182–86.

————. 1936. Pine and cherry from the Calvert Miocene. Torreya, **36**:124–27.

————. 1937. Tertiary floras of eastern North America. Bot. Rev., **3**:31–46.

————. 1939. A Miocene flora from the gorge of the Yumuri River, Matanzas, Cuba. Johns Hopkins Univ. Studies Geol., **13**:95–136.

BERTSCH, KARL. 1951. Geschichte des deutschen Waldes (3d ed.). Gustav Fischer, Jena.

BOLKHOVITINA, N. A. 1953. Sporovo-pyl'tsevaia kharakteristka melovykh otlozhenii tsentral'nykh oblastei SSSR (Spore and pollen characteristics of Cretaceous deposits of central regions of the U.S.S.R.). Trudy Akademiia Nauk S.S.S.R., Vol. 145, Geol. Series No. 61.

BOULAY, N. 1887. Notice sur la flore tertiaire des environs de Privas (Ardèche). Soc. Bot. de France Bul., **34**:227–29, 255–79.

BRAUN, E. LUCY. 1955. The phytogeography of unglaciated eastern United States and its interpretation. Bot. Rev., **21**:297–375.

BROWN, ROLAND W. 1934. The recognizable species of the Green River Flora. U.S. Geol. Survey Prof. Paper 185c: 45–77.

BUDANTSEV, L. I. 1957. Eotsenovaiia flora pavlodarskogo priirtysh'ia (Flore éocène dans le pri-Irtych de Pavlodar)–Sborn. Pamiati A. N. Krishchtofovich, ed. Inst. Bot. Komarov, Akad. Nauk SSSR: 177–98.

———— and I. N. SVESHNIKOVA. 1958. Tretichnaia flora Kaliningradskogo poluostrova (Pinaceae) (The Tertiary flora of the Kaliningrad Peninsula [II. Pinaceae]). Bot. Zhur. S.S.S.R., **44**:1154–58.

BUELL, MURRAY F. 1945. Late Pleistocene forests of southeastern North Carolina. Torreya, **45**:117–18.

CAIN, STANLEY A. 1944. Foundations of plant geography. Harper & Row, New York.

———— and LOUISE G. CAIN. 1948. Palynological studies at Sodon Lake. II. Size-frequency studies of pine pollen, fossil and modern. Amer. Jour. Bot., **35**:583–91.

————, LOUISE G. CAIN, and GEORGE THOMSON. 1951. Fossil pine pollen size-frequencies in Heart Lake sediments, Oakland County, Michigan. Amer. Jour. Bot., **38**:724–31.

CHANDLER, M. E. J. 1961. Palaeocene floras. London Clay Flora (Supplement). Brit. Mus. Nat. Hist., London.

CHANEY, R. W. 1936a. Plant distribution as a guide to age determination. Wash. Acad. Sci. Jour., **26**:313–24.

————. 1936b. The succession and distribution of Cenozoic floras around the northern Pacific basin. In Essays in geobotany in honor of William Albert Setchell. University of California Press, Berkeley. Pp. 55–85.

————. 1954. A new pine from the Cretaceous of Minnesota and its paleoecological significance. Ecology, **35**:145–51.

———— and DANIEL I. AXELROD. 1959. Miocene floras of the Columbian plateau. Carnegie Inst. Wash. Pub. 617.

————and HU HSEN HSU. 1940. A Miocene flora from Shantung province, China. Part II. Physical conditions and correlation. Geol. Survey China, Peiping (China Geol. Survey Paleontologia Sinica. New series A No. 1. Whole series No. 112). (Reprinted in Carnegie Inst. Wash. Pub. 507:85–140.)

———— and H. L. MASON. 1934. A Pleistocene flora from the asphalt deposits at Carpinteria, Calif. Carnegie Inst. Wash. Pub. 415:47–79.

———— and H. L. MASON. 1936. A Pleistocene flora from Fairbanks, Alaska. Amer. Mus. Nat. Hist., Amer. Mus. Novitates No. 887 (October 15, 1936): 1–17.

———— and E. I. SANBORN. 1933. The Goshen Flora of west central Oregon. Carnegie Inst. Wash. Pub. 439.

CHARLESWORTH, JOHN KAYE. 1957. The Quaternary era with special reference to its glaciation. 2 vols. (XLVII). E. Arnold, Ltd., London.

CHIGURIAEVA, A. A. 1952. Materialy k eotsenovoi rastitel'nosti pravoberezh'ia reki Dona (Materials on Eocene vegetation of the right bank of the river Don). Saratov Univ. Sci. Proc., 35:197-200.

CLEMENTS, F. E. 1936. The origin of the desert climax and climate. In Essays in geobotany in honor of William Albert Setchell. University of California Press, Berkeley. Pp. 87-140.

CLISBY, KATHRYN H., FRED FOREMAN, and PAUL B. SEARS. 1959. A pollen and sediment record of the Pliocene-Pleistocene in New Mexico. Proc. 9th Internatl. Bot. Cong., Montreal, 2:76. Abstract.

COCKERELL, T. D. A. 1908. Descriptions of Tertiary plants, II. Amer. Jour. Sci. 4th ser., 26:537-44.

———. 1934. An ancient foxtail pine. Nature [London], 133:573-74.

COEMANS, E. 1867. Description de la flore fossile du premier étage du terrain Crétacé du Hainaut. Brussels Acad. Roy. des Sci. Belg. Mém., 36:1-20.

COMBES, PAUL. 1908. Sur un néotype de Pinus (Pseudostrobus) defrancei Ad. Brong., du lutétien du Trocadéro (Paris). Comptes Rendus Acad. Sci., Paris. 146:206-7.

CONWENTZ, H. 1892. Untersuchungen über fossile Hölzer Schwedens. Kongl. Svenska Vetenskapsakademien Handlingar. series 4, 2403(13):13-25.

COUPER, R. A. 1958. British Mesozoic microspores and pollen grains: A systematic and stratigraphic study. Paleontographica Abt. B, 103:75-179.

CZECZOTT, HANNA. 1954. The past and present distribution of Pinus halepensis Mill. and P. brutia Ten. 8th Internatl. Cong. Bot., Paris and Nice, Papers, 8(sec. 2, 4-6): 196-97.

DANSEREAU, PIERRE. 1953. The postglacial pine period. Roy. Soc. Canada, Proc. and Trans. Series III, 47(Sec. 5):23-38.

DAUGHERTY, LYMAN H. 1941. The Upper Triassic flora of Arizona. Carnegie Inst. Wash. Pub. 526.

DAVIS, JOHN H., JR. 1943. The natural features of southern Florida, especially the vegetation and the Everglades. Fla. Geol. Survey Geol. Bul. 25.

DEEVEY, EDWARD S., JR. 1939. Studies of Connecticut lake sediments. I. A. post-glacial climatic chronology for southern New England. Amer. Jour. Sci., 237: 691-724.

DEPAPE, G. L. 1932. La flore tertiaire du Wei Tchang. Pub. du Mus. Hoang ho pai ho. No. 6. Quoted by Wulff (1944).

DIELS, L. 1910. Genetische Elemente in der Flora der Alpen. Bot. Jahrb., Beiblatt 102, 44:7-46.

DOBRYNIN, B. F. 1948. Fizicheskaia geografiia zapadnoi Evropy (Physical geography of USSR—European part and Caucasus.) Gos. ucheb. pedagog. izd-vo, Moscow.

DOROFEEV, P. I. 1955. Iskopaemaia shishka sosny iz sarmatskikh otlozhenii ta-manskogo poluostrova (Une pomme de pin fossile [Pinus Palibinii n. sp.] du Sarmatien de la presqu'île de Tamanj [Mer d'Azov]). Geol. Sborn., 3:326-29.

———. 1957. Materialy k poznaniiu zapadnosibirskoi tretichnoi flory (iskopaemaia flora s. Ekaterininskogo bliz g. Tary) (On the Tertiary flora of western Siberia [near Tara]) In Sbornik Pamiati. Afrikan Nikolaevicha Krishtofovicha (A memo-rial volume honoring A. N. Krishtofovich). Izd. Akademiia Nauk SSSR, Moscow. Pp. 277-312.

DUBOIS, GEORGES, and CAMILE DUBOIS. 1945. Tableau d'ensemble de l'histoire forestière flandrienne française. Comptes Rendus Acad. Sci., Paris, 221:634-36.

DUFFIELD, JOHN W. 1951. Interrelations of the California closed-cone pines with special reference to Pinus muricata D. Don. Unpublished Ph.D. disseration, University of California, Berkeley.

EMBERGER, LOUIS. 1944. Les plantes fossiles dans leurs rapports avec les végétaux vivants (éléments de paléobotanique et de morphologie comparée). Masson et Cie, Paris.

ENDO, S., and H. OKUTSU. 1939. Plant and animal life of Hokkaido. Inst. Geol. Paleontol. Tohoku Univ., 7(3):259.

ENGEL, A. 1943. Mécanisme et historique des migrations forestières de l'époque tertiaire à nos jours. Soc. Vaud. des Sci. Nat. Mém., 7(49):168–218.

ENGELHARDT, H. 1903. Tertiärpflanzen von Kleinasien. Beiträge zur Paläontologie und Geol. Österreich-Ungarns und des orients, 15(2–3):55–64.

ENGLER, A. 1882. Versuch einer Entwicklungsgeschichte der Pflanzenwelt, inbesondere der florengebiete seit der Tertiärperiode. Vol. II. Die extratropischen Gebiete der südlichen Hemisphäre und tropischer Gebiete. W. Engelmann, Leipzig.

―――― and K. PRANTL. 1926. Die naturlichen Pflanzenfamilien, Band 13—Gymnospermae. W. Engelmann, Leipzig.

ERDTMAN, O. G. E. 1926. On the immigration of some British trees. Jour. Bot., 64: 71–74.

――――. 1929. Some aspects of the post-glacial history of British forests. Jour. Ecol., 17:112–26.

FEINBRUN, W. 1959. Spontaneous pineta in the Lebanon. Bull. Israel Res. Council Sec. D, Bot., 7D(3–4):132–53.

FERRÉ, Y. DE. 1960. Une nouvelle espèce de pin au Viet-Nam, *Pinus dalatensis*. Soc. d'Hist. Nat. de Toulouse Bul., 95:171–80.

FLORIN, R. 1920. Einige chinesische Tertiärpflanzen. Svensk Bot. Tidskr., 14:239–43.

――――. 1933. Die von E. L. Ekman in Westindien gesammelten Koniferen. Arkiv för Bot., 25A:1–22.

――――. 1940. The Tertiary fossil conifers of south Chile and their phytogeographical significance. Svenska Vetenskapsakademiens Handlingar. Tredje Serien, Band 19, No. 2.

FLORSCHÜTZ, F. 1959. La végétation tardiglaciaire aux Pyrénées centrales françaises et en Espagne septentrionale. A, Pyrénées centrales. 9th Internatl. Bot. Congr., Montreal, Proc., 2:116. Abstract.

FONTAINE, WILLIAM M. 1893. Notes on some fossil plants from the Trinity division of the Comanche Series of Texas. U.S. Natl. Mus. Proc. Internatl. 16:261–82.

――――. 1905. The Jurassic flora of Douglas County, Oreg. In LESTER F. WARD, Status of the Mesozoic floras of the United States (U.S. Geol. Survey Monog. No. 48. Part 1), pp. 48–145.

FORDE, MARGOT BERNICE. 1963. Variation in the natural populations of Monterey pine (*Pinus radiata* Don) in California. Unpublished Ph.D. dissertation, University of California, Davis.

FRANCINI, ELEONORA. 1958. Ecologia comparata di *Pinus halepensis* Mill., *P. pinaster* Sol. e *Pinus pinea* L. sulla base del comportamento del gametofito femminale. Acad. Ital. di Sci. Forestali, Firenze, 7:107–72.

GAUSSEN, H. 1960. Les gymnospermes actuelles et fossiles. Tome 2, Vol. 1, Fasc. 6 Chapter XI, Généralités, Genre *Pinus*. Travaux du laboratoire forestier de Toulouse.

GODWIN, H. 1940. Pollen analysis and forest history of England and Wales. New Phytol., 39:370–400.

――――. 1956. The history of the British flora. Cambridge University Press, London. Pp. 275–81.

GOLUBEVA, L. V. 1958. Stratigraficheskaia skhema chetvertichnykh otlozhenii severozapadnoi chasti zapadno-sibirskoi nizmennosti e ee paleofitologicheskoe obosnovanie (A stratigraphic scheme for the Quaternary deposits of the northwestern part of the west Siberian lowlands and its paleo-floristic basis). Akad. Nauk S.S.S.R. Izv. Ser. Geol., 2:43–52.

GORBUNOV, M. G. 1958. Tretichnye sosny zapadnoi Sibiri (Tertiary pines of western Siberia). Bot. Zhur. S.S.S.R., 43:337–52.

GRAY, JANE. 1960. Temperate pollen genera in the Eocene (Claiborne) flora, Alabama. Science, 132:808–10.

GRAYSON, J. F. 1954. Evidence of four pine species from fossil pollen in Michigan. Ecology, 35:327–31.

HANSEN, HENRY P. 1942. The influence of volcanic eruptions upon post-Pliocene forest succession in central Oregon. Amer. Jour. Bot., 29:214–19.

———. 1943. Paleoecology of the sand dune bogs on the southern Oregon coast. Amer. Jour. Bot., 30:335–40.

———. 1947. Postglacial vegetation of the northern Great Basin. Amer. Jour. Bot., 34:164–71.

———. 1949. Postglacial forests in west central Alberta, Canda. Torrey Bot. Club Bul., 76:278–89.

———. 1950. Postglacial forests along the Alaska highway in British Columbia. Amer. Phil. Soc. Proc., 94:411–21.

HAYATA, B. 1905. On the distribution of the Formosan conifers. Bot. Mag. (Tokyo), 19:43–60.

HAYEK, AUGUST. 1928. Ein Beitrag zur Kenntnis der Vegetation und der Flora des thessalischen Olymp. Beih. Botanisches Zentralblatt, Abt. 2, 45:220–328.

HEER, OSWALD. 1868. Flora fossilis arctica. Vol. I. Part I. Die fossile Flora der Polarländer. Part II. Fossile Flora von Nordgrönland. A Creide Flora. I. Schuethess, Zürich.

———. 1869. Flora fossilis arctica. Vol. II. Die fossile Flora der Polarländer. Flora fossilis Alaskana. J. Wurster & Co., Zürich.

———. 1875. Flora fossilis arctica vol. III. Part III. Die fossile Flora der Polarländer. Nachträge zur miocenen flora Grönlands. J. Wurster & Co., Zürich.

———. 1876. Flora fossilis arctica. Beiträge zur Fossilen Flora Spitzbergens. Vol. IV. Part I. J. Wurster & Co., Zürich. Pp. 1–141.

———. 1878. Flora fossilis arctica. Die fossile Flora der Polarländer. Abt. 2. Beiträge zur fossilen Flora Sibiriens und des Amurlandes. J. Wurster & Co., Zürich. Also in Mem. Acad. Imp. des Sci. St. Petersburg Mem., 7th Ser., 25(6): 1–58.

HOLDEN, RUTH. 1913. Cretaceous Phytoscyla from Cliffwood, New Jersey. Amer. Acad. Arts and Sci. Proc., 48:607–24.

HOLLICK, ARTHUR. 1924. A review of the fossil flora of the West Indies, with descriptions of new species. N.Y. Bot. Gard. Bul., 12:259–323.

HOLLICK, ARTHUR, and EDWARD CHARLES JEFFREY. 1909. Studies of Cretaceous coniferous remains from Kreischerville, New York (N.Y. Bot. Gard. Mem. 3) III.

HUBBARD, GEORGE D. 1937. The geography of Europe. Appleton-Century-Crofts, Inc., New York.

HULTÉN, ERIC. 1937. Outline of the history of Arctic and boreal biota during the Quaternary period. Aktiebolaget Thule, Stockholm.

ILOFF, P. M., JR., and N. T. MIROV. 1956. Composition of gum turpentines of pines. XXV. A report on two white pines: Pinus koraiensis from Korea and P. peuce from Macedonia. Amer. Pharm. Assoc. Jour., Sci. Ed., 45:77–81.

ISIZIMA, W. 1936. A fossil pine cone. Jour. Geol. Soc. Japan, 43:805–7.

JONASSEN, H. 1950. Recent pollen sedimentation and Jutland heath diagrams. Thesis (Copenhagen). Reprinted from Dansk Bot. Arkiv. (Res. botanicae Danicae) Bind 13, Nr. 7, Copenhagen.

KANEHIRA, RYOZO. 1933. On the ligneous flora of Formosa and its relationship to that of neighboring regions. Lingnan Sci. Jour., 12:225–38.

KARAVAEV, M. N. 1960. Dva novykh vida Khvoinykh (Cathaya jacutica M i Pinus sukaczewii M.) iz tretichnykh otlozhenii tsentral 'noi Iakutii (Two new coniferous species [Cathaya jacutica M. sp. nov. and Pinus sukaczewi M. sp. nov.] discovered in the Tertiary deposits of central Yakutia). Moskov. Obsh. Isp. Prirody, Otd. Biol. Bul. (Soc. Nat. de Moscou, Sect. Biol. Bul.), 3:127–30.

KATS, N. I., and S. V. KATS. 1958. K istorii flory i rastitel' nosti severa zapadnoi Sibiri (History of the flora and vegetation of the north of western Siberia in the late glacial and postglacial ages). Bot. Zhur. S.S.S.R., 43(7):998–1014.

KAWASAKI, SHIGETARO. 1926. Geology and mineral resources of Korea. In The geology and the mineral resources of the Japanese empire. Part II. Imp. Geol. Survey of Japan. Pp. 109–28.

KNOWLTON, F. H. 1919. A catalogue of the Mesozoic and Cenozoic plants of North America (U.S. Geol. Survey Bul. 696). Government Printing Office, Washington, D.C.

KOCH, ESKE. 1959. Fossil *Pinus*—cone in late-Tertiary erratic from western Jutland (Denmark). Medd. Dansk Geol. Foren., 14(2):69–75.

KOLESNIKOV, B. P. 1935. Interesnye floristicheskie nakhodki v sviazi s istoriei rastitel-'nogo pokrova v basseine R. Gorin (Interesting floristic findings related to the history of vegetation in the basin of the river Gorin). Dalnevost. filial, Vladivostok. Věst. Akad. Nauk S.S.S.R., 14:138–44.

KORNILOVA, V. S. 1960. Nizhnemiotsenovaia flora Kushuka (Lower Miocene flora of Kushuk). 128, [42] p. 28 Akad. Nauk Kazakskoi S.S.R. Inst. Zoologii, Alma-Ata.

KRÄUSEL, R. 1929. Fossile Pflanzen aus dem Tertiär von Sud-Sumatra, Verhandl. Geologisch Mijnboawkundig Genootsch. Nederland en Koloniën. Geol. Serie 9: 1–42.

KREMP, G. O. W. 1959. Can expanding palynology escape taxonomic chaos? 9th Internat. Bot. Cong., Montreal, Proc., 2:206–7. Abstract.

KRISHTOFOVICH, A. 1930. Osnovnye cherty razvitiia tretichnoi flory Asii (General trends of development of Tertiary flora of Asia). Glav. Bot. Sada S.S.S.R. Izv., 29:391–401.

———. 1941. Prodromus florae fossilis. Paleontologia S.S.S.R. (Paleontology of U.S.S.R.). Vol. XII. Supplement Akad. Nauk S.S.S.R. Paleontological Inst.

———. 1956. Istoriia paleobotanikii S.S.S.R. (History of paleobotany of U.S.S.R.). Izd. Akad. Nauk S.S.S.R., Moscow.

———. 1959. Izbrannye trudy (Selected works). Vol. I. Izd. Akademii Nauk S.S.S.R., Moscow.

KULCZYŃSKI, STANISLAS. 1923. Das boreale und arktisch-alpine Element in der mittel-europäischen Flora. Bull. Intern. de l'Acad. Polon. Sci. et lettr. classe des sciences mathématiques et naturelles, sér. B, Sciences naturelles, 1923:127–214.

KUZNETSOV, N. I. 1909. Printsipy deleniia kavkaza na botaniko-geograficheskiia provintsii (Principles of dividing the Caucasus into botanicogeographical provinces). Zap. Akad. Nauk S.S.S.R. Fizikomatematichesk. otdel, Series 8, 24(1): 1–174.

LAMOTTE, ROBERT SMITH. 1944. Supplement to catalogue of Mesozoic and Cenozoic plants of North America 1919–37 (U.S. Geol. Survey Bul. 924).

LANGENHEIM, R. L., JR., C. J. SMILEY, and JANE GRAY. 1960. Cretaceous amber from the Arctic coastal plain of Alaska. Geol. Soc. Amer. Bul., 71:1345–66.

LECOMTE, H. 1924. Additions on subject of *Pinus krempfii* H. Lec. Mus. Natl. d'Hist. Nat., Paris, Bul., 30:321–25.

LECONTE, J. 1887. The flora of the Coast islands of California in relation to recent changes of physical geography. Bul. Calif. Acad. Sci., 2:515–20.

LESQUEREUX, L. 1883. Contributions of the fossil flora of the Western Territories. III. The Cretaceous and Tertiary floras. U.S. Geol. Survey of the Territories Rpt., 8:1–283.

———. 1895. Cretaceous fossil plants from Minnesota. Minn. Geol. and Nat. Hist. Survey Final Rpt. 3 (Pt. 1). Pp. 1–22.

LITTLE, ELBERT L., JR., and KEITH W. DORMAN. 1954. Slash pine (*Pinus elliottii*) including south Florida slash pine: Nomenclature and description. U.S. Forest Serv., Southeast. Forest Expt. Sta., Sta. Paper No. 36.

LONA, FAUSTO. 1954. Quaternary floristic modifications in Italy, particularly following pollen analysis. 8th Internatl. Cong. Bot., Paris, Proc., Sec. 2:261–62.

LÜDI, WERNER. 1953. Die Pflanzenwelt des Eiszeitalters in nördlichen Vorland der schweizer Alpen. Veröffentlichungen des Geobotanischen Institut Rübel in Zürich, 27 Heft.

MACGINITIE, H. D. 1953. Fossil plants of the Florissant beds, Colorado. Carnegie Inst. Wash. Pub. 599.

MALEEV, V. P. (MALEJEFF, W. P.). 1940. Rastitel'nost' prichernomorskikh stran . . . (Vegetation of Black Sea countries, etc.). Akad. Nauk S.S.S.R. Bot. Inst. Trudy, Ser. 3, Geobotanika, 4:135–249.

MALEJEFF, W. 1929. *Pinus pithyusa* (Stev.) und *Pinus eldarica* (Medw.), zwei relikt-Kiefern der taurisch-kaukasischen Flora. Mitt. Deutsch dendrol. Ges. Jahrbuch. Pp. 138–50.

MARCHESONI, VITTORIO. 1958. Importanza del pino nero dell' Abete del Tasso dell' Agrifoglio nella storia climatico-forestale dell' Appennino Umbro-Marchigiano, Monti e Boschi, 9:535–40.

MARTIN, PAUL S., and BYRON E. HARRELL. 1957. The Pleistocene history of temperate biotas in Mexico and eastern United States. Ecology, 38:468–80.

MASON, HERBERT L. 1927. Fossil records of some west American conifers. Carnegie Inst. Wash. Pub., 346:139–58.

———. 1932. A phylogenetic series of California closed-cone pines suggested by fossil record. Madroño, 2:49–55.

MENENDEZ AMOR, JOSEFINA. 1951. Una piña fósil nueva del Plioceno de Málaga. Bol. R. Soc. Esp. Hist. Nat., 49B(1–3):193–95.

——— and F. FLORSCHÜTZ. 1959. La végétation tardiglaciaire aux Pyrénées centrales françaises et en Espagne septentrionale. B. Espagne septentrionale. 9th Internatl. Bot. Cong., Montreal, II Abstracts, p. 260.

MERRILL, ELMER D. 1926. An enumeration of Philippine flowering plants (Philippine Dept. Agr. and Nat. Resources, Bur. Sci. Pub. No. 18). Vol. 4. Manila Bureau of Printing.

MIKI, SHIGERU. 1939. On the remains of *Pinus trifolia* n. sp. in the Upper Tertiary from central Honsyu in Japan. Bot. Mag. (Tokyo), 53:239–46.

———. 1956. Remains of *Pinus koraiensis* S. et Z. and associated remains in Japan. Bot. Mag. (Tokyo), 69:447–54.

———. 1957. Pinaceae of Japan, with special reference to its remains. Osaka City Univ. Inst. Polytech. Jour., series D, Biology, 8:221–72.

MIRANDA, F., and A. J. SHARP. 1950. Characteristics of the vegetation in certain temperate regions of eastern Mexico. Ecology, 31:313–33.

MIROV, N. T. 1951. Geography of Russia. John Wiley & Sons, Inc., New York.

———. 1955. Relationship between *Pinus halepensis* and other *Insignes* pines of the Mediterranean region. Bul. Res. Council Israel, Sec. D, Botany 5D:65–72.

MONTENEGRO DE ANDRADE, M. 1945. Contribuição da análise polínica para o conhecimento do género *Pinus* no Pliocénico superior Português. Bol. Soc. Geol. Portugal, 4(3):1–6.

NAHAL, I. 1960. La végétation forestière naturelle dans le Nordouest de la Syrie. Rev. for. Franç., 2:90–101.

NEIBURG, M. F. 1959. Paleobotanicheskoe obosnovanie Triasovykh uglenosnykh otolozhenii pechorskogo basseina (Paleobotanical basis for Triassic age of the coal-bearing strata in the Pechora Basin). Akad. Nauk S.S.S.R. Dok., 127:681–84.

NEISHTADT, M. I. 1957. Istoriia lesov i paleografiia S.S.S.R. v Golotsene (History of forests and paleogeography of the U.S.S.R. during the Holocene). Izd. Akad. Nauk S.S.S.R., Moscow.

———. 1960. Palinologiia v S.S.S.R., 1952–1957 gg. (Palynology in the U.S.S.R. from 1952 to 1957). Izd. Akad. Nauk S.S.S.R., Moscow.

NORDHAGEN, R. 1935. Zur spät quartären Geschichte der skandinavischen Flora (Beiträge zur Erforschung der eisfreien Refugien Norwegens). Proc. 6th Internatl. Bot. Cong., Amsterdam, 2:98–100. E. Brill, Leiden.

OMBONI, G. 1892. Frutto fossile di pino (*Pinus priabonensis* n. sp.) da aggiungersi alla flora tertiaria del Veneto. Nota. Atti R. Ist. Veneto Sci. Lett. ed Arti: series 7, 3:373–83.

PALIBIN, I. V. 1935. Etapy razvitiia flory prikaspiiskikh stran so vremeni melovogo perioda (Stages of development of Caspian flora from the Cretaceous period on). Sovet. Bot., 3:10–50.

——. 1937. Melovaia flora Daralageza (The Cretaceous flora of the Daralaghez Range). English summary. Trudy Bot. Inst. Akad. Nauk S.S.S.R., Series 1, 4: 171–98.

PENFOLD, A. R. 1935. The physiological forms of the eucalypts as determined by the chemical composition of the essential oils and their influence on the botanical nomenclature. Australasian Jour. Pharm., 16:168–71.

PENHALLOW, D. P. 1908. Report on Tertiary plants of British Columbia collected by Lawrence M. Lambe in 1906, together with a discussion of previously recorded Tertiary floras. Ottawa, Canada, Dept. Mines, Geol. Survey Branch. (No. 1013.)

PENNY, JOHN S. 1947. Studies on the conifers of the Magothy flora. Amer. Jour. Bot. 34:281–96.

PERKINS, GEORGE H. 1904. On the lignite or brown coal of Brandon and its fossils. Vt. State Geol. Rpt., 4:153–212.

PIERCE, RICHARD L. 1957. Minnesota Cretaceous pine pollen. Science, 125:26.

POSTHUMUS, O. 1931. De palaeontologie en stratigraphie van Nederlandisch Oostindië. Plantae. Leidsche geologische Meded., 5:485–508.

POTZGER, J. E. 1946. Phytosociology of the primeval forest in central-northern Wisconsin and upper Michigan, and a brief post-glacial history of the Lake Forest formation. Ecol. Monog., 16:211–50.

—— and ALBERT COURTEMANCHE. 1956. A series of bogs across Quebec from the St. Lawrence Valley to James Bay. Canad. Jour. Bot., 34:473–500.

—— and JAMES H. OTTO. 1943. Post-glacial forest succession in northern New Jersey as shown by pollen records from five bogs. Amer. Jour. Bot., 30:83–87.

—— and R. R. RICHARDS. 1942. Forest succession in the Trout Lake, Vilas County, Wisconsin area: A pollen study. Butler Univ. Bot. Studies, 5:179–89.

—— and B. C. THARP. 1947. Pollen profile from a Texas bog. Ecology, 28:274–80.

RAUP, HUGH M. 1946. Phytographic studies in the Athabaska–Great Slave Lake region. II. Arnold Arboretum Jour., 27:1–85.

REID, ELEANOR MARY. 1920. A comparative review of Pliocene floras, based on the study of fossil seeds. Geol. Soc. Quart. Jour., 76:145–69.

—— and M. E. J. CHANDLER. 1933. The London Clay Flora. Brit. Mus. Nat. Hist., London.

RIKLI, M. 1909. Die Arve in der Schweiz. Ein beitrag zur Waldgeschicte und Waldwirtschaft der Schweizer Alpen. Schweiz Naturf. Gesell., 44(I–XL):1–455.

RODRIGUEZ, F. BELLOT. 1950. El análsis polinico de las zonas higroturbosas de la Sierra Gerês en relación con las presencias de *Pinus pinaster* Sol. in Ait. y *P. silvestris* L. Agronomia Lusitania 12: 481–91.

ROEZL, B., ET CIE. 1857. Catalogue de graines de Conifères Mexicaines en vente chez B. Roezl et Cie Horticulteurs a Napoles près Mexico. Pour Automne 1857 et Printemps 1858. Imprimerie de M. Murguia, Mexico City.

——. 1858. Catalogue de graines et plantes Mexicaines à Napoles près Mexico. Pour Automne 1858 et Printemps 1859. Imprimirie Felix Malteste et Cie, Paris.

SAPORTA, GASTON DE. 1864. Etudes sur la végétation du sud-est de la France à l'époque tertiaire. Deuxieme partie. Flore des calcaries marnêux littoraux du bassin de Marseille. Ann. des Sci. Nat., Bot., 5th series, 3:5–152.

——. 1865. Etudes sur la végétation du sud-est de la France à l'époque tertiaire 2me partie. III. Flore d'Armissan et de Peyriac, dans le bassin de Narbonne (Aude). Ann. des Sci. Nat., Bot., 5th series, 4:5–264.

——. 1867. Etudes sur la végétation du sud-est de la France à l'époque tertiaire. Ann. des Sci. Nat., Bot., 5th series, 8:7–136.

SCHENK, A. 1888. Fossile Hölzer aus Ostasien und Aegypten. Bihang. till Kungl. Svenska Vetensk. Akad. Handl., 14(3):No. 2: 1–24.

SCHUCHERT, CHARLES. 1935. Historical geology of the Antillean-Caribbean region. John Wiley & Sons, Inc., New York.

——. 1955. Atlas of paleographic maps of North America with an introduction by Carl O. Dunbar. John Wiley & Sons, Inc., New York.

SEIFRIZ, WILLIAM. 1943. The plant life of Cuba. Ecol. Monog., 13:375–426.

SEWARD, A. C. 1941. Plant life through the ages (2d ed.). Cambridge University Press, London.

SHARP, AARON J. 1951. The relation of the Eocene Wilcox Flora to some modern floras. Evolution, 5:1–5.

SHAW, GEORGE RUSSELL. 1914. The genus Pinus (Arnold Arboretum Pub. No. 5). Riverside Press, Cambridge, Mass.

SHCHEKINA, N. O. 1953. Flora Buckaks'kogo viku na territorii Ukraini za danimi Sporovo-pilkovikh doslidzhen (Flora of Buchak time on the territory of the Ukraine according to investigations of pollen). Bot. Zhur., Kiev, 10:44–80.

SHILKINA, I. A. 1958. Iskopaemye drevesiny Goderdzskogo perevala (Fossil wood of the Goderdzi Pass). Akad. Nauk S.S.S.R. Bot. Inst. Trudy, Seria 8, Paleobotanika, 3:137–67.

SIEGFRIED, PAUL. 1961. Der Fund eines Wisentskeletts (Bison bonasus L.) in Gladbeck Westfalen. Neues Jahrb. f. Min., Geol. u. Paläontol., 112:83–105.

SITHOLEY, R. V. 1954. The Mesozoic and Tertiary floras of India: A review. 8th Internatl. Cong. Bot., Paris, 1:209–30.

SPOLJARÍC, Z. 1952. Anatomska i polenanalitska istrazivanja nekih lignita iz sjeverne Hrvatske (Anatomy and pollen investigation of lignites from northern Croatia). Sec. 2 Jugoslovenska Akad. Znanosti i Umjetnosti, Zagreb.

STEEVES, MARGARET W. 1959. The pollen and spores of the Raritan and Magothy formations (Cretaceous) of Long Island. Cambridge, Mass. Unpublished Ph.D. dissertation, Radcliffe College, Cambridge, Mass.

STEFFEN, H. 1937. Gedanken zur Entwicklungsgeschichte der arktischen Flora. Bot. Zentralblatt, Abt. B, Beihette, 56:409–47.

STEYERMARK, JULIAN A. 1950. Flora of Guatemala. Ecology, 31:368–72.

STOJANOFF, N. 1930. Versuch einer Analyse des relikten elements in der Flora der Balkanhalbinsel. Bot. Jahrb. von A. Engler, 63:368–418.

——— and B. STEFANOFF. 1929. Beitrag zur Kenntnis der Pliozänflora der Ebene von Sofia (Fossile Pflanzenreste aus den Ablagerungen bei Kurilo). Ztschr. Bulg. Geol. Ges., 1(3):3–115.

STRABO. 1917–32. The geography of Strabo, with an English translation by Horace Leonard Jones, in eight volumes. William Heinemann, Ltd., London.

STUDT, WERNER. 1926. Die heutige und frühere Verbreitung der Koniferen und die Geschichte ihren Arealgestaltung. Mitt. Inst. f. Alg. Bot., Hamburg, 6(2):167–308.

SUKACHEV, V. N. 1910. Nekotoryia dannyia k dolednikovoi flore severa sibiri (New data on the preglacial flora of the north of Siberia). Akad. Nauk Geologicheskii musei imeni Petra velikago Trudy, 4:55–62.

———, R. N. GORLOVA, E. P. METELTSEVA, and A. K. NEDOSEEVA. 1960. K poznaniiu pleistotsenov oi flory okrestnostei Moskvy (On the Pleistocene flora of the environment of Moscow). Dokl. Akad. Nauk S.S.S.R., 130:1120–23. (Available in English translation.)

SUSLOV, S. P. 1947. Fizicheskaia geografiia SSSR; zapadnaia Sibir', vostochnaia Sibir', Dal'nii vostok, sredniaia Aziia. Leningrad. Ucheb.-pedagog. izd-vo.

TAKHTADZHIAN, A. L. (ed.). 1963. Osnovy Paleontologii (Fundamentals of paleontology). Vol. XV. Golosemiannye i Pokrytosemennye (Gymnosperms and angiosperms). Gosad. nauchno–tekh. izd-vo lit. po geol. i okhrane NEDR, Moscow.

TEIXEIRA, C. 1944. Pinheiro fosil do Pliocénico de Rio Maior. Soc. Broteriana Bol., Series 2, 19(1):201–21.

TEMPLETON, BONNIE C. 1953. A new record of pine cone for the Miocene epoch. South. Calif. Acad. Sci. Bull., 52(2):64–66.

THOMSON, PAUL WILLIAM. 1954. New investigations about plant associations and swamp types in the Rhenish brown-coal layers. 8th Int. Cong. Bot., Paris, Rap. et Commun. (Proc.), 1:194–95.

TIKHOMIROV, B. A. 1941. O lesnoi faze v poslelednikovoi istorii rastitel'nosti severa Sibiri i ee reliktakh v sovremennoi tundre (On the forest phase in the post-glacial history of the North Siberia vegetation). (With English summary.) Materialy no istorii flory i rastitel'nosti S.S.S.R., Moscow. Pp.315–74.

————. 1949. Kedrovyi stlanik, ego biologiia i ispol'zovanie Moskva, Izd. Moskov. Obshch, Isp. Prirody (Materialy k poznaniia fauny i flory SSSR. Moskva, n.s. otdel. bot. vyp. 6).

TONGIORGI, EZIO. 1946. Sulle conifere fossili della Valle del Santerno (Romagna). Nuovo Gior. Bot. Ital. (N.S.), 53:695–97.

TRAVERSE, ALFRED. 1955. Pollen analysis of the Brandon lignite of Vermont (U.S. Bur. Mines Rpt. Invest. 5151). Washington, D.C.

TURRILL, W. BERTRAM. 1929. The plant life of the Balkan Peninsula. Oxford University Press, Fair Lawn, N.J.

UPHOF, J. C. T. 1938. Origin of the neotropical flora in the southeast of North America. Rev. Sudamer. de Bot., 5(3–4):49–64.

VIDAL, JULES. 1934–60. La végétation du Laos; 2me partie. Groupements, Végéteaux et Flore. Trav. du Lab. Forest. de Toulouse, Tome V, 1:121–582.

WARD, LESTER F. 1905. Status of the Mesozoic floras of the United States (U.S. Geol. Survey Monog. 48). Government Printing Office, Washington, D.C.

WEBER, C. A. 1905. Die Geschichte der Pflanzenwelt des norddeutschen Tieflandes seit der Tertiärzeit. 2d Internatl. Cong. Bot., Vienna, Proc. Pp. 98–116.

WEYLAND, H., and E. SCHÖNFELD. 1958. *Pinus marcoduriae* n. sp., eine neue Kieferform aus der Braunkohle der Ville. Palaeontographica Abt. B, 104(4–6):138–49.

WILSON, ERNEST HENRY. 1913. A naturalist in western China, with an introduction by Prof. Charles Sprague Sargent. Vol. I. Methuen & Co., Ltd., London.

WILSON, L. R., and R. M. WEBSTER. 1943. Microfossil studies of four southwestern Ontario bogs. Proc. Iowa Acad. Sci., 50:261–72.

WODEHOUSE, R. P. 1933. Tertiary pollen. II. The oil shales of the Eocene Green River formation. Torrey Bot. Club Bul., 60:479–524.

WULFF, E. V. 1944. Istoricheskaia Geografiia rastenii (Historical plant geography). Akad. Nauk S.S.S.R., Moscow.

ZAKLINSKAIA, E. D. 1953. Materialy k istorii flory i rastitel'nosti paleogena severnogo Kazakhstana v raione pavlodarskogo Priirtysh'ia (Materials on the history of flora and vegetation of northern Kazakhstan—about Pavlodar on the Irtysh). Akad. Nauk S.S.S.R. Inst. Geol. Nauk Trudy, Geologicheskaia seriia, 58:34–69.

ZAUER, V. V., E. H. KARA-MURZA, and M. A. SEDOVA. 1954. Osnovnye etapy v razvitii rastitel'nosti na territorii S.S.S.R. v Mezozoïskoe Vremia (po dannym palinologicheskogo analiza) (Main stages in development of vegetation in the U.S.S.R. during the Mesozoic time [based on palynological analyses]). Bot. Zhur. S.S.S.R., 39:238–41.

ZODDA. GIUSEPPE. 1903. Il *Pinus pinea* L. nel Pontico di Messina. Malpighia, 17(11–12):488–91.

# 3

# Geography

## INTRODUCTION

Information on general distribution of pines may be found in a series of maps assembled by Theodor Schmucker (1942). His maps are useful but they are small and sometimes not too accurate. For North America we have good, but somewhat obsolete, maps by Sudworth (1913). Sudworth's atlas is accurate enough for general purposes, but it was published about fifty years ago, and during this period some additional information became available.

In 1938, Munns published *The Distribution of Important Forest Trees of the United States*. This is an important contribution based on many years of collecting data. It has been used by workers in different branches of forestry throughout the world. In the Preface, the author modestly admitted that "The records of distribution of American forest trees are still incomplete." Twenty-six maps show distribution of that many North American pines. Distribution of some pines such as *P. clausa* No. 28 or *P. torreyana* No. 11 is not shown; *P. engelmannii* No. 53 and other pines are apparently included under *P. ponderosa* No. 14. This lumping together of several species gives an erroneous impression that *P. ponderosa* penetrates deeply into Mexico. In reality, except for its variety *arizonica*, which is considered in this book as an independent, essentially Mexican, species, *P. ponderosa* barely crosses the Mexican border in a few spots. Sudworth's and Munns's maps are used here as a basis for determining areas of North American pines; more recent information is added in many cases.

In this book, the distribution maps of Mexican pines are based chiefly on Martínez' *Los Pinos Mexicanos* (Martínez, 1948) and on Loock's *The Pines of Mexico and British Honduras* (Loock, 1950). Martínez' book contains many maps supported by the lists of herbarium specimens, with localities carefully indicated. Besides these two books, many other sources were used. These are indicated in the text.

Information on distribution of Mexican pines is far from being complete. For instance, there is the discovery of a white pine of southern Mexico that was designated as *"Pinus strobus* var. *chiapensis* No. 34." It was originally described by Martínez from Chiapas but later collected in several widely separated places both north and south of the type locality. New localities are being reported continually.

Information regarding areas of Eurasian and Mediterranean pines has been obtained from many different sources. Generally, distribution of pines in these two regions is well known.

In regard to Japan, Hayashi published a series of maps showing distribution of forest trees in that country. Among them are excellent and very detailed maps of Japanese pines (Hayashi, 1952, 1954). No doubt, these are the best maps of distribution of Japanese pines that have ever been prepared.

Our knowledge of Chinese pines is rather meager; fortunately, in 1947, Wu Chung-Lwen wrote a good account of this subject (Wu, 1947). Wang (1961) also supplied very useful information. Some data on pines of China have been obtained from recent Russian sources. These are mentioned in the proper place. Available maps of southeastern Asiatic pines are also very general. The author collected much information on that region during his trip there in 1961 and prepared detailed maps of some pines of that region.

There are some excellent maps showing distribution of pines in particular localities. Such are Ceballos and Ortuño's map of occurrence of *P. canariensis* on the Canary Islands (Ceballos y Ortuño, 1951) and the distribution map of *P. sylvestris* in Steven and Carlisle's monograph on *The Native Pine Woods of Scotland* (Steven and Carlisle, 1959). Very accurate maps are found in not too numerous monographs on individual pines such as *P. radiata* (Forde, 1962) and *P. sabiniana* No. 10 (Griffin, 1962).

In 1965, Critchfield and Little published a set of maps showing distribution of all species of pines. This publication is the most thorough and most reliable work in this field; nomenclature of the species has also been carefully checked and brought up to date (Critchfield and Little, 1965).

In his *Genus Pinus*, Shaw (1914) recognized 66 species; this book lists 105 species and several pines whose botanical status is uncertain. The discrepancy is caused by several circumstances. Since Shaw's monograph was published in 1914, many of his varieties, or mere synonyms, have been elevated to the status of independent species such as *P. jeffreyi* No. 13, *P. engelmannii* No. 53, and several others.

Several pines had not yet been described when Shaw prepared his *Genus Pinus*. These newly discovered pines include *P. kwangtungensis* No. 90, *P. dalatensis* No. 88, *P. strobus* var. *chiapensis* No. 34, *P. durangensis* No. 48, *P. cooperi* No. 51, and others.

As the taxonomy of the genus *Pinus* has not been settled yet (see Chapter 9), it is to be expected that in future revision of the genus—long overdue—several new species will appear, while some existing species will be invalidated. Accordingly, some of the maps presented here illustrating geographical distribution of pines are subject to revision.

It should be noted here that regional terms are often used in a geographical rather than political sense. For instance, geographically California extends to Oregon, to Nevada, and to Baja California. Therefore, typical California endemics are growing also in the above-mentioned places. Some Mexican pines cross the border and occur in California, Arizona, and New Mexico.

The purpose of this chapter is to show general areas occupied by the species of the genus *Pinus* rather than to present a detailed inventory of pine forests of the world. Accordingly, in this publication, the area of each species is shown in broad outline. In some instances, however, as in that of *P. merkusii* No. 101, within the general outline each authentic locality is shown. Where possible, locations of varieties are also indicated.

As regards selection of the types of projections, generally Goode's equal-area projections are used by permission; maps on other projections are employed only occasionally. How detailed a distribution map should be depends, of course, on the purpose for which it was prepared. If a study is of an ecological type, to show, for instance, recent decrease or increase of an area caused by activities of man (either destructive or beneficial),* the detailed maps are of utmost importance (see Chapter 6). As such maps have not been prepared in the past, we cannot say definitely, for instance, where *P. pinea* No. 73 is native and where it was planted in the Mediterranean region. Records of historians are often helpful. Such are Strabo's remarks made *circa* 60 B.C. on occurrence of pines in the Caucasus or the Balearics (see Chapter 2). But place names of the past always should be considered critically. How many places located amidst firs or spruces have been named "Whispering Pines"!

To understand the occurrence of a pine in a given part of the world, it is not enough to indicate its geographical coordinates. It is also important to show its altitudinal range. Sometimes insufficient information is available to show the exact limits of altitudinal range.

---

* Compare the complete destruction of *P. sylvestris* No. 69 in Denmark by primitive man with the expansion of *P. radiata* No. 19 from a small area in California into millions of acres in the Southern Hemisphere—also caused by man.

A pine species often is at its best only in the middle of its altitudinal range. In the lower and higher elevations, the species loses its prominence; the trees do not form a forest but, rather, are found as scattered groves, then as solitary trees, and eventually they disappear completely. Some pines may form good forests at the lower part of their altitudinal range.

A poorer appearance of the trees is noticeable when the genus reaches the northern limits of its distribution, but not necessarily so in its southern limits, because pines have been (and still are) advancing south, and, unless their advance is checked by man (through burning and grazing), they appear there numerous and healthy. I observed such pines at their southern limits in Nicaragua and in eastern Asia (see Chapter 6 page 431).

To describe what is inside a broadly outlined area is difficult. Pines may form there vigorous, continuous forests of one or several species, as in the American Southeast, or they may be scattered in a parklike fashion as is *P. sabiniana* No. 10, or they may form discontinuous groves (*P. merkusii* No. 101). Often, several pines occur in the same region, and each may grow in its particular ecological niche. For instance, in the Sierra Nevada of California, *P. sabiniana* is found at lower elevations; above it is a belt of *P. ponderosa* No. 14 with admixture of *P. lambertiana* No. 3. At 1800 to 2100 or more meters, the former is replaced by *P. jeffreyi* No. 13 and the latter by *P. monticola* No. 4. Still higher, chiefly in level places, there are pure groves of *P. contorta* No. 16, and, at the timberline, one finds *P. albicaulis* No. 1. On separate maps, the areas of these six species are found as occupying parts of the same general geographical area—the western slope of the Sierra Nevada. Superimposed, their irregular areas fit each other more or less neatly in a jigsaw manner, so that the whole western slope appears on the map as covered with pines. When one looks at a distribution map of a pine, it is always profitable to inquire in what manner the species is distributed within its outlined limits. Such information is not always available. In any pine forest, however continuous, there are treeless areas: swamps, rocky slopes, grasslands, burned or cultivated areas.

It is convenient for our purpose to divide the world (or rather its northern half) into several regions. The division is somewhat different from that used in Chapter 2 of this book. In the present chapter, Mexico and Central America are thus considered apart from northern America, but it was expedient, from the geographical point of view, to combine eastern and southeastern Asia. The geographical regions thus are as follows:

1. Western North America (Canada and the United States)
2. Eastern North America (Canada and the United States)

3. Mexico and the mountains of Central America
4. The Caribbean area including the southernmost part of Florida and the Caribbean Coast of Central America
5. Northern Eurasia
6. The Mediterranean area
7. Eastern Asia from Kamchatka to Indonesia, extending westward along the Himalaya and including the islands of Japan, Formosa, the Philippines, Hainan, and Sumatra

The seven regions are shown on the map in Fig. 3–1; the regions 1 to 4—North America, Mexico and Central America, and the Caribbean area —appear in greater detail on the map in Fig. 3–2.

## PINE REGION OF WESTERN NORTH AMERICA

Western North America is rich in pines. They grow from Alaska to the Mexican border, where they merge into the pine region of Mexico.
Longitudinally, western pines (*P. ponderosa* No. 14 and *P. contorta* No. 16) extend far east to the Black Hills of South Dakota, to north-central Nebraska, and to western Oklahoma (*P. ponderosa* No. 14).
The western North American pines are listed in Table 3–1.

**Table 3–1.** Western North American Pines

| Number | Species | Distribution |
|---|---|---|
| HAPLOXYLON | | |
| 1. | P. albicaulis | Widely distributed |
| 2. | P. flexilis | Widely distributed |
| 3. | P. lambertiana * | Chiefly California |
| 4. | P. monticola | Widely distributed |
| 5. | P. balfouriana | California |
| 6. | P. aristata | California to Colorado |
| 7. | P. monophylla * | Chiefly Nevada |
| 8. | P. edulis * | Widely distributed |
| 9. | P. quadrifolia * | Southern California—rare |
| DIPLOXYLON | | |
| 10. | P. sabiniana | California |
| 11. | P. torreyana | California |
| 12. | P. coulteri * | California |
| 13. | P. jeffreyi * | California, southern Oregon |
| 14. | P. ponderosa | Widely distributed |
| 15. | P. washoensis | Local in California and Nevada |
| 16. | P. contorta * | Widely distributed |
| 17. | P. attenuata * | California, southern Oregon |
| 18. | P. muricata * | Coastal California |
| 19. | P. radiata * | Coastal California |

* Also occurs in adjacent parts of Mexico.

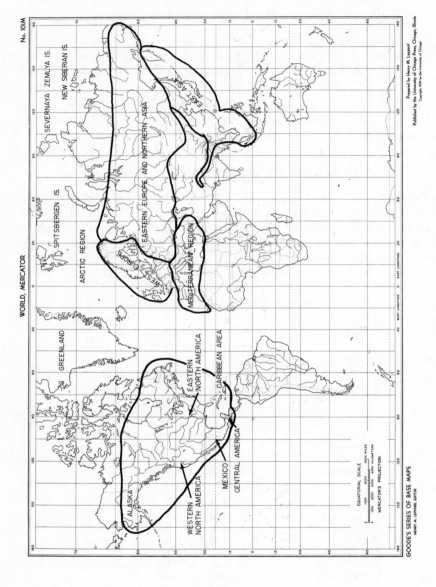

WORLD, MERCATOR

SEVERNAYA ZEMLYA IS.

NEW SIBERIAN IS.

SPITSBERGEN IS.

ARCTIC REGION

EASTERN EUROPE AND NORTHERN ASIA

EAST ASIA

WESTERN EUROPE

MEDITERRANEAN REGION

GREENLAND

EASTERN NORTH AMERICA

CARIBBEAN AREA

ALASKA

WESTERN NORTH AMERICA

MEXICO

CENTRAL AMERICA

EQUATORIAL SCALE

1000    2000    3000 MILES
1000  2000  3000  4000 KILOMETERS

MERCATOR'S PROJECTION

GOODE'S SERIES OF BASE MAPS

HENRY M. LEPPARD, EDITOR

Prepared by Henry M. Leppard
Published by the University of Chicago Press, Chicago, Illinois
Copyright 1939 by the University of Chicago

**Fig. 3–1. World pine regions.**

134

NORTH AMERICA                          No. 102

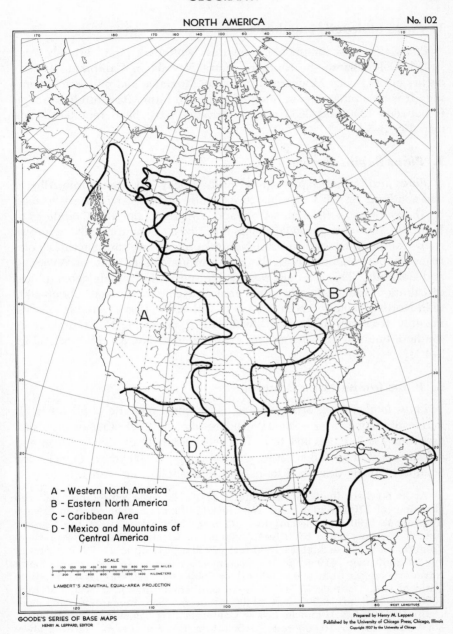

A – Western North America
B – Eastern North America
C – Caribbean Area
D – Mexico and Mountains of
     Central America

SCALE

LAMBERT'S AZIMUTHAL EQUAL-AREA PROJECTION

GOODE'S SERIES OF BASE MAPS
HENRY M. LEPPARD, EDITOR

Prepared by Henry M. Leppard
Published by the University of Chicago Press, Chicago, Illinois
Copyright 1937 by the University of Chicago

**Fig. 3–2.** Pine regions of America.

## 1. *Pinus albicaulis* Engelm.

*Pinus albicaulis,* commonly known as "whitebark pine," extends from British Columbia to the southern Sierra Nevada in California. It also occurs in the Rocky Mountains: in Idaho, Montana, and northern Wyoming. It is an alpine species, often of shrublike form. Its altitudinal range is between 1350 and 3650 m. No varieties have been reported. (See map, Fig. 3–3.)

## 2. *Pinus flexilis* James

*Pinus flexilis,* limber pine, grows in the Rocky Mountains from Alberta and southern British Columbia to its southern limits, which are formed by the canyons of the rivers Colorado, Arkansas, and Rio Grande (Dr. John W. Andresen, personal communication). Longitudinally, it grows from California to southwestern Nebraska and North and South Dakota. It grows most abundantly in the Rocky Mountains of western Wyoming and Colorado. This is a most remarkable species in its wide geographical distribution and in its altitudinal range, which varies from about 1000 m in North Dakota to about 3700 m in Colorado. It is a variable species. Possibly, it crosses in the Northwest with *P. monticola* No. 4, and, at its southern limits, it may merge into *P. strobiformis* No. 35. (See map, Fig. 3–4.)

## 3. *Pinus lambertiana* Douglas

*Pinus lambertiana,* or sugar pine, is the most majestic of all pines. It derives its name from a sugary exudate—monomethyl ether of $d$-inositol (see Chapter 7, pages 468–69). It reaches a height of about 70.0 m and a diameter of about 3.3 m. It may reach an age of 500 years. Fowells and Schubert (1956) described its habitat in the following words:

At its northern limits, about latitude 44°47′ N sugar pine grows between elevations of 1700 [520 m] and 3700 feet [1100 m]; farther south in Oregon from about 1100 feet [340 m] to 5400 feet [1650 m]. East of the Cascade summit it occurs up to 6500 feet [2900 m] in Klamath County. In northern California it grows as high as 7500 feet [2230 m] (latitude 41°23′ N.) and as low as 2000 feet [610 m] in the Sacramento canyon. In the central Sierra Nevada it ranges from 2000 [600 m] to 7800 feet [2400 m], as in Yosemite National Park (latitude 37°44′ N.). In southern California it occurs at from 4000 [1200 m] to 10,500 feet [4400 m] in the San Bernardino Mountains (latitude 34°15′ N.), and in Lower California it is common at elevations of 8000 [2400 m] to 10,000 feet [3100 m] in the San Pedro Martir Plateau (latitude 30°30′ N.).

The best stands of sugar pine occur in an elevational belt between 4500 [1400 m] and 6000 feet [1800 m] in the central Sierra, from the San Joaquin River north to the American River (latitudes 37° and 39° N.).

**Plate 3–1.** *Top: P. albicaulis* No. 1 near Bridgeport, California. Altitude slightly over 3000 m. (Photo by H. A. Jensen. Courtesy California Forest & Range Experiment Station, U.S. Forest Service.) *Lower left:* close-up of *P. albicaulis.* Photo by Duncan Dunning. Courtesy California Forest & Range Experiment Station, U.S. Forest Service.) *Lower right: P. lambertiana* No. 3 at an altitude of 2000 m in the Sierra Nevada, California. (U.S. Forest Service Photo.)

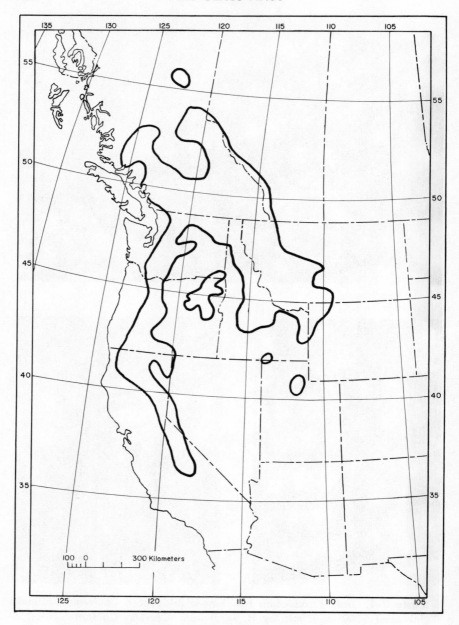

**Fig. 3–3.** Area of *P. albicaulis* Engelm. No. 1.

**Plate 3–2.** *Pinus flexilis* No. 2 east of Logan, Utah, 2478 m above sea level. (Photo by John W. Andresen.)

At the lower and middle elevations in the Sierra Nevada, sugar pine is most common on north and east facing slopes. In southern Oregon it grows on all aspects in equal abundance at lower elevations, but mostly on the warmer aspects at high ones.

Its altitudinal range, then, can be taken as 330 to 3200 m. But there are reports that, at the Cape Mendocino coast of California, this pine grows at much lower elevations.

Cones of this pine are the largest of all haploxylon-pine cones. They may reach 63 or more centimeters in length.

There is indication (G. L. Hayes, personal communication) that a variety of sugar pine is found on Ashland Peak (2100 m), in Oregon.

NORTH AMERICA

P. flexilis
P. strobiformis

**Fig. 3–4.** Areas of *P. flexilis* James No. 2 and *P. strobiformis* Engelm. No. 35.

**Plate 3–3.** *Pinus lambertiana* No. 3 in the Sierra Nevada, California. Altitude about 1850 m. This species may reach 70 m in height and over 3 m in diameter. (Photo by Clarence R. Quick.)

This small colony is situated 610 m above general and typical stands of the species. Whether this is a variety of *P. lambertiana*, or of *P. flexilis*, or a hybrid between the two species is not yet known. Except in this doubtful instance, *P. lambertiana* is rather stable morphologically, and no varieties of this species have yet been described.

Once I received a large cone of *P. lambertiana* whose scales were strikingly like those of *P. ayacahuite* of Mexico (Plate 9–2). Generally, however, *P. lambertiana* has no close resemblance to any other haploxylon pine, and it does not cross with any other American haploxylon pine. (See map, Fig. 3–5.)

### 4. *Pinus monticola* Douglas

*Pinus monticola* is commonly known as "western white pine." It grows chiefly in western Montana and northern Idaho. In Idaho it reaches its best development; hence it is often called "Idaho white pine." It extends to Washington and to southern British Columbia and southward to Oregon, central California, and adjacent parts of Nevada. Its altitudinal range is from sea level in Washington to 3350 m in the Sierra Nevada of California.

Apparently no varieties of *P. monticola* have been described. Chemical investigations, however, revealed a considerable variability throughout its extensive range (map, Fig. 3–6).

### 5. *Pinus balfouriana* Grev. & Balf.

*Pinus balfouriana* is a rare alpine haploxylon pine that, with *P. aristata*, forms Shaw's group *Balfourianae*. Its American name is "foxtail pine." It occurs in two disjunct localities. One is in the northern California ranges (Marble Mountains, Salmon Mountains, Scott Mountains, Trinity Alps, Yolla Bolly Mountains) at elevations between 2130 and 2440 m. In the other locality, about 500 km south, in the Sierra Nevada, it grows mainly at the sources of the Kings and Kern rivers at altitudes from about 2900 to 3650 m, either scattered, as in the north, or forming weird forests. Apparently it once occupied a more extensive area, but, since the end of the Tertiary, it has become separated into two localities. (See map, Fig. 3–7.)

There is evidence that *P. balfouriana* crosses with *P. aristata* (as suggested by Professor H. L. Mason, University of California, in a personal communication).

### 6. *Pinus aristata* Engelm.

*Pinus aristata* is commonly known as as "bristlecone pine." It is closely related to *P. balfouriana*, but its range is wider. It is scattered in the high

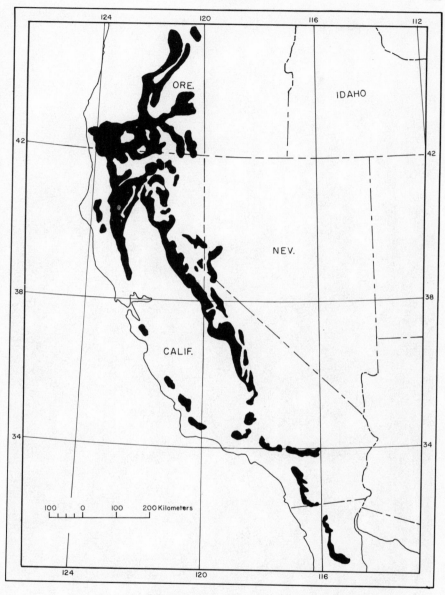

**Fig. 3–5.** Area of *P. lambertiana* Dougl. No. 3.

**Plate 3–4.** *Pinus monticola* No. 4, Coeur d'Alene National Forest, northern Idaho. (U.S. Forest Service photo.)

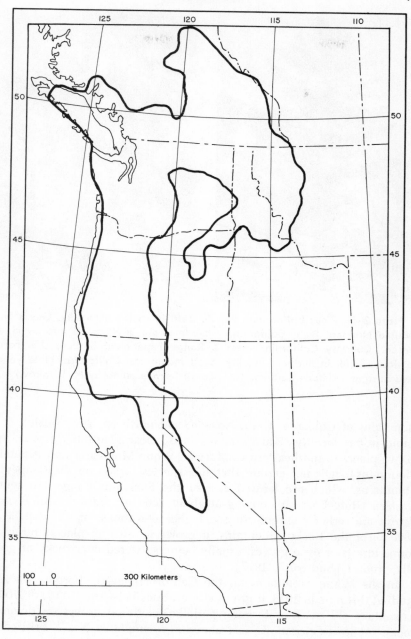

**Fig. 3–6.** Area of *P. monticola* Dougl. No. 4.

**Plate 3–5.** *Pinus balfouriana* No. 5. *Left:* in southern locality, Guyot Flat, Sequoia National Park, California. Altitude about 3000 m. (Photo by H. A. Jensen. Courtesy California Forest & Range Experiment Station, U.S. Forest Service.) *Right:* in northern locality, Scott Mountains, California. Note young trees at right. Altitude 2200 m. (U.S. Forest Service photo by N. T. Mirov.)

mountains of Colorado, Utah, Nevada, and northern New Mexico; it is found in one locality (San Francisco Peak) near Flagstaff, Arizona, and in two places in southeastern California (White Mountains and Panamint Mountains); it is not certain that this species occurs on the Grapevine Mountains, which are located east of the Panamint Range. In southwestern Utah, I saw it growing at about 2600 m admixed with *P. ponderosa* and other conifers. In the higher elevations, of about 2450 to 3300 m, of the Rocky Mountains, it grows in isolated places; rarely, it forms forests or even groves, usually being scattered over rocky or gravelly ground (Sudworth, 1917).

In the White Mountains on the California-Nevada border, where I studied this pine in 1948, it grows at elevations between 3100 and 3700 m as solitary old trees, or forming parklike, scattered groves on dolomite rocks. At lower elevations, just above *P. monophylla* No. 7, bristlecone pine grows together with not too numerous *P. flexilis* No. 2. It endures a great deal of drought. Apparently a semblance of annual rings is formed after every rather infrequent cloudburst. Little is known about the

**Plate 3–6.** *Pinus balfouriana* No. 5. *Top:* in southern Sierra Nevada near Mount Whitney. Altitude 2700–3600 m. Mature trees are from 10½ to, occasionally, 83 m tall and from 25 to 75 cm in diameter. (Photo by H. A. Jensen. Courtesy of California Forest & Range Experiment Station, U.S. Forest Service.) *Bottom:* in Scott Mountains, northern California, where this species does not form forests. Altitude 2400 m. (U.S. Forest Service photo by N. T. Mirov.)

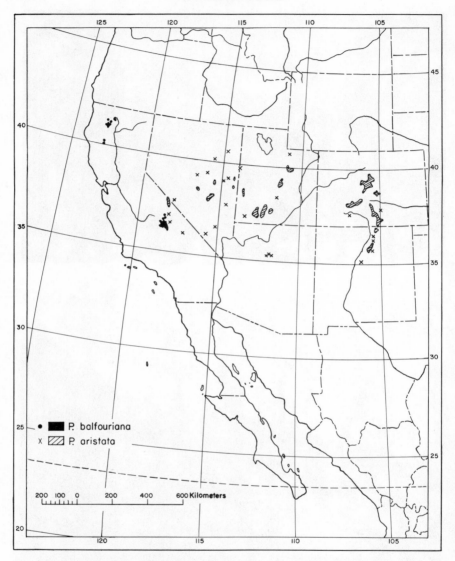

**Fig. 3–7.** Areas of *P. balfouriana* Grev. & Balf. No. 5 and *P. aristata* Engelm.
No. 6.

extreme age attained by this species (as Sudworth remarked in 1908
and 1917; see also Schulman, 1958; and see Chapters 5 and 6).

*Pinus aristata* is a Tertiary relict pine whose former (Pliocene) range
was much wider and whose occurrence was more frequent (cf. Axelrod
and Ting, 1960). Possibly it crosses with *P. balfouriana*. No varieties of
*P. aristata* have been described in the literature. (See map, Fig. 3–7.)

**Plate 3–7.** *Top: P. aristata* No. 6, southeast slope of Sheep Mountain, White Mountains, California. Altitude 3450 m. In the background are scattered trees of the same species. (Photo by Douglas Powell.) *Bottom: P. monophylla* No. 7, vicinity of Carson City, Nevada. Altitude 1800 to 2400 m. (Photo by R. C. Wilson. Courtesy California Forest & Range Experiment Station, U.S. Forest Service.)

To complete our consideration of haploxylon pines of western America, we should discuss the group *Cembroides*—the piñons, or nut pines, whose area is partly in the United States and partly in Mexico. There are seven species in this group; three are predominantly of southwestern America. These are *P. monophylla* No. 7, *P. edulis* No. 8, and *P. quadrifolia* No. 9. A fourth one, *P. cembroides* No. 36, although it occurs chiefly in Mexico, is also found sporadically in Arizona, southern New Mexico, and southwestern Texas. Its geography will be described later with that of other Mexican piñon pines: *P. pinceana* No. 37, *P. nelsonii* No. 38, and *P. culminicola* No. 39.

Piñons form a well-defined group, and their home is mainly in the Basin-and-Range Province of North America. Their habitat extends to the southwestern Pacific Coastal Ranges, the Colorado Plateau, and the Mexican Volcanic Plateau. They are small, scraggy trees of desert or semidesert environment. (See map, Fig. 3–8.) *P. cembroides* occurs only rarely in the United States.

### 7. *Pinus monophylla* Torr.

*Pinus monophylla* is a pine that has only one needle to a bundle; its common name is "singleleaf pine." It grows chiefly in Nevada, Utah, and the northern, somewhat larger, half of Arizona. In the northeast, it reaches southeastern Utah, and, in California, it is found chiefly east of the Sierra Nevada; from the southern-California ranges, it crosses the border into Baja California. It grows in desert ranges from 1200 to 2300 m in California; and, farther east, from 600 to 2100 m and up. It frequently forms pure, open stands that hardly can be called forests. Often it is intermixed with *Juniperus, Cercocarpus,* and other desert scrub. Its area in part overlaps with that of *P. edulis,* but whether or not they cross is uncertain. When the two grow together, each apparently maintains its own specificity. (See map, Fig. 3–8.)

### 8. *Pinus edulis* Engelm.

*Pinus edulis* is called "Colorado piñon." It is the only haploxylon pine that commonly has predominantly two needles to a fascicle (but see the discussion of *P. krempfii* on page 540 of Chapter 9). It grows in the Rocky Mountains region from Colorado and Utah, and extreme southern Wyoming, through Arizona and New Mexico to Trans-Pecos, Texas, and just across the border in the Mexican states of Baja California, Sonora, and Chihuahua. It occurs in a few spots in western Oklahoma and very rarely in southeastern California. In the Navajo country of Arizona, it grows on the arid mesas, forming rather scraggy, open forests either pure or with juniper. Its elevational range is between somewhat below 1500

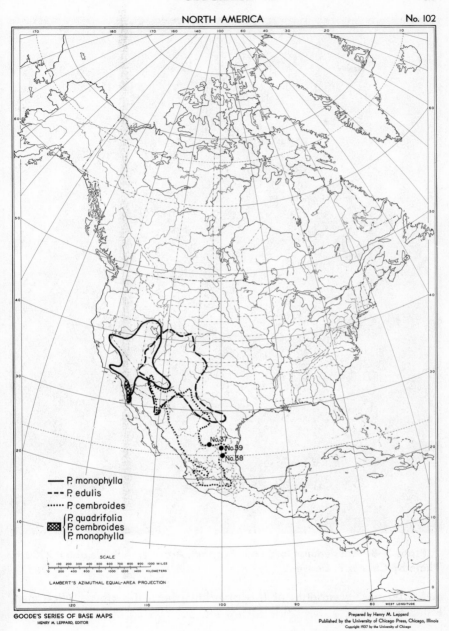

— P. monophylla

- - - P. edulis

··· P. cembroides

⊠ { P. quadrifolia
   { P. cembroides
   { P. monophylla

No. 37

No. 39

No. 38

SCALE

0  100  200  300  400  500  600  700  800  900  1000 MILES

0  200  400  600  800  1000  1200  1400  KILOMETERS

LAMBERT'S AZIMUTHAL EQUAL-AREA PROJECTION

GOODE'S SERIES OF BASE MAPS
HENRY M. LEPPARD, EDITOR

Prepared by Henry M. Leppard
Published by the University of Chicago Press, Chicago, Illinois
Copyright 1937 by the University of Chicago

**Fig. 3–8.** Areas of piñon pines. (*Pinus pinceana* Gordon No. 37, *P. nelsonii* Shaw No. 38, and *P. culminicola* Andresen & Beaman No. 39 are indicated by their numbers.)

**Plate 3–8.** *Pinus edulis* No. 8 near Flagstaff, Arizona. Altitude about 2200 m. (Photo by Chester F. Deaver.)

and 2700 m. No varieties of this pine have been described. (See map, Fig. 3–8.)

## 9. Pinus quadrifolia Parl.

*Pinus quadrifolia* is the rare Parry piñon of southern California and of adjacent parts of Baja California down to about 30° north. As a rule, it

**Plate 3–9.** *Left: P. quadrifolia* No. 9, Carrizo, Cleveland National Forest, San Diego County, California. Altitude 1000 m. (U.S. Forest Service photo.) *Right:* a vigorous old *P. sabiniana* No. 10, western foothills of Sierra Nevada. Altitude 150 m. (Photo by N. T. Mirov.)

has four needles per bundle, but clusters of three and sometimes five are also found on the same tree. Its elevational range is between 1150 and 1800 m.

Diploxylon pines of western North America are almost exclusively the pines of the geographical region of California, which includes adjacent parts of Oregon, Nevada, Baja California, and the nearby islands. Only two species grow also over an extensive area of the West beyond the geographical boundaries of California: *P. ponderosa* No. 14 and *P. contorta* No. 16. (See map, Fig. 3–8.)

### 10. *Pinus sabiniana* Dougl.

*Pinus sabiniana* is Digger pine—strictly a California species. Its home is in the dry foothills of the mountains surrounding the Central Valley. When young it is a straight, slender tree with lacy gray-green foliage; old trees are scraggy and forked, 15 to 23 m high.

Figures 3–9 and 3–10 are two maps of distribution of *P. sabiniana*. One (3–9) is from Sudworth (1913); the other (3–10) was taken from Griffin (1962). The first map shows general area of the species, sufficient for general geographical purposes. The second one, prepared about fifty years later, is more detailed. The much reduced range of *P. sabiniana* on

**Plate 3–10.** *Pinus sabiniana* No. 10. *Left:* typically straight and slender young tree of this species. *Right:* old tree on serpentine soil. Altitude about 150 m. (Photo by James Griffin.)

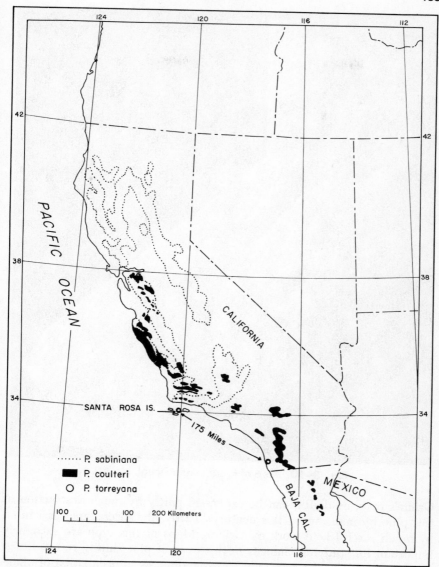

**Fig. 3–9.** Areas of *P. sabiniana* Dougl. No. 10, *P. torreyana* Parry No. 11, and *P. coulteri* D. Don No. 12

**Fig. 3–10.** Area of *P. sabiniana* Dougl. No. 10.

Griffin's map, no doubt, can be explained partly by much destruction of this pine by man during this century. Partly, the discrepancy is caused by much careful field work by Griffin. Maps of this type are extremely important for studying changes in the areas of pine during recent times. In some instances, the area may be expanding, as in occupation of abandoned cultivated land by pines in southeastern United States. Frequently, however, the area is reduced, as with *P. sabiniana*. It will be of considerable interest to compare Griffin's map with one made, say, fifty years from now. This phenomenon of changing extent and shape of area will be mentioned repeatedly throughout this discourse on geography of pines. It should be recalled that the Tertiary area of *P. sabiniana* extended farther south than the present area does (Axelrod, 1937). This pine's altitudinal range lies between 150 and 1500 m. It is a rather stable pine, and its subspecific variability is chiefly of a physiological nature.

## 11. *Pinus torreyana* Parry

*Pinus torreyana* (Torrey pine) is another Tertiary relic now found in two spots in southern California: near San Diego (about Del Mar) and on Santa Rosa Island. In its present natural habitat, *P. torreyana* is a low, crooked tree, 4.6 to 10.7 m, occasionally 15.0 m, high. Its altitudinal range is from sea level to 150 m. In cultivation, it reaches much larger

**Plate 3–11.** *Pinus torreyana* No. 11, about fifty years old, cultivated in Golden Gate Park, San Francisco, California. Note much superior form of the tree in comparison with native *P. torreyana* shown on the next plate. (Photo by Virginia Moore.)

**Plate 3–12.** *Top: P. torreyana* No. 11 in its natural habitat, near the ocean, southern California. (Photo by A. E. Wieslander. Courtesy U.S. Forest Service.) *Bottom: P. coulteri* No. 12, Cleveland National Forest, San Diego County, California. (U.S. Forest Service photo.)

size both in height and in diameter, displaying a peculiar candelabra-like form of several heavy stems and branches.

During the Tertiary period, the Torrey pine area was large. Mason (1927) found it in the Oligocene Bridge Creek Flora of Oregon. Possibly, the Oligocene and Miocene range of Torrey pine (or rather its predecessor, *P. trunculus* Dawson) extended to British Columbia. (See map, Fig. 3–9.)

## 12. *Pinus coulteri* D. Don

*Pinus coulteri* is closely related to the two preceding pines, and its area is restricted to the coastal ranges of California from San Francisco to the Mexican border; farther south, in Baja California, it occurs on the western slope of the San Pedro Martir Mountains, from San Vicente to Point San Quintin, i.e., about 30½° north. It grows at elevations of from 170 to about 2300 m. Martínez (1948) mentions its occurrence in Baja California in the Sierra del Pinal at an altitude of 1660 m. It is a tree of spreading crown, coarse needles, heavy, long lower branches, and the heaviest cones of all pines (see Chapter 5, page 381). *Pinus coulteri* crosses naturally with *P. jeffreyi*. (See map, Fig. 3–9.)

## 13. *Pinus jeffreyi* Grev. & Balf.

*Pinus jeffreyi*, commonly known as "Jeffrey pine," has been considered by some botanists (Jepson, 1923–25) as a variety of *P. ponderosa*, while other specialists (Sudworth, 1908) maintain it to be an independent species. This latter opinion has prevailed, and no botanists familiar with Jeffrey pine in its natural habitat call it a variety of *P. ponderosa* any more.

*Pinus jeffreyi* is essentially a California pine, extending beyond the administrative boundaries of the state to southern Oregon, western Nevada, and the San Pedro Martir Mountains of Baja California (see map, Fig. 3–11). Its Tertiary range was larger; Axelrod and Ting (1960) found it in Pliocene deposits of western Nevada, where it does not grow now. Its altitudinal range is from about 1000 to 3100 m. Jeffrey pine crosses naturally with *P. ponderosa* (Mirov, 1929) and also with *P. coulteri* No. 12, as reported in 1939 from southern California by Carl Meyer, then a student at the University of California.

## 14. *Pinus ponderosa* Laws.

*Pinus ponderosa* (ponderosa pine) is a western American species of wide distribution. Its area extends from British Columbia to near the Mexican border. Possibly, it crosses the international boundary to a few places in Chihuahua and Sonora. Duffield and Cumming (1949), who surveyed the area of San Pedro Martir in Baja California, came to the conclusion that *P. ponderosa* does not occur there.

Longitudinally, its area extends from the Pacific Coast eastward to elevations of about 2750 m in the Sierra Nevada. Farther east, it is found occasionally in higher elevations of desert ranges of the Great Basin. It crosses the Rocky Mountains, reaches the Black Hills and beyond in South Dakota, and goes surprisingly far east in central and northern Nebraska (at elevations of about 1000 m). In the Rocky Mountains,

**Plate 3–13.** *Left:* P. coulteri No. 12, Cuyamaca, San Diego County, California. Altitude about 1200 m. (Courtesy California Forest & Range Experiment Station, U.S. Forest Service.) *Center:* P. coulteri, San Benito Mountains, California. Altitude 750 m. (Photo by A. E. Wieslander. Courtesy California Forest & Range Experiment Station, U.S. Forest Service.) *Right:* a fine specimen of P. ponderosa No. 14 at middle altitude in the Sierra Nevada, California. Large trees may reach over 60 m in height and over 2 m in diameter. (U.S. Forest Service photo.)

160

**Plate 3–14.** *Top:* virgin stand of *P. jeffreyi* No. 13 and *P. ponderosa* No. 14, Shasta County, northern California. Altitude about 2000 m. Large tree at left is *P. ponderosa;* large tree at right is *P. jeffreyi.* Note difference in bark texture. (Photo by A. E. Wieslander. Courtesy California Forest & Range Experiment Station, U.S. Forest Service.) *Bottom:* *P. jeffreyi* on granite rocks in high mountains of the Sierra Nevada—Sentinel Dome, Yosemite National Park, California. Altitude about 2550 m. (U.S. Forest Service photo.)

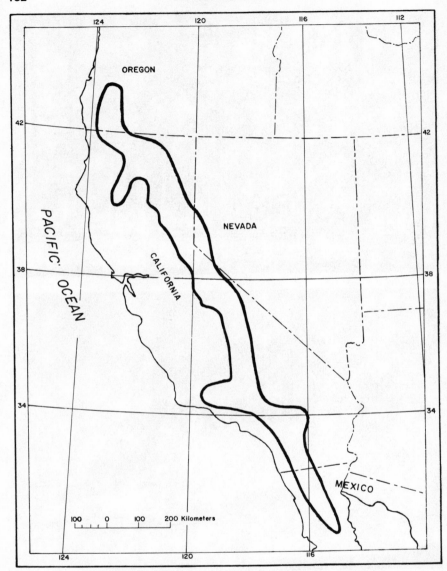

**Fig. 3–11.** Area of *P. jeffreyi* Grev. and Balf. No. 13.

forests of this pine are generally between 1500 and about 2600 m, but, in the southern Rockies, it may go as high as 3140 m. In the Laramie Mountains (Esterbrook), it forms forests at about 2000 m. In central Montana, it occurs at about 1500 m. The altitudinal range of *P. ponderosa* as a whole is from sea level to 3350 m.

*Pinus ponderosa* just crosses the border of Oklahoma. The Oklahoma colony consists of not more than 4000 trees. *Pinus ponderosa,* thus, is the most widely distributed species of the genus in North America.

The species is composed of several varieties, still little known. Generally, it is divided into the Pacific Coast variety (typical) and the Rocky Mountain form (var. *scopulorum*).

*Pinus ponderosa* crosses rarely with *P. jeffreyi.* Within the general boundaries of its area, the species has a rather spotty occurrence, generally on the middle slopes of the mountains, where it may form extensive forests. (See map, Fig. 3–12.)

## 15. *Pinus washoensis* Mason and Stockwell

*Pinus washoensis* is such a new discovery that the species has not acquired a common name yet. The official U.S. Forest Service check list (Little, 1953) suggests it be called "Washoe pine." It occurs in the upper reaches of Galena Creek, Nevada, east of Lake Tahoe, at an elevation of about 2100 to 2600 m (Mason and Stockwell, 1945).

Before exploration of the West, this pine had apparently been rather abundant, but, toward the end of the nineteenth century, it was almost completely exterminated, having been logged to supply lumber for the development of Nevada silver mines. It resembles very closely *P. ponderosa* in all morphological characters, but its small cones look like miniature *P. jeffreyi* cones. Its history and genealogy are not yet known. It appears that its present range in western Nevada is more extensive than was postulated by its discoverers. Moreover, it is not confined to the Pleistocene moraine and is not represented by "second growth" (young) trees only. Old trees intermingle with *P. jeffreyi* No. 13 (see Plate 3–15), "but the two species do not appear to hybridize at present" (Haller, 1959). Haller (1961) reported it also in the southern Warner Mountains of northwestern California. (See map, Fig. 3–13.)

## 16. *Pinus contorta* Dougl.

*Pinus contorta* has a well-established common name—"lodgepole pine." Some people call it "tamarack pine." It occurs at elevations ranging from sea level along the Pacific Coast to over 3350 m in the Sierra Nevada and the Rocky Mountains. It extends from 64° in the Yukon Territory to the San Pedro Martir Mountains of Baja California, latitude approximately 31°. Longitudinally, it extends from the Pacific Coast to the Black Hills of South Dakota. It is found in southwestern Saskatchewan. A little-known, isolated location is at the headwaters of Leidy Creek, White Mountains, southwestern Nevada, at elevations of 3100 to 3200 m (see

**Plate 3-15.** *Upper left and upper right: P. jeffreyi* No. 13 (*J*) and *P. washoensis* No. 15 (*W*) near Mount Rose, Nevada. Altitude about 2600 m. (*Photo by J. W. Duffield.*) *Bottom:* a fine virgin forest of *P. ponderosa* No. 14 in the Sierra Nevada, California. Altitude about 1500 m. Shrubs in foreground are *Ceanothus* and *Aristostaphylos*. (Courtesy California Forest & Range Experiment Station, U.S. Forest Service.)

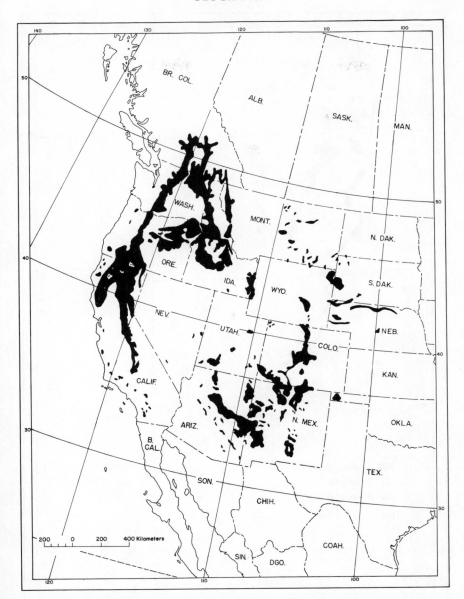

**Fig. 3–12.** Area of *P. ponderosa Laws.* No. 14.

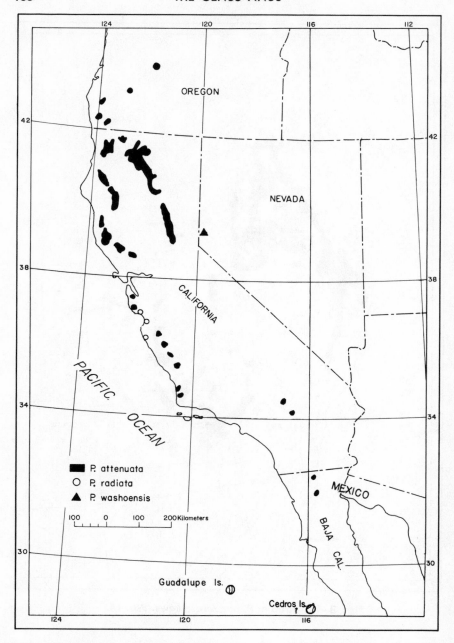

**Fig. 3–13.** Areas of *P. washoensis* Mason and Stockwell No. 15, *P. attenuata* Lemmon No. 17, and *P. radiata* D. Don No. 19.

**Plate 3–16.** *Pinus contorta* No. 16. *Top:* near Mount Lyell, Sierra Nevada, California. Altitude about 3000 m. (Photo by H. A. Jensen. Courtesy California Forest & Range Experiment Station, U.S. Forest Service.) *Bottom:* in the White Mountains of California, where it is very rare. Altitude 3050 m. (Photo by Douglas Powell.)

Plate 3–16). Critchfield (1957), in his monograph on *P. contorta,* described its complicated range in the following words:

(1) Along the Pacific coast, from Mendocino County, California, to southeastern Alaska, *P. contorta* occurs on low coastal bluffs, on sand dunes, in and around sphagnum bogs, and on other marginal sites. In this region its common name is beach or shore pine.

(2) In the Sierra Nevada–Cascade mountain chain, it is found at relatively high elevations, occupying a poorly defined zone slightly below timberline; it is also characteristic of mountain meadows and other moist sites down to moderate elevations. In the Sierra it used to be called tamarack, a common name now largely replaced by "lodgepole pine," and Sierra Nevada place names such as Tamarack, Tamarack Flat, and Tamarack Creek indicate its presence.

(3) In the Rocky Mountains, south to southern Colorado, it occupies a high-elevation zone just below the spruce-fir belt, but it is also widespread outside this zone because of its ability to revegetate burned-over areas. It was originally called lodgepole pine in this region, but this common name is now frequently used to designate the entire species.

These three distributional areas: coastal, Sierra-Cascade, and Rocky Mountain, are most distinct and widely separated at their southern extremities. North of the Canadian border the latter two are connected by extensive stands in the interior of British Columbia. The coastal strip is separated from the remainder of the range through most, and perhaps all, of its length, although there may be lateral connections between coastal and interior populations in the river valleys which dissect at right angles the Coastal Mountains of British Columbia and Alaska. Wood believes that the Skeena River valley, in northwest British Columbia, is one of the few places where the coastal and interior populations are contiguous.

Critchfield proposes that *P. contorta* consists of four subspecies: *contorta, bolanderi, latifolia,* and *murrayana.* (See Chapter 9, page 561.)

The extensive range of *P. contorta* overlaps the range of eastern American (largely trans-Canadian) *P. banksiana* in two places: around Edmonton, Alberta (Moss, 1949; Mirov, 1956), and in the Mackenzie region (Raup, 1947). Where the two come in contact, they cross, forming extensive hybrid areas. They have also been crossed artificially (Liddicoet and Righter, 1961).

Occurrence and distribution of *P. contorta* in the southwestern Mackenzie are not yet well known. To quote from Raup (1947):

It is presumed that the lodgepole and Jack pines overlap somewhere in the lower Liard country and on the foothills of the northern Rockies. Pines in the Liard valley above the "Liard Gap" all appear to be lodgepole, and it is supposed that those in the Mackenzie Mountains west of the South Nahanni R. are also of this species. No pines of any kind were seen at Brintnell L. and Prosild makes no mention of any along the Canol Road east of Macmillan Pass until he reaches the Mackenzie valley, where *Pinus banksiana* appears.

*Pinus contorta* was growing in western America during the Tertiary. *Pinus premurriana,* described by Knowlton from the Eocene strata of

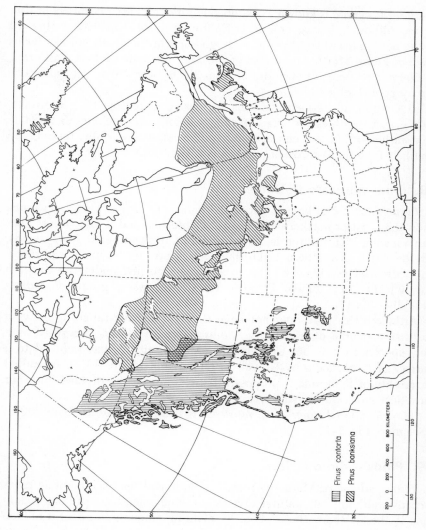

**Fig. 3–14.** Areas of *P. contorta* Dougl. No. 16 and *P. banksiana* Lamb. No. 32.

Pinus contorta

Pinus banksiana

200  0  200  400  600  800 KILOMETERS

Yellowstone Park (see Chapter 2, page 33 ), was, no doubt, an ancient *P. contorta* or its immediate predecessor. (See map, Fig. 3–14.)

## 17. *Pinus attenuata* Lemmon

*Pinus attenuata* is known as "knobcone pine." Its area is chiefly in California, although, like several other California pines, it extends northward to the mountains of southwestern Oregon and in the south goes as far as the San Pedro Martir Mountains of the Mexican state of Baja California. In Oregon, it occurs at altitudes of from 300 to over 600 m. In California, it may go as high as 1700 m.

In Oregon, it frequently forms "extensive pure forests" (Sudworth, 1908), and the trees are straight and well formed, reaching 18 to 24 or 25 m in height. In low elevations of California, it is scrubby, forked, and small; it is drought-resistant. (See map, Fig. 3–13.)

## 18. *Pinus muricata* D. Don

*Pinus muricata* is known under the name of "bishop pine." Its range is on the coast of northern and central California, and it also occurs near San Vicente, Baja California, and on Santa Cruz and Santa Rosa islands, off the coast of southern California. A variety of this pine was found on Cedros Island, lying off the coast of Mexico just under the thirtieth parallel (Durham, 1955). Possibly, the Cedros Island pine is *P. radiata* (Fielding, 1961).

Although this pine does not have a very extensive range, it shows a surprising degree of variability. *Pinus remorata* Mason, described as a new species from Santa Cruz Island (Mason, 1930), was reduced to a variety of *P. muricata* by Howell (1941). Duffield (1951), who studied variability of *P. muricata,* proposed that this species be divided into four varieties: *muricata, borealis, remorata,* and *cedrosensis.*

The elevational range of *P. muricata* is from sea level to about 300 m. (See map, Fig. 3–15.)

## 19. *Pinus radiata* D. Don

*Pinus radiata,* or Monterey pine, is unique and renowned among pines because, although its natural area is extremely small, its present expansion in the Southern Hemisphere by planting amounts to about a million hectares. It is a California endemic of relatively recent origin (Mason, 1932; Cain, 1944). It grows naturally in three localities on the coast: (1) on Point Pinos, south of Monterey Bay, from the sea over Huckleberry Hill to an elevation of about 370 m, extending about three miles inland; (2) on the coast of Santa Cruz County, from Point Año Nuevo to

**Plate 3–17.** *Left: P. attenuata* No. 17 near McCloud, Siskiyou County, California. *Right: P. muricata* No. 18 near Inverness, California. (U.S. Forest Service photos.)

171

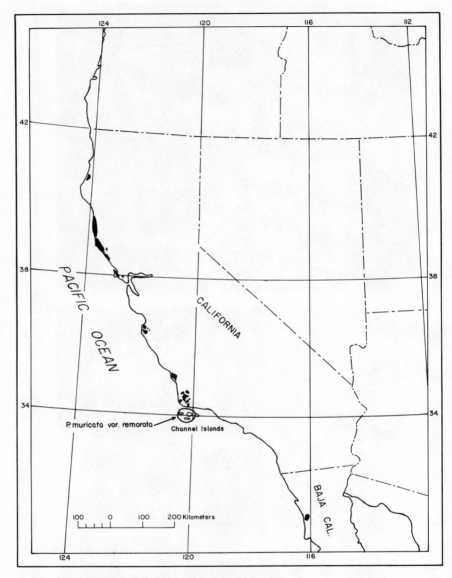

**Fig. 3–15.** Area of *P. muricata* D. Don No. 18. This species also occurs on Cedros Island (28° 15′ N., 115° 10′ W.), although Fielding (1961) suggests that the Cedros island pine may be *P. radiata* No. 19.

**Plate 3–18.** *Pinus radiata* No. 19 in California. *Left:* mature open-grown tree near inland edge of forest at Cambria. (Photo by Margot Forde.) *Right:* forest at about sea level, Monterey. (U.S. Forest Service photo.)

Big Creek; and (3) near Cambria, on the coast of San Luis Obispo County. It occurs also at 600 to 1200 m on Mexican Guadalupe Island off the coast of Baja California. In New Zealand, where it became the most important timber tree, it is known as *"Pinus insignis* Dougl." Its variability has been recently studied by Dr. Margot Forde, at the University of California (Forde, 1963). *Pinus radiata* crosses naturally with *P. attenuata.* (See map, Fig. 3–13.)

## PINE REGION OF EASTERN NORTH AMERICA

The eastern pine region of North America differs from the western region in that it has only one haploxylon pine, as compared with nine in the west. The number of diploxylon pines in the east is only slightly higher (twelve versus ten) than in the west.

There is one pine—*P. banksiana*—that may hardly be called an entirely eastern species, since it extends from the Atlantic Coast west to the Mackenzie River in the Northwest Territories of Canada.

In the West, especially in California, there are many endemic pines, occupying small areas; in the East, there are none, except perhaps *P. clausa* No. 28.

In the southern part of the region, there are found the extensive pine forests so aptly commented upon by Sargent when he contrasted these forests with scattered pine groves of eastern Asia (Sargent, in Preface to Wilson, 1913).

**Table 3–2.** Eastern North American Pines

| Number | Species | Distribution |
|---|---|---|
| HAPLOXYLON | | |
| 20. | *P. strobus* | From Newfoundland to northern Georgia |
| DIPLOXYLON | | |
| 21. | *P. resinosa* | Northeast |
| 22. | *P. palustris* | South, from southeastern Virginia to central Florida |
| 23. | *P. elliottii* | South, from South Carolina to central Florida |
| 24. | *P. taeda* | South, from southern New Jersey to central Florida |
| 25. | *P. echinata* | South, from southeastern New York to northern Florida |
| 26. | *P. glabra* | South Carolina to northern Florida |
| 27. | *P. virginiana* | Southeastern New York to northern Georgia |
| 28. | *P. clausa* | Florida to southern Alabama |
| 29. | *P. rigida* | From Ontario to northern Georgia |
| 30. | *P. serotina* | Southern New Jersey to central Florida |
| 31. | *P. pungens* | Appalachian region |
| 32. | *P. banksiana* | From Nova Scotia to the Mackenzie River |

## 20. *Pinus strobus* L.

*Pinus strobus* is called "eastern white pine." In Europe, where it is planted extensively, it is known as "Weymuth pine." Its area is larger than that of any other haploxylon pine of the New World. It extends from Newfoundland and Quebec west to central Ontario and southeastern Manitoba, south to Minnesota, northeastern Iowa, northern Illinois, northwestern Indiana, Ohio, Pennsylvania, and New Jersey, and south in the mountains to western North Carolina, northern Georgia, and Tennessee. It occurs locally in western Kentucky and western Tennessee (Little, 1953). (See map, Fig. 3–16.)

As *P. strobus* extends from north to south for at least 1900 km, and for about the same distance inland from the seacoast, one can expect some variability within the species. And, indeed, such variability does exist. Heimburger and Holst (1955) noted during their trip to the southern United States that *P. strobus* near Asheville, North Carolina, differs markedly in appearance from Canadian white pine; its needles are long and slender and of a more grayish color than in Canada. But generally *P. strobus* is not as variable as some other white pines such as *P. flexilis* No. 2 or *P. ayacahuite* No. 33. No varieties of *P. strobus* have been de-

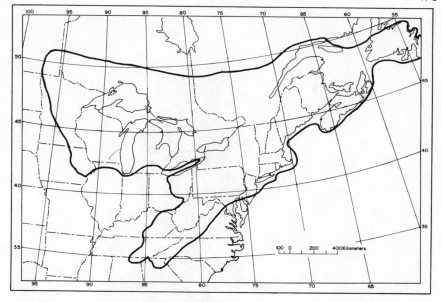

**Fig. 3–16.** Area of *P. strobus* L. No. 20.

scribed by botanists from its vast range in the United States and Canada.

*Pinus strobus* L. var. *chiapensis* Mart. No. 34, of Mexico, will be considered in the description of Mexican pines. Possibly, it will be elevated to the rank of an independent species.

The altitudinal range of *P. strobus* is from about 150 m and even lower to 1500 m; above 450 m in altitude, it is of limited occurrence.

## 21. *Pinus resinosa* Ait.

*Pinus resinosa* is one of the two representatives in the New World of Shaw's group *Lariciones*. The other is *P. tropicalis* No. 66 of the Caribbean area. *Pinus resinosa* is known in America as "red pine" or "Norway pine." It is a native of the northeastern part of the continent. Its area extends from Newfoundland and Quebec west to Ontario and southeastern Manitoba, and south to northeastern Minnesota, Wisconsin, Michigan, Illinois (Brenneman, 1956), northern Pennsylvania, New York, Connecticut, and Maine. Its latitudinal range is, thus, about 2400 km; longitudinally it extends for about 800 km. It occurs locally also in northeastern West Virginia. Its present main range (except West Virginia) from southeastern Wisconsin eastward lies within, or closely adjacent to, the area glaciated during the late Pleistocene (Rudolf, 1957, wherein is given a further bibliography on this pine). The altitudinal range of *P. resinosa* is between sea level and a little over 800 m (Rudolf, 1957). In West

**Plate 3–19.** *Pinus strobus* No. 20, South Barre, Massachusetts. (Photo by Martin H. Zimmermann.)

Virginia, it occurs in one place at 1150 to 1300 m above sea level. *Pinus resinosa* is very uniform morphologically. No varieties of this species have been described. (See map, Fig. 3–17.)

## 22. *Pinus palustris* Mill.

*Pinus palustris,* the longleaf pine of the Coastal Plain of the southeastern United States, extends from southeastern Virginia (north latitude

**Plate 3–20.** *Pinus resinosa* No. 21 in Chippewa National Forest, north-central Minnesota. *Top:* a mature wild stand. *Bottom:* well-managed forest with reproduction in openings. (U.S. Forest Service photo.)

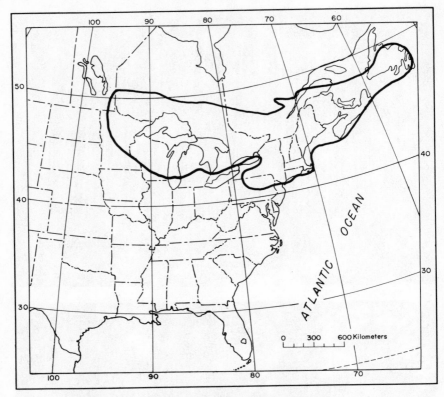

**Fig. 3–17.** Area of *P. resinosa* Ait. No. 21.

36° 31′) to Cape Kennedy, in central Florida, and across the peninsula
to a short distance from Tampa Bay and westward along the Gulf Coast
to the uplands that border upon the alluvial deposits of the Mississippi.
West of that river, longleaf pine forests continue to the Trinity River in
eastern Texas. Essentially, this pine grows at sea level. In Alabama,
however, it ascends the extreme southern spurs of the Appalachian Mountains to altitudes of about 450 to 600 m.

The geographical area of *P. palustris* extends from 76° to 96° west
longitude and from 20° 30′ to 36° north latitude. Its range is chiefly confined to the sandy and gravelly deposits of the Coastal Plain (Mohr,
1897). Since Mohr's time, the area of *P. palustris* and the continuity and
density of its forests have been greatly reduced. As no varieties of this
pine have been described, it might be taken that it is relatively stable. It
hybridizes naturally with *P. taeda* No. 24, the hybrid having been
described under the name of *P. sondereggeri* H. H. Chapman. (See map,
Fig. 3–18.)

**Plate 3–21.** *Pinus palustris* No. 22. (Photo by Southern Institute of Forest Genetics, Gulfport, Mississippi.)

## 23. *Pinus elliottii* Engelm.

*Pinus elliottii*, or slash pine, was known for some time as *"Pinus caribaea* Morelet." Originally it was named *"Pinus elliottii,"* and at one time it was known as *"Pinus heterophylla* Sudw." In 1952, it again became known as *"Pinus elliottii"* (Little and Dorman, 1952). This species now is subdivided into *P. elliottii* var. *elliottii* and *P. elliottii* var. *densa* No. 63, of southern Florida. The name *"Pinus caribaea* No. 62" has been retained

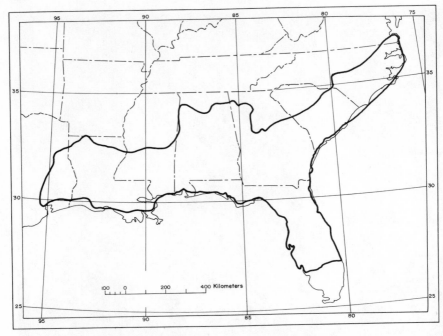

**Fig. 3–18.** Area of *P. palustris* Mill. No. 22.

only for the slash pine growing in the West Indies and Central America.

There are ample morphological justifications for segregating slash pine into the above three entities. The chemical characters of these three pines also are different.

The following account concerns only *P. elliottii* var. *elliottii*. Mohr (1897) described *P. elliottii* as a tree of the Coastal Plain of the subtropical region of North America east of the Mississippi River. Its area is from 33° north latitude in South Carolina along the coast to central Florida and southeastern Louisiana. Toward the west, the species extends along the Gulf Coast to the Pearl River Valley in southeastern Louisiana. (See map, Fig. 3–19.)

Its altitudinal range is from sea level to about 150 m.

*Pinus elliottii* itself is not a variable pine. No varieties of this pine have been described, besides the recently established variety *densa* (Little and Dorman, 1952). Perhaps variety *densa* deserves the rank of an independent species. Variety *densa* will be described as a Caribbean pine (No. 63), together with the other pines that are found in that region (see page 230).

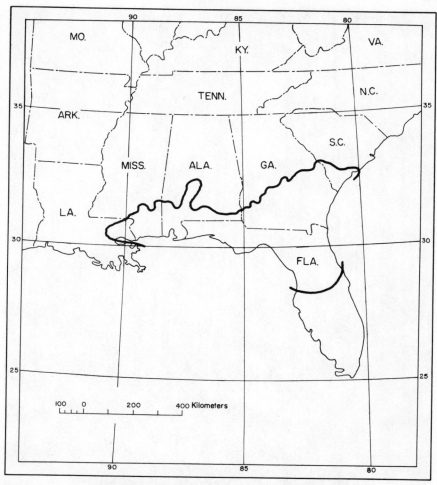

**Fig. 3–19.** Area of *P. elliottii Engelm.* No. 23.

## 24. *Pinus taeda* L.

*Pinus taeda* is the lobolly pine of the southeastern Coastal Plain and Piedmont from southern New Jersey south to central Florida (Cape Malabar), west to eastern Texas, and north in the Mississippi Valley to southeastern Oklahoma, Arkansas, and southern Tennessee. The Texas locations are separated from the main area, and trees there are more drought-resistant than those on the Coastal Plain. The altitudinal range of *P. taeda* is from sea level up to a little over 450 m. No varieties of this pine have been reported by botanists. It crosses naturally with *P. palus-*

**Plate 3–22.** Sixty-two-year-old *P. elliottii* No. 23, about 30 m tall. (U.S. Forest Service photo by D. O. Todd.)

*tris*, the hybrid being known as *"Pinus sondereggeri* H. H. Chapman." (See map, Fig. 3–20.)

## 25. *Pinus echinata* Mill.

*Pinus echinata* is the last of the "big four" southeastern American pines. It is known as "shortleaf pine." Its geographical area extends from southeastern New York and New Jersey to Pennsylvania, southern Ohio,

**Plate 3–23.** Fifty-year-old *P. taeda* No. 24 along roadway northwest of Crossett, Arkansas. (U.S. Forest Service photo by W. R. Mattoon.)

Kentucky, southern Illinois, and southern Missouri, south to eastern Oklahoma and eastern Texas, and east to Georgia. It barely crosses the Florida state line. In comparison with those of the other three pines, its area extends farther north, but its southern boundary does not go as far south. According to the map in Mohr's monograph on southern pines (Mohr, 1897), *P. echinata* does not occur along the main range of the Appalachian Mountains, and its distribution in the southern part and also in Kentucky and Tennessee is rather spotty. Its altitudinal range is from sea level to about 760 m. (See map, Fig. 3–21.)

No natural varieties of this pine have been reported.

## 26. *Pinus glabra* Walt.

*Pinus glabra* (spruce pine) is the least common pine of the southeastern United States. It grows either singly or in groups on the low terraces, mixed with hardwoods and with loblolly and shortleaf pines (Mohr, 1897). The general area of this pine is in the Coastal Plain between 31° and 33° north latitude, from South Carolina to northern Florida and west to southeastern Louisiana. *Pinus glabra* grows at sea level or slightly above it. (See map, Fig. 3–22.)

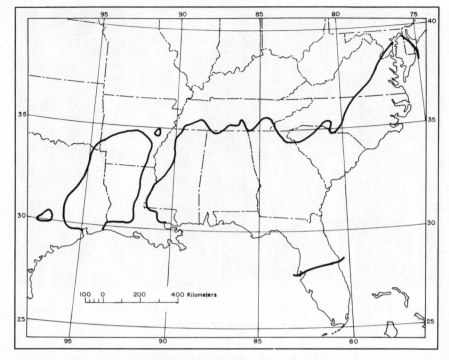

**Fig. 3–20.** Area of *P. taeda* L. No. 24.

## 27. Pinus virginiana Mill.

*Pinus virginiana* is so-called Virginia pine, also known locally as "New Jersey pine," "North Carolina pine," and "scrub pine." Virginia pine is generally a small tree. It is common on the Atlantic Coastal Plain; it is rare from Virginia south along the Appalachian Mountains and in the Ohio Valley. Its area extends from southeastern New York, New Jersey, Pennsylvania, Ohio, southern Indiana, and Kentucky south to northeastern Mississippi, Alabama, and northern Georgia. The altitudinal range of *P. virginiana* is between sea level and a little over 300 m. In Alabama, this pine was found at 325 m above sea level (Sargent, 1947). (See map, Fig. 3–23.)

No varieties of *P. virginiana* have been described by botanists. No natural hybrids of this pine are known.

## 28. Pinus clausa (Chapman) Vasey

*Pinus clausa* is known as "sand pine." Its range is almost entirely within Florida, where it occurs in two areas separated by about 200 km.

**Plate 3–24.** *Pinus echinata* No. 25 in Mississippi. (Photo by Southern Institute of Forest Genetics, U.S. Forest Service, Gulfport, Mississippi.)

The larger area is in central Florida, and the smaller one is in the western part of the state. On the Atlantic Coast, it reaches Fort Lauderdale, and, on the Gulf Coast, it extends to Tampa. It grows from sea level to about 60 m above it.

The western area of *P. clausa* is on the Gulf Coast between 85° and 87° west longitude; i.e., it extends westward into Alabama. *Pinus clausa* shows an interesting variability. The western race is characterized by

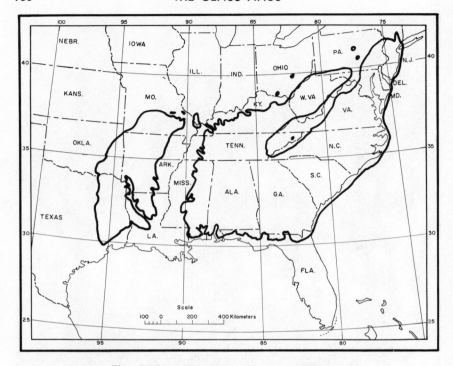

**Fig. 3–21.** Area of *P. echinata* Mill. No. 25.

cones that open when mature. In this respect, it is closer to the group *Australes*, to which the five previously described pines belong. The race of central Florida has cones like pines of the group *Insignes*. They open and release seed only after a severe fire sweeps through the forest. (See map, Fig. 3–24.)

## 29. *Pinus rigida* Mill.

*Pinus rigida* is known as "pitch pine." Its range is from central Maine, New York, and southeastern Ontario south to Pennsylvania, southern Ohio, West Virginia, Virginia, and the mountains of eastern Kentucky, eastern Tennessee, western North Carolina, and northern Georgia. The most northerly location of this pine is isolated in southern Quebec (Rouleau, 1955). (See Map, Fig. 3–25.)

*Pinus rigida* is a relatively variable species—small and scrubby in the north; in Pennsylvania reaching its best development, up to 30 m in height and 90 cm in diameter. It grows from sea level to an altitude of a little over 900 m, occasionally even higher (Harlow and Harrar, 1937). There are no named varieties of this pine.

**Plate 3–25.** *Pinus glabra* No. 26 with epiphytic bromelid (*Tillandsia*) on branches. (U.S. Forest Service photo by W. D. Brush.)

## 30. *Pinus serotina* Michx.

*Pinus serotina*, or pond pine, grows in the Coastal Plain from southeastern Virginia south to central and southeastern Alabama, and on Cape May, New Jersey (Wenger, 1958). (See map, Fig. 3–26.)

*Pinus serotina* is a pine of low elevations—not higher than 60 m above sea level.

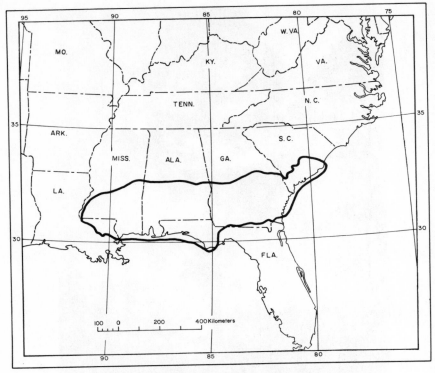

**Fig. 3–22.** Area of *P. glabra* Walt. No. 26.

Apparently it crosses naturally with *P. taeda* (Wenger, 1958). Artificially, it was crossed with *P. taeda* No. 24 (Harkin, 1957) and with *P. rigida* No. 29 (Liddicoet and Righter, 1960). Once it was considered as a variety of *P. rigida.*

### 31. *Pinus pungens* Lamb.

*Pinus pungens,* or Table Mountain pine, grows in the mountains from New Jersey, Pennsylvania, and West Virginia south to South Carolina, northern Georgia, and eastern Tennessee. This pine is most abundant in the southern part of its range, on the tablelands of the Alleghenies (Harlow and Harrar, 1937). Its altitudinal range is from sea level to a little over 900 m. It has no named varieties. (See map, Fig. 3–27.)

### 32. *Pinus banksiana* Lamb.

*Pinus banksiana,* or Jack pine, has an immense range, extending from Nova Scotia and central Quebec westward across Canada to northern Saskatchewan and the Northwest Territories, south to northern British

**Plate 3–26.** *Pinus virginiana* No. 27 forest in North Carolina Piedmont. (U.S. Forest Service photo by L. Della-Blanca.)

Columbia, central Alberta, southern Manitoba, and, in the northeastern United States, Minnesota, Wisconsin, Michigan, and Maine. It is local in northern Illinois, northwestern Indiana, northern New York, Vermont, and New Hampshire. According to Raup (1947), *P. banksiana* is common in the central and southern parts of the Mackenzie Basin, but records for the country below Great Slave Lake are based only on casual observation. It grows in Canada to latitude 64°, and even beyond that, on the sandy banks of the Mackenzie River.

It occurs commonly on the Simpson Islands and about the Northern Arm of Great Slave Lake. On [Preble's] route to the northward of Fort Rae it was seen in many places on the Grandin River, reaching a diameter of 18 inches, but not growing very tall. North of the height of land it was rare, but [Preble] saw many trees on a portage a few miles north of the outlet of Lake Hardisty.
On the Mackenzie it is common north to about latitude 64° 30'. . . . On the north slope of the Nahanni Mountains, 75 miles [121 km] below Fort Simpson, the species ascends to about 1,000 feet [300 m] and then becomes a dwarfed shrub and disappears. On the southern slopes of the same mountains it occurs as a fairly well-grown tree to about 2,000 feet [610 m] near the summit.[*]

[*] Preble, as quoted by Raup, 1947.

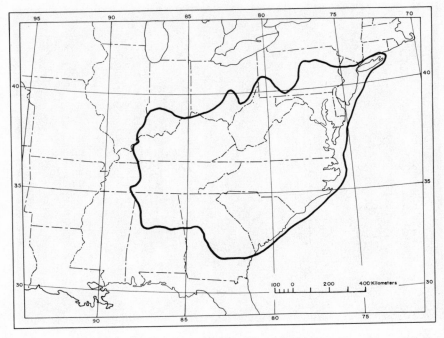

**Fig. 3—23.** Area of *P. virginiana* Mill. No. 27.

It occurs farther north than any other American pine. It is scrubby in the north but straight and tall in the southern parts of its range. It grows in areas characterized by warm to cool summers, very cold winters, rather low rainfall, light sandy soils, and level to rolling topography. It occurs on burned areas (Rudolf, 1958). Its altitudinal range is between sea level and a little over 600 m.

*Pinus banksiana* possesses a considerable intraspecific variability, but not as much as one would expect of a species occupying such a geographical range.

No varieties of this pine have been described by botanists. In Alberta, Canada, where *P. banksiana* meets the *P. contorta* No. 16 range, the two pines hybridize naturally (Moss, 1949, 1953; Mirov, 1956). Apparent overlap also takes place in the Mackenzie River area (Dr. Hugh M. Raup, personal communication). Generally, it is considered that, in these two places, the areas of *P. banksiana* and *P. contorta* overlap, but it might be that the overlap is formed by the hybrid swarm between the two areas of the species in the woodland, which previously had been within neither the *P. banksiana* nor the *P. contorta* area. (See map, Fig. 3–14, page 169.)

**Plate 3–27.** *Pinus clausa* No. 28 at about sea level in central Florida. (U.S. Forest Service photo by W. D. Brush.)

## PINE REGION OF MEXICO AND THE MOUNTAINS OF CENTRAL AMERICA

Information on geographical distribution of pines in Mexico is taken chiefly from *Los Pinos Mexicanos* by Martínez (1948), by far the most authoritative work on Mexican pines. In addition, various other sources have been used. These are indicated in the text.

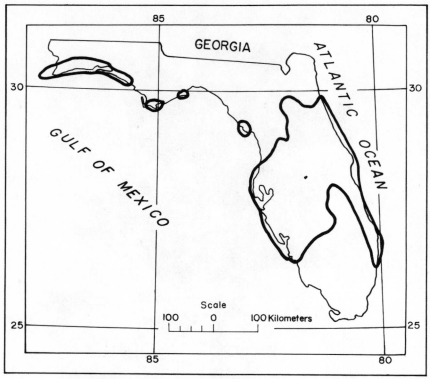

**Fig. 3–24.** Area of *P. clausa* (Chapman) Vasey No. 28.

The northern part of Mexico resembles the southwestern part of the United States in many ways. In fact, a vast area on both sides of the Mexican-American border is within the same geomorphological Basin-and-Range Province of North America (see map, Fig. 2–1, page 28). Accordingly, there is a certain overlap of geographical areas between the western North American pine region and that of Mexico. The group of seven piñon pines, for instance, belongs essentially to the Basin-and-Range Province. Only three of them are exclusively Mexican. Several western American pines—*P. jeffreyi* No. 13, *P. ponderosa* No. 14, *P. contorta* No. 16, *P. attenuata* No. 17, *P. muricata* No. 18, and *P. radiata* No. 19—penetrate into Mexico. At the same time, four species whose main areas lie in northern Mexico extend northward across the border; these are *P. strobiformis* No. 35, *P. arizonica* No. 43, *P. engelmannii* No. 53, and *P. chihuahuana*, No. 40.

In Table 3–3 are listed all effectively published pines of the region. There are seven haploxylon species, of which four are piñon pines, and twenty-two are diploxylon species. There are still some pines in Mexico

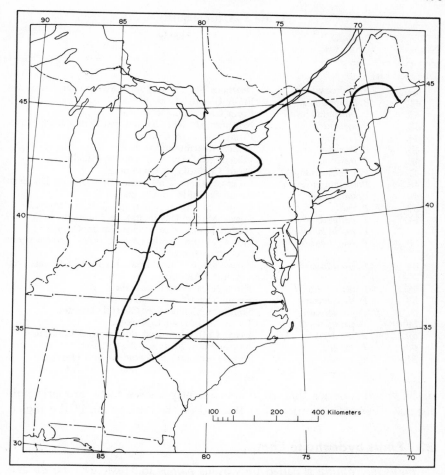

**Fig. 3–25.** Area of *P. rigida* Mill. No. 29.

**Table 3–3.** Pines of Mexico and the Mountain Regions of Central America

| Number | Species | Distribution |
|--------|---------|--------------|
| HAPLOXYLON | | |
| 33. | *P. ayacahuite* | From northern Mexico to Honduras |
| 34. | *P. strobus* var. chiapensis | Tropical southern Mexico and Guatemala |
| 35. | *P. strobiformis* | Northern Mexico; also in United States |
| 36. | *P. cembroides* | Large part of northern Mexico |
| 37. | *P. pinceana* | Rare; local in northeastern Mexico |
| 38. | *P. nelsonii* | Rare; local in northeastern Mexico |
| 39. | *P. culminicola* | Rare; local in northeastern Mexico |

**Table 3–3.** (Continued)

| Number | Species | Distribution |
|---|---|---|
| DIPLOXYLON | | |
| 40. | P. chihuahuana | Northern Mexico and southwestern United States |
| 41. | P. leiophylla | From Chihuahua to Oaxaca |
| 42. | P. lumholzii | From Chihuahua to Jalisco |
| 43. | P. arizonica | Northern Mexico; also southwestern United States |
| 44. | P. lawsonii | From Jalisco to Oaxaca |
| 45. | P. teocote | Widely distributed in Mexico |
| 46. | P. herrerai | Jalisco, Michoacan, Durango, Sinaloa |
| 47. | P. montezumae | From Coahuila to Guatemala |
| 48. | P. durangensis | From southern Chihuahua to southern Durango |
| 49. | P. hartwegii | From Coahuila to Chiapas |
| 50. | P. rudis | From Coahuila to Chiapas; Central America |
| 51. | P. cooperi | Sierra Madre Occidental in Durango |
| 52. | P. michoacana | Nuevo Leon, from Michoacan to Oaxaca |
| 53. | P. engelmannii | Sierra Madre Occidental; also in southwestern United States |
| 54. | P. pseudostrobus | Nuevo Leon, Tamaulipas, Jalisco to Chiapas, and Central America |
| 55. | P. tenuifolia | From Jalisco to Guatemala |
| 56. | P. douglasiana | From Nayarit to Oaxaca |
| 57. | P. oaxacana | Southern Mexico and Central America |
| 58. | P. pringlei | From Michoacan to Oaxaca |
| 59. | P. oocarpa | From Chihuahua and Sonora to Nicaragua |
| 60. | P. greggii | Northeastern Mexico |
| 61. | P. patula | From Queretaro to Veracruz and Oaxaca |

and Central America that are not sufficiently known to be properly published. These are mentioned at the end of the description of the region.

## 33. *Pinus ayacahuite* Ehren.

*Pinus ayacahuite* is called by various names in Mexico: "Pino de azucar" (i.e., sugar pine), "Acalocote," "Pinabete" (a name generally used for the genus *Abies*). Its area extends from the northern Mexican states of Sonora, Chihuahua, Coahuila, and Nuevo Leon to Guatemala. It occurs locally in Honduras (Santa Barbara Mountains), at an elevation of about 2700 m, and in one spot near the Honduran border at La Palma, Department of Chalatenango, San Salvador (Allen, 1962), at an elevation of about 2300 m. (See map, Fig. 3–28.)

*Pinus ayacahuite* is subdivided into three varieties: *brachyptera* Shaw, of the north, which apparently is the same as *P. strobiformis* Engelm. No. 35; *veitchii* Shaw of central Mexico; and *P. ayacahuite* proper, which, in accordance with the rules of nomenclature, should be designated as *Pinus ayacahuite* var. *ayacahuite* Ehren. It is essentially a pine of southern Mexico and Central America.

**Plate 3–28.** Open-grown *P. rigida* No. 29 near Westfield, Massachusetts. (U.S. Forest Service photo by C. R. Lockard.)

In Chihuahua, *P. ayacahuite* has been collected at 2300 to 2600 m; in Durango, it goes above 2800 m. Loock (1950) gave its range in the north as between 2400 and 2700 m. In Guatemala, it occurs between 2300 and 3200 m (Aguilar, 1961). In Chiapas, I collected it at about 2500 m.

## 34. *Pinus strobus* L. var. *chiapensis* Martínez

*Pinus strobus* var. *chiapensis* was described by Martínez in 1940 (Martínez, 1948). It has some resemblance to *P. strobus* L., of the eastern United States, but there are also differences in morphological characters such as fineness of the needles and heaviness of the cones (the average var. *chiapensis* cone is twice as heavy as that of *P. strobus* of the same length from the southern Appalachian Mountains). The general appearances of the two are also different.

The geographical area of this pine is not well known; it grows at altitudes between 500 and 2000 m. At Cascada de la Tamata, near Tlapa-

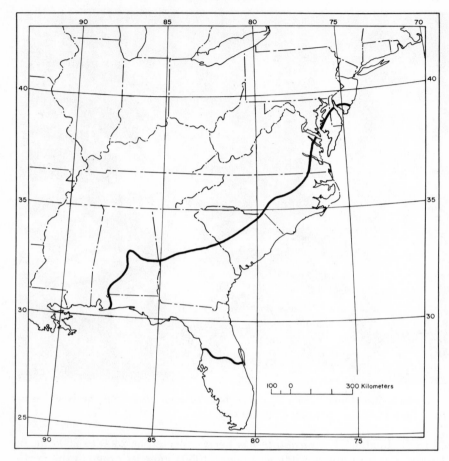

**Fig. 3–26.** Area of *P. serotina* Michx. No. 30.

coyan, Veracruz, it is found at altitudes of 500 to 600 m in a tropical environment, near coffee and banana plantations and orange groves. Apparently, it descends in many places down the escarpment of the Central
Mexican Plateau to tropical surroundings. New localities are being reported continually. Recently, it was found also in the Pacific-drainage
mountains of the Sierra Madre del Sur in the state of Guerrero. Schultes
(Martínez, 1948) observed pure stands of this pine of considerable size
between Teutila and Zautla, Cuicatlan District, Oaxaca, at 900 m above
sea level. Boone Hallberg (personal communication) said that this pine
occurs quite abundantly in the eastern part of Oaxaca as scattered individuals. One locality he mentioned is near Villa Alta, at an elevation of
1200 m. In Guatemala, it forms forests in the state of Huehuetenango

**Plate 3–29.** *Pinus serotina* No. 30 in a swamp (pocosin) in North Carolina. (U.S. Forest Service photo by C. F. Korstian.)

(near the Mexican border) up to 1900 m above sea level, but its lower limit there is not known (Schwerdtfeger, 1953). Aguillar (1961) mentions that it is especially abundant in the Departamento del Quiche. (See map, Fig. 3–28).

### 35. *Pinus strobiformis* Engelm.

*Pinus strobiformis* is a pine of northern Mexico, where it occurs in the mountains of Durango, Coahuila, and, especially, Chihuahua and Tamaulipas. It also grows in adjacent parts of the United States (Arizona, New Mexico, extreme southern Utah, and southwestern Colorado). Geographically, it is located between the areas of *P. flexilis* No. 2 and *P. ayacahuite* No. 32. Its altitudinal range is approximately 1650 to 3000 m. (See map, Fig. 3–4, page 140.)

### Mexican Piñon Pines

Seven species known as "piñon pines" form a well-defined group, *Cembroides* (Shaw, 1914). They are essentially pines of the arid environment

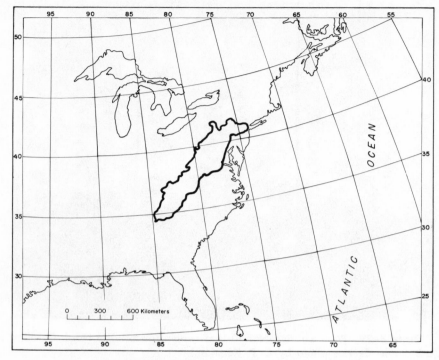

**Fig. 3–27.** Area of *P. pungens* Lamb. No. 31.

of the Basin-and-Range geomorphological province of North America. The areas of three species of this group—*P. monophylla* No. 7, *P. edulis* No. 8, and *P. quadrifolia* No. 9—have already been described under western American pines. *Pinus cembroides* Zucc. is predominantly a Mexican pine. The remaining three piñons considered here are strictly Mexican species, and they are of extremely limited distribution. The areas of all seven piñons are shown on the map in Fig. 3–8 (page 151).

### 36. *Pinus cembroides* Zucc.

*Pinus cembroides* occupies a large area in Mexico from Coahuila, Nuevo Leon (Zobel and Cech, 1957), Chihuahua, and Sonora as far south as the states of Tlaxcala and Puebla. It is also found in the extreme north and the extreme south of Baja California. In the United States, it occurs in southwestern New Mexico and southeastern Arizona. Its altitudinal range in the United States is from 1450 to 2300 m; in Mexico it is between 1800 and 2650 m (Loock, 1950; Martínez, 1948). (See map, Fig. 3–8, page 151.)

**Plate 3–30.** *Top: P. pungens* No. 31 on Holton Mountain, Tennessee. (U.S. Forest Service photo by E. S. Shipp.) *Bottom: P. banksiana* No. 32, Superior National Forest, northern Minnesota. (U.S. Forest Service photo.)

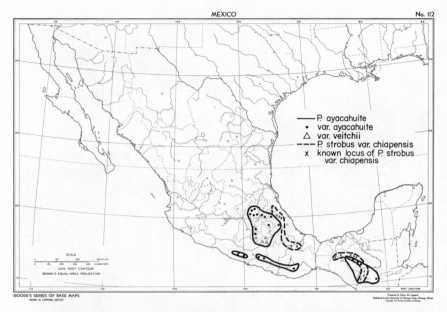

**Fig. 3–28.** Areas of *P. ayacahuite* Ehren. No. 33 and *P. strobus* var. *chiapensis* Martínez No. 34.

### 37. *Pinus pinceana* Gordon

*Pinus pinceana* is a very rare pine growing in dry ravines of desert ranges of the Sierra del Garambullo in the southeastern part of the state of Coahuila, Mexico; possibly in the adjacent parts of Nuevo Leon; and (subject to verification) near Camargo, Hidalgo. At Paso de Carneros, Coahuila, it is found at 2166 m. In the Sierra del Garambullo, Coahuila, I collected it at an altitude of 2100 to 2300 m above sea level. (See map, Fig. 3–8, page 151.)

### 38. *Pinus nelsonii* Shaw

*Pinus nelsonii* is a small bushy tree with long, pliant branches, gray bark, and sparse, gray-green foliage. It is a very rare pine, growing in a few restricted localities in the desert ranges of the Mexican states of Tamaulipas, Nuevo Leon, Coahuila, and San Luis Potosí at elevations of about 2000 to 2500 m. (See map, Fig. 3–8, p. 151.)

### 39. *Pinus culminicola* Andresen and Beaman

*Pinus culminicola* was first described in 1961. It occurs on Cerro Potosí Mountain, Nuevo Leon, Mexico, at an elevation of about 3600 m. Its ver-

**Plate 3–31.** *Left: P. ayacahuite* No. 33, Sierra María Tecúm, Guatemala. Altitude 3100 m. (Photo from Schwerdtfeger, 1953.) *Center and right: P. strobus var. chiapensis* No. 34, Cascada de la Tamata, near Tlapacoyan, Veracruz, Mexico. Altitude 500 m. (Photo by Norberto Sánchez-Mejorada.)

**Plate 3–32.** *Pinus strobiformis* No. 35, 20 m tall, in Escudilla Mountains near Springerville, Arizona. Altitude 2900 m. (Photo by John W. Andresen.)

tical range apparently is between 3350 and 3700 m. It differs from all other piñons by growing at extraordinarily high altitudes. No other piñon grows above 3000 m. *Pinus culminicola* grows in the same vicinity as *P. cembroides*, which occurs in abundance at the base of Cerro Potosí at about 2600 to 2700 m, but there is no evidence of hybridization between

**Plate 3–33.** *Pinus cembroides* No. 36, Coahuila, Mexico. Altitude 2300 m. (Photo by N. T. Mirov.)

the two pines (Andresen and Beaman, 1961). (See map, Fig. 3–8, page 151.)

The three rare Mexican piñons *P. pinceana, P. nelsonii,* and *P. culmini-cola* are geographically isolated from each other, and apparently there is no natural crossing between them. *Pinus pinceana* and *P. nelsonii* occasionally share their respective environments with *P. cembroides,* but there are no reports of their hybridization. These pines have no named varieties.

## Group Leiophyllae

*Pinus chihuahuana* Engelm., *P. leiophylla* Schiede and Deppe, and *P. lumholtzii* Rob. and Fern., form a small, well-defined group, *Leiophyllae,* of Shaw. These are the only diploxylon pines with deciduous bundle-sheaths, which are a general character of all haploxylon pines except *P. nelsonii.*

## 40. Pinus chihuahuana Engelm.

*Pinus chihuahuana* is essentially a three-needle Mexican pine. It grows chiefly in the states of Chihuahua, Sonora, and Durango. Southward, it

**Plate 3–34.** *Top: P. nelsonii* No. 38, Valle Hermoso, Tamaulipas, Mexico. Altitude 2000 m. (Photo courtesy Erasmo Cerda, Aramberri, Nuevo Leon, Mexico.) *Bottom: P. pinceana* No. 37, Sierra del Garambullo, Coahuila, Mexico. Altitude 2200 m. (Photo by N. T. Mirov.)

**Plate 3–35.** *Pinus culminicola* No. 39, 1 m tall, Cerro de Potosí, Nuevo León, Mexico. Altitude 3600 m. (Photo by John W. Andresen.)

extends to Nayarit, Zacatecas, and the northern part of Jalisco. In the north, it extends to the United States, where it occurs in the desert mountains of southeastern Arizona and southwestern New Mexico. It grows at between 2100 and 2700 m of altitude. In the United States, it has been recorded at approximate elevations of between 1670 and 2500 m. (See map, Fig. 3–29.)

### 41. *Pinus leiophylla* Schiede and Deppe

*Pinus leiophylla* is an entirely Mexican pine found in the states of Chihuahua and Durango and as far south as Veracruz and Oaxaca. Generally it grows in dry localities at high elevations, but occasionally it occurs at lower altitudes. It is closely related to *P. chihuahuana*, but it differs by having five needles to a bundle. Martínez (1948) recorded 2000 to 3660 m as its altitudinal range. On the slopes of Iztaccihuatl, state of Mexico, it occurs between 2165 and 2800 m. Loock (1950) gives 1500 m as the lowest limit of this pine. (See map, Fig. 3–29.)

**Plate 3–36.** *Left:* P. chihuahuana No. 40, south fork of Cave Creek, Coronado National Forest, Arizona. (U.S. Forest Service photo.) *Center:* P. leiophylla No. 41, Durango, Mexico. Approximate altitude 2100 m. (Photo by Gumersindo Borgo.) *Right:* P. lumholtzii No. 42, Durango, Mexico. Altitude 2500 m. (Photo by Cenobio Blanco.)

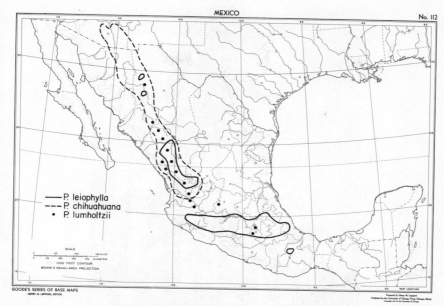

**Fig. 3–29.** Areas of *P. chihuahuana* Engelm. No. 40, *P. leiophylla* Schiede and Deppe No. 41, and *P. lumholtzii* Rob. and Fern. No. 42.

## 42. *Pinus lumholtzii* Rob. and Fern.

*Pinus lumholtzii* is a picturesque Mexican pine with bright green drooping foliage and cinnamon-red sheaths of the needle fascicles. Local people call it *"pino triste"* (sad pine) or *"pino barba caída"* (drooping-beard pine). In Nayarit, it is known under the name *"ocote dormido"* (sleeping pine). It grows in the western part of Mexico, from southern Chihuahua through Zacatecas to Jalisco. According to Martínez (1948), its altitudinal range is from 1600 to over 2300 m. I saw it at El Salto, Durango, at an altitude of about 2600 m above sea level. (See map, Fig. 3–29.)

## 43. *Pinus arizonica* Engelm.

*Pinus arizonica*, or Arizona pine, was discovered in Arizona, but its main range is in the Mexican states of Sonora, Chihuahua, and Durango. Its form *stormiae* Martínez occurs in the desert mountains of Coahuila and adjacent parts of Nuevo Leon. Shaw (1914) considered *P. arizonica* a variety of *P. ponderosa*. Martínez considered Arizona pine a valid species. Little (1953) designated this pine as a variety of *P. ponderosa* No

**Plate 3–37.** *Pinus arizonica* No. 43, Chihuahua, Mexico. (Photo by E. Flores Calderon.)

14. No doubt it is very closely related to *P. ponderosa* (see Chapter 9, page 559). Its altitudinal range in Mexico is 2000 to 2700 m. In the United States, it is found between 1900 and 2560 m above sea level. (See map, Fig. 3–30.)

## 44. *Pinus lawsonii* Roezl

*Pinus lawsonii* grows in the Mexican states of Jalisco, Michoacan, Morelos, Puebla, Guerrero, and Oaxaca. It is often confused with *P. teocote* No. 45 and *P. pringlei* No. 58. It is associated with *P. oocarpa* No. 59, *P. pringlei* No. 58, and *P. montezumae* No. 47. This pine grows rather sporadically in a subtropical environment at elevations ranging from 1200 to 3000 m. (See map, Fig. 3–31.)

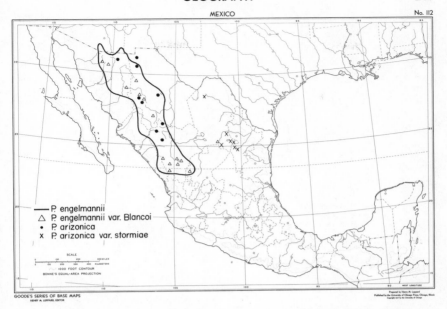

P. engelmannii
△ P. engelmannii var. Blancoi
• P. arizonica
x P. arizonica var. stormiae

**Fig. 3–30.** Areas of two pines of northern Mexico and their varieties.

## 45. *Pinus teocote* Schl. and Cham.

*Pinus teocote* is a pine of wide distribution. Its area extends from Tamaulipas, Nuevo Leon, Coahuila, and possibly southern Chihuahua to Chiapas. In the north, near Galena, Nuevo Leon, it occurs at 2500 to 2700 m. At Pinal de Amoles, Queretaro, it grows at 2000 to over 3000 m; at Yalagag, Oaxaca, at about 1700 to 3000 m. Generally, its vertical range is between 1500 and 3000 m. Occupying such a large area, *P. teocote* displays some variability. Shaw (1914) distinguished within it a variety, *macrocarpa*.

In the north *P. teocote* sometimes looks like *P. arizonica;* in the south some trees look like *P. lawsonii*. From Guatemala, Aguilar (1961) described *P. teocote* var. *guatemalensis*. (See map, Fig. 3–31.)

## 46. *Pinus herrerai* Martínez

*Pinus herrerai* was first collected in 1939 in the state of Jalisco, and its foliage was sent without cones to Dr. Maximino Martínez, who studied it. He first thought that the pine was related to *P. patula*, but later, receiving the cones, he decided that the pine in question was related to *P. teocote* but deserved the rank of an independent species. It is a three-needle pine. The needles are very flexible, soft, and delicate, and the cones are generally 2 to 3 cm long.

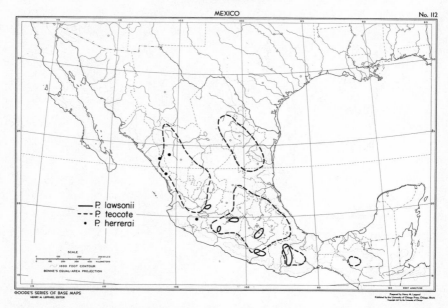

**Fig. 3–31.** Areas of *P. lawsonii* Roezl No. 44, *P. teocate* Schl. and Cham. No. 45, and *P. herrerai* Martínez No. 46.

*Pinus herrerai* occurs in Jalisco, Durango, Sinaloa, and Michoacan. Its altitudinal range is between 1200 and 2400 m. (See map, Fig. 3–31.)

### 47. Pinus montezumae Lamb.

*Pinus montezumae* is a complex species; Shaw (1914) was well aware of this when he wrote that "a monograph of this species . . . would be a valuable contribution to science." Since Shaw's time, a great deal of work has been done in studying the *P. montezumae* complex, chiefly by the late Dr. Maximino Martínez, who died in 1964. Several pines that were classified as *P. montezumae* in Shaw's *Genus Pinus* (1914) have been elevated to the rank of species. These are *P. hartwegii* No. 49, *P. rudis* No. 50, and *P. michoacana* No. 52.

*Pinus montezumae* (*sensu stricto*) occupies a large area; in the north, it expands through Jalisco and Michoacan to Chiapas. It also occurs in Guatemala (Schwerdtfeger, 1953). Its altitudinal range is probably between 900 and 3350 m. It reaches its best development at 2400 to 2800 m. In Guatemala, it is found between 1500 and 2500 m (Aguilar, 1961). This pine has not been found in Honduras. Martínez included in his treatise on pines (1948) a variety that he called "*Pinus montezumae* var. *lindleyi* Loudon"; it is found in Nuevo Leon (Zobel and Cech, 1957) and Coahuila

**Plate 3–38.** *Left: P. teocote* No. 45, Michoacan, Mexico. Altitude 2370 m. *Right: P. herrerai* No. 46, Hidalgo, Michoacan, Mexico. Altitude 2200 m. (Photos by Norberto Sánchez-Mejorada.)

and in central Mexico from Jalisco and Oaxaca to Veracruz. Forma *macrocarpa* Martínez occurs also in central Mexico from Michoacan to Veracruz. It also was reported from Chiapas.

Apparently, *P. montezumae* crosses with *P. hartwegii* (and possibly with other pines of the *montezumae* group) and also with *P. pseudostrobus*. It was crossed with *P. ponderosa* at the Institute of Forest Genetics, Placerville, California (Liddicoet and Righter, 1960). (See map, Fig. 3–32.)

### 48. *Pinus durangensis* Martínez

*Pinus durangensis* is a majestic pine, *"el pino real,"* growing in the state of Durango and possessing six, seven, or even eight needles in a fascicle. It was first described in 1938 by Cenobio E. Blanco and named by Martínez in 1942.

Shaw was aware of the existence of this pine. In *The Pines of Mexico* (1909), he included this pine under *P. montezumae,* but later, in his *Genus Pinus* (1914), he designated it as *P. ponderosa.*

**Plate 3–39.** *Left: P. montezumae* No. 47, Michoacan, Mexico. Approximate altitude 2000 m. (Photo by Norberto Sánchez-Mejorada.) *Right: P. durangensis* No. 48, 27 m tall, southeastern Durango, Mexico. Altitude 2700 m. (Photo by Gumersindo Borgo.)

*Pinus durangensis* resembles *P. montezumae*, but its cones are comparatively small, and its needles are more delicate. It also resembles *P. ponderosa*, but it lacks sharp prickles on the cone scales.

Its area extends along the Sierra Madre Occidental at elevations between 1800 and 2700 m from southwestern Chihuahua to the southern end of Durango. Zobel and Cech (1957) indicated its occurrence in Nuevo Leon. (See map, Fig. 3–33.)

## 49. *Pinus hartwegii* Lindl.

*Pinus hartwegii* was placed by Shaw (1914) under the name of *P. montezumae*. Standley (1920) and Martínez (1948), however, considered it an independent species. It grows from Coahuila to the state of Mexico and adjacent states, and it has also been reported from Veracruz, Oaxaca, and Chiapas, and, in the north, from Nuevo Leon (Zobel and Cech, 1957). It occurs at high elevations, being found near the line of permanent snow at its upper limit, approximately 3800 m. Its lower limit is at 2500 m. On

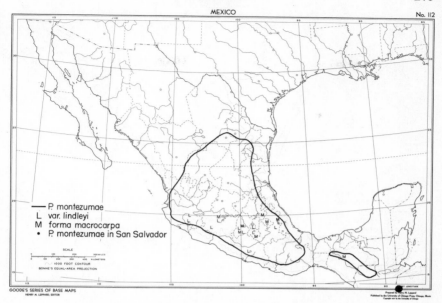

MEXICO                                    No. 112

P. montezumae
L  var. lindleyi
M  forma macrocarpa
•  P. montezumae in San Salvador

SCALE

1000 FOOT CONTOUR
BONNE'S EQUAL-AREA PROJECTION

GOODE'S SERIES OF BASE MAPS
HENRY M. LEPPARD, EDITOR

**Fig. 3–32.** Area of *P. montezumae* Lamb. No. 47.

the slopes of the two famous Mexican volcanoes—Popocatepetl and Iztaccihuatl—*P. hartwegii* forms pure stands at elevations ranging from about 2550 to 3500 m. Heilprin (1892) said that *P. hartwegii* exceeded 4300 m on the Sierra Negra near Orizaba. However, Martínez (1948) stated that the pine goes up to 3800 m. Possibly Heilprin's estimate was erroneous. (See map, Fig. 3–34.)

## 50. *Pinus rudis* Endl.

*Pinus rudis*, in the classification of Shaw (1914), was called *P. montezumae*. Martínez (1948), however, considered it to be a separate species. *Pinus rudis* and *P. montezumae* are closely related, and apparently they hybridize naturally; both species and many intermediate forms are often found in the same locality. *Pinus rudis* grows over a large territory from Coahuila, Nuevo Leon (Zobel and Cech, 1957), and Tamaulipas to Michoacan, and farther east to Puebla, Oaxaca, and apparently Chiapas. It extends even farther south and was reported (Schwerdtfeger, 1953) as growing in the mountains of Guatemala, adjacent to the Mexican state of Chiapas.

*Pinus rudis* most commonly grows at elevations between 2400 and 2750 m (Loock, 1950), but occasionally it ascends to extremely high alti-

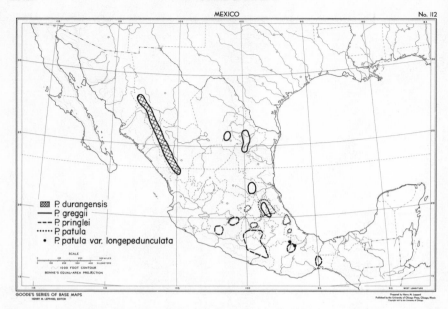

**Fig. 3–33.** Areas of *P. durangensis* Martínez No. 48, *P. pringlei* Shaw No. 58, *P. greggii* Engelm. No. 60, and *P. patula* Schl. and Cham. No. 61.

tudes. Martínez (1948) mentioned herbarium specimens from Tancítaro, Michoacan, collected at altitudes between 2833 and 3786 m, and Schwerdt-feger (1953) found this pine on the volcanoes of Guatemala, between 2800 and 4000 m, but a later publication (Aguilar, 1961) placed it be-tween 2300 and 4000 m above sea level. Din (1950) gave its vertical range as 2400 to 3600 m. Its altitudinal range is, then, between 2300 and 4000 m.

*Pinus rudis* possibly hybridizes naturally with *P. hartwegii*. Allen, in 1958, found a "handsome pine" growing at about 2300 m near La Palma, department of Chalatenango, San Salvador. He was not sure whether it was *P. rudis* or *P. hartwegii* (personal communication, 1962); probably it was *P. rudis*. (See map, Fig. 3–34.)

## 51. *Pinus cooperi* Blanco

*Pinus cooperi* is a newly discovered pine. It was originally described by Blanco in 1940 as *P. lutea*, probably because it is known locally as *"pino amarillo,"* i.e., yellow pine. As the name *"Pinus lutea"* had been given in 1788 to *P. taeda* No. 24, Blanco decided in 1949, on the suggestion of Dr. Elbert L. Little, Jr., to change its name from *"Pinus lutea"* to *"Pinus cooperi"* (Blanco, 1949). Martínez placed this pine near *P. rudis* No. 50.

**Plate 3–40.** *Left: P. hartwegii* No. 49, Mesa de Sandia, Durango, Mexico, where it is found at the altitudes between 2200 and 2750 m. (Photo by C. C. Robertson.) *Right: P. rudis* No. 50, Michoacan, Mexico. Altitude 2930 m. (Photo by Norberto Sánchez-Mejorada.)

*Pinus cooperi* grows in the mountain ranges of Durango, Mexico. At El Salto, Durango, it occurs at elevations of approximately 1800 to 2700 m. In the same locality also occurs a variety of this pine, *P. cooperi* var. *ornelasi* Martínez, characterized by coarser bark, longer needles, larger cones, and whiter wood than *P. cooperi* proper. Local people also distinguish these two pines and call variety *ornelasi* not *"pino amarillo"* but *"albacarrote."* The range of *P. cooperi* extends from southern Durango north to the southernmost part of Chihuahua. (See map, Fig. 3–34.)

## 52. *Pinus michoacana* Martínez

*Pinus michoacana* (see Plate 6–9, page 445) is a part of the complex that Shaw (1914) designated as *"Pinus montezumae"* (see Fig. 9–4, page 559). This species includes two varieties and two forms. *Pinus michoacana typica* occurs in Michoacan, Jalisco, and Oaxaca. In Michoacan, it may be found growing together with *P. montezumae;* possibly these two pines intercross. Forma *procera* Martínez has been reported from Urua-

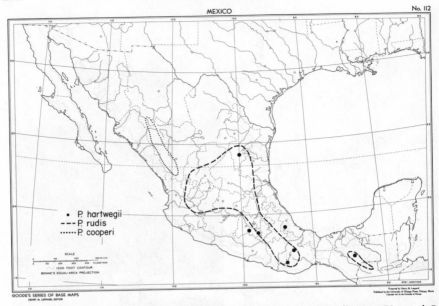

**Fig. 3–34.** Areas of *P. hartwegii* Lindl. No. *49*, *P. rudis* Endl. No. *50*, and *P. cooperi* Blanco No. *51*.

pan, Michoacan; Poncitlan and Tuxpan, Jalisco; and San Andreas, Ixtlahuaca, Etla, in the state of Oaxaca. Forma *tumida* Martínez has been found in a few spots in Oaxaca, Guerrero, and Chiapas. *Pinus michoacana* var. *cornuta* Martínez, which includes forma *nayaritana* Martínez, grows in the states of Nuevo Leon, Michoacan, Jalisco, Zacatecas, Durango, Mexico, Guerrero, Hidalgo, Morelos, Puebla, Oaxaca, Veracruz, and Chiapas. Its forma *nayaritana* Martínez is found in the southernmost part of Nayarit. *Pinus michoacana* var. *quevedoi* Martínez was described from several places in the southern part of San Luis Potosí.

The approximate vertical range of *P. michoacana,* according to Loock (1950), is between 1800 and 2400 m; judging by the herbarium data listed by Martínez (1948), it is from 1300 to 3000 m. Din's (1950) figures were 1200 to 3000 m. I have seen a magnificent old specimen of planted *P. michoacana* var. *cornuta* in the Tjibodas Botanical Garden, in central Java, at an altitude of 1425 m. (See map, Fig. 3–35.)

### 53. *Pinus engelmannii* Carr.

*Pinus engelmannii* is also known as *Pinus mayriana* Sudw., "*Pinus latifolia* Sarg.," "*Pinus macrophylla* Engelm.," and "*Pinus apacheca* Lemm." All these names indicate that this pine is believed by some botanists to

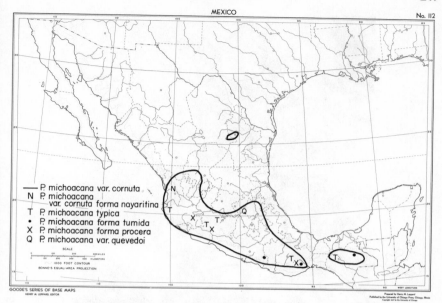

**Fig. 3–35.** Areas of *P. michoacana* Martínez No. 52 and its varieties.

be a valid species. Others, like Shaw (1914), consider that all these names are mere synonyms of *"Pinus ponderosa"* No. 14.

Its area is chiefly in the Sierra Madre Occidental of northwestern Mexico. In the north, its range extends to the United States, where it occurs in isolated mountain ranges of southeastern Arizona and southwestern New Mexico. In Mexico, it grows at about 1600 to 2400 m above sea level. In the southwestern United States, it occurs at altitudes between 1900 and 2500 m. Thus, its general vertical range is between 1600 and 2500 m.

Martínez (1948) described *P. engelmannii* var. *Blancoi*. It grows throughout the range of typical *P. engelmannii*; it also occurs near Nochistlan, Zacatecas, and in the Sierra del Ladrillal, near the town of Gral. Cepeda, Coahuila. (See map, Fig. 3–30, p. 209.)

## 54. *Pinus pseudostrobus* Lindl.

*Pinus pseudostrobus* is a pine of subtropical environment of Mexico and Central America. In Mexico, it was reported from Nuevo Leon (Zobel and Cech, 1957); it occurs in Tamaulipas, but its main range is from Jalisco to Chiapas. In Central America, it occurs in Guatemala and Honduras. In San Salvador, it is native only in one place near the Honduran border east of La Palma, department of Chalatenango, at an altitude of 1800 to 2300 m. In all other places in that republic, such as at

**Plate 3–41.** *Pinus engelmannii* No. 53, Durango, Mexico. (Photo by Cenobio Blanco.)

1200 m on the volcano San Salvador, it was planted (Allen, personal communication, 1962).*

The altitudinal range of typical *P. pseudostrobus*, according to Martínez (1948), is from 2300 to 3250 m. Loock (1950) gave the figures

* Mr. Allen made a survey of vegetation for the San Salvador government in 1958.

2100 to 3100 m. In Guatemala, it occurs from about 1500 up to about 2780 m (Allen, 1955). Din's (1950) lowest figure for the level of this pine was 1000 m.

Martínez described one form and four varieties of *P. pseudostrobus:* (1) Forma *protuberans* Martínez is found chiefly in Michoacan but also occurs in the states of Nuevo Leon (Zobel and Cech, 1957) and Mexico, in the Distrito Federal, and in Oaxaca. (2) Variety *coatepecensis* Martínez was collected near Xico, Veracruz, and near Teotitlan del Valle, Oaxaca. (3) Variety *estevezi* Martínez grows in isolated locations of northeastern Mexico, near Monterrey, Nuevo Leon, and in nearby parts of Coahuila (Artega), far away from the main concentration of the species and its other varieties. It occurs at elevations of about 1500 to 1800 m, in association with *P. greggii* and *P. rudis.* (4) Variety *apulcensis* (Lindley) Martínez is fairly common at 2100 to 2400 m in the mountains and cañons near Apulco, Hidalgo, and it has also been recorded from the states of Puebla, Tlaxcala, Mexico, and Veracruz (Loock, 1950). (5) Variety *oaxacana* Martínez has been elevated to the rank of species (No. 57) (Mirov, 1958). Forma *megacarpa,* a rare form, was described later by Loock (1950), from near the town of Hidalgo, Michoacan. "It is closely related to *P. pseudostrobus* forma *protuberans,* but the cones are bigger and the umbos not so prominent."

The above list of *P. pseudostrobus* varieties shows the complex nature of this species. To complicate the situation even more, Martínez, in describing varieties, often noticed further variability even within these. There is no doubt not only that different varieties of *P. pseudostrobus* intercross but also that the species itself hybridizes with other species such as *P. montezumae.* Some taxonomic complications of this pine are discussed in my paper on *P. oaxacana* (Mirov, 1958). (See also Larsen [1964] reference in Literature Cited section of Chapter 9.) The geography of this species and its varieties is shown on the map in Fig. 3–36.

## 55. *Pinus tenuifolia* Benth.

*Pinus tenuifolia* is closely related to *P. pseudostrobus,* of which Shaw considered it to be a variety. *Pinus tenuifolia* is a pine of the subtropical regions of Mexico. It grows primarily in the states of Jalisco, Michoacan, Sinaloa, and Guerrero. It is also found in Puebla, Veracruz, Oaxaca, and Chiapas and in the adjacent parts of Guatemala. It grows in association with *P. montezumae* No. 47, *P. pseudostrobus* No. 54, *P. leiophylla* No. 41, and *P. lawsonii* No. 44 at elevations of 1500 to 2400 m. In Oaxaca, it is found at about 2400 m (Loock, 1950). In Guatemala, it has been recorded at 1100 to 2400 m (Aguilar, 1961). (See map, Fig. 3–37.)

**Plate 3–42.** *Pinus pseudostrobus* No. 54. *Top, left and right:* in Michoacan, Mexico. (Photos by Norberto Sánchez-Mejorada.) *Bottom:* in Honduras. Altitude about 2000 m. Note epiphytes on trunk. (Photo by N. T. Mirov.)

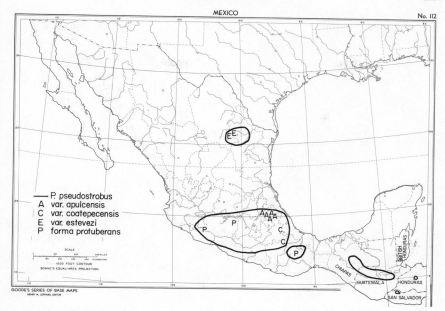

**Fig. 3–36.** Areas of *P. pseudostrobus* Lindl. No. 54 and its varieties.

## 56. *Pinus douglasiana* Martínez

*Pinus douglasiana*, like *P. tenuifolia,* is closely related to *P. pseudo-strobus.* Its needles are coarse and thick, 25 to 33 cm long, while those of *P. tenuifolia* are very soft and delicate.

*Pinus douglasiana* grows in the states of Nayarit, Sinaloa, Jalisco, Michoacan, Mexico, and Oaxaca. Martínez named it after Margaret Douglas, who was, to quote Martínez, *"dama norteamericana entusiasta admiradora de la flora Mexicana y protectora de los estudios de la misma."* It grows together with *P. tenuifolia* No. 55, *P. montezumae* No. 47, *P. leiophylla* No. 41, *P. lawsonii* No. 44, *P. oocarpa* No. 50, and *P. pseudostrobus* No. 54. Its best development is at an altitude of 1700 to 2400 m (Loock, 1950). Its vertical range is probably between 1500 and 2400 m. (See map, Fig. 3–37.)

## 57. *Pinus oaxacana* Mirov

*Pinus oaxacana* is a pine of the tropical highlands of southern Mexico and Central America. It is very common in the mountains of Oaxaca. It grows also in the states of Mexico, Puebla, Guerrero, Veracruz, and Chiapas. It also occurs in the highlands of Guatemala adjacent to Chiapas, and in Honduras. This pine is considered by Martínez as a variety of

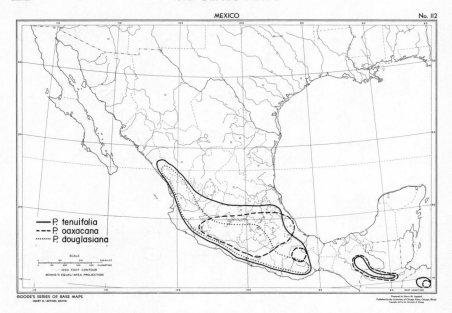

**Fig. 3–37.** Areas of *P. tenuifolia* Benth. No. *55, P. douglasiana* Martínez No. *56,* and *P. oaxacana* Mirov No. *57.*

*P. pseudostrobus,* but it differs so much from *P. pseudostrobus* in its morphological characters (especially in the shape and structure of the cone [see Plate 9–3]) and in composition of its turpentine that it deserves the rank of an independent species (Mirov, 1958). Apparently it crosses, on the one hand, with *P. pseudostrobus* and, on the other, with *P. montezumae.* It grows in association with *P. tenuifolia* No. 55, *P. pseudostrobus* No. 54, and *P. patula* var. *longepedunculata* No. 61. Apparently, its vertical range lies between 1500 and 2400 m above sea level. (See map, Fig. 3–37.)

### 58. *Pinus pringlei* Shaw

*Pinus pringlei* is a subtropical Mexican pine growing in the states of Michoacan, Mexico, Guerrero, and Oaxaca, at altitudes of 1500 to 2500 m above sea level (Martínez, 1948). Loock (1950) stated that it usually occurs at 1700 to 1800 m. According to Martínez, it is closely related to *P. oocarpa* No. 59. (See map, Fig. 3–33, page 214.)

### 59. *Pinus oocarpa* Schiede

*Pinus oocarpa* is a very variable and widely distributed, generally five-needle (except in the *trifoliata*) pine growing from Sonora and Chihua-

**Plate 3–43.** *Left: P. douglasiana* No. 56, Michoacan, Mexico. Altitude 1950 m. *Right: P. patula* No. 61, northeastern Puebla, Mexico. Altitude 2600 m. (Photos by Norberto Sánchez-Mejorada.)

hua to Central America. Its altitudinal range is from 900 to 2400 m. Besides its typical form, there are recorded four varieties of *P. oocarpa:* (1) forma *microphylla* Martínez, possessing very short fine foliage (Sinaloa, Zacatecas, Nayarit, and Jalisco); (2) var. *manzanoi* Martínez, which has asymmetrical cones and very short peduncles (found near Huasca, Hidalgo); (3) forma *ochoterenai* Martínez, distinguished by its slender cones that are not as heavy as those of the typical form, growing in the mountains of Chiapas and crossing the border of Guatemala; and (4) forma *trifoliata* Martínez, characterized by three needles in a fascicle (found in Durango at 1600 to 2000 m).

In Central America, *P. oocarpa* extends through Guatemala and Honduras to Nicaragua. It is found in the mountains of inner British Honduras (Standley and Record, 1936) at 900 m. Hunt (1962) wrote that Standley and Record were in error in reporting *P. oocarpa* from Baker Pine Ridge. According to Hunt, the only locality in which this pine occurs in British Honduras is on the high eastern part of Mountain Pine Ridge; there, it is variety *ochoterenai*. In northern San Salvador, near the Honduran border, it is found between 650 and 1500 m. In the vicinity of San Ignacio and La Palma, department of Chalatenango, San Salvador, it

**Plate 3–44.** *Pinus oocarpa* No. 59 in Nicaragua. *Top:* one of the southern-most outliers of upland pines, located southeast of Matagalpa. Burning is regular here, and there is no pine regeneration. *Bottom:* stand on a steep slope near Dipilto, Nueva Segovia. Note the deep gully erosion at the left. All the young pines at the right were killed by a fire a few weeks after this photo was taken. (Photos by William M. Denevan.)

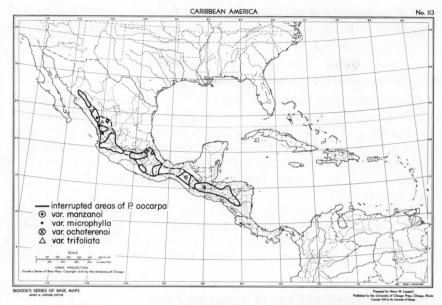

**Fig. 3–38.** Areas of *P. oocarpa* Schiede No. 59 and its varieties.

occurs at elevations between 1000 and 1200 m. Variety *manzanoi* also occurs there occasionally at 1200 m (Allen, 1962).

*Pinus tecumumani*, described by Schwerdtfeger (1953), possibly is a variety of *P. oocarpa*. Aguilar (1961) called it *Pinus oocarpa* forma *tecumumani* (see Chapter 9, page 563). Its area is in the departments of Baja Verapaz, Totonicapan, and Huehuetenango, Guatemala, where it occurs in small groves between 1900 and 2700 m above sea level. It grows either in pure stands or mixed with *P. pseudostrobus* No. 54 and *P. ayacahuite* No. 33. (See Chapter 9, page 563.)

*Pinus oocarpa* has the distinction of being the most southerly pine of the New World. The trees of this species begin to disappear on the south slope of the Cordillera Dariense, Nicaragua, at an altitude of about 1200 m. (See map, Fig. 3–38.)

## 60. *Pinus greggii* Engelm.

*Pinus greggii* has a limited range; it occurs in the northeastern part of Mexico, namely, in southeastern Coahuila, in adjacent parts of Nuevo Leon, and, farther south, in San Luis Potosí and in Hidalgo.

Its altitudinal range is between 1500 and 2700 m (Din, 1958). Near Saltillo, Coahuila, it grows at about 2500 m above sea level (Martínez, 1948). It has been crossed with *P. patula* No. 61 (Fielding, 1960).

Morphologically, it is closely related to *P. patula,* but it can be distinguished by its shorter, coarser, and erect rather than drooping needles. (See map, Fig. 3–33.)

## 61. *Pinus patula* Schl. and Cham.

*Pinus patula* (see Plate 3–43, page 223) is a pine of a rather limited distribution. This pine occurs in the states of Queretaro, Hidalgo, Mexico, Puebla, and Veracruz. It has been reported to grow in one locality in the state of Tamaulipas. It grows in the subtropical parts of the country, at elevations ranging from 1500 to 3000 m above sea level, where the climate is cool and humid. Loock (1950) gave its altitudinal range as from 1800 to 2700 m.

Variety *longepedunculata,* which Loock characterized by long cone stalks, was found in 1947 by Loock in the cool temperate zone of Oaxaca, at elevations of 1900 to 2000 m (Martínez, 1948). Its zone of distribution has not as yet been defined (Loock, 1950). (See map, Fig. 3–33.)

## Other Mexican and Central American Pines

In addition to those mentioned above, there are also several pines in Mexico and Central America that are difficult to identify. Zobel and Cech reported four such pines from the state of Nuevo Leon (Zobel and Cech, 1957) (see Fig. 9–6, page 564). Egon Larsen, of the New Zealand Forest Research Institute, who collected pine material in Mexico in 1961, wrote (personal communication, 1961) that, in the state of Guerrero, he encountered a pine that looked like *P. montezumae* and at the same time resembled *P. pseudostrobus* (see Fig. 9–6, page 564). In the state of Michoacan, Larsen (1964, reference in Literature Cited section of Chapter 9) found a pine that he named *"Pinus martinezii"* (see Chapter 9, page 559).

In Guatemala, Aguilar found a pine whose characteristics are intermediate between *P. montezumae* and *P. rudis.* He named it *"Pinus quichensis"* (Aguilar, 1961) (see Fig. 9–6, page 564.)

*Pinus coulteri* No. 12 and *P. jeffreyi* No. 13, whose ranges are essentially in California, cross the Mexican border into Baja California, where they are found in the San Pedro Martir Mountains (see maps, Figs. 3–9 and 3–11, pages 155 and 162).

## PINE REGION OF THE CARIBBEAN

In the Caribbean area are included not only the islands of the Caribbean Sea—the Bahamas, Cuba, Hispaniola—but also the southern part of Florida and the Gulf Coast of Central America. The pines of this area

(Table 3–4) are *P. caribaea, P. elliottii* var. *densa, P. occidentalis, P. cubensis,* and *P. tropicalis.* For the taxonomy and relationships of Caribbean pines, see Chapter 9, pages 554–56.

## 62. *Pinus caribaea* Morelet

*Pinus caribaea* grows in the Bahama Islands, western Cuba, Isla de Pinos, Honduras, Guatemala, Nicaragua, and British Honduras. Until recently, our southeastern slash pine, whose official name now is *"Pinus elliottii"* No. 23, was also known under this name. A pine of inner Honduras, found at altitudes of 600 to 900 m and often described aş *P. caribaea,* possibly is an independent species (Williams, 1955). I saw it in the Choluteca River Valley (see Plate 9–3, page 556).

Another locality of supposed *P. caribaea* is in British Honduras, on the "Mountain Pine Ridge" located at an altitude of about 1000 m in the southeastern part of that country (approximate position: 89° west and 17° north). It is difficult to say if the pine of the "Mountain Pine Ridge" (Romney, 1959) is the same species as the coastal *P. caribaea.*

In Guatemala, *P. caribaea* occurs near Poptun, Petén, at altitudes between 400 and 1000 m, and in three or four spots at Izabal and near Zacapa (Aguilar, 1961). In Nicaragua, it extends south to the vicinity of Bluefields.

**Table 3–4.** Pines of the Caribbean Area (Including Coast of Central America and Southern Part of Florida)

| Number | Species | Distribution |
|---|---|---|
| HAPLOXYLON | | |
| | None | |
| DIPLOXYLON | | |
| 62. | *P. caribaea* | Islands of the Caribbean and coast of Central America |
| 63. | *P. eliottii* var. *densa* | Southern Florida |
| 64. | *P. occidentalis* | Hispaniola and eastern Cuba |
| 65. | *P. cubensis* | Eastern Cuba |
| 66. | *P. tropicalis* | Western Cuba. This is one of the two *Lariciones* in the New World; the other is No. 21. |

Of interest is the occurrence of *P. caribaea* on Pine Cay (island) in the Caicos. Often referred to as "dwarf pine," it is not always a dwarf.

The altitudinal range of *P. caribaea* is taken as being from sea level to 300 m.

**Plate 3–45.** *Top: P. caribaea* No. 62 on Miskito Coast of Nicaragua, near Karawala, a little above sea level. (Photo by J. J. Parsons.) *Bottom: P. elliottii* var. *densa* No. 63, southern Florida, at about sea level, with natural reproduction. The seed trees are about twenty-five years old. (U.S. Forest Service photo.)

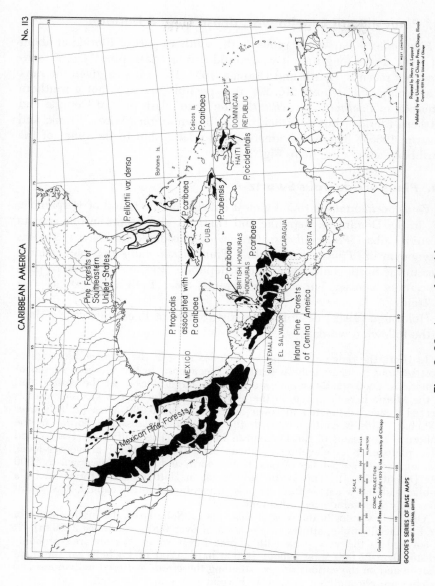

**Fig. 3–39. Areas of Caribbean pines.**

There are suggestions that *P. oocarpa* may cross with *P. caribaea* (Williams, 1955). (See map, Fig. 3–39.)

## 63. *Pinus elliottii* Engelm. var. *densa* Little & Dorman

*Pinus elliottii* var. *densa* grows in the southern part of Florida at about sea level. For a long time it was considered as "slash pine," i.e., *P. caribaea*, but recently (Little and Dorman, 1952, 1954) it was given the rank of a variety of *P. elliottii* No. 23. It is possible that it is not a southern extension of *P. elliottii* var. *elliottii* (the "true" slash pine of Georgia and northern Florida) but is, rather, of Caribbean origin (Mirov, Frank, and Zavarin, 1965). There is evidence of its relationship to the pines of the Caribbean area. (See map, Fig. 3–39.)

## 64. *Pinus occidentalis* Swartz

*Pinus occidentalis* is found almost entirely on the island of Hispaniola, i.e., in the Dominican Republic and Haiti. It also occurs in one spot in western Cuba. "*Pinus cubensis* Griseb." is considered by Shaw (1914) as a synonym of "*Pinus occidentalis.*" *Pinus occidentalis* occupies a large area in the north-central Dominican Republic. In the southwestern part, it occupies a lesser, but still considerable, area. Both areas extend west to Haiti.

Holdridge (1942) described the distribution of *P. occidentalis* in Haiti in the following words:

In Haiti, the range of the species includes most of the country, although in most sections it occurs only as scattered specimens. In the southern ranges of mountains, good stands of pine are found in large blocks. At the eastern end of the Morne la Selle range, in the section called Mornes des Commissaires is located a stand estimated to cover approximately 10,000 acres [a little over 4000 ha]. This is contiguous with the pine forest across the border in the Bahoruco Mountains of the Dominican Republic. The Haitian tract is located on a plateau at an elevation of about 5000 feet [1500 m] above sea-level, although scattered patches of pine to the north and south grow down to 2000 feet [about 610 m]. This is the only forest in Haiti which is traversed by a public road and when "le forêt de pins" is mentioned in the capital, it is almost invariably with reference to this unit.

Only a few miles to the west of this area La Selle Peak, the highest point of land in the Republic, attains an elevation of over 9000 feet [over 2700 m]. It is covered to the very peak with a pine forest which has an area probably greater than 25,000 acres [about 10,000 ha.]. West of La Selle on the main plateau and on the various ridges extending therefrom scattered individuals and patches are encountered to slightly beyond Furcy and Kenscoff.

Travelling still farther westward on the southwestern peninsula various, at present inaccessible, scattered patches in the Morne la Hotte range are found, but only near Pio Macayo are solid stands of pine found to be of any appreciable extent. Here, they ascend to 7000 feet [about 2100 m] on the peak and

**Plate 3–46.** *Pinus occidentalis* No. 64 in the Dominican Republic. *Top:* above Pedernales. *Bottom:* in San Juan Mountains. (Photos courtesy of Arnold Arboretum, Jamaica Plain, Massachusetts.)

occupy the sides and crests of precipitous ridges, which in combination with the very deep, intervening valleys make up a region which is very difficult to traverse and hence little known.

North of the Cul de Sac plain, which runs eastward from Port-au-Prince, many different mountain ranges occur and on all of these so far observed scattered trees of this pine have been seen. Only in the Montagnes du Nord, which come across the border between Monte Organise and Banica and extend northwestward, are there extensive areas of pine. Although this area has been invaded to a considerable extent by agriculturists so that the forest is very broken, there is nevertheless an area of about 40,000 ha. on which pine is the dominant feature of the landscape and thus it comprises an important forest section. In addition to this, the extensive central plateau should be mentioned since its so is very unproductive for agriculture and there remain a great many scattered pines, making it possible to develop this in the future as a solid block of pine which would probably be more profitable to the country than the present farming and grazing uses.

Generally *P. occidentalis* grows at elevations of from about 900 to over 2700 m. In Cuba, *P. occidentalis* occurs at from 300 to 1500 m (Smith, 1954). (See map, Fig. 3–39.)

### 65. *Pinus cubensis* Grisebach

*Pinus cubensis* is closely related to *P. occidentalis*. It grows in the eastern part of Cuba (Oriente), in the mountains, forming extensive stands in la Sierra de Nipe, Sierra de Cristal, Sierra de Moa, and Cuchillas de Toa. The altitudinal range of *P. cubensis* is from sea level to over 820 m (Smith, 1954). (See map, Fig. 3–39.)

### 66. *Pinus tropicalis* Morelet

*Pinus tropicalis* grows at sea level at Pinar del Rio, western Cuba, and on the Isla de Pinos, where it is associated with *P. caribaea*. It occurs on sandy savannas and in gravelly places on more or less rolling terrain below 150 m. (See map, Fig. 3–39.)

## PINE REGION OF NORTHERN EURASIA

The enormous pine region of northern Eurasia extends from Scotland through Scandinavia and across the northern part of the whole continent of Eurasia, almost to the coast of the Okhotsk Sea. In that entire expanse of land, there are found only three species of the genus *Pinus:* two haploxylon—*P. sibirica* and *P. pumila*, in the east—and one diploxylon—*P. sylvestris*, throughout the region (Table 3–5). As *P. sylvestris* occurs also in the Mediterranean region and *P. pumila* extends to the eastern Asiatic pine region, *P. sibirica* is the only pine species found exclusively in the pine region of northern Eurasia.

**Table 3–5.** Pines of Northern Eurasia

| Number | Species | Distribution |
|--------|---------|--------------|
| HAPLOXYLON | | |
| 67. | P. sibirica | Chiefly in Siberia, extending to northern Mongolia and to eastern Europe |
| 68. | P. pumila | Northeastern Siberia, extending to eastern Asia as far as central Japan |
| DIPLOXYLON | | |
| 69. | P. sylvestris | From Scotland to the Okhotsk Sea coast of Siberia and from Norway to northern Mongolia |

The three pines of this region grow from sea level to very high elevations. They also are the only pines of the genus that cross the Arctic Circle.

## 67. Pinus sibirica Mayr

"*Pinus sibirica*" was considered by Shaw (1914) a synonym of "*Pinus cembra*" No. 70. It occupies an area entirely different from that of *P. cembra*. It grows in plains, in river valleys, and in the mountains of both the northern part of European Russia and Siberia. One isolated location is on the Kola Peninsula, but it is not certain if this pine is native there. In northeastern Siberia, it is replaced by *P. pumila* No. 68, and, in the east, it is replaced by *P. koraiensis* No. 82. Russians call *P. sibirica* "Siberian cedar," which causes a great deal of confusion among geographers. In western Siberia, near Salegard, just west of the River Ob, *P. sibirica* crosses the Arctic Circle, but at the sixtieth meridian its northern boundary turns abruptly southwest. (See map, Fig. 3–47, page 324.)

In the Transbaikal region and in the Sayan Mountains of eastern Siberia, as well as in the Altai Mountains of western Siberia, there grows a variety of *P. sibirica* that has been called "*Pinus coronans* Litv." Apparently, this pine is a mountain variety of *P. sibirica*. In the Lake Baikal region of eastern Siberia, areas of *P. sibirica* and *P. pumila* No. 68 overlap. There the two pines intercross. The dwarf alpine form of *P. sibirica* is sometimes confused with *P. pumila* (Malyshev, 1960).

The altitudinal range of *P. sibirica* in the lowlands of western Siberia is from 100 to 200 m. It grows there on low watershed divides, in the river valleys, and in swampy plains where it is a dominant, growing together with *P. sylvestris* and *Picea* and *Abies*. Thus its "common" English name, "Siberian stone pine," is rather inappropriate.

In the Altai Mountains, *P. sibirica* grows at low elevations, up to 1000 m, mixed with *Abies*. Higher up, it forms pure, dense forests and

**Plate 3–47.** *Top: P. sibirica* No. 67 in subalpine zone of western Sayan Mountains, Siberia. (Photo by Komarov Botanical Institute, Leningrad, U.S.S.R. Courtesy of A. A. Iatsenko-Khmelevsky.) *Lower left: P. sylvestris* No. 69 in Sweden. (Photo by Bo Nilsson, National Board of Crown Forests and Lands, Stockholm. Courtesy of Sten Karlberg.) *Lower right: P. sylvestris,* Innsbruck, Austria. (Photo by Austrian Forest Research Institute, Schönbrunn.)

goes up to the timberline, which is at altitudes of from 1900 to 2400 m. The highest recorded altitude for *P. sibirica* there was 2580 m (Suslov, 1947).

In the Transbaikal, *P. sibirica* occurs at from 900 to 1900 m of altitude (Litvinov, 1913). In the Altai, the Sayans, and the mountains of northern Mongolia, a scrubby, trailing form of *P. sibirica* (forma *depressa*) occurs above the timberline, at 2100 m (Komarov, 1934).

*P. sibirica* also extends to northern Mongolia, where it occurs in Kentai Shan at 2200 to 2300 m (Wang, 1961).

## 68. Pinus pumila Regel

*Pinus pumila* is a very small tree, more often a creeping shrub, growing in the northeastern part of Siberia and in alpine parts of Japan, Korea, and Manchuria. Its northern limit is in the region of the Lower Lena, at 70° 31′ north. It is related to *P. sibirica*. Some botanists say that it is merely a dwarf variety of *P. sibirica;* others maintain that it deserves the rank of an independent species. Gaussen (1960) considers *P. pumila* to be closely related to *P. parviflora* (i.e., to *P. pentaphylla* No. 83), of Japan.

Its area extends to the region of eastern Asia (see page 263). On the peninsula of Kamchatka, it is abundant at 300 to 1000 m. In northern Hokkaido, it grows at altitudes between 50 and 1720 m; in central Honshu, between 1400 and 3180 m (Hayashi, 1954); and in Korea, between 900 and 2540 m (K. B. Yim, personal communication, Oct. 15, 1962). In northeastern Asia, *P. pumila* forms thickets above the forests of larch and (in the south) above *P. sylvestris,* and just below the barren tundra-like tops of the mountains. In the Verkhoyansk Mountains, the *P. pumila* belt lies at about 900 to 1000 m. In the upper reaches of the Omolon, it is found at 800 to 900 m above sea level. (See map, Fig. 3–47, page 265.)

## 69. Pinus sylvestris L.

*Pinus sylvestris* (Plate 3–47) is called, in English, "Scots" or "Scotch" pine. On the continent, it is known under many different names, but its most usual name is "common pine." It occupies an area larger than that of any other pine; longitudinally it grows from Scotland to the Pacific Coast of Siberia; latitudinally, from Norway (70° 29′ north) to Spain (37° north) and from Arctic Siberia to Mongolia; it also occurs in the Mediterranean region (see page 257). It is natural to expect that this species has many varieties because it grows over such a large area and under such different environmental conditions. In fact, *P. sylvestris* is a complex composed of several entities. Some botanists call these entities

**Plate 3–48.** *Pinus pumila* No. 68, Hokkaido, Japan. *Top:* foliage and cones at 1700 m. *Bottom:* at 1900 m. Thickets of this pine often cover large areas in a subalpine zone. (Photos by Yasaka Hayashi.)

"species"; others designate them as "varieties"; still others designate the whole complex as a single species, *P. sylvestris*. (For details, see Steven and Carlisle, 1959; Pravdin, 1964.)

From a geographical point of view, *P. sylvestris*, unlike *Picea excelsa* or *P. obovata*, is an interzonal tree. In eastern Russia and in Siberia, the main area of its distribution, this species may be found in the taiga zone, in the woodland belt, in grasslands of the south, and in the mountains. In the mesophytic environment, it behaves as a xerophyte does, preferring dry sandy areas. In arid areas such as steppes of western Siberia, it behaves as a mesophyte does, preferring places along the river courses. (See map, Fig. 3–50, page 277.)

*Pinus sylvestris* grows in Mongolia, near Hailar, on stabilized sand dunes (see Plate 6–4, page 428). In other places in Mongolia, it occurs near lakes and saline swamps in otherwise treeless grassland. Temperatures there may drop in winter to −50°C. In Mongolia also it occurs along river courses, on terraces, and on sand banks, and it is occasionally found in Mongolian taiga (Wang, 1961).

In northern Eurasia, *P. sylvestris* is generally a pine of low elevations; it rarely goes higher than 800 m and very seldom attains elevations above 1000 m. According to Suslov (1947), altitudinal distribution of *P. sylvestris* in different parts of Siberia is as follows:

| | |
|---|---|
| Western Siberia | 100 to   350 m |
| Altai | 350 to   700 m |
| Eastern Siberia | 300 to   650 m |
| Western Sayans | 400 to   850 m |
| Eastern Sayans | 650 to 1000 m |
| Transbaikal | 1000 to 2000 m |
| Tuva region | 500 to 1100 m |

In the Baltic region, it grows at sea level. In northern Norway, it goes up to 1050 m, while, in Austria, it may be found at elevations as high as 1200 m.

*Pinus sylvestris* grew in Ireland, England, and Denmark until relatively recently, but it was exterminated completely by primitive man. Stumps of this species are still found in the bogs of England and Ireland.

Schütt (1959) mentioned natural hybrids between *P. sylvestris* and different varieties of *P. montana* No. 76.

*Pinus sylvestris* in the Mediterranean region will be discussed later (page 257).

## PINE REGION OF THE MEDITERRANEAN

In studying the natural distribution of pines in the Mediterranean region (Table 3–6), one encounters difficulty in determining where a given species is natural and where it has been planted by former inhabitants such as Etruscans, Romans, ancient Greeks, or Arabs. No doubt, the region was previously more heavily forested; there is ample evidence that pines were more abundant in certain parts of the region, but it is doubtful if they ever formed dense, extensive forests similar, say, to pine forests of the American Southeast.

**Table 3–6.** Pines of the Mediterranean Region

| Number | Species | Distribution |
|---|---|---|
| Haploxylon | | |
| 70. | *P. cembra* | Alps to Carpathians |
| 71. | *P. peuce* | Balkans |
| Diploxylon | | |
| 72. | *P. canariensis* | Canary Islands |
| 73. | *P. pinea* | Portugal to Turkey |
| 74. | *P. nigra* | Widely distributed |
| 75. | *P. heldreichii* | Eastern Mediterranean (some in Italy) |
| 76. | *P. montana* | Pyrenees to Carpathians |
| 77. | *P. halepensis* | Widely distributed |
| 78. | *P. brutia* | Eastern Mediterranean |
| 79. | *P. pityusa* | Caucasus and eastern Mediterranean |
| 80. | *P. pinaster* | Widely distributed |
| 81. | *P. eldarica* | Endemic in Transcaucasia |

The Mediterranean pine region, as described in this book, is not restricted to the pines of coastal areas and islands; it includes also those of the Alps, the Carpathians, and the Canary Islands; the pines growing in those places are Mediterranean pines.

## 70. *Pinus cembra* L.

*Pinus cembra* is known in English as "Swiss stone pine." In Switzerland, it is called *"Arve"*; its German name is *"Zirbe,"* or *"Zirbekiefer"*; in Poland, it is known as *"limba"*; and Russians call it *"kedr"* (from the Greek *"kedros,"* i.e., "cedar"). It is a pine of high mountains of southern Europe, from the Alps to the Carpathians.

In Switzerland, *P. cembra* is found at from 1200 to 2585 m of altitude. In the middle altitudes between these limits, *P. cembra* sometimes forms fine forests. Rikli, in an excellent biological monograph on *P. cembra* (1909), gave for a locality near San Moritz, southeastern Switzerland, the tabulation shown at the top of the next page.

In the Tyrol, this pine forms forests at an altitude of about 1600 m. Single trees occur at higher elevations. In Poland and Czechoslovakia, it is found in a few places in the High Tatra mountain area of the Car-

|                   | Lower Limit | Upper Limit | Span   |
| ----------------- | ----------- | ----------- | ------ |
| Limits of forest  | 1650 m      | 2200 m      | 550 m  |
| Limits of trees   | 1450 m      | 2310 m      | 860 m  |

**Plate 3–49.** *Pinus cembra* No. 70. *Left:* in Tuxer Alps, southeastern Austria. Altitude 1800–2000 m. This tree is about two hundred years old. The exposure is southern and the soil calcareous shale. *Right:* in grove in Austrian Alps. Altitude 1700–1850 m. This pine locally is called "Zirbe." The exposure is northern and the soil podzolized with considerable iron content. (Photos by Austrian Forest Research Institute, Schönbrunn.)

pathians, between the eastern and western Beskids, and it is also found in the Ukrainian part of the Carpathians. (See map, Fig. 3–40.)

## 71. *Pinus peuce* Grisebach

*Pinus peuce* is a rare pine of southeastern Europe, morphologically similar to *P. griffithii* No. 91 (*P. excelsa*), of the Himalaya. *Pinus peuce* grows in a few places in the mountains of southern Yugoslavia and in the adjacent parts of Albania, Bulgaria, and Greece. Its northern limit is at 43° 10' north. The southern limit is at about 41° north. The lower altitudinal limit of *P. peuce* lies between 800 m and 1400 m, and the upper

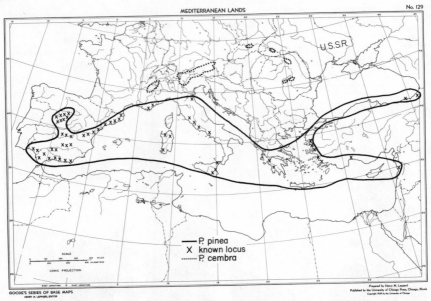

**Fig. 3–40.** Areas of *P. cembra* L. No. 70 and *P. pinea* L. No. 73.

one between 1800 and 2100 m. (See map, Fig. 3–41, and Plates 1–1 and 3–50.)

### 72. *Pinus canariensis* Smith

*Pinus canariensis* is a subtropical pine native to the Canary Islands. It grows on Grand Canary Island and Tenerife and occupies rather large areas at elevations from 1200 to 2200 m. The central part of Hierro Island is also occupied by forest of this pine. Some *P. canariensis* is found on Gomera Island (Ceballos y Ortuño, 1951).[*]

The area of *P. canariensis* is rather remote from the Mediterranean Sea. Although the distance from Gibraltar to the Canary Islands is between 1300 and 1400 km, this species is of the same origin as the other Mediterranean pines. A fossil pine similar to *P. canariensis* was found near Málaga, Spain (Wulff, 1944). The mountain ranges of northeastern Africa afforded it a route of migration to the Canary Islands. Its nearest relative, very similar in appearance, is *P. roxburghii* No. 93 (*P. longifolia*), of the Himalaya. (See map, Fig. 3–42.)

---

[*] Information about occurrence of pine on Grand Canary Island was obtained privately from Professor Ceballos.

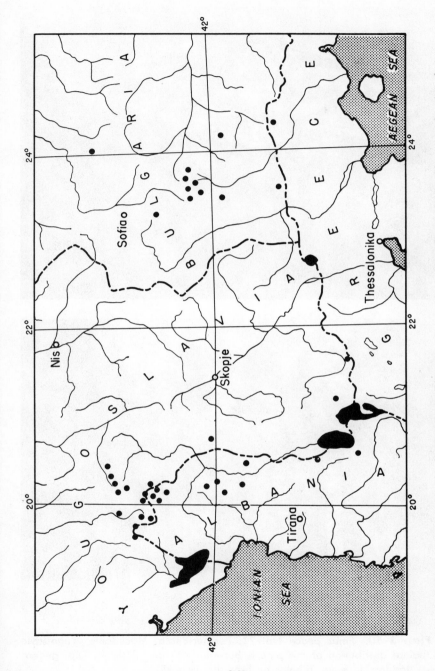

**Fig. 3–41.** Area of *P. peuce* Grisebach No. 71. (From Mirov, 1961; map supplied by Branislav Pejoski.)

**Plate 3–50.** *Pinus peuce* No. 71, Perister-Bitola, Macedonia, Yugoslavia. Altitudinal distribution of this pine is between 800 and 2100 m. *Top:* general view. *Bottom:* close-up. (Photos by Branislav Pejoski.)

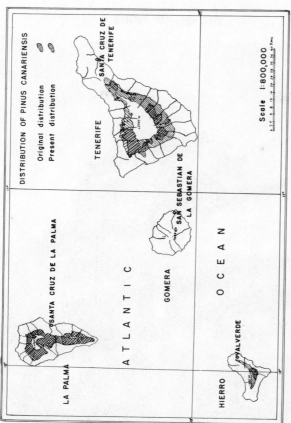

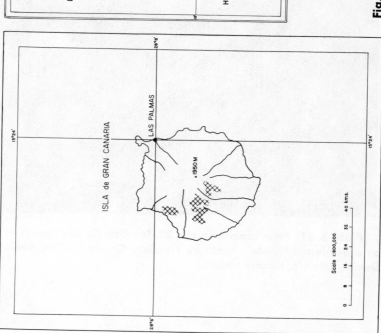

**Fig. 3–42.** Area of *P. canariensis* Smith No. 72.

**Plate 3–51.** *Pinus canariensis* No. 72, Tenerife, Canary Islands—an old pine on a deforested hillside. (Photo by Francisco Ortuño Medina, National Forest Service, Tenerife, Canary Islands.)

## 73. Pinus pinea L.

*Pinus pinea* is sometimes called "*P. sativa*," i.e., "planted pine." Its Italian name is "*pino domestico*," i.e., "cultivated pine," in opposition to "*pino silvestre*" (*Pinus sylvestris*), which means a "wild pine." (Compare with the Spanish "*flores silvestres*" for "wild flowers"; also see Chapter 1.) It is a difficult task to establish the natural area of *P. pinea*. This pine has been planted for its edible seeds (pinoli) since ancient times, and at present it is often impossible to tell if occurrence of this species in a given place is natural or whether the pine was planted there. Francini (1958) reviewed rather thoroughly the literature on its distribution. If we would follow Zangheri as quoted by Francini, we should accept that *P. pinea* was brought to Italy from the eastern Mediterranean, perhaps in the Etruscan period. Francini further mentioned that Parlatore, in 1867, following Endlicher, considered it to have originated on the island of Crete.

It is doubtful if *P. pinea* is indigenous in the great coastal pine region of Pisa-Villaregia, on the coast of the Tyrrhenian Sea. The same is true of the coastal *P. pinea* forest at Fregeni, near Rome. According to Francini, this forest was planted in 1666 on the initiative of Pope Clement IX and called "Pineta Clementina." Having been protected because of its decorative value and its edible nuts, *P. pinea* spread naturally from this original plantation. Even on the larger islands of the Tyrrhenian Sea, this pine apparently is not native, although, according to Francini, Briquet, in his *Prodromus of Corsican Flora,* said that it was indigenous to Corsica. Pavari (1955) was of the opinion that *P. pinea* was native near Mount Peloritani, in Sicily. His contention is supported by findings of fossil *P. pinea* (Zodda, 1903) near Messina.

After reviewing this problem thoroughly, Rikli, in his *Pflanzenkleid der Mittelmeerländer* (1943), wrote that it was impossible to distinguish between the original localities and the secondary places in the area occupied at the present time by *P. pinea*. He proposed that its origin was in the western Mediterranean region and particularly on the Iberian Peninsula, where this pine is found in larger groves and at higher altitudes than anywhere else. Extensive *P. pinea* forests are found in the warmer parts of Andalusia and Algarve and in western Portugal, and also in the interior plain of the Castillas. The Bay of Cádiz is surrounded with *P. pinea* forests, which extend to the mouth of the Guadalquivir.

Some time ago, large stands of *P. pinea* were found in the valleys of the Tejo and Sodotal in middle Portugal, but those were cut so intensively for shipbuilding and for making of railroad ties that no more *P. pinea* is found there.

**Plate 3–52.** *Left*: *P. pinea* No. 73 in Spain. This pine has been so extensively planted that it is difficult to say where it is native. (Photo by Instituto Forestal, Madrid.) *Right*: *P. nigra* No. 74, Baden, about 40 km from Vienna. This pine grows in the eastern Alps at altitudes of 200–400 m on very poor calcareous soils. (Photo by Austrian Forest Research Institute.)

According to Rikli, the eastern Mediterranean cannot be considered as the place of origin of *P. pinea;* it has been cultivated there, and its introduction by Fakhr-ed-din was relatively recent. Recently, Feinbrun (1959) reviewed the problem of distribution of *P. pinea* in Lebanon. She went there and found, southwest of Hemmana, near the village of Bmariam, *P. pinea* trees (locally called *"snobar"*) over 400 years old; i.e., they were there before Fakhr-ed-din's time. Hers was an excellent piece of research work. She thinks that *P. pinea* is native to Portugal, Spain, Corsica, the Tyrrhenian Coast of Italy, the Peloponnesus of Greece, and the coast of Asia Minor; it is not indigenous in Crete.

The easternmost locality of *P. pinea* is in northeastern Turkey on the west side of the Chorokh River Valley. This river, in its low reaches, is in the Soviet Union. The Turkish name of the river is "Coruh" or "Çoruh." *Pinus pinea* is found there near the Russian border, at an elevation of 150 to 600 m. Possibly it is native there, although Rikli doubts it.

*Pinus pinea* is not native to northern Africa.

To sum up, it is unknown exactly where *P. pinea* is native and where it is introduced. From paleobotanical records and from the excellent and most recent inquiry of Feinbrun, it appears that, before man came to the Mediterranean region, this pine had been growing, perhaps not too abundantly, from the Iberian Peninsula to the Levant. It is uncertain if it ever grew in Africa. Possibly it did during the Tertiary period, but there is no positive evidence of this.

*Pinus pinea* is a very stable species. The only known variety, *fragilis* Duhamel, is characterized by a soft and thin seedcoat. This variety is possibly a result of selection in cultivated plantations rather than a wild variety. *Pinus pinea* has never been crossed with any other species of pine.

The altitudinal range of *P. pinea* is from sea level to 1000 m on the south slope of the Sierra de Almijara near the Mediterranean Coast of Spain, between Málaga and Motril. On the eastern Mediterranean islands, it grows at altitudes between 150 and 600 m. (See map, Fig. 3–40.)

## 74. Pinus nigra Arn.

*Pinus nigra,* often called *"Pinus laricio* Poiret," is commonly known in Europe as "black pine." Local names are many; for example, Serbs call it *"tsrnog bor,"* i.e., "black pine."

Its area extends from Spanish Morocco to Asia Minor, southern France, northern Italy, Austria, the Balkan Peninsula, and Crimea, and it is found in one place on the Caucasian coast of the Black Sea, as well as on some islands of the Mediterranean, including Cyprus (see map, Fig. 3–43).

In the Dinaric Alps, the altitudinal range of *P. nigra* is from 550 to 600 m. In Corsica, *P. nigra* forests are found between 900 and 1200 m. Single trees may reach 1800 m of altitude. In the Sierra de Segura, southeastern Spain, this pine reaches an altitude of about 1200 m.

Several varieties are recognized within the species: *pallasiana* Lamb., native to Crimea; *austriaca* Endlich., of Austria; *calabrica* Loud., of Italy; *corsicana* Loud., of Corsica; and some others (Delevoy, 1949).

In Austria, *P. nigra* grows on poor dolomite and limestone soil at altitudes between 260 and 500 m and on better soils at 300 to 700 m. It may reach altitudes of 700 to 1200 m where it is intermixed with *P. sylvestris*. Single trees of this pine may be found as high as 1400 m above sea level.

Thus, the altitudinal distribution of *P. nigra* is between 250 and 1800 m.

### 75. *Pinus heldreichii* Christ

*Pinus heldreichii* was described in 1863 as an independent species. In 1914, Shaw placed it with *P. nigra*. In this publication, *P. heldreichii* is considered as a valid species.

*Pinus heldreichii* grows in northeastern Greece, in Albania, and in adjacent parts of Yugoslavia and Italy. *Pinus leucodermis* Antoine is considered here as a variety of *P. heldreichii*. This species hybridizes naturally with *P. montana* (Fukarek, 1960). (See map, Fig. 3–43.)

The basic altitudinal range of *P. heldreichii* is from 1000 to 1800 m in Yugoslavia, the highest occurrence being at 2300 m; in Greece, it ascends to 2500 m (Rikli, 1943).

### 76. *Pinus montana* Miller

*Pinus montana* ranges from the Pyrenees through the Alps and Apennines to the Carpathians (see map, Fig. 3–44). In the Jura Mountains of France, it is found in several localities at altitudes between 1300 and 1600 m and always in peat bogs. In the Vosges, the most known locality is Beliard, near Gerardmer. In the Massif Central, it occurs occasionally, also in peat bogs. In all of these places, *P. montana* is a botanical rarity. It occurs also in Austria, in the border mountains of Czechoslovakia, in the Tatra of Poland, in the Carpathian part of the Ukraine, and in Romania. This pine is rather variable. Its three major varieties are *mughus* (Scopoli) Zenari, *uncinata* Ramond, and *pumilio* (Haenke) Zenari; there are many horticultural forms. At the lower altitudes of its range, it intermingles and possibly crosses naturally with *P. sylvestris*.

**Plate 3–53.** *Upper left and upper right: P. heldreichii No. 75 var. leuco-dermis,* Métsovon, Greece. Altitude 1400 m. (Photos courtesy of Christos Moulopoulos.) *Bottom: P. montana No. 76 var. mughus,* Jakupica, Macedonia, Yugoslavia. Altitude 2000 m. (Photo by Branislav Pejoski.)

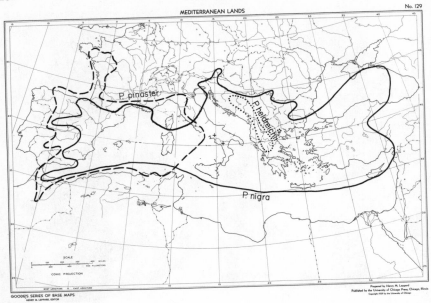

**Fig. 3–43.** Areas of *P. nigra* Arn. No. 74, *P. heldreichii* Christ No. 75, and *P. pinaster* Ait. No. 80.

In the Tatra, *P. montana* grows at elevations as high as 1950 m above sea level (Rubner and Reinhold, 1953). Rikli (1943) reported its habitat in the Mediterranean area at altitudes between 400 and 1500 m.

There are reports that in Bosnia it crosses naturally with *P. heldreichii* var. *leucodermis* (Fukarek, 1960). A natural cross between *P. montana* and *P. nigra* No. 74 was mentioned by Schütt (1959).

## 77. *Pinus halepensis* Miller

*Pinus halepensis* is the most widely distributed pine of the Mediterranean region (see map, Fig. 3–45). It occurs sparingly, sometimes forming more or less pure groves but more often mixed with Mediterranean scrub forest and maquis brush.

On the Iberian Peninsula, it is restricted to the Mediterranean Coast from Gibraltar to the northeast, continuing through the coastal parts of France and Italy. In two localities in Spain, it penetrates rather deeply inland; one toward Madrid, somewhat east of the city, and another north of Barcelona, along the foothills of the Pyrenees. It grows in the Balearic Islands, which in Strabo's time were known as "Pityusae" (i.e., "pine") islands (Strabo; reference in Literature Citations section of Chapter 2). In Italy, *P. halepensis* is very scarce, occurring along the coast of the

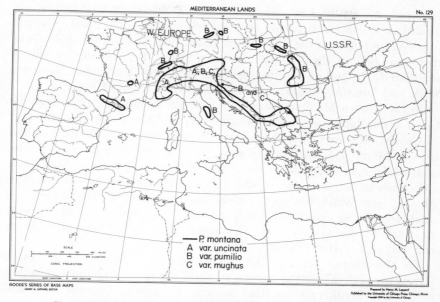

**Fig. 3–44.** Areas of *P. montana* Mill. No. 76 and its varieties.

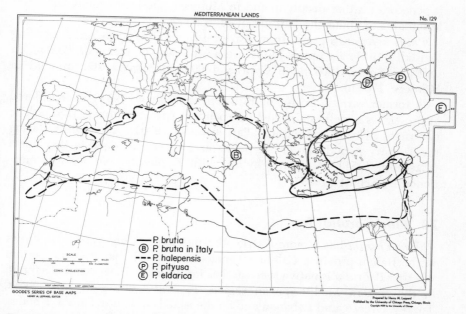

**Fig. 3–45.** Areas of *P. halepensis* Mill. No. 77, *P. brutia* Ten. No. 78, *P. pityusa* Steven No. 79, and *P. eldarica* Medw. No. 81.

Ligurian Sea and also in a few spots on the Adriatic Coast and in one locality of Calabria. It occurs on the French island of Corsica, where it forms a fine forest on the Cape Corse peninsula. In the area of Sardinia, it is found only on the small island of San Pietro. It grows on dry hills of southern Sicily, and on nearby small islands such as Pantelleria (between Sicily and Tunisia), Lampeduza, and Marettimo (west of Sicily).

In the eastern Mediterranean, *P. halepensis* occurs along the Adriatic Coast of the Balkan Peninsula (Yugoslavia) and also in the southern part of Greece. It grows on some islands of the eastern Mediterranean, but in Asia Minor it is surprisingly rare, being found only in one locality, above Adana, in the northeastern corner of the Mediterranean Sea. *Pinus halepensis* is native to the coastal regions of Syria but is not found in Aleppo, from which the species name is derived. In Jordan, it covers a small area, being associated with *Quercus, Cistus, Arbutus,* and *Pistacea.* In Israel, it is found only rarely, in places such as Mount Carmel, Hebron, and east of Tel Aviv (Zohary, 1947).

On the African coast of the Mediterranean, *P. halepensis* grows in Cyrenaica (Libya), in the maquis scrub of the Barce Peninsula, together with other Mediterranean trees such as *Ceratonia, Quercus ilex,* and *Cupressus sempervirens;* occasionally, it forms rather extensive, open forests. In Tunisia and Algeria, it grows also in the maquis brushfields; it penetrates rather deeply inland in Morocco, southwest along the Atlas Mountains to about the latitude of Marrakech.

*Pinus halepensis* grows from sea level to varying altitudes. According to Rikli (1943) its upper limits are as follows: in Dalmatia, 200 m; in southern Spain, 1000 m; in Cyprus, 1400 m; in Israel, 1000 m; and in Morocco, 1700 m.

A former variety, *brutia,* of *P. halepensis* (Shaw, 1914) is considered at present as a well-established independent species (Mirov, 1955). The two pines hybridize in nature (Papajoannou, 1936). Apparently, during the Tertiary period, the *P. halepensis* area extended much farther north (Czeczott, 1954). A natural hybrid with *P. pinaster* No. 80 was mentioned by Schütt (1959).

### 78. Pinus brutia Ten.

*Pinus brutia* has a more restricted range than *P. halepensis.* It grows in the Italian province Calabria (ancient Brutium), but it is not certain whether *P. brutia* is native there or was introduced. In its natural habitat, in the eastern Mediterranean region, *P. brutia* grows in Iraq, Syria, Turkey, Greece, and Lebanon and on the islands of Chios, Samos, Rhodes, Crete, and Cyprus. (See map, Fig. 3–45.)

**Plate 3–54.** *Upper left: P. halepensis* No. 77, Granada, Spain. (Photo by Instituto Forestal de Investigaciones y Experiencias, Madrid.) *Upper right: P. brutia* No. 78, Panorama, Thessalonike, Greece. Altitude 150–350 m. (Photo courtesy of Christos Moulopoulos.) *Lower left: P. brutia*, Seich Sou, Thessalonike, Greece. (Photo courtesy of Christos Moulopoulos.) *Lower right: P. brutia*, seventy-five years old, 25 m tall, between Elmali and Kas, in western Taurus, Turkey. Altitude 750 m. This a fast-growing "Yayla" (highland) form with a straight trunk. (Photo by Hannes Mayer, from Selik, 1959.)

The altitudinal range of *P. brutia* is approximately from 100 to 1500 m. In Turkey, it goes up to 750 m; occasionally, it reaches 1550 m altitude (Rikli, 1943).

Papajoannou (1936) described a variety of *P. brutia* from the island of Lesbos and named it "*Pinus brutia* var. *agrophiotii* Pap." *Pinus brutia* crosses with *P. halepensis.*

About 100 years ago, Tajiks brought home a handful of seeds of *P. brutia* from their pilgrimage to Mecca. In the *kishlak* (village) of Arbobi, in the Ghissar region of Tajikstan, U.S.S.R., there are still standing several specimens of this pine, reaching a height of 27 m (Gursky, 1957). This is mentioned as one instance of old introduction of Mediterranean pines into different regions that often makes determination of their native habitats extremely difficult.

### 79. Pinus pityusa Steven

*Pinus pityusa* was described in 1838 from near Pitsunda (ancient Pithyum: "*pithys*" in Greek means "pine"), on the eastern coast of the Black Sea. *Pinus pityusa* also has been reported from the island of Prinkipo (near Istanbul), from Thrace, from Anatolia, from Syria, and also from the island of Thasos, near the coast of eastern Thrace (Papajoannou, 1936), but this last information appears to be questionable. Shaw considered this pine to be *P. halepensis;* some, more recent, investigators believe that it is the same as *P. brutia. Pinus stankewiczii* (Suk.) Fom., which grows in two localities on the south coast of Crimea on dry marl soil of the slopes facing the sea, may be considered as *P. pityusa* Steven var. *stankewiczii* Suk. The vertical range of *P. pityusa* is from sea level up to 300 m. (See map, Fig. 3–45 and Plate 1–1.)

### 80. Pinus pinaster Ait.

*Pinus pinaster,* or *P. maritima,* is called "French maritime pine." Its area extends from southwestern France, near the mouth of the Loire River, up to Brittany, then to Portugal, through Spain and Italy, to the Dalmatian coast of Yugoslavia, and to Greece. It grows in a few spots in Morocco and Algeria, and along the Mediterranean Coast of France. It is also found on the islands of Corsica and Sardinia. (See map, Fig. 3–43, page 250.)

Unlike *P. nigra, P. pinaster* is a stable species. See, however, the discussion of *P. mesogeensis* Fieschi and Gaussen (page 553), which again is subdivided into several subspecies and varieties (Gaussen, 1960). Duff (1928) said that there are several races or geographical forms of this pine (the Corsican race, *pin de corté,* and var. *hamiltoni* of Corsica; the Atlantic race in the area from north of Bordeaux down to Portugal; and

**Plate 3–55.** *Pinus pityusa*, No. 79 at Pitsunda, ancient Pithyum, on the Black Sea coast of the Caucasus. (Photo by M. A. Kolosova.)

the Esterel race in the Esterel Mountains, in the Provence Alps, and occasionally along the Riviera on low hills and shallow, dry soil). *"Pin de Corté"* has been described by Fieschi and Gaussen as *P. mesogeensis* (see Fig. 9–6, page 564). According to these authors, the range of this pine is in the western Mediterranean, from Greece to Morocco. Its limits on the Iberian Peninsula have not yet been determined. These races, or strains (not necessarily botanical varieties), "differ principally in habitat, which at any time is a difficult thing to describe" (Duff, 1928). Varieties *aberdoniae* Loudon, *lemoniana* Loudon, and *minor* Loiseleur (Dallimore and Jackson, 1948) also do not appear to be very different from the typical *P. pinaster*. *Pinus pinaster* crosses naturally with typical *P. halepensis* (Schütt, 1959).

The altitudinal range of *P. pinaster* extends from sea level to about 400 m. In Corsica, fine forests of this pine are found between 400 and 900 m. In the Atlas Mountains of Morocco, it reaches the highest point of its vertical distribution, about 2000 m.

## 81. *Pinus eldarica* Medw.

*Pinus eldarica* is a rare pine found in one locality only, in a semi-desert environment southeast of Tbilisi, Georgia, Transcaucasia. This pine grows on the eastern extremity of the Choban-Dagh Range, along

**Plate 3–56.** *Pinus pinaster* No. 80. *Top:* a natural forest of the species, Landes, France. (Photo courtesy M. Debazac.) *Bottom:* at Chiavari, Corsica. (Photo by M. Toulgouat, Direction Générale des Eaux et Forêts.)

the south side of the Iori River. The *P. eldarica* area occupies only about 550 ha. It is located at altitudes of 200 to 600 m. A more or less pure pine stand occupies an area of 110 ha. This pine is considered to be an Oligocene relic. Previously, it occupied a larger area (Tutayuk, 1959). "*Pinus eldarica*" is considered by some authors as a synonym of "*Pinus brutia*" (Malejeff, 1929). (See map, Fig. 3–45, page 251.)

## Pinus sylvestris in the Mediterranean Region

*Pinus sylvestris* is essentially a pine of northern Eurasia (see No. 69, page 235), and its geographical distribution there took place chiefly during postglacial times (Bertsch, 1951) when this pine advanced from the southern refugia to western Europe, to the eastern European plain, and farther east.

Dissimilarly, in the Mediterranean region, *P. sylvestris* is always a relic of the Tertiary period. In Portugal, it is found only in the extreme north, in the Sierra do Gerez. In Spain, it forms forests in the Cordillera Central, in the Pyrenees, and in the Cordillera Iberica. It also occurs in the north of the peninsula, in the Cordillera Cantabrica, and in the south of Spain between 2° 30′ and 3° west longitude and between 37° and 37° 30′ north latitude, thus reaching the southernmost point of its distribution in the Mediterranean region.

In the Mediterranean part of France, *P. sylvestris* is found in the Pyrenees, at Cevennes, and in the Maritime Alps. In Italy, it occurs in the foothills of the Alps and in the northern Apennines. On the Balkan Peninsula, it is rather abundant in central Yugoslavia and to a lesser extent in Bulgaria and Greece (northeastern Macedonia). In Romania, its distribution along the Transylvanian Alps is rather sporadic. It extends north to the Carpathians. Farther east, the distribution of *P. sylvestris* is complicated by its taxonomy. There, several pines have been lumped together by some botanists (Shaw, 1914) under the name "*Pinus sylvestris*." Russian taxonomists consider several pines of the Caucasian region, extending to Turkey, as independent species (Komarov, 1934). What is generally considered *P. sylvestris* is represented in the Caucasus by variety *hamata* Sosn. (or *P. sosnowskyi* Nakai). This pine extends from the Black Sea coast, near Novorossisk, across the main Caucasian range to the Kakhetian range and to southwestern Transcaucasia (Adzhar-Imeretian range). It crosses the border of Turkey and continues through northern Anatolia as far west as 38½° north latitude, somewhat south of Afion. (See map, Fig. 3–46.)

Variety *hamata* also occurs on the south slopes of the Crimean Mountains, at altitudes from 1100 to 1300 m above sea level. The area occupied by variety *hamata* in the Caucasus corresponds exactly to the area

**Plate 3–57.** *Pinus eldarica* No. 81, Eller Oukhi, Azerbaijan, Transcaucasia, U.S.S.R. (Photo by B. K. Tutaiuk.)

**Plate 3–58.** *Pinus sylvestris* No. 69 in the Mediterranean region, on the southern slope of the main range of the Caucasus, where it is known as *"Pinus hamata Sosn."* (Photo by A. G. Dolukhanov.)

**Fig. 3—46.** Area of *P. sylvestris* L. No. 69 in the Mediterranean region. (See also Fig. 3—50, page 277.)

that was glaciated during the Ice Age (except, of course, upper portions of high mountains, which are still covered with ice). It appears that variety *hamata* was the pioneer invader of places newly liberated from ice after the end of glaciation.

It is of interest to mention that, while *P. sylvestris* of northern Eurasia possesses dextrorotatory turpentine, that of its variety *hamata* turns polarized light to the left (Lipsky, 1899). *Pinus sylvestris* turpentine I received from Greece was also laevorotatory; turpentine samples obtained from Spain and from Italy were dextrorotatory. This problem of differences in properties of turpentine of the northern and of the eastern Mediterranean *P. sylvestris* should be studied further; it might shed some light on the relationship of variety *hamata* to *P. sylvestris* of the western Mediterranean countries. A pine growing in the southwestern part of Transcaucasia and extending to Turkey, where it occurs from Ardahan to Kars and near Olty and Artvin, was listed by Shaw (1914) as *P. sylvestris* var. *armena*. It is a scrubby pine of high mountains reaching the subalpine zone. *Pinus kochiana* Klotzsch, also considered by Shaw as *P. sylvestris*, grows chiefly along the river Coruh (Chorokh) and sporadically near Ardahan, Turkey, and across the border in the Soviet Union. In many respects, it resembles *P. montana* No. 76, and its taxonomic status is still uncertain. In *Flora SSSR* (*Flora of the U.S.S.R.*) (Komarov, 1934), this pine is described as *P. kochiana* (see Chapter 9, page 552).

As for the altitudinal range of *P. sylvestris*, there are magnificent *P. sylvestris* forests in the Guadarrama Mountains at about 2100 to 2200 m, between Madrid and Segovia. On the northern slopes of the Sierra Nevada, southeast of Granada, it grows at 1600 to 2000 m of altitude. In southern France, it descends almost to the coast near Mentone. It forms forests in the southern Alps to an altitude of 1900 m and ascends mountains as high as 2000 to 2300 m (Rubner and Reinhold, 1953). In the Massif Central, it is found between 700 and 1200 m.

The lower vertical limit of distribution of *P. sylvestris* var. *hamata* in the Caucasus is at 500 m, and, on the Black Sea coast near the Turkish border, it is at 200 m. Its upper limit is, in the main range of the Caucasus, at timberline, at about 2500 to 2600 m.

In Transcaucasia, where it is sparse, it was noted by Rikli (1943) at 1280 m. In adjacent parts of Turkey (Rize province), where it occasionally reaches the Black Sea coast, its inland vertical range seldom starts lower than 1100 m; it grows up to 1700 m of altitude (Rikli, 1943). *Pinus sylvestris* and its variety *hamata* come in contact in Bulgaria (Cherniavski, 1954).

## PINE REGION OF EASTERN ASIA

During the Tertiary period, the pine region of eastern Asia extended farther north than it does now. At the present time in the south, it merges so gradually and imperceptibly into the pine region of southeastern Asia that it is better to consider the geography of pines of these two regions as one. In the north, the pine region of eastern Asia is separated by the deserts from the Siberian pine forests; only in its northeastern part is there contact between the two forest regions. *Pinus pumila* No. 68 has its main geographical area in northeastern Siberia, but it also occurs sporadically in eastern Asia as far south as Korea and the central part of Japan. In the south, the region extends as a narrow belt along the west slope of the Himalaya to eastern Afghanistan.

The total number of pines in the region is twenty-four including eleven haploxylon and thirteen diploxylon species (Table 3–7). More pine species are found in the northern part of eastern Asia; southward their number decreases as shown in Table 3–8.

The taxonomy of several pines of this region is not yet settled; moreover, its southern part (Indochina) has not yet been fully explored by

**Table 3–7.** Pines of Eastern Asia

| Number | Species | Distribution |
|---|---|---|
| HAPLOXYLON | | |
| 82. | *P. koraiensis* | Eastern Russia, Manchuria, Korea, Japan |
| 83. | *P. pentaphylla* | Japan |
| 84. | *P. himekomatsu* | Japan |
| 85. | *P. morrisonicola* | Formosa (Taiwan) |
| 86. | *P. armandi* | China, Japan, Formosa (Taiwan), Upper Burma |
| 87. | *P. bungeana* | Central China |
| 88. | *P. dalatensis* | Southern Viet Nam |
| 89. | *P. fenzeliana* | Hainan island |
| 90. | *P. kwangtungensis* | Southeastern China |
| 91. | *P. griffithii* | Himalaya (Yunnan to eastern Afghanistan) |
| 92. | *P. gerardiana* | Western Himalaya (to eastern Afghanistan) |
| DIPLOXYLON | | |
| 93. | *P. roxburghii* | Himalaya |
| 94. | *P. massoniana* | Southern China |
| 95. | *P. densiflora* | Japan, Korea, and Shantung (China) |
| 96. | *P. funebris* | Maritime Province (Russia) |
| 97. | *P. thunberghii* | Japan |
| 98. | *P. luchuensis* | Ryukyu Islands |
| 99. | *P. taiwanensis* | Formosa (Taiwan) |
| 100. | *P. hwangshanensis* | Southern China |
| 101. | *P. merkusii* | From Burma to the Philippines |
| 102. | *P. tabulaeformis* | Northern China |
| 103. | *P. yunnanensis* | Yunnan (China) |
| 104. | *P. khasya* | Assam (India), Burma, Thailand, Laos, and Viet Nam |
| 105. | *P. insularis* | Northern Luzon (Philippines) |

**Table 3–8.** Number of Pine Species in Different Countries of Eastern Asia

| Locality | Number of Species | | | Species' Numbers |
|---|---|---|---|---|
| | Hap-loxylon | Dip-loxylon | Total | |
| China [a] | 4 | 6 | 10 | 82, 86, 87, 90, 94, 95, 96, 100, 102, 103 |
| Japan [b] | 5 | 3 | 8 | 68, 82, 83, 84, 86, 95, 97, 98 |
| Formosa (Taiwan) | 2 | 2 | 4 | 85, 86, 94, 99 |
| Indochina | 2 | 3 | 5 | 88, 94, 101, 104, and *"pin du moyen Annam"* [c] |
| Hainan | 2 | 1 | 3 | 86, 89, 94 |
| Himalaya | 2 | 1 | 3 | 91, 92, 93 |
| Philippines | 0 | 2 | 2 | 101, 105 |
| Indonesia (Sumatra) | 0 | 1 | 1 | 101 |

[a] Including adjacent Korea and Maritime Province of U.S.S.R.
[b] Including Ryukyu Islands.
[c] Ferré, 1960.

botanists. New pines recently have been described there, and it may be possible that more will be discovered in the future. One difficulty of describing the geography of eastern-Asia pines is our insufficient knowledge of distribution of some Chinese pines. Some of the difficulties encountered will be mentioned in the description of individual species.

## 82. *Pinus koraiensis* Sieb. & Zucc.

*Pinus koraiensis* is a pine of the Amur and Maritime provinces of Russia, of Manchuria, and of Korea (see maps, Figs. 3–47 and 3–48); it occurs also on the island of Honshu, Japan. Its northern limit is at about 50° north latitude. It grows from the middle reaches of the Amur eastward in the river valleys on low, well-drained foothills and on relatively low mountains at altitudes of 600 to 900 m. Unlike the closely related *P. sibirica* No. 67, it does not grow in alluvial river valleys that are flooded in spring and during summer rains.

In the low Sikhote Alin Range, extending between the Ussuri River and the Sea of Japan, *P. koraiensis* grows abundantly as a dominant tree together with *Abies holophylla* in the lush, almost subtropical, broadleaf forests, on rich, moist soil, from almost sea level to 600 m of altitude (Suslov, 1947). In Manchuria, the habitat of *P. koraiensis* is similar to that of the above-described adjacent parts of Russia. In the Khingan Mountains, it grows at 600 to 900 m, descending to lower elevations as a component of Manchurian hardwood forests. Because of its valuable wood, it has been disappearing very rapidly.

In east-central Korea, *P. koraiensis* is seldom found below 600 m, and its upper limit is about 1200 m. Its southernmost range in Korea is in the Chiri-San Mountains, about 35° 15′ latitude north, where it grows between 1100 and 1500 m above sea level.

In Japan, *P. koraiensis* is local in the central part of Honshu island, occurring in several places, scattered among other conifers at altitudes of 2000 to 2500 m (Wilson, 1916). According to Hayashi (1952), it also occurs on Shikoku, though rarely, and its range there is not exactly known. The range of vertical distribution of *P. koraiensis* on northern Honshu is between 1200 and 1600 m; in central Honshu, at 1050 to 2600 m; and on Shikoku, from 1150 to 1400 m. It is rather unexpected to see it growing at lower elevations in the more southerly (Shikoku) location.

No varieties of *P. koraiensis* have been reported in the literature.

## *Pinus pumila* in eastern Asia

*Pinus pumila* Regel No. 68 already has been described as a pine of northern Eurasia. Originally, however, it was a species of eastern Asia,

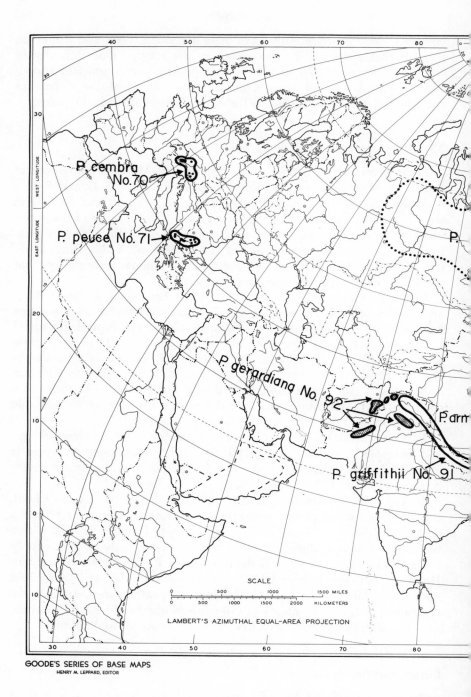

**Fig. 3–47.** Areas of haploxylon

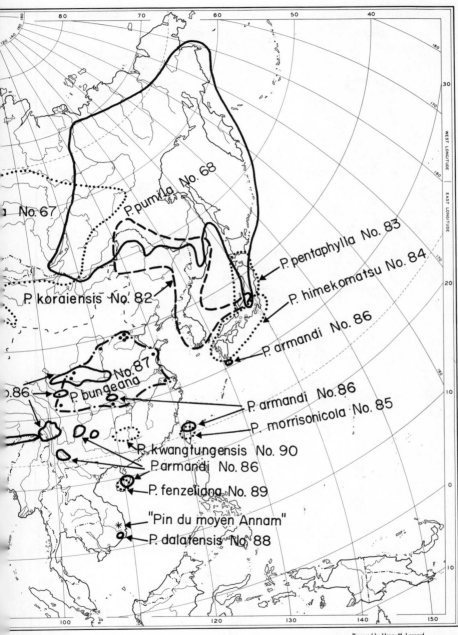

No. 67

P. pumila No. 68

P. koraiensis No. 82

P. pentaphylla No. 83

P. himekomatsu No. 84

P. armandi No. 86

No. 87

P. bungeana

.86

P. armandi No. 86

P. morrisonicola No. 85

P. kwangtungensis No. 90

P. armandi No. 86

P. fenzeliana No. 89

"Pin du moyen Annam"

P. dalatensis No. 88

Prepared by Henry M. Leppard
Published by the University of Chicago Press, Chicago, Illinois
Copyright 1940 by the University of Chicago

pines of eastern Asia.

**Fig. 3–48.** *Pinus koraiensis* Sieb. & Zucc. No. 82 in Korea and Japan.

Plate 3–59. *Pinus koraiensis* No. 82. *Left:* forest on Mount Senjo, in the Nagano prefecture, Japan. Altitude 1800 m. (Photo by Yosaka Hayashi.) *Right:* planted tree at Arnold Arboretum, Jamaica Plain, Massachusetts. (Courtesy Arnold Arboretum.)

closely related to *P. sibirica* No. 67, of northern Eurasia, and also to *P. pentaphylla* No. 83, of Japan. It expanded to northeastern Siberia relatively recently, after the glacial period. In eastern Asia, it is found in the mountains of Sihota Alin, Maritime Province of Russia, on the peninsula of Kamchatka, on the island of Sakhalin, on the Kurile Islands, in the high mountains of Manchuria and Korea, and on the Japanese islands of Hokkaido and Honshu. On the last-named island, it reaches its southernmost point of distribution, 35° 20′ north. (See map, Fig. 3–47.)

## 83. *Pinus pentaphylla* Mayr and 84. *Pinus himekomatsu* Miyabe and Kudo

*Pinus pentaphylla* and *P. himekomatsu* are generally considered by American botanists, following Shaw (1914), as *P. parviflora,* but the contemporary Japanese botanists (see Hayashi, 1954) who have studied *P. parviflora* more intensively are inclined to separate it into two species— *P. pentaphylla* Mayr, of the north of Japan, and *P. himekomatsu* Miyabe and Kudo, of the south of the country. In central Honshu, the two pines meet, overlap, and most likely intercross. The dividing line is approximately of an **S** shape from the intersection of the thirty-sixth parallel and the one hundred and thirty-sixth meridian on the coast of the Sea of Japan to the intersection of the thirty-eighth parallel and the one hundred and forty-first meridian (see map, Fig. 3–49). *Pinus pentaphylla* is the northernmost pine of the complex of species that extends to Hainan and to Viet Nam and that I designate tentatively, for convenience, as "*Pinus parviflora* complex" (see Chapter 9). *Pinus pentaphylla* is found on the Korean island of Utsurio-To (approximately 130½° east longitude and 37½° north latitude. (See also map, Fig. 3–47.)

It is difficult to ascertain the altitudinal range of the two pines, because Hayashi (1954) considers the two pines together. Subject to correction, I tabulated Hayashi's data as follows:

| Species | Locality | Altitudinal Range |
|---------|----------|-------------------|
| P. pentaphylla | S. Hokkaido | 60 to 800 m |
| P. pentaphylla | N. Honshu | 100 to 1800 m |
| P. himekomatsu | Central Honshu | 200 to 2500 m |
| P. himekomatsu | S. and W. Honshu | 100 to 1850 m |
| P. himekomatsu | Shikoku | 200 to 1700 m |
| P. himekomatsu | Kyushu | 400 to 1600 m |

According to the Japanese text of Hayashi, *P. pentaphylla* elevations are between 60 m and 2500 m, and *P. himekomatsu* grows between altitudes of 100 and 1850 m.

## 85. *Pinus morrisonicola* Hayata

*Pinus morrisonicola* is also known as "*Pinus formosana* Hayata" and "*Pinus formosensis* Hayata." A haploxylon pine of Formosa (Taiwan), it is closely related to *P. himekomatsu*, of Japan. Its home is throughout the island at altitudes of 300 to 2300 m. It is usually scattered on ridges, associated with hardwoods, seldom forming pure stands. It is possible (as the chemistry of this pine suggests) that it hybridizes in nature with *P. armandi* No. 86. (See map, Fig. 3–47.)

## 86. *Pinus armandi* Franchet

*Pinus armandi* is a widely distributed haploxylon pine of eastern Asia (see map, Fig. 3–47). On the continent, it is scattered over a wide but ill-defined area. To quote Wu (1947),

The main range of this pine forms a zone around the Red Basin. To the east and south, however, the distribution is rather discontinuous and occurrence is less abundant. Three main districts may be recognized. The first district is in

**Plate 3—60.** *Upper left:* P. pentaphylla No. 83, Mount Azuma, Fukushima prefecture, Japan. Altitude 1600 m. *Upper right:* P. pentaphylla, Mount Osawa, Nagano prefecture. Altitude 1850 m. *Bottom:* P. himekomatsu No. 84, Mount Kiyosumi, Chiba prefecture, Japan. Altitude 220 m. (Photos by Yosaka Hayashi.)

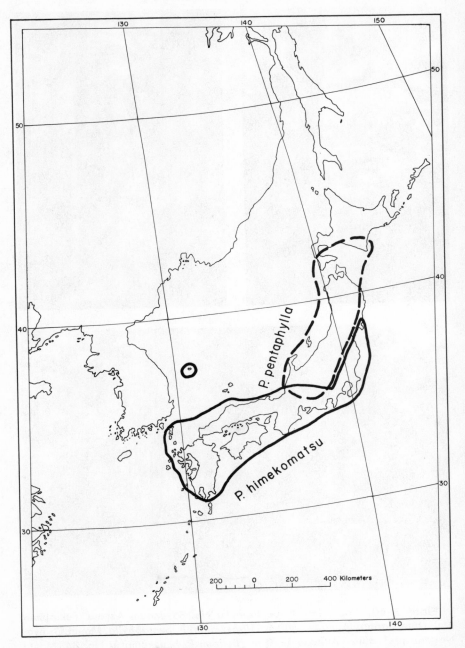

**Fig. 3–49.** Areas of *P. pentaphylla* Mayr No. 83 and *P. himekomatsu* Miyabe and Kudo No. 84.

**Plate 3–61.** *Left: P. morrisonicola* No. 85 at 2200 m. *Right: P. armandi* No. 86 at 2600 m. (Both photographed in central Formosa by Taiwan Forest Service.)

the Tsingling Range. It extends eastward to the Funiu Shan in Honan which is the east branch of the Tsingling Range. It grows at an elevation of 5,000 feet [about 1500 m] in central Tsingling as well as in the western part of the range. It has also been found in central and southwestern Kansu.

The next main district is located in southeastern Kansu, with a northern spur in Szechwan province. According to Rock, it is scattered in with *Abies* forest and sometimes grows on limestone cliffs in the forests of Wan Sang Ku.

The third, and most important region of this pine is in northern, northwestern and central Yunnan, and the southern part of former Sikang and southern Szechwan, at an elevation of 1400 to 3600 meters.

In upper Burma, *P. armandi* was found by Captain F. Kingdon Ward at Pawa Pass and at Phimaw Pass at about 26° and 25° 30′, respectively, on the Yunnan border about 145 km northeast of Myitkyina. The pines were growing scattered along ridges in *Tsuga-Quercus* forest at altitudes of 2100 m and up; also it was found in the Adung Valley at elevations of 1500 to 2400 m (Merrill, 1941). Near Kunming, Yunnan, *P. armandi* disappears below 1100 m (Fedorov *et al.*, 1956). On the Shweli-Salween divide, it grows in mixed forest at an elevation of about 3000 m.

Natural forests of *P. armandi* have been found in western Hupei and in the central part of Kweichow. This pine also occurs on Hainan island.

On Formosa, it is found in the central part of the island at 2300 to 3300 m, i.e., generally above *P. morrisonicola*. As regards occurrence of

*P. armandi* in Viet Nam, this apparently is an error (Ferré, 1960). Its variety occurs in an entirely different environment at an altitude of 180 m on the islands Yaku-Shima and Tanega-Shima, just south of the Kyushu island of Japan. It is known as *P. amamiana* Koidz.

## 87. *Pinus bungeana* Zucc.

*Pinus bungeana* is a rare three-needle haploxylon pine of the mountains of central China (see map, Fig. 3–47). It is found in a few spots in Shansi, Hopeh, Shensi, southeast Kansu, Honan, and neighboring parts of Hupeh and Szechwan (Sowerby, 1937; Wu, 1947). It is a picturesque tree with chalky white bark scaling off in small patches, resembling the bark of *Platanus* (see Plate 5–7). Chinese call it "bark-shedding tree" and plant it near temples and in cemeteries. Once it was more widely distributed than now, but it is doubtful if it was more abundant. In southeastern Shansi and Shensi, it usually grows with *P. tabulaeformis* No. 102. Pure open stands occur only on steep southern slopes. On Mount Taihang, it grows at an altitude of about 2750 m (Wu, 1947). Possibly in some reported localities at low elevations it is not native but planted.

Its altitudinal range is rather limited—probably between 1370 and 2800 m, although in Shantung it is found at an altitude of only 100 m above sea level.

## 88. *Pinus dalatensis* de Ferré

*Pinus dalatensis* is a haploxylon pine of southern Viet Nam. It is related to *P. griffithii* No. 91, but its pollen grains look like those of *P. peuce* (Ferré, 1960). Gaussen (1960) wrote that *P. dalatensis* appears to be closer to *P. strobus* than to *P. excelsa* (i.e., *P. griffithii*). Its area is not well known. It was collected at two localities (approximately $108\frac{1}{2}°$ east and $11\frac{1}{2}°$ north), but most likely it is found in other places in the same region (Ferré, 1960), at altitudes of 1500 to 2400 m. (See map, Fig. 3–47.)

## 89. *Pinus fenzeliana* Handel-Mazzetti

*Pinus fenzeliana* is considered by conservative botanists as *P. parviflora* var. *fenzeliana* Wu (Wu, 1956). But, since the epithet "*P. parviflora*" is not yet well established, *P. fenzeliana* will be considered here tentatively as a valid species.

*Pinus fenzeliana* occurs in the mountains of the south-central part of Hainan island, lying close to the coast of China and separated from the Luichow Peninsula of Kwangtung province by the narrow (15 to 24 km wide) Hainan Strait. There it grows scattered singly or in groups among

**Plate 3-62.** *Pinus bungeana* No. 87, Patung Hsien, western Hupei, China. *Left:* a tree about 15 m tall. Altitude about 1000 m. *Right:* on slate cliffs. Altitude 1300 m. Note white trunks (see also Plate 5-7). (Photos by E. H. Wilson. Courtesy Arnold Arboretum, Jamaica Plain, Massachusetts.)

other evergreen trees at altitudes varying from 1000 m to those of the summits of the highest mountains (about 1600 m). (See map, Fig. 3–47.)

## 90. *Pinus kwangtungensis* Chun

*Pinus kwangtungensis* is considered by Wu (1956) as the same pine as *P. fenzeliana*, and thus as a variety of *P. parviflora*. For the reason mentioned in describing *P. fenzeliana*, I prefer to consider this pine as a species until more information is available. Young *P. kwangtungensis* pines growing at the Institute of Forest Genetics, Placerville, California, certainly look too distinct (with much broader needles) to be called a variety of *P. parviflora*. *Pinus kwangtungensis* is found in southern Hunan at elevations between 1000 and 1800 m, where it is admixed with broadleaf forests. In Kwangsi, it is found on the Taining Shan at an elevation of about 1000 m. In Kwantung, it rarely forms pure stands, occurring as an admixture to hardwood forests above 700 m of altitude. (See map, Fig. 3–47.)

The last two haploxylon pines to be considered, *P. griffithii* No. 91 and *P. gerardiana* No. 92, and the first diploxylon pine, *P. roxburghii* No. 93, are the only pines of the Himalaya. *Pinus griffithii* is a species of high altitudes. *Pinus roxburghii* occupies lower elevations. The third one, *P. gerardiana*, is of limited distribution at the western end of the Himalayan chain.

## 91. *Pinus griffithii* McClelland

*Pinus griffithii* is a haploxylon pine also known as *"Pinus excelsa"* or *"Pinus wallichiana."* It grows, with some interruptions, along the Himalaya from southeastern Asia (western Yunnan and Upper Burma) to eastern Afghanistan (Troup, 1921; Vavilov, 1959) (see map, Fig. 3–47). It is absent from Sikkim. Ward found *P. griffithii* in the lower gorge country of Tibet at an altitude of about 2400 m in the temperate evergreen forest in the Zayul River gorge, associated with *P. khasya*, oak, maple, and *Ilex*. In northwestern Yunnan, it occurs in montane forest probably up to 3400 m (Wang, 1961).

In the western Himalaya, *P. griffithii* grows in almost continuous pure or mixed (with deodar and oak) stands from Garhwal to Kashmir. In the Simla Hills, pure forests occur chiefly between 1800 and 2600 m. In Kulu, pure stands of this pine are found occasionally as low as about 1370 m on northerly aspects. It also grows there in mixed stands with deodar and spruce at elevations between about 1700 and 2300 m.

In the Murree Hills, Rawalpindi, *P. griffithii* begins to appear in moist and cool places at about 1200 m; on the southern exposures, at

**Plate 3–63.** Left: *P. griffithii* No. 91, Himalaya, Punjab, India. Altitude 2500 m. Right: *P. gerardiana* No. 92 on abandoned cultivation, Punjab, India. Altitude 2400 m. (Photos by Indian Forest Research Institute.)

about 1700 m. Up to about 2000 m, it is mixed with *P. roxburghii*, and, at higher elevations, it grows either in pure stands or mixed with broad-leaf trees.

In the Takht-i-Sulaiman Range, it is associated with *P. gerardiana* No. 92. In northeastern Afghanistan, *P. griffithii* grows mainly above 2700 m with *P. gerardiana* and *Cedrus deodara*. At elevations chiefly between 2300 and 2600 m, it is admixed with oak and other broadleaf trees (Vavilov, 1959).

In Bhutan, *P. griffithii* grows generally between 2600 and 3000 m and as high as 3400 m of altitude and as low as less than 1800 m.

In Kashmir, it usually occurs between 1800 and 3000 m, sometimes descending below 1800 m (Troup, 1921). According to Ferré, it does not grow in Viet Nam as was previously supposed (Ferré, 1960).

No varieties of this species have been reported in the literature. In arboretums, *P. griffithii* apparently crosses naturally with *P. ayacahuite* No. 33 (Jackson, 1933).

## 92. *Pinus gerardiana* Wall.

*Pinus gerardiana* is a three-needle haploxylon pine growing in north-eastern Afghanistan, northern Baluchistan (in Pakistan), and adjacent

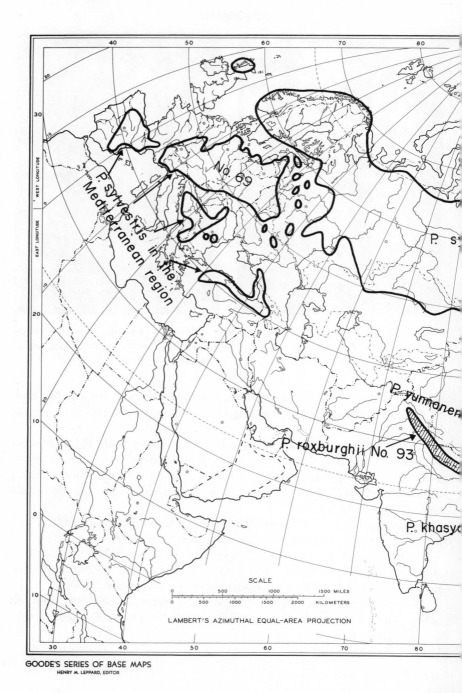

P. sylvestris in the Mediterranean region

No. 69

P. s...

P. yunnanen...

P. roxburghii No. 93

P. khasy...

SCALE

| 0 | 500 | 1000 | | 1500 MILES |
|---|---|---|---|---|
| 0 | 500 | 1000 | 1500 | 2000 KILOMETERS |

LAMBERT'S AZIMUTHAL EQUAL-AREA PROJECTION

GOODE'S SERIES OF BASE MAPS
HENRY M. LEPPARD, EDITOR

**Fig. 3–50.** Areas of diploxy...

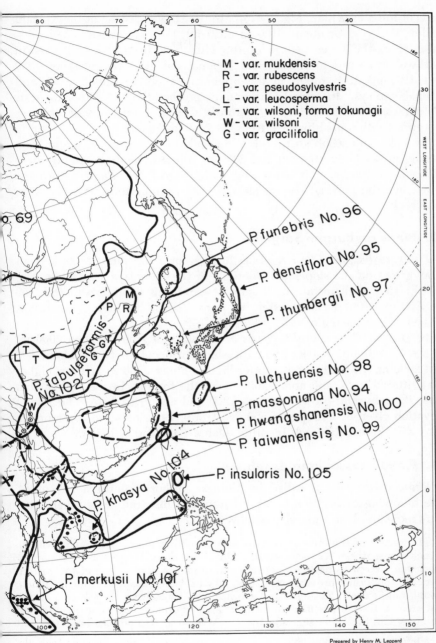

M - var. mukdensis
R - var. rubescens
P - var. pseudosylvestris
L - var. leucosperma
T - var. wilsoni, forma tokunagii
W - var. wilsoni
G - var. gracilifolia

No. 69

P. funebris No. 96

P. densiflora No. 95

P. thunbergii No. 97

P. tabulaeformis No. 102

P. luchuensis No. 98

P. massoniana No. 94

P. hwangshanensis No. 100

P. taiwanensis No. 99

P. khasya No. 104

P. insularis No. 105

P. merkusii No. 101

Prepared by Henry M. Leppard
Published by the University of Chicago Press, Chicago, Illinois
Copyright 1940 by the University of Chicago

...s of eastern Asia.

parts of India (see map, Fig. 3–47).* In the Haraib district of the Kurram Valley, it occurs at about 2100 to 3350 m. It is somewhat locally distributed in the inner valleys of the Himalaya from the Niti Pass in Garhwal westward to Chitral and beyond, chiefly between about 1800 and 3100 m. It is found in the upper parts of the Sutlej, Ravi, and Chenab valleys. In trans-Indus and in northeastern Afghanistan, it is sometimes intermixed with *P. griffithii* or *Cedrus deodara* (and in lower elevations with some broadleaf trees) at 2400 to 2700 m.

In Pakistan's Zhob district and in Takht-i-Sulaiman, *P. gerardiana* usually grows between 2200 and 2600 m, but it ascends to slightly over 3100 m. In places, it is associated with *P. griffithii. Pinus gerardiana* grows here on particularly dry sites, chiefly on limestone, sometimes on solid rocks.

## 93. *Pinus roxburghii* Sargent

*Pinus roxburghii* (*P. longifolia* Roxb.), or Chir pine, a diploxylon pine, grows on the slopes and foothills of the Himalaya (see map, Fig. 3–50), from Afghanistan to Bhutan, at elevations of approximately 450 to 2300 m, often forming extensive pure forests. At higher elevations, it ascends into the region of *P. griffithii.*

In Hazara, *P. roxburghii* grows at altitudes of from 1000 to 2000 m. In the Rawalpindi district and in Kashmir, it occurs between about 600 and 2000 m. In Garhwal, its upper limit is about 2300 m or even higher for scattered trees, and about 2000 m for the forests. In the Dehra Dun area, *P. roxburghii* grows between 1300 and about 2000 m. The lowest elevation given by Troup was 550 m (Troup, 1921; personal communications with Forest Research Institute, Dehra Dun, India, 1964).

## 94. *Pinus massoniana* Lamb.

*Pinus massoniana* is called by Chinese authors "southern red pine." The following description of its geographical distribution is taken from Wu's monograph on Chinese pines (Wu, 1947):

The region of this pine covers an area involving more than ten provinces. It includes southern Kiangsu, south Anhwei, southern Hupeh, a large part of Szechwan, except its northern and western border, a narrow belt of the eastern border of the former province of Sikang, all Checkiang, Kiangsi, Hunan, Fukien, Kwangtung, eastern Kwangsi, and southeastern Kweichow. In addition to the vast area on the continent, it crosses the sea to Formosa and Hainan. We find the Hwei Ho, the Hankiang, and the Ta Pa Shan as its northern boundary but

---

* Information regarding this pine is based on personal communication with the Forest Research Institute, Dehra Dun, India; Troup (1921); Said (1959); and Vavilov (1959). Edible nuts of this pine are called by natives "*Chil-ghus*" or "*Djil-ghus.*" The tree itself is called "*Chil*" (Vavilov, 1959).

**Plate 3–64.** *Pinus roxburghii* No. 93 in Nepal. Altitude about 1400 m. (Photo by A. A. Hasel. Courtesy Communications Media Division, U.S. Aid Mission to Nepal.)

including two islands: Formosa and Hainan. On the western and southwestern border of its range this species comes in contact with the region of Yunnan pine along an irregular but comparatively clearcut boundary.

Although *P. massoniana* covers such a vast area (see map, Fig. 3–50), its morphology is quite homogeneous throughout the whole range, no

**Plate 3–65.** *Pinus massoniana* No. 94, Omei Hsien, western Szechwan, China. Altitude about 400 m. (Photo by E. H. Wilson. Courtesy Arnold Arboretum, Jamaica Plain, Massachusetts.)

matter how divergent the climatic conditions are. There is no significant difference by which we may establish definite geographical or ecological varieties. See, however, Wu's discussion of *P. massoniana* var. *henrii* (Wu, 1956, pp. 23–28).

To quote further from Wu (1947):

Judging from the geographical distribution of *P. massoniana*, south Hunan is the geometrical center of the range of the species.

In Checkiang it usually occurs below 1,000 feet [310 m] either in pure stand[s] or associated with Chinese fir (*Cunninghamia lanceolata* Hook.), *Phyllostachys edulis* Houzeau de Lehaie, [and] *Cryptomeria japonica* D. Don. [In southern Checkiang, as well as in Fukien, it also sometimes associates with *Keteleeria*.]

Extensive unmanaged forests of *Pinus massoniana* associated with *Phyllostachys* and Chinese fir exist among mountainous districts of Anhwei, Kiangsi and northern Fukien below an altitude of 1,500 feet [about 450 m].

This pine is one of the common trees in the virgin forest of upper altitudes in northern Kwangsi. Pines over 100 years old were recorded in this province. Above an elevation of 3,300 feet [1000 m] in northern Kwangtung, the red pine grows everywhere, particularly on dry, thin soil, attaining diameters over two feet. [From Kwangtung it penetrates into Tonkin province of Viet Nam.]

In Hunan province, *Pinus massoniana* is the most abundant tree. It forms pure stands of small area here and there or is associated with other trees in mixed forests above 3,300 feet [1000 m] in altitude.

Around the Red Basin, mountain slopes below 1,000 m are often clad with *Pinus massoniana*. This pine is either scattered singly or in groups, or associated with other trees if the mountain is not entirely denuded. In northern Szechwan, near Wenchuan Hsien, a clump of old pine has been found around a lamasary.

In Kweichow province this pine is also quite common. In association with *Phyllostachys* and Chinese fir [*Cunninghamia*] it forms mixed forest in the lower valley of the Wu Kiang, and is also associated with oaks in the central valley. On the upper Wu Kiang above an altitude of 2,000 meters it decreases as the temperature becomes lower. Along the Yun Kiang the warm and moist climate provides suitable conditions for pine growth. Mixed forest of this pine with cypresses and broadleaved trees becomes common along the course of the Chishe or the Red River, which flows northeastward [?] to southern Szechwan. In the eastern part of the province where plantations of Chinese fir are both common and intensive, the red pine is grown only on poor, windy sites.

In the mountainous regions of western Hupeh, below the altitude of 1,500 meters this pine has been found mixed with hardwoods.

It occurs in the northern part of the island of Formosa, scattered in groups as a second-growth forest, and also on the coastal hills in the Taito prefecture. It is found also in the hills of Hainan island (Merrill, 1927). The altitudinal range of this pine in Formosa is between 300 and 1300 m; the general altitudinal range of *P. massoniana* is between 0 and 2000 m.

## 95. Pinus densiflora Sieb. & Zucc.

*Pinus densiflora* is known as "Japanese red pine." Its Japanese name is "*akamatsu*." Its area includes three of the main islands of Japan— Honshu, Shikoku, and Kyushu. Its northern limit is on the fourth, Hokkaido, at Mount Taramui, about 42° 41′ north. Its southern limit is on the island of Hakushima, near the southern tip of Kyushu. It also grows on the islands of the Tsushima group and on Oki Retto island.

**Plate 3–66.** *Left: P. densiflora* No. 95 in Tomakomai National Forest, Japan. Altitude 120 m. *Right: P. thunbergii* No. 97 in Kumamoto National Forest, Japan. (Photos by Japanese Forest Agency.)

On the mainland, *P. densiflora* is found in Korea and in Kiangsu and Shantung provinces of China. (See map, Fig. 3–50.)

Its altitudinal range (in Japan) is from sea level to 2300 m (Hayashi, 1952).

It crosses naturally with *P. thunbergii* No. 97 (Nakamura, 1955). It has been crossed with *P. sylvestris* No. 69, *P. taiwanensis,* and *P. thunbergii* (Wright, 1953), as well as with *P. nigra* No. 74 (Liddicoet and Righter, 1960).

### 96. *Pinus funebris* Kom.

*Pinus funebris* is closely related to *P. densiflora*. Its area is in northern Korea and adjacent parts of the Russian Maritime Province from the Korean border to the north shore of Lake Khanka. It was considered by Shaw (1914) as *P. sinensis* (i.e., *P. tabulaeformis*); other investigators (Komarov, 1934) have placed it closer to *P. densiflora*. It is a pine of low elevations (perhaps below 600 m); near the Russian-Korean border, it occurs at sea level. (See map, Fig. 3–50.)

## 97. Pinus thunbergii Parl.

*Pinus thunbergii* is Japanese black pine, or *karamatsu*. It grows predominantly along the coasts of Honshu, Shikoku, and Kyushu. It also occurs on the coast of southern Korea. Its northern limit is at about 41° 34′ north; its southern limit is on Takara island, south of Kyushu, at 29° north. Its range of vertical distribution in northern and middle Honshu is from sea level to 700 m and farther south up to 950 m (Hayashi, 1952). It hybridizes naturally with *P. densiflora* No. 95 (Nakamura, 1955).

The three pines to be discussed next—*P. luchuensis* No. 98, *P. taiwanensis* No. 99, and *P. hwangshanensis* No. 100—are considered by some scholars as one species—*P. luchuensis*—the other two being mere geographical races. Wu (1947) said that, in herbaria, all three look alike. I did not see living *P. hwangshanensis* during my visit to eastern Asia in 1961, but I saw *P. luchuensis* and *P. taiwanensis*. Under natural conditions, these two pines look quite different. I am inclined to consider the three pines as valid species: *Pinus luchuensis* Mayr, *P. taiwanensis* Hayata, and *P. hwangshanensis* Hsia. No doubt they are closely related, and possibly *P. taiwanensis* and *P. hwangshanensis* are closer to each other than to *P. luchuensis*. (See map, Fig, 3–50.)

## 98. Pinus luchuensis Mayr

*Pinus luchuensis* is a pine of Okinawa and of adjacent islands of the Ryukyu chain, which is located between Japan and Formosa (see map, Fig. 3–50). On the northernmost of the Ryukyu Islands—Oshima—the highest point is at about 700 m. From the sea to the mountain slopes, the land appeared to Wilson (1920) to be well forested, chiefly with pine. During World War II, most pine forests on Okinawa were destroyed. On the southern islands of the group, the forests were damaged less.

In the Ryukyu Islands, *P. luchuensis* is a tree of low elevation, usually of poor form, with irregular and knotty stems because of winds. In Formosa, where *P. luchuensis* is planted at low elevations—from sea level to 1000 m—it is a much better looking tree than in Okinawa but inferior to *P. taiwanensis* No. 99. (See Chapter 8, page 515.)

## 99. Pinus taiwanensis Hayata

*Pinus taiwanensis* is a pine of Formosa (Taiwan). It often forms pure stands over large areas in central ranges of the island, at elevations

**Plate 3–67.** *Left: P. luchuensis* No. 98 at sea level, Okinawa, Ryukyu Islands. (Photo by T. Wolf.) *Right: P. taiwanensis* No. 99, Ta Shu Shan, Formosa. Altitude about 2000 m. (Photo by Taiwan Forest Research Institute.)

of from 750 to 2800 m. It is a tree with a straight trunk, up to 80 cm in diameter and 35 m in height, not like the crooked and smaller *P. luchuensis.* (See map, Fig. 3–50.)

## 100. *Pinus hwangshanensis* Hsia

*Pinus hwangshanensis* is a pine of east-central China. It occurs west of western Hupeh at altitudes of about 1800 to 2400 m and extends south through Hunan, east to Kiangsi and Fukien, and then northeast through Chekiang and westward through Anhwei to Hupeh. It is uniformly confined to the higher elevations (above 900 m) and is of spotty distribution, being separated by distances of up to hundreds of miles (Wu, 1947). (See map, Fig. 3–50.)

## 101. *Pinus merkusii* De Vries

*Pinus merkusii* (see map, Fig. 3–50) grows in the Southern Shan States of Burma, at elevations of about 150 to 750 m. Its northern limits there are at about 20° north. In the hills between the Sittang and Salween rivers of Burma, and in northern Thailand, it is found in patches, or as single trees, below *P. khasya,* at elevations of 100 to 1000 m. It occurs sporadically in small groves near the Laotian border, east of Pitsanlooke, and also near Kanchanaburi, in the Bilauk Taung Range, about 175 m almost due west from Bangkok. In northern Thailand, I encountered *P. merkusii* in 1961 on the road from Chiang Mai to the Burmese border. I observed scattered mature and young trees intermixed with scrubby forest of oak, *Shorea,* and *Dipterocarpus.* It was February, a dry season of the year, and the soil, almost pure silica, was extremely dusty and appeared to be not too fertile. The elevation of the place was about 1000 to 1100 m.

The pine groves I saw between Pitsanlooke and Petchabam province, in central Thailand, not far from the Laotian border, were extensive pure stands of overmature trees much abused by man. Patches of *P. merkusii* are also found in the easternmost part of Thailand, extending along the fifteenth parallel across the Mekong to adjacent parts of Laos. In the central part of Laos, *P. merkusii* groves occur above Vientiane at 700 m and east of Xieng Khouang at similar altitudes. In the northeastern-most corner of Laos, in the region of Muong On Neua, there is a large forest of *P. merkusii*—about 10,000 ha. At a locality north of Paksé, it grows between 250 and 300 m above sea level. On the plateau Ta Hoi it is found together with *Dipterocarpus* at about 600 m ( Vidal, 1934–60).

In Cambodia, *P. merkusii* grows scattered with hardwoods in one spot not far from its occurrence in southeastern central Thailand (Sisaket) along the fourteenth parallel. Elevations of *P. merkusii* there are from 100 to 300 m. Farther south, in Pursat province, not far south of Tonle Sap (i.e., Lake Sap), at about the same elevation, is a stand of scattered *P. merkusii* mixed with deciduous hardwoods.

The third known locality of *P. merkusii* in Cambodia is on a high plateau ( 1000 m above sea level) at Kiri Rom in the southwestern part of the country (approximate latitude 12° 20′ north), where the pine grows in almost pure stands. No other pines have yet been found in Cambodia,[*] but possibly *P. khasya* might be discovered there.

In Viet Nam, *P. merkusii* is found on the plateau around Dalat, at elevations of about 500 to 1200 m. Generally, it grows on level ground, whereas *P. khasya* prefers slopes. According to Maurice Schmid,[†] *P. merkusii* may be found rarely at elevations below 500 m, but the trees there are generally scrubby and malformed. It may descend in places almost to sea level. At elevations of between 800 and 1200 m, it often grows together with *P. khasya,* but it seems that the two pines prefer different sites. As in many other places of Indochina, *Dipterocarpus obtusifolius* is a constant companion of *P. merkusii.* (See map, Fig. 3–51.)

[*] Information supplied by Cambodian Forest Service on January 21, 1961, courtesy of U.S. Operation Mission to Cambodia, Walter S. Astle, Forestry Advisor.

[†] Professor of Forestry, School of Agriculture and Forestry, Bao-Lôc, Lam Dong, Viet Nam. Personal communication.

**Plate 3–68.** *Pinus merkusii* No. 101. *Top:* in northwestern Thailand, near the southern border of the Shan States, of Burma. Altitude about 1000 m. (Photo by N. T. Mirov.) *Bottom:* tapped for oleoresin production in northern Viet Nam; note that the French method of tapping is used. (Photo courtesy A. A. Iatsenko-Khmelevsky.)

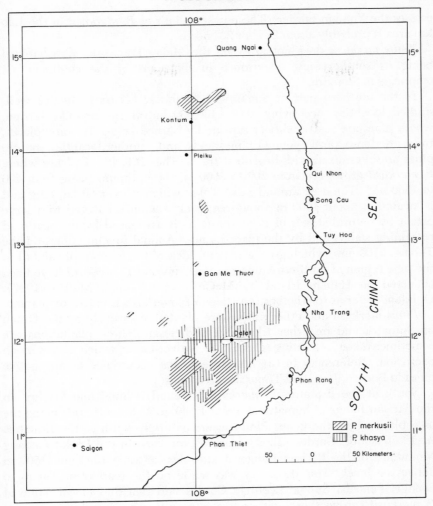

**Fig. 3–51.** *Pinus merkusii* De Vriese No. 101 and *P. khasya* Royle No. 104 in southern Viet Nam.

Farther north, *P. merkusii* grows sporadically in the mountains of Viet Nam, between the sea and the Laotian border, where some parts of the country have not yet been sufficiently explored.

On the parallel of Ho Thuong, there are considerable forests of this pine. Still farther north, *P. merkusii* is found in the Red River area at Lao Kai, close to the border of Yunnan. This locality is slightly farther north than the Muong Ou Nua locality of northern Laos and thus apparently is the northernmost known limit of *P. merkusii*. Possibly it crosses the Yunnan border. The northern limit of *P. merkusii* in the Lao Kai area is probably about 22½° or 23° north.

*Pinus merkusii* does not grow on the Malay Peninsula, Kanchanburi being its southernmost occurrence in that part of the continent. It reappears in Sumatra.

In the northern part of Sumatra, *P. merkusii* occurs in twelve well-studied localities, occupying about 130,000 ha. of savanna-like terrain, where pines are scattered over repeatedly burned areas. In some places, there are dense, pure (young) pine stands, and, in other localities, mature pines are intermixed with broadleaf trees. The altitudes of places where *P. merkusii* grows are from 200 to 2000 m, the optimum being from 400 to 1500 m.\* The area around Lake Toba, which is over 80 km long and is located at about 1000 m above sea level, was once covered to a large extent by natural stands of *P. merkusii,* as is evidenced by the scattered remaining stands and by the place names. Annual precipitation at Lake Toba is 2100 mm, which gives a general idea of the amount of rainfall in the pine region of northern Sumatra. Specimens of *P. merkusii* have been collected on Hainan island by McClure and Tsang (Merrill, 1927). Opinions differ as to whether the Hainan *P. merkusii* is native or planted.

*Pinus merkusii* and other pines were planted extensively by the Dutch on Sumatra and on other islands of Indonesia. These plantations are sometimes taken by visiting scientists as native stands, which causes much confusion. References in the literature to the occurrence of any native pines in Borneo, Java, and Timor are erroneous.

South of the Equator, *P. merkusii* is found in only one locality—in the Barisan Range of Sumatra at about 1° 40′ to 2° 6′ south, this being the only place where the genus *Pinus* occurs naturally south of the Equator. At 1° 55′ south, Cordes (1866) found *P. merkusii* in the Boekit Gedang Mountains of the Barisan Range at altitudes between 1000 and 1500 m above sea level. This discovery was made on the road from Tapan to Soengei Penoeh (Sungai Penuh). Cordes said that Sigi (local name of *P. merkusii*) grows there neither as a solitary tree nor in extensive stands but, rather, in groups among other trees. This locality is rather isolated; it is about 500 km from the nearest location in northern Sumatra. Cordes was not sure how far south of the road *P. merkusii* extended, but later collections indicate that it does not extend very far. Cordes' report of occurrence of *P. merkusii* has been questioned by several prominent botanists, but the investigations by the Dutch, and most recently by Indonesian explorers, supported by herbarium material, have verified Cordes' findings.† According to Van Steenis, *P. merkusii* in the Barisan

---

\* Unpublished report prepared by E. J. van Alphen de Veer, Forest Research Institute, Bogor, Java, Indonesia, obtained during my visit there in 1961.

† Personal communication with Professor C. C. G. T. Van Steenis and my study of collections at Herbarium Bogoriense with the kind permission of Anwari Dilmi, Director.

**Plate 3-69.** *Pinus merkusii* No. 101 on the island of Mindoro, in the Philippines. This is a scattered natural stand with grass ground cover, burned annually. (Photo by C. B. Tadeo, Philippine Bureau of Forestry.)

Range, at 2° 6′ south, is found on Mount Penawar, near Lake Kerintji, at 1500 to 2000 m above sea level.

*Pinus merkusii* is also found in two places in the Philippines—one on the island of Mindoro and the other in western Luzon. On Mindoro, *P. merkusii* grows in the northwestern part of the island. There, southwest of the high mountain chain extending north and south from Mount Halcon, *P. merkusii* is found in scattered groves along the ridges and slopes at about 300 m. The location is well drained and often extremely dry. In the vicinity of Santa Cruz, which is in the southern part of the pine's range, it descends to as low as 60 m (possibly even lower) above sea level. At the northern limit, it does not go lower than 900 m. Annual burning of the area destroys not only herbaceous vegetation but also the pine seedlings, so there is very little reproduction and no young pines—only overmature, widely scattered trees. A few other tree species occupy the bottom of "moist runs and stream valleys" (Merritt, 1908).

The other location is in the lower altitudes of the Zambales Mountains, which extend along the South China Sea coast from north of Manila to Lingayen Gulf. I visited this location in 1961. In the Zambales Moun-

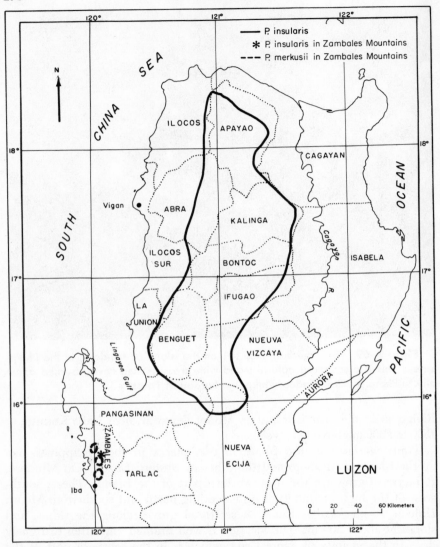

**Fig. 3–52.** *Pinus merkusii* De Vriese No. 101 and *P. insularis* Endlich. No. 105 on Luzon, in the Philippines.

tains, *P. merkusii* is found in three separate places, each occupying perhaps several square miles. These three places are approximately at the latitudes of (1) Candellaria, (2) Masinloc, and (3) Palauig (settlements along the coastal highway north from Iba). The pines are found along the crest and the knolls of the foothills of the mountains. (See map, Fig.

3–52.) Annual precipitation in these foothills is about 95 to 125 cm a year, but, perhaps because I visited this area during the dry season, the gravelly red ground looked extremely dry to me.

The main Zambales range is no higher than 1200 m and is covered with tropical broadleaf forest. The pine groves are at elevations of between 150 and 300 m, and some trees even are found at, or about, 90 to 100 m of altitude. These foothills are not more than 16 or 18 km from the coast of the South China Sea, and I could discern pines on the crests from the coastal highway between Palauig and Candellaria. The hills looked relatively bare; mature pines, with the crowns of some scorched by fire, were scattered in a parklike manner. Because of repeated burning, the ground was ashy with tufts of newly sprouted grasses (*Themeda triandra* and *Imperata* sp.). There were no pine seedlings and no young pines—only in the dry gulches were there some scrubby broadleaf trees.

The altitudinal range of *P. merkusii*, in round figures, is between 50 and 2000 m.

*Pinus merkusii* is not a very variable pine. It is easily recognizable throughout its discontinuous range by its two-needle clusters and by its narrow, cylindrical cones. Only in northern Viet Nam (northeast of the Red River) does it begin to look sufficiently different to be called "*Pinus tonkinensis*" (Chevalier, 1944).

In Sumatra, *P. merkusii* of different localities showed difference in response to insect attacks (Schütt, 1958). It is doubtful if these different populations are distinct races.

## 102. *Pinus tabulaeformis* Carrière

In Shaw's monograph (1914), *P. tabulaeformis* is called "*Pinus sinensis*." In the light of more recent investigations (Wu, 1947), it is preferable to use the name "*Pinus tabulaeformis*." The following account of its distribution (see map, Fig. 3–50, page 276) is based on information from Wu (1947):

*Pinus tabulaeformis* Carr. grows over a vast area in northern and north-central China. On the northern border of the western portion it is bounded by the dry climate. In central China the Han River is the demarcation between the region of *P. tabulaeformis* and that of *P. massoniana*. *P. tabulaeformis* extends, however, further south along the southwestern highland to northern Szechwan and northern Yunnan, and contacts with Yunnan pine [*P. yunnanensis* No. 103] forming an overlapping zone where the natural hybrid pine, *Pinus densata* Masters, grows. On the east side *P. tabulaeformis* extends to southern Manchuria limited more or less by the Liao Ho River.

In northwestern China, on the border of steppe and desert, *P. tabulaeformis* is found on the Ala Shan Range [at 1950 to 2500 m]. This mountain is now entirely separated from the main southern region of the pine by the arid desert

**Plate 3–70.** *Pinus tabulaeformis* No. 102 near Mao Chow, western Szechwan, China. Altitude 1800 m. (Photo by E. H. Wilson. Courtesy Arnold Arboretum, Jamaica Plain, Massachusetts.)

or semiarid steppe. The mountains on which this pine grows are the Shinlun Shan and Lien Cheng. They are adjacent to Ala Shan and are separated from one another by a distance of over 500 kilometers.

The distribution of *Pinus tabulaeformis* becomes more continuous as it extends eastward and southward. Comparatively extensive pine forests of this species, associated with *Pinus armandi* were found among the Tsingling Range, in southeastern Kansu [from 1000 to 2700 m altitude]. It has been reported that this pine grows among the Ta Pa Shan, and Chungnan Shan in Shensi. In Honan province, native forests of *P. tabulaeformis* have been badly destroyed.

*P. tabulaeformis* is also found in Sun Shan along the middle altitudinal belt. It grows on Taihang Shan within an altitude of 7,000–8,000 feet [from about 2100 to 2400 m]. *P. tabulaeformis* has also been found in the Mien Shan district and in Wu Tai Shan of Shansi province [growing in some places together with *P. bungeana* No. 87].

In Hopeh the distribution of *Pinus tabulaeformis* has a greater altitude range, beginning from level land [which is about 50 m above sea level, near Peking] up to 1400 m. Natural forests are found at Yang-Chia-Ping and Nan-Tai Shan on rocky dry sites. On northern slopes they form dense stands; on southern slopes they exist as scattered open stands. This pine extends eastward and northward to Jehol and Liaoning.

*Pinus tabulaeformis* is found in Maengsan county, Pyong Nam province, Korea, but, according to Korean foresters (K. B. Yim, personal communication October 15, 1962), this pine was introduced to Korea from northern China some 200 years ago.

*Pinus tabulaeformis* is an extremely variable species for which several varieties are recognized (Wu, 1947):

| Variety | Habitat |
|---|---|
| *mukdensis* Uyeki | Extreme east |
| *rubescens* Uyeki | Extreme east |
| *pseudosylvestris* Wu | Desert ranges of southern part of Outer Mongolia |
| *leucosperma* (Mas.) Wu | Alpine region of W. Kansu |
| *wilsoni,* forma *tokunagii* Wu | Ninghsia, Jehol, Hopeh |
| *gracilifolia* Wu | Scattered over the provinces of Kansu, Shansi, and Hopeh |

The variety *pseudosylvestris* possibly is a hybrid between *P. tabulaeformis* and *P. sylvestris* No. 69. The discontinuous distribution of *P. tabulaeformis* in the northwestern part of its region was attributed by Wu (1947) to the change of climate following the Ice Age. On the other hand, discontinuous distribution in the eastern part of its area may have been caused by human activities. Wu suggested that varieties of *P. tabulaeformis* are the result of climatic change in past geological time.

The altitudinal range of *P. tabulaeformis* appears to lie between 50 m and 3000 m. The reported hybrid between *P. tabulaeformis* and *P. bungeana* No. 87 (Teng, 1941) found in Honan is questionable. Probably it is a variety, *taihanshanensis* Yao, of *P. tabulaeformis*, described by Yao (1936).

Next to be considered are three diploxylon pines of southeastern Asia whose areas are difficult to ascertain and whose taxonomic relationship is still unsettled. These pines are *P. yunnanensis* No. 103, *P. khasya* No. 104, and *P. insularis* No. 105. In herbaria, the three pines are indistinguishable (Wu, 1956); on the basis of their geographical distribution, they perhaps deserve to be considered separate species. The difficulty of establishing the area of *P. yunnanensis* is that this pine merges into *P. khasya*, and there is an opinion (Wu, 1947) that *P. yunnanensis* and *P. khasya* of Khasi Hills, Assam, Naga Hills, Upper Burma, the Shan States, and adjacent parts of Thailand, and even perhaps, east-central Laos, are one species. On the other hand, Troup (1921) mentioned that turpentine of this pine from Assam contains a higher proportion of high-boiling-point terpenes than that of the pine from Burma, which indicates that *P. khasya* of Assam might be biologically different from the pine of Burma and thus from the pine of Yunnan. (See Chapter 9, page 554.)

### 103. *Pinus yunnanensis* Franchet

*Pinus yunnanensis* is a pine of the Yunnan-Kweichow Plateau of southwestern China. It occurs throughout the province of Yunnan, except the alpine region of the extreme northwestern corner, which is occupied by a putative hybrid between *P. yunnanensis* and *P. tabulae-formis* known as *P. densata* Masters, which, according to Wang, grows at an approximate altitude of 3900 m (Wang, 1961). Also there is no *P. yunnanensis* in the lowlands and ravines along deep mountain gorges at the southern and southwestern borders of Yunnan. It extends to the adjacent (southwestern) part of Kweichow, the southeastern part of Sikang, and a small part of southern Szechwan (Wu, 1947).

In the west, its area merges into that of *P. khasya*, and Wu (1947) has held the opinion that the two pines are actually the same species. However, this opinion is not shared by all botanists. In the vicinity of Kunming, Fedorov and his co-authors (1956) observed *P. yunnanensis* growing together with *P. armandi, Keteleeria*, and some broadleaf trees. They wrote that, to the southwest, toward Puerh, *P. yunnanensis* merges into *P. khasya*. Southwest of Kunming, toward the town of Yuankiang, which is on the Red River where the Yunnan Plateau is much dissected and the mountains are low, elevations run from 1500 to 3000 m, descending in the river valleys to 1000 m and, closer to the Red River itself, even to 500 m or lower. Along the road between the two towns, which runs at elevations of 1000 to 2000 m, there are parklike pine forests of *P. yunnanensis*—in places dense and extensive, but near habitations poor and badly culled (Lavrenko, 1960).

The altitudinal range of *P. yunnanensis* lies between 2750 and 3400 m (Wu, 1947; Wang, 1961). Wang mentioned that, on the tableland of central Yunnan, it attains its best development at 1600 to 2600 m either in pure stands or with *Keteleeria davidiana*. Forrest (as reported by Wu, 1947) found this pine on the eastern slopes of the Tali Range, in central Yunnan, at altitudes of 1700 to 3350 m.

In Sikang, pure forests of this pine are found between 2200 and 3500 m. We must assume that the altitudinal range of *P. yunnanensis* is between 1500 and 3500 m.

As has been mentioned above, *P. yunnanensis* possibly hybridizes naturally with *P. tabulaeformis* No. 102 (see map, Fig. 3–50, page 276).

## 104. *Pinus khasya* Royle *

*Pinus khasya* is known by this name in India, Thailand, Laos, and southern Viet Nam. In Burma, it is always called *"Pinus insularis"* (No. 105).

*Pinus khasya* extends from the mountains of the Indian Khasi states just east and south of the big bend of the Brahmaputra River (approximately 91° east; approximately 25° to 26° north) northeastward through the Naga Hills of Assam and farther, toward southeastern Sikang and Yunnan, merging gradually into the *P. yunnanensis* area. To the southeast of Khasi country, it extends to Manipur, to the mountains of Upper Burma, the Chin Hills, the Shan States, and the mountains between the Sittang and Salween rivers. It continues through Karenni country (still in Burma) to adjacent parts of Thailand and to Laos (in the vicinity of Luang Prabang and east of Xieng Khouang). Then, it reappears in the mountains of southern Viet Nam, not less than 800 km southeast of Xieng Khouang, approximately between 12° 30′ and 13° 45′ north and between 108° and 109° east (see map, Fig. 3–51, page 287).

In northern Thailand, across the Burmese border, *P. khasya* occurs in small patches, mostly in admixture with *Shorea*, oak, and *Dipterocarpus*. I visited that part of its general area during the dry (winter) season of 1961. The countryside looked extremely dry; the road, dusty; a bench mark on a summit amidst pines indicated 1347 m. Khasya pines appeared tall and stately, scattered among other drought-enduring trees, never forming pure stands. Only on the north slopes did the pines appear to be more prominent. At lower altitudes in some localities, there was *P. merkusii* No. 101.

Generally, in northern Thailand and in Laos, *P. khasya* grows only in patches in a few localities at elevations of, in the former, 1200 to 1400

---

* The name of this pine (like many names in that part of the world) is spelled in several different ways: *"khasya* Royle," *"keseya* Royle," *"kasya* Parl.," *"khasyana* Griffith," *"khasia* Engelm."

**Plate 3–71.** *Pinus khasya* No. 104. *Left:* at Kalaw, Southern Shan States, Burma. Altitude 1370 m. (Photo by E. W. Shields.) *Right:* on the Phukradung Plateau, Loey province, northeastern Thailand. Altitude 1250 m. (Photo by Thailand Royal Forest Department.)

m (my personal observation) and, in the latter, about 1000 to 1500 m near Xieng Khouang and somewhat lower (800 m) northwest of Luang Prabang.

In the Khasi Hills, *P. khasya* occurs at elevations of about 760 to 1900 m, thriving best at from 1200 to about 1500 m. It forms pure forests on plateaus and mountain slopes, but in damp places and along the banks of streams it is represented by scattered trees among broadleaf species (Troup, 1921).

In the Chin Hills, *P. khasya* forms forests from approximately 1300 to over 2400 m. There it usually grows with oak, alder, and other broadleaf trees. Between the Sittang and Salween rivers, it occurs between about 760 and 900 m, sometimes in pure stands but more often mixed with oaks and other hardwoods.

In the Northern Shan States, it is generally of scattered distribution, but, in the Southern Shan States, it forms rather large pure stands such as those in the former Lai Hka and Mong Kung states, at elevations of 1200 to 1800 m.

In central Viet Nam, *P. khasya* is scattered in the mountains at altitudes between 600 and 1800 m. At elevations of from 600 up to 1200 m, it is often associated with *P. merkusii*.

To sum up, the altitudinal range of *P. khasya* is between 600 and 2450 m.

*Pinus khasya* penetrates to Yunnan, where it forms groves resembling those of Laos, Thailand, Upper Burma, and Viet Nam (Fedorov *et al.,* 1956). Fedorov wrote that these pine groves of Yunnan reminded him of the pine woods of northern countries.

This rather lengthy description of *P. khasya* was necessitated by its importance for understanding of the evolution of pines in southeastern Asia. Apparently, this pine's spotty distribution and disjunct area are not necessarily results of human activity alone, but, rather, they reflect the part played by pines in the flora of the Tertiary period. This is clearly evident in southeastern Asia. (See maps, Figs. 3–50 and 3–51.)

## 105. *Pinus insularis* Endlich

*Pinus insularis* is known in the literature as "benguet pine." It forms pure, well-stocked, and extensive forests in the highlands of northern Luzon (i.e., the mountain provinces: Ilocos Sur, Abra, Nueva Viscaya, Nueva Ecija, Pangasinan, La Union, and Ilocos Norte). Reference to occurrence of *P. insularis* in Timor by Pilger is "a most aberrant and doubtless wrong record," according to Van Steenis (1950). Merrill found this pine in the Zambales Mountains (Foxworthy, 1911). *Pinus insularis* is considered by many to be the same species as *P. khasya*. Wu (1947) has held that *P. yunnanensis* should also be called *"Pinus insularis."* This problem is discussed further in Chapter 9, pages 553–554. The altitudinal range of *P. insularis* is from about 1000 to 2700 m, occasionally as high as 3000 m. It reproduces well and appears to be aggressive and expanding. It came to Luzon from the mainland of Asia (Merrill, 1926) either at the end of the Tertiary or, most likely, much later, during the cool periods at the time of the Ice Age in the north (cf. Vidal, 1934–60). (See maps, Figs. 3–50, 3–52, 3–53.)

## Pines of Uncertain Taxonomic Position

There are, in southeastern Asia, several more pines whose taxonomic positions are uncertain. These will be more fully discussed in Chapter 9.

*"Pin du moyen Annam"* (Ferré, 1960), a pine collected by Chevalier (foliage only) between Hué and Bolovens, in Viet Nam, latitude 15° 30' north (and in other localities) and reported by him to be *P. armandi* No. 86, is, in the opinion of De Ferré, not *P. armandi* but a pine more closely related to *P. pentaphylla* No. 83. It was found at an altitude of

**Plate 3–72.** *Pinus insularis* No. 105 at Senepsep, Benguet, Mountain Province, Luzon, Philippines. Altitude 2200 m. (Photo by Philippine Bureau of Forestry.)

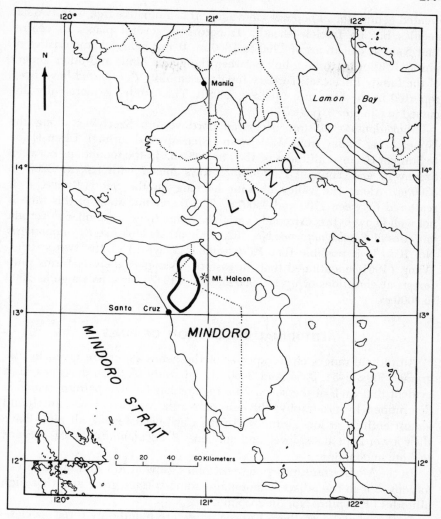

**Fig. 3–53.** *Pinus insularis* Endlich. No. 105 on Mindoro, in the Philippines.

1500 m. In the absence of cones from Chevalier's collection, it is impossible to describe this pine completely. It should be mentioned that the country north of Dalat, say, above the fourteenth parallel, has not been explored well by botanists. (See map, Fig. 3–47, page 264.)

*Pinus krempfii* Lecomte, discovered by Krempf in 1921 in southern Viet Nam, is a conifer growing in mixed broadleaf forests, occasionally together with *P. merkusii* and *P. khasya*, north and northeast of Dalat. It has been tentatively moved from the genus *Pinus* into the newly

created genus *Ducampopinus* Chevalier. It is a pinelike tree with two flat
needles but no fascicle sheath. It occurs in several places in central
Viet Nam at elevations of 1200 to 1800 m. It has many characteristics of
pines. It appears to be a link between the genus *Pinus* and other genera
of the family Pinaceae. Tertiary fossils resembling *P. krempfii* have been
reported in the literature (Jeffrey, 1908). This conifer is more fully discussed in Chapter 9, page 540.

*Pinus densata* Masters occurs in northwestern Szechwan along the
Upper Ming Valley from Wanchwan Hsien upward through Lifen Hsien
to Sunpan Hsien at altitudes of 1550 to 3000 m. In the mountains between
Szechwan and Yunnan, *P. densata* grows mixed with oak at 3200 to
3800 m. Along the valley of Kingshakiang, in the Snow Range, it is
scattered between 2700 and 3500 m. The taxonomic staus of this pine is
not well known. It is extremely variable. Some trees are similar to certain
varieties of *P. tabulaeformis* No. 102, while others look like *P. yunnanensis*
No. 103. It is possible that *P. densata* is a hybrid of the two species.
Wang (1961) mentioned that, in eastern Sikang, *P. densata* forms pure
forests at elevations of up to 3900 m. Wu (1947) gave its range as 2500
to 4000 m.

## ALTITUDINAL DISTRIBUTION OF PINES

Altitudinal ranges of 105 species of the genus *Pinus* are given in diagrams (Figs. 3–54, 3–55, and 3–56 *). In study of these diagrams, it is
evident that each of the seven pine regions has its own pattern, which is
determined by orography. In eastern North America, pines are found
almost entirely at low altitudes. In the Caribbean region, all pines have
their lower limit at sea level, and only one, *P. occidentalis* No. 64, ascends
to high mountains.

In the Mediterranean region, most pines grow at low and medium elevations, but in the adjacent mountains some species grow at rather high
altitudes (*P. cembra* No. 70: 2585 m).

In the whole of northern Eurasia, there are found only three species—
*P. sibirica* No. 67, *P. pumila* No. 68, and *P. sylvestris* No. 69, all having a
wide altitudinal range.

Vertical distribution of pines in eastern Asia is rather diverse; there
are some pines of low elevations descending to, or almost to, sea level.
These are pines growing in areas that appeared above the sea relatively
recently: shores of the Sea of Japan, Ryukyus, coastal parts of southern
China, and north to the Maritime Province of Russia. At the same time,
some pines occur in the very high altitudes of the relatively recently

* Very few pines grow exactly at sea level. In the diagrams, all species descending
below 150 m are considered to have their lower limit at sea level.

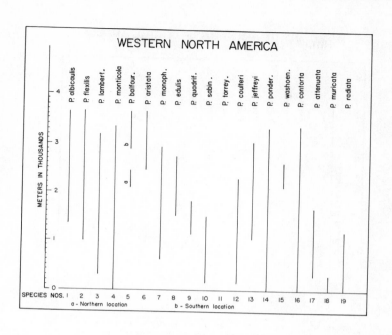

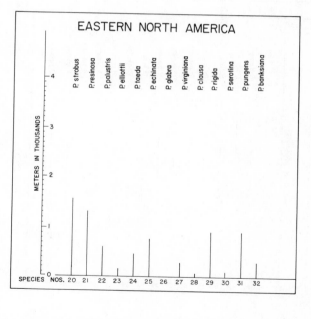

**Fig. 3–54.** Altitudinal ranges of individual pine species of western North America and eastern North America.

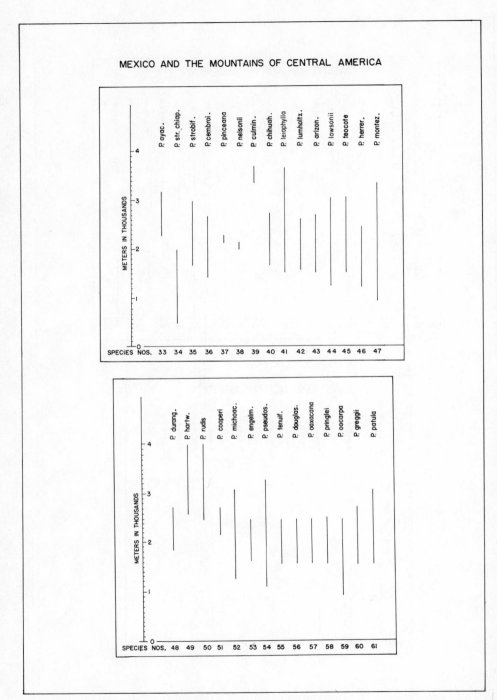

**Fig. 3—55.** Altitudinal ranges of individual pine species of Mexico and the mountains of Central America.

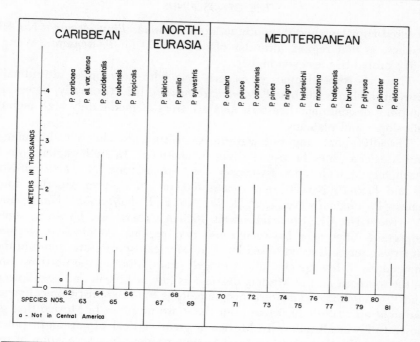

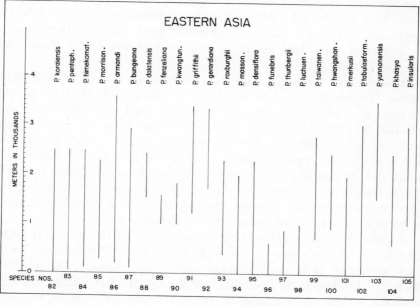

**Fig. 3–56.** Altitudinal ranges of individual pine species of the Caribbean region, northern Eurasia, the Mediterranean region, and eastern Asia.

303

elevated Himalaya and its continuation in Yunnan. *Pinus armandi* No. 86 reaches, in that region, altitudes of about 3500 m; *P. densata* (Wang, 1961) probably goes even higher.

There are several pines in eastern Asia with very broad altitudinal-distribution limits, such as *P. tabulaeformis* No. 102. Generally, however, the pines of continental eastern Asia are trees of moderately high mountain slopes and plateaus.

The altitudinal ranges of western American (i.e., chiefly Californian) and Mexican pines have one thing in common. In both regions pines reach very high altitudes; two species of Mexican pines (*P. hartwegii* No. 49 and *P. rudis* No. 50) may reach 4000 m. In western America, four pines (*P. albicaulis* No. 1, *P. flexilis* No. 2, *P. balfouriana* No. 5, and *P. aristata* No. 6) also reach about 4000 m. There are, however, some important differences between these two regions. While five western American pines descend to sea level, all Mexican species are found in the mountains. A few species, and strangely enough not in the northern but in the southern part of Mexico, descend as low as 1200 m and even lower, and *P. strobus* var. *chiapensis* occasionally is found amidst tropical vegetation at an altitude of 500 m. But there are no pines in Mexico that go down to lower altitudes. In Mexico, a great vertical expansion of pines, together with other environmental factors, resulted in rejuvenation of the genus that manifested itself in frequent intercrossing among different species, in extensive variability within the species, and in formation of an important secondary center of evolution of the genus *Pinus* (see Chapter 4, pages 341–44).

It is perhaps more revealing to compare not the entire altitudinal ranges of pine species but the zones of their optimal development. Middle points of vertical distribution of 107 species are given in Table 3–9 and are plotted in a chart, Fig. 3–57. In this chart, to the 105 pines accepted by the author as valid species are added 2 more pines: The first is *P. densata*, which usually is considered as a hybrid between *P. tabulaeformis* and *P. yunnanensis*, but whose altitudinal range surpasses that of both "parent" species (see page 300). The other pine added, the "pin du moyen Annam" (see page 545), has not yet been fully described as a valid species, but all indications are that it is one.

To take the middle point of altitudinal ranges of the species is rather arbitrary. Our own experience with the Pacific Coast *P. ponderosa* No. 14 (i.e., excluding its Rocky Mountain variety *scopulorum*) (Mirov, Duffield, and Liddicoet, 1952) shows that the optimal habitat for this pine is in the middle of its altitudinal range. It may be possible, however, that for at least some other pines the optimal habitat lies in somewhat lower altitudes than the midway point. Very little information is available on this subject. Figure 3–57 shows that, out of 107 species (including

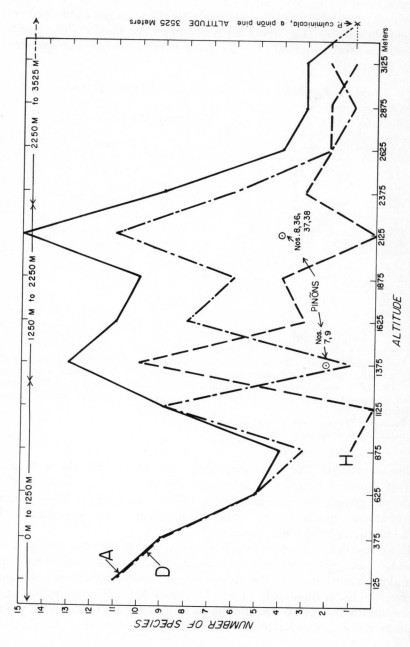

**Fig. 3–57.** Midpoints of altitudinal ranges of haploxylon pines (*H*), diploxylon pines (*D*), and all species of pines (*A*).

305

*P. densata* and De Ferré's "pin du moyen Annam"), only 20 (i.e., about 19 per cent) have their middle points of altitudinal ranges above 2250 m. Thirty-eight species (i.e., about 35 per cent) have their middle points between sea level and 1250 m; these pines may be classified as growing

**Table 3–9.** Middle Points of Altitudinal Distribution of Pines

| Middle Points of Altitudinal Ranges (Meters) | All Species | Haploxylon Pines | | Diploxylon Pines |
|:---:|:---:|:---:|:---:|:---:|
| | | Except Piñons | Piñons [a] | |
| 125 | 11 | | | 11 |
| 375 | 9 | | | 9 |
| 625 | 5 | | | 5 |
| 875 | 4 | 1 | | 3 |
| 1125 | 9 | 0 | | 9 |
| 1375 | 13 | 10 | 2 | 1 |
| 1625 | 11 | 3[b] | 0 | 8 |
| 1875 | 10 | 4 | | 6 |
| 2125 | 15 | 0 | 4 | 11 |
| 2375 | 9 | 3 | | 6 |
| 2625 | 4 | 2 | | 2 |
| 2875 | 3 | 2 | | 1[c] |
| 3125 | 3 | 1 | | 2 |
| 3375 | 1[a] | | 1[a] | |
| Total | 107 | 26 | 7 | 74 |

[a] Piñon pines are generally classified under haploxylon pines. However, they constitute a distinct geographical group of western American–Mexican arid-environment pines. One of them—*P. culminicola*—is found in an isolated locality in northeastern Mexico at an exceptionally high altitude for piñons; it is indicated on the chart separately.

[b] Including *"pin du moyen Annam."*

[c] Including *P. densata.*

at low elevations. The remaining 49 species, comprising about 46 per cent of the total number of species of the genus *Pinus*, have middle points of vertical distribution between 1250 m and 2250 m. Thus, about half of all pine species can be considered as having their optimal habitats in the moderately high mountains.

If we segregate all pines into haploxylon and diploxylon groups and consider piñon pines separately from haploxylon pines, we note that altitudinal distribution of the three groups follows somewhat different courses.* The 74 diploxylon pines (*D*, Fig. 3–57) follow, generally, the same pattern of vertical distribution as all pines (*A*), except that there are only three species having their middle points of vertical distribution

* There is an ecological, and perhaps a taxonomic (Rydberg, 1922), justification for considering the seven piñon pines as a separate group.

between 1250 and 1500 m. In contrast, the maximum distribution of haploxylon pines ($H$) is between these limits. There are eleven diploxylon pines whose home is at sea level (0 to 250 m). There are no haploxylon pines whose middle point of vertical distribution is below 875 m; they decidedly avoid lower altitudes. The upper limits of both haploxylon and diploxylon pines, however, are about the same: two haploxylon species and one diploxylon species at 2875 m and one haploxylon and two diploxylon at 3125 m. It is surprising to discover that many haploxylon pines, among which there are so many alpine species, have the middle points of their altitudinal distribution in the mountains at much lower elevations than the diploxylon pines.

The piñon pines, which originated in the southwestern (arid) parts of North America, and much later than the two other groups (see Chapter 2), have the middle points of their vertical distribution, as do most of the pines of the other two groups, between 1250 and 2250 m, except one newly described species—*P. culminicola* No. 39 (Andresen and Beaman, 1961), found in northeastern Mexico at an elevation of about 3600 m. Occurrence of a piñon pine at such a high altitude offers a possibility of studying migration of pines during the Tertiary period, when some of the haploxylon pines ascended the high mountains, while others (the piñons) adjusted to conditions of lower altitudes.

Three California pines—the haploxylon *P. monticola* No. 4 and the diploxylon *P. ponderosa* No. 14 and *P. contorta* No. 16—have the largest altitudinal spread, all three being found from sea level to 3500 m.

As a whole, the chart (Fig. 3–57) indicates that the most suitable environment for pines is the zone of middle elevations, and paleontological considerations (see Chapter 2) suggest that (barring local exceptions) such has been the condition throughout the history of the genus. From these altitudes, the genus has expanded downward to sea level and upward to formidable heights, reaching 4000 m.

## SUMMARY

The genus *Pinus* occupies an enormous area, expanding in the Old World from Scotland, Spain (*P. sylvestris* No. 69), and the Canary Islands (*P. canariensis* No. 72, longitude 18° west) to approximately 141° east longitude, almost to the shores of the Okhotsk Sea (*P. sylvestris* No. 69), i.e., an expanse of 159 degrees from the Atlantic to the Pacific. The latitudinal range is from 72° north (*P. sylvestris* in Norway) to 2° 6′ south (*P. merkusii* No. 101 in Sumatra), i.e., a span of over 74 degrees.

In the New World, the dimensions of the area of the genus *Pinus* are smaller. The longitudinal range is from about the sixty-second meridian west (*P. banksiana* No. 32) in Nova Scotia to the one hundred and thirty-seventh meridian west (*P. contorta* No. 16) in the Yukon territory, a span of 75 degrees—from coast to coast.

Latitudinally, pines extend in the New World from the sixty-fifth parallel (*P. banksiana* No. 32) in the Mackenzie River area of the Northwest Territories, Canada, to 11° 45′ north in Nicaragua, Central America, where *P. oocarpa* No. 59 descends from the mountains north of the Lake Nicaragua lowland and where *P. caribaea* No. 62 extends along the coast of the Gulf of Mexico, to just south of Bluefields. No pines in the New World are found north of the Arctic Circle or south of the Equator.

Within this enormous expanse of land, pine forests occur only intermittently, and pine species are not distributed uniformly. There are areas completely devoid of pines, such as the Great Plains, stretching between the western and eastern portions of the United States, and the expanse of grasslands in the southern Russian Ukraine and, farther east, the deserts of central Asia and Mongolia and the barren high country of Tibet. Some species spread over considerable areas; others are very local.

Latitudinal and longitudinal limits of the genus *Pinus* are shown below:

| Hemisphere | Latitude | Longitude | Expanse | |
|---|---|---|---|---|
| | | | Lat. | Long. |
| Eastern (Eurasia) | 72° N. to 2° 6′ S. | 141° E. to 18° W. | 74° 6′ | 159° |
| Western (America) | 65° N. to 12° 45′ N. | 62° W. to 137° W. | 52° 15′ | 75° |

With the exception of *P. merkusii*, which barely crosses the Equator in Sumatra, pines are not found in the Southern Hemisphere. Reports of their natural occurrence on Java, Borneo, and Timor are erroneous (see, for instance, Din, 1958, or Scharfetter, 1954). Some other conifers of the Southern Hemisphere (e.g., *Araucaria*) are sometimes called "pines," which causes confusion. Pines are, however, often planted south of the Equator.

A cursory glance at the area occupied by the genus *Pinus* (see map, Fig. 1–1, page 16) shows that pines are found chiefly in the southern part of the Northern Hemisphere. There are only a few species in the north. As one moves south, the number of pine species increases, reaches a maximum, and then decreases.

In the five charts in Figs. 3–58 and 3–59, the latitudinal distributions of (1) all pines, (2) diploxylon pines, and (3) haploxylon pines are shown separately, as well as those of the pines in the New World and the Old World.

Graph A shows the latitudinal distribution of all 105 species of the genus *Pinus* listed in Tables 1–1 (pages 18–20) and 1–2 (pages 20–22). *Pinus pumila* No. 68 and *P. sylvestris* No. 69 occur north of the

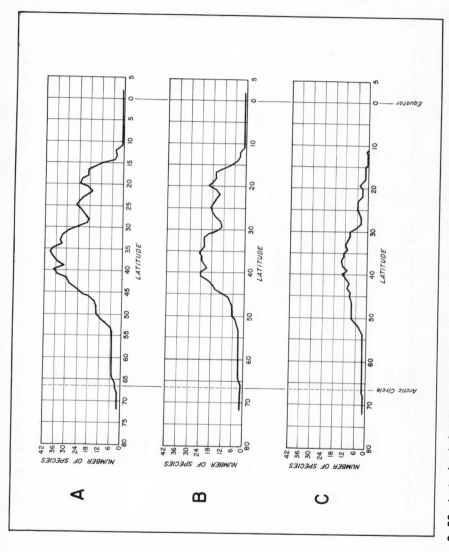

**Fig. 3–58.** Latitudinal distribution of all species of pines (A), diploxylon pines (B), and haploxylon pines (C).

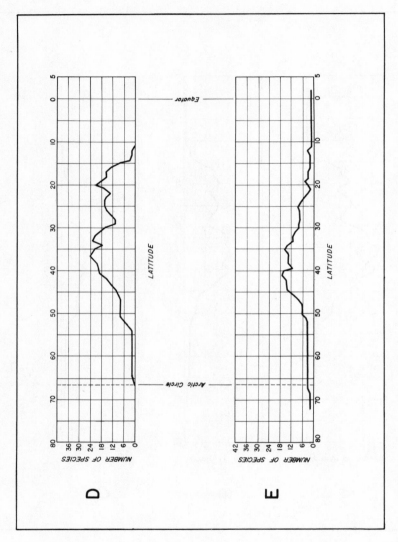

**Fig. 3–59.** Latitudinal distribution of pines in the New World (*D*) and the Old World (*E*).

310

Arctic Circle. *Pinus sibirica* No. 67 barely crosses the Arctic Circle between the Ob River and the Urals and then retreats south. There are only five species growing above the fifty-fourth parallel. Then the number of pines begins to increase rapidly when it reaches a maximum of 39 species at latitude 36°, which, in America, extends from central California (between San Francisco and Los Angeles) to northern North Carolina, and, in the Old World, from Gibraltar to central Japan. Farther south, the number of species decreases in a rather irregular manner, and, from the latitude somewhat north of Mexico City and the Burma-Thailand border (20°), it drops rapidly. At the twentieth parallel, there are no pines from Hispaniola in the Caribbean area eastward to the Southern Shan States, of Burma. At the twelfth degree of latitude north, in the vicinity of Bluefields, Nicaragua, and of Dalat, Viet Nam, all pines reach their southernmost limit except *P. merkusii*, which reappears at 5° north in Sumatra and continues intermittently on that island to 2° 6' south, thus being the only species of the genus *Pinus* to cross the Equator.

When we consider the two subgenera separately, we notice that, in the north, both haploxylon and diploxylon pines reach the same latitude —about 72°. Two haploxylon pines—*P. sibirica* No. 67 and *P. pumila* No. 68—and one diploxylon pine—*P. sylvestris* No. 69—cross the Arctic Circle. The southern limit for haploxylon pines and for all diploxylon species, except one, is at about 12° latitude. One species—*P. merkusii* No. 101— occurs farther south.

There are twenty-four diploxylon pines in the Old World, and more than twice as many (forty-nine species) in the New World. On the other hand, haploxylon pines are evenly distributed between Eurasia (seventeen species *) and America (fifteen species). Most of them are found between 30° and 45° north. Haploxylon pines go south to about the same latitude in both the New World and the Old World, approximately 15° in San Salvador and about 12° in Viet Nam. In northeastern Asia, one haploxylon pine, *P. pumila*, reaches a latitude of 70°. In America, haploxylon pines do not go that far north. The northernmost haploxylon pine in the New World is *P. albicaulis*, which reaches about 56° north.

Considering pines of the Old World, we notice that there are not as many species as in the New World—37 per cent of the total number of species in the genus *Pinus*. The maximum number of species of the genus *Pinus* in the Old World is at 41°–40° (i.e., on the parallel of Madrid, Ankara, and northern Korea). At these latitudes lie the Mediterranean region and a part of the region of eastern Asia. Along the fortieth parallel, there are no pines between the Caucasus and beyond the river Hwang (west of Peking). There is a lesser peak in the number of pines at the thirty-fifth parallel. Although at this latitude there are only a few pines

* Some may say fewer.

in the Mediterranean region, the number of species is increased by the three Himalayan pines (Nos. 91, 92, and 93) and by the pines of eastern Asia. The Old World is where the genus extends above the Arctic Circle and descends below the Equator. Further analysis of distribution data shows that there are more pine species in eastern Asia than in the rest of the Old World (twenty-four vs. fifteen species).

The Mediterranean region presents a very well-defined, compact area of twelve pines—two haploxylon and ten diploxylon species. All of these pines are Mediterranean endemics, isolated from the rest of the pines of the world. *Pinus montana*, however, goes north to the Vosges. There is only one species—*P. sylvestris* No. 69—essentially a pine of northern Eurasia, that also occurs in the Mediterranean region. In Spain, France, and Italy, it is considered as typical *P. sylvestris*, but, in the eastern Mediterranean (Caucasus and Asia Minor), it is represented by variety *hamata*, distinct enough to be considered by some botanists (Komarov, 1934) as an independent species, *P. hamata* Sosn. Apparently, it is only on the Balkan Peninsula that *P. sylvestris* and *P. sylvestris* var. *hamata* meet (Cherniavski, 1954). It is possible that *P. sylvestris* came to the Mediterranean region, as did the rest of the Mediterranean pines (or their immediate ancestors), from eastern Asia, reached the western Mediterranean, and then spread north. Postglacial migration of *P. sylvestris* to the northeast is discussed in Chapter 2. There are reports that, while northern *P. sylvestris* turpentine rotates polarized light to the right, *P. sylvestris* var. *hamata* of the eastern Mediterranean turns it to the left (Lipsky, 1899). The relationship of these two varieties of *P. sylvestris* of the Mediterranean region still awaits a thorough study, and a chemical approach (see Chapter 7, page 499, and Chapter 9, page 536) might help here.

Two Mediterranean pines closely resemble pines of eastern Asia. *Pinus canariensis* No. 72, an endemic pine of the Canary Islands, is closely related to *P. roxburghii* No. 93 of the Himalaya. *Pinus peuce* No. 71 of the Balkans is a close relative of *P. griffithii* No. 91, also of the Himalaya. Occurrence of a diterpene—cembrene (see Chapter 7)—in *P. peuce* links this species with the pines of eastern Asia and western America. The subject of chemical relationships of pines will be discussed in Chapter 8.

Another haploxylon pine occurring sparsely in the alpine habitats of the mountains separating the Mediterranean region from northwestern Europe is *P. cembra* No. 70. It is considered by some conservative botanists as the same species as *P. sibirica* No. 67. The relationship of these two pines deserves a closer investigation. It is possible that they had entirely different migration histories. On the whole, in the Old World, most pine species occur between 45° and 35°. Farther south, there are many arid areas.

In the New World (see diagram, Fig. 3–59) there are more pines than in the Old World, and there are more endemic and relict pines; such species, since they have limited latitudinal ranges, contribute to the irregular pattern of species distribution as seen in the diagram.

About two-thirds (63 per cent) of all pines are found in America; they occur from the Mackenzie River region and Alaska to San Salvador and Nicaragua. The maximum number of pines is between 35° and 15°. Between these limits are located the southern parts of eastern and western United States pine regions and those of Mexico with adjacent parts of Central America. There are also more species in western North America (nineteen species, growing mostly in California) than in its eastern part (thirteen species). The greatest number of pines, however, is found in Mexico (twenty-nine species, five of them extending to the United States). Of this number, only seven species are haploxylon (four piñons and *P. ayacahuite* No. 33, *P. strobus* var. *chiapensis* No. 34, and *P. strobiformis* No. 35).

Eastern United States pines possess interesting geographical-genetic features; they do not vary as much as the western American pines, and they do not cross as readily as Mexican pines. They are conservative pines that are settled in their migration from the northwest; still vigorous, they, nevertheless, have reached the most advanced stage of evolution of the genus. Western American pines are a strange mixture of relics (*P. sabiniana, P. aristata, P. torreyana,* and others) that have lost their capacity to expand. At the same time, the West possesses vigorous and variable pines such as *P. ponderosa* No. 14 that have still been advancing when human activities have not interfered.

In California and Mexico combined, there are found forty-four species of pines, or nearly half of all the pines. The two regions somewhat overlap. Northern Mexico and the southwestern United States geographically are very similar. The real Mexican pine region begins farther south of the international border, roughly from Monterrey, in the east, to the middle of the state of Sinaloa, in the west.

Although the western United States (chiefly California) is also rich in pines, there is a significant difference between the two regions. In California, there are found many endemics and Tertiary relics of extremely limited distribution; *P. sabiniana* No. 10 and *P. torreyana* No. 11 are good examples. In the tropical highlands of Mexico, there are many young and vigorous species with a great capacity for hybridization and for intraspecific variability. The secondary center of evolution and speciation of the genus *Pinus* is located there. The origin of this center is relatively recent; it is of the Tertiary period; in the more northern parts of the world, pines already were growing in the Mesozoic era.

Leaving aside the secondary center of evolution of pines in the highlands of Mexico, we notice another startling feature of the geography of pines: forty-three species are distributed rather evenly on both sides of the Pacific. If the four or five (Nos. 35, 36, 43, 49, 53) Mexican pines are considered also as western American species, there are twenty-four pines in western America and twenty-four pines in eastern Asia. This seems to indicate that the area of origin of the genus was located in the north, where America and Asia were connected by a broad stretch of land sometimes called "Beringia." This conclusion is reached after consideration of the geographical distribution of living pines. Paleobotanical evidence and chemical considerations are given elsewhere in this book (Chapters 2 and 8, respectively).

Pines grow from sea level to the very high mountains. About half of all species, however, occur at the moderate altitudes. Mountain slopes and plateaus are the habitats pines prefer. Indications are (see Chapter 2) that the ancestral home of the genus *Pinus* was also in the mountains.

In discussing distribution of pines, it is well to keep in mind Sargent's remark, in the Introduction to Wilson's book on western China (Wilson, 1913), that extensive pine forests are not found all over the Northern Hemisphere but are more common in the New World. Also we should remember Krishtofovich's suggestion (1959) that pines began to form extensive forests rather recently, chiefly during the Quaternary. Previously, pines were merely admixed sparingly with broadleaf or mixed forests. In the places where climate has not changed much since the end of the Cretaceous, pines seldom have formed extensive forests; more often they occur as relatively small groves or even as single, scattered trees. I have noticed this in southeastern Asia, and apparently such sporadic distribution of pines there has not always been caused by recent destruction of pine forests.

One difficulty in delineating exactly the limits of areas of some species of the genus *Pinus* is their widespread capacity to hybridize. In Chapter 4, the genetic behavior of the genus is discussed more fully; it is sufficient to state here that, while some pines maintain their specific status well, (e.g., *P. massoniana* No. 94 and *P. lambertiana* No. 3), others intercross widely and often unexpectedly. *Pinus ponderosa* No. 14, an extremely complex and widely distributed species of the western United States, crosses with the complex Mexican species *P. montezumae*, and *P. montezumae* crosses with the complex species *P. pseudostrobus*. Under these circumstances, it is impossible to give the exact area of the thirty-six pines (forms, varieties, and species) involved in this hybridization. *Pinus ponderosa* also crosses with several other pines.

Again, two pines of eastern Asia—*P. tabulaeformis* No. 102 and *P. yunnanensis* No. 103—overlap and cross, and the apparent result of this cross is known as "*Pinus densata*." Furthermore, *P. yunnanensis* merges in the western part of its area into *P. khasya,* and the two are considered by some as a single species. But, even if they are different species, they certainly hybridize in the area of their overlap or contact. There are other examples of natural hybridization in pines; these are mentioned in the descriptions of the individual species involved. To indicate accurately areas occupied by such pines is a difficult task.

Apparently, hybridization between two adjacent pines does not always require an areal overlap. A hybrid swarm may occur in an area located between the areas of two species, in places that might have been disturbed by fire or by grazing of wild cattle or, later, of domestic stock.

## LITERATURE CITATIONS

AGUILAR G, J. IGNACIO. 1961. Pinos de Guatemala (3d ed.). Ministerio de Agric. Direc. Gen. Forestal. Guatemala [City], Guatemala.

ALLEN, PAUL H. 1955. The conquest of Cerro Santa Barbara, Honduras. Ceiba, 4:253–70.

ANDRESEN, JOHN W., and JOHN H. BEAMAN. 1961. A new species of *Pinus* from Mexico. Arnold Arboretum Jour., 42:437–41.

AXELROD, DANIEL I. 1937. A Pliocene flora from the Mount Eden beds, southern California. Carnegie Inst. Wash. Pub. 476. Pp. 125–83. 1938.

——— and WILLIAM S. TING. 1960. Late Pliocene floras east of the Sierra Nevada. Univ. of Calif. Pub. Geol. Sci., 39(1):1–118.

BERTSCH, KARL. 1951. Geschichte des deutschen Waldes. 3. Aufl. Gustav Fischer, Jena.

BLANCO, CENOBIO E. 1949. *Pinus cooperi blanco,* sp. nova. Mex. Inst. Biol. Ann., 20:185–87.

BRENNEMAN, WILLIAM S. 1956. Red pine indigenous to Illinois? Jour. Forestry, 54:775.

CAIN, STANLEY A. 1944. Foundations of plant geography. Harper & Row, New York.

CEBALLOS Y FERNANDEZ DE CORDOBA, LUIS Y FRANCISCO ORTUÑO MEDINA. 1951. Estudio sobre la vegetación y la flora forestal de las Canarias Occidentales. Inst. Forest. de Invest. y Exper. Madrid.

CHERNIAVSKI, P. 1954. Beliiat bor v Bulgariia [*Pinus hamata* in Bulgaria]. Gorsko Stopanstvo, 10:257–62.

CHEVALIER, AUGUST. 1944. Notes sur les conifères de l'Indochine. Rev. de Bot. Appl. et d'Agr. Trop., 24:7–34.

CORDES, J. W. H. 1866. Het geslacht *Pinus* in 't Zuidelijk halfrond. Natuurkundig tijdschrift voor Nederlandsch Indie, 29:130–35.

CRITCHFIELD, WILLIAM B. 1957. Geographic variation in *Pinus contorta.* (Maria Moors Cabot Foundation. Pub. No. 3). Harvard Univ., Cambridge, Mass.

——— and ELBERT L. LITTLE, JR. 1965. Geographic distribution of the pines of the world. U.S. Dept. Agr. Misc. Pub. 991.

CZECZOTT, H. 1954. The past and present distribution of *Pinus halepensis* Mill. and *Pinus brutia* Ten. Papers, 8th Internatl. Cong. Bot., Paris, Sec. 2, 4/6. Pp. 196–97.

DALLIMORE, W., and A. BRUCE JACKSON. 1948. A Handbook of Coniferae (3d ed.). Edward Arnold, Ltd., London.

DIN, AUNG. 1958. Pines for tropical areas. Unasylva, 12(3):121–33.

DUFF, C. E. 1928. The varieties and geographical forms of *Pinus pinaster* Soland in Europe and South Africa. (Union So. Africa Forest Dept. Bul. 22.)

DUFFIELD, JOHN WARREN. 1951. Interrelationships of the California closed-cone pines with special reference to *Pinus muricata* D. Don. Unpublished Doctor's thesis, University of California, Berkeley.

———— and W. C. CUMMING. 1949. Does *Pinus ponderosa* occur in Baja California? Madroño, 10:22–24.

DURHAM, GEORGE. 1955. The pines of Cedros. Pacific Discovery, 8(6):22–24.

FEDOROV, A. A., I. A. LINCHEVSKII, and M. E. KIRPICHNIKOV. 1956. V tropikakh i subtropikakh kitaia (In the tropics and subtropics of China). Bot. Zhur., 41: 1235–62.

FEINBRUN, NAOMI. 1959. Spontaneous pineta in the Lebanon. Israel Res. Council Bul., 7D(3/4):132–53.

FERRÉ, Y. DE. 1960. Une nouvelle espèce de pin au Viet-Nam, *Pinus dalatensis*. Bul. Soc. Hist. Nat. de Toulouse, 95:171–80.

FIELDING, JOHN M. 1960. The role of exotic species in forest tree improvement. 5th World Forestry Cong., Proc., 2:742–46.

————. 1961. The pines of Cedros Island. Austral. Forestry, 25(2):62–65.

FORDE, MARGOT BERNICE. 1963. Variation in the natural populations of Monterey pine (*P. radiata* Don) in California. Unpublished Doctor's thesis, University of California, Davis.

FOWELLS, H. A., and G. H. SCHUBERT. 1956. Silvical characteristics of sugar pine, Berkeley, Calif. Calif. Forest and Range Expt. Sta. (U.S. Forest Serv.) Tech. Paper No. 14.

FOXWORTHY, FRED W. 1911. Philippine gymnosperms. Philippine Jour. Sci., C. Botany, 6:149–77.

FRANCINI, ELINORA. 1958. Ecologia comparata di *Pinus halepensis* Mill., *P. pinaster*, Sol., e *Pinus pinea* L. sulla base del comportamento del gametofito femminile. Ann. Accad. Ital. Sci. Forestali, 7:107–72.

FUKAREK, P. 1960. Nova svojta borova u Bosni (Prethodno suopštenje) (A new race of pine in Bosnia (preliminary communication)). Šumarski (Zagreb, Yugoslavia) List, 84:152–56.

GAUSSEN, H. 1960. Les gymnospermes actuelles et fossiles. Fasc. VI. Généralités, genre *Pinus*. (Trav. Lab. Forest. Toulouse.) Part III. Pinoidenes, 1 Abietaceae, chap. 11.

GRIFFIN, JAMES R. 1962. Intraspecific variation in *Pinus sabiniana* Dougl. Unpublished Doctor's thesis, University of California, Berkeley.

GURSKII, A. V. 1957. O snovnye itogi introduktsii drevesnykh rastenii SSSR (A summary of the introduction of woody plants into the U.S.S.R.). Izd. Akad. Nauk S.S.S.R., Moscow.

HALLER, JOHN R. 1959. The role of hybridization in the origin and evolution of *Pinus washoensis*. Abstr. Proc. 9th Internatl. Bot. Cong., 2:149.

————. 1961. Some recent observations on ponderosa, Jeffrey and Washoe pines in northeastern California. Madroño, 16:126–32.

HARKIN, D. A. 1957. Every seedling from selected seed. Jour. Forestry, 55:842–43.

HARLOW, WILLIAM M., and ELWOOD G. HARRAR. 1937. Textbook of dendrology. McGraw-Hill Book Co., New York.

HAYASHI, YASAKA. 1952. The natural distribution of important trees indigenous to Japan. Conifers, Report 2. Bul. Govt. Forest Expt. Sta. No. 55, Meguro, Tokyo, Japan. In Japanese, English summary.

————. 1954. The natural distribution of important trees indigenous to Japan. Conifers, Report 3. Bul. Govt. Forest Expt. Sta. No. 75. In Japanese, English summary.

HEILPRIN, ÁNGELO. 1892. The temperate and alpine floras of the giant volcanoes of Mexico. Amer. Phil. Soc. Proc., 30:4–22.

HEIMBURGER, C., and M. HOLST. 1955. Notes from a trip to the southern United States, January 1953. Forestry Chron., 31:60–73.

HOLDRIDGE, L. R. 1942. The pine forests of Haiti. Caribbean Forester, 4(1):16–21.

HOWELL, JOHN THOMAS. 1941. The closed-cone pines of insular California. Leaflets Western Bot., 3:1–8.

HUNT, D. R. 1962. Some notes on the pines of British Honduras. Empire Forestry Rev., 41:134-45.

JACKSON, A. BRUCE. 1933. A new hybrid pine. Gard. Chron., Series 3, 93:152-53.

JEFFREY, EDWARD C. 1908. On the structure of the leaf in Cretaceous pines. Ann. Bot., 22:207-20.

JEPSON, WILLIS LINN. 1923-25. A manual of the flowering plants of California. Assoc. Students Store, University of California Press, Berkeley.

KOMAROV, V. L. (ed.). 1934. Flora SSSR (Flora of the U.S.S.R.). Vol. I. Izd. Akad. Nauk S.S.S.R., Leningrad.

KRISHTOFOVICH, A. N. 1959. Izbrannye trudy (Selected works). Vol. I. Izd. Akad. S.S.S.R., Moscow.

LAVRENKO, E. M. 1960. O rastitel'nosti savann po reke krasnoi na iuge provintsii Iun'nana (KNR) (On the savanna vegetation along the Red River in the south of Yunnan province. Chinese People's Republic). With English summary. Moskov. Obsch. Isp. Prirody, Otd. Biol. Biul. Trudy, 3:157-70.

LIDDICOET, A. R., and F. I. RIGHTER. 1961. Trees of the Eddy Arboretum. Institute of Forest Genetics, Placerville, Calif. (Rev. ed.) (U.S. Forest Serv.) Pacific Southwest Forest and Range Expt. Sta., Misc. Paper No. 43.

LIPSKII, V. I. 1899. Flora Kavkaza. Trudy Tiflis. Bot. Sad., 4:1-584.

LITTLE, ELBERT L., JR. 1953. Check list of native and naturalized trees of the United States (Including Alaska) (U.S. Department of Agriculture Handbook No. 41). Government Printing Office, Washington, D.C.

—— and KEITH W. DORMAN. 1952. Slash pine (Pinus elliottii), its nomenclature and varieties. Jour. Forestry, 50: 918-23.

—— and KEITH W. DORMAN. 1954. Slash pine (Pinus elliottii), including South Florida slash pine: Nomenclature and description. (U.S. Forest Serv., Southeast. Forest Expt. Sta., Sta. Paper No. 36.

LITVINOV, D. I. 1913. Pinus coronans sp. n.—Gornyi sibirskii kedr (Mountain Siberian pine). Akad. Nauk S.S.S.R. Bot. Muzei Trudy, 11:20-26.

LOOCK, E. E. M. 1950. The pines of Mexico and British Honduras. (So. Africa Dept. Agr. and For. Bul. 35.)

MALEJEFF, W. 1929. Pinus pithyusa (Stev.) and Pinus eldarica (Medw.) zwei relict-Kiefern der taurish-kaukasischen Flora. Mitt. Dtsch. dendr. Ges. (Jahrb.) Pp. 138-50.

MALYSHEV, L. I. 1960. Oshibochnoe mnenie o proizrastanii kedrovogo stlanika (Pinus pumila [Pall] Rgl.) v Saianakh. (Erroneous opinion on occurrence of Pinus pumila [Pall] Rgl. in the Savans.) Bot. Zhur., 45:737-79.

MARTÍNEZ, MAXIMINO. 1948. Los pinos mexicanos (2d ed.). Ediciones Botas, Mexico [City].

MASON, H. L. 1927. Fossil records of some west American conifers. Carnegie Inst. Wash. Pub. 346. Pp. 139-58.

——. 1930. The Santa Cruz Island pine. Madroño, 2:8-10.

——. 1932. A phylogenetic series of California closed-cone pines suggested by the fossil record. Madroño, 2:49-55.

—— and W. PALMER STOCKWELL. 1945. A new pine from Mount Rose, Nevada. Madroño, 8:61-63.

MERRILL, ELMER D. 1926. An enumeration of Philippine flowering plants. Vol. IV. (Philippine Islands, Bur. Sci. Pub. 18.) Bureau of Printing, Manila.

——. 1927. An enumeration of Hainan plants. Lingnan Sci. Jour., 5:1-186.

——. 1941. The upper Burma plants collected by Capt. F. Kingdon Ward on the Vernay-Cutting Expedition, 1938-39. Brittonia, 4:20-188.

MERRITT, M. L. 1908. The forests of Mindoro. (Bur. Forestry Bul. 8.) Bureau of Printing, Manila.

MIROV, N. T. 1929. Chemical analysis of the oleoresins as a means of distinguishing Jeffrey pine and western yellow pine. Jour. Forestry, 27:176-87.

——. 1955. Relationships between Pinus halepensis and other insignes pines of the Mediterranean region. Israel Res. Council Bul. 5D, Sec. D, Bot. Pp. 65-72.

————. 1956. Composition of turpentine of lodgepole × jack pine hybrids. Canad. Jour. Bot., 34:443–57

————. 1958. *Pinus oaxacana,* a new species from Mexico. Madroño, 14:145–50.

————, J. W. DUFFIELD, and A. R. LIDDICOET. 1952. Altitudinal races of ponderosa pine: A 12-year progress report. Jour. Forestry, 50:825–31.

————, EDITH FRANK, and EUGENE ZAVARIN. 1965. Chemical composition of *P. elliottii* var. *elliottii* turpentine and its possible relation to taxonomy of several pine species. Phytochemistry, 4:563–68.

MOHR, CHARLES. 1897. The timber pines of the southern United States (rev. ed.). (U.S. Dept. Agr., Div. Forestry, Bul. No. 13.) Government Printing Office, Washington, D.C.

MOSS, E. H. 1949. Natural pine hybrids in Alberta. Canad. Jour. Res. Sec. C, Bot. Sci., 27:218–29.

————. 1953. Forest communities in northwestern Alberta. Canad. Jour. Bot., 31: 212–52.

MUNNS, E. N. 1938. The distribution of important forest trees of the United States. (U.S. Dept. Agr. Misc. Pub. 287.) Government Printing Office, Washington, D.C.

NAKAMURA, K. 1955. On the seedlings of *Pinus densi-thunbergii.* Jap. Forestry Soc. Jour., 37:251–52. (In Japanese.)

PAPAJOANNOU, JOHANNES. Über Artbastarde zwischen *Pinus brutia* Ten. und *P. halepensis* Mill. in Nordostchalkidiki (Griechenland). Forstwiss. Centbl., 58: 194–205.

PAVARI, A. 1955. Sul trattamento delle fustaie di pino domestico (*Pinus pinea* L). Atti Cong. Naz. Selvicoltura, Florence, March 18, 1954, 1:69–97.

PRAVDIN, L. F. 1964. Sosna obyknovennaia [*P. sylvestris*] Izmenchivost, vnutrividovaia sistematika, i selektsiia (Common pine [*P. sylvestris*], its variability, intraspecific systematics and selections). Akad. Nauk S.S.S.R. Laboratoria Lesovedrniia. Nauka, Moskva.

RAUP, HUGH M. 1947. The botany of southwestern Mackenzie. Sargentia, 6:1–275.

RIKLI, M. 1909. Die Arve in der Schweiz. Neue Denkschr. Schweiz. Naturf. Gesell., 44:1–455.

RIKLI, MARTIN ALBERT. 1943. Das Pflanzenkleid der Mittelmeerländer. 3 vols. Hans Huber, Bern.

ROMNEY, D. H. (ed.). 1959. Land in British Honduras: Report of the British Hond. Land Use Survey Team (A.C.S. Wright, D. H. Romney, R. H. Arbuckle, V. E. Vial.). (Colon. Off. Res. Pub. No. 24.)

ROULEAU, ERNEST. 1935. *Pinus rigida* Miller in Quebec. Rhodora, 57:299.

RUBNER, K., and F. REINHOLD. 1953. Das näturliche Waldbild Europas. Paul Parey, Hamburg.

RUDOLF, PAUL. 1957. Silvical characteristics of red pine (*Pinus resinosa*). (U.S. Forest Serv., Lake States Forest Expt. Sta. Paper No. 44.)

————. 1958. Jack pine (*Pinus banksiana*) (U.S. Forest Serv., Lake States Forest Expt. Sta. Paper No. 61.)

RYDBERG, P. A. 1922. Flora of the Rocky Mountains and adjacent plains (2d ed.). Privately printed, New York.

SAID, M. 1959. *Pinus gerardiana* (Chilgoza) in the Zhob District. Pakistan Jour. Forestry, 9(2):118–23.

SARGENT, CHARLES SPRAGUE. 1890. The silva of North America. Vol. XI. Coniferae (*Pinus*). Peter Smith, Gloucester, Mass.

SCHARFETTER, RUDOLF. 1954. Ein Beitrag zur Biographie der Gattung Pinus. Festschrift für Erwin Aichinger, I: 43–49 In: Janchen, Erwin. Festschrift für Erwin Aichinger zum 60 Geburtstag. Springer Verlag, Vienna.

SCHMUCKER, THEODOR. 1942. The tree species of the Northern Temperate Zone and their distribution. Silvae Orbis, 4:54–80.

SCHULMAN, EDMUND. 1958. Bristlecone pine, oldest known living thing. Natl. Geog. Mag., 113(March):354–72.

SCHÜTT, P. 1958. Züchtung mit Kiefern. Teil 1. Individualunterschiede und Provenienzversuche. Mitt der Bundesforschungsanstalt für Forst-und Holzwirt. Reinbek bei Hamburg. No. 40 Forstgenetik und Forstpflanzenzüchtung.

———. 1959. Züchtung mit Kiefern Teil 2. Kreuzungen, Resistenzzüchtung und Zytologie. Mitt. Bundesforsch. Forst-und Holzwirt. No. 42 Forstgenetik und Forstpflanzenzüchtung. Pp. 1–40.

Schwerdtfeger, Fritz. 1953. Informe al govierno de Guatemala sobre la entomologia forestal de Guatemala. Vol. I. Los pinos de Guatemala. Org. de las Naciones Unidas Agr. y Aliment. Informe FAO/ETAP No. 202, Rome.

Shaw, George Russell. 1909. The pines of Mexico. (Arnold Arboretum Pub. No. 1.) J. R. Ruiter & Co., Boston.

———. 1914. Genus Pinus. (Arnold Arboretum Pub. No. 5.) Riverside Press, Cambridge.

Smith, Earl E. 1954. The forests of Cuba. (Maria Moors Cabot Foundation Pub. No. 2.) Cambridge, Mass.

Sowerby, Arthur De Carle. 1937. The white-barked pine (Pinus bungeana Zuccarini) in North China. Roy. Hort. Soc. Jour., 62:443–45.

Standley, Paul Carpenter. 1920–26. Trees and shrubs of Mexico. U.S. Natl. Mus. Contrib. U.S. Natl. Herbarium, 23: Pts. 1–5.

——— and S. J. Record. 1936. The forests and flora of British Honduras. (Field Mus. Nat. Hist., Chicago, Pub. 350, Bot. Ser. 12.)

Steenis, C. G. G. J. van (ed.). 1950. Flora Malesiana, series I. Spermatophyta. Vol. I.

Steven, H. M., and A. Carlisle. 1959. The native pinewoods of Scotland. Oliver and Boyd, Ltd., Edinburgh.

Strabo. 1917–32. The Geography of Strabo with an English translation by Horace Leonard Jones. 8 vols. G. P. Putnam's Sons, Inc., New York.

Sudworth, George B. 1908. Forest trees of the Pacific slope. Government Printing Office, Washington, D.C.

———. 1913. Forest atlas: Geographic distribution of North American trees. Part I. Pines. Government Printing Office, Washington, D.C.

———. 1917. The pine trees of the Rocky Mountain region. (U.S. Dept. Agr. Bul. 460.) Government Printing Office, Washington, D.C.

Suslov, S. P. 1947. Fizicheskaia geografiia SSSR; zapadnaia Sibir; vostochnaia Sibir; Dal'nii vostok, sredniaia Aziia Leningrad. Ucheb. pedagog. izd-vo.

Teng, S. G. 1941. Silviculture of Kansu trees. Bot. Bul. Acad. Sinica, 1:221–42.

Troup, R. S. 1921. The silviculture of Indian trees. Vol. III. Oxford University Press, Fair Lawn, N.J.

Tutaiuk, V. K. 1959. O nekotorykh Pokazateliakh ekologicheskoi prisposovlennosti dikorastushchei el'darskoi sosny (Pinus eldarica Medw.) (On indicators of ecological adaptation of native Pinus eldarica). Bot. Zhur. Akad. Nauk, S.S.S.R., 44:185–93.

Vavilov, N. I. 1959. Zemledel'cheskii Afganistan (Agricultural Afghanistan). Acad. Nauk S.S.S.R., Moscow.

Vidal, Jules. 1934–60. La végétation du Laos 2ᵐᵉ Partie: Groupements végéteaux et Flore. Trav. Lab. Forest. Toulouse Tome V, Vol. I. Pp. 121–582.

Wang, Chi-Wu. 1961. The forests of China. (Maria Moors Cabot Foundation Publ. No. 5.) Harvard University, Cambridge, Mass.

Wenger, Karl F. 1958. Silvical characteristics of loblolly pine (Pinus taeda L.). (U.S. Forest Serv., Southeast. Forest Expt. Sta. Paper No. 98.)

Williams, L. 1955. Pinus caribaea. Ceiba, 4:299–300.

Wilson, Ernest Henry. 1913. A naturalist in western China with an introduction by Professor Charles Sprague Sargent. Vol. I. Methuen & Co., Ltd., London.

———. 1916. The conifers and taxads of Japan. (Arnold Arboretum Pub. No. 8.) Harvard University Press, Cambridge, Mass.

———. 1920. The Liukiu Islands and their ligneous vegetation. Arnold Arboretum Jour., 1:171–86.

Wright, Jonathan W. 1953. Summary of tree breeding experiments by the Northeastern Forest Exp. Sta. 1947–1950. (U.S. Forest Serv., Northeast. Forest Expt. Sta. Paper No. 56.)

Wu Chung-Lwen. 1947. The phytogeographic distribution of pines in China. Unpublished Master's thesis, Yale University, New Haven.

———. 1956. The taxonomic revision and phytogeographical study of Chinese pines. Acta phytotaxonom. Sinica, 5: 131–64. In Chinese, English summary.

Wulff, E. V. 1944. Istoricheskaia geografiia rastenii (Historical plant geography). Akad. Nauk S.S.S.R., Moscow.

Yao, T. Y. 1936. A statement of the hybrid *Pinus tabulaeformis* var. *taihanshanensis* recently discovered at Taihanshan, Honan, China. Agr. Assoc. China, Jour., 144: 67–68.

Zobel, Bruce, and Franklin Cech. 1957. Pines from Nuevo Leon, Mexico. Madroño, 14:133–44.

Zodda, Guiseppe. 1903. Il *Pinus pinea* L. nel Pontico di Messina. Malpighia, 17(11–12):488–91.

Zohary, M. 1947. A vegetation map of western Palestine. Jour. Ecol., 34:1–19.

# 4

# Genetic Aspects

## GENERAL CONSIDERATIONS

To a non-specialist, genetics of the genus *Pinus* may appear simple. All pine species so far examined (and most likely all existing pines) have the same number of chromosomes—$n = 12$; $2n = 24$. Sax and Sax (1933) found that chromosomes of all species of *Pinus* examined were morphologically similar. "One of the 12 chromosomes is somewhat heterobrachial and the others have approximately median fiber attachments."

Mehra and Khoshoo (1956) reported that no pines have chromosomes with terminal or subterminal centromeres. Of a total of thirty-seven species examined (Plate 4–1), the number of species with median and submedian chromosomes was twelve. Species within the genus differed in the number and nature of secondary constriction and satellites. All species examined had essentially the same karyotype.

Santamour (1960) extended the examination of chromosomes of the genus *Pinus* and reported that generally their morphology agrees with that reported by Sax and Sax (1933) and by Mehra and Khoshoo (1956). All chromosomes examined belonged to the class in which the shorter arm is one-half, or more than one-half, the length of the longer arm. Only one chromosome, considered by Sax and Sax as heterobrachial, illustrated in their karyotype picture of *P. parviflora*, would not fall into the median-submedian (centromere) category of Mehra and Khoshoo.

Sax (1960) extended the cytological studies of pines to the $F_1$ hybrids of several Haploxylon pines (*P. griffithii* No. 91,* *P. strobus* No. 20, *P. parviflora* (i.e., Nos. 83 or 84), and *P. holfordiana* × *P. parviflora*.†

* Numbers after the specific names of pines refer to Table 1–2 in Chapter 1.
† *Pinus holfordiana* is a pine discovered in the arboretum at Westonbirt, England, having morphological characters intermediate between *P. ayacahuite* No. 53 and *P. parviflora*, which might have been either *P. pentaphylla* No. 83 or *P. himekomatsu* No. 84, or even a hybrid between these two species.

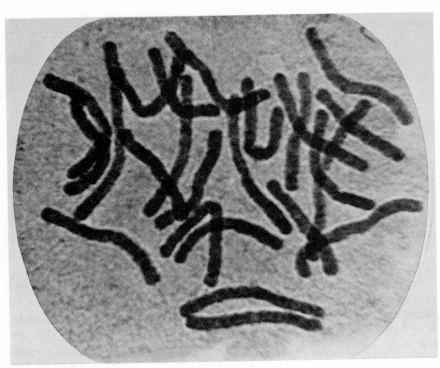

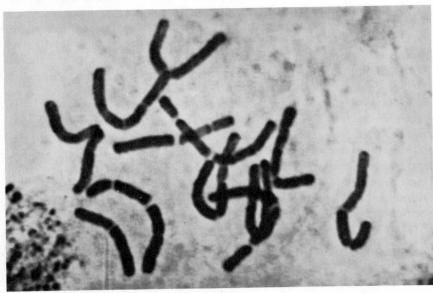

**Plate 4–1.** Chromosomes. *Top:* of *P. gerardiana* No. 92 (root tips; 2n = 24). (From Mehra and Koshoo, 1956.) *Bottom:* of *P. densiflora* No. 95 (endosperm squash; n = 12). (Photo by P. N. Mehra.)

Meiosis was nearly normal; the hybrids were vigorous and the fertility relatively high. Apparently, changes in chromosome structure were not important as a barrier to crossing between the pine species. Sax remarked that although the species studied have been isolated geographically for very long periods, measured by millions of years, they were found to be similar in chromosome constitution and in genetic compatibility. This chromosomal stability of pines became evident when attempts were made to induce polyploidy in them (see below).

In reviewing the literature on karyotypes of pines, Saylor (1961) remarked that Aass in Norway found no cytological abnormalities in "morphologically atypical" *P. sylvestris*. Aass, however, observed secondary constriction in the chromosomes and detected two pairs of the chromosomes that appeared smaller than others. Saylor also mentioned studies at Vidaković of natural hybrids between *P. sylvestris* No. 69 and *P. nigra* No. 74 (1958).* Difference in length between the smallest and the largest somatic chromosomes was found to be greater in *P. sylvestris* than in *P. nigra*.

In the most recent study of chromosome morphology of *P. sylvestris* (Pravdin 1964), karyotypes of *P. sylvestris* were found to be about the same throughout the range of the species, except for one population of the subspecies *kulundensis* from the Tuva country (51 degrees North, 96 degrees East). The Tuva pine karyotype was compared with the "standard" *P. sylvestris* karyotype of Sweden. While in the Swedish pine there are five pairs of chromosomes (I, II, VI, VII, and X) with secondary constrictions, the Tuva population has only three pairs (I, II, and VI). In the Swedish pine, the chromosomes XI and XII have submedial centromeres; thus, one arm is shorter than the other. In the Tuva population, all chromosomes have arms of equal length. Difference between the long and the short chromosomes is more pronounced in the Tuva pine than in the Swedish pine. Moreover, the Swedish material has only two short chromosomes (XI and XII), while the Tuva pine has four (IX, X, XI, and XII).

Saylor (1961) found that there was not much difference in the number and in the position of secondary constrictions in *P. strobus* No. 20, *P. taeda* No. 24, *P. palustris* No. 22, *P. virginiana* No. 27, and *P. resinosa* No. 21. No intraspecific difference was detected in any of the pines studied. Four species possessed "remarkably similar karyotypes and only *P. resinosa* had haploid karyotype somewhat different: there were two heterobrachial chromosomes instead of one."

It appears from the above review that among the pines there is a high degree of uniformity in chromosome morphology. Until recently, the karyotype picture of Mexican pines was totally unknown. In 1962, Luna

* There are several varieties of *P. nigra*.

published some data on a rare piñon pine, *P. pinceana* No. 37. In both meiotic divisions, the chromosomes were found to be long and intertwined, extending throughout the cytoplasm. However, in some cases, they formed a mass so contracted that precise chromosome count was difficult (Luna, 1962). The diploid number of chromosomes was 24.

Zinnai (1952) reported finding five tetraploid seedlings in transplant beds of *P. densiflora* No. 95. They amounted to 0.08 per cent of all transplants.

Attempts have been made to induce artificial polyploidy in pines. Mirov and Stockwell (1939) treated germinating seeds or established seedlings of *P. ponderosa* No. 14 with colchicine * and obtained a small percentage of malformed, presumably polyploid seedlings; some of these died young. The chromosome number varied from 24, which is normal in somatic tissue, to about 96. Spindle formation was inhibited in some cells, and formation of the cell wall was lacking or was vestigial. Some other abnormalities were described. Depressed growth of all seedlings was observed. (See Plate 4–2.)

Komissarov (1947) reported that colchicine-induced polyploid pines have invariably been dwarfed, malformed, or slow growing.

Machado (1943) was able to induce polyploidy in *P. pinaster* No. 80 seedlings both by soaking seeds in 1 per cent colchicine solution and by immersing young seedlings, or, again, by placing a drop of 1 per cent colchicine in gelatin on the terminal bud. To quote Machado (in translation), "*P. pinaster* appears to be very sensitive to the action of the alkaloid." His results, however, were essentially the same as reported by Mirov and Stockwell.

Hyun (1954) repeated the colchicine treatment experiment on a much larger scale. Some polyploids were obtained; these were of a different nature. Some were perfect tetraploids; others were mixoploids consisting of $3n$ and $4n$ tissues; still others were mixoploids consisting of $2n$ and $4n$ tissues. Some of the treated seedlings reverted to the diploid condition, but others maintained the polyploid condition for one or two years. It is difficult to say what will be the nature of these seedlings in the future. In 1962, i.e., ten years after the experiment was discontinued, some transplants looked malformed, while others appeared to be as normal as average diploids. At ten years of age, treated transplants looked no more vigorous than average untreated transplants of the same age.

The above described experiments with artificial induction of polyploidy show that pines are extremely resistant to any attempts to change the orderly behavior of their chromosomes. Pines are equally resistant to

---

* Colchicine is found in a lily family plant *Colchicum autumnale;* it prevents formation of the wall between the dividing cells.

**Plate 4–2.** Colchicine-treated seedlings of *P. ponderosa* No. 14. *Top:* survived seedlings with abnormal cotyledons. *Bottom:* an abnormal seedling among normal ones. (Photos by F. H. Schumacher. Courtesy California Forest & Range Experiment Station, U.S. Forest Service.)

the action of X rays.* The absence of polyploids among pines and the difficulties encountered in creation of artificial polyploids probably caused Mehra and Khoshoo (1956) to remark that polyploidy has played no part in the evolution of pines. Evolution of pines apparently has been caused chiefly by gene mutations. Gustafsson (1960), after careful consideration of mutations in forest trees (including pines), arrived at the conclusion that although mutations are the driving force in evolution, very little is known about this phenomenon in forest trees.

## COMPLEXITY IN PINE GENETICS

To a geneticist, uniformity in the number and morphology of chromosomes makes genetic studies of the genus *Pinus* difficult, for specific, valuable characteristics are missing. Genetic complexity of the genus is especially evident in the relationship among its species. There are many definitions of the term "species." It is sufficient to quote here Cain's (1944) definition to the effect that "species are naturally evolved populations with distinct genetic constellations the members of which interbreed but [are] not usually crossbred with members of other specific populations." † He, however, cautions that many species do not conform with this definition. Certainly, in the genus *Pinus,* the nature of species is quite different from that suggested by many scholars working chiefly with the angiosperms.

## HYBRIDIZATION AMONG PINES

The most striking genetic feature of the genus *Pinus* is its irregularity in respect to hybridization. Many species, often belonging to distant generally accepted groups, intercross freely and produce fertile hybrids; there are also many species, often of the same taxonomic group, that possess strong barriers to intercrossing with other species.

Examples of interspecific crossings in diploxylon pines are numerous. *Pinus ponderosa* No. 14 has been crossed with *P. montezumae* No. 47 (Liddicoet and Righter, 1960), which is a complex species. There is evidence that *P. montezumae* crosses with some species or varieties of its own complex, such as *P. hartwegii* No. 49 or *P. rudis* No. 50, and also with the species of another complex group known to conservative botanists as *P. pseudostrobus.* For instance, there is evidence that *P. montezumae* crosses naturally with *P. oaxacana* No. 57 (Mirov, 1958). *Pinus ponderosa* also crosses naturally with *P. jeffreyi* No. 13, *P. washoensis* No. 15, *P. engelmannii* No. 53, and *P. arizonica* No. 23.

* Unpublished experiments of the author.
† See also Chapter 10.

Another example of wide intercrossing is presented by the diploxylon pines of China. *Pinus tabulaeformis* No. 102 of northern China (an extremely variable species) crosses in its southwestern limits with *P. yunnanensis* No. 103 of Yünnan Province, resulting in the hybrid known as *P. densata* Masters. *Pinus yunnanensis* imperceptibly merges into *P. khasya* No. 104 of upper Burma. Some botanists (Wu, 1947) think that these two pines are the same species and that they are identical with *P. insularis* No. 105 of the Philippines; in fact, in Burma (but not in adjacent Thailand), *P. khasya* is "officially" called *P. insularis*. These pines are closely related, and no doubt *P. yunnanensis* and *P. khasya* intercross naturally, and *P. insularis* probably could be crossed with the two if brought in contact with them.

Most haploxylon pines also display this capacity of hybridization. *Pinus strobus* No. 20 can be crossed with *P. monticola* (Righter, 1945). *Pinus monticola* most likely crosses naturally with *P. flexilis*. The latter crosses naturally with *P. strobiformis* No. 35, and *P. strobiformis* merges into the complex species of Mexican *P. ayacahuite,* whose varieties no doubt intercross. On the other hand, *P. flexilis* No. 2 can be crossed with *P. griffithii* No. 91 of the Himalaya. *Pinus monticola* No. 4 has been crossed with *P. peuce* No. 71 of the Balkans.

In spite of the widespread interspecific hybridization within the genus *Pinus,* there are some species that are difficult to cross. *Pinus lambertiana* No. 3 does not cross naturally with any other North American pine, and its hybridization with Mexican *P. ayacahuite* No. 33 has not been proved yet (although the two pines most likely will be crossed sooner or later). However, *P. lambertiana* has been crossed with *P. koraiensis* No. 82 and *P. armandi* No. 86 of eastern Asia (Stone and Duffield, 1950). (See Plate 4–3.) Other western endemics and California relics also are resistant to interspecific crossing. These are *P. albicaulis* No. 1, *P. balfouriana* No. 5, and *P. aristata* No. 6, although the last two little-known pines possibly do cross. *Pinus sabiniana* No. 10 and *P. torreyana* No. 11 are difficult to cross.

In eastern Asia, *P. bungeana* No. 87 and *P. gerardiana* No. 92 (the two species comprising Shaw's [1914] group *Gerardianae* within the subgenus *Haploxylon*) have not been crossed with any other pines.

Of the Mediterranean region pines, *P. pinea* No. 73 possesses sufficient genetic differences to prevent its hybridization with other pines.

As a whole, although a great advance has been made in the field of interspecific hybridization among pines (chiefly at the Institute of Forest Genetics, U.S. Forest Service, Placerville, California), our knowledge on this subject is far from being complete. This is especially true with the Mexican and southeastern Asiatic species. Haploxylon pines appear to intercross more freely than diploxylon species, but even among the

**Plate 4–3.** *Pinus armandi* No. 86 × *P. lambertiana* No. 3 hybrid at the Institute of Forest Genetics, Placerville, California. Age, twelve years. On the right in back is *P. lambertiana*. Crossability of the two pines ties up genetically a California haploxylon pine with haploxylon pines of eastern Asia. *Pinus lambertiana* has not yet been crossed with any American pine. (U.S. Forest Service photo.)

former, there are found formidable barriers yet unexplainable, though highly suggestive from the evolutionary point of view. Why, for instance, does not *P. lambertiana* No. 3 cross naturally—and so far it has not been crossed artificially—with any American pines, while it has been crossed with two Asiatic pines?

In the subgenus *Diploxylon*, there are many species that are similar in morphology and purportedly closely related that cross with difficulty or not at all. Dr. G. Ledyard Stebbins of the University of California is of the opinion that genetic barriers between species of the subgenus *Dip-*

*loxylon* are more highly developed than in most genera of woody plants.

In many experiments with hybridization of species of the genus *Pinus,* it was found that the hybrids are fertile and have normal meiosis. Stebbins comments that this is also true of some other woody genera such as *Quercus* but different from most herbaceous plants.

It suggests that for some reason the kind of genetic isolation barriers which arise most easily in *Pinus* are mutations which affect cross compatibility between species, rather than small chromosomal changes which influence chromosomal pairing and fertility of the $F_1$ hybrids. This is in agreement with the observations of similarity in chromosome number and morphology throughout the genus.[*]

## BARRIERS TO HYBRIDIZATION

Barriers to interspecific hybridization of pines, as in any other group of plants, may be classified as follows:

A. External barriers
   1. Geographical isolation
B. Internal barriers
   2. Difference in time of pollen ripening
   3. Failure of pollen tube to reach the ovule
   4. Failure of seedling to reach maturity

Geographical isolation imposes an efficient barrier to the intercrossing of several pines. It is obvious that two pines isolated from each other for many million years and separated by oceans for thousands of miles cannot cross; the surprising fact is that when geographically distant pines are brought together, they often cross easily, either with the assistance of man or even voluntarily. Such is the case of *P. strobus* No. 20 of North America and *P. griffithii* No. 91 of the Himalaya, or *P. nigra* No. 74 of Europe and *P. thunbergii* No. 97 of Japan. The ease with which geographically separated pines hybridize in cultivation shows that some pines, isolated for an enormously long time, some since the Cretaceous period and perhaps even from the Jurassic, have not developed any differences in their genetic mechanism that would have made them incompatible to their relatives, distant both in space and in time. No doubt geographical barriers can be broken occasionally when, for instance, a hurricane might carry pine pollen (and even seeds) over long distances, such as from the Caribbean islands to Florida; [†] but, by and large, such contacts, especially trans-Pacific ones, are most unlikely.

Difference in the time of pollen ripening occurs occasionally among sympatric pines. A good example was described by Forde (1962). *Pinus*

[*] Dr. G. Ledyard Stebbins, personal communication.

[†] Viability of pine pollen is maintained much longer than in many other trees.

*attenuata* No. 17 and *P. radiata* No. 19 grow together at Año Nuevo, a locality not far south of San Francisco. Artificially, these two pines are the easiest to cross, and the cross is outstanding for its fertility. In spite of previous suggestions (Bannister, 1958), Forde was unable to find much introgression of *P. attenuata* to *P. radiata*. She explained the almost complete absence of hybrids between the two pines at Año Nuevo by the difference in their pollen-shedding periods. *Pinus radiata* usually sheds pollen in that locality early in February; *P. attenuata* does not begin until approximately one month later. There may be a slight overlap in pollen discharge between individual trees of the two species, but the phenological barrier is sufficient to prevent substantial interspecific pollination. According to Forde, the phenological barrier between *P. radiata* No. 19 and *P. muricata* No. 18 is even greater than between *P. radiata* and *P. attenuata* No. 17. *Pinus muricata* generally sheds its pollen at the beginning of April, i.e., about two months after *P. radiata*.

Forde's observations are somewhat at variance with Focke's suggestion (as discussed by Stebbins, 1959, p. 232) that an overlap in flowering is more inducive to hybridization (of angiosperms) than when both parental species are in full bloom at the same time. Of course, what is valid for flowering plants may not be applicable to pines.

Another example is perhaps *P. khasya* No. 104 and *P. merkusii* No. 101, which the author observed in Thailand. The former grows at higher elevations than the latter (see Chapter 3); their areas often overlap. But oddly enough, *P. khasya* sheds its pollen from two to three weeks earlier than *P. merkusii;* this difference in time of pollen shedding apparently constitutes a sufficient barrier to hybridization of these two pines. Unfortunately, nobody yet has attempted to cross these two pines artificially to prove that the different time of pollen shedding is the only barrier to the crossing of the two pines.

Failure of the pollen tube to reach the ovule is one of the most important obstacles to hybridization of some sympatric species of pines; another obstacle is the failure of the seedlings to reach maturity. McWilliam (1959) studied interspecific incompatibility in pines using both the anatomical and the biochemical approach. After interspecific pollination of *P. nigra* No. 74, the development of the gametophyte and fertilization showed no major deviation from the normal course. In the unpollinated ovule, its breakdown occurred about one month after the female conelet became receptive. He ascribed the breakdown of the ovule to the lack of some growth factor that, in the pollinated ovule, probably initiated growth of the pollen tube in the nucellus. In spite of suggestive reports by several investigators of occurrence of parthenocarpy (i.e., development of cones but not fertile seeds), McWilliam was unable to observe it during his experiments, nor could he induce it artificially. The causes of incompatibility in attempted crosses of *P. nigra* No. 74 with several pines (*P. caribaea* No. 62 × *P. nigra*, *P. resinosa* No. 21 × *P. rigida* No. 29, *P. nigra* × *P. rigida*, *P. resinosa* × *P. nigra*, and *P. nigra* × *P. resinosa*) were, according to McWilliam, related to inability of the pollen tube to function normally in the nucellar tissue of a foreign pine. Apparently here also, as in the unpollinated ovule, a special growth factor was involved. McWilliam thought that amino acids in the ovules of different pines had something to do with their incompatibility. Although all of the fifteen amino acids investigated were present in the ovules of both species, their concentrations varied; in *P. nigra*, there was five times as much arginine as in P. *resinosa*. It should be noted, however, that these two pines had been crossed at the Institute of Forest Genetics in 1955, but the published report appeared only after careful checking much later (Liddicoet and Righter, 1960). Although the mechanism blocking fertilization in pines probably is more complicated than reported, McWilliam's research was in the right direction, and it opened an avenue for future work. Many internal barriers, no doubt, will be removed when biochemistry of the growing pollen tube and chemical response of the ovule are better understood.

It should be kept in mind that failure to cross two species in any investigation may be caused by inadequate technique rather than by the intrinsic incompatibility of the two pines to cross. For instance, *P. lambertiana* No. 3 was successfully crossed with other species only after many previous unsuccessful efforts.

Regarding the failure of seedlings to reach maturity as a barrier protecting two species, its presence and its importance was recently discussed by Haller (1962) in his paper on variation and hybridization in *P. ponderosa* and *P. jeffreyi*. Haller argued that *P. ponderosa* and *P. jeffreyi* are old, stable species that have been subjected to natural selection for a long time and have developed "precise adaptations" to their environment. The hybrid seedlings lack such adaptations and are not able to compete successfully with the parents. According to Haller, most of the hybrid seedlings are eliminated in their youth. He sampled five- to ten-year-old trees in two localities of a *P. ponderosa–P. jeffreyi* forest. Out of fifty individuals sampled, no hybrids were detected.

Haller's contention that almost all germinated hybrid seeds never reach maturity finds support in the experience of the author. Once he tapped pines in a mixed *P. jeffreyi–P. ponderosa* forest to obtain *n*-heptane for standardization of motor fuel by the Ethyl Gasoline Corporation (Carruthers, 1956). As *n*-heptane is a specific compound present in *P. jeffreyi* but absent in terpene-bearing *P. ponderosa*, it was easy to identify "heptane pines." Out of the total number of 12,000 tapped trees, only two or perhaps three were found to be chemical hybrids, containing both *n*-heptane and terpenes. The morphological characters of these chemically intermediate trees were also intermediate between *P. jeffreyi* and *P. ponderosa.*

## ROLE OF HYBRIDIZATION IN EVOLUTION OF PINES

Stebbins (1959), who discussed the role of hybridization in evolution, said that it depends not necessarily on the frequency with which hybrids occur in nature, but on the effects that the hybrids may have on genetic variability in natural populations. Following Stebbins' argument, it can be assumed that since interspecific hybrids of pines are generally fertile, they may take an important part in evolution. Moreover, there is a possibility that progeny of partly sterile hybrids are more fertile than the hybrids themselves, and the fertility is often increased in subsequent generations. Stebbins suggested that ". . . in spite of the tendency of the majority of segregates to resemble one or the other of their original parents, the progeny of interspecific and interracial hybrids may nevertheless affect profoundly the course of evolution." To quote further from Stebbins' article, ". . . the interspecific hybridization is not necessarily a 'blind alley' which leads only to worthless sterile offspring or to restoration of the parental types; some hybrids are fertile, constant, stable, and genetically isolated from one or both of their original parents." This was well demonstrated by Rollins (1954) who experimented with two species of *Lesquerella* (*Cruciferae*). In Tennessee, he has observed populations of *L. densipila* × *L. Lescurii* hybrids that were completely fertile and capable of survival without backcrossing to either parental species. Rollins concluded that interspecific hybrids are not always only agents of gene transmission through introgression to the parental species, but ". . . they are also important as a pool of recombined genes to be screened by the forces of evolution." The interspecific hybrid populations, independently of their parental species, may be the source of evolutionary genetic material upon which natural selection can operate and thus give rise to new species.

There are very few studies of genetic behavior of pine hybrids in the field. Interesting is the case of natural hybridization between *P. contorta* No. 16, a western American pine descending to the plains from the Canadian Rockies, and *P. banksiana* No. 32, a northeastern American species extending to Alberta, Canada, and to the Mackenzie River (Raup, 1947), where its area overlaps the area of *P. contorta* and where the two pines cross. The hybrid swarm of Alberta in the vicinity of Edmonton was first described by Moss (1949) and studied by Mirov (1956). Mirov's studies were concerned with distribution of two different terpenes in the hybrid swarm. Of the trees examined in the hybrid swarm, 47.9 per cent had morphological characters of *P. contorta*, 23.3 per cent were intermediate, and 28.8 per cent looked like *P. banksiana*. The chemical nature of the trees in the hybrid swarm followed a different pattern; this topic is discussed in Chapter 7. Here it is pertinent only to describe the locality of the Alberta hybrid swarm.

In early postglacial times what is today the overlap area probably was an extensive grassland, or perhaps a parkland or grove area. The black soils now found frequently in the area could not have developed under postglacial conifer forests. Moss concluded that the forest is gradually encroaching upon the grassland. All investigators agree that the area has been greatly disturbed by fires, which became more frequent with the advent of primitive man. Although Moss [1949] considers the disturbing influence of bison and domestic animals only of local importance, nevertheless, judging by the information available for other grasslands regions [Berg, 1950] the influence of once-numerous hoofed wild animals in disturbing the prehistoric grasslands should not be disregarded. We may visualize the Alberta overlap area since the retreat of the ice as having been repeatedly disturbed by fires, by wild cattle, and by possible subsequent surface erosion especially in sandy places. The area offered conditions favorable to the appearance of a lodgepole × jack pine hybrid swarm [Anderson, 1949]. It might be possible that the two pines never overlapped, but merely approached each other when hybrids were first formed. The hybrid swarm then might have originated in a disturbed area not previously occupied by either parent.

There is no botanical evidence at present of a preglacial hybridization between the two pines. Apparently there had been no preglacial contact between lodgepole pine and jack pine; at least no fossil records are available that would indicate such contact. No signs of hybridization between these two pines have been reported in any part of their respective ranges other than the Alberta overlap area [although perhaps hybridization also occurs in the Mackenzie River area (Raup, 1947)].

Pines of an intermediate character are found occasionally west of and beyond the overlap area, as for instance near Seebe, between Calgary and Banff. There are also reports of intermediate forms in Saskatchewan. Both of these localities are not too far from the overlap area of Alberta.*

It is difficult to decide at present whether some introgression of the hybrids into one or both species has been in progress at the Alberta location. The genetic nature of the *P. contorta* × *P. banksiana* hybrid swarm of Alberta still awaits investigation.

## GENETIC AFFINITY OF PINES

Genetic affinity of pines in relation to their modern classification will be considered in Chapter 9. Here we will discuss the genetic relationship of pines without attempting their rearrangement.

If the genus *Pinus* is divided into two subgenera, (1) the subgenus *Haploxylon*, including the seven piñon pines, and (2) the subgenus

* Mirov, 1956.

*Diploxylon,* a certain correlation may be noticed between these major taxonomic categories and the capacity of pines to intercross.

1. The subgenus *Haploxylon,* consisting of thirty-two pines, has very broad limits of intercrossing. Artificial hybridization of some pines in the subgenus has not been attempted yet so the genetic behavior of *P. gerardiana* No. 92, *P. bungeana* No. 87, *P. aristata* No. 6, *P. balfouriana* No. 5, and *P. albicaulis* No. 1 is not known. But the rest of the *Haploxylon* pines, excluding the piñon pines, intercross rather freely. Difficulty has been encountered with *P. lambertiana,* which does not cross with North American pines but which has been crossed with two Asiatic pines (*P. armandi* and *P. koraiensis*).

The piñon pines, Nos. 7, 8, 9, 36, 37, 38, and 39 (Table 1–2), have not been hybridized artificially; under natural conditions, they possibly intercross, but Dr. Elbert L. Little, dendrologist of the U.S. Forest Service who studied the piñons intensively, has informed the author that in the overlap areas of different piñons, he was unable to detect any intermediate forms.* A biosystematical study of piñon pines accompanied with hybridization tests is much needed.

2. The subgenus *Diploxylon* is very heterogeneous as far as its genetic relationships are concerned. There are species, presumably closely related, that possess strong barriers to intercrossing, and again there occur species belonging to different groups and morphologically very different that cross naturally.

Group *Longifoliae* consists of two species: *P. roxburghii* No. 93 of the Himalaya and *P. canariensis* No. 72 of the Canary Islands. Brought together, these two pines apparently cross spontaneously. It is not known whether or not they cross with other pines.

The group *Leiophyllae* consists of three Mexican pines: *P. chihuahua* No. 40, *P. leiophylla* No. 41, and *P. lumholtzii* No. 42. Numbers 40 and 41 intercross naturally (Martínez, 1948). There are no reports of natural hybridization of *P. lumholtzii* with *P. chihuahua* and *P. leiophylla.*

Group *Pineae* consists of only one species, *P. pinea* No. 73. This pine does not cross with any other pines.

In Shaw's group *Macrocarpae,* two species, *P. sabiniana* No. 10 and *P. torreyana* No. 11, possess formidable barriers to crossing with pines of any other group, while the third pine, *P. coulteri* No. 12, hybridizes naturally with *P. jeffreyi* No. 13, which, according to Shaw (1914), belongs to the group *Australes* (Zobel, 1951).

In Shaw's group *Lariciones, P. nigra* of the Mediterranean region and nearby mountains crosses well with *P. thunbergii* No. 97 of Japan. *Pinus resinosa* No. 21 has been successfully crossed with *P. nigra* No. 74 (Critchfield 1963b).

* Personal communication.

*Pinus sylvestris* No. 69 of Eurasia was crossed by Wright (1953) with *P. densiflora* No. 95 of Japan. There is a report of a successful cross between *P. sylvestris* and *P. patula* No. 61 of Mexico (achieved in Germany using *P. patula* pollen from planted trees in Natal, South Africa (South Africa University 1955). *Pinus patula* is a pine of the group *Insignes*. This report should be verified.

Among Asiatic *Lariciones* pines, *P. tabulaeformis* No. 102 crosses naturally with *P. yunnanensis*. The hybrid was described as *P. densata* Masters. *Pinus yunnanensis* No. 103 apparently crosses with *P. khasya* No. 104, and probably only geographical barriers prevent intercrossing this pine with *P. insularis* No. 105 of Luzon. *Pinus taiwanensis* No. 99, *P. luchuensis* No. 98, and *P. hwangshanensis* No. 100 probably intercross, but it should be proven experimentally. Generally, pines of eastern Asia are still awaiting biosystematical investigation. *Pinus merkusii* No. 101 apparently does not cross with other pines of southeastern Asia (Nos. 103, 104, and 105).

No work has been done as yet with the genetic relationship of *P. tropicalis* No. 22, the only *Lariciones* pine of the Caribbean region. It might be possible that it hybridizes with other pines of the region (which belong to the group *Australes*), or had been hybridized in the past with some Mexican pines.

The group *Australes*, a strictly New World group, is rather heterogeneous. Critchfield (1963a) reviewed compatibility of the United States pines of this group. Southeastern American pines were found to be highly incompatible with western American pines. Within the southeastern species of the group *Australes*, there are also evidences of strong isolation mechanisms; for instance, *P. glabra* No. 26 is strongly isolated genetically from all other species of *Australes* (Critchfield, 1963a). *Pinus echinata* No. 25 and *P. palustris* No. 22 are extremely difficult to cross. *Pinus rigida* No. 29 of Shaw's group *Insignes* is impossible to cross with *P. elliottii* No. 23, but it was crossed with *P. echinata* No. 25 and *P. taeda* No. 24.

The relationship of Mexican pines of the group *Australes* has been little studied, although natural intercrossings are known within the *P. montezumae* complex or the *P. pseudostrobus* complex and between the two complexes.

As regards genetic relations of pines of the group *Insignes*, the western species of this group (*P. contorta* No. 16, *P. muricata* No. 18, *P. radiata* No. 19, and, to a certain extent, *P. attenuata* No. 17) have been studied well (Duffield, 1951; Critchfield, 1957; Forde, 1962). Forde concluded that there are in existence strong isolation barriers within the group *Insignes*. According to her, Duffield's statement that *P. attenuata, P. muricata,* and *P. radiata* "had been brought into all three possible combinations, is only partially correct." Under natural conditions, *P. radiata* is reluctant to cross with *P. attenuata*. Other investigators, however, have found that on the Monterey Peninsula, *P. muricata* and *P. radiata* hybridize freely.*

*Pinus contorta*, essentially a western American *Insignes* pine (although it reaches the Dakotas), crosses naturally with *P. banksiana*, a pine of the same group extending from Alberta, Canada, to the Atlantic Coast (Moss, 1949). But *P. banksiana* has sufficient genetic barriers to prevent its crossing with an eastern *Insignes* pine, *P. virginiana*.

Of the eastern American species of this group, *P. rigida* No. 29 and also *P. serotina* No. 30 have shown a close relationship with the pines of the group *Australes* (Nos. 24 and 25). Mexican *Insignes* have not been studied well. *Pinus greggii* No. 60 apparently crosses naturally with *P. patula* No. 61.

## SELF-FERTILIZATION IN PINES

Selfing occurs in pines, but there apparently are in operation some genetic or biochemical factors that are responsible for various types of inbreeding depressions in the offspring. Johnson's (1945) experiments in self-fertilization of *P. strobus* No. 20, *P. resinosa* No. 21, and *P. sylvestris* No. 69 demonstrated that there was no appreciable difference in seed set in open-, cross-, or self-pollinated cones of *P. strobus*. The other two pines, however, showed a marked reduction of seed set for self-pollinated cones.

Mortality of *P. resinosa* germinating seedlings from damping-off fungi, possibly caused by self-fertilization, was so high that no future experimentation was possible with this pine. Survival of *P. strobus* and *P. sylvestris* seedlings was much higher; they were examined when they were four years old. Progenies of these two self-fertilized pines showed less average growth, weight gain, and general vigor of growth than comparable cross- or open-pollinated seedlings. About one-quarter of all seedlings of *P. strobus* were chlorophyll deficient (Johnson, 1945).

Righter (1945) reported that in the selfing test of *P. jeffreyi* No. 13, a high percentage of seedlings resulting from the self-pollination were, on the average, much smaller than the backcross progeny from the same tree. Deleterious effects of inbreeding in pines also have been reported by Mergen (1954) and by Wright and Gabriel (1958).

Bingham and Squillace (1955) studied self-compatibility in *P. monticola* No. 4. They found that in controlled pollination, the percentage of cones that matured was the same for selfs and outcrosses, but the selfs

---

* Personal comment of Professor William J. Libby, University of California.

contained 50 per cent less seeds and most of these were hollow. Those that appeared normal gave from 7 to 13 per cent less germinability, and the resulting seedlings, on the average, exhibited less height growth.

The same team of investigators (Squillace and Bingham, 1958) also studied selective fertilization in *P. monticola* No. 4. In the three tests involving different parents, crossing exceeded selfing in two of them, but the reverse was true in the third test. It was concluded that some trees may have a low degree of self-compatibility, while in others it may be relatively high. "In a highly self-fertile tree, crossing exceeded selfing when its own pollen was mixed with that from one tree, while the reverse was true when its own pollen was mixed with that of another tree." Studies of Fowler (1962) indicated that *P. resinosa* was little affected by selfing. Some effects of inbreeding in pines are discussed by Righter (1962).

It should be emphasized, however, that self-fertility is not a prerequisite to inbreeding. It is entirely possible that a certain degree of inbreeding goes on within the species of the genus *Pinus*, and at present we can only speculate what would be the results of prolonged inbreeding within two species of pines and subsequent interspecific crossing.

## HETEROSIS IN PINES

Righter (1962) came to the conclusion that "heterozygosity appears to be obligate in *P. taeda* No. 24, *P. ponderosa* No. 14, *P. jeffreyi* No. 13, and *probably in all* pines." He also agreed with Bingham and Squillace (1955) that the degree of self-fertility varies from tree to tree. There are numerous reports of heterosis in artificially produced interspecific hybrids of pines, but the disturbing fact is that some hybrids possessed heterosis in one location and not in another. Righter gives, as an example, experiments with crossing *P. monticola* No. 4 and *P. strobus* No. 20 by Bingham, Squillace, and Patton (1956). In the state of Washington, home of *P. monticola*, the three-year-old hybrids of this pine were taller than *P. strobus*, while in Wisconsin, home of *P. strobus*, this latter pine outgrew the hybrid. In Righter's own tests (Righter, 1945), the seed parent, *P. monticola*, grew at a high altitude of the Sierra Nevada, California; pollen of *P. strobus* came from the east, and the tests were made at about 900 m above sea level, i.e., in an entirely different environment than that of the mother tree. The hybrids displayed pronounced vigor, and they outgrew the *P. monticola* × *monticola* progeny.

Duffield and Snyder (1958) demonstrated that *P. nigra* × *P. resinosa* hybrids were superior to their parents, and Righter illustrated superiority of this hybrid over the parents with a photograph (Righter, 1962). (See Plate 4–4.)

**Plate 4–4.** Hybrid vigor shown by *P. nigra* No. 74 × *P. resinosa* No. 21.
The four tall seedlings are hybrids; the remainder are wind-pollinated offspring
of both parents. (U.S. Forest Service photo.)

Buchholz (1945) observed embryonic heterosis in the *P. contorta* ×
*P. banksiana* hybrid. The hybrid embryos were, stage by stage, intermediate in size between those of the parents, but the hybrid embryos
grew faster and reached comparable stages in their development more
quickly than did the embryos of the parents. Later reports from the
Institute of Forest Genetics indicated that the hybrid maintained its
superiority in growth rate for over twenty years in Placerville, California,
where, however, environmental conditions are very different from those
of both parents (Righter, 1962).

In view of the above findings, it appears that heterosis is a well-established phenomenon in pines. The maintenance of heterozygosity undoubtedly has played an important part in evolution of pines. On the
other hand, self-fertility is apparently not uncommon in pines.

## GENETIC VARIABILITY OF PINES

Variability is present in any species of the genus *Pinus*, and it goes
down to the individual level. There are no two trees exactly alike either

morphologically or chemically (cf. Chapter 7). Zobel (1961 and earlier papers) contributed much to the studies of variability of morphological characters in pines. Variability may be caused by hybridization among individual trees belonging to different species. This situation was demonstrated by the study of the hybrid swarm in Alberta, Canada (Mirov, 1956). On the other hand, in a pine forest composed of only one species, where there is no possibility of interspecific hybridization, the variability of individual trees is caused by intercrossing between individual members of the population. In both cases, however, it is important to keep in mind that it is not the species or varieties that hybridize naturally or are hybridized artificially; it is the individual trees that cross one with another.

*Pinus ponderosa* No. 14 and *P. jeffreyi* No. 13 are partially sympatric; where their areas overlap, they grow in mixed stands. Haller (1962) concluded that both pines are highly variable and that variation is displayed by single individuals, between individuals, and between populations. A similar statement can be made about almost any species in the genus *Pinus*. The opinion of the author is that *P. ponderosa* is much more variable than *P. jeffreyi*. The former is a younger, more aggressive species, whose area extends to Nebraska, Oklahoma, and the Trans-Pecos region of Texas; it includes several named and more yet unnamed varieties. *Pinus jeffreyi* is a California endemic, old, and rather conservative and stable pine (Mirov, 1938). Haller's study, however, has revealed a trend very significant for all pines—that even such old and stable species as *P. jeffreyi* nevertheless show considerable, if somewhat restrained, variability. It has been known for a long time that the two pines hybridize naturally (Mirov, 1932), and it has been puzzling how these two pines have maintained their specificity in a mixed forest. Haller found that there is no evidence that they have tended to merge during the last few thousand years. He arrived at an important conclusion:

. . . that recent mutations, as a source of variability, have not played an important role in adaptability and thus in survival of the two species. Their adaptability has been caused by hybridization; there has been a constant exchange of genes between the two species, . . . but their over-all variability may still remain constant because of continuous elimination of variants from the population, either by change or by natural selection.

Even in the most genetically stable pines, one finds some variability. A good example is *P. sabiniana* No. 10. Apparently, it does not cross naturally with any other species (it has been crossed experimentally with *P. torreyana*). Griffin (1962) found that even in *P. sabiniana* there can be detected slight variability manifesting itself in occasional change of number of needles, in short shoots, or in somewhat different germination patterns in seed from different places.

Variability in species of the genus *Pinus* can be roughly measured by the number of named varieties within a species. While some (usually widely distributed) species contain several named varieties, others, also widely distributed, have no described varieties.

In the Mediterranean region, six species out of twelve are variable. *Pinus nigra* No. 74 is extremely variable (*P. heldreichii* No. 75 has been considered by some to be a variety of *P. nigra*); *P. montana* No. 76 and *P. brutia* No. 78 together with No. 79 and 81 may be considered as variable species. *Pinus pinea* No. 73 has one variety, but possibly it has been induced by man. The remaining five pines, Nos. 70, 71, 72, 73, and 80, are relatively stable. *Pinus halepensis* No. 77 hybridizes naturally with *P. brutia* No. 78.

In northern Eurasia, *P. sylvestris* No. 69 is very variable; *P. sibirica* No. 67 is moderately variable (three varieties of this pine have been described).

Among the diploxylon pines of eastern Asia, there are some stable species. *Pinus merkusii* No. 101 possesses no conspicuous variability over its extensive and discontinuous distribution. One variety has been described from the extreme northwest of the area of *P. merkusii* (Chevalier, 1944). *Pinus massoniana* No. 94 occupies an enormous area of southern China approaching closely the area of *P. yunnanensis*, yet it has only one, uncertain variety. On the other hand, *P. tabulaeformis* No. 102 of northern China has several named varieties. Variability of *P. yunnanensis* No. 103 is not well known. In the northeast, the area of this pine overlaps the area of *P. tabulaeformis*, forming a hybrid known as *P. densata*. In the southwest, *P. yunnanensis* merges into *P. khasya* No. 104. *Pinus roxburghii* No. 93 of the Himalaya has no named varieties.

Among haploxylon pines of eastern Asia, *P. bungeana* No. 87 and *P. koraiensis* No. 82 are conservative and stable; so are the two Himalayan species, *P. griffithii* No. 91 and *P. gerardiana* No. 92. In contrast, *P. armandi* No. 86 is variable. The complex of haploxylon pines extending from southern Hokkaido through Formosa and Hainan to southern China and southern Vietnam, according to some botanists (Wu, 1947), consists of several varieties of *P. parviflora*. It is, rather, a series of vicarious species: *P. pentaphylla* No. 83, and *P. himekomatsu* No. 84, both of Japan; *P. morrisonicola* No. 85 of Formosa, *P. fenzeliana* No. 89, *P. kwangtungensis* No. 90 of southern China, and possibly the *pin du moyen Annam* (Ferré, 1960). Variability within the "*P. parviflora* complex" is very little known. *Pinus pumila* No. 68 has no named varieties; possibly this pine is closer to *P. pentaphylla* than to *P. sibirica* No. 67 as generally thought (Gaussen, 1960).

Variability of Caribbean pines is little known. *Pinus caribaea* No. 62 of Central America requires more study.

Out of nineteen species of western American species, *P. ponderosa* No. 14, *P. contorta* No. 16, and *P. flexilis* No. 2, although they have not many named varieties, can be classified as variable pines. *Pinus muricata* No. 18, a pine of limited distribution along the California Coast, is surprisingly variable. As a result of his studies of variation in *P. muricata*, Duffield (1951) came to the conclusion that this pine can be separated into two forms: the northern, from northern California to Sonoma County; and the southern, south of San Francisco Bay to Baja California. Duffield found a greater variability in the northern populations than in the southern. The Inverness population, located between the northern and the southern localities, was also found to be rather polymorphic. The remaining fifteen species, or an overwhelming majority, have no described varieties, and it is not expected that new ones will be described in the future, with the possible exception of *P. monticola* No. 4.

With two or three exceptions, eastern American pines have no described varieties. Recently, Little and Dorman (1952) described *P. elliottii* var. *densa* No. 63. It is possible that this pine is a Caribbean species that has reached Florida relatively recently. Probably, it crosses with *P. elliottii* of the more northern part of the Southeast. *Pinus strobus* has no recognized varieties in Canada or in the United States. *Pinus strobus* L. var. *chiapensis* Martínez of tropical Mexico needs thorough study. Possibly, it is an independent species. *Pinus clausa* (Chapman) Vasey shows some variability in opening of its cones, but no attempt has been made to describe the western race as a variety.

## UNIQUENESS OF TROPICAL HIGHLANDS OF THE NEW WORLD

In the tropical highlands of Mexico, we see a striking difference between the genetic setup of pines of that region on the one hand and the two other regions of continental North America on the other. Field observations indicate that the pine region of the Mexican–Central American tropical highlands is characterized by almost total absence of relics, incapable of crossing with other species as is the case of the western pine region of America. In comparison with the eastern United States, where there are only two named varieties, both subjects of a further investigation (see pines No. 20 and No. 23 in Chapter 3), in Mexico we find many pine species that intercross freely and where there are many varieties, named and unnamed.

Excluding four piñon pines (Nos. 36, 37, 38, and 39; see Table 1–2), which belong to the arid region of Mexico, there are in that country only three haploxylon species, all of Shaw's (1914) group *Strobi*. Of these, *P. strobiformis* No. 35 is a pine of the range-and-basin province, and *P. strobus* var. *chiapensis* No. 34 is a tropical pine of relatively low elevations; it grows along the escarpments of the Mexican and Central American plateaus. Therefore, the only haploxylon species that is a component of the pine forests of the Mexican–Central American highlands is *P. ayacahuite* No. 33.

On the other hand, diploxylon pines are numerous in the Mexican highlands. In Mexico, there are twenty-one or twenty-two species of this subgenus. (*Pinus oaxacana,* described by the author, is listed by Martínez as a variety of *P. pseudostrobus.*) Martínez (1948) described thirteen varieties and eight forms of diploxylon pines. Some of his species, such as *P. douglasiana* and *P. tenuifolia,* are considered by conservative American botanists (Shaw, 1914) as varieties of *P. pseudostrobus.* Martínez has been criticized for establishing too many species and naming too many varieties, but this criticism is not well founded. All collectors who recently explored Mexico (Loock, 1950; Schwerdtfeger, 1953; Zobel and Cech, 1957; Mirov, 1958; Hinds and Larsen, 1961) either describe new species and varieties (*P. patula* var. *longepedunculata,* Loock; *P. oaxacana,* Mirov) or comment on the variability of Mexican pines. Larsen not only agrees with Martínez that *P. douglasiana* is a species different from *P. pseudostrobus,* but believes that there is a pine in Michoacan somewhat resembling *P. douglasiana,* which deserves the rank of an independent species named *P. martinezii* (Larsen 1964).

Zobel and Cech (1957) have encountered, in northeastern Mexico, several apparently new varieties. Paul Allen, of the United Fruit Company, Tela, Honduras, in describing pines of San Salvador, hesitated to classify a pine that looked like both *P. rudis* No. 50 and *P. hartwegii* No. 49.[*] Schwerdtfeger (1953) described a new *P. tecumumani* from Guatemala (unfortunately in a manner unacceptable to taxonomists), whose appearance suggests that it is a new species. Standley and Steyermark (1958) attempted to classify this pine but could not arrive at any definite conclusion. A pine in the inland mountains of Honduras that goes under the name of *P. caribaea* No. 62 is possibly a new undescribed species.

To sum up, everyone who has collected recently in Mexico is convinced that Martínez is a rather conservative botanist and that in the future more varieties and even perhaps more species will be described from Mexico.[†] The existence of diversity and variability of pines of the subgenus *Diploxylon* in the tropical highlands of Mexico is well established.

The abundance of pine species in Mexico, their widespread inter-

---

[*] Personal communication.

[†] Andresen and Beaman (1961) recently described a new piñon pine, *P. culminicola.*

specific hybridization, and their pronounced intraspecific variability all bespeak that in the tropical highlands of Mexico and Central America, there has developed a secondary center of evolution and speciation of the genus *Pinus*. *Pines* occupied the region not earlier than the middle Tertiary period. Although the folded mountains of Mexico appeared above water at the end of the Cretaceous period, there have occurred, in the Tertiary period, approximately during the Miocene epoch, volcanic activities; as a result, lava covered by far the greater part of Mexico. Accordingly, the tropical highlands of Mexico became available to colonization by plants during the second half of the Tertiary period (Wulff, 1944). Pines, as individual trees, had penetrated to Mexico along the escarpments of the plateau earlier in the Tertiary period. Being pioneer invaders throughout their history, the pines took advantage of the newly exposed terrain of the plateau, advanced there, and formed extensive forests (see Chapter 2).

Stebbins (1959) postulated that for major advancement in evolution, a group of plants (population) with a high degree of variability must be placed in a diversified environment. As far as pines are concerned, such conditions have existed in the highlands of Mexico since the second half of the Tertiary period. The habitat there seems to have been extremely favorable for forming hybrid swarms of many species in many places. The topography also has been favorable to hybridization among pines, since the tropical zone there is located very close to the high mountains. Although the climate is diversified, ranging from humid hot lowlands (*tierra caliente*) to the cool to cold of high mountains (*tierra fria*), it is seldom too severe for pines, and the growing season is long. Precipitation is chiefly in summer; it is abundant and favorable to the survival and development of pine seedlings. The diversity of habitat of Mexican tropical highlands proved to be favorable to the origin and development of agricultural plants. It has also been inducive to development and speciation of pines. However remote these two groups of plants are, some of the underlying factors causing this phenomenon may have been the same. Some may say that the habitat of agricultural plants—cucurbits, beans, and maize—and their ancestors is the low and intermediate altitude valleys, while the habitat of pines is the mountain slopes. However, this argument is not valid. Cultivation in the Mexican highlands goes up the steep slopes of the mountains well above the valley floor into and beyond pine forests. Every traveler notices *milpas* located high in the mountains—in many cases to their tops. In Guatemala, near Chichicastenango, at about 2500 m altitude, agricultural crops, peaches, and young pines are growing in the same habitat. Again, in Chiapas, at about the same altitude, there are magnificent groves of *P. montezuma*. These are located

**Plate 4–5.** Highlands of Mexico. Patches of pines intermingle with culti-vated land near Zacapoaxtla, in northeastern Puebla, at altitudes of 2000–3000 m. The two trees at the left are *P. patula* No. 61. (Photo by Norberto Sánchez-Mejorada.)

in lush green valleys covered partly by pines and partly by cornfields. There are many more examples of places where agricultural plants and pines share the same environment.

It is entirely possible that in the highlands of Mexico and Central America, the predecessors of agricultural plants and the pines shared the same environment since the second half of the Tertiary period. Pines in their development apparently have been as much benefited by this envi-ronment as have the agricultural plants—hence, the astonishing variability among the pines in that region.

**Plate 4–6.** Pine forest at 2400 m in Chiapas, Mexico. Overmature *P. monte-zumae* No. 47 on the floor of an agricultural valley, intermingling with fields of maize and beans. (Photo by N. T. Mirov.)

## SUMMARY

From a genetic point of view, the genus *Pinus* appears deceivingly simple; all species have the same number of chromosomes of relatively uniform morphology. The complexity of the genus arises from its widespread interspecific hybridization.

Some species do have efficient barriers that prevent their crossing; these may be geographical, phenological, or developmental. On the other hand, many recognized species intercross freely, and their hybrids are fertile. Genetic affinity of species in the two subgenera of the genus is not completely known, but what has been found so far proved to be useful in the classification of pines (see Chapter 9).

Self-pollination has been observed in several species of the genus *Pinus*, while heterosis is a well-established phenomenon among pines. These two factors should be considered against the background of paleogeography of the genus. When populations of pines were separated during transgressions of the seas, they were subjected to conditions favorable to inbreeding. When the land masses were reunited and the inbred populations were brought in contact again, heterozygosity might have been developed.

Hybridization has played an important part in evolution of the pines. Judging by the number of named varieties (as a first approximation), intraspecific variability of many pine species is low. On the other hand, many species are extremely variable, and their variability extends beyond their specific boundaries. Such variable species of the genus *Pinus* are numerous in Mexican–Central American highlands where a secondary center of evolution and speciation has developed.

The main cause of *genetic variability* in pines as observed in the field is mutation. Hybridization affects the distribution, and to some extent the frequency of the mutant genes. The main cause of *variability* of pines is the environment.

## LITERATURE CITATIONS

ANDERSON, E. 1949. Introgressive hybridization. John Wiley & Sons, Inc., New York.

ANDRESEN, JOHN W., and JOHN H. BEAMAN. 1961. A new species of *Pinus* from Mexico. Arnold Arboretum Jour., 42:437–41.

BANNISTER, M. H. 1958. Evidence of hybridization between *Pinus attenuata* and *P. radiata* in New Zealand. Roy. Soc. New Zeal. Trans. and Proc., 85:217–25.

BERG, L. S. 1950. Natural regions of the U.S.S.R. The Macmillian Co., New York.

BINGHAM, R. T., and A. E. SQUILLACE. 1955. Self-compatibility and effects of self-fertility in western white pines. Forest Sci., 1:121–29.

———, A. E. SQUILLACE, and R. F. PATTON. 1956. Vigor, disease resistance and field performance in juvenile progenies of the hybrid *Pinus monticola Dougl.* × *P. strobus L.* Ztschr. Forstgenetick u. Forstpflanzenzüchtung., 5(4):104–12.

BUCHHOLZ, J. T. 1945. Embryological aspects of hybrid vigor in pines. Science, 102:135–42.

CAIN, STANLEY A. 1944. Foundations of plant geography. Harper & Row, New York.

CARRUTHERS, GUY. 1956. Our strange debt to the "'gasoline tree." Westways, 48 (January):14–15.

CHEVALIER, A. 1944. Notes sur les Conifères de l'Indochine. Rev. de Bot. Appl. et d'Agr. Trop., 24(Jan.–March, 1944):7–34. (Also called Bul. No. 269–271.)

CRITCHFIELD, WILLIAM B. 1957. Geographic variation in *Pinus contorta*. (Maria Moors Cabot Foundation, Pub. No. 3.) Harvard University, Cambridge, Mass.

———. 1963a. Hybridization of the southern pines in California. (South. Forest Tree Improvement Com. Pub. 22.) Forest Genet. Workshop, Macon, Ga. Pp. 40–48.

———. 1963b. The Austrian × red pine hybrid. Silvae Genetica, 12:187–92.

DUFFIELD, JOHN W. 1951. Interrelationships of the California closed-cone pines with special reference to *Pinus muricata* D. Don. Unpublished Ph.D. dissertation, University of California, Berkeley.

——— and E. BAYNE SNYDER. 1958. Benefits from hybridizing American forest trees. Jour. Forestry, 56:809–15.

FERRÉ, Y. DE. 1960. Une nouvelle espèce de pin au Viet-Nam, *Pinus dalatensis*. Soc. Hist. Nat. Bul., 95:1–10 (also called p:171–80).

FORDE, MARGOT BERNICE. 1963. Variation in the natural populations of Monterey pine (*Pinus radiata* Don) in California. Unpublished Ph.D. dissertation, University of California, Davis.

FOWLER, D. P. 1962. Initial studies indicate *Pinus resinosa* little affected by selfing. Proc. 9th Northeastern Forest Tree Improvement Conf. Syracuse, N.Y., Aug. 23–25, 3–8, 1961.

GAUSSEN, H. 1960. Les gymnospermes actuelles et fossiles. Fasc. VI. Les Coniférales Généralités, Genre *Pinus*. Toulouse (City) Univ. Lab. Forest. Trav., Tome 2, Vol. I, Chap. XI.

GRIFFIN, JAMES RICHARD. 1962. Intraspecific variation in *Pinus sabiniana* Dougl. Unpublished Ph.D. dissertation, University of California, Berkeley.

GUSTAFSSON, AKE. 1960. Polyploidy and mutagenesis in forest-tree breeding. 5th World Forestry Cong. Proc., **2**:793–803.

HALLER, JOHN R. 1962. Variation and hybridization in ponderosa and Jeffrey pines. Calif. Univ., Pubs. Bot., **34**:123–66.

HINDS, H. V., and E. LARSEN. 1961. Collecting tree seed in Mexico. Empire Forestry Rev., **40**:43–53.

HYUN, SIN KYU. 1954. Induction of polyploidy in pines by means of colchicine treatment. Ztschr. f. Forstgenetik u. Forstpflanzenzüchtung, **3**:25–33.

JOHNSON, L. P. V. 1945. Reduced vigour, chlorophyll deficiency, and other effects of self-fertilization in *Pinus*. Canad. Jour. Res. Sect. C, Bot. Sci., **23**:145–49.

KOMISSAROV, D. A. 1947. Osobennosti poliploidnoi sosny (Pinus silvestris L.) Poluchennoi pri pomoshchi kolkhitsina (Polyploid *Pinus sylvestris* obtained by treatment with colchicine). Dok. Akad. Nauk S.S.S.R., **58**:2077–80.

LARSEN, EGON. 1964. A new species of pine from Mexico. Madroño, **17**:217–18.

LIDDICOET, A. R., and F. I. RIGHTER. 1961. Trees of the Eddy Arboretum, Institute of Forest Genetics, Placerville, Calif. (U.S. Forest Serv., Pacific Southwest Forest and Range Expt. Sta. Misc. Paper No. 43. Berkeley, Calif.

LITTLE, ELBERT L., JR., and KEITH W. DORMAN. 1952. Slash pine (*Pinus elliottii*) its nomenclature and varieties. Jour. Forestry, **50**:918–23.

LOOCK, E. E. M. 1950. The pines of Mexico and British Honduras. (So. Africa Dept. Forestry, Bul. No. 35.) Pretoria.

LUNA, CARLOS LUIS DIAZ. 1962. Estudio chromosomico de *Pinus pinceana* Gordon. Inst. Nac. de Invest. y Exper. Agron. y Forest. Bol. No. 4.

MACHADO, DOMINGOS PEREIRA. 1943. Inducão de poliploides no *Pinus pinaster* Sol. e no *Quercus suber* L. Lisboa (City) Inst. Super. de Agron. An., **14**:185–87.

McWILLIAM, J. R. 1959. Interspecific incompatibility in *Pinus*. Amer. Jour. Bot., **46**:425–33.

MARTÍNEZ, MAXIMINO. 1948. Los pinos Mexicanos (2d ed.). Ediciones Botas, Mexico [City].

MEHRA, P. N., and T. N. KHOSHOO. 1956. Cytology of conifers. I. Jour. Genet., **54**: 165–85.

MERGEN, F. 1954. Selection and breeding of slash and longleaf pine at Lake City, Florida. Internatl. Union Forest Res. Organizations Cong. Proc., **11**(1953):481–87.

MIROV, N. T. 1932. A note on Jeffrey and western yellow pine. Jour. Forestry, **30**: 93–94.

———. 1938. Phylogenetic relations of *Pinus jeffreyi* and *Pinus ponderosa*. Madroño, **4**:169–71.

———. 1956. Composition of turpentine of lodgepole × jack pine hybrids. Canad. Jour. Bot., **34**:443–57.

———. 1958. *Pinus oaxacana*: A new species from Mexico. Madroño, **14**:145–50.

——— and P. STOCKWELL. 1939. Colchicine treatment of pine seeds. Jour. Hered., **30**:389–90.

MOSS, E. H. 1949. Natural pine hybrids in Alberta. Canad. Jour. Res., Sect. C, Bot. Sci., **27**:218–29.

PRAVDIN, L. F. 1964. Sosna obyknovennaia: [*P. sylvestris*] Izmenchivost, vnutrividovaia sistematika i selektsiia (*Pinus sylvestris*: Variability, intraspecific systematics, and selection). Akad. Nauk. S.S.S.R. Laboratoria Lesovedrniia, Nauka, Moscow.

RAUP, HUGH M. 1947. The botany of southwestern Mackenzie. Arnold Arboretum of Harvard University, Sargentia VI, Cambridge, Mass.

RIGHTER, F. I. 1945. *Pinus*: The relationship of seed size and seedling size to inherent vigor. Jour. Forestry, **43**:(2):131–37.

——. 1962. Evidence of hybrid vigor in forest trees. In Tree growth, ed. by T. T. KOZLOWSKI. The Ronald Press Co., New York. Pp. 345–55.

ROLLINS, REED C. 1954. Interspecific hybridization and its role in plant evolution. Internatl. Cong. Bot., Paris, Proc., 1(Sect. 9):172–80.

SANTAMOUR, F. S., JR., 1960. New chromosome counts in *Pinus* and *Picea*. Silvae Genetica, 9(3):87–88.

SAX, KARL. 1960. Meiosis in interspecific pine hybrids. Forest Sci. 6:135–138.

—— and HALLEY JOLIVETTE SAX. 1933. Chromosome number and morphology in the conifers. Arnold Arboretum Jour., 14:356–75.

SAYLOR, L. C. 1961. A karyotypic analysis of selected species of *Pinus*. Silvae Genetica, 10:77–84.

SCHWERDTFEGER, FRITZ. 1953. Informe al gobierno de Guatemala sobre la entomologia forestal de Guatemala. Vol. I. Los pinos de Guatemala. Organ. de las Naciones Unidas Agr. y Alimente, No. 202, Rome.

SHAW, GEORGE RUSSELL. 1914. The genus *Pinus*. (Arnold Arboretum Pub. No. 5.) Houghton Mifflin Co., Boston.

SOUTH AFRICA, UNIVERSITY OF. 1955. Hybrid between *P. sylvestris* and *P. patula*. (Annual report of Department of Forestry, University of South Africa for the year ending 31st March, 1954.) P. 38.

SQUILLACE, A. E., and R. T. BINGHAM. 1958. Selective fertilization in *Pinus monticola* (Dougl. I. Preliminary results. Silvae Genetica, 7(6):188–96.

STANDLEY, PAUL, and JULIAN Á. STEYERMARK. 1958. Flora of Guatemala. Fieldiana: Bot., 24:1. Chicago Nat. Hist. Mus.

STEBBINS, G. LEDYARD. 1959. The role of hybridization in evolution. Amer. Phil. Soc. Proc., 103:231–51.

STONE, E. C., and J. W. DUFFIELD. 1950. Hybrids of sugar pine by embryo culture. Jour. Forestry, 48(3):200–201.

VIDAKOVIČ, M. 1958. Investigations on the Intermediate Type between the Austrian and Scots pine. Silvae Genetica, 7:12–19.

WRIGHT, JONATHAN W. 1953. Summary of tree-breeding experiments by the Northeastern Forest Experiment Station 1947–1950. (U.S. Forest Serv. Northeast. Forest Expt. Sta. Paper No. 56.) Upper Darby, Pa.

—— and W. J. GABRIEL. 1958. Species hybridization in the hard pines, series sylvestres. Silvae Genetica, 7:109–15.

WU, CHUNG-LWEN. 1947. The phytogeographical distribution of pine in China. Unpublished A.M.F. thesis. Yale University, New Haven.

WULFF, E. V. 1944. Istoricheskaia geografiia rastenii (Historical plant geography). Izd. Akad. Nauk S.S.S.R., Moscow.

ZINNAI, I. 1952. Tetraploid plants of Japanese red pine (*Pinus densiflora* Sieb. et Zucc.) discovered in transplant beds. Jap. Soc. Forestry Jour., 34(6):185–87.

ZOBEL, BRUCE. 1951. The natural hybrid between Coulter and Jeffrey pines. Evolution, 5:405–13.

——. 1961. Inheritance of wood properties in conifers. Silvae Genetica, 10:65–70.

—— and FRANKLIN CECH. 1957. Pines from Nuevo Leon, Mexico. Madroño, 14(4):133–44.

# 5

# Morphology and Reproduction

The purpose of this chapter is to describe the pine tree, its external and internal morphology, and to trace its development, in general terms, from seed to seed. Because of the limits of this book, developmental aspects of pine structures and their comparison with those of other conifer genera are not considered. For fundamental aspects of pine anatomy, the reader is referred to appropriate texts, especially to the books by Esau (1953, 1960), Foster and Gifford (1959), and Chamberlain (1935).

A pine tree, as we see it, consists of a tapering column of wood, called the stem or trunk, enveloped in a sheath of bark (Plate 5–1). The trunk supports branches that carry the crown of narrow, needle-like leaves. A pine tree may be as high as 75 m (*P. lambertiana* No. 3). The tree has a root system that serves for anchoring the stem and for obtaining water and minerals from the soil.

Botanically, the pine tree is described as a sporophyte (see page 380). When it reaches physiological maturity, it develops male and female organs; microsporangia and megasporangia, respectively, are borne in separate strobili (cones) on the same tree. After pollination, the microsporangia are shed, while the small megasporangiate cones persist and develop into the pine cone, which contains seed. Under proper conditions, the seed germinates and develops into a seedling; it passes through a juvenile stage and becomes again a mature pine tree capable of bearing cones and producing seeds.

Seed crops occur, not annually, but at intervals of two or three or even more years. Seed-bearing capacity decreases with old age, but it does not cease entirely, and pines continue to produce seeds until their death. Longevity of some pines, such as *P. radiata* No. 19, is not over 150 years,

**Plate 5–1.** *Left: P. ponderosa* No. 14 at about 1800 m in the Sierra Nevada, California. This species may reach a height of 60.0 m and a diameter of 2.4 m. Thickness of bark at the lower part of the trunk may be 10 cm. (Photo by A. E. Wieslander. Courtesy California Forest & Range Experiment Station, U.S. Forest Service.) *Right: P. lambertiana* No. 3 on its way to a sawmill. When alive, it was 64 m tall and 2 m in diameter. (U.S. Forest Service photo by Henry Fowler.)

while in *P. lambertiana* No. 3, the life span reaches 600 years. According to recent findings, *P. aristata* No. 6 may live as long as 4600 years (Schulman, 1958).

## THE STEM

### The Apex

The primary growth of the pine shoot is the result of the activity of an apical meristem. The latter is located at the uppermost tip of the shoot (Plate 5–2) as well as at the tip of each branch. The actual shoot apex is sometimes referred to as the growing point. Division of the meristematic cells is not limited to the apex but also takes place at some distance from the apical meristems. Cell elongation also takes place at some distance from the apex (Foster, 1949).

The apical meristem is not an unorganized mass of embryonic cells; it is a structure where different regions can be discerned and where certain differentiation in cells exists that manifests itself in later organization of the stem (Esau, 1960).

The initial cells and their immediate derivatives are called *promeristems*. These derivatives differentiate into primary meristems that are precursors of the basic systems of plant organization: *protoderm,* from which epidermal tissues are formed; *procambium,* which gives rise to the primary vascular (conducting) tissue; and *ground meristem,* from which originate ground (fundamental) tissues (parenchyma, sclerenchyma, and collenchyma).

Later in the development of the plant, the cells of permanent tissues may again become capable of division, giving rise to secondary meristems: vascular cambium and cork cambium or phellogen. Vascular cambia, however, more usually are derived directly from procambial tissue. In pine, a very small portion of the cambium is of interfascicular origin. "Wood, which is very largely secondary xylem, is a product of the vascular cambium." Topographically, the apical meristems are primary meristems, and the lateral are secondary meristems (Esau, 1953).

Primary meristematic tissue located in places other than apical meristems, between the regions of already differentiated tissues (for example, at the base of secondary needles), is called intercalary meristem (see Needles, p. 370). From development of meristems, in a complicated process of maturation, involving changes in structure and physiology, the whole body of a pine tree is formed.

Relatively little is known about apical meristems of the genus *Pinus.* In Clowes' (1961) treatise on the apical meristems, pines are mentioned only in passing. Studies of apical meristems of *P. sylvestris* No. 69 by

**Plate 5–2.** *Left:* 1–2, dormant buds of *P. lambertiana* No. 3; 3–5, stages of development of young shoot (note male strobili on 5); 6, dormant bud of *P. ponderosa* No. 14. *Right:* median longitudinal section of winter bud (young shoot with unexpanded internodes) of *P. lambertiana*. The terminal bud scales at the base of the bud and the portions of the scales subtending short shoots were removed. (Photos from Sacher, 1954.)

Gifford and Wetmore (1957) have shown that there are no basic differences between the vegetative apex and the reproductive apex, which supposedly arises from a modified portion of the former. In reality, both categories of the apical meristem, at least in *P. sylvestris*, are similar in their structure. The shoot apices of pines, as judged by evidence obtained by Sacher (1954) for *P. lambertiana* No. 3, a haploxylon pine, and *P. ponderosa* No. 14, a diploxylon pine, exhibit a cytohistological zonation that Esau discussed in her *Plant Anatomy* (1953) and which she later illustrated with a photomicrograph of *P. strobus* in her *Anatomy of Seed Plants* (1960). Sacher accepted Esau's concept that evolution of conifers involved a refinement of the meristem in the sense that it became simpler, with less diversity in growing zones and at the same time with a more precise separation of zones of surface and volume growth, each derived from independent initials (Esau, 1953). Within the genus *Pinus*, then, the subgenus *Haploxylon*, as represented by *P. lambertiana* No. 3 with its more diversified meristem, is more primitive than the subgenus *Diploxylon*, as exemplified by *P. ponderosa* No. 14, for the diploxylon pines have a less distinctly defined central mother cell zone and possess a more refined apical meristem (Sacher, 1954). As Sacher suggested, further studies with other species of the genus are desirable.

In 1963, Romberger reviewed anatomical, physiological, and morphogenic aspects of meristems, growth, and development of woody plants. In Romberger's book, the reader will find valuable information on organization of gymnosperm shoot apices. Pines are mentioned on several occasions.


## The Wood

**Sapwood and Heartwood.**   In a transverse section of a pine stem, one can see two distinct parts. Outside are tissues commonly called "bark" (see p. 362); inside is the xylem, or wood. These two elements of the stem have their origin in a layer of lateral meristem located between them called vascular cambium.

The vascular cambium develops from a primary meristematic tissue (the procambium), and it characteristically differentiates into primary vascular tissues (i.e., primary xylem and phloem).

In pines (as in other gymnosperms and in most dicotyledonous angiosperms), after the completion of primary differentiation, procambium remains active and develops into vascular cambium. In other words, procambium and cambium are really two stages of development of the vascular meristem.

Initial cells or initials of the vascular cambium as shown for *P. strobus* (Bailey, 1920) are of two kinds: the fusiform initials and the ray initials. The former are long, tapering cells that may be several hundred times longer than their diameter; these give origin to the tracheids of the xylem and to the sieve cells of the phloem. Variability in the size of the fusiform initials is very great.

In contrast, the ray initials are as long as they are wide; from them are formed the horizontal elements of the xylem and the phloem; they are much smaller than the fusiform initial cells. Both types of the initial cells are mononucleate, but while the ratio of the nucleus to the cytoplasm in the ray initials is nearly constant, it varies much in the fusiform initials.

The size of tracheids is determined partly by the size of the fusiform initials and partly by changes taking place during the differentiation of the xylem (Bailey, 1920). Length of fusiform initials increases with the axis, but after the length reaches a certain limit, it becomes constant.

Vascular cambium is not visible to the naked eye. What is often called, by foresters, the *cambium layer* in reality is the cambium and the adjacent regions of inner bark, or phloem, and of immature xylem. Since the actual cambium is usually not precisely identifiable, some botanists prefer not to designate the single layer of meristematic cells alone, but to use the term cambium in a broader sense to denote the entire zone of cell division of both the wood and the bark sides of the layer of initials (Bannan, 1962). The outer bark of pine sloughs off, the wood accumulates, and the diameter of the tree expands; in *P. lambertiana* No. 3, it may reach over 3 m.

In the wood part of the stem, one can discern the outer, lighter part, or sapwood, and the inner part, or heartwood, which is darker than the sapwood. The central part of the stem contains a parenchymatous pith clearly seen in cross-sections of young trees. All wood of young pines is functional; it is called sapwood. Its ray parenchyma cells, the tracheids, after they have lost their protoplasts, are active, serving as a water-conducting system. As a pine tree grows older, the cells of the ray parenchyma begin to die, first in the innermost growth layers; the tracheids cease to conduct water. Gradually, from year to year, the sapwood is converted into heartwood. The heartwood does not contain living cells; it becomes resinous and is enriched with polyphenolic compounds; it does not conduct water, and it serves mainly as a support for the tree.

The width of the sapwood changes with the age of the tree. The whole of a, say, twenty-year-old pine, excluding the remains of the pith, is sapwood. In old, slow-growing trees, the sapwood is very narrow.

**Growth Rings.** On the transverse section of a pine trunk, one notices concentric circles commonly called annual rings (Plate 5–3). The annual ring pattern is caused by formation of vigorously grown, thin-walled cells in the early wood; as the season progresses, the growth slows down, and in the late wood the cell walls become thicker. The term "annual ring" is not accurate; it originated in the northern countries where the periods of summer growth and winter rest are well defined, but even in countries where growth and rest periods alternate, formation of rings does not always coincide with the calendar year. Nevertheless, it is common to ascertain the age of a pine tree by counting its "annual rings." Larson (1956) believes, however, that this practice is often open to criticism. Occasionally, abnormalities occur; these are caused by adverse environmental conditions. Abnormalities include discontinuous rings, missing rings, extremely narrow rings, and no "annual rings" at all. Glock (1937) defined discontinuous rings as follows: "a ring locally present, is one present only in part on the sample or portion of the tree under study; the ring does not surround the entire stem as a continuous sheath. An absent ring is defined as one wholly missing from the sample." Only by examining an entire cross-section of a pine can one say which rings are discontinuous. Long ago, Hartig (1869) noticed that in a lopsided tree, the greatest number of rings would occur on the stem side possessing the largest portion of the crown. Subsequent investigations have also re-

**Plate 5–3.** *Left:* a rapidly growing *P. taeda* No. 24. *Right:* a slowly growing *P. palustris* No. 22. (U.S. Forest Service photo.)

vealed the occurrence of distorted, discontinuous, or missing rings in trees (Harper, 1913; Nägeli, 1935).

When the above-mentioned difficulties are taken into consideration, radial growth increments may be used to indicate the age of a pine. Using growth rings methodology, Schulman (1958) found that the oldest pine he encountered was *P. aristata* and that its age was over 4600 years. Schulman's conclusions on longevity of pines have been supported by the $C^{14}$ analysis of this pine.* and extended to other pines (Ferguson and Wright, 1963).

The determination of dates of events and intervals of time by comparative studies of the sequence of growth rings is known as dendrochronology (McGinnies, 1963).

Pines do not grow naturally in ever-humid tropics. When planted there, the radial growth of the trees is apparently continuous and often erratic; no definite annual rings are discerned, and it is extremely difficult to judge the age of the trees by counting their growth layers (see Chapter 6, Plate 6–3).

**Internal Morphology of Wood.**   The wood of pines consists mostly of elongated cells—tracheids. New tracheids are formed by the division

* C. W. Ferguson, personal communication.

of their mother cells in the cambium. The newly formed tracheids do not remain alive very long; as soon as their walls are thickened, cells lose their protoplasm and die. Wood parenchyma is absent in pines. Some preliminary and not too certain analyses seemed to indicate that wood parenchyma is present in *P. krempfii*, but these findings still require verification (Chapter 9, page 541).

The function of tracheids is twofold: they are strength-giving elements, and they comprise a system conducting water and minerals from the roots to the leaves. Water is transmitted in pines in a tortuous way—not through vessels with their perforations at the end as in broadleaf trees (angiosperms), but from one tracheid to another, laterally through the bordered pit pairs situated on the walls of the tracheids.

In the tracheid tissue, as seen in the transverse section, vertical resin canals are found. In pines, these canals, in active stages of oleoresin production, are lined with thin-walled, unpitted, and unlignified cells that are chief producers of oleoresin in pines (see Chapter 7). In the family Pinaceae, the thin-walled epithelial cells of resin canals occur only in the genus *Pinus*.

In *P. balfouriana* No. 5 and *P. aristata* No. 6, and also in the piñon pines (Nos. 7, 8, 9, 36), there occur thick-walled epithelial cells; these are, however, not very conspicuous, being interspersed among the usually thin-walled cells (Bailey, 1909).

Resin ducts are formed as intercellular spaces by separation of resin-producing parenchyma cells. There are indications that resin ducts develop as a response to injury, which may be quite remote from the place of the duct formation. This has been found by Bailey and Faull (1934) in *Sequoia sempervirens*, by Thomson and Sifton (1925) in *Picea*, and by Bannan (1936) in *Abies*. In pines, however, resin ducts are not necessarily a result of injury. Nevertheless, pines are very sensitive to wounding. The effect of wounding on formation of resin ducts is especially conspicuous in commercial turpentining operations. After a wound is inflicted, many resin ducts are formed above it. Resin ducts are much less frequent in the early wood than in the late wood. Available information regarding the development and structure of resin canals in the family Pinaceae and structural changes that occur during transformation of sapwood into heartwood is still inadequate. Comprehensive and reliable investigations are still greatly needed.

When sections of wood are further observed, there becomes evident another element, namely, the rays (Plates 5–4, 5–5, and 5–6). The rays are composed of living parenchyma cells and of marginal and interspersed tracheids that are devoid of protoplasts. The rays extend from the vascular cambium, i.e., from the periphery, toward the center. They are of two kinds: uniseriate, formed by one row of parenchyma cells; and

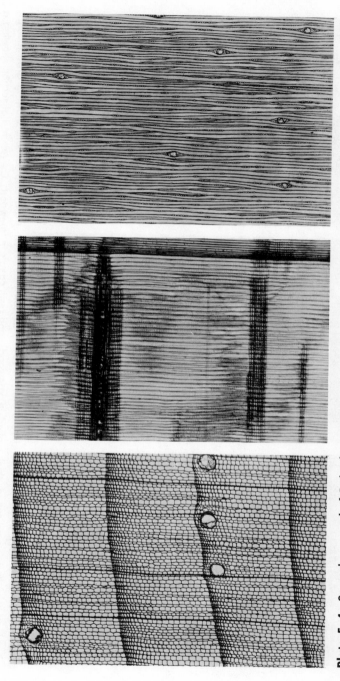

**Plate 5-4.** Secondary wood of *P. lambertiana* No. 3 (a haploxylon pine). *Left:* transverse section, showing growth rings, thin-walled tracheids of earlywood, thick-walled tracheids of latewood, and resin canals in the latewood, showing part of a growth ring and two kinds of rays (one with a horizontal resin canal). *Center:* radial section, *Right:* tangential section, showing tracheids with numerous rays, uniseriate and fusiform (with resin canals). (All × 20.) (U.S. Forest Service photos.)

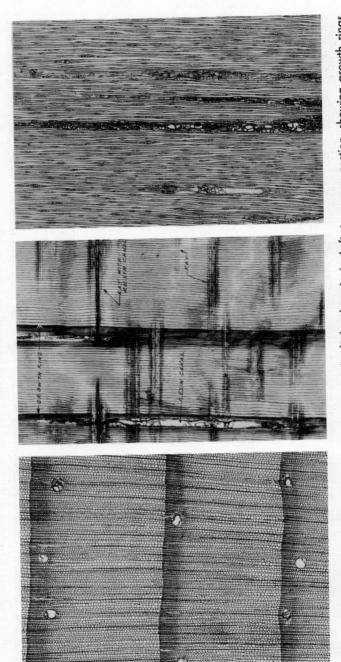

**Plate 5–5.** Secondary wood of *P. ponderosa* No. 14 (a diploxylon pine). *Left:* transverse section, showing growth rings, tracheids (thin-walled in earlywood, thick-walled in latewood), and resin canals in latewood. *Center:* radial section showing a growth ring, tracheids with bordered pits on their sides, rays, and resin canals. *Right:* tangential section, showing tracheids, vertical resin canals, and rays, both uniseriate and fusiform (with resin canals). (All × 20.) (U.S. Forest Service photos.)

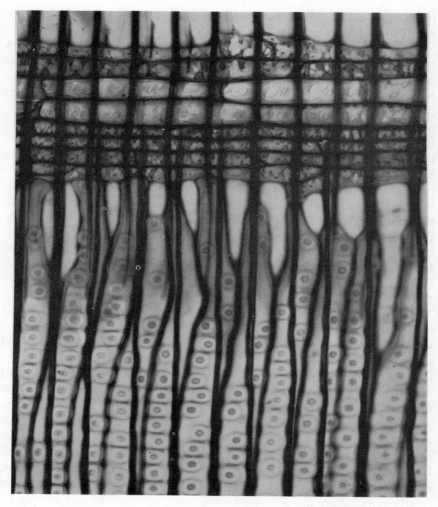

**Plate 5–6.** Radial section of secondary wood of *P. echinata* No. 25, showing ray tracheids with dentate walls and two rows of ray parenchyma with pits of different sizes and forms (× 225). (U.S. Forest Service photo.)

fusiform, composed of two or three, rarely four, rows. In the center of a fusiform ray is located a horizontal resin duct. The horizontal resin ducts of the rays intercross with the previously described vertical resin ducts of the sapwood forming an efficient oleoresin-producing system. The ray tracheids have small bordered pits on their walls, which may be smooth or dentate. On the parenchyma cells, the pits are large and simple, single, and of different shapes; in some groups of pines, the pits are roundish and more or less bordered.

In haploxylon pines, marginal and interspersed tracheids of the rays have smooth walls; there are also well-developed tangental pits in the ray tracheids formed at the end of the year's growth. Diploxylon pines possess dentate or reticulate tracheids of the rays; no tangental pits develop on the ray tracheids at the end of a year's growth. Generally, pines have very large pits, quite different from the round, small "*Picea*-like" pits. In piñons, and in foxtail (Nos. 5 and 6) pines, and in certain of the diploxylon species, the pits are smaller, approaching *Picea* type. Morphology of rays has been found useful in classification of pines.

There are two monographs on wood structure of the genus *Pinus:* one by Greguss (1955), recently translated from Hungarian into English; the other written in Russian (Budkevich, 1961). In Greguss' monograph, twenty-two haploxylon and forty-eight diploxylon pines are described; the text is illustrated with excellent photomicrographs. In a tabulated form, Greguss gives dimensions of tracheids, rays, and ray cells; diameter of resin ducts; number and diameter of pits; type of ray parenchyma cells, their diameter, and also some other anatomical features.

Apparently, not enough material was examined to make the presented data statistically reliable. Nomenclature of pines in Greguss' book is conspicuously out of date; for instance, *P. virginiana* is called by its old name, *P. inops*.

Budkevich, in her book on wood structure of Pinaceae (1961), devoted considerable space to the genus *Pinus*. Twenty-two haploxylon and fifty-one diploxylon pines were described, i.e., about the same number as in Greguss' monograph. But the two lists are not exactly identical. There are about ten species listed by Greguss that are omitted by Budkevich, and there is about the same number of pines in her book that are absent from Greguss' volume. Therefore, the two books, to a certain extent, complement each other. There are unavoidable discrepancies in the two treatises, and there are also conflicting interpretations of certain characters, such as pinoid types of pits. Apparently, the concept of the pinoid type of pits is different with the two investigators.

In the genus *Pinus*, the evolution of pits in ray parenchyma has been toward merging several pits into one large pit (some call it *fenestriform type*). Pinaceae, other than the genus *Pinus*, have true secondary walls in ray parenchyma and simple unbordered pits adjacent to bordered pits. This is two *Picea*-type pitting ("piceoid" of some authors). In Taxoidaceae and Cupressaceae, pitting is superficially like that in *Picea*, but since in these two families there are only thick primary walls in the ray parenchyma cells, no such pitting is visible.

Within the family Pinaceae, in the genera other than *Pinus,* in the cross-field, i.e., the areas of contact between parenchyma and tracheids (as seen in radial sections), the simple pits of the ray parenchyma cells are adjacent to small bordered pits having narrow, slitlike orifices. This is called *Picea*-type pitting.

In the genus *Pinus* where there are observed various stages of disappearance of the secondary walls in the ray parenchyma cells, variation in appearance of pits is considerable. *Picea*-type pits occur only in certain species; they become variously modified in others. Apparently, failure to understand fundamental differences in wall structure of different conifers is responsible for the confusion in interpretation of pitting in pines by different authors.* (See Plate 5–6.)

**Ultrastructure of Tracheids.** Judging from a recent communication by Esau (1963), studies of the ultrastructure of plant cells in general are not too abundant. This is even more true of pines. Some of the available information on the electron microscopy of pine wood tracheids will be summarized below.

In 1951, Kobyashi and Utusumi (as quoted by Harada, 1953) observed, on the inner lumen surface of the tertiary walls of *P. densiflora* No. 95 tracheids, "curious increscences" measuring 0.03 to 0.4 microns in diameter. In the same year, Liese (1951) independently discovered similar structures on the lumen surface of *P. sylvestris* tracheids; he called them warts. Harada and Miyazaki (1952) observed identical warts on the pit border of *P. densiflora.* Harada was not able to see clearly the warts on the lumen surface of the haploxylon pines, and judging from Liese's photomicrographs, they also are not very conspicuous on the walls of the bordered pits of at least some haploxylon pines (Liese, 1956).

Liese (1956) extended studies of the lumen warts to thirteen haploxylon and sixty-three diploxylon species of pines (including some varieties). This was a preliminary study in which one sample of wood represented each species, the material having been obtained from different European wood-testing laboratories. Liese found many differences in structure and distribution of warts on the inner surface of bordered pits among the species he analyzed. Unfortunately, there was much overlap of the characteristics of the warts of different species, which was understandable in view of the material he used in his studies.

The nature of the warts in *P. radiata* No. 19 was further studied by Wardrop, Liese, and Davis (1959). Judging by their results with *Actinostrobus,* the warts consist of a membrane lining the cell lumen and the spherical bodies within, measuring 0.1 to 0.5 microns in diameter. These

* Personal communication with Dr. I. W. Bailey, 1964–65.

bodies showed strong absorption of ultraviolet light; the membrane itself did not.

## The Bark

What is commonly called *bark* is a highly complex array of tissues varying in composition at successive stages of development of the stem. The "bark" is composed of epidermis, cortex, and phloem. Old stems having a rough outer appearance contain, in addition to phloem, cork cambia, periderms, and dead external tissue (the rhytidome) cut off by periderms. The inner bark is composed mainly of the secondary phloem and comprises several seasons' growth. It consists of several elements:

1. The conducting elements of the inner bark are long sieve cells arranged in radial rows of about ten cells. They have numerous sieve areas, usually at the radial sides. Esau (1960) describing the phloem of conifers in general says, "only a narrow band of conductory tissue, approximately one growth layer, may be in active state; the rest is no longer conducting; . . . collapse of the sieve cells gives the tissue a distorted appearance; . . . rays assume a wavy course."

2. The parenchyma cells of inner bark are vertically extended and arranged in increments in radial rows often of single cells or up to three cells. The parenchyma cells of inner bark often contain calcium oxalate crystals.

3. Sclerenchyma cells are usually absent in the inner bark of pines. Albuminous or erect cells are conspicuous in the rays; they are present in almost every ray section close to the cambial region; farther from it, they are mostly collapsed.

4. The uniseriate rays are numerous. Both uniseriate and fusiform rays occur in the inner bark of pines. Fusiform rays are common, especially abundant in the haploxylon pines, and contain horizontal resin canals. There are vertical resin ducts in the inner bark, but there are no fibers.

The secondary phloem of four haploxylon (Nos. 2, 3, 4, and 6) and eight diploxylon (Nos. 10, 13, 14, 15, 17, 18, 19, and 73) (see Table 1–2) pine species was studied by Srivastava (1963). The material was collected from well-identified trees, all native to California except planted *P. pinea* No. 73 of unknown origin.

In the secondary development of the issues outside the vascular cambium, the cortex (which is a primary tissue adjacent to the epidermis) and epidermis itself are crushed and sloughed away and replaced by the periderm. Periderm is tissue originating from a secondary meristem, *phellogen* or cork cambium, from which parenchyma-like phelloderm develops centripetally, and the phellum or cork centrifugally. All the bark region from the last-formed periderm is called outer bark or rhytidome (Chang, 1954). The outer bark includes alternate layers of periderm and of secondary phloem. The outermost part of the outer bark in the older trees is made of hard plates of rhytidome divided by fissures of varying depth. Outside appearance of the bark is different in the two subgenera. In the subgenus *Haploxylon*, branches and young stems are smooth and without fissures, resembling the bark of firs. In the subgenus *Diploxylon*, branches and young stems are rough, either scaly or fissured. There are some exceptions, however. The bark of young stems of *P. glabra* No. 26 and *P. halepensis* No. 77, for instance, is smooth.

It is difficult to differentiate among the species of the subgenus *Haploxylon* by their bark, although in some instances it is feasible (Plate 5–7). The bark of *P. monticola* No. 4 is broken into small square or rectangular blocks of dark gray, or purple-gray color. The bark of *P. lambertiana* No. 3 can be distinguished from that of *P. monticola* No. 4 by wideness of its plates, which are of a rich red-brown color, and by its short and broad parenchyma cells containing large-size starch grains and long sieve cells, usually about 4.5 mm long. Chang (1954) reports that a gelatinous substance may be extracted by "acidic alcohol" from the inner bark of *P. lambertiana*. Apparently, the chemical nature of this gelatinous substance has not been analyzed. Possibly, it contains water-soluble polysaccharides. (See Chapter 7.)

## THE ROOT

The development of the tissues of pine roots follows the general patterns described in the textbooks of anatomy. There is the usual growing tip with its four zones: (1) the root cap, (2) the apex with its region of cell division, (3) the region of elongation, and (4) the region of maturation, also called the region of root hairs. Behind the root tip is the region of secondary growth.

The apex in the root is not terminal as it is in the shoot, but subterminal. It initiates not only the axial growth, but also the growth of the root cap. The structure of the root apex is much simpler than that of the shoot, for there are no leaves on the roots and because root branches originate beyond the region of most active growth (Esau, 1953). For the most recent review of organization of root structure in pines, consult Romberger (1963).

In the cross-section of a primary root, the following structures are recognized: the epidermis, the cortex, and the vascular cylinder.

The epidermis is not a stable structure in pine roots. Root hairs arise from the epidermal cells when the roots possess this structure. Later,

**Plate 5–7.** Bark patterns of several pine species. *Top: P. merkusii* No. 101. (Photo by C. B. Tadeo, Philippine Bureau of Forestry.) *Bottom:* two views of *P. bungeana* No. 87. Bark pattern of this pine resembles that of *Platanus.* (Photos courtesy Arnold Arboretum, Jamaica Plain, Massachusetts.)

**Plate 5–7** (continued). *Top: P. pinaster* No. 80. (Photo by M. Debazac.) *Lower left: P. aristata* No. 6 (U.S. Forest Service photo by N. T. Mirov.) *Lower right: P. peuce* No. 71. (Photo by Branislav Pejoski.)

the epidermis disintegrates, and the outer surface of the root becomes covered with collapsed cells that tend to slough off in long shreds. In older, long roots, there is no layer that could be designated as epidermis; instead, there is a general transition from the crushed outer elements to the inner living cells of the cortex. In this instance, the root hairs originate from the second or third layer of cortex (Aldrich-Blake, 1930). The cortex is located under the epidermis; its innermost layer is the endodermis.

The central part of the root is occupied by the vascular cylinder with its vascular tissue and the associated parenchyma. The vascular tissue is surrounded with pericycle, which is meristematic. The phloem is arranged in strands along the outer part of the vascular cylinder, near the pericycle. The xylem occupies the center of the cylinder and extends outward in the form of strands alternating with phloem strands. The number of strands varies in the genus. Polyarch roots with as many as seven strands occur in pines (Esau, 1953).

In the region of elongation in the root tip, differentiation of tissues is just beginning; the cortex is set off from the pericycle, and alternate protoxylem and protophloem strands are evident.

In the zone of maturation, metaxylem develops inwardly from the original strands of protoxylem, finally meeting in the middle at about which time the protophloem becomes disorganized and the cambium becomes evident. There may be discerned one or two resin canals just outside the protoxylem strands, or there may be none. With future growth, secondary thickening begins, and, on account of formation of the periderm, collapse of the cortex takes place. With development of the secondary phloem, the remnants of the primary phloem are crushed and disappear.

When pine roots go into a resting period, either because of winter cold or summer drought, development of the periderm extends toward the top of the root and may entirely enclose it, forming the so-called "winter root cap." The process is complicated; the result is that the whole tip is enclosed in a suberized layer. When growth is resumed, the living cells have to break through this protective layer to re-establish the active growing point.

At the beginning of its growth, a pine seedling has an unbranched taproot developed from the radicle end of the embryo. Short branches, however, begin to appear soon. During the first growing season, the taproot penetrates into soil to a varying depth (See Fig. 5-4.) In a one-year-old *P. ponderosa* No. 14 seedling, the ratio shoot weight: taproot weight is as low as 1, but in later years, it is 2 or even 3. In a mature pine tree, only about 10 per cent of the whole wood mass of the tree comprises the root system. In some species, the root system is well developed, with a strong taproot deeply penetrating into the ground; in others, it is rather shallow. When a developing taproot meets some obstacle, such as hardpan or permanently frozen ground, a superficial root system develops. Generally, however, the genus *Pinus* is characterized by a well-developed taproot.

The main side roots do not exhibit constant, positive geotropism as the taproot does. The lesser side roots branch profusely, forming short roots. These are small, slow-growing roots, frequently dichotomously branched and almost always forming mycorhiza.*

Adventitious roots in young stems commonly originate in the interfascicular parenchyma and in older stems in the vascular rays near the cambium (Esau, 1960). Satoo (1952, 1955, 1956) found that in the seedling cuttings of four diploxylon species—*P. densiflora* No. 95, *P. thunbergii* No. 77, *P. sylvestris* No. 69, and *P. pinaster* No. 80—adventitious roots originated in the callus tissue near the cut surface of the cutting. In *P. strobus* No. 20, which is a haploxylon pine, the roots had their origin in the bud traces. Mergen (1955) reported that in the "air-layered" slash pine, adventitious roots originated from the base of the wound-induced xylem. Experimenting with eight-year-old *P. contorta* No. 16 in Korea, Yim (1961) found that the roots originated from the cambium, or near to it, in the secondary xylem and also from the callus parenchyma.

As Theophrastus (see Chapter 1) implied a long time ago, pines generally do not reproduce themselves vegetatively. In nature, pine stems very seldom develop roots. In their rooting capacity, pines vary greatly. The easiest to root artificially are cuttings of *P. radiata* No. 19; the most difficult to strike roots is, perhaps, *P. lambertiana* No. 3 (Plate 5–8).

In pine forests, roots of different trees occasionally intergraft. Natural subterranean grafting is one of the means of spreading infection (Esau, 1960) among the trees of a forest. Foresters often notice in the woods so-called "living stumps" that are intergrafted below the ground with standing trees and stay alive. Such stumps develop a callus covering the periphery, thus protecting the vascular cambium. Lanner (1961) gives references to several articles on this subject and also describes his own observations on living stumps of several conifers, among them *P. lambertiana* No. 3 and *P. ponderosa* No. 14. Apparently underground intergrafting of roots in pines is a more common phenomenon than generally supposed.

---

* Recently, spelling of this word has been simplified by dropping one *r*. As regards the plural of mycorhiza, Harley (1959) ends it with *s*, while some authors prefer to use *ae*.

**Plate 5–8.** *Left:* two trees in center are *P. radiata* No. 19, twenty-three years old, propagated by cuttings, which in this pine strike roots relatively easily. Rooting capacity of pines decreases rapidly with age. *Right:* branch of *P. lambertiana* No. 3 rooted by air-layering method. This pine is difficult to propagate vegetatively.

## Mycorhiza

Mycorhiza is a fungus-root that is formed by association of fungus with a higher plant. It occurs in several conifers, but it is the best developed and the most studied in the genus *Pinus*.

Pines may live without mycorhiza. Seedlings grown in nutrient solution do not develop mycorhizal roots, but in nature, mycorhiza is always found in pines, although in rich soils it is apparently not necessary. An association of a fungus and a pine is very important in the life of the tree, and the interested reader is referred to Harley (1959) where, besides basic presentation of the subject, an extensive bibliography is given. It is generally accepted that the benefits of mycorhiza to a pine tree apparently are brought about by an increase of absorbing area of the mycorhizal roots for soil nutrients (Slankis, 1958). Physiology and ecology of mycorhiza will be discussed in Chapter 6.

In the genus *Pinus*, the mycorhiza is predominantly of an ectotropic type, the fungal mycelium being generally external, forming a sheath that completely envelops the short lateral roots (Plate 5–9). The fungus hyphae penetrate the intercellular spaces of cortical cells of the root, forming a so-called Hartig net, though developing occasional intracellular

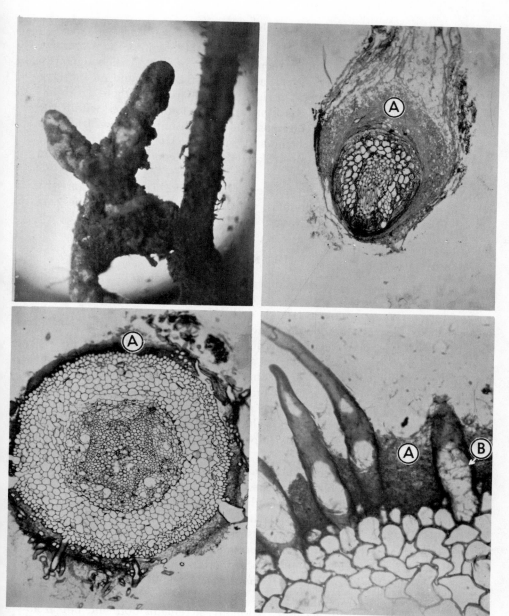

**Plate 5–9.** Mycorhiza on *P. lambertiana* No. 3. *Upper left:* appearance of mycorhiza on one-year-old seedling (× 34). *Upper right:* cross-section of a root growing in association with mycorhizal fungus *Boletus variegatus*, showing loose fungus mantle (A) (× 120). *Lower left:* mantle of *Boletus badius* (A) surrounding tap root (× 60). *Lower right:* intracellular penetration of *Boletus badius* into root hairs and epidermal cells (B); A is fungus mantle (× 450). (Photos by Jane Murdock Ulrich.)

hyphae (Hatch and Doak, 1933). While in other conifers the mycorhiza is of a racemose type, in the genus *Pinus* alone, it is dichotomously branched (Harley, 1959). Occasionally, mycorhiza is found on the long roots, but it does not develop a sheath or a Hartig net there (Aldrich-Blake, 1930). Apparently, the root-cap formation continues within the mycorhizal sheath, but its outermost cells, which in non-mycorhizal roots slough off in the soil, are decomposed within the sheath. Clowes (1954) found this for *Fagus,* but most likely the same conditions also exist in pines.

Different species of fungi may enter into mycorhizal association with pines. Most common mushrooms, which include some edible ones, are also the common mycorhizal fungi.

## THE NEEDLES

Primary leaves, or needles, appear above the cotyledons (see Juvenile Stage, p. 389) very shortly after germination and assume the functions of foliage. They are always single and different in appearance from the secondary leaves; these latter may appear in fascicles in the axils of primary leaves, occasionally even during the first growing season. Within two or three years, primary leaves are completely replaced by secondary leaves, remaining on the shoot only as scarious bracts. On the lower part of the shoot, these scarious bracts are without axillary buds; on the upper part of the shoot, the bracts subtend the axillary buds from which develop the secondary needles. The scarious bracts are very important in separating the genus *Pinus* into the two subgenera *Haploxylon* and *Diploxylon.*

The secondary (permanent) leaves or needles of pines are borne on short shoots (brachyblasts) in the axils of primary leaves. When they are approximately 250 microns high, their apical growth ceases. Further growth results from cell division in the intercalary meristem at the base of the needles. A dwarf shoot consists generally of a cluster of needles, ranging mostly from two in *P. sylvestris* No. 69, *P. contorta* No. 16, and others, to five; in *P. monophylla* No. 7, there is only one secondary needle, and the number of needles in *P. durangensis* No. 48 is generally six, but sometimes is seven or even eight. At the base of the needles, a short shoot apex is centrally located. Normally, it remains dormant, but in an emergency, caused by excessive defoliation or by any other kind of sudden shock, it can be activated; if this is the case, it begins to grow and develops into a long shoot (Plate 5–10). The origin of the branch originating from a short shoot can be easily discerned by the presence at its base of secondary needles of the shoot instead of a subtending primary leaf. These needles are somehow changed in appearance, be-

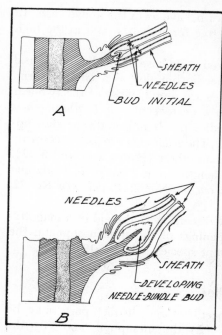

**Plate 5–10.** Short shoots of *P. ponderosa* No. 14. *Left:* two longitudinal sections, showing bud initial (A) and developing bud (B). (Redrawn from Cooperrider, 1938.) *Right:* grafted short shoot, showing developing bud. (Photo by N. T. Mirov.)

coming short, broad, and heavy. They persist for a long time and are never shed as are ordinary needles (Cooperrider, 1938). (See Plate 5–10.) Debazac (1962) lists thirty-three pines (species and some varieties) in which development of short shoot buds was observed. It appears then that this phenomenon may occur in time of distress in any species of pine.

The scales of the short shoot bud elongate into a basal sheath that is persistent in the needle fascicle of all diploxylon pines except *P. leiophylla* No. 41, *P. chihuahuana* No. 40, and *P. lumholtzii* No. 42. In contrast, the basal fascicle sheath of all haploxylon pines, except *P. nelsonii* No. 38, is deciduous.

In some pines, such as *P. strobus* No. 20 or *P. palustris* No. 22, needles fall at the end of the second growing season; in other species, they persist longer—for three, four, or five years, and up to twelve to fourteen years in *P. balfouriana* and *P. aristata*.

The shedding of needles of pines is influenced by the environment. Weidman (1939) reported that in a plantation in northern Idaho, *P. ponderosa* needles remained on the tree for three or four years. In its natural habitat, in low altitudes, needles behave as in the above case. In medium altitudes, they remain on the tree for six years; and in the high altitudes, even for eight years.

A needle bundle (fascicle) is enclosed at its base in a cylindrical basal sheath, thus a cross-section of each needle bundle has a circular form. *Pinus monophylla* No. 7 solitary needles are round; those of the two-leaf pines are semicircular; and so on. In a cross-section of *P. durangensis* (having six, seven, or even eight needles per bundle), the needles appear as very narrow segments indeed. The segments are not necessarily of the same size; some are narrower than others (Plates 5–11 and 5–12).

Pine needles vary greatly in their length—from 2 cm in *P. banksiana* No. 32 to 40–50 cm or more in *P. michoacana* No. 52, *P. palustris* No. 22, and *P. engelmannii* No. 53.

On the surface of needles, one may discern, with the aid of a magnifying glass, rows of dots; these are openings of the sunken stomata; the shape of the openings varies in different species (Plate 5–12).

## Internal Characters of Pine Needles

On the cross-section of a pine needle, three distinct parts may be recognized: (1) the dermal tissue, (2) the mesophyll, and (3) the vascular part containing the vascular tissues (Plates 5–11 and 5–12). The dermal tissue is derivative of protoderm; it consists of a layer of small thick-walled epidermal cells whose outer walls are covered with a thick layer of cutin, which is a highly polymerized mixture of lipids and waxes. The outer layers of the mesophyll (ground tissue) are known as hypodermis; it may consist of one or several layers of thin-walled cells. When the cells of the outer row are thin-walled and those of the inner row are thick-walled, the hypodermis is called biform. In multiform hypodermis, the cell walls gradually become thicker toward the center of the needle. When the walls of all cells of the hypodermis have the same thickness, the hypodermis is called uniform. Sometimes the cells of the epidermis and the hypodermis are similar in appearance.

The stomata in the genus *Pinus*, as revealed in the cross-section of a needle, are sunken well into the hypodermis, with subsidiary cells arching over them. The walls of the subsidiary cells and of the guard cells are partly lignified and partly free of lignin. Difference in the structure of the walls of these cells is apparently responsible for the opening and closing of the stomata.

The openings and the cavities leading to the stomata are lined and often filled to a varying degree with a whitish substance whose chemical and physical nature is interpreted variously by different investigators (Esau, 1953). The stomata may be located on all surfaces of the needles,

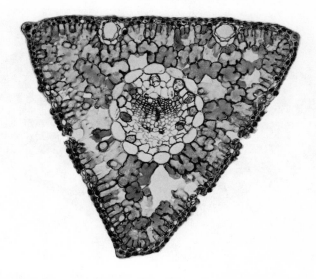

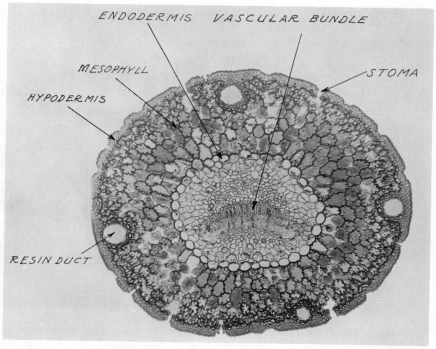

**Plate 5–11.** Cross-sections of needles of two haploxylon pines, showing single vascular bundles. *Top: P. strobus* No. 20. (Photo by Adriance S. Foster.) *Bottom: P. monophylla* No. 7 (U.S. Forest Service photo.)

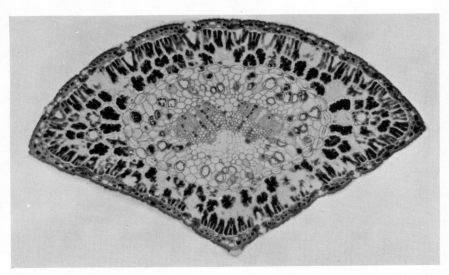

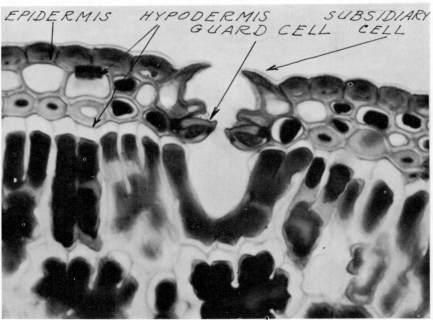

EPIDERMIS    HYPODERMIS    SUBSIDIARY
GUARD CELL    CELL

**Plate 5–12.** *Pinus radiata* No. 19 (a diploxylon pine). *Top:* cross-section of a needle (× 66). Note two vascular bundles. *Bottom:* cross-section through part of a needle, showing stoma (× 415). (Photos by Margot Forde.)

as in all diploxylon pines, or they may be absent on the outer surfaces of the needles, as in some of the haploxylon pines. Edges of pine needles may be smooth or serrated.

Florin (1931), in his fundamental work on morphology of conifers, studied the structure of epidermis and of stomata of many conifers. As regards the genus *Pinus*, it is represented only by two or three species. He considered morphology of stomata to be useful for the study of evolution of conifers.

*Mesophyll* is largely photosynthesizing parenchyma occupying the middle (and the largest) part of the needle. In pines, it is not differentiated into palisade and spongy parenchyma; it consists of uniform green tissue having tortuous cell walls; it does not vary much with species of the genus. In the mesophyll are located resin ducts, which may occupy different positions in respect to the dermal and the vascular regions of the needle. When the ducts are touching the cells of the dermal region, they are called external; when they touch the vascular region, they are internal; those that are located fully in the mesophyll tissue are known as medial ducts. The resin ducts, large enough to touch both the hypodermis and the endodermis, form a septum; such ducts are called septal resin ducts.

The number of resin ducts in pines varies from two (occasionally one or even none in *P. contorta* No. 16 var. *contorta*) to many. The resin ducts are surrounded with thin-walled, resin-secreting epithelial cells; these are enclosed in a sheath of sclerenchymatous fibers possessing thickened, lignified walls. The outermost layer of mesophyll is sclerenchyma. The hypodermal sclerenchyma, mesophyll resin canals, and endodermis are formed from the ground meristem (Sacher, 1954).

**The Vascular Region.** The central part of a pine needle is occupied with vascular and associated tissues. These are surrounded, and separated from the mesophyll, by one layer of relatively thick-walled cells called endodermis. The walls of the endodermis cells in most pine species are of uniform thickness. In some species, however, the outer walls of the endodermis are thickened, while in a few pines (Nos. 10, 11, 12, and 72—see Table 1–2 in Chapter 1), the cells of the endodermis may be both thin- and thick-walled.

The vascular bundle of haploxylon pines is single; in the diploxylon pines, it is double. The two parts of the double vascular bundle occupy varying positions in relationship to one another. In some species, they are distinct and situated well apart; in others, they are almost completely merged into one bundle. This apparent *merger* is never constant in diploxylon pines, and generally there is no difficulty in distinguishing the two subgenera of the genus *Pinus* by this character (Shaw, 1914). The vascular bundle, either single or double, is surrounded with transfusion tissue that consists of dead, thin-walled, lignified tracheids and of living parenchyma cells (Huber, 1947). The vascular bundle is separated almost entirely by sclerenchyma from the transfusion cells.

Coulter and Rose (1886), Doi and Morikawa (1929), Harlow (1931), Sutherland (1934), and others contributed a great deal to our knowledge of the anatomy of pine needles.

The most comprehensive examination of needle characteristics of pine hybrids was undertaken by Keng and Little (1961). They investigated gross morphology and internal morphology of forty-two pine hybrids, including one natural hybrid, thirty-four first generation artificial interspecific hybrids and also two trihybrids, three backcrosses, and two intraspecific hybrids. The material was obtained from the plantation of the Institute of Forest Genetics, Placerville, California, and thus was well documented. Internal morphology of needles was found to be useful in identification of hybrids of young pines. However, Keng and Little found it impossible to identify positively from needle characters alone the hybrids between certain closely related species.

## INITIATION AND DEVELOPMENT OF STAMINATE AND OVULATE STROBILI

Description of ontogeny of reproductive organs in pines may be found either in general textbooks such as Holman and Robbins (1927) or in more specialized treatises, such as Chamberlain's (1935), with its extensive list of references.

In pines, the male strobili (catkins) and female strobili (conelets) are found on the same tree. Only occasionally a tendency is observed in individual trees toward dominance of masculinity or femininity. Generally, male strobili are in the position of the short shoot and are predominantly borne on the lower branches of the tree and on the side branchlets. The female strobili are located in the upper part of the crown and are in the position of a long shoot, taking the place of a subterminal or lateral bud. Exceptions to this general arrangement, however, are frequent. Abnormal flowering habits in pines are described by Chamberlain (1935).

### The Male Strobilus

In temperate climates, initiation of male (microsporangiate) strobili occurs generally toward the end of the growing season. In the Himalaya, for instance, initiation of pollen "catkins" of *P. roxburghii* takes place in early September, while in *P. griffithii* it occurs at the middle of October

**Table 5–1.** Date of Cone Initiation for Certain Species of *Pinus* (from Gifford and Mirov, 1960)

| Author and Date of Publication * | Geographical Location | Species | Date of Cone Initiation | |
|---|---|---|---|---|
| | | | Megasporangiate or Ovulate | Microsporangiate |
| Strasburger, E., 1872 (data from Mergen and Koerting, 1957) | | *P. pumilio* (*P. montana*) No. 76 | Late August | Early August |
| Ferguson, M. C., 1940 | Mass., U.S.A. | *P. strobus* | Not found as late as November 20 | Not found in fall |
| | | *P. rigida* | | October or November |
| | | *P. austriaca* (*P. nigra* No. 74) | | October or November |
| Coulter, J. M., and C. J. Chamberlain, 1910 | Chicago, Ill., U.S.A. | *P. laricio* (*P. nigra* No. 74) | Late fall and winter | Not reported |
| Doak, C. C., 1935 | From widely separated regions of U.S.A. and neighboring islands | Seven species | Mid-August | End of July |
| Little, E. L., Jr., 1938 | Flagstaff, Ariz., U.S.A. | *P. edulis* No. 8 | August–September | August–September |
| Mergen, F., and L. E. Koerting, 1957 | Lake City, Fla., U.S.A. | *P. elliottii* No. 23 | Late August | Mid-July |
| Wareing, P. F., 1958 | Oakmere, Cheshire, England | *P. sylvestris* No. 69 | | |
| | | 1951—Tree 1 | August 22 | August 10 |
| | | 1951—Tree 3 | September 12 | No data |
| | | 1952—Tree 1 | August 14 | August 1 |

* References in Gifford and Mirov (1960).

**Plate 5–13.** Branch of *P. edulis* No. 8, with male strobili (A). (Photo by Chester F. Deaver.)

to the beginning of November. Other data on the initiation of the microsporangiate cones are given in Table 5–1, p. 377.

The male strobilus consists of an axis on which microsporophylls are borne. On the under side of each microsporophyll are found two microsporangia or pollen sacs that, in moderate climates, open in the spring and discharge vast quantities of pollen (Plate 5–13). The time of pollination varies with the species and with the climate. We shall return to this subject later (see Chapter 6). Each pollen grain has an air sac or bladder on each side. These bladders are formed between intine and exine. Some information on morphology of pollen grains of pines may be found in Wodehouse's (1959) treatise on pollen (Plate 5–13).

Campo-Duplan (1950) contributed much to elucidation of pollen morphology of the genus *Pinus*. Earlier researches on the subject are reviewed in her book. Her own material was procured either from herbarium specimens or from the arboretum of *L'Ecole des Barres,* in north-central France. Pollen of fifty-five pine species and one variety was examined. She was primarily interested in size of the pollen grains, and she showed that generally the genus *Pinus* possessed the smallest pollen grains of all genera of the family Pinaceae. Regarding use of pollen grains for identification of pines, see Chapter 9, p. 529.

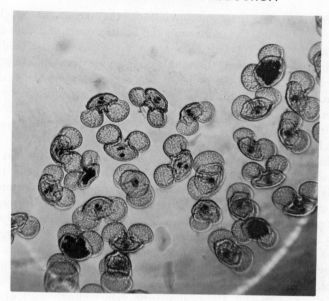

**Plate 5–14.** Pollen grains of *P. ponderosa* No. 14 (× 200). (Photo by F. I. Righter. Courtesy California Forest & Range Experiment Station, U.S. Forest Service.)

## The Female Strobilus

Dates of initiation of female conelets of some pine species are given in Table 5–1, p. 377. Francini (1958), who studied Mediterranean pines, found that *P. halepensis* No. 77 and *P. pinaster* No. 80 begin to develop female cones in the fall, while *P. pinea* No. 73 begins its division at the beginning of the summer (*"au seuil de l'été"*). She said that this is because *P. halepensis* and *P. pinaster* are old Mediterranean species, while *P. pinea* is a later migrant that has not adjusted its physiology to the Mediterranean climate. She did not say from where this pine migrated. Initiation of female cones of *P. roxburghii* No. 93 occurs in the Himalaya in early February (Konar, 1960).

The female conelet (megasporangiate strobilus) consists essentially of an axis upon which ovuliferous scales are arranged. The scales of a conelet may be entire, as in *P. cembra* No. 67, or tuberculate, as in *P. tropicalis* No. 66; short mucronate, as in *P. sylvestris* No. 69, or long mucronate, as in *P. aristata* No. 6, or spinescent as in *P. pungens* No. 31 (Shaw, 1914). On the upper face of the ovuliferous scale of the conelet are located two ovules (megasporangia) that, at the time of pollination, appear as pearly white swellings. Each of these consists of a mass of cells called the nucellus enclosed in a cover or integument. In pines, the ovules are inverted; i.e., their micropyle faces the axis of the conelet. As a result of this position, the embryo of the mature seed of *Pinus* appears erect, the radicle being toward the sharp pointed base of the seed.

At the time of pollination, the scales of the megasporangiate strobilus are slightly separated, and the pollen grains enter between the scales and lodge on micropilar exudate. The exudate is a weak solution of sugars (McWilliam, 1958). A closer chemical analysis of it is desirable. The pollen grain comes in contact with the nucellus and germinates; the pollen tube begins to grow and penetrates the nucellus.

Meanwhile, in the ovule, a megaspore mother cell is formed in the nucellus and soon undergoes two successive divisions. During the first of these divisions, the twenty-four chromosomes (the diploid number in all pines) are reduced one-half. Of the four megaspores so formed, only one develops, giving rise to the female gametophyte commonly called endosperm. It has a haploid number (i.e., twelve) of chromosomes.

Nearly a year after pollination, two to six archegonia are formed at the micropylar end of the endosperm a few weeks prior to fertilization. In each archegonium, one egg cell develops.

During the first season, the pollen tube grows slowly and penetrates only a little distance into the nucellar tissue. In temperate regions, with the advent of winter, it ceases to grow but resumes development in the spring. The length of time for maturation of pine seed in temperate climates is, then, usually two growing seasons with a winter rest period between.

In the wet-tropical regions of low elevations, the process of seed maturation is greatly distorted, for there are no cold winters and no spring revival of life (Mirov, 1962); the growing season is continuous. Accordingly, it takes the seed only a little over one year to mature. Apparently, there have been no embryology studies of development of the seed in the wet-tropical pines.

When the pollen tube, after its winter rest or after a period controlled by some internal physiological process, reaches the female gametophyte, fertilization takes place. One of the sperm nuclei of the pollen tube that has a haploid (twelve) number of chromosomes is fused with the ovule nucleus, which is also haploid, forming a zygote with a diploid (twenty-four) number of chromosomes. Formation of the zygote signifies the beginning of a sporophyte generation. After fertilization, two mitotic divisions of the zygote take place, and thus four nuclei are formed. Four to eight embryos are the result of the subsequent divisions of these nuclei. Since there may be six archegonia within a single ovule and each zygote can initiate eight embryos, as many as forty-eight embryos may be formed. In reality, usually only one embryo is developed to maturity—occasionally two.

Polyembryony in mature seed involving two embryos or more is rare in pines. In one test (Johnstone, 1940), polyembryony was found to be the most frequent in *P. monticola* No. 4 (2.14 per cent of all seedlings examined) and least frequent in *P. muricata* No. 18 (0.02 per cent).

Since multiple embryos in pines come from a single egg by the splitting of the product of a single fertilization, this type of polyembryony is called cleavage polyembryony (Buchholz, 1918). In conifers, besides pines, it occurs also in *Larix, Picea,* and *Pseudotsuga.*

Embryogeny, including polyembryony in pines, was a subject intensively investigated by Buchholz (1946, and his other publications). Francini (1958) studied the embryogeny of Mediterranean pines; in America, we have a classical study on embryogeny of *P. strobus* by Ferguson (1901). For a more recent treatment of the subject, see Spurr (1949) and Foster and Gifford (1959).

In the regions such as the middle elevations of the Sierra Nevada, above Placerville, California (altitude about 800 m), the female strobili of *P. ponderosa* No. 14 continue to grow throughout the late fall and winter (Gifford and Mirov, 1960). Outdoor temperatures there frequently are high enough for growth to occur. Sustained growth of strobili through the winter is in agreement with results reported by Mergen and Koerting (1957) for *P. elliottii* No. 23 in northern Florida.

## Structure of Mature Cone

After the union of the sperm and the ovule nuclei is consummated, the megasporangiate cone (female strobilus) begins to grow rapidly; it changes its color from red or purple to green and later to brown (Plate 5–15). In the temperate climates, it reaches maturity at the end of the second summer (counting from the time of pollination at the beginning of the previous growing season). Only in three species (*P. chihuahuana* No. 40, *P. leiophylla* No. 41, and *P. pinea* No. 73) does it take three growing seasons for cones (and seeds) to mature.

Pine cones vary much in size—from minute ones of *P. montana,* which may be only 2–3 cm in length and in diameter, to the huge cones of *P. lambertiana,* reaching 50 and even 60 cm in length and about 10 cm in diameter. In weight, pine cones vary from about 2 gm (*P. montana* No. 76 var. *Mughus*) to over 1100 gm (*P. coulteri* No. 12).

The ovuliferous scales of the female strobilus are enlarged to form cone scales. The exposed part of a cone scale is called apophysis. The end part of the apophysis (which represents the exposed part of the scales in the female strobilus at the time of fertilization) becomes the umbo of the mature cone (Fig. 5–1). The umbo of all diploxylon pines is dorsal; the umbo of haploxylon pines is terminal in the pines of Shaw's

**Plate 5–15.** Cones and conelets. *Left: P. culminicola* No. 39—*A,* female conelets at beginning of second growing season; *B,* mature cones at end of season. (Photo by John H. Beaman.) *Right: P. ponderosa* No. 14—*A,* preceding year's female conelet; *B,* current year's conelet, soon after pollination in spring. (Photo by G. F. Shockley. Courtesy California Forest & Range Experiment Station, U.S. Forest Service.)

subsection *Cembra,* but is dorsal in the species of the subsection *Paracembra.*

Morphology of the apophysis, and especially of the umbo, varies considerably in different species of pines (Fig. 5–1) and thus has a diagnostic value.

Shaw (1914) describes the mature pine cone as having the following structure: The axis of the cone is a woody cylinder enclosing a wide pith and covered with a thick cortex. From the wood of the axis extend three strands (vascular bundles) that subdivide into smaller strands converging toward the umbo. If a scale of a pine cone is srtipped of the soft brown fundamental parenchymatous tissue, immersed in water, and subsequently dried, there is at first flexion toward the cone axis and then away from it. The tissues of the cone scale, especially the vascular bundles, are hygroscopic; since their greatest thickness is on the adaxial surface of the scale, there is a much greater strain on that side of the scale, tending to force the scales apart when they are ripe and dry, and

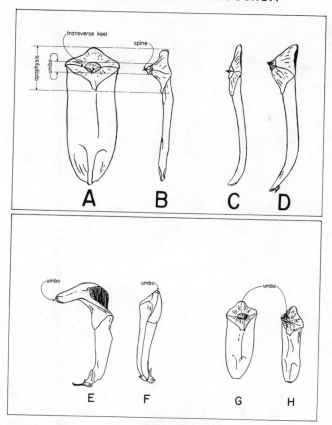

**Fig. 5–1.** Cone scales of pines: A—dorsal view and B—side view, showing apophysis and armed umbo of *P. engelmannii* No. 53 var. blancoi; C—flattened apophysis of *P. hartwegii* No. 49; D—salient, pyramidal apophysis of *P. michoacana* No. 52; E—terminal umbo of *P. strobiformis* No. 35 (note elongated apophysis); F—terminal umbo of *P. strobus* var. *chiapensis* No. 34; and G and H—dorsal umbo of *P. montezumae* No. 47. (After Martínez, 1948.)

subsequently closing and opening the cone on rainy and sunny days and releasing the seeds.

## THE SEED

The mature seed of a pine consists essentially of an embryo embedded in the female gametophyte, a fleshy tissue with reserve food. This in turn is enclosed in a seed coat, the outer layer of which, apart from the membranous wing, is hard or stony. Seeds of various pine species differ

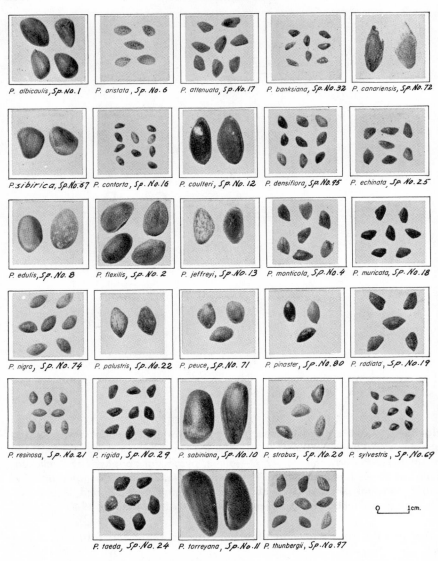

**Plate 5–16.** Seeds of twenty-eight pine species. (From U.S. Department of Agriculture, 1948. Name "*P. cembra* var. *sibirica*" has been changed to "*P. sibirica*." Species numbers added refer to Tables 1–1 and 1–2.)

much in size (Plate 5–16). The smallest of all pine seeds are those of *P. banksiana* No. 32 and *P. contorta* No. 16; they average about 220,500 per kg. The smallest seeds of European pines are those of *P. montana* No. 76; and of Mexican pines, those of *P. teocote* No. 45. At the other end of the scale, 1 kilogram contains only about 1100 *P. torreyana* No. 11 seeds, or 1550 *P. sabiniana* No. 10 seeds. Seeds of these two species, because of their large size, are excellent for experimental purposes.

## The Embryo

The later stages of embryo development and organization in *P. strobus* were investigated by Spurr (1949, 1950). Before the root initials are apparent, the embryo consists of a cylindrical mass of cells with a rounded apex, and continuing at the lower end with the suspensor system.

A root apex becomes morphologically defined with the appearance of the root initials. The upper and largest part of the embryo is referred to as the hypocotyl-shoot axis; the lower part, between the root apex and suspensor, is the root cap. The root cap becomes highly organized; a well-defined column or central region is formed, as contrasted with the periphery of the root cap. In full-grown pine embryos, the root cap is a relatively long structure as compared to the root caps in many angiosperms.

Tissue systems in the hypocotyl-shoot axis are initiated very early. The upper part of the embryo, which gives rise to the cotyledons and to the conical epicotyl, is interpreted by Spurr as a shoot apex.

Two interesting histological features of the pine embryo (Spurr, 1950) are the secretory cells and resin duct cells. Some individual elements of the former, each with a single nucleus, may extend from a deep level in the hypocotyl to near the tip of a cotyledon. In the mature embryo, secretory cells may approach 2 mm in length. The resin duct cells in the mature embryo are associated with the procambium and are the fore-runners of the resin ducts or canals of the seedling.

The mature embryo has the appearance of a blunt spindle occupying the central part of the seed (Fig. 5–2). It has multiple cotyledons that obscure a small conical epicotyl. It makes up a rather small part of the total seed—about 5 per cent in *P. lambertiana* No. 3, or in *P. jeffreyi* No. 13.

At the radical end of the embryo are the remnants of the suspensor cells, a thin coiled thread that is very conspicuous in certain pines and is located on the narrower (micropylar) end of the seed.

## The Endosperm

The embryo is imbedded in the tissue of the female gametophyte commonly called the endosperm. It is similar in its function to the endosperm of the angiosperms in its nutritive nature, although basically different in origin.

In pines (as in other gymnosperms), double fertilization does not take

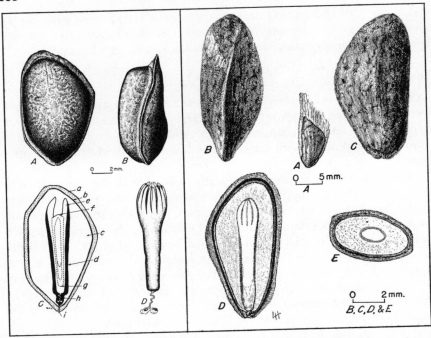

**Fig. 5–2.** Internal structure of pine seeds. *Left:* P. *lambertiana* No. 3—A and B, exterior view in two planes; C, longitudinal section (a, seed coat; b, nucellus; c, endosperm; d, embryo cavity; e, cotyledons; f, plumule; g, radicle; h, suspensor; i, micropyle); D, embryo. *Right:* P. *ponderosa* No. 14—A, exterior view of seed with wing fragment; B and C, exterior views of seed in two planes; D, longitudinal section; E, cross-section. (From U.S. Department of Agriculture, 1948.)

place as in the angiosperms, and the "endosperm" (female gametophyte) has the haploid number of chromosomes instead of being triploid as in many angiosperms (see Plate 4–1, page 322).

On the micropylar end of a pine seed, there are attached to the endosperm some remnants of the nucellus, forming a brown papery cup. The endosperm is completely covered with a dry membranous cover, representing the remains of the inner, fleshy layer of the integument, which, during the development of the seed, becomes partly absorbed and partly crushed by the growth of the endosperm. Tissue of the endosperm is composed of cells filled with substances that provide nutrition for the embryo: droplets of fats and proteins that are found in the form of aleurone grains and as components of the cell nuclei. Carbohydrates are found in the endosperm of pine seeds in varying amounts; starch may be present as well as monosaccharides, disaccharides, and hemicelluloses;

cellulose is present as a structural material. As much as 7 per cent starch is reported in *P. cembra* No. 67 seed (Schulze and Rongger, 1899); but, on the other hand, according to our analyses, starch is found only in minute quantities in *P. jeffreyi* No. 13 or *P. lambertiana* No. 3. Seeds of *P. monophylla* No. 7 appear to be exceptionally rich in starch.

Work with excised embryos indicates that the endosperm also protects these from bacterial and fungal attacks to which the naked embryos are very susceptible.

## The Seed Coat

The endosperm is enclosed in the seed coat or testa, which is derived from the integument of megasporangium, i.e., a tissue belonging to the mother tree. Accordingly, the qualities of the seed coat are inherited from the female parent alone.

In pines, the outer covering of the integument (spermoderm) remains attached to the seed of most species as a membranous wing.

The seed coat consists of rows of uniform isodiametric stone cells connected with narrow pit canals. In some pines (*P. sabiniana* No. 10), the seed coat is extremely hard; in others, it is almost papery; in all, it is permeable to water.

Only eleven species of pines, all haploxylon, have wingless seeds: Nos. 1, 7, 8, 9, 36, 37, 38, 39, 67, 68, 82. Only in one pine species—*P. koraiensis* No. 82—is the spermoderm entire. In *P. cembra* No. 70 (and presumably in *P. sibirica* No. 67 and *P. pumila* No. 68), it is wanting on the central side of the seed, but on the dorsal side, it adheres partly to the seed itself and partly to the cone scale.

The seeds of *P. albicaulis* No. 1 and of the piñon pines (Nos. 7, 8, 9, 36, 37, 38, 39) are "quite bare of membranous cover" (Shaw, 1914). *Pinus flexilis* No. 2 and *P. strobiformis* No. 35 have seeds with a rudimentary wing; the latter pine is sometimes described as *P. ayacahuite* var. *brachyptera*. The other two varieties of *P. ayacahuite* No. 33 have a well-developed wing—short in var. *vetchii* and long in *P. ayacahuite* proper.

In all other pines, seed wings are well developed. They are either adherent (in all winged haploxylon pines except *P. balfouriana* No. 5) or articulate, i.e., easily detachable (in all diploxylon pines except *P. pinea* No. 73, *P. roxburghii* No. 93, and *P. canariensis* No. 72).

## JUVENILE STAGE

When fertilization is completed, the seed develops and ripens. When internal and external conditions are proper, the seed germinates. The physiology of germination will be considered in Chapter 6.

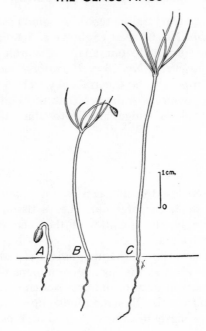

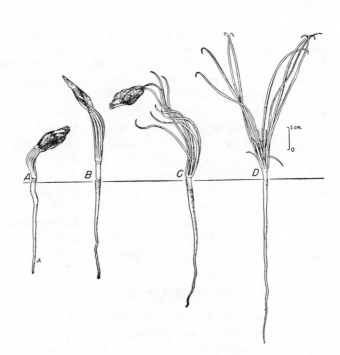

The first sign of germination is a longitudinal splitting of the seed coat near the narrow (micropylar) end of the seed; it is caused by inbibition of water and later by the growing embryo. The primary root begins to grow downward; the part of the plantlet between the root and the cotyledons, the hypocotyl (Fig. 5–3), elongates and, if the seed is not buried too deeply, is drawn out of the soil with the partially (but not entirely) exhausted endosperm and the cotyledons still inside the seed coat (Fig. 5–3). In a few days, the cotyledons pull out of the seed and spread out like fronds of a miniature palm (Fig. 5–3). The number of cotyledons in the genus *Pinus* varies from three (*P. contorta* No. 16, *P. banksiana* No. 32, and *P. sylvestris* No. 69) to eighteen (*P. lambertiana* No. 3 and *P. sabiniana* No. 10), and possibly more in other yet unexamined species. There is a general tendency of species with larger seeds to have more cotyledons. The number of cotyledons of some pine species is given in Table 5–2. It is partly based on Butts and Buchholz (1940) data, partly on personal observations.

The cotyledons, when they are still embedded in the endosperm, are yellowish-white, occasionally greenish. As soon as they emerge, they turn green; they possess stomata and are able to photosynthesize. The hypocotyl, however, is often of a red color, caused by the presence of an anthocyanin, malvidin, which also to a certain extent may appear in the cotyledons (see Chapter 7).

The following tabulation (after Ferré, 1952) provides some information regarding number of resin ducts in cotyledons and in primary leaves of pine seedlings.

| Sections | Cotyledons | Primary Leaves |
|----------|------------|----------------|
| *Cembra* | 2 | 2 |
| *Paracembra* | 2 | 2–3? |
| *Pinaster* | 0 | 2 |
| *Parapinaster* | 3 | 2–3 |

**Fig. 5–3.** Germinating seedlings. *Top:* normal development of pine seedling, exemplified by *P. resinosa* No. 21—A, after one day; B, after seven days; C, after thirty days. *Bottom:* Retarded development of the shoot of *P. palustris* No. 22—A, after one day; B, after two days; C, after five days; D, after thirty-two days. This type of retarded seedling development also occurs in several other species. (See Chapter 6, pages 417–418.) (From U.S. Department of Agriculture, 1948.)

**Table 5–2.** Number of Cotyledons in Pines *

| Species and Reference Number | Cotyledons |
|---|---|
| HAPLOXLON PINES | |
| P. *balfouriana* No. 5 | 5 to 9 |
| P. *aristata* No. 6 | 5 to 9 |
| P. *quadrifolia* No. 9 | 6 to 8 |
| P. *albicaulis* No. 1 | 7 to 9 |
| P. *monophylla* No. 7 | 6 to 10 |
| P. *flexilis* No. 2 | 6 to 9 |
| P. *monticola* No. 4 | 7 to 9 |
| P. *strobus* No. 20 | 7 to 10 |
| P. *lambertiana* No. 3 | 11 to 18 |
| DIPLOXYLON PINES | |
| P. *banksiana* No. 32 | 3 to 6 |
| P. *contorta* No. 16 | 3 to 8 |
| P. *echinata* No. 25 | 4 to 7 |
| P. *glabra* No. 26 | 5 to 6 |
| P. *muricata* No. 18 | 4 to 6 |
| P. *resinosa* No. 21 | 5 to 7 |
| P. *rigida* No. 29 | 4 to 8 |
| P. *sylvestris* No. 69 | 3 to 8 |
| P. *virginiana* No. 27 | 4 to 8 |
| P. *attenuata* No. 17 | 5 to 8 |
| P. *radiata* No. 19 | 5 to 9 |
| P. *taeda* No. 4 | 5 to 9 |
| P. *elliottii* No. 23 | 5 to 10 |
| P. *engelmannii* No. 53 | 8 to 10 |
| P. *montezumae* No. 47 | 7 to 10 |
| P. *palustris* No. 22 | 6 to 11 |
| P. *ponderosa* No. 14 | 6 to 11 |
| P. *jeffreyi* No. 13 | 7 to 13 |
| P. *coulteri* No. 12 | 9 to 14 |
| P. *arizonica* No. 43 | 10 to 12 |
| P. *torreyana* No. 11 | 12 to 14 |
| P. *sabiniana* No. 10 | 12 to 18 |

* Data are from Butts and Buchholz (1940) and personal observations of the author.

Hill and De Fraine (1909) reported that *P. halepensis* and *P. coulteri* had no resin canals in their cotyledons, which is in accordance with de Ferré's data, for both these pines belong to the subsection *Pinaster*. But the cotyledons of *P. sylvestris, P. montana,* and *P. contorta,* which are also *Pinaster* pines, have one resin duct. It seems that more systematic studies should be made to obtain a complete picture on resin ducts in cotyledons and primary leaves of pines.

A period of several weeks after germination is the most critical time in the life of a pine. This is a succulent stage of development. In California, in about two weeks after germination, the hypocotyl and the

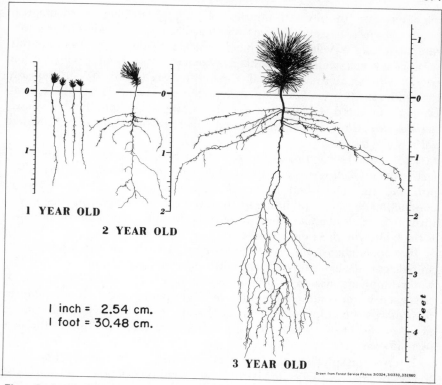

1 YEAR OLD

2 YEAR OLD

I inch = 2.54 cm.
I foot = 30.48 cm.

3 YEAR OLD

*Drawn from Forest Service Photos 310324, 310330, 332860*

**Fig. 5–4.** The development of the seedling root system of *P. ponderosa* from initial taproot to one with high and low spreading laterals. First-year seedling taproots as long as 51 inches (i.e. about 130 cm) have been recorded where the growing tip met no obstructing soil layers. (From Curtis and Lynch, 1957.)

cotyledons reach their full size, and above them appears a tuft of primary leaves. Secondary leaves, commonly called needles, which have been described earlier (p. 370), may appear occasionally at the end of the first growing season, but usually during the second year (Fig. 5–4).

## SUMMARY

From a morphological point of view, pines appear to us as large-size trees, both in height and in diameter. They are long-lived, and they have a well-developed taproot that provides a secure anchorage for their big stems. When circumstances demand, pines may survive with superficial root systems. At their maturity, pines possess thick bark, which protects them from fire damage and from other injuries. Pines possess a well-developed resin-producing system that makes them more resistant to infections and to physical injuries. The most striking morphological feature of pines, however, is their xeromorphism. Pine needles have a low ratio of surface to volume; they have a thick cuticular layer, an epidermis with heavy cell walls, and sunken stomata whose front cavities often contain whitish alveolar material, apparently wax (Esau, 1953). Beneath the epidermis is a well-developed hypodermis, several layers thick, containing elongated sclerenchyma cells, arranged longitudinally. Thus, needles are strong and rigid. Annual shoots of pines are often covered with waxy bloom.

The internal structure of the pine stem reveals the inner cylinder of heartwood, which serves as support for their massive bodies. Outside the pith and the heartwood is located sapwood whose chief function is conduction of water and minerals from the root to the crown. The structure of "bark" is complex. In mature trees, its outer part (the rhytidome) is thick and rough in most species.

Pine roots almost always are mycorhizal, and this provides pines with an efficient mechanism to obtain nutritional elements from the soil. The water-supplying system of pines is not as highly specialized as the more advanced water-conducting system of angiosperms, but it is adequate to their more economical requirements of water. The most vulnerable stage in development of pines is the period from germination through the first several years of their life.

Internal morphological characters of pines are extremely important in classification of pines; this latter subject will be discussed in Chapter 9.

## LITERATURE CITATIONS

ALDRICH-BLAKE, R. N. 1930. The plasticity of the root system of Corsican pine in early life. (Oxford Forestry Mem. 12.) Oxford University Press, Fair Lawn, N.J.

BAILEY, IRVING W. 1909. The structure of the wood in the Pinaceae. Bot. Gaz., 48:47–55.

———. 1920. The cambium and its derivative tissues. II. Size variations of cambial initials in gymnosperms and angiosperms. Amer. Jour. Bot., 7:355–67.

——— and A. F. FAULL. 1934. The cambium and its derivative tissues. IX. Structural variability in the redwood, *Sequoia sempervirens*, and its significance in the identification of fossil woods. Arnold Arboretum Jour., 15:233–54.

BANNAN, M. W. 1936. Vertical resin ducts in the secondary wood of the Abietinae. New Phytol., 35:11–46.

———. 1962. The vascular cambium and tree-ring development. In Tree growth, ed. by THEODORE T. KOZLOWSKI. The Ronald Press Co., New York. Pp. 3–21.

BUCHHOLZ, JOHN T. 1918. Suspensor and early embryo in *Pinus*. Bot. Gaz., 66:185–228.

———. 1946. Volumetric studies of seeds, endosperms and embryos in *Pinus ponderosa* during embryonic differentiation. Bot. Gaz., 108:232–44.

BUDKEVICH, E. V. 1961. Drevesina sosnovykh: Anatomicheskoe Stroenie i kliuchi dlia opredeleniia rodov i vidov (Wood of Pinaceae: Anatomical structure and keys for identification of genera and species). Leningrad, Izd. Akad. Nauk S.S.S.R. Leningradskoe otd-nie.

BUTTS, DOROTHY, and J. T. BUCHHOLZ. 1940. Cotyledon number in conifers. Ill. State Acad. Sci. Trans., 33(2):58–62.

CAMPO-DUPLAN, M. VAN. 1950. Recherches sur la phylogénie des abiétinées d'après leurs grains de pollen. Trav. Lab. Forest. de Univ. Toulouse, Tome II, Sect. 1, Vol. IV, Article 1.

CHAMBERLAIN, CHARLES JOSEPH. 1935. Gymnosperms, structure and evolution. Johnson Reprint Corp., New York.

CHANG, YING-PE. 1954. Bark structure of North American conifers. (U.S. Dept. Agr. Tech. Bul. 1095.) Government Printing Office, Washington, D.C.

CLOWES, F. A. L. 1954. The root cap of ectotropic mycorrhiza. New Phytol., 53: 525–29.

———. 1961. Apical meristems. (Bot. Monog. v-2.) Blackwell Scientific Publications, Oxford, England.

COOPERRIDER, C. K. 1938. Recovery processes of ponderosa pine reproduction following injury to young annual growth. Plant Physiol., 13:5–27.

COULTER, JOHN M., and J. H. ROSE. 1886. Synopsis of North American pines based upon leaf-anatomy. I, II. Bot. Gaz., 11:256–62, 302–9.

CURTIS, JAMES D., and DONALD W. LYNCH. 1957. Sylvics of ponderosa pine. Intermountain Forest and Range Experiment Station, Forest Service, U.S. Department of Agriculture, Misc. Pub. 12, Ogden, Utah.

DEBAZAC, E. F. 1962. Note sur le bourgeon interfasciculaire et les aiguilles surnuméraires chez les pins. (Soc. Bot. de France Bul., 109(1–2): 1–5.

DOI, TOHEI, and KIN-ICHI MORIKAWA. 1929. An anatomical study of the leaves of the genus *Pinus*. Kyushu Imp. Univ., Dept. Agr. Jour., 2:149–98.

ESAU, KATHERINE. 1953. Plant anatomy. John Wiley & Sons, Inc., New York.

———. 1960. Anatomy of seed plants. John Wiley & Sons, Inc., New York.

———. 1963. Ultrastructure of differentiated cells in higher plants. Amer. Jour. Bot., 50:495–506.

FERGUSON, C. W., and R. A. WRIGHT. 1963. Tree rings in the western Great Basin. Nev. State Mus. Anthrop. Papers, No. 9. Pp. 10–16.

FERGUSON, MARGARET C. 1901. The development of the egg and fertilization in *Pinus strobus*. Ann. Bot., 15:435–79.

FERRÉ, Y. DE. 1952. Les formes de jeunesse des abiétacées. Trav. Lab. Forest. de Toulouse Univ. tome II, Sect. 1, Vol. III, Art. 1.

FLORIN, R. 1931. Untersuchungen zur Stammesgeschichte der Coniferales und Cordaitales. Kung. Svenska Vetensk. Akad. Handl. Ser. 3, 10(1):1–588.

FOSTER, ADRIANCE S. 1949. Practical plant anatomy (2d ed.). D. Van Nostrand Co., Inc., Princeton, N.J.

——— and ERNEST M. GIFFORD, JR. 1959. Comparative morphology of vascular plants. W. H. Freeman & Co., San Francisco.

FRANCINI, ELENORA. 1958. Ecologia comparata di *Pinus halepensis* Mill., *Pinus pinaster* Sol. e *Pinus pinea* L. sulla base del compartamento del gametofito feminile. Ann. Acad. Ital. Sci. Forest., 7:107–72.

GIFFORD, ERNEST M., JR., and N. T. MIROV. 1960. Initiation and ontogeny of the ovulate strobilus in ponderosa pine. Forest Sci., 6:19–25.

——— and RALPH H. WETMORE. 1957. Apical meristems of vegetative shoots and strobili in certain gymnosperms. Natl. Acad. Sci. Proc., 43:571–76.

GLOCK, WALDO S. 1937. Principles and methods of tree-ring analysis. (Carnegie Inst. Wash. Pub. 486.) Washington, D.C.

GREGUSS, PÁL. 1955. Identification of living gymnosperms on the basis of xylotomy. (Akademia Kiado, Budapest.)

HARADA, HIROSHI. 1953. Electron-microscope investigation on the wart-like (particle) structure of conifer tracheids. Jap. Forestry Soc. Jour., 35:393–96.

——— and Y. MIYAZAKI. 1952. The electron-microscopic observation of the cell wall of conifer tracheids. Jap. Forestry Soc. Jour., 34:350–52.

HARLEY, J. L. 1959. The biology of mycorrhiza. Leonard Hill, Ltd., London.

HARLOW, W. M. 1931. The identification of the pines of the United States, native and introduced, by needle structure. (N.Y. State Col. Forestry, Syracuse Univ., Tech. Pub. No. 32.)

HARPER, A. G. 1913. Defoliation: Its effects upon the growth and structure of the wood of *Larix*. Ann. Bot., 27:621–42.

HARTIG, R. 1869. Das Aussetzen der Jahresringe bei unterdrückten Stämmen. Ztschr. Forst. u. Jagdw., 1:471–76.

HATCH, A. B., and K. D. DOAK. 1933. Mycorrhizal and other features of the root system of *Pinus*. Arnold Arboretum Jour., 14:85–99.

HILL, T. G., and E. DE FRAINE. 1909. On the seedling structure of gymnosperms. Ann. Bot., 23:189–227.

HOLMAN, RICHARD M., and WILFRED W. ROBBINS. 1927. A textbook of general botany for colleges and universities. John Wiley & Sons, Inc., New York.

HUBER, B. 1947. Zur Mikrotopographie der Saftströme im Transfusiongewebe der Konifernnadel. Planta, 35:331–51.

JOHNSTONE, A. R. 1940. Further studies on polyembryony and germination of polyembryonic pine seeds. Amer. Jour. Bot., 27:808–11.

KENG, HSUAN, and ELBERT L. LITTLE, JR. 1961. Needle characteristics of hybrid pines. Silvae Genetica, 10:131–46.

KONAR, R. N. 1960. The morphology and embryology of *Pinus roxburghii* Sar. with a comparison with *Pinus wallichiana* Jack. Phytomorphology, 10:305–19.

LANNER, RONALD M. 1961. Living stumps in the Sierra Nevada. Ecology, 42:170–73.

LARSON, P. R. 1956. Discontinuous growth rings in suppressed slash pine. Trop. Woods, 104:80–89.

LIESE, WALTER. 1951. Demonstration electronenmikroskopischer Aufnahmen von Nadelholzhoftüpfeln. Ber. Deut. Bot. Gesell., 64:31–32.

———. 1956. Zur systematischen Bedeutung der submikroskopischen Warzenstruktur bei der Gattung *Pinus* L. Holz als Roh- und Werkstoff, 14:417–24.

McGINNIES, W. G. 1963. Dendrochronology. Jour. Forestry, 61:5–11.

McWILLIAM, J. R. 1958. The role of the micropyle in the pollination of *Pinus*. Bot. Gaz., 120:109–17.

MERGEN, F. 1955. Vegetative propagation of slash pine. (U.S. Forest Serv. Southeast. Forest Expt. Sta. Paper No. 54.) Asheville, N.C.

——— and L. E. KOERTING. 1957. Initiation and development of flower primordia in slash pine. Forest Sci., 3:145–55.

MIROV, N. T. 1962. Phenology of tropical pines. Arnold Arboretum Jour., 43:218–19.

NÄGELI, W. 1935. Aussetzende und auskeilende Jahrring. Schweiz. Ztschr. f. Forstw., 86:209–15.

ROMBERGER, J. A. 1963. Meristems, growth, and development in woody plants. (U.S. Dept. Agr. Tech. Bul. 1293.) Government Printing Office, Washington, D.C.

SACHER, J. A. 1954. Structure and seasonal activity of the shoot apices of *Pinus lambertiana* and *Pinus ponderosa*. Amer. Jour. Bot., 41:749–59.

SATOO, W. 1952. Origin and development of adventitious roots in seedling cuttings of conifers. I. Bul. Tokyo Univ. Forests No. 43. Pp. 59–81. In Japanese.

———. 1955. Origin and development of adventitious roots in seedling cuttings of conifers. II. Bul. Tokyo Univ. Forests No. 48. Pp. 115–28. In Japanese.

———. 1956. Anatomical studies on the root cuttings in coniferous species. Bul. Tokyo Univ. Forests No. 51. Pp. 109–58. In Japanese, with English summary.

SCHULMAN, EDMUND. 1958. Bristlecone pine, oldest known living thing. Natl. Geog. Mag., 113:354–72.

SCHULZE, E., and N. RONGER. 1899. Über die Bestandteile der Samen von *Pinus cembra* (Zirbelkiefer oder Arve). Landw. Vers. Sta., 51:189–204.

SHAW, G. P. 1914. The genus *Pinus*. (Arnold Arboretum Pub. No. 5.) Houghton Mifflin Co., Boston.

SLANKIS, V. 1958. The role of auxin and other exudates in mycorrhizal symbiosis of forest trees. In The physiology of forest trees, ed. by KENNETH V. THIMANN. The Ronald Press Co., New York. Pp. 427–43.

SPURR, A. R. 1949. Histogenesis and organization of the embryo in *Pinus strobus* L. Amer. Jour. Bot., **36**:629–41.

———. 1950. Organization of the procambium and development of the secretory cells in the embryo of *Pinus strobus* L. Amer. Jour. Bot., **37**:185–97.

SRIVASTAVA, LALIT M. 1963. Secondary phloem in the Pinaceae. Calif. Univ., Pubs. Bot., **36**:1–142.

SUTHERLAND, M. 1934. A microscopical study of the structure of the leaves of the genus *Pinus*. New Zeal. Inst. Trans. and Proc., **63**:517–68.

THOMSON, R. B., and H. B. SIFTON. 1925. Resin canals in the Canadian spruce (*Picea canadensis* [Mill]) B.S.P.: An anatomical study especially in relation to traumatic effects and their bearing on phylogeny. Roy. Soc. London, Phil. Trans., Ser. B, **214**:63–111.

WARDROP, A. B., W. LIESE, and G. W. DAVIS. 1959. The nature of the wart structure in conifer tracheids. Holzforschung, **13**:115–20.

WEIDMAN, R. H. 1939. Evidences of racial influences in a 25-year test of ponderosa pine. Jour. Agr. Res., **59**:855–87.

WODEHOUSE, R. P. 1959. Pollen grains. Hafner Publishing Co., New York. Pp. 256–61.

YIM, KYONG BIN. 1961. Air-layering of lodgepole pine and origin of adventitious roots. Forest Sci., **7**:227–31.

# 6

# Physiology and Ecology

## PHYSIOLOGY

Many articles have been written on the physiology of pines. To discuss all of them would be a formidable task. Basic information on this subject may be found in Kramer and Kozlowski (1960) and in Kozlowski (1956).

In April, 1957, an international symposium on the Physiology of Forest Trees was held at Harvard Forest (Thimann, 1958). In June of the same year, a symposium on Forest Tree Physiology took place at the Ohio Agricultural Experiment Station, Wooster, Ohio, and its results were published (*Ohio Journal of Science*, 1957). Both of these symposia contributed much to our knowledge of the physiology of pines.

A little later, Mirov and Stanley (1959) published an article on the physiology of pines. In 1960, a symposium on tree growth was held in Tucson, Arizona. It also included some information on pines (Kozlowski, 1962b). The publications mentioned above helped materially in the preparation of this chapter. Other sources were also used.

Of over one hundred species of the genus *Pinus*, only a few have been used for experiments in plant physiology. In Europe, *P. sylvestris* No. 69 has been the most common experimental pine. In the eastern United States, *P. taeda* No. 24 and *P. strobus* No. 20 have been the most frequently used; and in the western United States, the pines most used have been *P. ponderosa* No. 14 and *P. lambertiana* No. 3. In the northeastern United States and in Canada, the experimental pines are *P. strobus* No. 20, *P. resinosa* No. 21, and *P. banksiana* No. 32. In Japan, most plant physiological work has been done with *P. densiflora* No. 95 and *P. thunbergii* No. 97. In New Zealand and Australia, research on physiology of pines has been almost entirely with planted California pine *P. radiata* No. 19. Other pines have been used occasionally.

It is important to keep in mind that the experimental material for physiological research on pines is almost always obtained from wild forests and thus is always genetically heterogeneous; the physiological performance of pines even of the same species varies from one individual to another. Also, the slow growth and large size of pines complicate experimental work; most physiological studies of pines have been done with seedlings.

## Nutrition

The most important macroelements obtained by pines from the soil are nitrogen and phosphorus—then follow: potassium, sulfur, magnesium, and calcium (Plate 6–1). Iron is indispensable; small quantities of other elements are also necessary, although little is known about deficiency symptoms caused by microelements except zinc deficiency in *P. radiata* No. 19 cultivated in Australia (Kessel and Sloate, 1938). The reader will find a great deal of instructive information on mineral nutrition of pines in publications by Howell (1932a), Mitchell (1939), Chandler (1943), Hobbs (1944), White (1954), and Fowells and Krauss (1959). The most recent and very thorough study of pine nutrition (of *P. sylvestris*) is that of Ingestad (1962).

Nutritional experiments have shown that pines, perhaps because they are slower growing than annuals, can be cultivated at much lower concentrations of nutrients than agricultural plants (Howell, 1932b). In the author's unpublished experiments, equally good results were obtained when *P. ponderosa* seedlings were grown in full Hoagland solution (Hoagland and Arnon, 1939), and also in a solution diluted to one-tenth of that commonly used in experiments with agricultural crops. That pines are moderate in their requirements for minerals is also seen from Sucoff's (1962) experiments with *P. virginiana* No. 27 seedlings. Deficiency symptoms were evident only when potassium concentration dropped below 4 ppm and that of calcium, below 3 ppm. Incidentally, he found no major differences in nutrient requirements between *P. virginiana* and *P. taeda* No. 24.

Deficiency symptoms in pines manifest themselves in about the same way as in most other plants (Mitchell, 1939): Nitrogen-deficient seedlings are stunted and their needles are of a pale yellow color; phosphorus-deficient foliage turns purple; iron-deficient plants are chlorotic; potassium-deficient pines also bear the signs of chlorosis, especially in the tips of young leaves, which later fade and become brown (Ingestad, 1962). Sucoff (1961) reported purple discoloration in potassium-deficient seedlings of *P. taeda* No. 24 and *P. virginiana* No. 27. Needle tips of magnesium-deficient plants turn brown. Visual symptoms, however, cannot always be considered as a reliable indication of deficiency of one mineral or another. Sometimes a severe insect infestation or a fungous disease

**Plate 6–1.** Calcium-deficient *P. banksiana* No. 32. Note beads of exuded resin and contorted needles—typical symptoms. (By permission Pulp and Paper Institute of Canada. Photo by Stewart D. Swan.)

may be mistaken for mineral deficiency in the soil (Sucoff, 1961). E. L. Stone (1953) found that in *P. resinosa* No. 21, deficiency of magnesium caused only reduction of growth. Only when extreme deficiency occurred were symptoms evident. The author observed similar behavior in *P. ponderosa* No. 14 seedlings.

Of all major elements, calcium deserves special consideration. In Pessin's (1937) experiment, calcium deficiency produced no apparent injurious effect in *P. echinata* No. 25 seedlings. The response of *P. elliottii* No. 23 seedlings to calcium deficiency was also indefinite; only the length of the roots was affected. Calcium deficiency, however, hindered development of *P. taeda* No. 24 seedlings. In *P. palustris* No. 22, the needles of calcium-deficient plants appeared less vigorous. Davis (1949) was able to detect effects of calcium deficiency on *P. taeda* seedlings; their terminal buds were small, there was poorer development of needles and the root tips did not appear healthy. Sucoff (1961) noticed resin exudation on the needles of calcium-deficient *P. taeda* and *P. virginiana* seedlings. Swan (1963) described resin droplets and contorted needles in calcium-deficient *P. banksiana* No. 32 seedlings (Plate 6–1).

In repeated (unpublished) experiments conducted by the author in 1939, eliminating calcium in the nutrient solution did not affect the growth of *P. ponderosa* No. 14 seedlings; calcium deficiency symptoms could be induced only when a special technique was applied (i.e., purified salt, Pyrex dishes); the seedlings grown with this precaution in calcium-free solution had poorer root development than the control plants. No resin exudation on the needles was observed. It should be noted that the environments of eastern American pines (No. 24 and No. 27) and that of *P. ponderosa* of the West are very different.

Judging by the response of pines to calcium in nature, the genus *Pinus* has a wide range of tolerance for this element. Apparently, some species can live with a minimum of this element in the soil in one locality and tolerate an excess of calcium in another (Ingestad, 1962).

As to the distribution of different elements in tissues of pines, there are indications that boron, silicon, manganese, aluminum, iron, and copper accumulate in the tips of *P. strobus* No. 20 and *P. resinosa* No. 21 needles, while phosphorus, magnesium, lead, silver, calcium, and zinc are uniformly distributed; concentration of potassium is lower in the tip and high in the base of the needle (Sayre, 1957).

Most nutritional experiments with pines have been conducted in greenhouses, using potted plants. When the experiments are performed with older trees in a forest, the situation becomes more complicated. To correlate mineral nutrition (including nitrogen, which in a forest is almost always of biological origin) with growth of the trees, one has to consider not only the species but also the climate, the soil, and the composition of the forest. Leyton (1958) and Reuther, Embleton, and Jones (1958) have discussed many problems of nutritional studies of conifers (and among them of pines) growing in a forest.

Sometimes deficiency of an element is not caused by its absence in, but rather by the properties of the soil. The lateritic clay soils may contain considerable amounts of $PO_4$, but it is adsorbed by the colloidal particles of the soil and is not readily available to the pines. Rennie (1955) gives a broad estimate of the uptake of K, P, and Ca by mature broadleaf forest, spruce-pine forest, and pine forest (*P. sylvestris*). Pine forest requires less K, P, and Ca than do hardwoods or a pine-spruce forest. All three types of forest take up considerably less K and P, but the amounts of Ca are not much less compared with agriculture crops. This statement is apparently valid only for the particular environment and for one pine species. In other places and with other species, the requirements for the three elements might be different. We know as yet too little of the nutritional requirements of mature pines.

The nutritional balance of a pine tree in a forest may be somewhat judged by analysis of its foliage. But it should be kept in mind that mineral content of pine needles varies in different parts of the crown (Leyton and Armson, 1955), in the needles of different ages (Leyton, 1957), and also at different times of the year (Chandler, 1939).

## Mycorhiza

The morphology and anatomy of mycorhizae in pines have been described in Chapter 5. Their physiology is briefly discussed here. Melin (1962) found that more than forty species of fungi may enter into symbiotic relations with *P. sylvestris* alone; thus, there are not mycorhizal fungi, but only a mycorhizal state (Kelley, 1950).

Larger quantities of minerals are absorbed by mycorhizal roots than by those deprived of mycorhiza. This has been demonstrated by Hatch (1937) for *P. strobus* seedlings, by Routien and Dawson (1943) for *P. echinata* (growing in poor soil), and by other investigators. Hatch (1937) suggested that mycorhizal roots of pine exert selectivity for cations; later, J. M. Wilson (as quoted by Harley, 1959) showed this experimentally for mycorhizal roots of beech, and no doubt his findings are applicable to pines. Harley (1959) discussed at length the physiology of salt absorption by mycorhizal pines; for further information on this subject, the reader is referred to this valuable source. Why are mycorhizal roots beneficial for absorption of larger quantities of minerals? Hatch (1937) thinks that mycorhizal roots possess a large absorbing area; others suggest that fungi may stimulate the metabolic processes in the pine roots and thus increase intake of nutrients (McComb and Griffith, 1946). There also is the possibility that mycorhiza is beneficial to pines because it may protect the trees from the pathogenic fungi (Melin, 1925). Mycorhiza even may increase the drought resistance of pines (Cromer, 1935).

Fungi also are benefited by their symbiosis with pines. When not associated with pines, they may lack the capacity of producing cellulose-hydrolyzing enzyme and are thus unable to obtain sugars to sustain them

(Slankis, 1958). It has also been demonstrated that when mycorhizal fungi are not in association with tree roots, the fungi are not capable of producing fruit bodies (several publications quoted by Slankis, 1958). There was also evidence that the symbiosis makes certain vitamins and certain amino acids available for use by the mycorhizal fungi (Hacskaylo, 1957).

Slankis is of the opinion that auxin somehow is involved in formation of mycorhiza (Slankis, 1958). Auxin, exuded from mycorhizal fungi, causes morphological deviations of short roots. Depending on concentration, it stimulates or inhibits the elongation of long roots and determines the general pattern of the root system.

Ulrich (1959), who investigated effects of auxins on mycorhizae of *P. lambertiana* No. 3, came to the conclusion that the mycorhiza-forming fungi could be divided into three groups. Fungi of the first group produced indole–acetic acid (IAA) even without tryptophane, if provided with a medium favoring rapid growth; the slow-growing species required tryptophane to produce IAA. The second group (consisting of two unrelated species) apparently had an active IAA-oxidizing system, converting the auxin into other indole compounds. To the third group belonged species of the genus *Amanita*, which produced IAA along with many other indole compounds. IAA alone, however, did not cause dichotomy in pine roots; neither did it cause formation of mycorhizae. The presence of fungi alone (i.e., without IAA) was somewhat detrimental to the health of the pine roots (Ulrich, 1960). In Ulrich's experiments, $10^{-4}$M indole–acetic acid inhibited root elongation of *P. lambertiana* seedlings; lower concentrations had no noticeable effect. Dichotomous branching of some short roots was caused by $10^{-5}$M and $10^{-6}$M indole-acetonitrile; and $10^{-6}$M 2,4-dichlorophenoxyacetic acid (2,4-D) had very little effect except to cause swelling of the meristems of short roots during the two weeks the roots were bathed in the $10^{-5}$ 2,4-D solution. Naphthalene acetic acid at a concentration of $10^{-6}$M initiated many lateral root primordia (Ulrich, 1962).

There are, in soil, some substances inhibitory to mycorhizal fungi; these not only are produced by soil microorganisms, but also may be present in the decomposing pine needles of the forest ground cover. Hacskaylo (1957), in his discussion of Melin's paper on physiological aspects of mycorhizae in forest trees (Melin, 1962), postulated the following sequence in the mycorhizal relationship of trees: (1) secretion of some growth regulator by the fungi, causing change in morphology of the short roots; (2) secretion of growth-promoting metabolites, essential to the growth of the mycorhizal fungi (these unknown metabolites have been designated by Melin as "Factor M"); (3) secretion of enzymes by the hyphae of the fungi, enabling them to form the mantle and to penetrate into the intercellular space of the root, and in pines, to a limited extent, into the cells; (4) exchange of materials between the tree and the fungus.

Symbiosis of pines with fungi probably has played an important part in the history of pines. The ecology of mycorhizae will be mentioned later in this chapter.

## Photosynthesis

Among the early researches on photosynthesis of pines should be mentioned publications of Ivanov and his associates in Russia. References to these publications may be found in one of Ivanov's papers published in German, entitled "Über die Arbeit des Assimilationsapparates verschiedener Baumgarten" I. Kiefer [Pine] (Iwanoff and Kossowitsch,* 1929). These authors concluded that pines must be placed among species that possess high photosynthetic capacity (calculated per unit of area).

In the United States, important researches on photosynthesis of pines have been made by Kramer and his associates (Kramer and Clark, 1947; Kramer and Decker, 1944). A general review was recently presented by Kramer (1958a). The rate of photosynthesis in *P. taeda* No. 24 was found to increase with light intensity to the maximum intensity of applied light; this was attributed to the limited penetration of light to shaded areas when it was of low intensity. Lower efficiency of pines (*P. taeda* No. 24) in comparison with that of broadleaf trees (*Quercus*) was attributed to shading of each needle by others nearby. The capacity of pines to accumulate the products of photosynthesis at low levels of light intensity perhaps explains how pines sometimes establish themselves and survive under the canopy of a forest (Bormann, 1955). In the shade, needles photosynthesize more efficiently because they have greater chlorophyll content. Pisek and Tranquillini (1954) found this in fir, and probably it is so also in pine. The maximum photosynthesis in *P. strobus* No. 20 was recorded at 5461 Å and 5780 Å (Burns, 1942). This is more toward the blue end of the spectrum than reported for broadleaf trees.

It has been known for a long time that pines have the capacity to photosynthesize in winter, although opinions differ on this subject. According to some investigators, photosynthesis continues in pines throughout the winter (Zacharowa, 1929); others have found that in the northern climates, it practically ceases with the advent of cold weather and is resumed in the spring (Ivanov and Orlova, 1931). In winter, the slowdown of photosynthesis is caused by inactivation of the chloroplasts. Their appearance and their position in the cell are changed by the low temperatures. With increasing temperatures, the normal shape and dis-

---

* This is a German way to spell the authors' names.

tribution of the chloroplasts are restored. The low temperatures in winter (and excessively high temperatures in summer) inactivate the chloroplasts and decrease the photosynthesis; respiration is not affected by high and low temperatures in the same way as is photosynthesis. More recent studies of seasonal conditions of chloroplasts were made by Parker and Philpott (1961), who examined *P. strobus* No. 20 cells under electron microscope. In winter, a network of reticulum occurred in all living cells, aparently enmeshing mitochondria as well as chloroplasts, and in sieve cells extending through the plates. Winter-type chloroplasts appeared as distinct, intact entities, closely appressed to one another in the folds or sides of the cells.

Freeland (1944) found that *P. sylvestris* No. 69 and *P. nigra* No. 74 still photosynthesize at −6°C, and respiration was detectable down to −19°C. Kramer (1958a) suggested that in the warmer parts of the world, such as southeastern America, pines apparently carry on considerable photosynthesis throughout the year. *Pinus echinata* accumulates considerable amounts of carbohydrates during the winter (Hepting, 1945). However, the net rate of photosynthesis depends on the rate of respiration and translocation, the carbon dioxide availability (Decker, 1947), and age of the needles. The maximum rate is reached after completion of needle growth in the first year and a subsequent decline in the two- and three-year-old needles (Freeland, 1952). The trend of decline in the needles that may remain on the trees of some pine species for a longer time (see Chapter 5, p. 371) is apparently unknown.

Decker (1947), who reviewed the problem of relationship between $CO_2$ concentration and photosynthesis, concluded that the rate of photosynthesis increases linearly with the $CO_2$ concentration in the range from 0.45 to 0.5 mg per liter of air. Huber (1952) found that $CO_2$ content of the atmosphere at ground level is at a maximum in the early afternoon and that this condition extends several hundred feet into the air. Local conditions affecting $CO_2$ in the air are numerous (Kramer, 1958a).

It may be concluded a priori that mineral deficiencies may affect photosynthesis in pines. Apparently, no studies of this kind have been attempted with the genus *Pinus*, but Kramer (1958a) summarized what has been done in this field with other trees. Deficiency in both the macroelements and the microelements greatly reduces photosynthesis in many fruit trees, and we may expect the same in pines. This area needs investigation.

To photosynthesize, pines, as well as other plants, have to keep their stomata open. Under these circumstances, the trees lose water in transpiration. When available soil moisture decreases and the transpiration becomes excessive, the stomata close earlier in the afternoon and photosynthesis is decreased (Kramer, 1958a). In young *P. taeda* No. 24 seedlings, photosynthesis is decreased considerably long before the permanent wilting point has been reached (Kozlowski, 1949). Even in cool and moist climates, photosynthesis was found to increase after rains (Iwanoff and Kossowitsch, 1929).

Pines are more drought-resistant than many other conifers; they have the capacity to continue photosynthesis under much drier summer conditions than, for instance, *Picea* (Stålfelt, 1921). Moreover, pines seem to have the capacity to lose more water from their protoplasm than other conifers, which permits them to keep their stomata open and thus to continue photosynthesis longer (Dobroserdova, 1962).

## Photoperiod

Apparently, Bogdanov (1931) was the first to experiment, in 1928, with the effect of photoperiod on pines. His material was *P. sylvestris* No. 69 seedlings of southern origin. The seedlings grown under natural long days in a northern locality (18½ hours in June and 14½ hours at the end of August) completed their growth in July; then the terminal buds became active again, and thus two flushes of growth resulted in one season. Seedlings from the same locality growing under their natural 9-hour photoperiod developed normally (i.e., with one flush of growth). Later, photoperiod experiments were expanded to different species. Seedlings of *P. taeda* No. 24, a species of southern latitudes (see Chapter 3), were found to make slightly less growth under days shortened to 8.5 hours than under normal days (14½ hours in June and 9½ hours in December). Under a 14½-hour photoperiod, or in continuous daylight, the seedlings grew well throughout the year (Kramer, 1936). A little later, it was discovered that addition of red irradiation (680 to 1400 m$\mu$) during daylight hours was more beneficial to the seedlings than the addition of blue light. Under supplementary blue light, a stunting effect resulted (Phillips, 1941).

There are numerous other early publications on photoperiod in pines, and the results described in them are often contradictory. Some of the earlier studies on photoperiod had many shortcomings. Equipment was often poor; the effect of temperature was not separated from the effect of light; quality of light was rarely considered. When pine seedlings were grown under long-day conditions, the effects of photoperiods were probably confounded with the effects of photosynthesis. The number of experimental plants was often small, and variation in individual response was great. Vaartaja (1954) was one of a very few investigators who mentioned the individual variation of pine seedlings in their reaction to photoperiod, a problem that recently has been touched upon also by Hellmers (1963).

Downs and Borthwick (1956) fully realized the shortcomings of previous (though very valuable) work when they started to experiment with seedlings of (chiefly) *P. sylvestris* No. 69, and also *P. virginiana* No. 27 and *P. taeda* No. 24, using much better light and temperature controls. They demonstrated that normal seasonal height growth in the seedlings consists of elongation of elements initiated in the bud the year before. Under long photoperiods, however, the new structures elongated as fast as they were formed, so that at a 14-hour photoperiod, the growth was somewhat erratic; the rate of growth at a 16-hour photoperiod was perhaps even faster than at 14-hour daylight, but they noticed "several periods of growth stoppage," possibly caused by disturbing the balance between initiation of structures and their elongation.

Generally speaking, pines of moderate climates do not grow continuously when they are subjected to a long-day treatment as some broadleaf trees do. On the contrary, they stop growth, form terminal buds, and, after a period of inactivity, resume growth again. This has been proved experimentally (Borthwick, 1957) and has been observed repeatedly under natural conditions. Flushes of growth in pines are not necessarily caused by photoperiod alone. Temperature, water, and nutrition also play important parts in the termination and resumption of growth in pines.

Wareing (1950, 1951) has contributed much to our knowledge of photoperiod in pines. He experimented with *P. sylvestris* No. 69. Under a short photoperiod of 10 hours as opposed to a long photoperiod of 15 hours, duration of growth of the first-year seedlings was reduced, fewer needles were formed, and the length of internodes and needles was reduced. The root/shoot ratio and the appearance of roots were not affected.

Maximum growth of the seedlings was attained at the 20-hour photoperiod. The growth was considerably less under continuous light. The rates of leaf production and stem elongation were greatly accelerated by the introduction of one 4-hour dark period, as compared with continuous illumination; when the two 4-hour dark periods were introduced, there was a further increase in leaf number and in stem elongation.

Cambial activity of one-year-old seedlings was maintained longer under a 15-hour photoperiod than under a 10-hour photoperiod. It was concluded that in the fall, when daylight is reduced to 10 hours, cambial activity ceases. Nutrition was also apparently involved in the cessation of growth. In the spring, cambial activity begins when days are as short as in the autumn.

Wareing (1951) suggested that two systems seem to operate in pine seedlings during the dark period: (1) a growth hormone, formed during the preceding light period, is active during the first hours of darkness; and (2) a growth inhibitor becomes effective after 4 hours of darkness.

Downs (1962) reviewed briefly, but well, the effect of photoperiod on growth of pines. It appears from his own experiments with *P. radiata* No. 19, *P. elliottii* No. 23, *P. rigida* No. 29, *P. banksiana* No. 32, *P. strobus* No. 20, and *P. aristata* No. 6 that they all had the best height growth and the highest fresh weight under continuous light. He used photoperiods of 8, 12, 14, 16, and 24 daylight hours. All but one (No. 32) and partially Nos. 20 and 29 of these seven species are found naturally in the lower lattitudes where days during the growing period are relatively short (see Chapter 3 and Table 6–1).

**Table 6–1.** Effect of Photoperiod on Seven Species of Pines (Modified from Downs, 1962)

| Species | Total Growth (cm) Under Different Daylight Hours | | | | | Latitude Range (degrees *) | Altitude Range (meters *) |
|---|---|---|---|---|---|---|---|
| | 8 | 12 | 14 | 16 | 24 | | |
| *P. radiata* | 66 | 71 | 78 | 77 | 121 | 35–37.5 | 0–370 † |
| *P. elliottii* | 10 | 23 | 29 | 31 | 56 | 30–33.5 | 0–150 |
| *P. rigida* | 8 | 12 | 26 | 23 | 39 | 31.5–46 | 0–900 |
| *P. banksiana* | 3 | 5 | 10 | 14 | 25 | 41.5–65 | 0–600 |
| *P. strobus* | 1 | 4 | 4 | 7 | 31 | 34–51 | 0–1500 |
| *P. resinosa* | 1 | 3 | 6 | 8 | 15 | 39.5–52 | 0–1300 |
| *P. aristata* | 2 | 4 | 6 | 10 | 19 | 35–41 | 2500–3700 |

* Approximate.
† On the mainland.

In Downs's experiments, the temperate-climate pines stopped growth on day lengths of 12 hours or less. Their vegetative growth was definitely benefited by long days. On the other hand, *P. radiata* behaved as a tropical tree in that it did not completely stop shoot elongation and did not set dormant buds.

Experience with other pines planted in humid tropics also indicates a continuous growth of shoots. More about this will be said later, under Growth, page 411 of this chapter.

The concept of the mechanism governing long-day and short-day effect on plants changed drastically when it was found that a brief interruption of the dark period has the same effect as a long or continuous day.

Zahner (1955) experimented with the effect of interrupted photoperiod on pines. Control seedlings of *P. taeda* No. 24 were grown under 9½ hours of daylight followed by 14½ hours of darkness. These were compared with the seedlings whose dark period was interrupted in the middle by 30 minutes of 200-watt light. The seedlings with the interrupted night made more than twice the height growth, began growing 2 to 4 weeks earlier, and continued growth to September, while control seedlings "almost ceased to grow early in June." Apparently, in Zahner's experiments, as Wareing had suggested, a growth-inhibiting substance was formed during the dark period. The inhibitor was unstable at the end of the short dark period and was destroyed by light.

The mechanism of photoperiod is complicated; it was found that certain plant pigments are responsible for growth and for flowering. The pigments are activated and inactivated by the light of different wavelengths (Downs, 1962).

Hellmers (1959) reports that a long photoperiod (20 hours) appears to promote bud opening in *P. coulteri* No. 12 (although it is a southern species grown naturally at latitudes between 32 and 38 degrees where its buds open early in March when days are of a duration of between 11 and 12 hours). That is perhaps why Hellmers remarked that "a short photoperiod (9 hours) does not completely inhibit bud opening" of this pine. It is not clear why one should expect inhibition of bud opening of this pine by a short photoperiod, as its buds open in its habitat under naturally short days. Moreover, it is not certain whether the photoperiod alone is responsible for breaking dormancy of buds in pines. In nature, terminal buds are formed in the fall when days become short; but in the spring, the buds become active even though the day length may still be shorter than that which induced their formation. Apparently, the low winter temperature caused the changes necessary for resuming growth; i.e., here thermoperiod was involved. This was shown for *P. resinosa* seedlings by Gustafson (1938).

In one experiment (Ikemoto, 1961), *P. densiflora* No. 95 seedlings responded differently at different times of the year to the same number of daylight hours. In December, under continuous illumination, they began to grow in about 7 days; those under "natural" daylight (which at the latitude of Kyoto, where the experiments were conducted, is about 10½ hours) began to grow 3 weeks later. In January, however, both groups of seedlings began to grow in 1 week.

As has been already mentioned, all experiments on photoperiod in pines were concerned with vegetative growth of very young seedlings. How the photoperiod affects older pines, we do not know.

We do not yet know how different photoperiods or combinations of dark and light hours affect flowering of pines. Thus far, no initiation of flowers has been induced by any artificial manipulations of pines that have not already reached the flowering stage. After this stage is reached, seed production has been induced by such practical measures as girdling or fertilizing. Some pines may produce flowers very early in life, but apparently this is caused by factors other than photoperiod.

In 1956, the author inspected many northern and southern pines growing in the Eddy Arboretum, Placerville, California, at latitude 38 degrees
and altitude about 1000 m, and found that when northern (long-day)
pines were moved to that more southern locality, their flowering habits
were not changed. For example, *P. sylvestris* No. 69 is a prolific seed
producer both in its home at 72 degrees latitude and also at 38 degrees
latitude. Moreover, *P. sylvestris* apparently grows well and develops
flowers when cultivated in the Quinta Equinoccial Experimental Station
located exactly on the Equator in Ecuador, South America (Acosta-Solís,
1954).

Similarly, when "short-day" tropical pines were moved north, for instance, *P. patula* from 17 degrees to 38 degrees lattitude, they also did not
change their natural flowering habits and continued to bloom under much
longer daylight hours of California summer (Mirov, 1956b).

Wareing (1958) also could not find any evidence that photoperiod
controls reproduction of pines. Lately there have been reports to the
contrary (Longman, 1961), but results do not appear to be conclusive.
It is entirely possible that in the future, when physiology of flowering in
pines is better understood, some artificial ways of inducing flowering will
be found. Under natural conditions, however, flowering of the genus
*Pinus* is not affected by changing photoperiod. Pines are neither short-day

**Table 6–2.** Flowering of Northern Pines Cultivated at Eddy Arboretum, Institute
of Forest Genetics, Placerville, Calif., 38 degrees 44 minutes North Latitude [1]
(from Mirov, 1956b)

| | Northern Latitude of Natural Range, Degrees | | Flowering at Age 28–30 Years | |
| --- | --- | --- | --- | --- |
| | From | To | Male Flowers [2] | Female Flowers |
| *P. banksiana* | 41.5 | 65 | Abundant | Abundant |
| *P. sylvestris* var. *lapponica* [3] | 60 | 70 | Abundant | Abundant |
| *P. sylvestris* var. *rigensis* | 57 | 58 | Abundant | Abundant |
| *P. resinosa* | 39 | 52 | Moderate | Moderate |
| *P. montana* (several varieties) | 40 | 50 | Abundant | Abundant |
| *P. nigra* (several varieties, except *mauretanica* [4]) | 40 | 41 | Abundant | Abundant |

[1] *Pinus cembra* and *P. peuce* are both northern pines; the former is not represented
at the Eddy Arboretum; the latter is too young to flower.

[2] Additional information has been published on catkin development and pollen
shedding of pines at the Institute (Duffield, 1953).

[3] Seed source: Finland.

[4] Latitudinal range of *P. nigra* var. *mauretanica* is more southern than the latitude
of Placerville. This variety also flowers profusely at the Institute.

**Table 6–3.** Flowering of Southern Pines Cultivated at the Eddy Arboretum, Institute of Forest Genetics. Placerville, Calif., 38 degrees 44 minutes North Latitude (from Mirov 1956)

| Species | Latitude of Natural Range, Degrees | | Flowering Habits at Age 28–30 Years | |
|---|---|---|---|---|
| | From | To | Male Flowers | Female Flowers |
| P. arizonica | 25 | 34.5 | Scarce | Scarce |
| P. bungeana | 25 | 35 | Abundant | Abundant |
| P. canariensis [1] | 28 | 29 | None | None |
| P. cembroides | 18 | 34 | Moderate | Moderate |
| P. clausa | 26.0 | 30.5 | None | None |
| P. coulteri | 28 | 37 | Abundant | Moderate |
| P. elliottii | 30 | 33.5 | Moderate | Moderate |
| P. engelmannii | 24 | 32.5 | Moderate | Scarce |
| P. excelsa | 25 | 35 | Moderate | Moderate |
| P. gerardiana | 29 | 35 | Moderate | Moderate |
| P. glabra | 29.5 | 33.5 | Light | Light |
| P. greggii | 20 | 26 | Moderate | Moderate |
| P. leiophylla | 17 | 28 | Abundant | Abundant |
| P. longifolia | 25 | 35 | Moderate | Scarce |
| P. luchuensis | 29 | 29.5 | Moderate | Moderate |
| P. massoniana | 22.5 | 38 | Moderate | Moderate |
| P. montezumae [2] | 15 | 25 | Scarce | Scarce |
| P. muricata | 35 | 39 | Abundant | Abundant |
| P. palustris [3] | 27 | 37 | None | None |
| P. patula | 19 | 21 | Abundant | Abundant |
| P. quadrifolia | 30 | 33 | Moderate | Moderate |
| P. radiata | 35 | 37.5 | Abundant | Abundant |
| P. remorata | 29 | 29.5 | Abundant | Abundant |
| P. serotina | 28 | 37.5 | Abundant | Abundant |
| P. taeda | 28 | 38.5 | Moderate | Moderate |
| P. taiwanensis | 22 | 24 | Moderate | Moderate |
| P. torreyana [3,4] | 33 | 34 | Scarce | Scarce |
| P. yunanensis | 24 | 26 | Moderate | Moderate |

[1] Repeatedly damaged by cold at the Institute. At Berkeley, Calif. (latitude 37 degrees 52 minutes North Latitude), produces male and female strobili in abundance.
[2] Older trees of P. montezumae produce cones as far north as 45 degrees north latitude.
[3] Repeatedly damaged by snow at the Institute.
[4] Trees of P. torreyana of same age at Berkeley produce both male and female strobili.

plants nor long-day plants; they are neutral. Perhaps expansion of the genus from the northern regions, where there is continuous daylight during the growing season, toward the Equator, where the length of day is always equal to the length of night, was possible at least partly because pines are (*sensu stricto*) photoperiodically neutral.

From Vaartaja's (1959, 1962) experiments with pines it appears that besides the complicated interplay of light, temperature, composition of soils, nutrition, and other external factors, there may be an endogenous rhythm in pines that determines their phenology. Sometimes it enhances, often it conflicts with photoperiodicity in pines. It is well to keep in mind Chailakhian's (1954) suggestion that photoperiodic response is a complicated phenomenon and that it involves many other factors besides the length of light hours.

## Thermoperiod

Karschon (1951) was the first to apply Went's (1948) term—thermoperiodicity—to pines. Precise experiments, in which the effect of temperature on pines is separated from that of light and in which thermoperiod itself is accurately controlled, have been possible only when modern plant-growth chambers and greenhouses became available. In one of the first experiments, using such installations, it was found that one-year-old *P. taeda* No. 24 seedlings made their best growth when the days were warmer than the nights, and poorest growth when the nights were as warm as the days (Kramer, 1957, 1958b). During the second year of experimentation it was found that increased day temperature was accompanied by increased shoot growth; an increase in night temperature caused decreased growth (Kramer, 1958b). It was demonstrated that the difference between day and night temperatures, within certain limits, was more important than the actual temperature. Essentially, these conclusions were in accordance with ideas postulated by Went (1948).

Hellmers experimented with the thermoperiod of seedlings of several pines. *Pinus taeda* No. 24 behaved as reported by Kramer, i.e., its growth was found to be best when the days were warm and the nights were cool. The tallest seedlings were those grown under conditions of maximum day-night temperature difference. For *P. sabiniana* No. 10 night temperature was more important than day temperature; the seedlings grew the best when maintained under constant 17°C temperature day and night (Hellmers, 1962). Ecological observations, however, indicate that in the vicinity of Placerville, California, elevation about 1000 m, where this pine makes its best growth, the days during the growing period, say, from March to June, are warm to hot while the nights are generally cool.

Again, in *P. jeffreyi* No. 13 and *P. brutia* No. 78 the daily heat sum was the dominant factor regulating growth (Hellmers, 1962). A year later Hellmers reviewed thoroughly the whole problem of thermoperiod in pines, added more results of his own experiments with *P. jeffreyi*, and came to the unavoidable conclusion that the thermoperiod is a very complex phenomenon. All experiments were performed with two-year-old seedlings, but even at this tender age it was evident that different parts of the plantlet have different temperature requirements. Most likely the different stages of later development of a pine tree also have their own thermoperiod design. Light intensities also play an important part in the thermoperiodic response, as shown by Pisek and Winkler (1959) for *P. cembra* No. 70.

It appears from Hellmer's review that, so far, thermoperiod experiments with pine seedlings have produced somewhat inconsistent results. Hellmer's own tests with *P. jeffreyi* seedlings showed that the total daily degree-hours appeared to be the best measure to determine maximum dry-weight production. The necessity of having days warmer than nights was only a secondary factor. Under conditions of equal total daily degree hours, warm nights and cool days favored root growth. The reversed conditions favored top growth. Different parts of the seedlings—terminal buds, needles, branches, roots—had their own thermal regimen and most of the variability among the seedlings was apparently caused by genetic differences. This was a very important observation, often disregarded in this kind of experiment.

The importance of the interrelation between thermoperiod and photoperiod in pines is seen from Downs' (1962) experiments with *P. taeda* No. 24 seedlings. They continued to grow with long days and 4.5°C nights, but stopped growth on 8-hour days and 4.5°C nights. With 26°C or 15.5°C nights and an 8-hour day the seedlings stopped growth sooner at 15.5°C than at 26°C.

## Growth

In temperate climates there is a periodicity in the growth of pines. Growth is of an intermittent character and different parts of a tree grow at different times. There is a definite growth pattern in each species and there is a considerable variation in this pattern among individual pines (Kozlowski, 1963a). In the spring the roots are first to begin growing, followed by the leader, then by the vascular cambium and the needles (Kienholz, 1934). The cyclic periodicity of pine growth was attributed to depletion of nutritional material in the tree. There are, of course, many other factors influencing periodicity of growth in pines. Mikola (1962) found that radial growth of *P. sylvestris* No. 69 depends chiefly on the temperature of the growing season; in southern Finland growth ceases every year about the middle of August. It was noted that the earlier growth starts in the spring, the broader is the latewood portion of the whole growth ring.

The material necessary for the apical growth comes from a different source. Rutter (1957) found that in England, where height growth of *P. sylvestris* seedlings is completed by the middle of June, the old needles showed a significant decrease in dry weight. Importance of old needles as a source of nutrition of young shoots was also shown by Neuwirth (1959). Thus, height growth of uninodal pines depends on the carbohydrate accumulation and on the environmental conditions of the previous season. In the multinodal shoots only the height growth of the first flush depends on events of the past season. On the other hand, diameter growth of pines (as well as the height growth following the first flush) depends chiefly on the products of current photosynthesis, with only slight use of stored food reserve at the beginning of the season.

Kozlowski (1962a) emphasized the importance of redistribution of carbohydrates at the time of flowering and seed production. No data are given for pines, but, judging by results obtained with beech when nutrients are spent in production of seeds, it unfavorably affects the width of annual rings.

Seasonal growth of four species of pine was studied by Friesner (1942) in the eastern United States (Indiana). Terminal shoots of *P. strobus* No. 20, *P. banksiana* No. 32, *P. resinosa* No. 21, and European *P. sylvestris* No. 69 were measured weekly. *Pinus banksiana* and *P. sylvestris* reached maximum elongation early in May; *P. strobus* and *P. resinosa*, somewhat later in the month. In all four species elongation came to a standstill, or nearly so, some time in June and July, but after a brief period of inactivity elongation of the shoots was resumed and continued until the end of September.

A similar sequence of activity was observed by the present writer throughout a growing season in development of annual shoots of young specimens of *P. ponderosa* No. 14 at an altitude of about 1000 m in the Sierra Nevada of California. The spring growth started early in March and reached its maximum at the end of May when some terminal shoots were as long as 55 cm. At that time the terminal buds appeared to be well formed and inactive. Needles began to appear at the middle of April and reached their full length by the middle of July; then the buds began to elongate again and toward fall, when it became cooler, some of them were already 3 or 4 cm long. Their elongation apparently ceased in winter and resumed next spring. Of course, the timetable of development varies from year to year.

In the regions of temperate climate the late summer flushes of growth are caused by drought in the early summer followed by late rains. This happens not every year and not in all trees, as shown by Carvell (1956) for *P. resinosa* No. 21. In contrast, in *P. ponderosa* No. 14, as described above, elongation of terminal buds of the leader and of the branches occurs every year and in all young trees of normal vigor; thus it may be considered a part of the growth pattern of this species.

**Physiology of Forming Growth Rings.** The physiology of growth ring formation is little known (see Chapter 5, p. 354). Nutritional factors are much involved in their formation, their width, and the ratio between the fast-growing cells of earlywood and the slow-growing cells of latewood. The change from earlywood to latewood may be a response to a changed auxin level (Wareing, 1958; Larson, 1962).

Larson (1962) has reviewed the problem of physiology of annual growth layers well and he showed by his own experimentation with *P. resinosa* No. 21 how intimately the terminal growth of a shoot (and hence auxin production) and photoperiod are connected with the formation of growth rings. A renewed activity in the annual shoot, or even an application to the decapitated shoot with indoleacetic acid, resulted in a false ring formation. Photoperiod coupled with auxin production is also involved in the formation of growth rings of young *P. resinosa*. Latewood was initiated at the termination of height growth, following exposure to short days. The young pines growing under long-day conditions continued formation of earlywood cells (Larson, 1962). These researches bring to mind Vaartaja's (who also worked with *P. resinosa*) conclusions that, besides other mechanisms governed by photoperiod, there apparently exists in pine an endogenous rhythm determining cessation and resumption of growth of xylem cells that form growth rings. It is perhaps this endogenous rhythm, the result of a complicated hormone-nutrition inherited mechanism, that causes occasional appearance of more or less conspicuous growth layers even in the warm and humid regions where pines are planted (Plate 6–3).

As a result of their investigation of *P. resinosa* No. 21, Duff and Nolan (1953) arrived at the conclusion that the endogenous rhythm, that is, an hereditary trait, is more important in the northern habitats of pines than the environment in the growth pattern of this pine. There is also a marked daily rhythm in shoot elongation and more growth occurs during the night (Kozlowski, 1963a).

But even in the more northern climate, with abundant summer rains, this endogenous rhythm might often be distorted by external factors. More than one annual ring can be formed during a growing season. Sokolov and Artiushenko (1957) observed up to seven flushes of growth in *P. sylvestris* No. 69 and in *P. banksiana* No. 32 that resulted in renewed activity of the cambium and caused formation of additional growth rings (Plate 6–2). In semi-arid parts of the world, such as the southwestern United States, where precipitation during the growing season is in the form of occasional violent cloudbursts, several rings may be formed in pines during one year. These are called false annual rings; there also may be found partial growth rings or lenses.

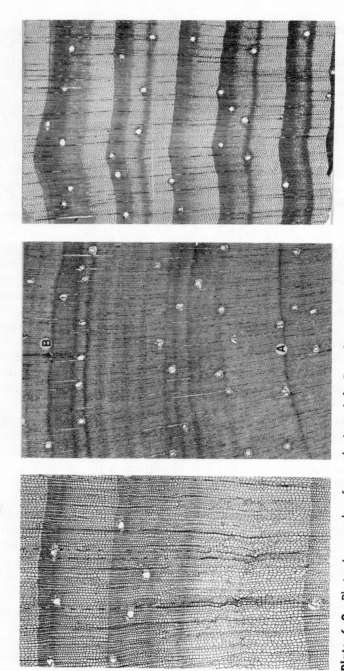

**Plate 6–2.** Photomicrographs of growth rings. *Left:* P. radiata No. 19. Two false rings were caused by variations in available water. *Center:* P. merkusii No. 101. The wood between A and B may have been formed during two successive years. *Right:* Five years' growth of P. leiophylla No. 41, showing more than five growth rings. (Photos by I. W. Bailey.)

414

Perhaps the effect of summer cloudbursts on growth of woody plants in the arid countries could be illustrated with formation of growth layers in planted specimens of *Simmondsia californica*, a Sonoran desert shrub of the American Southwest and the adjacent parts of Mexico (Mirov, 1952). A plantation of Simmondsia was started at Riverside, California, in 1940 and twelve years later had to be abandoned. During these twelve years the bushes were irrigated three times a (rainless) summer. Upon examination, the cross-section of these twelve-year-old specimens showed an average of thirty-six growth layers of a highly irregular character (Plate 6–3c).

Naturally pines occur rarely if ever, in the humid tropics, i.e., in habitat of evenly distributed and abundant rainfall, uniformly high temperatures, and high air humidity. When planted in such environment some pine species do not form distinct "annual rings." In Plate 6–3b is shown a cross-section of a five-year-old *P. radiata* No. 19, planted on the island of Hawaii at an altitude of about 1600 m. In the young plant there was resemblance of a growth ring, but there was no differentiation between the earlywood and the latewood. Later development of the seedling was rather erratic, although there was a tendency to form growth layers. Ronald M. Lanner * writes that different pine species and even different individuals of the same species respond differently to the warm, humid climate of Hawaii. *Pinus contorta* No. 16 at an altitude of about 2400 m has very distinct annual rings, while *P. radiata* at the same place shows no ring development. It is tempting to speculate that since pines originated in the temperate climate of the north (see Chapter 2), then perhaps the pattern of forming concentric growth layers may be considered as an ancestral, genetically fixed capacity. In the course of evolution of the genus, under pressure of the environment, some pines deviated from this pattern of wood formation (see Chapter 2, pages 85–86). Much is yet to be done on this interesting problem. Growth of pines planted decades ago in steaming lowlands of Java (Mirov, 1962) should be studied; Mexican *P. chiapensis* No. 34, growing naturally in low elevations (down to 500 m) sometimes with palms and amidst coffee and banana plantations, perhaps offers good material for studying aberrant wood formation in pines. Hawaii, where pine plantations are well established, also is a suitable place for this kind of research.

Regarding the absence of annual rings in some fossil tropical pines, see Chapter 2, page 86.

**Role of Auxin in Growth of Pines.** Czaja (1934) detected auxin in the tips of *P. sylvestris* No. 69 and *P. heldrechii* No. 75 and Zimmermann (1936) found it in *P. strobus* No. 20. In *P. ponderosa* No. 14 and *P. tor-*

* U.S. Forest Service, Hilo, Hawaii, who sent the *P. radiata* material to the author.

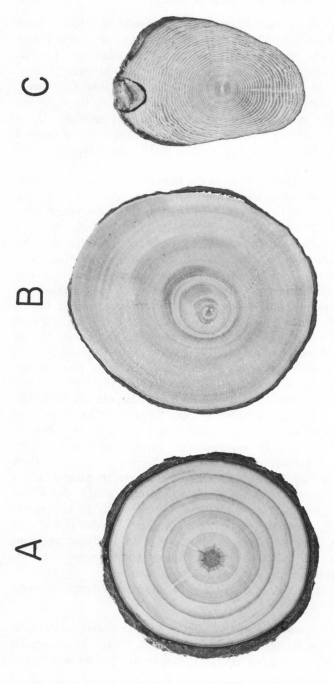

**Plate 6-3.** Growth rings. A: *P. ponderosa* No. 14 grown in the Sierra Nevada, California, at an altitude of about 800 m. The tree, when cut, was six years old. During the first three summers, which were rainless, the seedling was repeatedly irrigated; this caused formation of weak additional growth layers. Generally, however, the number of seasonal growth rings indicates the age of the tree. B: *P. radiata* No. 19, five years old, planted in Hawaii at an altitude of about 1600 m in a wet tropical climate. Its growth layers are not definite and do not permit determination of the age of the tree. C: *Simmondsia californica* (a species of arid environment) twelve years old, irrigated three times every summer. Its growth layers do not permit determination of its age. (Photos by N. T. Mirov.)

416

*reyana* No. 11 the lowest concentration of auxin was found in the upper-most part of the shoot. With increase of distance from the tip the con-centration of auxin increased and reached a maximum near the base of the present-year shoot. In *P. ponderosa* auxin concentration was always higher in fast-growing than in slow-growing young pines. Free auxin was evenly distributed both in the xylem and phloem parts of the annual shoot but bound auxin was found only in the xylem part (Mirov, 1941). Later investigations of auxin in pines indicated that there exists an inter-action between growth-promoting and growth-inhibiting substances. In terminal buds of *P. palustris* No. 22 seasonal variations in amounts of growing substances (IAA) and of a growth inhibitor apparently regulate the winter rest period of the buds (Allen, R. M., 1960). A similar growth promoting-growth inhibiting system was found in the buds and shoots of *P. pinaster* No. 80 (Couvy, 1962). An interplay of growth substances and a growth inhibitor was investigated also in *P. thunbergii* No. 97 (Ogasawara and Kondo, 1962).

**"Grass Stage" in Pine Seedlings.** Some pines of Mexico, of the Caribbean region, and of the southeastern United States have, in the juvenile stage, a peculiar inhibition of height growth. The seedling develops secondary foliage but there is no internodal elongation of the shoot and the plant appears as a tuft of "grass" on a stocky, carrot-like root. Sometimes the seedling remains in this dwarfed stage for several years (up to fifteen and more) and then begins to grow normally and rapidly, especially when exposed to abundant light (Pessin, 1944). *Pinus palustris* No. 22 possesses the most pronounced "grass stage"; other pines having it in a greater or lesser degree are: *P. montezumae* No. 47, *P. michoacana* No. 52, *P. tropicalis* No. 66, *P. elliottii* var. *densa* No. 63, *P. engelmannii* No. 53, some varieties of *P. pseudostrobus* No. 54, and (subject to verification), *P. merkusii* No. 101 from Burma and Viet Nam but not from Sumatra.

Attempts have been made by many to break the grass-stage dormancy of *P. palustris* seedlings. In 1948 the writer grafted a terminal bud of this pine, about 3 cm wide and 3 cm long, on a *P. elliottii* No. 62 (a species not having a grass stage) transplant of the same diameter. The graft took, but the operation did not break the dormancy of the bud; the plant remained in the grass stage for 10 years (see Brown, 1958, p. 525). It appeared from this simple test that the dormancy resided in the bud and not in the root of *P. palustris*. Brown (1958) subjected the problem to a thorough investigation and concluded that apices of *P. palustris* seedlings in the grass stage produce no auxin; no polar auxin transport was detected; when indole–acetic acid was applied, it was neither transported nor inactivated by the apices. That auxin physiology is involved in the grass-stage condition was proved beyond doubt, but the mechanism involved is not yet known. The presence or absence of a grass stage has a certain significance for the taxonomic relationship of the above-mentioned pines (Chapter 9).

## Age and Reproduction

Both male and female strobili may be produced in pines at a very young age. Righter (1939) tabulated the minimum ages of "flower" production of fifty-seven pine species (including some varieties) cultivated in the Arboretum of the Institute of Forest Genetics, Placerville, California, at an altitude about 820 m above sea level. Observation was continued for 8 years. The average minimum age for ovulate strobili production was 5.2 years. Some species such as *P. densiflora* No. 95 produced conelets at an age of 2 years, others, such as *P. griffithii* No. 91 or *P. patula* No. 61, delayed conelet production until the age of 7 years. *P. lambertiana* No. 3 was the only species that did not produce conelets for the whole 8-year period. Further observations have shown that this species reaches reproductive age at about 25 years.

As regards precocity of pollen production, *P. sinensis* (i.e., *P. tabulaeformis* No. 102) was the earliest—1 year. Quite a few species had not started to produce pollen even when they were 8 years old. The average minimum age for pollen production was found to be 4.4 years.

These statistics do not mean, however, that after the initial outburst of reproductive activity pines always continue to produce staminate or ovulate strobili.

It is common for many pine species, after their initial outburst of "flowering" at a tender age, to have a long period of vegetative growth before their permanent reproductive stage is reached at a much older age.

## Senescence in Pines

The terminal shoot is chronologically of the same age at any stage of the life span of a pine tree. At the beginning of the growing season in temperate climates the uppermost part of the stem, between the last whorl of branches and the terminal bud, is always "one-year" (or rather one growing season) old. Physiologically, however, it is not so. A one-year-old shoot of a young pine of most species, say 2 or 3 years of age, when used as a cutting will strike roots easily; a one-year-old shoot taken from an old tree cannot be rooted, even with optimal auxin treatment (see Thimann and Behnke-Rogers, 1950). Apparently profound physiological and biochemical changes take place in the tip of old trees (inadequate hormone content, poor mineral nutrition, poor water supply). The terminal shoots of old trees physiologically display signs of senescence.

Very little is known of what changes have occurred in the protoplasm of the apical tissues of old pines that make them differ from those of young trees.

## Water Movement

The movement of water to the crown of pine trees (to a height of over 60 m in *P. ponderosa* No. 14) is usually explained on the basis of the Dixon-Joly water cohesion theory. Objections to this theory are many and these have been reviewed in several publications (Greenidge, 1957; Swanson, 1957) and in general texts on tree physiology (Kramer and Kozlowski, 1960).

Work with radioisotopes (Fraser and Mawson, 1953) and researches with dyes (Vité, 1959; Vité and Rudinsky, 1959) indicate that water movement is not straight up the tree but is spiral. The movement of water is slow, through bordered pits located on the sides of the tracheids. Many pine species have been examined by Vité and Rudinsky. There was a striking difference between the two subgenera. In three haploxylon pine species (Nos. 2, 3, 4) the spiral movement of water was found to follow a left-turning pattern; the five diploxylon pines examined possessed a right-turning pattern. One haploxylon pine, *P. aristata* No. 6, followed the diploxylon (right-turning) pattern and the two piñon pines (species Nos. 7 and 8) were found to have a water-conducting pattern comparable neither to that of the haploxylon nor the diploxylon pines. Kozlowski and Winget (1963) observed considerable variation in the rotation of the water stream among individual trees. The pattern of water movement is caused by the spiral arrangement of the tracheids. In *P. banksiana* No. 32 the pattern of water movement was to either the left or right, in *P. strobus* No. 20 the pattern was predominantly to the left, and in *P. resinosa* No. 21 predominantly to the right.

As could be expected, the environmental conditions, the age, the growth rate, and especially the genetically controlled individuality affect the nature of water movements in pines. Gibbs (1958), who studied seasonal water content of many tree species, also obtained some information on one pine, *P. strobus* No. 20. There were observed great variations among individual trees and the results, when averaged, gave a curve that was entirely different from the curves of seasonal variation in water content of other tree species. The maximum water content of *P. strobus* was in September and the minimum was in May. Other pine species, and from different climatic regions, should be studied to obtain a more complete picture of water-content pattern in pines. It is felt that researches in this area may contribute to the problem of evolution (and especially the survival) of the genus from Mesozoic time until present days. Water economy of pines of arid habitat, such as southwestern American piñon pines (Nos. 7, 8, 36, 37, 38, 39), offers material for a very interesting study.

## Transpiration

In comparison with other branches of pine physiology, little is known about transpiration in pines. As pines have no lenticels and as their leaves are well protected with cuticular wax (see Chapter 7), most water loss in pines is through their stomata.

According to Kramer and Kozlowski (1960), at the end of the summer *P. taeda* seedlings lose, through the stomata, 4.65 to 5.08 grams per square decimeter of leaf surface per day; this is two or three times less than in the seedlings of broadleaf trees. On the other hand, under the influence of certain microelements, water-holding capacity became much lower in pine seedlings than in the seedlings of broadleaf species, so that the former could lose more water without harm to the protoplasm than the latter (Dobroserdova, 1962).

Polster (1950) estimated that average daily transpiration of a *P. sylvestris* forest amounts to about 23,500 liters per ha. which is considerably less than the 43,000 liters for *Picea excelsa* and 53,000 for *Pseudotsuga taxifolia* (i.e., *P. menziesii*). What transpiration rates are in pines of the arid regions of the southwestern American (species Nos. 7, 9, or 10) or in the tropical pines, such as Nos. 63, 94 or 101, is not known; neither are there available data on transpiration of *P. sylvestris* in the Arctic as compared with that in the dry areas in Mongolia where this species is occasionally found.

Pines are xeromorphic plants (see Chapter 5); they can withstand a great deal of drought without wilting. Whether they are also physiologically drought-resistant plants (cf. Maximov, 1931) is not known. Experiments of Dobroserdova (1962) with influence of boron and molybdenum on loss of water by pine seedlings suggest that they are. Ecological considerations seem to support this conclusion. Experiments with *P. jeffreyi* No. 13 and *P. ponderosa* No. 14 seedlings (Stone, Edward C., 1958) indicated that they are capable of surviving a considerable period of time after the soil moisture is reduced to the ultimate wilting point.

Do pines have the capacity to absorb moisture from the atmosphere? This moisture may be supplied in the form of rain, fog, or dew. While fog is definitely useful in supplying moisture to pines, it is not certain that dew is. For further information the reader is referred to a presentation of this subject by Stone (1958) and comments of several other investigators, following Stone's article.

## Translocation of Mineral and Organic Substances

Studies of the movement of mineral solutes in pine have been greatly facilitated through the use of radioisotopes. $P^{32}$ was shown to move more rapidly across the lateral roots than in the stems of *P. taeda* seedlings (Moreland, 1950). The anatomy of the root cells and their active protoplasmic stream versus that of the stem might help explain such observations. However, other factors are also undoubtedly involved. Melin and Nilsson (1958) showed that transpiration markedly affected the rate of movement of $P^{32}$ from the fungus to the host tissue. Ferrell and Huber (1952) compared the rates of movement of $Ca^{45}$ and $P^{32}$ in pole-blighted and in healthy *P. monticola* No. 4 trees; they found that the radioactive elements moved more rapidly in the blighted than in the healthy trees. This fact was attributed to the higher rate of transpiration in the diseased trees.

Wikberg (1956) found that shoots of *P. sylvestris* No. 69, which absorbed $P^{32}$ through the roots, accumulated most of it in meristematic regions in phloem and cambium. The concentration was considerably lower in the xylem and cortex. This raises the question of whether or not the xylem is always the main stream for translocation of all elements. Since phosphate is often bound to sugars, it is quite possible that movement of this element is at least partly through the phloem.

In *P. radiata* the major constituent of the nitrogen fraction of xylem sap is in the form of glutamine. No nitrates were detected (Bollard, 1957). Glutamine is the most abundant amino acid in *P. taeda* No. 24 xylem sap in all seasons of the year. The time of greatest translocation of amino acids in xylem of this pine is when transpiration is maximal (Barnes, 1962). These studies have been extended to other pines and in all of them (Nos. 20, 21, 23, 24, 25, and 27) the main component of the organic nitrogen of the xylem sap was glutamine. Aspartic acid, serine, alanine, γ-aminobutyric acid, and glycine were detected in smaller and respectively decreasing amounts (Barnes, 1963). The complexity of the processes involved in translocation of photosynthetic products from the foliage to roots of pines was demonstrated in studies of *P. resinosa* No. 21 and *P. strobus* No. 20 seedlings by Nelson (1964) working in Ontario, Canada. The main form in which the photosynthate was translocated was sucrose; translocation was markedly affected by light: When pines were growing under low light, translocation to the roots came to a standstill. Physiological activity of the roots was not the controlling factor in the rate of translocation in *P. strobus* seedlings.

Seasonal variations in translocation in *P. strobus* are considerable; the greatest translocation was observed in May. It stopped completely in June and July and was resumed later, reaching a lesser peak in October. The processes involved in translocation are those of assimilation of carbon dioxide, the synthesis of new compounds, their mixing with compounds already present in the cells, local utilization of the sugars, their transfer from mesophyll to the vascular system, translocation, and longitudinal and radial distribution and storage in any tissues. Mycorhiza markedly increased translocation of photosynthate (Nelson, 1964).

## Germination and Viability of Pine Seeds

In some pine species (Nos. 16, 17, 19) that have serotinous cones, i.e., those which on maturity remain closed, seed viability may be preserved within the cone for an amazingly long time. This is well illustrated by studies of *P. banksiana* No. 32 by Schantz-Hansen (1941).

| Age of Seed, years | Germination, Per Cent |
|---|---|
| < 1 | 66.2 |
| 1 | 79.6 |
| 2 | 73.0 |
| 3 | 69.7 |
| 4 | 73.8 |
| 5 | 77.0 |

The above data show that in 5 years there was no decrease in viability of the seeds of this species, as long as they remained in the cone. In the author's experience, a *P. attenuata* No. 17 cone kept at room temperature for twenty-seven years yielded germinable seed. There are records of much longer viability of pine seeds, but it is difficult to say how reliable they are.

Seeds of all pine species (unless they are placed in conditions favorable for germination, or sufficiently dried and kept at extremely low temperature) will suffer changes and eventually will lose their viability. Seeds of haploxylon pines (*P. lambertiana* is a good example) lose their viability faster than seeds of diploxylon pines (Mirov, 1937). Storage at low temperature (say 5° C) preserves viability for a longer time than at room temperature.

Information on chemical composition of food reserves of pine seeds will be found in Chapter 7. Suffice it to say here that about one-half of all the stored food of pine endosperm consists of triglycerides of oleic, linoleic (chiefly), and linolenic acids. The amount of saturated acids in pine seeds is very small.

Apparently, loss of viability in pine seeds is somehow connected with changes taking place in the unsaturated fatty acids (Mirov, 1944; Kaloyereas, 1958). Although there are many other factors causing loss of germination of pine seeds (such as deterioration of nucleoproteins), rancidity of fats develops much earlier in storage than deterioration of other storage material.

In moist, well-aerated soil, seeds of some pine species germinate in the course of several days, while seeds of other pines do not germinate unless they are subjected for a prolonged period to a low temperature and adequate moisture. Commonly this pregermination period, which requires temperatures just above 0° C, is called a "rest period," "dormancy," or "after-ripening." At least for pines these terms are misleading, for this is not a period of rest but a period when profound pregermination changes take place in the seed: Enzyme activity increases, the storage substances of the endosperm are hydrolized and moved to the embryo. Apparently some auxin trigger mechanism is also involved (Cholodny, 1935). This period also should not be called "after-ripening," for it is not the last stage of ripening of the seed (i.e., synthesis of stored food) but rather the first stage of germination (i.e., hydrolysis of the stored material). It would be more proper to call it a "period of incipient germination." The length of the period varies with species—in some it is very short; in others it is prolonged. In those diploxylon pines that do not germinate promptly it is about three months, while in those haploxylon species whose seeds are refractory, the optimum period of incipient germination is about 150 days. There is not always a correlation between need for prolonged period of incipient germination and the climate. *Pinus banksiana* No. 32 of northern America, or *P. ponderosa* No. 13 of Montana, where winter temperatures may drop occasionally to −60° C or −65° C, does not need a prolonged low temperature period to hasten germination; on the other hand, *P. sabiniana* No. 10 of the foothills of California mountains, where winters are mild, requires such temperatures. In other words, it is not the subfreezing temperatures of the winter but rather the higher spring temperatures (approximately 0° C to 5° C) that are important. When all biochemical processes incipient to germination are completed, the embryo begins to grow and emerges from the seed coat.

For practical considerations of germination behavior of pine seeds the reader is referred to the U.S. Forest Service *Woody Plant Seed Manual* (1948), where information on germination requirements of seeds of many pine species is assembled.

**Effect of Light on Germination of Pine Seed.** The usual practice for germinating pine seeds is either to cover them with soil, where they are deprived of light, or to put them on a moist blotter covered with a bell jar, in which case they are exposed to light. Seeds of many pine species germinate well in both instances. Nevertheless, light, when applied experimentally, may play an important part in germination of some pine seeds. Sarvas (1950), for instance, reported that in the presence of light seeds of *P. sylvestris* No. 69 germinated earlier and germination was far better than that of seeds kept in darkness. Truly spectacular discoveries have been made at the U.S. Department of Agriculture Experimental Station, Beltsville, Maryland, on the effect of red and infrared light on germination of pine seeds.

Before discussing this topic it is necessary to mention the action of red and far-red light on plants in general (Borthwick, 1957; Downs, 1962). The initiation and cessation of growth in plants can be controlled under certain conditions mainly by red light (wave lengths 5500 Å to 7000 Å) and its action can be negated in many cases, and even reversed, by immediately subsequent far-red irradiation (7000 Å to 7500 Å). Specific effects of the red radiant energy include inhibition of flowering of short-day plants, promotion of flowering of long-day plants. Red–far-red irradiation also is involved in formation of certain plant pigments and in promotion of seed germination.

A classical example of influence of red and far-red is *P. virginiana* No. 27. Germination of seeds of this pine (Toole *et al.*, 1961) was promoted by a single brief period of irradation by red and inhibited by far-red radiant energy. It is possible that seeds of other pine species also can be manipulated in a similar way to induce their germination. This method would be especially interesting to apply to the above-mentioned refractory seeds.

Whether or not red light plays any part in natural germination of certain pine seeds is not known. As far as *P. virginiana* is concerned, its seeds belong to that category which germinates equally well in light and in darkness; neither does it require any pretreatment (U.S. Forest Service *Woody Plant Seed Manual*, 1948).

## Radiosensitivity of Pines

Very little is known on the effects of ionizing radiation on pines. Mergen and Stairs (1962) reviewed what has been done in this area of research. As could be expected, most of the experiments have been done with seedlings. Several investigators have shown that species of the genus *Pinus* are unusually sensitive to ionizing radiation; this may be due in part to the relatively large cell nuclei of pines. In one experiment *P. strobus* No. 19 seeds were exposed for several hours to $Co^{60}$ radiation of 50 to 100 r. Growing seedlings were affected more than dormant ones.

Some tests with mature trees of *P. rigida* No. 29 (Sparrow and Woodwell, 1962) showed that while irradiation with $Co^{60}$ at dosage of 5 r a day for 8 months did not produce noticeable damage, the same dosage for a period of 7 years killed many trees. The surviving trees showed morphological aberrations. Pine seeds also have been subjected to ionizing radiation. A dosage of 2000 r killed the seeds of *P. palustris* No. 22 and *P. taeda* No. 24. Some experiments also have been performed with *P. elliottii* seeds: those subjected to $Co^{60}$ irradiation of 5000 r germinated to the extent of 90 per cent; those that received 25,000 r showed only 10 per cent germination (May and Posey, 1958). The considerable variation in the results of the irradiation of pine seeds is apparently due in part to differences in the methods used. Mergen and Stairs themselves studied the effect of $Co^{60}$ radiation on a mature *P. rigida* forest located near the source of the gamma irradiation. The trees received approximately 2 to 4.5 r a day during 1960 and 1961. This low-intensity prolonged exposure of *P. rigida* to irradiation caused its cones to decrease in size; seed germination was found to be lower than of the non-irradiated seed. The decrease of germination was found to be associated "not with the total dose which has accumulated in the seed but with the total dose that the individual trees had accumulated prior to and during seed formation." The resulting irradiated one-month-old seedlings were much smaller than the control plants. As a result of irradiation, flower phenology was retarded by one to two weeks. The harmful effects of irradiation were found to be both genetic and physiological in nature. There was observed an increase in pollen abortion, reduced pollen tube growth, and other abnormalities.

## Physiology of Pine Pollen

Pine pollen is known for its viability; it can be stored under ordinary temperature conditions for several weeks. Stored at low temperatures and low humidity it retains its viability for several years. Under natural conditions a prolonged preservation of viability does not appear to serve any particularly useful purpose unless the pollen grains settle on pine foliage and are later carried to the female strobili by air currents or by rain.

Germinating pine pollen has been used in many recent pine enzyme studies. Presence of phosphohexokinase was demonstrated (Axelrod *et al.*, 1952), and evidence for the glycolytic pathway was found in *P. ponderosa* No. 14 pollen (Hellmers and Machlis, 1956). This anaerobic pathway has been shown to be supplemented during pollen germination, in part, by the aerobic hexose–monophosphate pathway (Stanley, 1958). Apparently, boron plays an important part in physiology of pine pollen, especially in its germination and in its growth (Stanley and Lichtenberg, 1963).

## Respiration

All live processes of pines like all higher organisms depend on the energy of respiration. For the basic treatment of this subject the reader is referred to Kramer and Kozlowski (1960). As far as pines are concerned, some peculiarities in respiration of pines (in winter or under snow cover) are mentioned elsewhere in this chapter. By far most work on respiration in pines has been done with their seeds. Gross respiration, and respiratory quotient and oxygen absorption have often been used as indices of the substrates being utilized by germinating pine seeds (Stone, 1948; Hatano, 1957b). However, the respiratory variations within pine seeds with different water content and physiological maturity of the seeds (Hatano, 1957b) render interpretation of such measurements questionable. A similar difficulty was also faced by Kozlowski and Gentile (1958) in attempting to measure the respiration of pine buds.

## ECOLOGY

### General Considerations

The whole subject of silviculture and forest management is based on ecologic principles. Accordingly, ecological literature on commercially important pines is very large. To review it all would be beyond the scope of this book; only salient points pertinent to the genus *Pinus* as a whole, illustrated with ecological traits of some species, will be discussed here.

In studies concerned with the ecology of pines we encounter two approaches: experimental and observational. Experimental ecological studies based on physiology and other exact sciences usually deal with a small number or even with single trees. Often physiological studies of this kind, conducted under controlled environment, cannot be applied to field conditions. In experimental studies a tree is considered as an individual, while in the forest its life is determined not only by its own physiological processes, but also by those of its competitors. This is the study of "ecosystems"; a subject of "biogeocoenology" (Mirov, 1965). It seems that frequently an observational field study can be more exact than a laboratory experiment, simply because it can consider most of the factors that influence tree growth instead of only a few. By clever observation, some variables can be held constant in nature and tree performance studied as a function of only that (or those) variable(s) that is (or are) allowed to vary. Such studies require the skills of an ecological physiologist who should be as much at home in a forest as he is in a laboratory.

Pines are components of many ecological associations. They occur as extensive forests of a single species, or they are found with other pine species, other conifers, or both evergreen and deciduous broadleaf trees. Some pines have restricted habitats. For example, *P. monophylla* No. 7 is essentially a tree of arid slopes at a considerable altitude (600 to about 3000 m), *P. sabiniana* No. 10 is a species of extremely hot and dry foothills in California mountains, while both *P. albicaulis* No. 1 and *P. cembra* No. 70 are alpine species. Other species are found in quite diverse habitats. *Pinus contorta* No. 16 grows at sea level along the coast of the Pacific Ocean, but it is also found in high mountain bogs and on well-drained mountain slopes. *Pinus bungeana* No. 87 or *P. armandi* No. 86 occurs in many floristic regions and in diverse habitats. *Pinus ponderosa* No. 14 not only transects several of Merriam's "Life Zones" (Jepson, 1925, p. 4) in California but also grows in entirely different environments in the Rocky Mountains, the Navajo country, and the Black Hills of South Dakota. *Pinus sylvestris* No. 69 can be found on dunes and limestone cliffs as well as in grasslands and in swamps (Plate 6–4). It is an intrazonal pine; in the forest zone it is a xerophyte, forming pure stands on dry porous sandy soil. In the grasslands of southern Siberia it is a mesophyte growing along the rivers. Often explanation for such tolerances as those shown by *P. contorta* and *P. sylvestris*—i.e., their occurrence in excessively dry or wet sites—is that they are excluded from favorable sites by more highly competitive species. However, populations of a given species found in diverse ecological niches are often, if not always, different biological entities, which are known to taxonomists as subspecies, varieties, or forms, and to biosystematists as ecotypes and other "infraspecific units." More will be said in Chapter 9 about the species concept with respect to the genus *Pinus*. As in all preceding chapters, we shall consider here Linnaean species only.

Ecological behavior of pines is well illustrated by the description of *P. rigida* No. 29 of the eastern United States published by McQuilkin (1935, p. 1003):

Pitch pine is to be regarded as a member of that widespread fraternity which, demanding little except a place in the sun, must find its place as a rule in the left-over, unfavorable areas that will not support the "nobler" species. Such are the sterile, fire-scorched sands of the Coastal Plain, or the wind-swept ridges of the mountains, both of which are typical pitch pine sites. It invades burned-over areas, abandoned fields, and clearings, where individuals may persist [note this], but where if the conditions are favorable, reproduction soon becomes impossible in competition with other species. Although its competitive capacity is low, its tolerance of a wide range of site factors is remarkable. Sandy soils over clay, fertile or infertile, drained or saturated, situations xeric or mesic or hydric—all are acceptable to this indiscriminating species.

**Plate 6–4.** *Pinus sylvestris* No. 69 in different habitats. *Top:* on eroded chalk hills, Voronezh province, U.S.S.R. (Photo by A. Dubiansky, from Morozow, 1928.) *Center:* in a moss bog, Leningrad province, U.S.S.R. (Photo courtesy of Komarov Botanical Institute, Leningrad.) *Bottom:* in western section of central grassland of northeastern provinces, China. (From Wang, 1961. Courtesy of U.S. Department of Agriculture.)

This excellent description of the ecology of *P. rigida* may be used, with local modifications, for describing many other species of diploxylon pines in many different regions. But it should be noted that there are also "nobler species" such as *P. lambertiana* No. 3 that prefer better sites for their growth.

In eastern Asia pines occur in groves or as single trees in forests of floristically different groups. When the broadleaf components of such forests are destroyed, these pine supply seed to invade the available area (Wu, 1950). That is apparently what Sargent (in Wilson, 1913) had in mind when he wrote that in

. . . eastern continental Asia there is nothing to compare with the great maritime pine belt which extends from southern Virginia to eastern Texas; and the great forests of *Pinus strobus* L., which once extended from northern New England and eastern Canada to northern Minnesota, are poorly replaced in northeastern Asia by trees of *P. koraiensis* S. & Z. scattered over comparatively restricted area of eastern Siberia and Korea.

In Central America the combination of temperature and edaphic factors provides more natural habitats for growth of pines at the higher elevations than the lower altitudes (Denevan, 1961). This also has been observed by the author in southeastern Asia and finds support in the present altitudinal distribution of pines. In other words, pines are generally adapted to relatively cool, temperate, fairly moist conditions. Deviations from this general generic pattern are not too frequent; they are of a local nature.

Generally, it is at the lower altitudes where pines enter into competition with other conifers and both deciduous and evergreen broadleaf trees. The competition of pines with other genera in the course of plant succession follows many different patterns in different parts of the extensive range of the genus *Pinus*. In northern countries of the Old World pure stands of *P. sylvestris* on poor sandy soils regenerate well without any interference of other trees, but on more fertile and moist soils they may be replaced by birch and aspen and by spruce. Gradually pine may occupy the ground and the cycle is repeated. Plant succession involving *P. sylvestris* is well described in several Russian publications of Morozow that appeared at the beginning of the present century and later in Morozow's book translated into German (Morozow, 1928).

The part played by pines in plant succession in North America is mentioned many times by Clements in his classical treatise on plant succession (Clements, 1916). The diverse behavior of North American pines in plant succession is amazing. Sometimes they represent mere stages in the succession of plants. For example, in northeastern America, *P. banksiana* No. 32 and *P. resinosa* No. 21, and later *P. strobus* No. 20, appear after annual and perennial grass stages and in turn are replaced by broadleaf trees. Under other circumstances pines may form a "fire subclimax." *Pinus contorta* No. 16 may establish itself as a permanent climax on a given site (Plate 6–12). The *P. ponderosa–Pseudotsuga* climax in the Rocky Mountains (Clements, 1916) is such a case.

## Northern and Southern Boundaries of the Genus *Pinus*

The environmental factor limiting the northern advance of pines is not the low winter temperature per se. Pines can withstand temperatures of $-50°$ C or $-60°$ C and even lower, and at such temperatures a drop of ten or twenty degrees probably would not matter much. It is the cool and short summers, the frozen ground preventing penetration of roots to deeper layers of soil, and the severe dessicating winter winds that check advance of pines north (Obolensky, 1956).

Pines grow farther north in Siberia than in North America because of the different climate. The Eurasian continent is larger than the American continent and is subject to greater climatic extremes; the winters are colder, but the summers are much warmer in Siberia than in America at the same latitude. In Europe the Gulf Stream ameliorates the climate so that pines go as far as 72 degrees north on the Scandinavian Peninsula. In North America pines disappear at the 65th parallel while in northern Eurasia three pine species (Nos. 67, 68, and 69) cross the Arctic Circle (Plate 6–5).

The southern extent of pines in northern Africa, the Levant, and the southern parts of western and eastern Siberia is limited by lack of moisture and high concentration of salts in the soil. Between Siberia and the Himalaya lie extensive deserts. Pines do occur in the Himalaya, to which they penetrated from eastern Asia.

Why pines do not occur in India south of the Himalaya is not easy to say. There are places in Ceylon and along the Malibar coast of India and inland in Orizza, Baluchistan, and in other places where altitudes run high enough to provide suitable habitats for pines. It is possible that the southward migration of pines there was checked by the broad valleys of the great rivers, by excessive monsoon rains, by the hot humid climate of the lowlands, and later, possibly, by human activities (Map, Fig. 6–1).

In southeastern Asia, southward migration of pines along the mountain ranges was unobstructed until the end of the Pleistocene (Chapter 2, pp. 63–69, and Fig. 2–4). Along the mountain ranges they penetrated to Yunnan, the Himalaya, Indochina, Thailand, and as far as the middle of Sumatra. Penetration of pines to Sumatra is recent; the only species growing there (*P. merkusii*) is not endemic to Sumatra but occurs also in several places on the continent and in localities more northern than

**Plate 6–5.** *Top: P. banksiana* No. 32 at about sea level, Snare River, Northwest Territories (Mackenzie River area), latitude 63° 31′ north, only 1° 10′ from the northern limit of the species. (Photo by C. S. Lord, Geological Survey of Canada, courtesy A. E. Porslid, Chief Botanist, Department of Northern Affairs and National Resources of Canada.) *Bottom: P. sylvestris* No. 69 in northern Finland, where forest merges into tundra in the valley of the river Kevo, at 69° 40′ north. The scrubby deciduous trees are *Betula pubescens* var. *tortuosa.* (Photo by Risto Sarvas.)

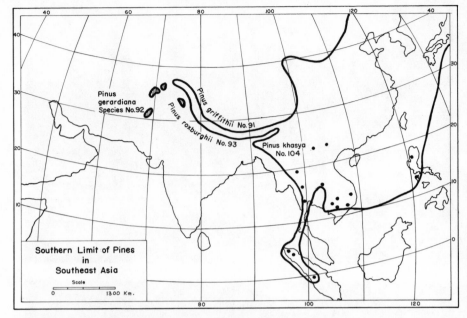

**Fig. 6–1.** Southern limits of pines in Asia. Black dots indicate actual occurrence of *P. merkusii* No. 101, the most southern of all pines.

those on the island. It does not form extensive forests but occupies a rather small area and there are suitable habitats farther south on the island which are not occupied by pines. It is entirely possible that human activities have been instrumental in stopping the southward advance of pines in Sumatra (cf. Denevan, 1961).

In the New World, too, there are no major environmental barriers to the southward movement of pines. They recently reached Nicaragua (Plate 6–6) (Denevan, 1961), and no doubt sometime in the future pines will cross the Nicaraguan Lowland as they crossed the Tehuantepec in the past and will continue their southward trek along the mountains of Costa Rica or along the coast. At present, their advance has been checked by human activities—burning and grazing—but from a geological point of view, this is a minor and temporary obstacle (cf. Chapter 2 and Fig. 6–2).

Beyond their natural limits of occurrence, pines have been successfully grown in Australia, New Zealand (Plate 6–13, page 453), South Africa, and South America (to Argentina).

To understand better the survival of the genus *Pinus* from the Mesozoic era to the present time it is pertinent to discuss individually the various ecologic factors that affect pine growth and distribution.

**Plate 6–6.** *Top:* P. *caribaea* No. 62 and palmetto near Karawala, on the coast of Nicaragua, not far from the southern limit of the genus *Pinus*. (Photo by J. J. Parsons.) *Bottom:* end of pines in the mountains of inner Nicaragua. Above the town of Matagalpa, P. *oocarpa* No. 59 descends along the south slope of the Cordillera Dariense to about 1200 m. (Photo by N. T. Mirov.)

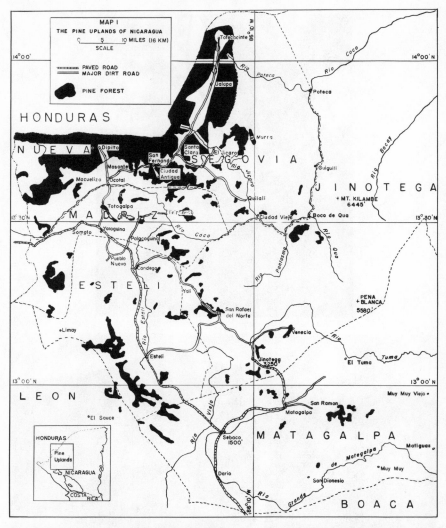

**Fig. 6–2.** Southern limits of pines *(P. oocarpa* No. 59) in the mountains of Nicaragua. (After Denevan, 1961.)

## Drought Resistance

In Chapter 5 it was mentioned that pines are xeromorphic trees. Their leaves are narrow and their water loss is reduced by heavy, waxy cuticula. The surface/volume ratio of the leaves is small; the stomata are deeply sunk; the sclerenchyma tissues are developed sufficiently to assure their rigidity (Shields, 1950). Physiologically pines are drought-resistant plants (page 420); they can withstand a shortage of water without harm more readily than the broadleaf mesophytic trees (Stone, Edward C., 1958; Muelder *et al.*, 1963). Ecologically most of the pine species are xerophytes. They may occur in the dry environment of the Mediterranean region (Chapter 3), in the grasslands of Mongolia (Plate 6–4c), or in extremely arid localities of western America and in high altitudes. The capacity of xerophytes to withstand low temperatures has been mentioned by Wulff (1944) in his discussion of Hooker's analysis of the *Flora of India*. At the same time many pine species, such as those of the eastern United States or of eastern and northern Eurasia, are trees of a mesic habitat where their xeromorphism also may serve them well, for instance, when an unusual drought occurs.

Pines do not occur naturally at low elevation in humid tropical regions. Such an environment is suitable for their somewhat erratic growth but not for their reproduction (see Phenology, page 451).

An exceptional pine species is *P. strobus* var. *chiapensis* No. 34, which descends to 500 m altitude, to the upper edge of the low-elevation, humid tropics along the escarpment of the central Mexican plateau bordering the Gulf of Mexico. But even there, there is a pronounced (recuperative?) dry season in winter.

In regions other than deserts, tundra, and the tropical, humid lowlands, pines may be found in nearly any conceivable habitat. They ascend mountains to 4000 meters (No. 50) and they descend to sea level (No. 23 or No. 69). The xeromorphy of pines appears partly to explain their adaptability to diverse habitats. Their drought resistance also helps them to survive in habitats where water is abundant, but not available because of its physical or chemical condition. When the atmosphere is sufficiently warm in spring, but the soil is still frozen, as often happens in northern habitats, a water shortage for normal functioning of pines may be as real as it is in arid regions. When the soil is saturated, respiratory functions of roots are impaired and water cannot be absorbed (Zak, 1961). This condition of edaphic physiological dryness has been observed in *P. sylvestris* and most likely it exists, at least partially, in other species growing in places covered the year around with shallow warm water. A good example is *P. elliottii* No. 23 (Plate 6–8).

## Soils

Pines are found on many different types of soil. In the north they grow on podzols, on sands, and also on moister and richer clay soils. For instance, *P. sibirica* No. 68 forms fine pure forests in alluvial river valleys subject to flooding early in summer. Farther south pine forests often occur on lateritic soils. In high altitudes pines may grow in bogs (*P.*

**Plate 6–7.** *Top: P. nigra* No. 74 on limestone, Frauenstein, near Mölding, Austria. (Photo by Austrian Forest Research Institute.) *Bottom: P. aristata* No. 6 on dolomite, White Mountains, California. Altitude 3000–3400 m. (U.S. Forest Service photo by N. T. Mirov.)

*contorta* No. 16), on granite (*P. albicaulis* No. 1) or on dolomites (*P. aristata* No. 6), and on other parent material (Plate 6–7). Pines grow also on calcareous soils and on other types of pure limestone (*P. nigra* No. 74; *P. sylvestris* No. 69). The capacity of some pine species to grow on soils almost entirely deprived of calcium already has been mentioned (p. 399). Different pine species respond differently to an excess of calcium in soils. Nearly one hundred years ago Fliche and Grandeau (1873, 1877) reported that *P. nigra* could survive in calcareous situations while *P. pinaster* No. 80 could not.

There is a considerable difference among southeastern American pines in their tolerance to calcium and magnesium. *Pinus palustris* No. 22 is less tolerant than *P. taeda* No. 24, and *P. echinata* No. 25 is the most tolerant of the three. Application of lime to hill soil of the *P. palustris* belt in Mississippi is reputed to have caused disappearance of this pine and its replacement by oaks (Hilgard, 1880).

Occasionally pines occur on outcrops of serpentine. This mineral is rich in magnesium and it also contains considerable quantities of chromium, nickel, and manganese. The soils derived from serpentine rocks contain these three microelements in concentrations lethal to most plants. *Pinus sabiniana* No. 10 occurs on both serpentine and non-serpentine soils while *P. lambertiana* does not tolerate serpentine (Mason, 1946). Thus it appears that adaptability of the genus *Pinus* to diverse edaphic conditions has contributed greatly to its survival and expansion of range.

## Mycorhiza

In Chapter 5 we saw that normally the feeding roots of pine are composed partly of tree tissues and partly of fungus hyphae. In the opinion of Harley (1959) pines are organisms as dual as lichens. The physiological role of mycorhiza has been mentioned earlier in the present chapter.

Mycorhizae are found in pines growing under very diverse environmental conditions, although it should be remarked that most mycorhiza studies have been made on the pine species of temperate climates. What the mycorhizal mechanism is of pines of arid regions, such as *P. monophylla* No. 7 of Nevada or *P. sylvestris* No. 69 of Mongolia, apparently is not known.

Mycorhizae need air for development (Zak, 1961). It is not known how they function on pines growing in swamps and ponds (as *P. elliottii* and other pines occasionally do) where the roots may be submerged in water throughout the growing season. McQuilkin (1935) described three *P. rigida* trees growing in saturated soil with roots below the water table. Two of these trees bore mycorhizae on submerged roots. He also cites findings by Bondois (1913) and others who failed to find mycorhizae on submerged roots. Zak * has said that he has never seen mycorhizae on submerged roots.

It would be interesting to examine the development of the mycorhiza on roots of *P. contorta* No. 16 growing in mountain swamps. The oxygen content of water there is higher than in the swamps and ponds of the southeastern United States, and this might be conducive to better development of mycorhizae in *P. contorta*. Would it be different in pines growing in swamps as compared with those growing on well-drained mountain slopes? Some clues as to the behavior of *P. contorta* roots in water-saturated soils are given by Gail and Long (1935). Tap roots of the seedlings of this species grown in saturated soil appeared inhibited, but there were many short, stubby laterals just below the surface of the water that were explained as an adaptation to oxygen deficiency. Unfortunately, no mention was made of mycorhizal development.

It has been generally assumed (Slankis, 1958) that the beneficial effects of mycorhizae are due to an increase in root surface area. However, Harley (1959) has said that ". . . a simple increase of the area does not explain the success of mycotrophs in difficult sites. . . . The fungal sheath which is interposed between the host root and the soil calls the tune in the activities of absorption from the soil."

It is precisely there, in poor soils, where mycorhiza is the most beneficial for pines. No doubt this unique symbiosis between a tree and a fungus—so exceptionally well developed in pines—has played an important role in survival and migration of pines.

## Soil and Air Salt Content

The endurance of pines to soil salinity and salt spray in the air is an interesting ecological phenomenon. Generally pines do not come close to the sea shore; they stop some distance from the water on the mountain slopes or cliffs so that they are not much affected by sea salt carried on the wind or infiltrated in the soil. *Pinus sylvestris* No. 69 comes very close to sea level along the coasts of the Baltic Sea, but water salinity there is lower than on the open ocean coast. *Pinus elliottii* No. 23 grows along the coast of the Mississippi Sound and on offshore islands very close to the edge of the water, but again, salinity of water in the Sound is much less than in the open Gulf of Mexico (Plate 6–8). Spray damage to the foliage there is only sporadic. *Pinus strobus* No. 20, on the coast of New England, was observed to be very susceptible to salt spray. During the hurricane of 1938 the wind carried salt water for more than forty miles inland causing damage to the needles of this pine. Planted *P. syl-*

* Personal communication.

**Plate 6–8.** *Pinus elliottii* No. 23. *Top:* near Mississippi Sound, Gulf of Mexico. *Bottom:* near salt marsh, Ocean Springs, Mississippi. (U.S. Forest Service photos.)

*vestris* was also damaged there by salt spray while *P. nigra* No. 74 was found to be the most resistant to it (Wallace and Moss, 1939).

*Pinus radiata* No. 19 and *P. torreyana* No. 11 grow close to the ocean; presumably these pines are resistant to salt spray. Perhaps this is also true of *P. thunbergii* of Japan, *P. luchuensis* No. 98 of the Ryukyus, or *P. massoniana* No. 94 of China, and of some other pines (Chapter 1, Plate 1–1).

Excessive concentration of any salt in the soil is, of course, detrimental to the life of pines. This is especially evident along the southernmost limits of pine distribution (*P. sylvestris*) in Eurasia.

## Light

Pines are light-enduring trees. Although in their youth they may stand some shading, toward maturity they require an abundance of light. In the course of evolution of the genus and its expansion from the original moderate altitudes, the light requirements of some pine species appear to have undergone considerable change. Species that ascended high mountains became exposed to much ultraviolet light; species that descended to low altitudes became protected from excess short-wave radiation by a thicker layer of atmosphere. Although the primeval pines endured bright sunlight (see Chapter 2), some species, such as *P. sibirica* No. 67 or *P. strobus* No. 20, later developed a certain tolerance to shading. In fact, it appears that continuous bright sunshine may be actually harmful to certain pines. *Pinus strobus* No. 20 becomes chlorotic when transplanted to the Sierra Nevada of California, and thus exposed to continuous bright sunlight throughout the summer. On the coast, however, near San Francisco, where cloudiness during summer months is considerable, this pine maintains its dark green color and grows well. Water regimen also is responsible for ill behavior of *P. strobus* in interior California, but according to our observations the light seems to be the main factor that determines its poor performance there.

## Temperature

The endurance of some species of the genus *Pinus* to extreme temperatures is truly remarkable. In the winter *P. ponderosa* No. 14 or *P. banksiana* No. 32 may tolerate temperatures of $-65°C$. *Pinus sylvestris* No. 69 in Siberia endures even lower temperatures. On the other hand, some species in inner California (*P. sabiniana* No. 10, *P. coulteri* No. 12) may withstand summer temperature of 45°C or 50°C.

However, pines from low elevations in the tropics are sensitive to cold. For instance, *P. canariensis* No. 72 is damaged when the temperature drops to even a few degrees below freezing. Some species from tropical highlands, however, can withstand relatively low temperatures. One example is *P. patula* No. 61, which is known to survive winter cold of −10°C. Occasionally pines may be damaged by cold even in their native habitat; for instance, needles of *P. ponderosa* at 2000 m in Sierra Nevada of California are sometimes damaged in winter by blasts of cold wind. The damage apparently is caused by desiccation of the foliage.

## Snow Cover

Tikhomirov (1949) observed that *P. pumila* No. 68, which forms low trailing thickets in northeastern Asia, has the capacity of bending toward the ground when temperatures are low and straightening up again when the air becomes warm. By bending low the pine has a better chance of being covered with snow and thus protected from cold. Similar stem bending was described also for *P. montana* No. 76 var. *mugus* in the eastern Carpathians. It was also observed that, when the bent branches of this pine are pressed against moist ground, they occasionally developed roots, a phenomenon rare in pines (Barykina *et al.*, 1963). During the winter pines may be covered with snow of varying depth for a more or less prolonged time. In pine forests at moderate altitudes seedlings may be buried under snow every winter until they reach a height greater than that of the snow depth. In alpine habitats even mature trees may be covered with snow, for example, *P. montana* var. *mughus* No. 76, *P. pumila* No. 69, *P. albicaulis* No. 1, and other dwarfed species of high altitudes. Some pines may remain under snow for at least six months every year. The physiology and ecology of such buried trees are not well known. Under a deep layer of snow the soil may not be frozen, while the insulating snow cover protects the pines from low air temperatures. By judging from observations on development of herbaceous plants under snow (Iashina, 1960), it is probable that alpine species of pines also undergo some physiological development under these conditions. It is known that pines photosynthesize during warmer spells in winter. They are probably capable of assimilating carbon dioxide under a snow cover provided that they are not buried so deep as to prevent penetration of light and air. With a deeper snow cover, of course, the physiological functions of pines probably come almost to a standstill as in tall pines with their foliage above the snow when air temperature drops well below freezing; although the causes for suspension of physiological functions may be not identical in pines remaining above the snow and those buried under it. Tranquillini (1959) noted that respiration of young *P. cembra* No. 70 buried under snow is continued, but at a very much smaller rate. Research on the physiology and ecology of pines hibernating under snow promises to be interesting.

## Insects and Fungi

It is difficult to estimate the importance of insects and fungi to the development of the genus *Pinus*. Insects may cause a great deal of damage, especially to trees weakened by some other factors: drought, fire, cold. The most terrifying account of insect damage is the description by Suslov (1947) of an infestation of *P. sibirica* No. 67 forests in the East Sayan Mountains of Siberia.

An infestation by a moth (*Dendrolimus sibiricus*) defoliated and killed hundreds of square miles of forest. One could hear the sound of millions of caterpillars chewing upon pine foliage; one could not get a drink of water from a stream because its surface would be covered and polluted with a thick layer of dead caterpillars. The stench of dead insects in the infested localities was hard to bear. Wild life—sable and squirrel—left the infested area, thus depriving the people of hunting revenues. The regeneration of such areas has been very slow and was successful only in places where a few seed trees survived the epidemic and subsequent fires that ravaged the region.

We have seen, in the discussion of mycorhiza, that fungi can be not only beneficial, but also indispensable for the normal development of pines. There are, however, many fungi that are harmful. Only two are mentioned as examples. A rust (*Cronartium ribicola*), which attacks only haploxylon pines, originated in the Old World and some pine species, such as *P. sibirica* No. 67 or *P. peuce* No. 71, are more or less immune to it. In America it causes considerable damage to pines. *Fomes annosus* (Boyce, 1962) (see Chapter 5, p. 367), which is transmitted through intergrafted roots, may also cause serious damage to pine forests.

Harmful fungi may retard expansion of pine forests. But both insects and fungi, no matter how much local damage they cause to pine forests, are essentially local in effect.

## Grazing

Grazing generally is associated with activities of man. It now plays a very important and harmful part in ecology of pine forests. Grazing by sheep and goats (and to a lesser extent, cattle) is detrimental to regeneration of pine forests in many parts of the world. It is presently often the main cause of checking establishment and advance of pines. On the other hand, in prehistoric times grazing of wild animals possibly played an important part in keeping the woodland areas open and the sod disturbed, thus receptive to pine invasion (see Mirov, 1956a, p. 455, on possible role of wild cattle in establishment of pines).

Pines possess an efficient mechanism for recuperation after browsing by animals, as shown by Cooperrider (1938); (see Chapter 5, p. 370); nevertheless, excessive and repeated grazing causes irreversible damage.

## Birds and Rodents

Some birds feed on pine seeds and sometimes destroy a considerable part of the seed crop. Clements (1916, p. 65) once examined the seed crop of *P. flexilis* No. 2 and found that ". . . the toll taken by nutcrackers, jays and squirrels [was] so complete that no viable seed has been found in hundreds of mature cones examined." On the other hand, jays and nutcrackers (*Nucifraga*) are considered as very important agents in dissemination of the (wingless) seeds of *P. sibirica* No. 67 in northern Eurasia (Mirov, 1951, p. 114; see reference in Literature Citations, Chapter 2).

A good example of the difficulty, slowness, and probability of dispersal of pine seed by birds is *P. coulteri* No. 12, which is found on the coastal ranges of central California, but is naturally absent in Sierra Nevada. When, in 1926, man introduced this pine to a Sierra Nevada site located above the town of Placerville at about 1000 m altitude and a little over 100 km from the nearest native *P. coulteri*, this pine reproduced itself naturally quite well and thus may be considered as established in the new habitat. Why this species had not previously crossed the relatively short distance from the coast to the Sierra Nevada is difficult to say. There have been reported periodic invasions of the Pacific Coast ranges by the Clark nutcracker (*Nucifraga columbiana*), a species of the Sierra Nevada pine forests (Davis and Williams, 1957), but apparently its role in dispersal of *P. coulteri* seed was extremely small. All in all, birds, rodents, and occasionally larger mammals, although they play a part in the biology of pine forests, are of local importance only.

## Topography, Water, and Wind

Cones may roll downhill and thus help the pines to expand to lower elevations. Water dispersal of pine seeds might have been important in some localities along the streams. Pine seeds can endure salt water for only a very short time, thus dispersal by water from one sea island to another is out of the question.

Wind is probably the major factor in dispersing pine seeds for long distances, such as from one island to another in the Caribbean area. But even so, pines migrated this manner only in exceptional cases.

## Pines as Pioneers

When the effect of glaciation on distribution of pines was discussed in Chapter 2, it was repeatedly mentioned that after recession of ice, pines were among the pioneers invading newly exposed areas. In the New World the pioneer invaders were *P. contorta* No. 16, *P. banksiana* No. 32, and to a lesser extent *P. strobus* No. 20. In northern Eurasia the pioneer invader was *P. sylvestris* No. 69. In the Caucasus Mountains the present area of *P. sylvestris* (*P. hamata*) coincides neatly with the area that was covered with ice. Only rarely did *P. sibirica* No. 67 act as a post-glacial pioneer. The pioneer invader capacity of many pine species has been evident throughout the Quaternary period, including present times.

*Pinus sylvestris* is being gradually replaced in the northern Kola Peninsula by birch and in the south, east, and west by spruce. Thus the process of plant succession on the area exposed by the retreat of the ice is still continuing. As recent investigations show, the chief cause of disappearance of pines at present is change of climate from dry to moist (Solonevich, 1940).

Mineral soil may be exposed and made available to pines by many factors other than retreating glaciers: by volcanic activity (as this writer observed shortly after eruption of Paracutin Volcano in Michoacan, Mexico; Plate 6–9), by avalanches, by man abandoning his cultivation (a common cause in eastern United States and in southeastern Asia, known in the latter as shifting cultivation), and on sand dunes and on the banks of newly constructed roads.

In northern California *P. muricata* No. 18 occurs only on the windward side of *Sequoia sempervirens* forest; it also invades the coastal pastures where soil is disturbed by livestock. Apparently this pine is more abundant now than previously because of human activities: fire, grazing, and land-clearing. On the other hand, in the southern parts of its area (see No. 18 in Chapter 3), *P. muricata* finds enough places with poor soil to occupy without depending on fire and land-clearing (Duffield, 1951). *Pinus radiata* No. 19 has recently increased in area with the help of lumbering of Douglas-fir and clearing the land (Forde, 1962).

## Fire

Of all the factors exposing ground to invasion by pines, fire has played an extremely important part in the expansion of pine forests from their original mountain habitats to lower elevations and in their spread there (Plate 6–9). In some parts of the world fire has become a permanent factor in the ecology of pine forests. An example of plant succession in relation to fire in pine forests of temperate climates is the *P. sibirica* forests of the Altai Mountains of western Siberia. Such forests have a considerable admixture of fir, spruce, and larch that are often destroyed by fire. Because of slow decay, dead snags remain standing for 30 to 40 years. Regeneration of pine is extremely slow there. During the first few years the burned area becomes covered with *Calamagrostis* (*Stipa*) *splendens*, *Epilobium angustifolium*, and raspberry (*Rubus*) brambles. Later, birches

**Plate 6–9.** *Top:* effect of volcanic eruption on pine forest. Volcano Parícutin in action near Uruápan, Michoacan, Mexico. Lava flow destroyed forest near volcano and covered soil with layer of ashes, killing pine seedlings. By 1960, area was reoccupied by young pines. Surviving old pines are *P. michoacana* No. 52. (Photo by N. T. Mirov.) *Bottom:* fire in *P. insularis* No. 105 forest in northern Luzon. (Photo by Philippine Forest Bureau.)

and aspen appear. They remain dominant for many years; eventually, however, fir and spruce begin to suppress them and gradually *P. sibirica* will assume the dominant place. Above 4000 m, however, *P. sibirica*, together with larch, invades the burned-over areas without intermediate birch-aspen stages, for birch and aspen do not grow above such altitude (Suslov, 1947). *Pinus sibirica* maintains prominence until the next fire.

In New Jersey the upland pine forests are composed of *P. rigida* No. 29 and *P. echinata* No. 25, while *P. taeda* No. 24 and *P. serotina* No. 30 grow on the eastern shore. Succession in both places is about the same. Pines usually form pure stands on old field sites. When the pines are 15 to 20 years old, one can discern hardwoods in the understory. As the pines mature, the hardwoods increase in size and number. In all cases the "climax" would be a mixed hardwood forest and would have no pines (Little, 1953). It is stated, however, that the original "climax" upland forests in New Jersey consisted of open stands of large pitch (No. 29) and shortleaf (No. 25) pines (Little *et al.*, 1948).

In pine forests of temperate climates plant succession caused by fire is slow. There the pine stage may be taken by some investigators as a "climax" that is defined by ecologists as a "terminal community . . . in a dynamic equilibrium with the prevailing climate" (Cain, 1944, p. 478; see reference in Literature Citations, Chapter 2). It is better not to call those pine forests where fire was involved climaxes, subclimaxes, fire climaxes, or plagioclimaxes (Radley, 1960), but rather to refer to them as a "pine stage" in the plant succession in a given area. The length of this stage depends on intensity and frequency of fires. It is easier to note effects of fire on pines of the forests of more southern regions, especially where a dry season, however short, alternates with a rainy season. There plant succession proceeds at a much faster pace.

The effect of fire on forests has been observed in many countries at low altitudes: India, southeastern China, United States, Mexico, Central America. Lyell (1849) remarked more than a hundred years ago that the area of *P. palustris* in Georgia in the United States has been expanding because of the Indian custom of burning the grass, and, by this practice, killing the broadleaf trees that are more susceptible to fire than pines.

In Honduras (Lake Yojoa area) pines are apparently of secondary origin, being a result of clearing and burning of broadleaf forests, a practice going back to Mayan times (Allen, Paul H., 1955). On the Caribbean coast of Nicaragua the role of fire, involving the pine stage, was well studied by Parsons (1955), Radley (1960), and Taylor (1962, 1963). The upland pine forests of Nicaragua and their relation to fire were investigated by Denevan (1961); similarly pine forests of inner Honduras were described by Johannessen (1959) (Plates 6–10 and 6–11).

**Plate 6–10.** *Top:* grass fire on pine-covered slopes near Ocotal, Nueva Se-govia, Nicaragua. (Photo by William M. Denevan.) *Bottom: P. merkusii* No. 101, Zambales Mountains, Luzon, Philippines. This pine occurs here in three places along the low foothills (altitudes 150–300 m) about 16 km from the shore of the South China Sea. Repeatedly burned. No reproduction was noticed. (Photo by N. T. Mirov.)

**Plate 6–11.** *Top:* open stand of *P. caribaea* No. 62, "inland form," with the understory being burned. Site is near the Rio Tapalchi, a tributary of the Rio Poteca, in eastern Nueva Segovia, Nicaragua. Annual precipitation here is over 180 cm. *Bottom:* dense stand of *P. oocarpa* No. 59 east of Matagalpa, Nicaragua, which has been protected from fire for two or three years. There is no pine regeneration in the thick understory of grasses, ferns, and leguminous weeds. If burning is not resumed, hardwood trees will grow from the moist, shaded understory and eventually replace the pines. (Photos by William M. Denevan.)

Even at low latitudes, however, pines are not always able to establish themselves immediately on burned areas or on abandoned cultivated land. In the mountain cloud forests of interior Honduras, when cultivation is abandoned, on better soils the forest is replaced by weedy broadleaf trees; pines and oaks occupy only poorer sites (Johannessen, 1959). Durland (1922) mentioned that burned selva in the Dominican Republic is not invaded by *P. occidentalis* No. 64 but instead by various broadleaf shrubs: *Cecropia, Jambosa,* and others.

Plant succession on newly available areas is a complicated process and cannot be considered in detail here. Plant succession involving pines does not necessarily imply the presence of large denuded areas, for pines can be regenerated in many types of existing forests. There are always openings under a broadleaf canopy formed by the fall of old trees or by rocky outcrops where pines can germinate and grow. Moreover, since during their young stages some pine species are fairly tolerant to shading (Morozow, 1928; cf. p. 402, reference to Bormann, 1955), they may perpetuate themselves without the operation of major catastrophic factors to prepare open areas for them. Nevertheless, fire still may be considered as a major ecological factor in the reproduction of pine forests at low altitudes.

**Pine Savannas.**    Fires are responsible, if not for the origin, then surely for the perpetuation of pine associations known as savannas. The term "savanna" came from South America where it originally meant grassy plains (*llanos*). Ecologists describe many different types of savannas, but commonly, however, mean by it an open forest with grass, a transition type of vegetation between woodland and grassland.

Parklike *P. ponderosa* No. 14 in the Navajo country of Arizona, or scattered piñon pine trees in Nevada, or again open groves of *P. contorta* No. 16 in Alberta (Canada) or *P. sylvestris* No. 69 in the southern parts of Siberia may fall into this definition. Some consider even rather dense *P. oocarpa* forests of steep mountain slopes or alluvial valleys of Central America as savannas (Taylor, 1963; Johannessen, 1959). By this definition, pine savanna may be found in any part of the world, in any climate, and on any topography; thus, the term *savanna* still is not clearly defined in ecological literature.

In the present discussion, pine savanna means any open pine forest of the neotropical and paleotropical parts of the world where terrain is predominantly level or gently sloping and where the climate is characterized by a more or less prolonged dry period. Under these conditions a pine savanna represents a stage in plant succession caused primarily by fire. Pine savannas vary according to the floristic composition of successional stages (grasses and broadleaf shrubs and trees) and the species of pines themselves. A pine savanna with *P. elliottii* var. *densa* No. 63 is found in Florida, while in Central America it contains *P. caribaea* No. 62 (Parsons, 1955). The writer observed a *P. merkusii* No. 101 savanna on the flats and knolls of the lower slopes of the Zambales Mountains, Luzon, facing the South China Sea (Plate 6–10). The same type of pine savanna is found on the Island of Mindoro (see Chapter 3). *Pinus merkusii* savannas also occur on Sumatra. Recent Russian visitors to China describe savannas in Yunnan where the pine component was represented by "*P. insularis*" No. 105 (Federov *et al.*, 1956), i.e., *P. khasya* No. 104 (see Chapter 9).

Since today the main cause of forest fires is man, one is inclined to disregard lightning as another cause and to conclude that pine savannas are of recent origin. In many places they must be because, for instance, the frequency of lightning fires in the tropics is very small (Denevan, 1961); but the frequency is small only when measured by the span of a human lifetime. Moreover, lightning is a very common cause of forest fires in many places, such as the mountains of California. Through the thousands of years prior to the Holocene (see Chapter 2), lightning fires no doubt were numerous. It appears that fire, among other factors— windfall, floods, epidemics—played the most important part in establishing the pine savanna stage of plant succession, although probably the process proceeded at a much slower pace than now.

Radley (1960) diagrammed plant succession in a pine savanna of the eastern coast of Nicaragua (Miskitia); it may be described as follows: 1) selva burns out; 2) pioneer pine appears; 3) broadleaf shrubs (*Curatella*) appear under the pines; 4) young selva species appear; 5) pines are gradually replaced by the selva—old solitary pines tower over the canopy of the selva; 6) selva matures and remains dominant until next fire. Denevan (1961) found that in the mature selva of the Nicaraguan uplands the solitary pines towering over the canopy of broadleaf trees are much older than the selva.

It is possible that these solitary pines in Central America are components of a well-developed selva, just as they are components of broadleaf forests of eastern Asia.

When fires are frequent, they are harmful to pines. In the Zambales Mountains of Luzon, where the pine savanna is burned every year, the author was unable to find a single pine seedling. In the Miskitia savanna of Nicaragua, or in Florida (where people use to burn "piney woods" several times a year), repeated fires are detrimental to pine regeneration.

On the other hand, when pine savanna is protected by man from fire, it is gradually converted into broadleaf forest (Radley, 1960). Holdridge (1953) stated that when fires are spaced at intervals of 5 to 20 years, the pines maintain themselves as dominants, i.e., the pine stage appears as a "climax."

## Man's Role in Destroying and Expanding Pine Forests

In the Holocene a powerful new environmental agent appeared—Man —who both destroyed and expanded pines. Pine forests of England, Ireland, and Denmark apparently were destroyed by man very soon after the glacial period. Later man destroyed large areas of pine forests throughout the Northern Hemisphere.

But in more recent times man has expanded the area of the genus *Pinus*, mainly in the Southern Hemisphere. At present close to two million hectares of planted pine forests exist in South America, South Africa, Australia, and New Zealand. The most frequently planted species is *P. radiata* No. 19 of California, which, in its natural habitat, occupies a very limited area (Chapter 3; Plate 6–13).

In the Old World man has planted pines for a long time. We saw in Chapter 3 that in the Mediterranean region today it is almost impossible to determine where *P. pinea* No. 73 is native and where it was introduced by man. *Pinus brutia* No. 78 in southern Italy (ancient Brutium) apparently was introduced by man from eastern Mediterranean countries.

Another example of the expansion of pine forests by man is found in the afforestation of the southwestern part of France with *P. pinaster* No. 80, started at the beginning of the nineteenth century. More than one million hectares have been planted. It is sometimes difficult to ascertain without consulting records which forest is natural and which is planted. It is also impossible to decide how far *P. bungeana* has been expanded by man to lowlands in China.

## Phenology

In the temperature zone pines shed their pollen during the season of the year designated as spring. Pollination occurs at that time and the ovulate strobili begin to develop; in the North their development ceases in the fall, but in the warmer parts of the zone it continues throughout the ensuing winter. Ovules are fertilized the next spring, the cones develop throughout the second growing season, and the seeds ripen in the fall. The time elapsing between pollination and ripening of the seed is thus about 15 months and embraces two summers and one winter. The closer to the Equator, the earlier pine pollen flies. Many local environmental and genetic factors determine the time of pollen shedding. *Pinus radiata* No. 19 sheds pollen in March both in its natural environment on the Pacific Coast and at low elevations in the Sierra Nevada. It is inter-

**Plate 6–12.** *Top:* P. contorta No. 16 forest at 2600 m in the Sierra Nevada, California, cut over in 1870. The photo was taken about eighty years later. Signs of destruction remain, but pines gradually reoccupy the area. (Photo by R. C. Wilson. Courtesy California Forest & Range Experiment Station, U.S. Forest Service.) *Bottom:* slope near Santa Clara, Nueva Segovia, Nicaragua, originally pine-covered but now used for pasture. A single pine stump is in the foreground, while pines line the ridge in the background. Here, pine regeneration has been prevented or at least delayed by human activity. (Photo by William M. Denevan.)

**Plate 6–13.** Planted forest of *P. radiata* No. 19 in New Zealand. In its home (see map, Fig. 3–13, page 166), its total area is only 6500 hectares. About 630,000 hectares of this pine have been planted elsewhere. (Photo by Peter Godwin. With permission of Breckell and Nicholls, Ltd., Auckland, New Zealand.)

454 THE GENUS *PINUS*

esting that when *P. radiata* is planted in the southern hemisphere, for example, in New Zealand where it is known as *P. insignis* Dougl., it sheds pollen when it is spring there, i.e., during August or September.

A changed photoperiod does not prevent flowering of pines; they are photoperiodically neutral (see p. 408 of this chapter). Nevertheless, the closer to the Equator, the more irregular is flowering in pines. Other factors such as thermoperiodicity are involved there. Even in the southern parts of the United States, pines—for instance, *P. elliottii* No. 23, in southern Texas or in northern Florida—shed their pollen sometimes as early as the end of January. Farther south, in the highlands of Mexico and Central America, early "flowering" of pines becomes a widespread phenomenon, and its relation to the four seasons of the year becomes really distorted.

The author had occasion to observe *P. oocarpa* No. 59 at the southernmost limit of pine distribution in Nicaragua on a mountain south slope at 1220 m above sea level. It was the middle of February; the trees had just completed "blooming" (probably at the end of January) and numerous female strobili were still pink and tender, just having passed their receptive stage. The trees also possessed many full-sized cones, still green in color but already containing ripe seeds. Squirrels were busy cutting the cones and eating the fresh seeds. It is evident that the timetable of events leading to the production of seeds was considerably distorted.

During springtime in Nicaragua there is no upsurge of life as there is in the North; tropical pines never cease to grow. We cannot make the statement that in the mountains of Nicaragua it takes two growing seasons, or two calendar summers, for seeds to mature. The ovulate strobili continue to develop, apparently without much winter slowing, for there is no winter and it takes the strobili only a little over one year to mature. This is why a Honduran botanist once told the writer that in his country only one year is required for *P. oocarpa* to produce seed.

In Indonesia, late in February and early in March of 1961, the author observed still more distortion in the flowering of pines. The pine there was *P. merkusii* No. 101, moved from the mountains of northern Sumatra (about 3° north latitude) to the mountains and lowlands of Java (about 6° south latitude).

In the mountains of Java (elevation about 1500 m) near Bandung, *P. merkusii* shed pollen twice a year: in January–February, and in July–August. Better seeds are obtained from the latter pollination.

A twenty-year-old pine plantation at sea level was visited by the author on February 25, 1961. It was a fully stocked forest of tall trees with well-developed canopy and dense herbaceous ground cover. The forest ranger produced phenological records taken for several years. These records showed that *P. merkusii* pollen was ripened and dispersed intermittently all year round, ovulate strobili emerging from the buds; mature cones were also recorded throughout the year. No healthy seeds were found in the cones. However, *P. khasya* No. 104, a pine of Burma and Indochina growing naturally at elevations higher than those of *P. merkusii*, neither produced pollen nor developed ovulate strobili in this same plantation. High air humidity may be detrimental to normal seed production of this pine in the humid and hot lowlands of Java. No seedlings were observed in or near the forest (Mirov, 1962).

Distortions in flowering schedule of planted pines also have been observed in Hawaii (approx. 17 degrees north latitude) by Ronald M. Lanner of the U.S. Forest Service.* At the end of August, *P. contorta* was shedding pollen at an elevation of about 2400 m. *Pinus thunbergii* No. 97 may show every possible stage of male and female flowers at a given time. Vegetative growth of many pines also was observed to be modified in the humid climate of Hawaii; the leaders did not branch, their growth was continuous, and the stems were covered with scaly primary leaves subtending the needle fascicles. Some pines, under these conditions, lacked clear "annual" rings, common to the pines of temperate climates (Plate 6–3b).

All these observations show that humid, tropical habitats are not suitable for normal development of pines. Species of the genus *Pinus* do not grow naturally in such an environment. When they are planted, their flowering is distorted (by factors other than photoperiod) and their vegetative growth, although lush, is erratic.

## SUMMARY

Physiologically, the genus *Pinus* is a flexible group of plants. Mineral requirements of different species vary considerably. Some pines occur on limestone and dolomite; others grow in soils containing but little calcium. Generally mineral and nitrogen requirements of pines are much lower than those of agricultural plants and of broadleaf trees. Nevertheless, pines do not avoid rich soils and readily invade abandoned cultivation. Mycorhiza is highly beneficial in nutrition of pines. Pines are light-enduring trees. Their photosynthetic capacity is high and, because they are evergreen, they are capable of assimilating carbon dioxide even during winter months when the weather is warm. Productivity of winter photosynthesis, of course, depends on the climate of the habitat. The remarkable light endurance of pines could not have developed in warm and cloudy lowlands of the Mesozoic era; it could only have developed in the uplands.

* Personal communication, 1963.

Photoperiodically the genus *Pinus* is neutral. "Flowering" of pines is not affected by change of daylight hours, which possibly has contributed to the wide spread of the genus from the long-day northern regions to the short-day tropical parts of the world.

Response of pines to the thermal regimen of the habitat seems to indicate that they develop best in the regions where days are warm and nights are cool; there are possible exceptions, but these do not change the general picture.

Growth of pines is a complicated phenomenon depending on the environment and on the physiology of the tree. There exists in pines an endogenous rhythm determining the beginning and the end of seasonal growth; possibly this rhythm developed in northern habitats. Environment distorts this rhythm and more so with decreasing latitudes. The conflict between the rhythm and the environment is especially noticeable in the wet tropics where pines are occasionally planted.

The water-conducting system of pines is less advanced compared with that of broadleaf trees. But it is apparently equally or even more efficient, for it permits water to be delivered to heights surpassed only by few angiosperm trees. The mechanism of water movement in pines is not yet fully explained.

In their germination behavior pines may be divided into two large groups: the species whose seeds germinate promptly, and the species whose seeds need prolonged conditioning at low, but not freezing temperatures, and sufficient moisture. Delayed germination is especially important in dry climates.

Increased atmospheric ionizing radiation of recent times undoubtedly will affect growth and development of pines; how widespread its influence will be is difficult to say, but there are indications of pines being rather sensitive to irradiation. When located near the source of radioactivity, pines are definitely affected by it.

The physiology of pine pollen is little known. Empirical studies show its long viability; recent inquiries indicate the importance of boron in its germination. Research on germination and growth of the pollen tube through the nucellus of the ovule promises to be important in the understanding of incompatibility in hybridization between some pines.

In general pines have a broad ecological amplitude. Many species of the genus are interzonal trees; their adaptability to different environments is great. There are certain limiting factors, however, that determine the northern and southern boundaries of the genus of pines. In the North it is the low summer temperatures of the tundra; in the South it is either the aridity of the deserts or the humidity of the lowlands.

Ecologically, pines are basically drought- and light-enduring trees. Some pines of high elevations may remain under heavy snow cover for a long period of time; the physiology of their life under these conditions is little known.

Remarkable is the pioneer capacity of pines to occupy denuded or disturbed areas caused by glaciation, volcanic activities, and grazing. Apparently fire has been a very important factor in the life of pines throughout geological ages. Fire is responsible for perpetuation of pine savannas.

In dispersal of pine seeds wind appears to be the most important factor, but even so, it is of only local importance. Only under certain climatic conditions (high winds) can pine seeds be carried over long distances.

A new and important environmental factor of recent times is man, who both destroyed pine forests and expanded them.

Phenological observations indicate that humid tropical lowlands are not suitable for normal development of pines.

## LITERATURE CITATIONS

Acosta-Solís, M. 1954. La forestacíon artificial en el Ecuador central. Escuela Politécnica Nac., Quito.

Allen, Paul H. 1955. The conquest of Cerro Santa Barbara, Honduras. Ceiba, 4: 253–70.

Allen, R. M. 1960. Changes in acid growth substances in terminal buds of longleaf pine saplings during the breaking of winter dormancy. Physiologia Plant., 13:555–58.

Axelrod, Bernard, Paul Saltman, Robert S. Bandurski, and Rosemund S. Baker. 1952. Phosphohexokinase in higher plants. Jour. Biol. Chem., 197:89–96.

Barnes, Robert L. 1962. Glutamine synthesis and translocation in pine. Plant Physiol., 37:323–26.

———. 1963. Organic nitrogen compounds in tree xylem sap. Forest Sci., 9:98–102.

Barykina, R. P., L. V. Kudriashov, and A. N. Klasova. 1963. Stroenie i formirovanie stlanikov u Pinus mughus Scop. i Juniperus sibirica Burgsd. v vostochnykh Karpatakh (Structure and development of Pinus mughus Scop. and Juniperus sibirica Burgsd. in eastern Carpathians). Bot. Zhur. S.S.S.R., 48:949–64.

Bogdanov, P. 1931. O fotoperiodizme u drevesnykh pogod (On photoperiodism in woody species.) Trudy i Issledovaniia po Lesnomy Khoziaistvu i Lesnoi Promysh., 10:21–55. With German summary.

Bollard, E. G. 1957. Translocation of organic nitrogen in the xylem. Austral. Jour. Biol. Sci., 10:292–301.

Bondois, G. 1913. Contribution à l'étude de l'influence du milieu aquatique sur les racines des arbres. Ann. des Sci. Nat., Bot., Ser. 9, 18:1–24.

Bormann, F. H. 1955. Ecological implications of changes in the photosynthetic response of Pinus taeda L. seedlings during ontogeny. Ecol. Soc. Amer. Bul., 36: 81.

Borthwick, H. A. 1957. Light effects on tree growth and seed germination. Ohio Jour. Sci., 57:357–64.

Boyce, John S., Jr. 1962. Fomes annosus in white pine of North Carolina. Jour. Forestry, 60:553–57.

Brown, Claud L. 1958. Studies in the auxin physiology of longleaf pine seedlings. In The physiology of forest trees, ed. by Kenneth V. Thimann. The Ronald Press Co., New York. Pp. 511–25.

Burns, G. Richard. 1942. Photosynthesis and absorption in blue radiation. Amer. Jour. Bot., 29:381–87.

Carvell, Kenneth L. 1956. Summer shoots cause permanent damage to red pine. Jour. Forestry, 54:271.

Chailakhian, M. K. 1954. Problema fiziologicheskoi prirody protsessov zatsvetaniia vysshikh rastenii (Problem of the physiological nature of the flowering processes of higher plants). Zhur. Obshch. Biol., 15(4):269–87.

Chandler, Robert F., Jr. 1939. The calcium content of the foliage of forest trees. (N.Y. Agr. Expt. Sta., Ithaca, Mem. No. 228.)

————. 1943. Amount and mineral nutrient content of freshly fallen needle litter of some northeastern conifers. Soil Sci. Soc. Amer. Proc., 8:409–11.

Cholodny, N. 1935. Über das Keimungshormon von Gramineen. Planta, 23:289–312.

Clements, Frederic E. 1916. Plant succession. (Carnegie Inst. Wash. Pub. 242.)

Cooperrider, C. K. 1938. Recovery processes of ponderosa pine reproduction following injury to young annual growth. Plant Physiol., 13:5–27.

Couvy, J. 1962. Présence d'une substance de croissance et d'un inhibiteur dans les bourgeons et les pousses de première année chez *Pinus pinaster* Sol. Évolution de ces substances au cours de l'année. Comptes Rendus Acad. Sci., Paris, 254(14): 2643–45.

Cromer, D. A. 1935. The significance of the mycorrhiza of *Pinus radiata*. (Australia Forest Bur. Bul. 16.)

Czaja, A. T. 1934. Der Nachweis des Wuchsstoffes bei Holzpflanzen. Ber. Deut. Bot. Gesell., 52:267–71.

Davis, D. E. 1949. Some effects of calcium deficiency in the anatomy of *Pinus taeda*. Amer. Jour. Bot., 36:276–82.

Davis, John, and Laidlow Williams. 1957. Irruptions of the Clark nutcracker in California. Condor, 59:297–307.

Decker, J. P. 1947. The effect of air supply on apparent photosynthesis. Plant Physiol., 22:561–71.

Denevan, William M. 1961. The upland pine forests of Nicaragua. Calif. Univ., Pub., Geog., 12:251–320.

Dobroserdova, I. V. 1962. Vliianie makroelementov na vodnyi rezhim seiantsev nekotorykh drevsnykh porod (Influence of microelements on water regimen of seedlings of some woody plants). Physiol. Rast., 9:582–88.

Downs, Robert Jack. 1962. Photocontrol of growth and dormancy in woody plants. In Tree growth, ed. by Theodore T. Kozlowski. The Ronald Press Co., New York. Pp. 133–48.

———— and H. A. Borthwick. 1956. Effects of photoperiod on growth of trees. Bot. Gaz., 117:310–26.

Duff, G. H., and N. J. Nolan. 1953. Growth and morphogenesis in the Canadian forest species. I. The controls of cambial and apical activity in *Pinus resinosa* Ait. Canad. Jour. Bot., 31:471–513.

Duffield, John W. 1951. Interrelations of the California closed-cone pines with special reference to *Pinus muricata* D. Don. Unpublished Ph.D. dissertation, University of California, Berkeley.

Durland, W. D. 1922. The forests of the Dominican Republic. Geog. Rev., 12:206–22.

Fedorov, A. A., I. A. Linchevsky, and M. E. Kirpichnikov. 1956. V tropikakh i subtropikakh Kitaia (In the tropics and subtropics of China). Bot. Zhur., 41:1235–62.

Ferrell, W. K., and E. E. Huber. 1952. The use of radioisotopes in forest tree research. Idaho Forester, 34:42–45.

Fliche, P., and L. Grandeau. 1873. De l'influence de la composition chimique du sol sur la végétation du Pin Maritime (*Pinus pinaster* Soland.) Ann. de Chim. et de Phys. Series 4. Vol. XXIX. Pp. 383–414.

———— and ————. 1877. Recherches chimiques sur la composition des feuilles du

Pin noir d'Autriche. Ann. de Chim. et de Phys. Series 5. Vol. XI. Pp. 224–43.

FORDE, MARGOT. 1962. Variation in the natural populations of Monterey pine (*Pinus radiata* Don) in California. Unpublished Ph.D. dissertation, University of California, Berkeley.

FOWELLS, H. A., and ROBERT W. KRAUSS. 1959. The inorganic nutrition of loblolly pine and Virginia pine with special reference to nitrogen and phosphorus. Forest Sci., 5:95–112.

FRASER, D. A., and C. A. MAWSON. 1953. Movement of radioactive isotopes in yellow birch and white pine as detected with portable scintillation counter. Canad. Jour. Bot., 31:324–33.

FREELAND, R. O. 1944. Apparent photosynthesis in some conifers during the winter. Plant Physiol., 19:179–85.

———. 1952. Effect of age of leaves upon the rate of photosynthesis in some conifers. Plant Physiol., 27:685–90.

FRIESNER, R. C. 1942. Elongation of the primary axis in four species of pines. Abs. in Ind. Acad. Sci. Proc., 51:73–74.

GAIL, F. W., and E. M. LONG. 1935. A study of site, root development and transpiration in relation to the distribution of *P. contorta*. Ecology, 16:88–100.

GIBBS, R. DARNLEY. 1958. Patterns in the seasonal water content of trees. In The physiology of forest trees, ed. by KENNETH V. THIMANN. The Ronald Press Co., New York. Pp. 43–69.

GREENIDGE, K. N. H. 1937. Ascent of sap. Ann. Rev. Plant Physiol., 8:237–56.

GUSTAFSON, FELIX G. 1938. Influence of the length of day in the dormancy of tree seedlings. Plant Physiol., 13:655–60.

HACSKAYLO, EDWARD. 1957. Micorrhizae of trees with special emphasis on physiology of ectotrophic types. Ohio Jour. Sci., 57:350–57.

HARLEY, J. L. 1959. The biology of mycorrhiza (Plant sci. monog.) Leonard Hill, Ltd., London.

HATANO, K. 1957a. Alpha-keto acids in pine seeds. (Bul. Tokyo Univ. Forests No. 53.) Pp. 135–38.

———. 1957b. Über die Abhangigkeit der Atmungsintensität vom Wassergehalt bei keimenden Kiefernsamen verschiedener Keimfähigkeit. Forstwissenschaftliches Centbl. 76(11–12):376–81.

HATCH, A. B. 1937. The physical basis of mycotrophy in *Pinus*. (Black Rock Forest Bul. 6.)

HELLMERS, HENRY. 1959. Photoperiodic control of bud development in Coulter pine and Bigcone Douglas-fir. Forest Sci., 5:138–41.

———. 1962. Temperature effect on optimum tree growth. In Tree growth, ed. by THEODORE T. KOZLOWSKI. The Ronald Press Co., New York. Pp. 275–87.

———. 1963. Some temperature and light effects in the growth of Jeffrey pine seedlings. Forest Sci., 9:189–201.

——— and L. MACHLIS. 1956. Exogenous substrate utilization and fermentation by the pollen of *Pinus ponderosa*. Plant Physiol., 31:284–89.

HEPTING, G. R. 1945. Reserve food storage in shortleaf pine in relation to little-leaf disease. Phytopathology, 35:106–19.

HILGARD, E. W. 1880. Cotton production in the United States. U.S. Census Office. 81 pp. In 10th census of the U.S. 1880, Vol. V. U.S. Census Office.

HOAGLAND, D. R., and D. I. ARNON. 1939. The water-culture method for growing plants without soil. (Calif. Agr. Expt. Sta. Cir. 347.)

HOBBS, C. H. 1944. Studies on mineral deficiency in pine. Plant Physiol., 19:590–602.

HOLDRIDGE, LESLIE R. 1953. Curso de ecologia vegetal. Inst. Interamericano de Cien. Agr. San José, Costa Rica.

HOWELL, JOSEPH, JR. 1932a. Relation of western yellow pine seedlings to the reaction of the culture solution. Plant Physiol., 7:657–71.

———. 1932b. The effect of the concentration of the culture solution on seedlings of ponderosa pine. Jour. Forestry, 30:829–30.

HUBER, BRUNO. 1952. Tree physiology. Ann. Rev. Plant Physiol., 3:333–46.

IASHINA, A. V. 1960. K metodike izucheniia podsnezhnogo razvitiia rastenii (On methods of studies on development of plants under snow). In Geografiiia snezhnogo pokrova (Geography of snow cover), pp. 106–12. Akad. Nauk S.S.S.R. Inst. Geog., Moscow.

IKEMOTO, AKIO. 1961. Effect of day-length upon breaking of dormancy in one-year-old seedlings of *Pinus densiflora*. Jap. Forestry Soc. Jour., 43:162–65.

INGESTAD, TORSTEN. 1962. Macro-element nutrition of pine, spruce and birch seedlings in nutrient solutions. Meddel. Stat. Skogsforskningsinst., 51:1–150.

IVANOV, L. A., and I. M. ORLOVA. 1931. K voprosy o zimnem fotosinteze nashikh khvoinykh (On winter photosynthesis of our conifers). Zhur. Russ. Bot. Obshch., 16:139–57.

IWANOFF (IVANOV), L. A., and N. L. KOSSOWITSCH. 1929. Über die Arbeit des Assimilationsapparates verschiedenen Baumarten. I. Die Kiefer (*Pinus sylvestris*). Planta, 8:427–64.

JEPSON, WILLIS LINN. 1925. A manual of the flowering plants of California. Assoc. students, University of California, Berkeley.

JOHANNESSEN, CARL L. 1959. The geography of the savannas of interior Honduras. Unpublished Ph.D. dissertation, University of California, Berkeley.

KALOYEREAS, SOCRATES A. 1958. Rancidity as a factor in the loss of viability of pine and other seeds. Jour. Amer. Oil Chemists' Soc., 35:176–79.

KARSCHON, R. 1951. Photopériodicité et thermopériodicité chez le pin sylvestre. Schweiz. Ztschr. f. Forstw., 102:268–75.

KELLEY, A. P. 1950. Mycotrophy in plants. Chronica Botanica Co., Waltham Mass.

KESSEL, S. L., and T. N. SLOATE. 1938. Pine nutrition. (West. Austral. Forests Dept. Bul. No. 50.)

KIENHOLZ, RAYMOND. 1934. Leader, needle, cambial and root growth of certain conifers and their interrelations. Bot. Gaz., 96:73–92.

KOZLOWSKI, THEODORE T. 1949. Light and water in relation to growth and competition of Piedmont forest tree species. Ecol. Monog., 19:207–31.

———. 1956. Tree physiology bibliography. Compiled in cooperation with U.S. Forest Service [n.p.].

——— (ed.). 1962. Tree growth. The Ronald Press Co., New York.

———. 1963. Growth characteristics of forest trees. Jour. Forestry, 61:655–62.

——— and A. C. GENTILE. 1958. Respiration of white pine buds in relation to oxygen availability and moisture content. Forest Sci., 4:147–52.

——— and C. H. WINGET. 1963. Patterns of water movement in forest trees. Bot. Gaz., 124:301–11.

KRAMER, P. J. 1936. The effect of variation in length of day on the growth and dormancy of trees. Plant Physiol., 11:127–37.

———. 1957. Some effects of various combinations of day and night temperatures and photoperiod on the height growth of loblolly pine seedlings. Forest Sci., 3:45–55.

———. 1958a. Photosynthesis of trees as affected by their environment. In The physiology of forest trees, ed. by KENNETH V. THIMANN. The Ronald Press Co., New York. Pp. 157–86.

———. 1958b. Thermoperiodism in trees. In The physiology of forest trees, ed. by KENNETH V. THIMANN. The Ronald Press Co., New York. Pp. 573–80.

——— and W. S. CLARK. 1947. A comparison of photosynthesis in individual pine needles and entire seedlings at various light intensities. Plant Physiol., 22:51–57.

——— and J. P. DECKER. 1944. Relation between light intensity and rate of photosynthesis of loblolly pine and certain hardwoods. Plant Physiol., 19:350–58.

——— and THEODORE T. KOZLOWSKI. 1960. Physiology of trees. McGraw-Hill Book Co., New York.

LARSON, PHILIP R. 1962. Auxin gradients and the regulation of cambial activity. In Tree growth, ed. by THEODORE T. KOZLOWSKI. The Ronald Press Co., New York. Pp. 97–117.

LEYTON, L. 1957. The mineral nutrient requirements of forest trees. Ohio Jour. Sci., 57:337–45.

———. 1958. The relationship between the growth and mineral nutrition of conifers. In The physiology of forest trees, ed. by KENNETH V. THIMANN. The Ronald Press Co., New York. Pp. 323–47.

——— and K. A. ARMSON. 1955. Mineral composition of the foliage in relation to the growth of Scots pine. Forest Sci., 1:210–18.

LITTLE, SILAS, JR. 1953. Prescribed burning as a tool in forest management in the northeastern states. Jour. Forestry, 51:496–500.

———, J. P. ALLEN, and E. B. MOORE. 1948. Controlled burning as a dual-purpose tool of forest management in New Jersey's pine region. Jour. Forestry, 46:810–19.

LONGMAN, K. A. 1961. Factors affecting flower initiation in certain conifers. Linn. Soc. London, Proc., 172. Sess., 1959–60, Part. I, pp. 124–27.

LYELL, SIR CHARLES. 1849. A second visit to the United States of North America. Harper and Row, New York.

McCOMB, A. L., and J. E. GRIFFITH. 1946. Growth stimulation and phosphorus absorption of mycorrhizal and non-mycorrhizal white pine and Douglas fir seedlings in relation to fertilizer treatment. Plant Physiol., 21:11–17.

McQUILKIN, WILLIAM E. 1935. Root development of pitch pine, with some comparative observations on shortleaf pine. Jour. Agr. Res., 51:983–1016.

MASON, HERBERT L. 1946. The edaphic factor in narrow endemism. II. The geographic occurrence of plants of highly restricted patterns of distribution. Madroño, 8:241–57.

MAXIMOV, N. A. 1931. The physiological significance of the xeromorphic structure of plants. Jour. Ecol., 19:272–82.

MAY, J. T., and H. G. POSEY. 1958. The effect of radiation by Cobalt-60 gamma rays on germination of slash pine seed. Jour. Forestry, 56:854–55.

MELIN, E. 1925. Untersuchungen über die Bedeutung der Baummykorrhiza. Eine ökologisch-physiologische Studie. G. Fischer, Jena.

———. 1962. Physiological aspects of mycorrhizae of forest trees. In Tree growth, ed. by THEODORE T. KOZLOWSKI. The Ronald Press Co., New York. Pp. 247–63.

———and H. NILSSON. 1958. Translocation of nutritive elements through mycorrhizal mycelia to pine seedlings. Bot. Notiser, 111:251–56.

MERGEN, FRANÇOIS, and G. R. STAIRS. 1962. Low level chronic gamma irradiation of a pitch pine–oak forest: Its physiological and genetical effects on sexual reproduction. Radiation Bot., 2:205–16.

MIKOLA, PEITSA. 1962. Temperature and tree growth near the northern timber line. In Tree growth, ed. by THEODORE T. KOZLOWSKI. The Ronald Press Co., New York. Pp. 265–74.

MIROV, N. T. 1937. The relation of some internal factors to the germination of seeds of Pinus jeffreyi Murr. and Pinus lambertiana Dougl. Unpublished Ph.D. dissertation, University of California, Berkeley.

———. 1941. Distribution of growth hormone in shoots of two species of pine. Jour. Forestry, 39:457–64.

———. 1944. Possible relation of linoleic acid to the longevity and germination of pine seed. Nature, 154:218–19.

———. 1951. Geography of Russia. John Wiley & Sons, Inc., New York.

———. 1952. Simmondsia or Jojoba: A problem in economic botany. Econ. Bot., 6:41–47.

———. 1956a. Composition of turpentine of lodgepole × Jack pine hybrids. Canad. Jour. Bot., 34:443–57.

———. 1956b. Photoperiod and flowering of pines. Forest Sci., 2:328–32.

———. 1962. Phenology of tropical pines. Arnold Arboretum Jour., 43:218–19.

———. 1965. Review of fundamentals of forest biogeocoenology by V. N. SUKACHEV and N. V. DYLIS. Science, 148:828.

——— and R. G. STANLEY. 1959. The pine tree. Ann. Rev. Plant Physiol., 10:223–38.

MITCHELL, H. L. 1939. The growth and nutrition of white pine (Pinus strobus L.)

seedling in cultures with varying nitrogen, phosphorus, potassium and calcium: With observations on the relation of seed weight to seedling yield. (Black Rock Forest Bul. No. 9.)

MORELAND, D. E. 1950. A study of the translocation of radioactive phosphorus in loblolly pine (*Pinus taeda* L.) Elisha Mitchell. Sci. Soc. Jour., 66:175–81.

MOROSOW (MOROZOV), G. F. 1928. Die Lehre vom Walde. Translated from Russian edition of 1923, Uchenie o lese. J. Neumann, Neudamm.

MUELDER, D. W., D. O. HALL, and R. G. SKOLMEN. 1963. Root growth and first-year survival of *Pinus ponderosa* in second-growth stands of the Sierra Nevada. (Calif. Forestry and Forest Prod. No. 32.) Calif. Univ., School of Forestry, Berkeley.

NELSON, C. D. 1964. The production and translocation of photosynthate—$C^{14}$ in conifers. In The formation of wood in forest trees, ed. by M. H. ZIMMERMAN. Academic Press, Inc., New York. Pp. 234–57.

NEUWIRTH, GERHARD. 1959. Der $CO_2$—Stoffwechsel einiger Koniferen während des Knospenaustriches. Biol. Zentr., 78:559–84.

OBOLENSKII, V. M. 1956. Usloviia geograficheskago raspostraneniia sosny obyknoven-noi (Conditions of geographical distribution of *Pinus sylvestris*). Trudy Brianskogo sel'sko-Khoziastvo Inst., 7:17–20.

OGASAWARA, R., and Y. KONDO. 1962. Studies on auxins and inhibitors in *Pinus thun-bergii*. II. Existence of indolocetic acid. Tottori Soc. Agr. Sci., Tottori 14. Pp. 102–6. In Japanese.

PARKER, J., and D. E. PHILPOTT. 1961. An electron microscopic study of chloroplast conditions in summer and winter in *Pinus strobus*. Protoplasma, 53(4):575–83.

PARSONS, JAMES J. 1955. The Miskito pine savanna of Nicaragua and Honduras. Assoc. Amer. Geog. Ann., 45:36–63.

PESSIN, L. J. 1937. The effect of nutrient deficiency on the growth of longleaf pine seedlings. (U.S. Forest Serv. South. Forest Expt. Sta. Occas. Paper 65.)

———. 1944. Stimulating the early height growth of longleaf pine seedlings. Jour. Forestry, 42:95–98.

PHILLIPS, J. E. 1941. Effect of day length on dormancy in tree seedlings. Jour. Forestry, 39:55–59.

PISEK, A., and W. TRANQUILLINI. 1954. Assimilation und Kohlenstoffhaushalt in der Krone von Fichten (*Picea excelsa* Linn.) und Rotbuchenbäumen (*Fagus sylvatica*). Flora, 141:237–70.

——— and E. WINKLER. 1959. Licht- und Temperaturabhängigkeit der $CO_2$ Assimilation von Fichte (*Picea excelsa* Link), Zirbe (*Pinus cembra* L.) und Sonnenblume (*Helianthus annuus* L.). Planta, 53(5):532–50.

POLSTER, H. 1950. Die physiologischen Grundlagen der Stofferzeugung im Walde. Bayerischer Landwirtschafts-verlag, Munich.

RADLEY, JEFFREY. 1960. The physical geography of the east coast of Nicaragua. Unpublished Master's thesis, University of California, Berkeley.

RENNIE, P. J. 1955. The uptake of nutrients by mature forest growth. Plant and Soil, 7:49–95.

REUTHER, WALTER, TOM W. EMBLETON, and WINSTON W. JONES. 1958. Mineral nutrition of tree crops. Ann. Rev. Plant Physiol., 9:175–206.

RICHTER, F. I. 1939. Early flower production among the pines. Jour. Forestry, 37: 935–38.

ROUTIEN, J. B., and R. F. DAWSON. 1943. Some interrelationships of growth, salt absorption, respiration, and mycorrhizal development in *Pinus echinata* Mill. Amer. Jour. Bot., 30:440–51.

RUTTER, A. J. 1957. Studies in the growth of young plants of *Pinus sylvestris* L. I. The annual cycle of assimilation and growth. Ann. Bot., 21:399–426.

SARVAS, RISTO. 1950. Effect of light on the germination of forest tree seeds. Oikos, 2:109–19.

SAYRE, J. D. 1957. Spectographic techniques and analyses of pine needles. Ohio Jour. Sci., 57:345–49.

SCHANTZ-HANSEN, T. 1941. A study of Jack pine seed. Jour. Forestry, 39:980–90.

SHIELDS, L. M. 1950. Leaf xeromorphy as related to physiological and structural influences. Bot. Rev., 16:399–447.

SLANKIS, VISVALDIS. 1958. The role of auxin and other exudates in mycorrhizal symbiosis of forest trees. In The physiology of forest trees, ed. by KENNETH V. THIMANN. The Ronald Press Co., New York. Pp. 427–43.

SOKOLOV, C. I., and Z. T. ARTIUSHENKO. 1957. Ivanovy pobegi u sosny. (Llama shoots in pine). Bot. Zhur., 42:741–45.

SOLONEVICH, K. I. 1940. O regressii areala sosny na kol'skom poluostrove (Regression of pine area on the Kola Peninsula). Akad. Nauk S.S.S.R. Bot. Inst. Trudy. Ser. 3 Geog. Bot., 4:97–133.

SPARROW, A. H., and G. M. WOODWELL. 1962. Prediction of the sensitivity of plants to chronic gamma irradiation. Radiation Bot., 2:9–26.

STÅLFELT, M. G. 1921. Till kännedomen om förhallandet mellan solbladens och skuggbladens kohlhydrats-produktion. Meddel. f. Statens Skogsforsokanst, 18: 221–80.

STANLEY, ROBERT G. 1958. Gross respiratory and water uptake patterns in germinating sugar pine seed. Physiologia Plant., 11(3): 503–15.

——— and ELIZABETH A. LICHTENBERG. 1963. The effect of various boron compounds on in vitro germination of pollen. Physiologia Plant., 16:337–46.

STONE, EDWARD C. 1948. Auxin and respiration changes during stratification of sugar pine (Pinus lambertiana Dougl.) seed and their relation to subsequent embryo growth. Unpublished Ph.D. dissertation, University of California, Berkeley.

———. 1958. Dew absorption by conifers. In The physiology of forest trees, ed. by KENNETH V. THIMANN. The Ronald Press Co., New York. Pp. 125–53.

STONE, EDWARD L. 1953. Magnesium deficiency in some northeastern pines. Soil Sci. Soc. Amer. Proc., 17:297–300.

SUCOFF, EDWARD I. 1961. Potassium, magnesium and calcium deficiency symptoms of loblolly and Virginia pine seedlings. (U.S. Forest Serv. Northeast. Forest Expt. Sta. Paper No. 164.)

———. 1962. Potassium, magnesium, and calcium requirements of Virginia pine. (U.S. Forest Serv. Northeast. Forest Expt. Sta. Paper No. 169.)

SUSLOV, S. P. 1947. Fizicheskaia geografiia SSSR; zapadnaia Sibir', vostochnaia Sibir', Dal'nii vostok, sredniaia Aziia. Leningrad, Ucheb.-pedagog. izd.vo.

SWAN, H. STEWART D. 1963. The scientific use of fertilizers in forestry. In Trend: The activities of the Pulp and Paper Research Institute of Canada, Montreal, Quebec. Pp. 9–13.

SWANSON, C. A. 1957. Translocation in Trees. Symposium on Forest Tree Physiol. Ohio Agr. Expt. Sta., Wooster, Ohio, June 13–14, 1957. Ohio Jour. Sci., 57(6): 321–70.

TAYLOR, B. W. 1962. The status and development of the Nicaraguan pine savannas. Caribbean Forester, 23(1): 21–26.

———. 1963. An outline of the vegetation of Nicaragua. Jour. Ecol., 51:27–54.

THIMANN, KENNETH V. (ed.). 1958. The physiology of forest trees. The Ronald Press Co., New York.

——— and J. BEHNKE-ROGERS. 1947. The use of auxins in the rooting of woody cuttings. (Maria Moors Cabot Found. Pub. No. 1.)

TIKHOMIROV, B. A. 1949. Kedrovyi stlanik: Ego biologiia i ispol'zovanie (Pinus pumila Regl.: Its biology and utilization). (Materialy k poznaniiu fauny i flory SSSR. Nov. Ser. Otdel botanicheskii. VI. P. 6.)

TOOLE, VIVIAN K., E. H. TOOLE, S. B. HENDRICKS, H. A. BORTWICK, and A. G. SNOW. 1961. Responses of seeds of Pinus virginiana to light. Plant. Physiol., 36:285–90.

TRANQUILLINI, WALTER. 1959. Die Stoffproduktion der Zirbe (Pinus cembra L.) an der Waldgrenze während eines Jahres. II. Zuwachs und $CO_2$ Bilanz. Planta, 54:130–51.

U.S. FOREST SERVICE. 1948. Woody plant seed manual. (U.S. Dept. Agr. Misc. Pub. No. 654.) Government Printing Office, Washington, D.C.

ULRICH, JANE MURDOCK. 1959. Auxin production by some mycorrhizal fungi and its relation to the morphology of sugar pine roots. Unpublished Ph.D. dissertation, University of California, Berkeley.

————. 1960. Effect of mycorrhizal fungi and auxins on root development of sugar pine seedlings (*Pinus lambertiana* Dougl.) Physiologia Plant., 13:493–504.

————. 1962. Wurzelmorphogenese der Sämlinge von *Pinus lambertiana* (Dougl.) bei Anweisenheit von Mykorrhizapilzen oder auxinen. Internationales Mykorriza-symposium, Weimar, 1960. Gustave Fischer, Vienna. Pp. 165–73.

VAARTAJA, OLLI. 1954. Photoperiodic ecotypes of trees. Canad. Jour. Bot., 32:392–99.

————. 1959. Evidence of photoperiodic ecotypes in trees. Ecol. Monog., 29:91–111.

————. 1962. Ecotypic variation in photoperiodism of trees with special reference to *Pinus resinosa* and *Thuja occidentalis*. Canad. Jour. Bot., 40:849–56.

VITÉ, J. P. 1959. Observations on the movement of injected dyes in *Pinus ponderosa* and *Abies concolor*. Boyce Thompson Inst. Contrib., 20: 7–26.

———— and J. A. RUDINSKY. 1959. The water-conducting systems in conifers and their importance to the distribution of trunk injected chemicals. Boyce Thompson Inst. Contrib., 20:27–38.

WALLACE, RAYMOND H., and A. E. Moss. 1939. Salt spray damage from recent New England hurricane. 15th Natl. Shade Tree Conf. Proc., 112–19.

WAREING, P. F. 1950. Growth studies in woody species. I. Photoperiodism in first-year seedlings of *Pinus sylvestris*. Physiologia Plant., 3:258–76.

————. 1951. Growth studies in woody species. III. Further photoperiodic effects in *Pinus sylvestris*. Physiologia Plant., 4:41–56.

————. 1958. Reproductive development in *Pinus sylvestris*. In The physiology of forest trees, ed. by KENNETH V. THIMANN. The Ronald Press Co., New York. Pp. 643–54.

WENT, F. W. 1948. Thermoperiodicity. In Vernalization and photoperiodism: A symposium. Chronica Botanical Co., Waltham, Mass. Pp. 145–57.

WHITE, D. P. 1954. Variation in the nitrogen, phosphorus and potassium contents of pine needles with season, crown, position, and sample treatment. Soil Sci. Soc. Amer. Proc., 18:326–30.

WIKBERG, E. 1956. The distribution of water soluble radioactive substances in plant tissue: Some experiments with an autoradiographic method. (Kungl. Skogshög-skolans Bul. No. 24.)

WILSON, ERNEST HENRY. 1913. A naturalist in western China. With an introduction by Prof. Charles Sprague Sargent. Vol. I. Methuen & Co., Ltd., London.

WU, CHUNG-LWEN. 1950. Forest regions of China with special references to natural distribution of pines. Unpublished D. F. thesis, Duke University, Durham, N.C.

WULFF, E. V. 1944. Istoricheskaia geografiia rastenii (Historical plant geography). Izd. Akad. Nauk S.S.S.R., Moscow.

ZACHAROWA, T. M. 1929. Über das Gasstoffwechsel der Nadelholzpflanzen im Winter. Planta, 8:68–83.

ZAHNER, R. 1955. Effect of interrupted dark period on height growth of two tree species. Forest Sci., 1:193–95.

ZAK, BRATISLAV. 1961. Aeration and other soil factors affecting southern pines as related to littleleaf disease. (U.S. Dept. Agr. Tech. Bul. 1248.)

ZIMMERMANN, W. A. 1936. Untersuchungen über die räumliche und zeitliche Verteilung des Wuchsstoffes bei Bäumen. Ztschr. f. Bot., 30:209–52.

# 7

# Chemical Aspects

## INTRODUCTION

Pines have long been regarded by man as useful trees producing lumber, pitch, tar, and edible seeds. With the advent of modern chemistry numerous inquiries have been made into the composition of various products of pines, at least of those species that are, or were, abundant and easily accessible.

At present we have information on the chemistry of many products: cellulose, lignin, phenolic compounds of wood and bark, turpentine and rosin, essential oils of foliage, and minor components such as alkaloids. A great many of these investigations have been made chiefly for industrial purposes, and in many instances their results cannot be used in biology. Nevertheless, industrial findings on various pine materials have produced very valuable scientific information. Purely scientific research on chemical components of pines is, to a large degree, a continuation of earlier industrial and pharmaceutical investigations.

It is beyond the scope of this book to consider the extensive literature on research dealing with the products obtained from pines. Some of these products will be mentioned, but only briefly. For the rest, the reader is referred to the appropriate texts, to the recent excellent review by Rowe (1962), and to several journals dealing with wood products. The author's purpose is limited to consideration of the chemical aspects of pines insofar as these are useful in understanding the general picture of the origin, development, and relationship of different species of the genus.

In the field of wood chemistry it is customary to divide all compounds found in pines into two groups: (1) cell wall components, and (2) extraneous materials.

Cell walls of tissues in all higher plants include cellulose (usually about 45 per cent), lignin (up to 30 per cent), and hemicellulose. The cell wall also contains small amounts of minerals and possibly very small amounts of pectins.

Since these cell wall components are also omnipresent in the genus *Pinus*, they do not serve for differentiation of pine species; thus these components will be defined only briefly. It is the extractives that often serve to help in chemical, and often in botanical, differentiation of pines.

The extraneous materials, or extractives, of pines are those components that can be removed from the cells by means of neutral organic solvents (ether, alcohols, petroleum ether, benzene, chloroform, methylene chloride, etc.) or with *cold* distilled water (but not with hot water because it attacks the cell wall components). The extractives give certain characteristic properties to wood—e.g., color, odor, fungicidal properties, durability, etc. For a more complete discussion of wood extractives, the reader is referred to Hillis (1964).

There may be other materials in pines, such as mineral deposits (calcium oxalate, silica, etc.), which are not extractable.

## CELL WALL COMPONENTS

### Cellulose

In its pure chemical state, cellulose is a linear polymer composed of anhydroglucose units linked through the 1,4-positions by glycosidic bonds having the $\beta$-configuration. The essential difference between the various types of cellulose is physical in nature; i.e., it is governed by variations in molecular chain length and in the spatial organization of groups of molecular chains.

### Lignin

The nature of lignin is very complicated; it is not known yet if it is a single substance or not. Apparently lignin of the genus *Pinus* is not different from the lignins of other conifers. For an exposition of the intricate structure of lignin, see Pearl (1964).

According to Erdtman (1959), lignin has no great taxonomic value except in the delimitation of large taxonomic categories such as gymnosperms and angiosperms. It was known from early researches that some of the lignin reactions were caused by the syringil group. It was found that angiosperms give a positive test to the presence of syringaldehyde while gymnosperms do not (Creighton, Gibbs, and Hibbert, 1944).

A glycoside of coniferyl alcohol, coniferin, is found in the cambium sap of pines. When Korchemkin (1949) kept cambium sap under aseptic conditions, he obtained a highly methylated precipitate, giving positive reaction for lignin. It should be noted * that, since the conducting phloem is near the cambium, it is impossible to collect cambial sap without collecting the phloem-originating material.

## Hemicelluloses

Hemicelluloses are polysaccharides; they are usually separated from the cellulose by extraction with alkalies. Not all the polysaccharides come from the cell wall. Many can be removed by cold-water extractions. On hydrolysis they yield xylose, mannose, arabinose, and galactose (Normann, cited in Wise, 1944) as well as glucose, rhamnose, and uronic acids; in general, they are not readily extracted from lignified tissues—the presence of lignin always complicates studies of carbohydrates in wood (Hamilton and Thompson, 1959).

In *P. banksiana* No. 32 are found the following proportions of hemicellulose polysaccharides: galactan, 2.2 per cent; mannan, 16.0 per cent; araban, 2.1 per cent; and xylan, 10.7 per cent. Galactomannan polysaccharide, which amounts to 10.6 per cent of the oven-dried weight of total content of neutral sugar residues, is found chiefly in *P. strobus* No. 20 wood (Timell, 1957).

Foreman and Englis (1931) isolated and identified galactose and arabinose in *P. palustris* No. 22. Arabinogalactan was reported in the wood of *P. contorta* No. 16 (Laidlaw and Smith, 1962).

Anderson (1944) reported that the pentosan content of three western American pines was about the same in the sapwood and the heartwood for each species and that there was not much difference between the species.

*Pinus banksiana* No. 32 arabinogalactan was studied by Bishop (1957). The structure of arabinogalactan of *P. jeffreyi* No. 13 was determined by Wadman, Anderson, and Hassid (1954). It was found to be a highly branched molecule with *l*-arabinose residues in the terminal positions. Furthermore, it was found to be polydisperse: its average molecular weight was about 100,000. A highly soluble polymer, a branched galactoglucomannan, was detected in a mixed sample of *P. elliottii–P. palustris* wood by Hamilton et al. (1958).

Hamilton and Thompson (1959) reviewed the status of our present knowledge of hemicelluloses: While the celluloses of hardwoods (angiosperms) and softwoods (gymnosperms, chiefly conifers) are very similar in physical and chemical properties, there is a considerable difference between the two categories of plants with respect to hemicelluloses. Angiosperms have 20 to 30 per cent of hemicelluloses, the main constituent being 4-O-methyl-glucuronoxylan, with a high ratio of D-xylose to

---

* Personal communication from Martin H. Zimmermann.

4-*O*-methyl-*D*-glucuronic acid. There are also present small amounts of mannose, galactose, and arabinose. On the other hand, conifers (and among them pines) contain from 15 to 20 per cent of hemicelluloses composed chiefly of glucomannan, a component that is difficult to extract. There are also found smaller amounts of 4-*O*-methyl-D-glucuronoarabinoxylan.

Studies of hemicelluloses in pines have been done chiefly for industrial purposes. Sometimes pulp of two species was mixed, as has always been the custom in handling southeastern American pines. No comprehensive work covering the hemicelluloses of the genus *Pinus* has as yet appeared in the literature.

Great advances have been made in the last decade in the study of hemicelluloses and in determining their structures. For the fundamental aspects of hemicellulose research, the reader is referred to the most recent review on this subject by Hirst (1962).

## EXTRANEOUS MATERIALS

### Simple Sugars

Free mono- and oligosaccharides are found in all plants, where they are used for building the plant body and for maintaining its physiological processes. Different parts of a plant differ markedly in amounts of simple sugars; this has been shown by Smith and Zavarin (1960). It does not appear that simple sugars are of any taxonomic value in the genus *Pinus*.

### Cyclitols

It has been known for a long time that *P. lambertiana* No. 3 * of California, commonly known as sugar pine, exudes from its trunk a sugary substance which was used by the Indians as a food and medicine. Wiley (1891) related that this sugary substance, obtained in California in the middle of the nineteenth century, was examined in France by Berthelot, who named it pinite. According to Wiley, Maquenne published a paper in 1889 on "a new sugar with an aromatic nucleus," which he named beta-pinite and which he claimed was obtained from the *Pinus lambertiana* growing in Nebraska—an error quite easy to understand, considering the remoteness of America from France. Later it was found that pinite, or pinitol, was a cyclitol, a monomethyl ether of *d*-inositol, $C_6H_6(OH)_5OCH_3$. The structures of pinitol and sequoyitol are given below.

* Numbers after species refer to Table 1–2.

OH   OH

OCH₃   OH
OH
OH

OH   OH

OH

OCH₃
OH
OH

PINITOL *
5-Methyl Ether
of *d*-Inositol

SEQUOYITOL †
5-Methyl Ether of
*meso*-Inositol

*Pinus ayacahuite* No. 33 of Mexico, called in some places pino de azucar (i.e., sugar pine), also exudes large quantities of pinitol. Roezl (1858) mentions that *Pinus bonapartea* Roezl is known for its sugary exudate found in abundance on the bark of the tree; it is now known as *P. ayacahuite.*

Much work has been done by Arthur B. Anderson and his associates on extraction of pinitol from *P. lambertiana* (Anderson, MacDonald, and Fischer, 1952). In the course of these investigations it was found that besides pinitol, the wood of this pine contained small quantities of other cyclitols—a *meso*-inositol sequoyitol and a trace of *d*-inositol. The last two substances were absent in sapwood of the above-mentioned pine (Ballou and Anderson, 1953).

Lindstedt (1951) encountered some difficulties in identifying pinitol chromatographically in pines; therefore he was not sure whether it was characteristic for the whole subgenus *Haploxylon*. Pinitol was found in six haploxylon pines, but not in any pines of the subgenus *Diploxylon* for the species examined.

Plouvier (1952, 1953, 1958, 1960), however, reported later the presence of pinitol and sequoyitol in the needles of many gymnosperms, including both subgenera of the genus *Pinus*. He also experienced difficulty in extracting these cyclitols. In some instances it was possible to obtain the cyclitols only after fermentation (*"fermentation et défécation"*). His material, at least for some species, came from trees planted in the Bois de Boulogne.

Pinitol and *meso*-inositol were reported by Assarsson and Theander (1958) from the needles of *P. sylvestris.*

* Arthur B. Anderson, D. L. MacDonald, and Hermann O. L. Fischer, *Amer. Chem. Soc. Jour.,* 74:1479–80 (1952).

† L. Anderson, E. S. DeLuca, A. Bieder, and G. G. Post, *Amer. Chem. Soc. Jour.,* 79:1171 (1957).

## Phenolic Glycosides

In his thorough survey of occurrence of chemical compounds in plants, Hegnauer (1962) does not mention any phenolic glucosides in pines. In the nearest genus *Picea*, however, two substances of this class are mentioned: piceine and pungenine. Their structural formulae are given below.

PICEINE °                    PUNGENINE †

Judging by the presence of coniferin in the cambial sap of pines (Korchemkin, 1949), and also by Paris' remark (Swain, 1963, p. 343) that piceine, the β-D-glucoside of *p*-hydroxyacetophenone, occurs in *Pinus*, it appears possible that phenolic glycosides are not totally absent in pines.

## Polyphenolic Compounds

**Heartwood Polyphenols.** Erdtman and his co-workers published a series of articles on the composition of polyphenolic compounds of many conifers and among them of pines.

In 1951, two papers appeared. One, by Lindstedt and Misiorny (1951), summarized results of investigations of forty-eight *Pinus* species by paper partition chromatography. This paper includes not only Lindstedt and Misiorny's investigations, but also earlier researches of Erdtman, who originated the project and has been guiding it for many years. In the same year (1951), Lindstedt published his "General Discussion" of the results. Lindstedt mentioned that ". . . generally only one wood sample from each species [except *P. griffithii*] has been investigated and this, of course, limits the possibility of drawing general conclusions." Samples of *P. griffithii* from the Himalaya and from England (cultivated) gave identical chromatograms, indicating that change of environment had not changed the composition of the flavonoids. A very valuable observation was made that ". . . the percentage of each constituent may however vary within rather wide limits for different samples of the same species."

° T. Kariyone *et al.*, *Pharm. Soc. Japan Jour.*, 79:394 (1959).
† A. C. Neish, *Canad. Jour. Biochem. Physiol.*, 35:161 (1957).

For instance, the content of pinosylvin phenols of *Pinus sylvestris* taken from different parts of Sweden varied between 0.4 and 1.3 per cent. Later, Erdtman (1955) remarked that statistical studies tend to indicate that there are local races of this pine. In the Pyrenees it contains large amounts of pinosylvin phenols; in Sweden the content is higher for the north and south than for the central part of the country. The branches contain more pinosylvins than the trunks; the central part of the heartwood usually contains more pinosylvin monomethyl ether than the periphery.

Four substances—pinosylvin, its monomethyl ether, pinocembrin, and pinobanksin—are very common in both subgenera, *Haploxylon* and *Diploxylon* (Chapter 1, p. 14). In the subgenus *Diploxylon* these compounds form the main part of the polyphenolic constituents (Erdtman, 1959). Only two haploxylon pines—*P. lambertiana* and *P. peuce*—contain no pinosylvin phenols. Lindstedt (1951) attributed this to possible individual variations, but it should be noted that these two species possess many other unexpected chemical characteristics.

Erdtman and his co-workers discovered an interesting chemical difference between the two subgenera, coinciding well with their anatomical differences (from which the two had been named; see Chapter 5, page 375). The subgenus *Haploxylon* possesses a much more complex composition of heartwood flavonoids. The haploxylon pines are characterized by occurrence of stilbenes and flavanones with their respective hydrogenation and dehydrogenation products, the dibenzyls and the flavones.

Erdtman (1959) suggested that in haploxylon pines there exists ". . . an oxidation-reduction system responsible for transferring hydrogen from the flavones to the stilbenes." To quote further from Erdtman, ". . . it is possible that these chemical differences are due to a loss mutation, in which case the haploxylon pines would be forerunners of the diploxylon pines." This was an extremely valuable suggestion. Although both subgenera already existed during the Jurassic period, there are other indications, such as present geographic distribution of haploxylon pines (see Chapter 3), that they might have been the forerunners of diploxylon pines.

In the *Strobi* group of the haploxylon pines (see Table 9–1) are found flavones and flavanones containing a methylphloroglucinol nucleus. These are strobopinin, cryptostrobin, strobochrysin, and strobobanksin. It is interesting that, in *P. lambertiana,* Anderson (1952) found cinnamic acid, which is considered to be closely related biosynthetically to the flavonoids.

The two haploxylon pines, *P. bungeana* and *P. gerardiana,* form the group *Gerardianae.* They are similar morphologically and were found to be similar in their flavonoid composition. Within this group *P. bungeana* has strobopinin; *P. gerardiana* has not. They contain pinosylvins but no dihydropinosylvins, and pinocembrin but not chrysin, i.e., they possess the chemical characters of diploxylon pines. On the other hand, these two species contained pinobanksin, which was found in all seventeen haploxylon pines analyzed (four with question marks) and strobobanksin, which was present in three pines of the group *Strobi*, but absent in the other haploxylon groups. Thus, chemically, the group *Gerardianae* occupies an intermediate position between the haploxylon and diploxylon pines.

In the subgenus *Diploxylon* the most striking feature is the uniformity of the polyphenolic compounds. Intriguing is the presence of the usual compounds of haploxylon pines, pinostrobin and alpinone (discovered previously in *Alpina japonica*, a plant of the ginger family), in the heartwood of diploxylon pine *Pinus clausa* No. 28. This pine grows in northern Florida and westward to the extreme south of Alabama. It is never associated with *P. strobus*, the only haploxylon pine of the eastern United States. Thus, Erdtman's suggestion that possibly the abnormal tree was a hybrid with a pinostrobin pine was not justifiable. Moreover, diploxylon pines do not hybridize with haploxylon pines.

Hata and Sogo (1954) investigated *P. thunbergii;* it was found to contain exactly the same polyphenols as in previously analyzed *P. densiflora; P. armandi* was found to contain all polyphenols listed by Erdtman (1955) as occurring in haploxylon pines except the most common, pinostrobin and tectochrysin; and in *P. pentaphylla* var. *himekomatsu* (which is close, if not identical to *P. parviflora* of Erdtman), Hata and Sogo found pinostrobin and strobobanksin, which were reported by Erdtman as absent in *P. parviflora*.

Kondo, Ito, and Miyoshi (1955b) investigated wood polyphenols of haploxylon pine, *P. pumila* No. 68, and found pinosylvin, its monomethyl ether, dihydropinosylvin monomethyl ether, pinocembrin, pinobanksin, chrysin, tectochrysin, and strobopinin. Pinostrobin, found in almost all haploxylon pines, was absent.

Kondo, Ito, and Miyoshi (1955a) isolated and identified in *P. koraiensis* heartwood: pinitol, chrysin, pinocembrin, pinosylvin, and pinosylvin monomethyl ether, all reported by Erdtman. In *P. parviflora* (i.e., either *P. pentaphylla* No. 83 or *P. himekomatsu* No. 84), they isolated and identified, among other polyphenols, strobobanksin. As a whole, with few exceptions, the difference in polyphenols between the two subgenera, *Haploxylon* and *Diploxylon*, is clearly indicated (see Table I in Erdtman, 1959).

Mahesh and Seshadri (1954) found in the heartwood sample of *P. griffithii* No. 91 from Simla, western India, five new compounds: one chalcone, two flavonols, and two stilbenes.

All told, about fifty-two species out of more than one hundred and five have been investigated for their polyphenols, chiefly by Erdtman and his co-workers. Occurrence of these compounds in the remaining species is being investigated.

**Sapwood Polyphenols.**  Linstedt and Misiorny (1951) found that the content of polyphenols in the sapwood is always very low. Traces of the most common heartwood phenols have also been found in the sapwood. Lindstedt (1951) concluded that these compounds are generated in the cambium, transported via the medullary rays through the sapwood, and accumulated in the heartwood.

Jorgensen (1961) showed that pinosylvin phenols in *P. resinosa* No. 21 are formed in sapwood at sites of fungal or mechanical damage; apparently these were not transported from cambium.

**Bark Polyphenols.**  Early investigations of *P. ponderosa* No. 14 bark polyphenols were rather confusing. A yellow pigment (Kurth and Hubbard, 1951), named ponderosin by Ramanathan and Venkataraman (1954), later was found to be a mixture of quercetin and myricetin. Besides quercetin there were detected in *P. ponderosa* bark the following polyphenols: a quercetin pentamethyl ether pinoquercetin, and a flavonol pinomyricetin hexamethylquercetin (Kurth, Ramanathan and Venkataraman, 1955).

In 1956 Hergert analyzed *P. contorta* bark. The yield and nature of bark extractives of this pine are shown in Table 7–1. The yellow and brown waxes were apparently of a complex nature (see p. 480). Later, Hergert expanded his studies and, in 1957, he was able to report on flavonoids and tannin precursors of *P. elliottii* No. 23 from northern Flor-

**Table 7–1.** Yield and Nature of *P. contorta* Bark Extractives *

| Substance | Yield (%)[a] | | |
|---|---|---|---|
| | I [b] | II [c] | III [d] |
| Yellow wax, resin acids | 3.41 | 6.94 | 6.23 |
| Brown wax, oxidized resin acids | 2.29 | 2.87 | 2.14 |
| Flavonoids, phenolic wax | 2.86 | 0.90 | 1.01 |
| Tannin and carbohydrate | 12.95 | 16.42 | 19.01 |
| Phlobaphene [e] | 2.30 | 2.02 | 1.82 |
| Sum | 23.81 | 28.15 | 30.21 |

* From Hergert (1956).
[a] Yield based on oven-dry weight of unextracted bark.
[b] Bark obtained from Grays Harbor, Washington.
[c] Bark from Mt. Hood National Forest, Oregon.
[d] Bark from Ochoco National Forest, Oregon.
[e] Phlobaphenes are amorphous and colloidal red phloroglucinol tannins.

ida and *P. monticola* No. 4 from Washington. Some *P. monticola* samples contained substituted stilbenes in the inner bark (Hergert, 1957, 1960).

In the flavonoid group obtained by ethyl ether extraction, Hergert found myricetin, a hexahydroxyflavone, in about 2 per cent yield of the bark and comprising 90 per cent of the total flavonoid fraction. Small amounts of a flavone, quercetin, were also detected. In the flavanone fraction he found dihydroquercetin (taxifolin), dihydromyrcetin, aromadendrin, and pinobanksin. Table 7–2 shows the complexity of polyphenols obtained from the bark of the two pines. Hergert found only traces of catechin and leucocyanidins in *P. elliotti* bark. In the heartwood of this pine he found no catechin; only traces of polymeric leucocyanidins.

Hergert came to the conclusion that the polymeric tannins are primarily derived from leucocyanidins and from catechin. He made a plausible effort to find the significance of polyphenols in the taxonomy of conifers. Although any attempt to distinguish between genera on the basis of flavonoids of the bark was unsuccessful, he was able to separate "yellow pine" from other conifer genera on the basis of contents of myricetin and other flavonols in its bark and pinobanksin and related compounds in its heartwood.

**Table 7–2.** Polyphenols from Bark of Two Pines *

| Compound | *P. elliottii* | *P. monticola* |
|---|---|---|
| Dihydromyricetin | + | – – |
| Dihydromyricetin glucoside | + | – – |
| Dihydroquercetin | + | + |
| Dihydroquercetin glucoside | + | + |
| Dihydrokaempferol | + | – – |
| Pinobanksin | + | – – |
| Myricetin | + | – – |
| Quercetin | + | – – |
| Gallocatechin | + | – – |
| Catechin | + | + |
| Leucocyanidin A | + | + |
| Leucocyanidin B | + | + |
| Leucodelphinidin (s-) | + | – – |
| Gallic acid | T | – – |
| Protocatechuic acid | + | + |
| Phloroglucinol | + | + |
| Caffeic acid (*trans-*) | + | + |
| Ferulic acid (*trans-*) | + | + |
| Coniferylaldehyde | + | + |
| Vanillin | + | + |
| Unknown stilbenes | – – | 5 † |

* After Hergert (1960).
+ = compound present.
T = trace of compound present.
† = five different stilbenes present.

Hergert deserves to be commended for his awareness of the biological significance of chemical compounds recovered from trees and for indicating the locality and species from which the material was obtained.

**Polyphenols of Pine Needles.** Takahashi and his co-workers (1960) have made a survey of the occurrence of flavonoids (in glucoside form) in about thirty-five species of pines. There are, in their report, unavoidable discrepancies, such as occurrence of quercetin in *P. nigra* Arnold and its absence in the same species presented under the name of *P. laricio* Poir. Generally, quercetin and kaempferol were found in many species while myricetin was detected only in three pines: *P. halepensis* No. 77, *P. muricata* No. 18, and *P. sabiniana* No. 10.

Taxifolin was found in the needles of only one species, *P. koraiensis* No. 82 (Takahashi *et al.*, 1965). It is hoped that the remaining species of the genus will be investigated for occurrence of flavonoids in their needles.

**Polyphenols in Pine Pollen.** Polyphenolic substances of pollen of eight pine species—*P. taeda* No. 24, *P. strobus* No. 20, *P. resinosa* No. 21, *P. elliottii* No. 23, *P. banksiana* No. 32, *P. ponderosa* No. 14, *P. echinata* No. 25, and *P. palustris* No. 22—have been studied by Strohl and Seikel

**Table 7–3.** Distribution of Phenolic Acids in Pine Pollen *

| Pollens | p-Hydroxybenzoic | p-Coumaric (cis) | p-Coumaric (trans) | Vanillic | Protocatechuic | Gallic | Ferulic |
|---|---|---|---|---|---|---|---|
| *P. taeda* No. 24 | +++ | ++ | ++ | ++ | ++ | + | + |
| *P. strobus* No. 20 | ++ | +++ | +++ | ± | + | − | ++ |
| *P. resinosa* No. 21 | +++ | ++ | ++ | ++ | ++ | + | + |
| *P. elliottii* No. 23 | +++ | ++ | ++ | ++ | ++ | − | + |
| *P. banksiana* No. 32 | +++ | ++ | ++ | ++ | + | + | + |
| *P. ponderosa* No. 14 | +++ | +++ | +++ | − | ++ | + | ± |
| *P. echinata* No. 25 | ++ | ++ | ++ | − | + | + | + |
| *P. palustris* No. 22 | +++ | ++ | ++ | ++ | ++ | ++ | ± |

* After Strohl and Seikel (1965).
+++ = highest concentration.
++ = high concentration.
+ = low concentration.
± = very low concentration.
− = absent.

(1965). They found the ether extractives to be the richest in polyphenols. Seven hydroxyacids of a phenolic nature have been detected by paper chromatography. These are shown in Table 7–3. It is seen that all but two of the six acids were found in the pollen of all eight pines. Vanillic acid was absent only in *P. ponderosa* No. 14 and *P. echinata* No. 25. Gallic acid was absent in *P. strobus* and *P. elliottii*.

Strohl and Seikel also identified in the pollen two flavonols, dihydroquercetin and dihydrokaempferol. These were found in a greater or lesser degree in all eight pines; only dihydroquercetin was definitely not present in *P. strobus* pollen (being replaced by another unidentified flavonol).

The yellow color of pine pollen has repeatedly been shown not to be carotene (Strain, 1935; Euler *et al.*, 1945; Karrer *et al.*, 1950). Rather it appears to be due to flavonoids.

The benzene extractives of pollen contained *p*-coumarate esters. *P. taeda* No. 24 (a diploxylon pine) pollen was richest in these compounds while *P. strobus* No. 20 (a haploxylon pine) had almost none. In *P. taeda* pollen, Strohl and Seikel detected a flavanone, naringenin.

The phenolic acids and the coumarate esters varied little with the species of pine, but the flavonoid fraction had sufficient variation to warrant further study.

It should be recalled that Hisamichi (1961) found quercetin and isorhamnetin (3: 5: 7: 4'-tetrahydroxy-3'-methoxyflavone) in pollen of *P. densiflora* No. 95 and *P. thunbergii* No. 97.

**Polyphenols of Seedlings and Conelets.** Red coloration of pine seedlings of some species and red or purple coloration of pine conelets are caused by a group of flavonoids called anthocyanins. In 1956 and 1959 Krugman published two papers which covered well our present knowledge of occurrence in pines of these substances and their precursors, leucoanthocyanins. According to Krugman, Gertz, as early as 1906, reported the presence of anthocyanins in (presumably young) cones of pines; Robinson and Robinson, in 1934, found an anthocyanin in the conelets of *P. griffithii* No. 91; Hayashi and Abe have identified an anthocyanin, chrysanthemin, in reddish-purple staminate cones of *P. thunbergii*. Leucoanthocyanins are widely distributed in pines. Robinson and Robinson were the first who reported (in 1932) on the presence of leucoanthocyanin in wood of a pine (probably *P. sylvestris* No. 69). When they hydrolyzed a leucoanthocyanin obtained from the cones of *P. sylvestris* they detected an aglycone, cyanidin. According to Krugman, cyanidin-yielding leucoanthocyanins have also been identified by Bate-Smith in wood of *P. pinaster* No. 80, and by Hill in *P. radiata* No. 19. Krugman himself worked with *P. lambertiana* No. 3. He found no leucoanthocyanins in the "endosperm" (female gametophyte) of the resting seed, but its embryo contained both in the hypocotyl and in the cotyledons the precursors which, upon hydrolysis, yielded cyanidin and delphinidin. In subsequent development of the embryo Krugman found three aglycones (cyanidin, delphinidin, and malvidin) but in the cotyledons he found only two: cyanidin and delphinidin. Red color (caused by malvidin) appeared first in the hypocotyl, giving an intense coloration, but later the pigment decreased there and increased in the cotyledons. As the seedling grew older, red pigment disappeared first in the cotyledons and then in the hypocotyl and, after two months from germination, coloration disappeared completely. No malvidin was detected; only cyanidin and delphinidin were present. Judging from the behavior of leucoanthocyanins and anthocyanins during the development of *P. lambertiana* No. 3 seedlings, Krugman concluded that the former are not direct precursors of the latter: the two pigment groups are synthesized independently.

In his 1959 paper Krugman made a partial survey of leucoanthocyanin distribution in the genus *Pinus*. Xylem and phloem of young branches and needles of thirty-seven species, one variety, and six hybrids were tested separately for presence of leucoanthocyanins. Roots of seedlings of seven species and thirteen samples of pine pollen were also investigated. Leucoanthocyanins which upon hydrolysis yielded cyanidin and delphinidin were detected in needles and phloem of roots of all pines (xylem and phloem not separated); xylem of the stems contained only cyanidin-yielding leucoanthocyanins. Apparently there were no seasonal variations in presence or distribution of leucoanthocyanins in young pines (Krugman, 1959).

Hergert (1960) found leucocyanidins A and B and leucodelphinidin in bark of *P. elliottii* No. 23 and *P. monticola* No. 4 (Table 7–2).

That is apparently all we know at present regarding anthocyanin pigments in pines. Presence of pigments in pines is most conspicuous in the female strobili (conelets) at the time between their emergence from the buds and their pollination. In some species the conelets are russet-brown, in others they are carmine-red, and in still others, such as *P. balfouriana* No. 5 they are of a deep purple, almost blue, color. A systematic investigation of distribution of pigments among species of the genus *Pinus* might prove to be interesting.

Another type of coloration in pine seedlings occurs when they are deprived of phosphorus: the plants turn dark purple. The same phenomenon is observed in forest nurseries with the advent of winter; it is called "bronzing" and apparently it is not uncommon among conifers.

To sum up, although some commendable work has been done with anthocyanins in pines, especially by Krugman, and some exploratory tests have been made with pine pollen pigments, the whole field of distribution of these substances among the species of the genus *Pinus* still awaits investigation.

## Fats

Pine seeds are rich in fats, some species containing as much as 50 per cent fat, chiefly in the "endosperm" (female gametophyte). The seed fats consist mainly of triglycerides of unsaturated acids: oleic, linoleic, and linolenic, predominantly the second one. Saturated fatty acids occupy a subordinate position, amounting to not more than 10 per cent or so of the total.

Ivanov (1915, 1926, 1937), in his very extensive studies of the evolution of plants and composition of their seed oil, investigated several species of pines. Ivanov came to the conclusion that the degree of unsaturation of seed oil depends on the climate. It is commonly measured by the "iodine number," which is the number of grams of iodine absorbed by 100 grams of oil. Tropical families generally possess more species with low iodine numbers, while plants of northern latitudes are characterized by high iodine numbers, i.e., by high percentages of unsaturated fatty acids; the oils of some tropical plants (*Aleurites* for instance) are highly unsaturated. There were some discrepancies, but these are always present when one deals with biological material.

Ivanov's general conclusion was that northern pines possess seed oils with higher degree of unsaturation than the pines from southern regions. Unfortunately, his data for pines are not very accurate. Most of the material was obtained from the trees cultivated in the Mediterranean area (presumably in the Crimea) and the original home of the species is not indicated.

Our tests of seed oil of *P. ponderosa* No. 14 or *P. jeffreyi* No. 13 from different altitudinal belts of the Sierra Nevada in California failed to show any correlation between increase of unsaturated fatty acids and increase of altitude (unpublished data; see Table 7–4). But we have found that these two species, growing at the same altitude (i.e., under the same temperature regimen), differ considerably in the degree of unsaturation of their seed oil. *Pinus jeffreyi*, a relict pine of limited distribution, repeatedly showed less unsaturated fatty acids (iodine number between 130 and 137) than *P. ponderosa* (iodine number between 148 and 154) which is an aggressive and widely distributed species and still expanding (see Chapter 3, pine No. 14).

Iodine numbers determined by several workers are given in Table 7–5.

Ivanov's suggestion that northern species possess higher iodine number than southern pines is, broadly speaking, correct. Ivanov also apparently was right in that southern pines do not have much linolenic acid

**Table 7–4.** Iodine Numbers of *Pinus ponderosa* and *P. jeffreyi* Seed Oil from Altitudinal Belts of the West Slope of the Sierra Nevada, California *

| Altitudinal Belts (feet)† | Species | Iodine Numbers of Seed Oil | Number of Samples |
|---|---|---|---|
| 0–1000 | *P. ponderosa* | 148.4–149.0 | 2 |
| 1000–2000 | *P. ponderosa* | 148.4–153.1 | 3 |
| 2000–3000 | *P. ponderosa* | 151.1–153.3 | 4 |
| 3000–4000 | *P. ponderosa* | 149.5–150.2 | 4 |
|  | *P. jeffreyi* | 136.8–137.7 | 2 |
| 4000–5000 | *P. ponderosa* | 150.6–151.3 | 2 |
| 5000–6000 | *P. ponderosa* | 152.1–153.6 | 3 |
|  | *P. jeffreyi* | 131.3–135.3 | 3 |
| 6000–7000 | *P. ponderosa* | 151.7–152.0 | 2 |
|  | *P. jeffreyi* | 131.8–135.2 | 3 |
| 7000–8000 | *P. jeffreyi* | 139.2–142.8 | 2 |
| 8000–9000 | *P. jeffreyi* | 130.6–135.0 | 3 |

\* Unpublished data.
† Mirov, Duffield, and Liddicoet (1952).

**Table 7–5.** Iodine Numbers of Seed Oil of Several Pine Species

| Species | Natural Range Latitudinal Degrees | Natural Range Altitudinal Feet | Iodine Number [h] |
|---|---|---|---|
| *P. pumila* [a] | 34 –72 | 0–10,000 | 146 |
| *P. sylvestris* | 34 –72 | 0– 8,500 | 160 |
| *P. cembra* (i.e. *P. sibirica*) [b] | 43 –67 | 0–10,000 | 146–155 |
| *P. ponderosa* [c] | 31.5–51.5 | 0–11,000 | 148–154 |
| *P. jeffreyi* [c] | 30.5–43 | 3,500–10,000 | 131–137 |
| *P. lambertiana* [c] | 31 –45 | 1,000–10,500 | 150 |
| *P. pinea* [d] | 32 –42 | 0– 3,500 | 118–121 |
| *P. sabiniana* [e] | 34.5–41.5 | 500– 5,000 | 120 |
| *P. gerardiana* [f] | 29 –35 | 6,000–11,000 | 121–125 |
| *P. monophylla* [g] | 31.5–43 | 2,000– 9,000 | 108 |
| *P. edulis* [d] | 29 –41 | 5,000– 9,000 | 105 |

[a] N. J. Hasebe, *Chem. Soc. Japan*, **64**:967 (1943).
[b] S. L. Ivanov and S. B. Reznikova, *Schr. Zent. Biochem. Forsch. Inst.*, **3**:239 (1933).
[c] Author's unpublished data.
[d] H. Kaufmann and Fu-Ying Liu, *Fette u. Seifen*, **47**:409 (1940).
[e] J. J. Semb, *Amer. Pharm. Assoc.* **24**:609 (1935).
[f] I. Hardikar, *Jour. Indus. Chem. Soc.*, **5**:63 (1928); David Hooper, *Agr. Ledger* (*India*) 17 (1912).
[g] M. Adams and A. Holme, *Indus. Engin. Chem.*, **5**:(4) 285 (1913).
[h] As only approximate values were sought, the method of determining iodine numbers is not indicated.

in their seeds. It is interesting to mention that Dillman and Hopper (1943) found for cultivated flax that a higher degree of unsaturation (presence of linolenic acid) occurs in the arid parts of the northern hemisphere.

McNair, who carefully analyzed available data for many plants, came to the same conclusion as Ivanov, that northern plants possess more unsaturated fats in their seed than tropical plants (McNair, 1929, 1930, 1934).

It appears highly desirable to expand the investigation of seed fats to all species of the genus *Pinus*, and also to study individual variations within the species.

Pollen of *P. taeda* contains about 7.5 to 9 per cent lipids, chiefly triglycerides of oleic, linoleic, and palmitic acids. The triglycerides are not easily extracted unless the pollen grains are crushed. Lipids which were easily extracted amounted to 1.6 per cent of the dried pollen; these were probably part of the outer coat of pollen grain and were mainly $C_{28}$ and $C_{26}$ alcohols, octacosanol and hexacosanol, with small amounts of wax esters and free acids (Scott and Strohl, 1962). There is also a brief report on identifying twelve fatty acids in *P. ponderosa* No. 14 and *P. contorta* No. 16 pollen by Ching and Ching (1962). Myristic, stearic, oleic, and linolenic acids predominated (75.7 per cent in pine No. 14 and 73.6 in pine No. 16).

## Waxes

Chemically, waxes are esters of higher fatty acids and higher aliphatic alcohols; but the waxy substances of plants also contain alkanes, and minute amounts of other substances, such as terpene alcohols, aldehydes, ketones, and estolides.

Needles and young shoots of pines are covered with waxy bloom of varying intensity. Some species appear decidedly pruinose. As was already mentioned, wax also has been found in the bark and in the pollen of some pines. Estolides (or etholides) is the name given by Bougault and his associates (1908, 1911, 1928) to those waxy substances, which comprise a long chain of polyesters of hydroxy-acids (Bougault and Cattelain, 1928); on one end of this chain molecule is a hydroxyl group and on the other end a carboxyl group. The estolides have the following formula (Hegnauer, 1962):

$$HO-CH_2-(CH_2)_n-C- \left[ -O-CH_2-(CH_2)_{n_1}-C- \right]_x$$
$$\overset{\|}{O} \qquad \overset{\|}{O}$$
$$-O-CH_2-(CH_2)_{n_2}-COOH$$

When estolides are saponified, juniperic (16-hydroxyhexadecanoic) and sabinic (12-hydroxydecanoic) acids are obtained (Bougault, 1911).

Kariyone and Isoi (1956) also found sabinic and juniperic acids in *P. thunbergii* needle wax. They thought that their waxy substance was of the nature of estolide.

Tong (1954) extracted 1.75 to 2 per cent wax from *P. sylvestris* needles. The main products of extraction were juniperic acid and sabinic acid; the remainder contained lower fatty acids, phenols, and resins.

In the bark of *P. densiflora,* Hata and Sogo (1957) found 52.4 per cent lignoceric acid, 5.4 per cent hydroxypalmitic acid, 11.6 per cent lignoceryl alcohol, and 1.77 per cent phytosterols.

As a whole, waxes of pines are little known; they are found in many different parts of trees and possibly in some cases they might be of considerable taxonomic significance. Eglinton *et al.* (1962), who worked with alkanes, have shown well how composition of the wax coating of some *Crassulaceae* can be used for taxonomic purposes.

## Alkaloids

In 1955 Tallent, Stromberg, and Horning conducted a botanical survey of alkaloids in the families that previously had not been investigated for this group of compounds. Pines were included in this survey. Generally, it had been assumed that the genus *Pinus* was alkaloid-free, but the survey has shown that the leaves of nine pine species out of twenty-seven examined (of a total number of more than one hundred five species in the genus *Pinus*) do contain alkaloids (Tallent, Stromberg and Horning, 1955). From leaves of *P. sabiniana* two alkaloids were isolated: $(+)$-$\alpha$-pipecoline and a new organic base, $C_9H_{17}N$, to which the name of pinidine was given (Table 7–6).

In a subsequent paper, Tallent and Horning (1956) determined the structural formula of pinidine, shown below.

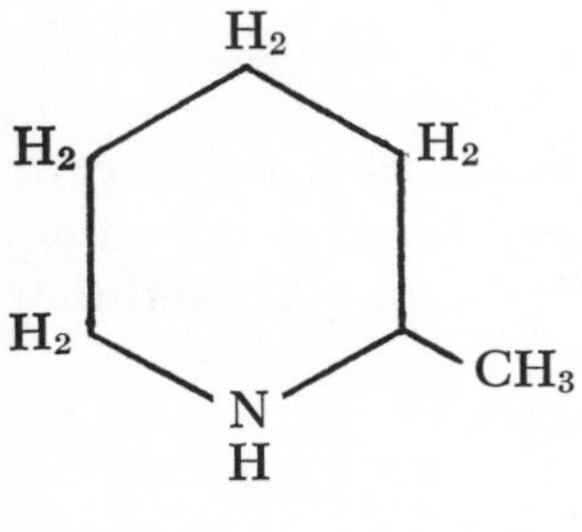

$\alpha$-PIPECOLINE                                      PINIDINE

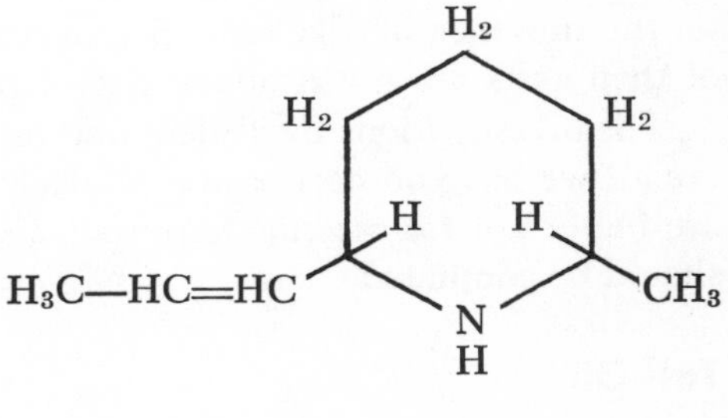

**Table 7–6.** Presence of Alkaloids in the Needles of the Genus *Pinus* Species *

| Species | Source | Mayer's soln. | Silico-tungstic acid soln. | Author's Remarks |
|---|---|---|---|---|
| | | | Alkaloid Test Reagents | |
| *P. attenuata* Lemmon No. 17 | Calif. | – | + | |
| *P. caribaea* Morelet No. 62 | Cuba | – | – | |
| *P. coulteri* D. Don No. 12 | Calif. | + | + | |
| *P. jeffreyi* Balfour No.13 | Calif. | + | + | |
| *P. monophylla* Torr. No. 7 | Calif. | – | + | |
| *P. muricata* D. Don No.18 | Calif. | – | – | |
| *P. pinceana* Gordon No. 37 | Calif. (?) | + | + | Mexican pine |
| *P. radiata*, D. Don No. 19 | Calif. | – | + | |
| *P. remorata* Mason No. 18 | Calif. | – | + | Var. of *P. muricata* |
| *P. sabiniana* Dougl. No. 10 | Calif. | + | + | |
| *P. torreyana* Parry No. 11 | Calif. | – | + | |
| *P. tropicalis* Morelet No. 66 | Cuba | – | – | |
| *P. virginiana* Miller No. 27 | Md. | – | – | |
| *P. ayacahuite* Ehrenb. No. 33 | Mexico | – | – | |
| *P. cembroides* Zucc. No. 31 | Mexico | – | – | |
| *P. chihuahuana* Engelm. No. 40 | Mexico | – | – | |
| *P. edulis* Eng. No. 8 | Mexico(?) | – | – | Southwestern U.S. pine |
| *P. hartwegii* Lindl. No. 49 | Mexico | – | – | |
| *P. lawsonii* Roezl No. 44 | Mexico | – | – | |
| *P. leiophylla* Schlect & Cham. No. 41 | Mexico | – | – | |
| *P. lumholtzii* Rob. & Fern. No. 42 | Mexico | – | – | |
| *P. montezumae* Lindl. No. 47 | Mexico | – | – | |
| *P. oocarpa* Schiede No. 59 | Mexico | – | – | |
| *P. ponderosa* Dougl. No. 14 | Mexico(?) | – | – | Western U.S. pine. |
| *P. quadrifolia* Sudw. No. 9 | Mexico(?) | – | – | Chiefly Calif. |
| *P. teocote* Schlecht & Cham. No. 45 | Mexico | – | – | |
| *P. tenuifolia* Benth. No. 55 | Mexico | – | + | |

* From Tallent, Stromberg, and Horning (1955).

Kariyone *et al.* (1956) added to Tallent and Horning's list information on the presence of alkaloids in four additional species of pines. Results of their tests are given at the top of page 483.

The investigations by Tallent and his co-workers and of Kariyone *et al.* are all we have on occurrence of alkaloids in pines. These investigations are important for taxonomic purposes (see p. 537, Chapter 9), and they should be continued.

## Tall Oil

From what had once been a waste material of the kraft pulping process of pine wood, a valuable chemical by-product known as tall oil

| Species | Mayer's soln. | Dragendorf's soln. | Wagner's soln. | Picric acid | Tannic acid | Silicotungstic acid |
|---|---|---|---|---|---|---|
| *P. resinosa* No. 21 | ++ | ++ | + | + | − | ± |
| *P. nigra* var. *corsicana* No. 74 | ++ | ++ | ++ | ++ | | |
| *P. pinea* No. 73 | + | + | + | | | |
| *P. armandi* var. *amamiana* No. 86 | ++ | + | + | | | |

++ = abundant; + = present; ± = uncertain.

is now recovered. Tall oil can be defined as that mixture of resin acids and fatty acids (mostly unsaturated), together with unsaponifiables, which is the product of the acidification of the soap skimmings from the black liquor of the alkaline pulping industry. The composition of tall oil varies: from 30 to 50 per cent fatty acids, 40 to 60 per cent resin acids, and 6 to 10 per cent unsaponifiables. This latter group contains such components as fatty acids, sterols, waxes, neutral terpenoids, lignin- and terpene-degradation products, and other miscellaneous substances. The fatty acids are derived chiefly from the sapwood triglycerides. Tall oil rosin comes predominantly from the heartwood as well as from the resin canals. The variation in the composition of tall oil can be attributed to species pulped as well as to regional and seasonal differences in source. Although the constituents of tall oil are similar to those found in the pine wood, the composition, both qualitative and quantitative, undergoes extensive change during processing.* Current references for this subject are found in the review by Rowe (1962).

Although tall oil is a very important industrial product, it cannot be used for taxonomic purposes. It is a mixture of many classes of substances and often of several species of the genus *Pinus*. Also, it changes chemically during pulping.

## Volatile Oil of Pine Needles

Pine needles have varying numbers of resin ducts (see Chapter 5). When severed, these ducts exude oleoresin that appears to be much thinner, i.e., richer in volatile oil, than the oleoresin obtained from the resin ducts of sapwood. The resin ducts of needles are not connected with the resin ducts of wood; the composition of volatile oil obtained from

---

* The above information on tall oil was supplied by Dr. D. F. Zinkel, U.S. Forest Products Laboratory, Madison, Wisconsin.

the needles differs considerably from the composition of volatile oil obtained from the wood.

Pine needles are distilled for production of commercial essential oil, mostly in the countries where labor is cheap. The raw material—needles with varying admixture of twigs—is bulky; the yield of essential oil is very small, amounting to less than 0.5 per cent of the weight of fresh material and even lower. A product of different species and even of different genera (*Abies, Picea*) is often sold under the name of "pine needle oil" (Guenther, 1952). The composition of needle volatile oil of a pine species is more complicated than the composition of turpentine obtained from the wood of the same species. Sandermann (1939–1940) found in the needle oil of *P. sylvestris* from Sweden: $\alpha$-pinene, $\beta$-pinene, $\beta$-dipentene, $\alpha$- and $\beta$-phellandrene, cuminaldehyde, anisaldehyde, cryptone (4-isopropyl-2-cyclahexen-*l*-one), tertiary terpene alcohols, bornyl acetate, *l*-cadinene, tertiary sesquiterpene alcohols, phenols, and a fatty acid, $C_{13}H_{25}COOH$.

Hunt (1912) distilled needle oil of several western American pines and found that yield of the oil was very poor. Results of his investigations were these:

P. *ponderosa* No. 14   0.11% of the weight of twigs and needles
P. *lambertiana* No. 3   0.115%
P. *contorta* No. 16   0.158%
P. *sabiniana* No. 10   0.188%

When needles of *P. ponderosa* were carefully separated from the twigs, the yield of volatile oil in the needles was 0.075 per cent. The poorer yield from *P. sabiniana* probably was due to the presence of *n*-heptane, which is highly volatile (B.P., 98° C) and readily lost.

Schorger (1919), who analyzed material distilled by Hunt, found the following components in the needle-and-twig oil of pines from western North America:

P. *ponderosa:* *l*-$\alpha$-pinene, 2%; *l*-$\beta$-pinene, 75%; dipentene, 6%; borneol, 7%; bornyl acetate, 2%; "green oil" (probably alcohols and sesquiterpenes), 3%.

P. *lambertiana:* furfural, trace; *l*-$\alpha$-pinene, 22%; *l*-camphene, 21%; 1-$\beta$-pinene, 39–40%; dipentene, 4–5%; ester, as bornyl acetate, 1.5%; borneol, 3.5%; sesquiterpenes (?), 1%.

P. *sabiniana:* *n*-heptane, 3%; *l*-$\alpha$-pinene, 58–59%; *l*-limonene, 18%; ester (as bornyl acetate), 3.5%; free alcohol (as borneol), 6%; methyl chavicol (?), "green oil," 2–3%.

P. *contorta:* furfural, trace; *l*-$\alpha$-pinene, 3%; *l*-$\beta$-pinene, 49–50%; *l*-$\beta$-phellandrene and dipentene, 19%; methyl chavicol (percentage not given); cadinene, 7%.

Schorger also analyzed needle oil of two southeastern American pines, *P. palustris* and *P. elliottii* var. *elliottii*, with the following results:

*P. palustris* (needles): furfural, trace; *l*-α-pinene, 2%; *l*-camphene, 12–13%; *l*-β-pinene, 50%; dipentene, 5%; borneol, 9.8%; bornyl ester, 2%; *d*-cadinene, 11%. The combined acids were caprylic, probably with heptanoic and caproic acids.

*P. palustris* (needles and twigs): furfural, trace; *l*-α-pinene, 8–9%; *l*-camphene, 13–14%; *l*-β-pinene, 44%; dipentene, 5%; borneol, 10%; bornyl ester (as acetate), 2.4%; *d*-cadinene, 10–11%.

*P. elliottii* var. *elliottii* (classified by Schorger as *P. heterophylla*) (needles and twigs): furfural, trace; *l*-α-pinene, 4%; *l*-camphene, 10%; *l*-β-pinene, 35–36%; dipentene, 8%; borneol, 11.4%; bornyl ester (as acetate), 3.5%; *d*-cadinene, 18–19%. The combined acids were probably caproic and caprylic acids.

However general and incomplete were Schorger's reports, they showed that all pine needle samples analyzed by him contained more β-pinene than α-pinene with the exception of the "heptane pine"—*P. sabiniana;* that camphene was a common ingredient; that borneol and bornyl esters were always present. His "green oil" probably contained many oxygenated compounds—alcohols and aldehydes. The sesquiterpene fraction was not fully investigated.

Schorger attributed the presence of *n*-heptane in *P. sabiniana* material to an admixture of twigs. It is known that *P. sabiniana* wood oleoresin contains no terpenes, but consists of *n*-heptane. It would be interesting to ascertain if its needles (and those of *P. jeffreyi,* another heptane pine; cf. Schorger, 1919) do contain *n*-heptane or not.

Very little is known about the non-volatile part of pine needle oleoresin. Reports of Enzell and Theander (1962) on presence of a new diterpene acid, pinifolic acid, suggests that the rosin acids in pine needles are different from those of stem oleoresins.

Cvrkal (1958) experimented with physical properties of *P. sylvestris* No. 61 needle oil in relation to genetic variability of the species. He reported that he was able to tell whether or not different pine stands found in different environments belonged to the same physiological variety.

Zanini, Dal Pozzo, and Dansi (1961) reported that commercial pine-needle oil from *Pinus montana* consisted of α-pinene, about 10%; β-pinene, less than 5%; limonene, about 4%; *l*-β-phellandrene, about 17%; Δ³-carene, about 20%; bornyl acetate, 5.45%.

A plausible effort was made by Savory (1962) when he attempted correlation of composition of needle oil for settling the taxonomy of two southeastern Asiatic pines—*P. khasya* No. 104 and *P. insularis* No. 105. Some botanists maintain that these two pines—one of the continent

(Assam, Burma, Thailand, Viet Nam) and the other of northern Luzon, Philippines—are two different species. Others believe that the two pines are the same species. Savory, working at Oxford University under Dr. L. Leyton, compared the two pines morphologically and chemically. Savory's material came from the plantations of North Rhodesia. He extracted the material with petroleum ether and then separated the terpenes from troublesome fat and wax by steam distillation. The yield of volatile oil was high, amounting probably to about 1.8 per cent of the weight of the needles. Savory has proven morphologically that his material of *P. insularis* and *P. khasya*, obtained from the plantations in North Rhodesia, belongs to the same species. His comparison of needle oils with the "gum turpentines" of the two pines, however, was not warranted. Not all components of pine needle oil of the two species have been determined, and from Savory's results with the volatile oils it is impossible to say whether the two pines were the same species or not. His approach was wise and modern in that he tried several different methods to establish the taxonomic relation of the two pines. He mentioned, quite correctly, that Simonsen and Rau (1922) probably overlooked $\beta$-phellandrene in the turpentine of *P. khasya*.

To sum up, earlier investigations of pine needle oil were unacceptable for biological purposes. Either the botanical source of material was not certain, or, as in Schorger's work, the analyses, although suggestive, were not complete. Only a few species have been investigated, and variability within a species has not been ascertained. Savory's work suggests a very interesting line of research.

## Oleoresin

Droplets of oleoresin may be found in any living parenchyma cells of pines. Most oleoresin, however, is produced in the thin-walled epithelial cells of the sapwood surrounding the resin canals (see Chapter 5). When a pine is wounded, the resin canals are severed. The oleoresin, squeezed from the epithelial cells into the resin canals, may be gathered in receptacles attached below the wound.

Oleoresin can be separated into two components: rosin and turpentine.[*] In industrial practice this is done by steam distillation. What is volatile with steam is called turpentine; what remains as "pot residue" is called rosin. The dividing line between the two components is arbitrary; it depends on the conditions of distillation. Generally, only monoterpenes (with a small and varying admixture of other substances, such as sesquiterpenes) are removed. Most of the sesquiterpene and diterpene hy-

[*] For terminology pertinent to oleoresin and allied products see Glossary of Terms (Appendix 3) of the author's "Composition of Gum Turpentines of Pines" (Mirov, 1961).

drocarbons and their derivatives are left as the "pot residue" and are considered a part of the rosin. In pine species used commercially as a source of turpentine and rosin (such as *P. elliottii* No. 23, *P. pinaster* No. 80, *P. montezumae* No. 47, and others) these substances are found in very small quantities; in other species, however (*P. albicaulis* No. 1, *P. flexilis* No. 2, *P. armandi* No. 86, and others) the sesquiterpene and diterpene hydrocarbons fraction is large.

The author has, perhaps arbitrarily, considered sesquiterpene and diterpene hydrocarbons as components of turpentine. Accordingly, these substances are not included in the consideration of rosin, which will presently follow.

Oleoresin composition of pine phloem is little known. In the bark of young stems of some pine species oleoresin accumulates in little pustules or blisters. Apparently chemistry of the product collected from such blisters is different and more complex than that obtained from the sapwood.

**Rosin.** The rosin obtained from oleoresin and from stumps of southeastern United States is composed to about 90 per cent by diterpene resin acids and to 10 per cent by non-acid compounds, generally reported as unsaponifiable material. This latter contains, depending on the conditions of distillation, varying amounts of before-mentioned sesquiterpenes and diterpenes. Rosin also is obtained from tall oil (see p. 482).

Balaš (1927) lists the following unsaponifiable substances in the rosin of *P. palustris* No. 22: a $C_{27}H_{56}$ hydrocarbon, a tricyclic diterpene, a diterpene alcohol, a sesquiterpene alcohol, an amorphous brittle resene. Many other as yet unidentified compounds have been reported in various pine rosins.

Resin acids of pines are generally tricyclic diterpene monocarboxylic acids. Their empirical formula is $C_{19}H_{29}COO_{19}$.

Resin acids can be classified into two groups: the abietic and pimaric. The abietic-type acids possess an isopropyl side chain in their skeleton, and they differ in the number and position of their double bonds. The pimaric-type acids, on the other hand, possess a vinyl and methyl side chain instead, and they differ from one another in their stereochemistry as well as in position of the double bonds. The exact structure of the pimaric acids is not fully elucidated (Rowe, 1962).

Much work has been done with the occurrence of different resin acids in oleoresins (and in processed rosin) of several species of pines—usually those which are considered to be either actual or potential sources of commercial rosin.

According to Harris (1948), the principal constituent of resin obtained from carefully collected oleoresin of southeastern American pines (*P.*

*palustris* No. 22 and *P. elliottii* No. 23) is levopimaric acid. But in processing (usually at high temperatures) the original acids rearrange their structure. This is caused chiefly by isomerization to more stable structures.

In addition to the pimaric acids, there were also found the following primary acids: neoabietic, isopimaric, abietic, and dehydroabietic acids. The first two of these four acids were described by Harris and his associates (Harris and Sanderson, 1948a, 1948b).

Palustric acid, which was originally found by Loeblich, Baldwin, and Lawrence (1955) in *P. palustris* No. 22, was isolated also from the oleoresin of *P. densiflora* No. 95 (Miyazaki and Yasue, 1956).

Oleoresin of *Pinus nigra* No. 74 (var. *pallasiana* from the Crimea) was found to consist mainly of pimaric, abietic, and neoabietic acids (Bardyshev and Cherches, 1958a). In *Pinus sibirica* No. 67 isopimaric acid was detected (Bardyshev and Cherches, 1958b). Expanding their investigation of *P. sibirica* further, Bardyshev, Cherches, and Kokhanskaia (1961) reported that the rosin of this pine contained abietic, neoabietic, and isopimaric acids and considerable amounts of a $C_{20}H_{30}O_3$ acid. So-called "cedar" acid of *P. sibirica* rosin * (reported by previous investigators) was found to be a mixture of this $C_{20}H_{30}O_3$ acid, abietic acid and, possibly, of some other resin acids.

Bardyshev, Cherches, and Kokhanskaia (1960) found in the rosin of *Pinus massoniana* No. 94 the following acids: pimaric, 42 per cent; abietic, 20 per cent; neoabietic and palustric, 25 per cent; dehydroabietic and abietic, 3 to 4 per cent; and up to 10 per cent of fatty acids. No details are given about the origin of the rosin of this Chinese pine. Apparently it was a commercial product; its unusually high percentage of fatty acids may have been caused by contamination. Generally, pine rosins do not contain fatty acids.

It appears to be profitable for taxonomic purposes to inquire into the unsaponifiable part of pine rosins. As Balaš showed and as we repeatedly found in our laboratory, there are almost always in the rosin small amounts of neutral substances that might be important for taxonomy. The nature of lactones reported in pine rosins is yet to be investigated (Balaš, 1927).

From the above, it appears that there is not very much difference in resin acids of oleoresins of different pines. In fact, according to Hegnauer (1962), oleoresins of all conifers are rather uniform in the composition of their resin acids. See, however, the most recent, important discovery by Dauben and German (1966) of lambertianic acid in *P. lambertiana* oleoresin. This new acid is a bicyclic diterpene acid con-

---

* Russians call *Pinus sibirica* Siberian cedar, which causes a great deal of confusion in literature.

taining a furan ring possessing a normal configuration, and it belongs to the series containing agathic acid and sciadopic acid found in other conifer genera quite remote from the genus *Pinus*.

**Turpentine.** The composition of pine turpentines has been studied from a biological point of view more completely than that of any other class of chemical substances. It is therefore pertinent to dwell in detail upon the subject of turpentine components and their occurrence and distribution among the species of the genus *Pinus*. What has been found for terpenes and associated non-terpene volatile compounds can be also applied to the other groups of substances.

The steam-volatile part of the oleoresin, called turpentine, is not a chemically pure substance. It consists, generally, but not always, of cyclic hydrocarbons, monoterpenes of an empirical formula $C_{10}H_{16}$. There is almost always an admixture of sesquiterpenes ($C_{15}H_{24}$) and sometimes of non-terpene substances.

The history of investigations concerned with the chemical composition of pine turpentines is reviewed in the author's publication, "Composition of Gum Turpentines of Pines" (Mirov, 1961). The turpentines of *P. nelsonii* No. 38 and *P. occidentalis* No. 64 were later analyzed (Mirov, Zavarin, and Bicho, 1962). All told, the turpentine composition of ninety-four species and two varieties has been reported by the writer and his associates.

In the course of normal growth of a pine the inner parts of the sapwood are gradually converted into heartwood. The oleoresin which is found in heartwood, chiefly in stumps, can be recovered. The wood is chipped, the chips are extracted with some appropriate solvent, and the extractive is subjected to distillation. Turpentine obtained from the wood in this manner is called wood turpentine; its composition often differs from that of oleoresin turpentine, commonly called "gum turpentine," of the same species although the chief ingredients of both are usually the same (Goldblatt and Burgdahl, 1952).

Sebe (1935a) gives the following list of wood turpentine components of *P. formosana* (*P. morrisonicola* No. 85):

| | |
|---|---|
| *l*-α-pinene | α-terpineol |
| *l*-β-pinene | *l*-borneol |
| camphene | *l*-camphor |
| cineol | a terpineol ester |
| dipentene and limonene | fenchyl alcohol |
| α- and β-phellandrene | *d*-thumbelene (or goyoditerpene, later |
| *p*-cymene | renamed thunbergene; it is identi- |
| terpinolene | cal with cembrene; see page 497) |

Possibly some of these compounds, such as camphor, were of secondary origin.

Bark terpenes of pines are very little known. *P. contorta* No. 16 bark contains large amounts (21 per cent of the benzene extract) of diterpenes, chiefly a diterpene alcohol, 13-epimanool ($\Delta^{8(20),14}$-labdadien-3-$\alpha$-ol), and lesser amounts of three other diterpenes with the labdane skeleton, hydroxyepimanool, contortolal, and contortadiol (Rowe and Scroggins, 1964).

Sulfate turpentine is obtained as a pulping by-product, by condensation of the relief gases from the pulp cook. Over 50 per cent of the United States turpentine production is from this source. The composition of sulfate turpentine is similar to that of gum turpentine, although some alteration takes place during processing. Sometimes in industrial practice more than one pine species is pulped and cooked. Then the sulfate turpentine is a mixture of the turpentines of the species used in processing.

Bardyshev and his co-workers (Bardyshev, Skridan, Roman, and Kostianova, 1961) distilled turpentine from one-thousand-year-old *P. sylvestris* No. 69 stumps buried in a peat bog. The composition of the turpentine was found to be somewhat different from that of turpentine obtained from recent stumps or from oleoresin of living trees. Nevertheless, there was a surprisingly high amount of the main ingredients of present-day *P. sylvestris* turpentine, i.e., 16 per cent of $\alpha$-pinene and 14 per cent of $\Delta^3$-carene. We have accumulated ample evidence that if a terpene compound is found in the oleoresin of a pine it also will be found in the stumpwood of the pine. The reverse is not always true because stumpwood turpentine contains some secondary products not present in the oleoresin of living trees.

STABILITY OF TURPENTINE COMPOSITION. It has often been reported that the composition of turpentine of a pine varies considerably. The nature, extent and causes of this variability have been little understood and seldom discussed. For a better understanding of the chemistry of pine turpentines (and this applies to all classes of chemical substances found in plants) it is necessary to discuss briefly what is known about stability and variability of their composition. To begin with, three questions will be considered:

1. Does the turpentine composition of an individual tree change during the growing season?
2. Does the composition change when a pine is planted outside its natural range?
3. Does a change of environment in a given region affect the composition of turpentine of a pine?

To study variability in physical properties—and thus the variability in chemical composition—investigators of the past often selected optical rotation of turpentine. Variability of optical rotation depends on three factors: (1) different proportions of levorotatory and dextrorotatory terpenes in a turpentine, (2) different amounts of the levorotatory and the dextrorotatory antipodes of the same terpene, and (3) different amounts of an optically active compound and an optically inactive compound (such as an alkane).

Herty (1908) investigated optical variability in turpentine samples obtained throughout two seasons from several individual *Pinus elliottii* No. 23 and *P. palustris* No. 22 trees. He found considerable variation among individual trees, but very little within an individual tree. Herty's investigation was followed by similar experiments of the French workers, Dupont and Barraud (1925), who studied a European pine, *P. nigra*. They found that although the rotatory power of the composite samples varied with the method of obtaining the oleoresin and with the time of the year, the chemical composition of the turpentine remained about the same. Here follow some examples of variability of optical rotation of *P. nigra* turpentine:

| | Sample 10 | Sample 11 | Sample 12 |
|---|---|---|---|
| Third gathering | −42.36° | −39.90° | −46.63° |
| Fourth gathering | −33.90° | −40.45° | −41.75° |
| Fifth gathering | −25.35° | −29.98° | −48.00° |

Although the optical rotation of the samples (more than forty) varied considerably (from −25 to 48°), all of them were levorotatory.

Oudin (1939), working with *P. pinaster* turpentine, found that the optical rotation of commercial lots was −30°, and varied only within 1 degree. In individual trees, the optical rotation varied from +16.20 to −41.0°; that is, some trees possessed dextrorotatory, and other trees levorotatory, turpentine. In individual trees, variations from one year to another and from one gathering of the oleoresin to another were relatively small. Oudin's "dextrorotatory pines" were less frequent than the "levorotatory pines." There were no morphological differences between the two.

Black and Thronson (1934), studying six *P. elliottii* No. 23 and six *P. palustris* No. 22 trees, found that during a single season the optical properties of turpentines of individual trees of both species did not follow any orderly course. Optical rotation of turpentine of one *P. elliottii* tree actually changed from minus to plus for a span of two weeks, but later returned to the original levorotatory state.

As the result of an inquiry into seasonal variability of *P. ponderosa* turpentine in the Sierra Nevada of California, we found considerable difference in optical rotation among individual trees (Fig. 7–1). This character varied little throughout a growing season, and, as in Black and Thronson's experiment, the variation did not follow any orderly course. Recent vapor chromatography tests of *P. ponderosa* turpentine have

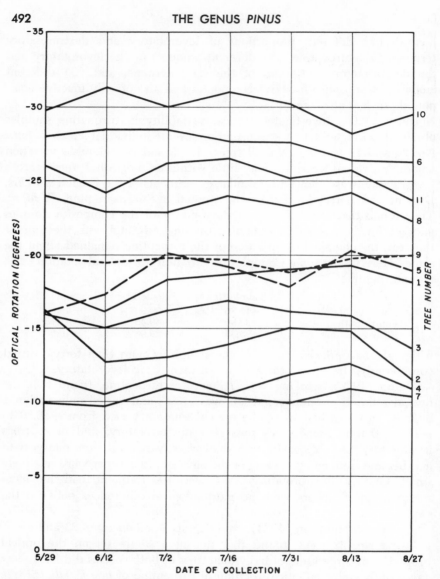

**Fig. 7–1.** Seasonal variability of optical rotation in several individual trees of *P. ponderosa* No. 14. (From Mirov, 1961.)

shown only slight change in quantity of different terpenes during a growing season (Dr. Richard H. Smith, U.S. Forest Service, personal communication).

To sum up, all evidence seems to indicate that turpentine composition in individual pine trees varies little throughout a growing season.

Then does the chemical composition of turpentine change when a pine is planted outside its natural range? Scheuble (1942) reported that *P. jeffreyi,* a California pine whose turpentine consists chiefly of *n*-heptane, also yields chiefly *n*-heptane when cultivated in Austria. In our experience, the *P. pinea* terpene fraction consists almost entirely of *l*-limonene both in Italy, where it is native, and in California, where it is cultivated in parks, as well as in Australia and in South Africa, where it is occasionally planted. Examples of this stability in turpentine composition are numerous; these two are sufficient to demonstrate that the composition of turpentine is a genetically fixed character.

Finally, when one physiological form [*] of a pine grows under different ecological conditions within its habitat, the chemical composition of its turpentine remains unchanged. Krestinsky and his co-workers (1932) found that *P. sylvestris* turpentine obtained from different ecological types of a forest in the same locality possessed the same physical properties and the same chemical composition. Apparently these workers dealt with the same physiological form of *P. sylvestris.* On the other hand, Penfold (1935) was able to distinguish, in one locality, several physiological forms of *Eucalyptus.*

SPECIFICITY OF TURPENTINES. Some pines, supposedly closely related, may possess turpentines of different composition; on the other hand, it is known that two species taxonomically remote may have turpentines of almost identical composition. The high-boiling sesquiterpene fractions from such pines may differ, but knowledge of the composition of these fractions is still too incomplete to permit any conclusions.

The chemical composition of turpentine is not always correlated with the generally accepted taxonomic position of a pine. One reason for absence of relationship is our still incomplete knowledge of chemical composition of pine turpentines. Another reason is that there is still disagreement among botanists as to the classification of pines (cf. Chapter 9).

But the most important cause of discrepancy between the taxonomy of any group of plants (which is based chiefly on morphology) and chemical composition of extraneous chemical compounds found in that group apparently lies in the evolution of plants. It could be dangerous to assume that evolution of chemical characters and of morphological characters have been parallel. Most likely morphological and chemical characters have followed different paths of development.

[*] The term "physiological form" was suggested by Penfold (1935) to denote subspecific entities having the same morphological appearance but differing in chemical composition of essential oils.

VARIABILITY OF COMPOSITION WITHIN A SPECIES.   When the physical characters (which reflect the chemical composition), even of composite samples of turpentine, are studied, it is easy to notice that some species vary but little throughout their environmental range, whereas others vary greatly. *Pinus merkusii* No. 101, which grows over a wide range in Burma and in Indonesia, is rather uniform in the physical characters of its turpentine (Mirov, 1948; see, however, Chapter 9, page 553).

By way of contrast, another widely distributed pine, *P. ponderosa*, varies widely in physical characters and chemical composition of its turpentine. Several "physiological varieties" (cf. Penfold, 1935) of *P. ponderosa* have been identified.

Within a species, the optical rotation of some populations is rather uniform, but in other populations it is rather variable (Table 7–7). As was mentioned before, this variability is caused either by the presence of different antipodes of the same terpene or by varying proportions of different (dextrorotatory and levorotatory) terpenes. For instance, some individual trees of *P. washoensis* No. 15 contained turpentine composed predominantly of dextrorotatory $\Delta^3$-carene; others contained more levorotatory $\beta$-pinene.

Individual variability in composition of turpentine may be caused by hybridization of two pine species or varieties. This situation was demonstrated by the study of turpentine from individual trees of the hybrid swarm in Alberta, Canada (Mirov, 1956). On the other hand, in a pine forest composed of only one species where there is no possibility of interspecific hybridization, the variability in chemical characters of individual trees is apparently caused by crossing among individual members of the population. On the whole, individual variation in composition of turpentine is only one manifestation of variability among the individual trees of a forest. The ever-present variability in a population of forest trees is of prime importance in the development of subspecific taxa as well as in the evolution of the genus. It is not the species or varieties that hybridize naturally or are hybridized artificially; it is the individual trees that cross one with another. For interesting discussion of chemical individuality in man, the reader is referred to several publications of Dr. Roger J. Williams, especially his *Biochemical Individuality* (Williams, 1956). His findings are also applicable to forest trees.

COMPONENTS OF TURPENTINE.   Composition of oleoresin of pine turpentines was summarized in one of the writer's publications (Mirov, 1961). Here it is sufficient to mention that about thirty major components are found in turpentine of the genus *Pinus*. Some pines have turpentines consisting almost entirely of one chemical compound. Such are *P. pinea,* possessing almost pure limonene turpentine, or *P. attenuata* No. 17, whose

**Table 7-7.** Optical Rotation ($[\alpha]_{5780}^{25}$) of Turpentine Obtained from Individual Trees of Several Pine Species *

| Tree No. | P. engelmannii Arizona | P. washoensis Nevada | P. quadrifolia California | P. monticola N. Idaho | P. ponderosa Sierra-Nevada, Calif. | P. ponderosa SW Utah | P. ponderosa Priest River, Idaho | P. ponderosa McNary, Ariz. | P. ponderosa Santa Cruz, Calif. | P. ponderosa Manitou, Colo. |
|---|---|---|---|---|---|---|---|---|---|---|
| 1 | +27.5 | - 1.6 | + 5.3 | -30.2 | - 9.1 | -17.7 | + 2.5 | +11.3 | -12.5 | + 7.7 |
| 2 | +18.7 | - 6.6 | +23.5 | -18.8 | -11.2 | +16.3 | + 4.5 | +11.3 | -32.3 | + 8.0 |
| 3 | +12.7 | + 1.0 | +27.7 | -33.7 | -12.2 | +10.3 | + 1.0 | +11.0 | -19.0 | + 3.0 |
| 4 | + 7.0 | + 8.1 | +20.2 | -16.0 | -12.5 | + 9.0 | + 4.2 | +14.4 | -20.2 | + 5.5 |
| 5 | + 1.0 | +10.1 | + 8.5 | -23.3 | -12.7 | +23.3 | - 6.0 | +16.0 | -17.0 | + 5.3 |
| 6 | - 1.0 | + 4.4 | +26.0 | -29.7 | -13.9 | +20.8 | - 2.7 | +10.3 | -21.8 | + 5.3 |
| 7 | - 2.3 | + 6.8 | +22.5 | -29.2 | -15.2 | +14.2 | - 4.0 | +11.0 | -18.8 | + 4.2 |
| 8 | ± 0.0 | + 1.7 | +28.3 | -29.3 | -16.0 | - 4.5 | + 3.0 | +10.5 | -19.7 | +10.2 |
| 9 | .0 | + 8.0 | +15.2 | -29.3 | -16.1 | -16.0 | -10.2 | +16.2 | -16.7 | + 7.8 |
| 10 | .0 | + 7.9 | +23.8 | -27.8 | -17.7 | +17.2 | + 4.2 | +26.8 | -19.3 | + 1.3 |
| 11 | + 5.0 | .0 | — | -69.0 | -18.7 | + 8.7 | -10.7 | — | — | - 2.5 |
| 12 | + 8.7 | - 9.7 | — | — | -19.7 | + 3.3 | - 6.0 | — | — | - 8.8 |
| 13 | +10.0 | + 1.3 | — | — | -19.8 | + 3.5 | - 5.1 | — | — | - 3.5 |
| 14 | + 8.0 | + 3.7 | — | — | -20.5 | + 1.9 | -13.2 | — | — | 6.2 |
| 15 | + 6.0 | + 3.4 | — | — | -21.2 | + 6.2 | — | — | — | -13.4 |
| 16 | + 4.0 | + 4.2 | — | — | -21.2 | + .7 | — | — | — | - 1.5 |
| 17 | + 1.4 | + 3.1 | — | — | -22.7 | - 7.3 | — | — | — | — |
| 18 | + 8.0 | + 8.4 | — | — | -22.8 | + 1.5 | — | — | — | — |
| 19 | +18.0 | + 4.8 | — | — | -24.3 | .0 | — | — | — | — |
| 20 | +30.4 | — | — | — | -25.5 | - 3.0 | — | — | — | — |
| 21 | +40.7 | — | — | — | -25.6 | +22.8 | — | — | — | — |
| 22 | +47.0 | — | — | — | -26.7 | -27.2 | — | — | — | — |
| 23 | +49.0 | — | — | — | -27.1 | + 9.0 | — | — | — | — |
| 24 | +46.0 | — | — | — | -29.9 | +19.5 | — | — | — | — |
| 25 | +49.0 | — | — | — | -30.9 | + 2.7 | — | — | — | — |
| 26 | +46.0 | — | — | — | -33.5 | -13.0 | — | — | — | — |
| 27 | +49.6 | — | — | — | -39.1 | +13.8 | — | — | — | — |

* From Mirov (1961).

turpentine is over 95 per cent α-pinene. Other components are of a sub-ordinate type; there are some exceptions. All species of pines, except two, contain terpenes in their turpentines. The exceptional species are California pines—*P. jeffreyi* No. 13 and *P. sabiniana* No. 10. The "turpentine" of these two species consists almost entirely of an alkane, *n*-heptane, with small admixture of aliphatic aldehydes; no terpenes are present. Heptane is also found as an admixture to the terpenes in three pines of Mexico (Nos. 47, 54, and 57). Another alkane, *n*-undecane, occurs in several pine species.

Often the components of turpentines occur in relatively small amounts and only in few species. Such are, for instance, β-myrcene (up to 5 per cent) or a phenol ether, methyl chavicol (up to 3 per cent). Some components are found in such minute quantities that they can be detected only by using such sensitive methods as vapor chromatography. Occasionally there are found rare components that have been detected only in one species. Examples of these are ethyl caprylate in the turpentine of *P. edulis* (Mirov and Iloff, 1956) or a bicyclic terpene, sabinene, which occurs in some varieties of *P. muricata* No. 17 (Blight and McDonald, 1963; Forde and Blight, 1964).

Sesquiterpenes, and especially diterpene hydrocarbons, are not abundant in pine oleoresins, but occasionally they are found in large quantities. Some pines, such as *P. armandi,* possess as much as 15 per cent, while *P. flexilis* has up to 20 per cent of sesquiterpene and diterpene hydrocarbons. On the whole, sesquiterpene and diterpene hydrocarbon fractions of pine oleoresins are as yet poorly explored (cf. Mirov, 1961, Appendix 1, pages 146–150).

Later investigations extended analytical studies of pine turpentines (Mirov, Zavarin, and Bicho, 1962; Williams and Bannister, 1962; Blight and McDonald, 1962; Forde and Blight, 1964; and others). Some advances have been made recently in elucidation of structure of the sesquiterpene and diterpene hydrocarbons of pine turpentines. Albicaulol, originally described from *P. albicaulis* No. 1 (Haagen-Smith, Wang, and Mirov, 1951) was found to be identical with δ-cadinene and δ-cadinol (Dauben *et al.*, 1961). Torreyol and sesquigoyol (Sebe, 1940) also proved to be identical with δ-cadinol (Pentegova, Motl, and Herout, 1961). A bicyclic sesquiterpene of *P. pinceana* No. 37 turpentine, named maderene (Mirov, 1951), was found later to be β-caryophyllene. Apparently the same sesquiterpene with admixture of humulene is found in *P. pinea* No. 73 (Wm. G. Dauben, personal communication).

Of recent discovery (Nayak and Dev, 1963) is a tetracyclic sesquiterpene, longicyclene, which is found in higher boiling fractions of *P. roxburghii* No. 93 (formerly known as *P. longifolia*) together with a tricyclic sesquiterpene, longifolene. Structural formulae of the two are shown below.

LONGIFOLENE *

LONGICYCLENE †

In analyzing turpentine of *P. armandi* (Mirov and Iloff, 1955) we found that it contains two diterpenes: one which gave a maleic anhydride adduct, and another which was originally found in *P. albicaulis* turpentine (Haagen-Smith, Wang, and Mirov, 1951) and which was named cembrene. Mirov and Iloff (1955) ventured to say that the diterpene thumbelene, previously isolated by Sebe (1935a, 1935b; see tabulation on p. 489) was probably the same as cembrene. Later we found that it also is present in *P. koraiensis* No. 82 of East Asia and *P. peuce* No. 71 of the Balkans (Iloff and Mirov, 1956). Dauben, Thiessen, and Resnick (1962) described cembrene as a 14-membered ring diterpene hydrocarbon having the following structure:

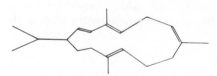

CEMBRENE ‡

In the same year Kobayashi and Akiyoshi (1962) reported structure of a diterpene hydrocarbon, thumbelene, or thunbergene, from stumpwood of *P. thunbergii* No. 97. The structure was identical to that of cembrene (cf. Sebe's data on *P. morrisonicola* No. 85 wood turpentine, p. 489).

Very little information is available on the composition of turpentines of pine hybrids and of varieties.

*Pinus ponderosa* No. 14 and *P. jeffreyi* No. 13 grow together and occasionally cross naturally (see Chapter 3), and they have been crossed artificially. *Pinus ponderosa* is essentially a bicyclic terpene pine; *P. jeffreyi* possesses no cyclic terpenes, the volatile part of its oleoresin containing mostly *n*-heptane. The hybrids between the two species investigated by the writer were found to contain terpenes to about 75 per cent and *n*-heptane to 25 per cent.

*Pinus banksiana* No. 32 and *P. contorta* No. 16 meet and hybridize naturally in western Canada, forming a hybrid swarm. Turpentine of the former consists of a monocyclic terpene, *l-β*-phellandrene, with addition

* After Hegnaver (1962).
† Modified after Nayak and Dev (1963).
‡ Dauben, Thiessen, and Resnick (1962).

of small quantities of bicyclic terpenes; turpentine of the latter is composed mostly of two bicyclic terpenes, α-pinene and β-pinene. The artificial hybrid was found, by the author, to contain a mixture of *l*-β-phellandrene and bicyclic terpenes. In the hybrid swarm, turpentine samples of individual trees also contained a mixture of *l*-β-phellandrene and bicyclic terpenes, ranging from almost pure phellandrene in some trees to a complete absence of it (Mirov, 1956).

Turpentine composition of *P. attenuata* × *P. radiata* hybrids was studied by Forde (1964). The results of her investigations suggest that the major difference between the turpentines of these two species is controlled by a single gene, ". . . but since variation in $F_1$ hybrids and those within the range of wild *P. radiata* is of a continuous nature, a multifactorial system of modifiers is probably present in this species."

Williams and Bannister (1962), using vapor chromatography method, detected in planted *P. contorta* (origin not given) turpentine a trace of camphene and small quantities of β-pinene, myrcene, and Δ³-carene. Hergert, in a letter (1964), said that he found in oleoresin of this pine "at least fifty terpene compounds (up to $C_{30}$) present, depending upon locality and duration of distillation." In some localities Δ³-carene content was very high; in the northwestern coastal variety this terpene was completely absent.

## SUMMARY

From the foregoing survey of chemical compounds found in pines it appears certain that extraneous substances are more useful than cell wall components for taxonomic investigations of the genus *Pinus*. Most of the extraneous substances (terpenes, polyphenols) are widespread, being found in all species of the genus *Pinus;* others, such as alkaloids, have been detected, so far, in only a few species. Most of the extraneous substances, however, are found in relatively small amounts.

On the whole, very few complete systematic investigations of occurrence of extraneous substances in pines have been made thus far. Polyphenols and terpenes have been studied more extensively than any other group of extraneous substances of pines, but composition of the higher boiling fractions of the terpenes, consisting of sesquiterpenes and diterpenes, is still insufficiently known. Diterpene acids have been considered generally similar in all species of pines, although recent discovery of a new diterpene acid (Dauben and German, 1966), having a rather unusual structure, seems to open new possibilities in investigations of these compounds. Heartwood polyphenols have been analyzed in about one half of the total number of species of the genus.. Bark polyphenols are known only for the pine species used in pulp and paper industry. Composition of seed fats is known only for a few species and what is known should be re-examined. Waxes of pines are little known.

In available studies of extraneous compounds of pines, sampling is almost always inadequate. Usually one sample from one tree is used as a criterion for ascertaining occurrence of a certain compound in a species. Composite samples taken from many trees give a better picture of specificity of a compound, but they give no information on individual trees. The fact—often disregarded—is that there is variability within a species and that often there are no two trees alike in chemical composition of their extraneous substances. Sometimes individual variation is small; often it is so considerable as to cause misunderstanding and confusion. Nevertheless, more work has been done on extraneous substances of pines than perhaps for any other group of plants. What is known gives us hope that further studies of occurrence of these substances in pines, especially of polyphenols, seed fats, waxes, and terpenes, may be very interesting and useful in the taxonomic studies of the genus. Future studies should be concerned both with species and with populations. Individual variability should always be considered. Data presented in this chapter show that distribution of chemical compounds among the pines may often be used for taxonomic purposes.

## LITERATURE CITATIONS

ANDERSON, ARTHUR B. 1944. Chemistry of western pines. Indus. Engin. Chem., 36: 662–63.

———. 1952. Occurrence of cinnamic acid in sugar pine (*Pinus lambertiana* Dougl.). Amer. Chem. Soc. Jour., 74:6099.

———, D. L. MACDONALD, and HERMANN O. L. FISCHER. 1952. The structure of pinitol. Amer. Chem. Soc. Jour., 74:1479–80.

ASSARSSON, ANDERS, and OLOF THEANDER. 1958. The constituents of conifer needles. I. Low molecular weight carbohydrates in the needles of *Pinus silvestris*. Acta Chem. Scand., 12:1319–22.

BALAŠ, F. 1927. Chemistry of natural resins and resin acids. Časopis Českoslov. Lékárnictva, 7:320–38.

BALLOU, CLINTON E., and ARTHUR B. ANDERSON. 1953. On the cyclitols present in sugar pine (*Pinus lambertiana* Dougl.). Amer. Chem. Soc. Jour., 75:648–50.

BARDYSHEV, I. I., and K. A. CHERCHES. 1958a. Smolianye Kisloty zhivitsy sosny Krymskoi. (Resin acids from the Crimean pine *Pinus pallasiana* Lamb.) Zhur. Prikl. Khim., 31:1122–26.

——— and K. A. CHERCHES. 1958b. Komponents Smolianykh Kislot zhivitsy Kedra sibirskogo—*Pinus sibirica* (Rupr.) Mayr. (Isodextropimaric acid from Siberian cedar—*Pinus sibirica* [Rupr] Mayr.) Dok. Akad. Nauk S.S.S.R., 120:1025–26.

———, K. A. CHERCHES, and Z. F. KOKHANSKAIA. 1960. O Prirode Smolianykh Kislot i Svoistvakh Kanifoli is Zhivitsy sosny Masona—*P. massoniana*. (The nature of resin acids and properties of rosins from oleoresins from *P. massoniana* oleoresin.) Zhur. Prikl. Khim., 33(4):884–90.

———, K. A. CHERCHES, and Z. F. KOKHANSKAIA. 1961. K Voprosy o Prirode Smolianykh Kislot Zhivitsy Kedra Sibirskogo *Pinus sibirica* (Rupr.) Mayr. (The nature of resin acids in the oleoresin from *P. sibirica*.) Zhur. Prikl. Khim., 34(5):1147–51.

——, A. I. Skridan, L. V. Roman, and S. S. Kostianova. 1961. Khimicheskii sostav sukhoperegonnogo skipidara poluchennogo iz sosnovykh pnei, prolezhav-shikh v techenie tysiacheletie v torfianykh zalezhakh (Composition of dry distilled turpentine from pine stumps aged 1000 years in peat bog). Zhur. Prikl. Khim., 34:440–45.

Bishop, C. T. 1957. Constitution of arabogalactan from Jack pine (*Pinus banksiana* Lamb.). Canad. Jour. Chem., 35:1010–1119.

Black, A. P., and S. M. Thronson. 1934. Oleoresin from individual trees of slash and longleaf pine. Indus. Engin. Chem., 26:66–69.

Blight, Margaret M., and I. R. C. McDonald. 1963. Note on *l*-sabinene from *Pinus muricata*. New Zeal. Jour. Sci. and Technol., 6:229–31.

Bougault, J., and L. Bourdier. 1908. Sur les cires des conifères: Nouveau groupe de principes immédiats naturels. Compt. Rend., 147:1311–13.

——. 1911. Nouvelles recherches sur les cires des conifères. Jour. Pharm. Chim., 3:101–3.

—— and E. Cattelain. 1928. Nouvelles recherches sur les étholides des cires de conifères. Compt. Rend., 186:1746–48.

Ching Te May and Kim K. Ching. 1962. Fatty acids in pollen of some coniferous species. Science, 138:890–91.

Creighton, R. H. J., R. Darnley Gibbs, and H. Hibbert. 1944. Studies on lignin and related compounds. LXXV. Alkaline nitrobenzene oxydation of plant materials and application to taxonomic classification. Amer. Chem. Soc. Jour., 66:32–37.

Cvrkal, Harymir. 1958. Ein Beitrag zur Untersuchung der Waldkieferaborten (*Pinus silvestris* L.) Sborn. Českoslov. Akad. Zemedel. Ved. Sborn. Lesnictvi Rocnik, 4(4):213–28.

Dauben, William G., and W. F. German. 1966. The structure of lambertianic acid. A new diterpene acid. Tetrahedron, 22:679–83.

——, William E. Thiessen, and Paul R. Resnick. 1962. Cembrene, a 14-membered ring diterpene hydrocarbon. Amer. Chem. Soc. Jour., 84:2015–16.

——, Boris Weinstein, Peter Lim, and Arthur B. Anderson. 1961. The structure of δ-cadinol. Tetrahedron, 15(1–4): 217–22.

Dillman, A. C., and T. H. Hopper. 1943. Effect of climate on the yield and oil content of flaxseed and on the iodine number of linseed oil. (U.S. Dept. Agr. Tech. Bul. 844.) Government Printing Office, Washington, D.C.

Dupont, George, and M. Barraud. 1925. Sur l'essence de térébenthine du pin noir d'Autriche (*P. laricio* austriaca). Proc.-Verb. Soc. Sci. Phys. Naturelles de Bordeaux, Année 1923–24. Pp. 6–12.

Eglinton, G., A. G. Gonzalez, R. J. Hamilton, and R. A. Raphael. 1962. Hydrocarbon constituents of the wax coating of plant leaves: A taxonomic survey. Phytochemistry, 1:89–102.

Enzell, C., and O. Theander. 1962. The constituents of conifer needles. II. Pinifolic acid: A new diterpene acid isolated from *Pinus sylvestris* L. Acta Chem. Scand., 16(3):607–14.

Erdtman, Holger. 1955. The chemistry of heartwood constituents of conifers and their taxonomic importance. 156–180 Separatum, Experientia Supplementum Birkhäuser Verlag. Basel/Stuttgart. Also as 14th Internatl. Cong. Pure Appl. Chem., Zurich, 1955, Proc. Pp. 156–80.

——. 1959. Conifer chemistry and taxonomy of conifers. In Symposium II. Biochemistry of wood. Proc. 4th Internatl. Cong. Biochem., Vienna, 1958, 2:1–28.

Euler, H. v., L. Ahlström, B. Högberg, and I. Pettersson. 1945. Coenzyme, Enzyme, Wuchsstoffe und Reizstoffe in Pflanzenorganen. I. Arkiv. Kem. Min. Geol. 19A Heft No. 4. Pp. 1–15.

Forde, Margot B. 1964. Inheritance of turpentine composition in *P. attenuata* × *radiata* hybrids. New Zeal. Jour. Bot., 2:53–59.

—— and Margaret M. Blight. 1964. Geographical variation in the turpentine of Bishop pine. New Zeal. Jour. Bot., 2:44–52.

Foreman, E. Leon, and D. T. Englis. 1931. Isolation and identification of a polysaccharide from southern yellow pine. Indus. Engin. Chem., 23:415–16.

GUENTHER, ERNEST. 1952. The essential oils. Vol. VI. D. Van Nostrand Co., Inc., Princeton, N.J. Pp. 217–53.

HAAGEN-SMIT, A. J., TIAO-HSIN WANG, and N. T. MIROV. 1951. Composition of gum turpentines of pines. XIII. A report on *Pinus albicaulis*. Amer. Pharm. Assoc. Jour. Sci. Ed., **40**:557–59.

HAMILTON, J. K., E. V. PARTLOW, and N. S. THOMPSON. 1958. The behavior of wood hemicelluloses during pulping. I. Examination of the xylose-containing hemicelluloses associated with hardwood and softwood pulps. Tappi, **41**:803–11.

—— and N. S. THOMPSON. 1959. A comparison of the carbohydrates of hardwoods and softwoods. Tappi, **42**:752–60.

HARRIS, GEORGE C. 1948. Resin acids. V. The composition of the gum oleoresin acids of *Pinus palustris*. Amer. Chem. Soc. Jour., **70**:3671–74.

—— and THOMAS F. SANDERSON. 1948a. Resin acids. I. An improved method of isolation of resin acids: the isolation of new abietic-type acid, neoabietic acid. Amer. Chem. Soc. Jour., **70**:334–39.

—— and THOMAS F. SANDERSON. 1948b. Resin acids. III. The isolation of dextropimaric acid and a new pimaric-type acid, isadextrapimaric acid. Amer. Chem. Soc. Jour., **70**:2079–81.

HATA, K., and M. SOGO. 1954. Detection of the phenolic substances of *Pinus densiflora, P. thunbergii, P. pentaphylla* var. *himekomatsu* and *P. armandi*. J. Jap. Forest Soc., **36**:8–11.

—— and MURAO SOGO. 1957. Chemical studies on the bark I on the extractives, especially on wax from the outer bark of Japanese red pine (*P. densiflora*, S et Z.) Jour. Jap. Forestry Soc., **39**:102–6.

HEGNAUER, R. 1962. Chemotaxonomie der Pflanzen. Part I (including gymnosperms). Birkhaüser Verlag, Basel.

HERGERT, HERBERT L. 1956. The flavonoids of lodgepole pine bark. Jour. Organic Chem., **21**:534–37.

——. 1957. Flavonoids and tannin precursors of yellow and white pine. Amer. Chem. Soc., Abs. Papers, 131st Mtg., Amer. Chem. Soc. P. 6E.

——. 1960. Chemical composition of tannins and polyphenols from conifer wood and bark. Forest Prod. Jour., **10**:610–17.

HERTY, C. H. 1908. The optical rotation of spirits of turpentine. Amer. Chem. Soc. Jour., **30**:863–67.

HILLIS, W. E. (ed.). 1962. Wood extractives and their significance to the pulp and paper industries. Academic Press, Inc., N.Y.

HIRST, E. L. 1962. Chemical structure of hemicelluloses. Pure and Appl. Chem. **5**:53–66.

HISAMICHI, SUIJI. 1961. Microchemical investigation on the distribution of pollen flavonoid components. J. Pharm. Soc. Japan, **81**:446–52.

HUNT, G. M. 1912. Steam distillation of needles, twigs and cones of western conifers. U.S. Dept. of Agr. Forest Serv. Dist. 5, Unpublished Rpts.

ILOFF, P. M., JR., and N. T. MIROV. 1956. Composition of gum turpentines of pines. XXV. A report on two white pines: *Pinus koraiensis* from Korea and *P. peuce* from Macedonia. Amer. Pharm. Assoc. Jour., Sci. Ed., **45**:77–81.

IVANOV, S. L. 1915. Physiologische Merkmale der Pflanzen; ihre Variabilität und ihre Beziehung zur Evolutions Theorie. Bot. Centbl. Beiherte., **321**:66–80.

——. 1926. Die Evolution des Stoffes in der Pflanzenwelt und das Grundgesetz der Biochemie. Ber. Deut. Bot. Gesell. **44**:31–39.

——. 1937. Klimaticheskaia izmenchivost' khimicheskogo sostava rastenii (Climate variability of chemical composition in plants). Akad. Nauk S.S.S.R. Izv. Otd. Mat. i Estest. Nauk Ser. Biol. Pp. 1789–1800.

JORGENSEN, ERIK. 1961. The formation of pinosylvin and its monoethyl ether in the sapwood of *Pinus resinosa* Ait. Canad. Jour. Bot., **39**:1765–72.

KARIYONE, TATSUO, and KOICHIRO ISOI. 1956. Studies of plant waxes. VIII. Leaf wax of *Pinus thunbergii* Parl. Pharm. Soc. Japan Jour., **76**:473–74.

——, MITSUO TAKAHASHI, AYA NITTA, and YOSHINAO TSUNEHISA. 1956. The alkaloids of coniferous plants. I. Pharm. Soc. Japan Jour., **76**:611.

KARRER, PAUL, C. H. EUGSTER, and M. FAUST. 1950. Über das Auftreten von Carotinoiden in Pollen und Staubbeuteln verschiedener Pflanzen. Helvetica Chim. Acta, 33(2):300–301.

KOBAYASHI, HIROSHI, and SABURO AKIYOSHI. 1962. Thunbergine: A macrocyclic diterpene. Chem. Soc. Japan Bul., 35:1044–45.

KONDO, TAMIO, HIROYUKI ITO, and TOMOZO MIYOSHI. 1955a. Wood extractives. II. On the heartwood of *Pinus koraiensis* S. et Z. Bul. Govt. For. Exp. Sta. No. 78: 79–83.

――――, HIROYUKI ITO, and TOMOZO MIYOSHI. 1955b. Wood extractives. III. Heartwood of *Pinus pumila*. Govt. For. Exp. Sta. Tokyo. Bul. 79. Pp. 110–12.

KORCHEMKIN, F. I. 1949. Metilirovannye veshchestva kambial'nogo soka sosny (Methylated substances of cambium sap of pine). Biokhimiia, 14:256–58.

KRESTINSKY, V., S. MALEVAKAIA, and F. SOLODKY. 1932. Vyiasnenie vliianiia geograficheskych faktorov tipov lesa na sostav zhivichnykh skipidarov iz *Pinus silvestris* (On influence of geography factors and forest types on composition of gum turpentine of *Pinus silvestris*). Zhur. Prikl. Khim., 5:950–57.

KRUGMAN, STANLEY. 1956. The anthocyanin and leuco-anthocyanins of sugar pine seedlings. Forest Sci., 2:273–80.

――――. 1959. The leuco-anthocyanin distribution in the genus *Pinus*. Forest Sci., 5:169–73.

KURTH, E. F., and JAMES K. HUBBARD. 1951. Extractives from ponderosa pine bark. Indus. Engin. Chem., 43:896–900.

――――, V. RAMANATHAN, and K. VENKATARAMAN. 1955. The coloring matters of ponderosa pine bark. Current Sci., 24:157.

LAIDLAW, R. A., and G. A. SMITH. 1962. Arabinogalactans of *Pinus contorta*. Chem. and Indus. No. 10. P. 462.

LINDSTEDT, GÖSTA. 1951. Constituents of pine heartwood. XXVI. A general discussion. Acta Chemica Scand., 5:129–38.

―――― and ALFONS MISIORNY. 1951. Constituents of pine heartwood. XXV. Investigation of forty-eight *Pinus* species by paper partition chromatography. Acta Chem. Scand., 5:121–28.

LOEBLICH, VIRGINIA M., DORIS E. BALDWIN, and RAY V. LAWRENCE. 1955. The isolation of a new resin acid from gum rosin—palustric acid. Amer. Chem. Soc. Jour., 77:2823–25.

McNAIR, J. B. 1929. The taxonomic and climatic distribution of oils, fats and waxes in plants. Amer. Jour. Bot., 16:832–41.

――――. 1930. A study of some characteristics of vegetable oils. Field Mus. Nat. Hist., Chicago, Pub. 276 Bot. Ser., 9(2):47–68.

――――. 1934. The evolutionary status of plant families in relation to some chemical properties. Amer. Jour. Bot., 21:427–52.

MAHESH, J. V. B., and T. R. SESHADRI. 1954. Chemical components of commercial woods and related plant materials. II. The heartwood of *Pinus excelsa* Wall. Jour. Sci. Indus. Res. (India) 13B:835–41.

MIROV, N. T. 1948. The terpenes (in relation to the biology of genus *Pinus*). Ann. Rev. Biochem., 17:521–40.

――――. 1951. Composition of gum turpentines of pines. XIV. A report on three Mexican pines: *Pinus ayacahuite*, *P. cembroides*, and *P. pinceana*. Amer. Pharm. Assoc. Jour., Sci. Ed., 41:673–76.

――――. 1956. Composition of turpentine of lodgepole × jack pine hybrids. Canad. Jour. Bot., 34:443–57.

――――. 1961. Composition of gum turpentines of Pines. (U.S. Dept. Agr. Tech. Bul. 1239.) Government Printing Office, Washington, D.C.

――――, J. W. DUFFIELD, and A. R. LIDDICOET. 1952. Altitudinal races of ponderosa pine: A 12-year progress report. Jour. Forestry, 50:825–31.

―――― and P. M. ILOFF, JR. 1955. Composition of gum turpentines of pines. XXIV. A report on two Asiatic pines: *Pinus armandi* and *P. bungeana*. Amer. Pharm. Assoc. Jour., Sci. Ed. 44:424–27.

———— and P. M. ILOFF, JR. 1956. Composition of gum turpentines of pines. XXVIII. A report on *Pinus edulis* from eastern Arizona, *P. tropicalis* from Cuba, and *P. elliottii* var. *densa* from Florida. Amer. Pharm. Assoc. Jour., Sci. Ed., **45**: 629–34.

————, EUGENE ZAVARIN, and JOSEPH G. BICHO. 1962. Composition of gum turpentines of pines: *Pinus nelsonii* and *Pinus occidentalis*. Jour. Pharm. Sci., **51**:1131–35.

MIYAZAKI, MAKOTO, and MORITAMI YASUE. 1956. Natural resins. I. Isolation of palustric acid from oleoresin of *Pinus densiflora*. Govt. Forest Expt. Sta., Tokyo Mokuzai Gakkaishi, **2**(5):210–12. In English.

NAYAK, U. RAMDAS, and SUKH DEV. 1963. Longicycline: The first tetracyclic sesquiterpene. Tetrahedron Letters No. 4. Pp. 243–46.

OUDIN, A. 1939. Les variations du pouvoir rotatoire de l'essence de térébenthine du pin maritime et la notion d'individualité chimique. Assoc. Franç. pour l'Avanc. des Sci. Rap. Commun. Pin Maritime, 62d Cong. Archaron, Sept. 22–27, 1938. Pp. 123–125.

PEARL, IRWIN A. 1964. Century-old puzzle. Chem. Engin. News, **42**(27):81–93.

PENFOLD, A. R. 1935. The physiological forms of the eucalypts as determined by the chemical composition of the essential oils and their influence on the botanical nomenclature. Australasian Jour. Pharm., **16**:168–71.

PENTEGOVA, V. A., O. MOTL, and V. GEROUT. 1961. O vydelenii (t)-δ-kadinola iz zhivitsy Pinus sibirica R. Mayr i ego identichnosti s torreolom i seskvigoiolom (On obtaining +δ-kadinola from oleoresin of *Pinus sibirica* [R] [?] Mayr and its identity with torreol and sesquigoyol). Dok. Akad. Nauk S.S.S.R., **138**:850–51.

PLOUVIER, VICTOR. 1952. Sur la recherche du pinitol chez quelques conifères et plantes voisines. Compt. Rend., **234**:362–64.

————. 1953. Sur le pinitol des conifères et le québrachitol des acéracées; recherche de ces deux itols dans quelques autres familles. Compt. Rend., **236**:317–19.

————. 1958. Sur la recherche d'éthers méthyliques des inositols dans quelques groupes botaniques. Compt. Rend., **247**:2423–26.

————. 1960. Nouvelles recherches de cyclitols dans quelques groupes botaniques; Signification phylogénétique du séquoyitol. Compt. Rend., **251**:131–33.

RAMANATHAN, V., and K. VENKATARAMAN. 1954. Synthetical experiments in the chromone group. XXX. A synthesis of 3:5:8:3':4'-pentahydroxyflavone and its non-identity with ponderosin. Indian Acad. Sci. Proc., **39**(Sect. A): 90–97.

ROEZL, B., ET CIE. 1958. Catalogue de graines et plantes mexicaines. Imprimerie Felix Maleteste et Cie., Paris.

ROWE, JOHN W. 1962. Progress in chemical conversion. Forest Prod. Jour., **12**: 124–40.

SANDERMANN, WILHELM. 1939–40. Über das schwedische kiefernadel Öl und seine Bestandteile. Seifensieder-Zeitung, **66**:803, 833, 863 (1939); **67**:15, 45 (1940).

SAVORY, B. M. 1962. The taxonomy of *Pinus khasya* (Royle) and *Pinus insularis* (Endlicher). Empire Forestry Rev., **41**(1):67–80.

SCHEUBLE, RUDOLF. 1942. Die ungewöhnliche Zusammensetzung der Terpentinöle von *Pinus sabiniana* und *jeffreyi*. Ein Beitrag zur Klärung des Gegenstandes. Centbl. f. das Gesam. Forstw., **68**:64–69.

SCHORGER, A. W. 1919. Contribution to the chemistry of American conifers. Wisc. Acad. Sci., Arts, Letters, Trans., **19**:728–66.

SCOTT, R. W., and MARY JANE STROHL. 1962. Extraction and identification of lipids from loblolly pine pollen. Phytochemistry, **1**:189–93.

SEBE, YEIGAI. 1935a. The wood turpentine oil from *Pinus formosana* Hayata. I. Chem. Soc. Japan Jour., **56**:1118–36.

————. 1935b. The wood turpentine oil from *Pinus formosana* Hayata. II. Chem. Soc. Japan Jour., **56**:1137–41.

————. 1940. On "Sesquigoyol," a sesquiterpene alcohol of high melting point. Chem. Soc. Japan Jour., **61**:1269–74.

SIMONSEN, JOHN LIONEL, and MADYAR GOPAL RAU. 1922. The essential oil from the oleoresin of *Pinus khasya*. Indian Forest Rec., **9**(4): 112–15.

SMITH, LESLIE V., and EUGENE ZAVARIN. 1960. Free mono- and oligo-saccharides of some California conifers. Tappi, 43:218–221.

STRAIN, H. H. 1935. Carotene. IX. Carotenes from different sources and some properties of α- and β-carotene. Jour. Biol. Chem., 111:85–93.

STROHL, MARY JANE, and MARGARET K. SEIKEL. 1964. Polyphenols of pine pollens: A survey. Phytochemistry, 4:383–99.

SWAIN, T. (ed.). 1963. Chemical plant taxonomy. Academic Press, Inc., New York.

TAKAHASHI, MITSUO, IKO TOKUZO, AKIHIKO MIZUTANI, and KOICHIRO ISOI. 1960. Constituents of the plants of Coniferae and allied orders. XLIII. Distribution of flavonoids and stilbenoids of Coniferae leaves. Jour. Pharm. Soc. Japan, 80: 1488–92.

TALLENT, W. H., and E. C. HORNING. 1956. The structure of pinidine. Amer. Chem. Soc. Jour., 78:4467–69.

———, V. L. STROMBERG, and E. C. HORNING. 1955. *Pinus* alkaloids: The alkaloids of *P. sabiniana* Dougl. and related species. Am. Chem. Soc. Jour., 77:6361–64.

TIMELL, T. E. 1957. Carbohydrate composition of ten North American species of wood. Tappi, 40:568–72.

TONG, S. TRAVIS. 1954. Macrocyclic compounds from pine needle wax. Soap, Perfumery and Cosmetics, 27(1):58–61.

WADMAN, W. H., ARTHUR B. ANDERSON, and W. Z. HASSID. 1954. The structure of an arabogalactan from Jeffrey pine (*Pinus jeffreyi*). Am. Chem. Soc. Jour., 76: 4097–4100.

WILEY, H. W. 1891. Pine tree sugar. Am. Chem. Soc. Jour., 13:228–37.

WILLIAMS, ALETTE L., and M. H. BANNISTER. 1962. Composition of gum turpentines from twenty-two species of pines grown in New Zealand. Jour. Pharm. Sci., 51: 970–75.

WILLIAMS, ROGER J. 1956. Biochemical individuality: The basis for the genetotrophic concept. John Wiley & Sons, Inc., New York.

WISE, LOUIS E. (Ed.). 1944. Wood chemistry. Reinhold Publishing Corp., New York.

ZANINI, C., A. DAL POZZ, and A. DANSI. 1961. Principal components of oil from dwarf pine needles. Bol. Chim. Farm., 100:83–92.

# 8

# Chemical Geography

## GENERAL REMARKS

Geographical distribution of blood groups proved to be useful in studies of the origin and migration of different races of man (Candela, 1942; also see Map 14, p. 72, Mirov, 1951). In a similar manner the geographical distribution of chemical constituents could prove as useful in studies of the genus *Pinus* (Mirov, 1961b).

Some may say that distribution of blood types among the human races is a recent phenomenon while the distributional pattern of chemical substances found in pines has been in the making for over a hundred million years. But most likely blood types have been developing also for a long time, even before the advent of man.

The volatile portion of the oleoresin is chosen as the most suitable for the purpose of studying the chemical geography of pines. This choice is based on the extent of reliable data as well as on the evidence of useful relationships between chemical constitution and botanical classifications (Chapter 9, page 536).

Data on occurrence of turpentine components of the genus *Pinus* may be found in Mirov (1961a).

The chemical composition of turpentines of species rather than of individual trees is considered in this chapter. It has already been mentioned in Chapter 7 that variation in the chemical composition of turpentine may be considerable. For instance, in *P. monticola* No. 4 as a species, limonene plays a subordinate part, but there are encountered occasional individual trees whose turpentine contains a very large percentage of this terpene. *Pinus ponderosa* No. 14, whose range extends from British Columbia to the Mexican border of the United States and from the Pacific Coast to western Nebraska, is a $\Delta^3$-carene species. There occur, however, individual trees where this terpene is wanting. In *P. sylvestris*

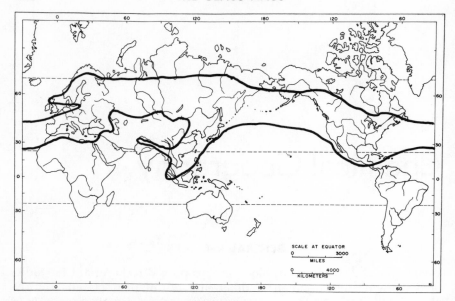

**Fig. 8–1.** Geographical distribution of α-pinene in the genus *Pinus*. This terpene is found in almost all pine species and, thus, is distributed throughout the area of the genus.

No. 69, no matter where it is found, a composite sample of turpentine always contains Δ³-carene. In one instance, however (Krestinsky and Bashenova-Kozlovskaia, 1930), an individual pine is described that yielded turpentine containing no Δ³-carene but consisted mostly of β-phellandrene. In considering individual variability that is encountered in any biological study, it is wiser to base the conclusions of geographical distribution of chemical components not on individual trees, but rather on the populations.

When components of pine turpentines are put on a geographical map, a certain pattern in their distribution becomes evident. First we shall consider bicyclic terpenes, which are more widely distributed than any other components of pine turpentines.

## BICYCLIC TERPENES

Geographical distribution of α-pinene coincides with the area of the genus *Pinus* as a whole. This terpene is not found (unless there are traces) in *P. albicaulis* No. 1, *P. sabiniana* No. 10, *P. jeffreyi* No. 13, *P. torreyana* No. 11, *P. washoensis* No. 15, and in some varieties of *P. contorta* No. 16. If α-pinene is absent in these species, it is present in other pines of the same regions (Fig. 8–1).

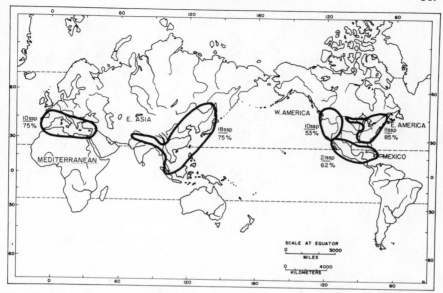

**Fig. 8–2.** β-Pinene is widely distributed. More species with this terpene are found in eastern North America and in Eurasia than in western America and Mexico.

The second most widely found pine terpene, β-pinene, has a strange geographical distribution. It is present in quantities larger than a trace in more than fifty pine species, generally (but not always) being associated with α-pinene. It occurs in all but two pine species of the eastern United States, in all but two Mediterranean pines, and in all except six eastern Asiatic pines. It is present in turpentines of ten out of nineteen western American pines and in twenty-one pines out of thirty-four pines of Mexico, including the five Caribbean species (Fig. 8–2).

**Table 8–1.** β-Pinene Distribution by Regions

| Region | Total Number | Species β-Pinene Absent | | Species β-Pinene Present | |
|---|---|---|---|---|---|
| | | Species | Per Cent | Species | Per Cent |
| Western America | 19 | 9 | 47 | 10 | 53 |
| Mexico and Caribbean | 34 | 13 | 38 | 21 | 62 |
| Eastern Asia | 24 | 6 | 25 | 18 | 75 |
| Mediterranean region | 12 | 2 | 17 | 10 | 83 |
| Eastern America | 13 | 2 | 15 | 11 | 85 |
| Northern Eurasia | 3 | 0 | 0 | 3 | 100 |

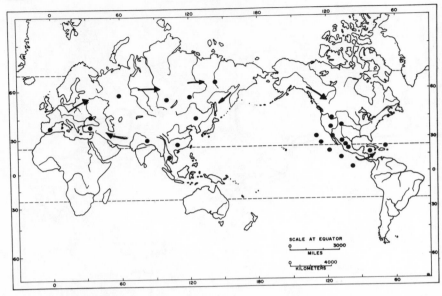

**Fig. 8–3.** Δ³-Carene is essentially an eastern Asiatic and western American terpene. It may be postulated that it came to the Caribbean area from western America via Mexico, whereas it came to northern Eurasia from eastern Asia via the Mediterranean region (cf. Chapter 2). This terpene is found in many species of *Pinus*. (See Mirov, 1961.)

When the above data are presented in tabulated form, it is seen that there is a higher percentage of β-pinene pines in the eastern United States, Mediterranean region, and northern Eurasia than in western America, Mexico with the Caribbean area, and eastern Asia. The author is not prepared to give any explanation of this pattern of distribution (Table 8–1).

The third major bicyclic terpene of the genus *Pinus*—Δ³-carene—is found in four species of western America, including *P. ponderosa* No. 14, in eight species of Mexico, and in two species of the Caribbean islands. The geographical area of Δ³-carene in the New World thus extends latitudinally from western Canada to Central America, continuing into the Caribbean islands; longitudinally it extends from the Pacific Coast of western America to western Nebraska.

In the Old World Δ³-carene is found in three southeastern Asiatic pines —*P. roxburghii* No. 93, *P. merkusii* No. 101, *P. yunnanensis* No. 103 (in the latter only 2 per cent; unpublished data), and in the three widely distributed pines of northern Eurasia—*P. pumila* No. 68, *P. sibirica* No. 67, and *P. sylvestris* No. 69. In the Mediterranean region Δ³-carene occurs, besides *P. sylvestris*, only in two, perhaps three, pines of the eastern part

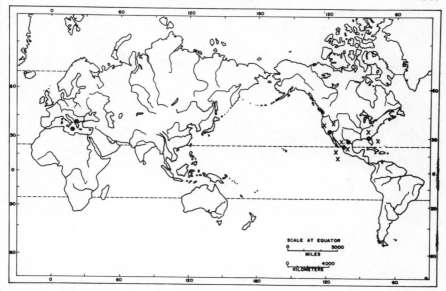

**Fig. 8–4.** *L*-Limonene (dots) and methyl chavicol (crosses). "Limonene pines" are found in the southern parts of the *Pinus* area. These are Nos. 11, 30, 37, 42, 75, and 80. In small quantities, this terpene is found in over thirty species. Methyl chavicol is found only in New World pines (Nos. 13, 14, 24, 42, 49, 52, 61, and 63, and in the higher boiling fractions of 22 and 23) (see Table 1–2).

of the region: *P. brutia* No. 78, *P. pityusa* No. 79, and most likely *P. eldarica* No. 81. Occurrence of $\Delta^3$-carene is shown on the map, Fig. 8–3.

$\Delta^3$-Carene does not occur in the eastern United States (including adjacent parts of Canada); neither is it found in the Mediterranean area save for the above-mentioned exceptions.

A bicyclic terpene, sabinene, recently discovered independently in southern varieties of *P. muricata* No. 18 of California by the New Zealand workers (Chapter 7, page 496) and by the U.S. Forest Service researchers (unpublished report), has the distinction of being found in large quantities only in this species of the genus *Pinus* (Fig. 8–12).

## MONOCYCLIC TERPENES

Turning to the three monocyclic terpenes of pines, terpinolene is not restricted to any particular area, occurring sporadically and in very small amounts. Limonene also has a scattered distribution, being found in relatively small amounts in many species and in many parts of the northern hemisphere and occasionally in large amounts in individual trees of these species. In several pine species, however, this terpene is found in

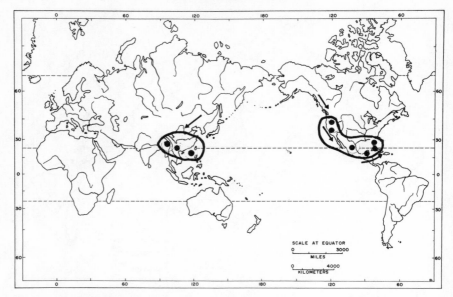

**Fig. 8–5.** β-Phellandrene (dots) is found in three pine species of southeastern Asia (Nos. 102, 104, and 105) and in six western American pines (Nos. 12, 16, 23, 61, 62, and 63) (see Table 1–2).

very large quantities and always in its levorotatory form. The "limonene pines" are tabulated below, showing their geographical occurrence.

| Species | Occurrence | Limonen in Turpentine (per cent) |
|---|---|---|
| *P. pinceana* No. 37 | N. E. Mexico | 80 |
| *P. lumholtzii* No. 42 | N. W. Mexico | 75 |
| *P. pinea* No. 73 | Mediterranean | Over 95 |
| *P. heldreichii* No. 75 | Balkans | Up to 58 |
| *P. serotina* No. 30 | S. E. United States | 90 |
| *P. torreyana* No. 11 | California | 75 |

It is seen from the above tabulation and from the map, Fig. 8–4, that the six "limonene pines" are limited to the southern part of the area occupied by the genus *Pinus*.

The third monocyclic terpene, *l*-β-phellandrene, is relatively rare, being found in eight or nine species of pines, but its geographic distribution is interesting (Fig. 8–5). It is not found in the turpentine of eastern American pines, except *P. elliottii* No. 23 and its newly described variety,

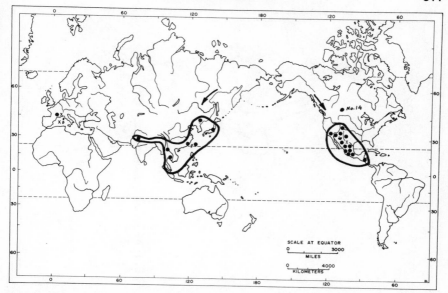

**Fig. 8–6.** Sesquiterpenes: longifolene (dots) and caryophyllene (crosses) in species Nos. 37, 73, and 80 (see Table 1–2).

*densa* No. 63. Occurrence of β-phellandrene in *P. elliottii* No. 63 requires a thorough investigation. More about this will be said in Chapter 9.

β-Phellandrene comprises the largest part of *P. contorta* No. 16 turpentine; in some populations the entire turpentine is composed of this terpene. Its occurrence extends to Mexico, where it is found in *P. patula* No. 61, and it occurs in Central America from where it extends into the Caribbean area and possibly to southern Florida (*P. elliottii* var. *densa* No. 63). In eastern Asia, β-phellandrene is found in *P. tabulaeformis* No. 102, *P. khasya* No. 104, and *P. insularis* No. 105.

## SESQUITERPENES AND DITERPENES

Longifolene is a tricyclic sesquiterpene (see Chapter 7), rather widely distributed among the species of the genus *Pinus* (Fig. 8–6). So far it has been found in twenty-three pine species: seven of eastern Asia (including *P. roxburghii* No. 93 of the Himalaya); one in the Mediterranean region (No. 80) and fourteen in western America and Mexico (including one species, No. 62, of Central America). Minute amounts of longifolene were reported in a Caribbean pine—*P. occidentalis* No. 64 (Mirov, Zavarin, and Bicho, 1962).

No longifolene has been reported from the eastern United States and adjacent parts of Canada. A sesquiterpene, caryophyllene, was found in

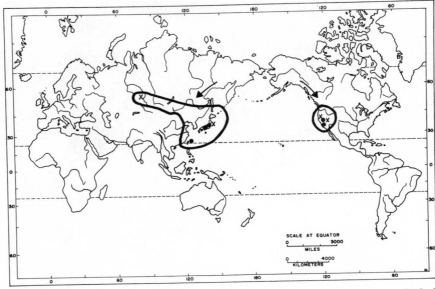

**Fig. 8–7.** A sesquiterpene, δ-cadinene (dots), and a sesquiterpene alcohol, δ-cadinol (crosses).

two Mediterranean pines (Nos. 80 and 73) and in one Mexican pine (No. 37).

δ-Cadinene is found in two western American pines, *P. albicaulis* No. 1 and *P. flexilis* No. 2, and in eastern Asia in either *P. pentaphylla* No. 83 or *P. himekomatsu* No. 84, reported as *P. parviflora*.

A sesquiterpene alcohol, δ-cadinol, is found in America in *P. albicaulis* No. 1 and probably in *P. lambertiana* No. 3; and in Asia in *P. parviflora* (i.e., Nos. 83 and 84), *P. armandi* No. 86, *P. morrisonicola* No. 85, and *P. sibirica* No. 68. It is possible that δ-cadinene also will be found in the tails of *P. peuce* No. 71 turpentine (Fig. 8–7).

Even more striking is the geographical distribution of a diterpene hydrocarbon, cembrene, whose discovery and nomenclature were described earlier in this book (Chapter 7). So far, cembrene has been found only in one haploxylon pine of western America (*P. albicaulis* No. 1), but there is evidence that it is also found in turpentine of *P. flexilis* No. 2 of the same region.

In eastern Asia it is found in haploxylon pines of Japan, in Formosa, on the mainland in Korea, China, and the Russian Far East. It was also discovered in *P. peuce* No. 71 of the Balkans. A diterpene alcohol is apparently also present in the turpentine of this pine. *Pinus peuce* is a well-known Tertiary relic of the Balkans and paleobotanists believe that it

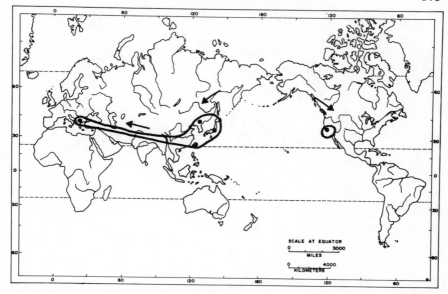

**Fig. 8–8.** A diterpene hydrocarbon, cembrene, is found in species Nos. 1, 71, 82, 86, and 89 (see Table 1–2).

came there from eastern Asia via the ancient mountain ranges north of and parallel to the present Himalaya.

Unpublished reports from Dauben's laboratory (University of California, Berkeley) indicate that traces of cembrene are found in the Mediterranean *P. pinea* No. 73, a diploxylon pine possessing seed characters and wood anatomy similar to the eastern Asian haploxylon pines of the group *Gerardianae* (Fig. 8–8). Akiyoshi (1937) reported occurrence of cembrene in stumpwood of *P. thunbergii* No. 97 (see Chapter 7).

## ALKANES

*n*-Undecane is found in three eastern Asiatic pines, three western American pines, and two Mexican pines; thus it is found on both sides of the Pacific (Fig. 8–9).

*n*-Heptane is found in nine species of pines. Its geographical distribution is restricted to western America, including Mexico (Fig. 8–10).

While *n*-undecane is found in pines in small proportions, *n*-heptane occurs in much larger amounts. The volatile part of oleoresin (Chapter 7) of two California pines, *P. jeffreyi* No. 13 and *P. sabiniana* No. 10, consists almost entirely of *n*-heptane; the tails contain aliphatic aldehydes.

Traces of *n*-heptane were reported in *P. nelsonii* No. 38 of northeast

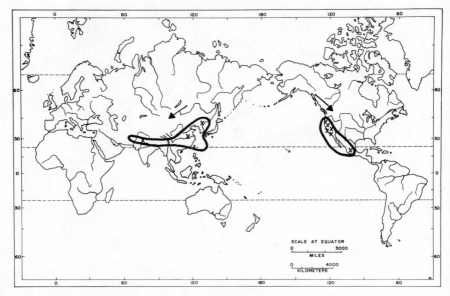

**Fig. 8–9.** An alkane, *n*-undecane, is found in five western American, one Mexican, and three eastern Asiatic species of *Pinus* (Nos. 4, 11, 12, 14, 35, 57, 82, 86, and 91) (see Table 1–2).

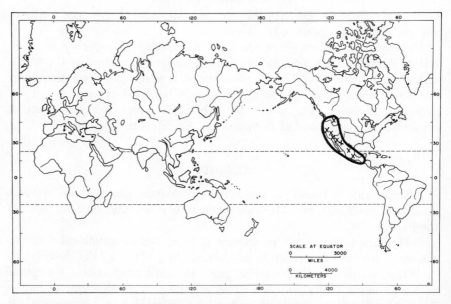

**Fig. 8–10.** An alkane, *n*-heptane, whose distribution is restricted to western America, extending to Mexico (species Nos. 4, 10, 12, 13, 33, 35, 47, and 57) (see Table 1–2).

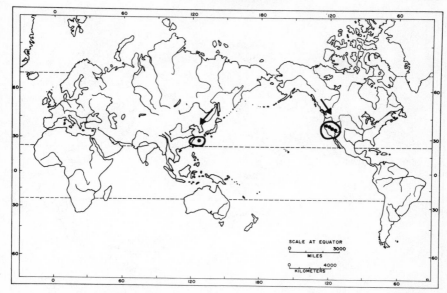

**Fig. 8–11.** Aldehydes are found in four species of *Pinus* in western America, Nos. 10, 11, 12, and 13, and in one species, No. 98, in the Ryukyus, in eastern Asia (see Table 1–2).

Mexico and in *P. occidentalis* No. 64 of Haiti (Mirov, Zavarin, and Bicho, 1962).

## OTHER COMPONENTS OF PINE TURPENTINES

Aliphatic aldehydes are found in four relict California pines and also in *P. luchuensis* of the Ryukyu Islands (Fig. 8–11). None has been yet detected in other regions of the genus *Pinus*.

The only aliphatic ester occurring in pine turpentines, ethyl caprylate, is found only in one pine, western American *P. edulis* No. 8. There is an indication that it also occurs in *P. monophylla* No. 7 (Fig. 8–12).

Of the two olefinic open-chain terpenes ($C_nH_{2n-4}$), occurring in turpentines, $\beta$-myrcene is found in small quantities (not more than five per cent) in seven pine species; three of America and four of Eurasia, except the southeastern part of the continent. The other olefine, ocimene, is restricted to the southwestern United States (Fig. 8–12).

Only three terpene esters have been found in pine turpentines: two of these, bornyl formate in *P. canariensis* No. 72 and terpinyl acetate in *P. albicaulis* No. 1 of western America, are rare and local. The third one, bornyl acetate, has been detected in two western American pines (Nos.

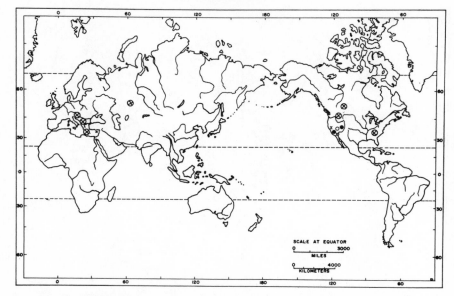

**Fig. 8–12.** Geographical distribution of several components of pine turpentine: a terpene, sabinene (uncircled crosses), in No. 18; an aliphatic ester, ethyl caprylate (circle), in No. 8; and two olefinic, open chain terpenes—ocimene (dots), in Nos. 8 and 9; and myrcene (circled crosses), in Nos. 8, 14, 24, 69, 71, 74, and 77 (see Table 1–2).

4 and 5), in three eastern Asiatic pines (Nos. 82, 86, and 99) and in a Balkan pine, *P. peuce* No. 71 (Fig. 8–13).

Methyl chavicol, a phenolic ether, is an unusual component of pine turpentines. Its geographic distribution is restricted to America. In the eastern part of the continent it is found to the extent of 1 per cent in *P. serotina* No. 30 and *P. taeda* No. 61 and as a trace in the high-boiling fractions of *P. palustris* No. 22 and *P. elliottii* No. 23. In four western American and six Mexican pines it occurs in somewhat larger quantities, amounting to 2, 3, and even 5 per cent of the weight of the turpentine (Fig. 8–4). It is also found in two Caribbean species, Nos. 63 and 64.

## CONCLUSIONS

In considering the geographical distribution of the components of pine turpentines as presented on the maps (Figs. 8–1 to 8–13), one will notice that two of these components, α-pinene and, to a somewhat lesser extent β-pinene, are widely distributed throughout the geographical area of the genus *Pinus*.

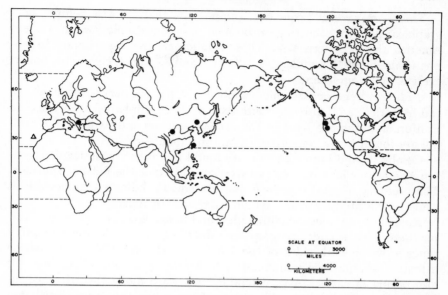

**Fig. 8–13.** Geographical distribution of terpene esters of the genus *Pinus:* bornyl formate (triangle) in No. 72; bornyl acetate (dots), in Nos. 4, 5, 71, 82, 86, and 89; and terpinyl acetate (crosses) in No. 1 (see Table 1–2).

Distribution of the third major component of pine turpentines, $\Delta^3$-carene, requires further comment. In the New World this bicyclic terpene is found in western America, extending to Mexico and Central America; it is absent in eastern America.

In the Old World $\Delta^3$-carene occurs in eastern Asia, from which it extends both northwest (species Nos. 67 and 68) and southwest along the Himalaya as far as the eastern Mediterranean area (species Nos. 78 and 79). It is also found in *P. sylvestris* No. 69, which is both a Mediterranean and northern Eurasiatic pine and which occurs over an enormous area (see Chapter 3, No. 69). This particular case has to be considered in context with paleogeography of *P. sylvestris*. It is possible that originally $\Delta^3$-carene came to western Europe from eastern Asia via the Mediterranean region. During the glacial age *P. sylvestris* perished in northern Europe, being preserved in the more southern refugia. After the postglacial reinvasion of *P. sylvestris*, $\Delta^3$-carene extended to the northern parts of Europe and eastward across northern Asia until it reached almost the Pacific Coast of Siberia. Paleogeographical history of $\Delta^3$-carene in *P. sylvestris* may be entirely different from that of $\Delta^3$-carene in *P. sibirica* No. 67 and *P. pumila* No. 68, which both expanded from the east of Asia in a northwesterly direction (see Chapter 2).

518 THE GENUS PINUS

There are several turpentine components that form a definite geographical pattern, occurring on both sides of the Pacific, i.e., in western America and in eastern Asia. These compounds are: $\beta$-phellandrene, aliphatic aldehydes, longifolene, $\delta$-cadinene, and $\delta$-cadinol, cembrene, bornyl acetate, and n-undecane.

$\beta$-Phellandrene occurs chiefly both in western America–Mexico–Central America and also in southeastern Asia; aliphatic aldehydes, in California and in the Ryukyu Islands. $\delta$-Cadinene and its alcohol $\delta$-cadinol are found in western America and in Japan.

Cembrene and bornyl acetate are found in western America and eastern Asia from where they extend westward as far as the Balkan Peninsula. The presence of cembrene in P. pinea seems to indicate that possibly it came to the Mediterranean region from eastern Asia.

An alkane, n-undecane, although found in small quantities in pine turpentines, has a wide geographical distribution. Undecane-containing pines grow on both sides of the Pacific. In the New World undecane extends from northwestern America to Mexico and Central America. It also occurs in eastern Asia, extending westward along the Himalaya as far as eastern Afghanistan. The other alkane, n-heptane, is not distributed on both sides of the Pacific. Pines containing this hydrocarbon are found in California and in Mexico. Might it be possible that in their migration south, pines lost n-heptane in eastern Asia and in northwestern America; and that it "survived" only in the more southern latitudes?

The monotopic origin of the chemical components of turpentine appears to be as feasible as the monotopic origin of species. The majority of botanists believe that a species can originate only in one place (Cain, 1944). According to Jhering (1928), there are at distant places no diphyletic, independently arising species of plants and animals. Perhaps this dictum can also be extended to the occurrence of chemical substances in pine species. Critics may say that there is a great difference between the origin of such a complex entity as a species and the origin of a chemical compound. But the difference is only relative. Development of a chemical compound in plants is also a complicated process; it involves many stages of biochemical reactions, each one being regulated by a special enzyme system.

When a chemical compound is formed in a plant, it is transmitted to the future generations. For pines this has been shown repeatedly (Chapter 7). Even if we assume that these components of pine turpentines originated in situ in the two different regions—eastern Asia and western America—their presence would indicate a certain evolutionary programming that originated in a common ancestral area.

It seems logical to conclude that a complex organic chemical compound such as the unusual 14-carbon-ring diterpene, cembrene, developed in one place rather than to assume that it would have appeared here and there independently in many places. If it be so, we could expect to find cembrene also in other regions of the world such as eastern America or western Europe. If we would study distribution of cembrene on the map, Fig. 8–8, in context with the paleobotanical record of *P. peuce*, we would see that this compound could be traced to eastern Asia. In order to come to eastern Asia as well as to California, it could come only from the North. The same reasoning may be applied also to several other chemical compounds found in the genus *Pinus*: an intricate sesquiterpene, longifolene, or rarely encountered aldehydes, or an alkane, *n*-undecane.

Not all compounds of pine turpentines are found only on both sides of the Pacific; $\Delta^3$-carene, for instance, is more widely distributed. When its geographical occurrence is considered in context with Cenozoic migration of pines, certain conclusions as to its origin in space seem to be permissible. Essentially, $\Delta^3$-carene is a compound of eastern Asia–western America; its occurrence in the Mediterranean region can be traced to Tertiary migration from eastern Asia and its present distribution throughout northern Eurasia apparently is of recent (postglacial) origin.

Thus it appears that several chemical compounds found in pines show a certain distribution pattern. This pattern indicates that the genus *Pinus* originated in the north, possibly in an area now covered by the Bering Sea, and it also suggests possible migration routes of pines.

Considered alone, this approach is possibly not sufficient to determine the area of primary development of pines and the routes of their migration; in context with other evidence discussed in this book it seems to be of a certain significance.

## LITERATURE CITATIONS

AKIYOSHI, S. 1937. Turpentine oils of Japan and her neighboring countries. Imp. Indus. Res. Inst. Rpt., Osaka, Japan, 17:1–102. In Japanese.

CAIN, STANLEY A. 1944. Foundations of plant geography. Harper & Row, New York.

CANDELA, P. B. 1942. The introduction of blood-group B into Europe. Human Biol., 14:413–43.

JHERING, H. VON. 1928. Die phyto-geographischen Grundgesetze. Bot. Jahrb., 62: 113–54.

KRESTINSKY, V., and L. BASHENOVA-KOZLOVSKAIA. 1930. O levovrashchaiushchem zhivichnom skipidare iz *Pinus silvestris* (On influence of geography factors and forest types on composition of gum turpentine of *Pinus silvestris*). Zhur. Prikl. Khim., 3:681–89.

MIROV, N. T. 1951. Geography of Russia. John Wiley & Sons, Inc., New York.

————. 1961a. Composition of gum turpentines of pines. (U.S. Dept. Agr. Tech. Bul. No. 1239.) Government Printing Office, Washington, D.C.

————. 1961b. Biochemical geography of the genus *Pinus*. Recent Advances Bot., 1:72–77. (From lectures presented to the 9th Internatl. Bot. Congr., Montreal, 1959.)

————, EUGENE ZAVARIN, and JOSEPH G. BICHO. 1962. Composition of gum turpentines of pines: *Pinus nelsonii* and *Pinus occidentalis*. Jour. Pharm. Sci., 51:1132–35.

# 9

# Taxonomy

## RECENT TRENDS IN CLASSIFICATION OF PINES

Shaw published *The Genus Pinus* in 1914. In a somewhat extended form his classification is presented in Table 9–1. Since Shaw's time several changes have been suggested for a more logical classification of pines. Shaw himself later made certain changes in his system when he eliminated his group *Flexiles* (*P. flexilis* No. 2, *P. strobiformis* No. 35, and *P. armandi* No. 86), merging it with the group *Strobi* (Shaw, 1924).

Shaw was the first to use evolutional characters in the classification of pines; the transition of the cone from a symmetrical one of weak tissues, indehiscent to dehiscent bearing a wingless seed, to a heavy asymmetrical cone that remains closed at maturity and retarded in opening (serotinous) with elaborate forms of winged seeds. Duffield (1952), however, was of the opinion that the significance of the asymmetrical serotinous cone was overemphasized by Shaw.

Based chiefly on Bailey's researches on wood anatomy of pines (see references in Chapter 5), Shaw used all available information on the structure of the rays. In Shaw's section *Haploxylon* (Table 9–1), the ray tracheids have smooth walls. In the subsection *Cembra*, ray parenchyma cells have large pits; in the subsection *Paracembra* they have small pits. In the section *Diploxylon*, ray tracheids have dentate walls, and within this section, pines of the subsection *Lariciones* have ray parenchyma cells with large pits, while in the species of all other subsections, ray parenchyma cells have small pits. Shaw found very few inconsistencies in dentation of the ray tracheid walls. *Pinus bungeana* and *P. gerardiana*, both haploxylon pines, resembled, in the above characters, a diploxylon pine, *P. pinea*. Shaw also detected evidence of transition from small to large pits in *P. merkusii* No. 101 and made reference in this respect to Bailey (1910, see Chapter 5). Bailey's explanation of the evo-

**Table 9–1.** Species of the Genus *Pinus* According to Classification by Shaw (1914) (somewhat expanded)

|  | Reference Numbers As Used in This Book (see Table 1–2) |
|---|---|
| A. Subgenus (Section) *Haploxylon* | |
| Subsection CEMBRA | |
| Group *Cembrae* | |
| P. *koraiensis* Sieb. & Zucc. | 82 |
| P. *cembra* L. | 70 |
| ° P. *sibirica* Mayr | 67 |
| ° P. *pumila* Regel | 68 |
| P. *albicaulis* Engelm. | 1 |
| Group *Strobi* | |
| P. *flexilis* Jam. | 2 |
| ° P. *strobiformis* Engelm. | 35 |
| P. *armandi* Franch. | 86 |
| P. *ayacahuite* Ehr. | 33 |
| P. *lambertiana* Dougl. | 3 |
| ° P. *pentaphylla* Mayr | 83 |
| ° P. *himekomatsu* Miyabe & Kudo | 84 |
| ° P. *dalatensis* de Ferré | 88 |
| ° P. *morrisonicola* Hayata | 85 |
| ° P. *fenzeliana* Hand.-Maz. | 89 |
| P. *peuce* Griseb. | 71 |
| P. *griffithii* McClell. (P. *excelsa* Wallich) | 91 |
| P. *monticola* Dougl. | 4 |
| P. *strobus* L. | 20 |
| ° P. *strobus* L. var. *chiapensis* Mart. | 34 |
| ° P. *kwangtungensis* Chun. | 90 |
| Subsection PARACEMBRA | |
| Group *Gerardianae* | |
| P. *bungeana* Zucc. | 87 |
| P. *gerardiana* Wall. | 92 |
| Group *Balfourianae* | |
| P. *balfouriana* Grev. & Balf. | 5 |
| P. *aristata* Engelm. | 6 |
| Group *Cembroides* | |
| P. *cembroides* Zucc. | 36 |
| ° P. *edulis* Englem. | 8 |
| ° P. *quadrifolia* Sudw. | 9 |
| ° P. *monophylla* Torrey | 7 |
| P. *pinceana* Gordon | 37 |
| P. *nelsonii* Shaw | 38 |
| ° P. *culminicola* And. & Beam. | 39 |
| B. Subgenus (Section) *Diplyoxylon* | |
| Subsection PARAPINASTER | |
| Group VII *Leiophyllae* | |
| P. *leiophylla* Schiede & Deppe | 41 |
| ° P. *chihuahuana* Engelm. | 40 |
| P. *lumholtzii* Rob. & Fern. | 42 |

**Table 9–1.** (Continued)

| | Reference Numbers As Used in This Book (see Table 1–2) |
|---|---|
| Group VIII. *Longifoliae* | |
| P. *roxburghii* Sarg. (*P. longifolia* Roxb.) | 93 |
| P. *canariensis* Smith | 72 |
| Group IX. *Pineae* | |
| P. *pinea* L. | 73 |
| Subsection PINASTER | |
| Group *Lariciones* | |
| P. *resinosa* Ait. | 21 |
| P. *tropicalis* Morelet | 66 |
| P. *massoniana* Lamb. | 94 |
| P. *densiflora* Sieb. & Zucc. | 95 |
| * P. *funebris* Kom. | 96 |
| P. *thunbergii* Parl. | 97 |
| P. *sylvestris* L. | 69 |
| P. *montana* Miller | 76 |
| P. *luchuensis* Mayr | 98 |
| * P. *taiwanensis* Hayata | 99 |
| * P. *hwangshanensis* Hsia | 100 |
| P. *merkusii* DeVriese | 101 |
| P. *nigra* Arn. | 74 |
| * P. *heldreichii* Christ | 75 |
| P. *tabulaeformis* Carr. (*P. sinensis* Lamb.) | 102 |
| * P. *yunnanensis* Franch. | 103 |
| * P. *khasya* (Royle) | 104 |
| P. *insularis* Endl. | 105 |
| Group *Australes* | |
| * P. *jeffreyi* Grev. & Balf. | 13 |
| P. *ponderosa* Laws. | 14 |
| * P. *washoensis* Mason & Stockwell | 15 |
| P. *palustris* Mill. | 22 |
| P. *caribaea* Mor. | 62 |
| * P. *elliottii* Engelm. (*P. caribaea* Morelet) | 23 |
| * P. *elliottii* var. *densa* Little & Dorman | 63 |
| P. *taeda* L. | 24 |
| P. *echinata* Miller | 25 |
| P. *lawsonii* Roezl | 44 |
| P. *arizonica* Engelm. | 43 |
| P. *teocote* Schl. & Cham. | 45 |
| * P. *herrerai* Martínez | 46 |
| P. *montezumae* Lamb. | 47 |
| * P. *durangensis* Martínez | 48 |
| * P. *hartwegii* Lindl. | 49 |
| * P. *rudis* Endl. | 50 |
| * P. *cooperi* Blanco | 51 |
| * P. *michoacana* Martínez | 52 |
| * P. *engelmannii* Carr. | 53 |
| P. *pseudostrobus* Lindl. | 54 |
| * P. *oaxacana* Mirov | 57 |
| * P. *tenuifolia* Benth. | 55 |

**Table 9–1.** (Continued)

| | Reference Numbers<br>As Used in This<br>Book<br>(see Table 1–2) |
|---|---|
| * *P. douglasiana* Martínez | 56 |
| *P. occidentalis* Swartz. | 64 |
| * *P. cubensis* Griseb. | 65 |
| *P. glabra* Walter | 26 |
| Group *Insignes* | |
| *P. pringlei* Shaw | 58 |
| *P. oocarpa* Schiede | 59 |
| *P. halepensis* Miller | 77 |
| * *P. brutia* Tenore | 78 |
| * *P. pityusa* Steven | 79 |
| * *P. eldarica* Medw. | 81 |
| *P. pinaster* Ait. | 80 |
| *P. virginiana* Miller | 27 |
| *P. clausa* Vasey | 28 |
| *P. rigida* Miller | 29 |
| *P. serotina* Michx. | 30 |
| *P. pungens* Lambert | 31 |
| *P. banksiana* Lambert | 32 |
| *P. contorta* Dougl. | 16 |
| *P. greggii* Engelm. | 60 |
| *P. patula* Schl. & Cham. | 61 |
| *P. muricata* D. Don | 18 |
| *P. attenuata* Lemmon | 17 |
| *P. radiata* D. Don | 19 |
| Group *Macrocarpae* | |
| *P. torreyana* Parry | 11 |
| *P. coulteri* D. Don | 12 |
| *P. sabiniana* Dougl. | 10 |

* An asterisk (*) before the species name denotes a pine that either was not considered by Shaw as a valid species, or has been described since Shaw's *Genus Pinus* was published.

Not included in the above list, but mentioned in the text, are the following pines: *P.* sp. of Inner Honduras; *P. tecumumani, P. quichensis* Aguilar, *P. teocote* var. *guatemalensis* Aguilar, *P. amamiana, P. krempfii,* "*pin du moyen Annam,*" *Pinus* sp. of Guerrero, Mexico, *P. martinezii* in Michoacan, Mexico, *P. densata* Masters—supposedly a natural hybrid between *P. yunnanensis* No. 10 and *P. tabulaeformis* No. 102 and occupying a prominent place in the landscape of Yunnan. Other numerous varieties are mentioned in describing species in Chapter 3.

lution of pitting in pines was mentioned in Chapter 5. Shaw also used many other morphological characters for the classification of pines: shape of cone scales, position of resin ducts in the needle, form and method of attachment of seed wing.

Pilger (1926) was the author of the genus *Pinus* in Engler and Prantl's *Pflanzenfamilien.* Some eighty to ninety species ("*viele zahlreiche Arten beschrieben!*") were taken as the components of the genus *Pinus.* These were divided as in Shaw's system, into two large groups—subspecies *Haploxylon* and *Diploxylon* of Koehne (1893)—and further subdivided into eleven sections as follows:

**Table 9–2.** Classification of Pines According to Pilger (1926)

|  | Reference Numbers As Used in This Book (see Table 1–2) |
|---|---|
| Subgenus *Haploxylon* Koehne | |
| Section 1. *Cembra* Spach. | |
| P. *cembra* L. | 67 and 70 |
| P. *pumila* Regel | 68 |
| P. *koraiensis* Sieb. & Zucc. | 82 |
| P. *albicaulis* Engelm. | 1 |
| P. *armandi* Franch. | 86 |
| P. *flexilis* James | 2 |
| Section 2. *Strobus* Sweet ex. Spach. | |
| P. *lambertiana* Dougl. | 3 |
| P. *ayacahuite* Ehren. | 33 |
| P. *monticola* Dougl. | 4 |
| P. *strobus* L. | 20 and 34 |
| P. *peuce* Griseb. | 71 |
| P. *excelsa* Wall. | 91 |
| P. *parviflora* Zieb. & Zucc. | 83 and 84 |
| P. *formosana* Hayata | 85 |
| P. *uyematsui* Hayata | 85 |
| Section 3. *Paracembra* Koehne | |
| Undersection *Gerardianae* | |
| P. *gerardiana* Wall. | 92 |
| P. *bungeana* Zucc. | 87 |
| P. *cembroides* Zucc. | 36 |
| P. *edulis* Engelm. | 8 |
| P. *monophylla* Torrey | 7 |
| P. *quadrifolia* Sudw. | 9 |
| P. *pinceana* Gord. | 37 |
| P. *nelsonii* Shaw | 38 |
| Undersection *Balfourianae* | |
| P. *krempfii* Lecompte (see pp. 540–543) | No number is assigned to this pine |
| P. *balfouriana* Murray | 5 |
| P. *aristata* Engelm. | 6 |
| Subgenus *Diploxylon* Koehne | |
| Section 4. *Sula* | |
| P. *longifolia* Roxb. | 93 |
| P. *canariensis* Smith | 72 |

**Table 9–2.** (Continued)

|  | Reference Numbers<br>As Used in This<br>Book<br>(see Table 1–2) |
|---|---|
| **Section 5. *Eupitys*** |  |
| *P. maritima* Lamb. | 80 |
| *P. tropicalis* Morelet | 66 |
| *P. resinosa* Ait. | 21 |
| *P. massoniana* Lamb. | 94 |
| *P. densiflora* Sieb. & Zucc. | 95 |
| *P. sinensis* Lamb. | 102 |
| *P. silvestris* L. | 69 |
| *P. montana* Miller | 76 |
| *P. merkusii* Jungh | 101 |
| *P. thunbergii* Parl. | 97 |
| *P. luchuensis* Mayr | 98 |
| *P. nigra* Arnold | 74 |
| *P. leucodermis* Antoine | 75 |
| **Section 6. *Banksia*** |  |
| *P. pungens* Lamb. | 31 |
| *P. muricata* D. Don | 18 |
| *P. banksiana* Lamb. | 32 |
| *P. contorta* Douglas | 16 |
| *P. clausa* Vasey | 28 |
| *P. virginiana* Miller | 27 |
| *P. echinata* Miller | 25 |
| *P. glabra* Walter | 26 |
| *P. halepensis* Miller | 77 |
| **Section 7. *Pinea*** |  |
| *P. pinea* L. | 73 |
| **Section 8. *Australes*** |  |
| *P. palustris* Miller | 22 |
| *P. caribaea* Morelet | 62 |
| *P. occidentalis* Swartz | 64, 65 |
| *P. lawsonii* Roezl | 44 |
| *P. oocarpa* Schiede | 59 |
| *P. pringlei* Shaw | 58 |
| **Section 9. *Khasia*** |  |
| *P. insularis* Endl. | 105 |
| *P. khasya* Royle | 104 |
| **Section 10. *Pseudostrobus*** |  |
| *P. lumholtzii* Rob. & Fern. | 42 |
| *P. leiophylla* Schlicht. & Cham. | 40, 41 |
| *P. teocote* Schl. & Cham. | 45 |
| *P. montezumae* Lamb. | 47 |
| *P. pseudostrobus* Lindl. | 54 |
| *P. torreyana* Parry | 11 |
| *P. ponderosa* Dougl. | 14 |
| *P. jeffreyi* Balf. | 13 |

**Table 9–2.** (Continued)

|  | Reference Numbers As Used in This Book (see Table 1–2) |
|---|---|
| *P. engelmannii* Carr. | 53 |
| *P. arizonica* Engelm. | 43 |
| Section 11. *Taeda* | |
| *P. patula* Schl. & Cham. | 61 |
| *P. greggii* Engelm. | 60 |
| *P. serotina* Michx. | 30 |
| *P. rigida* Miller | 29 |
| *P. taeda* L. | 24 |
| *P. attenuata* Lemmon | 17 |
| *P. radiata* D. Don | 19 |
| *P. sabiniana* Dougl. | 10 |
| *P. coulteri* D. Don | 12 |

In comparison with Shaw's system, Pilger's classification shows some changes. Some of Shaw's varieties were given the rank of species; *P. krempfii* was added and placed close to *P. balfouriana* No. 5 and *P. aristata* No. 6; *P. uyematsui* (our No. 85) was also added; *P. khasya* No. 104 was separated from *P. insularis* No. 105. But the chief difference between the two systems is in the grouping of the diploxylon pines. Pilger eliminated the group *Leiophyllae*, created a new group *Khasia*, rearranged species in the remaining group, and devised new names for the groups.

Pilger's classification is based on the number of needles in the short shoot, on the morphology of seed wing, and the position of the resin ducts in the needles. The weakness of Pilger's system is the excessive reliance on needle number (Duffield, 1952). As compared with Shaw's classification, it is a step backward; nevertheless it is widely used in Europe.

Martínez (1948) added much to our knowledge of Mexican pines. He recognized in Mexico thirty-nine species, eighteen varieties, and nine forms (some extending to the United States). He divided them into nine sections following, as much as available information permitted, Shaw's arrangements from the most primitive to the most advanced. Martínez has been unjustly considered a "splitter." The difficulty of identifying pines in the Mexican highlands has been recognized by many; it is caused by a very broad intercrossing of species. As indicated in Chapter 4, a secondary center of speciation is located in the Mexican–Central American highlands; it is extremely difficult positively to identify some species there. It is pertinent to remember that Roezl (1857, 1858; see reference in Literature Citations, Chapter 2) listed about ninety species of Mexican pines, no doubt having been overwhelmed and confused with their diversity. Even now botanists and foresters still collect specimens of new pines (in Mexico and Central America): species, varieties, and varieties of varieties (see reference to Zobel and Cech [1957] in Literature Citations, Chapter 4). Martínez certainly should not be considered a "splitter"; he was rather conservative and has brought order into the taxonomy of Mexican pines. As in other pine regions, the greatest uncertainty in classifying Mexican pines lies in the subgenus *Diploxylon*, but even there, Martínez effected a very sensible arrangement. Martínez' classification is prepared with a great deal of thought and foresight. His established sections: I, *Piñoneros*; 11, *Ayacahuite*; III, *Leiophylla*; IV, *Teocote*; V, *Pseudostrobus*; VI, *Montezumae* (subdivided into groups *Montezumae, Rudis,* and *Michoacana*); VII, *Ponderosa*; VIII, *Serotinos*; and IX, *Coulteri* can be easily incorporated into the general system of Shaw-Duffield.

Duffield (1952) made a major contribution to the classification of pines when he applied to it results of the hybridization work done at the Institute of Forest Genetics, U.S. Forest Service, Placerville, Calif. (see Table 9–3), by Righter and his associates.

Duffield's rearrangements were concerned with Shaw's subsection *Pinaster,* which is composed of the groups *Lariciones, Australes, Insignes,* and *Macrocarpae. Pinus halepensis* No. 77 and *P. pinaster* No. 80 were moved from the group *Insignes* to Group X, *Lariciones. Pinus halepensis* was moved to Group X because of the position of the resin canals and also because its turpentine "fits more consistently into the *Lariciones* than into the *Insignes.*" There are also valid reasons for moving *P. pityusa* No. 79 (mentioned by Duffield) and *P. eldarica* No. 81 and *P. brutia* No. 78 (not mentioned by him but very closely related to *P. pityusa*), to the group *Lariciones.*

Duffield divided Shaw's group *Australes* into two groups; XI, the eastern group composed of species Nos. 22, 23, 24, 25, and 26, to which he transferred *P. rigida* No. 29, *P. serotina* No. 30, *P. pungens* No. 31, *P. occidentalis* No. 64; and the western group consisting of Nos. 13, 14, 43, 44, 45, 47, 53, and 54, designated as Group XII.

Shaw's group *Macrocarpae* was moved provisionally *in corpore* into Group XII.

*Pinus contorta* No. 16, *P. banksiana* No. 32, *P. virginiana* No. 27, and *P. clausa* No. 28 of Shaw's group *Insignes* formed a separate Group XIII; what remained of Shaw's group *Insignes* formed Duffield's Group XIV consisting of *P. radiata* No. 19, *P. muricata* No. 18, *P. attenuata* No. 17, *P. greggii* No. 60, *P. pringlei* No. 58, *P. patula* No. 61, and *P. oocarpa* No. 59.

Duffield's rearrangement of pines was criticized by Gaussen (1955, 1960). The chief objection seems to be (in Gaussen's own words *"peut-*

**Table 9–3.** Rearrangement of Species in Shaw's Subsection *Pinaster* by Duffield (1952), Based on Hybridization Experiments.

| | Reference Numbers as Used in This Book (see Table 1–2) | | Reference Numbers as Used in This Book (see Table 1–2) |
|---|---|---|---|
| **Group X** | | **Group XII** | |
| P. resinosa | 21 | P. teocote | 45 |
| P. tropicalis | 66 | P. lawsonii | 44 |
| P. massoniana | 94 | P. montezumae | 47 |
| P. densiflora | 95 | P. pseudostrobus | 54 |
| P. sylvestris | 69 | P. ponderosa | 14 |
| P. montana | 76 | P. latifolia | 53 |
| P. luchuensis | 98 | P. arizonica | 43 |
| P. thunbergii | 97 | P. jeffreyi | 13 |
| P. nigra | 74 | P. torreyana | 11 |
| P. merkusii | 101 | P. sabiniana | 10 |
| P. sinensis | 102 | P. coulteri | 12 |
| P. insularis | 105 | | |
| P. khasya | 104 | **Group XIII** | |
| P. leucodermis | 75 | P. banksiana | 32 |
| P. halepensis | 77 | P. contorta | 16 |
| P. pinaster | 80 | P. virginiana | 27 |
| | | P. clausa | 28 |
| **Group XI** | | | |
| P. caribaea (i.e., P. elliottii) | 23 | **Group XIV** | |
| P. palustris | 22 | P. radiata | 19 |
| P. echinata | 25 | P. muricata | 18 |
| P. taeda | 24 | P. attenuata | 17 |
| P. glabra | 26 | P. greggii | 60 |
| P. occidentalis | 64 | P. pringlei | 58 |
| P. rigida | 29 | P. patula | 61 |
| P. serotina | 30 | P. oocarpa | 59 |
| P. pungens | 31 | | |

NOTE: In Group X, *P. sinensis* is our *P. tabulaeformis* No. 102, *P. leucodermis* is our *P. heldreichii* No. 75. To Group X should be added the following pines: *P. funebris* No. 96, *P. taiwanensis* No. 99, *P. hwangshanensis* No. 100, *P. yunnanensis* No. 103, *P. brutia* No. 78, *P. pityusa* No. 79 and *P. eldarica* No. 81. In Group XI *P. caribaea* No. 62 includes *P. elliottii* No. 23 and its var. *densa* No. 63; *P. occidentalis* includes *P. cubensis* No. 65. In Group XII *P. latifolia* is *P. engelmannii* No. 53. To Group XII should be added the following species: *P. herrerai* No. 46, *P. durangensis* No. 48, *P. hartwegii* No. 49, *P. rudis* No. 50, *P. cooperi* No. 51, *P. tenuifolia* No. 55, *P. douglasiana* No. 56, *P. oaxacana* No. 57, *P. washoensis* No. 15, and *P. michoacana* No. 52.

*être inattendue et révolutionnaire"*) that success of hybridization lies (to quote Gaussen again) in the *"nature éveillée ou dormante des caractères au moment de la fécondation"* (Gaussen, 1960), and, because of such erratic behavior, cannot be used as a criterion indicating affinity of pines.

Subsequent analyses of hybridization experiments in pines, however, have amply supported Duffield's proposal (Critchfield, 1963).

The research group at the Laboratoire Forestier de Toulouse, under the leadership of Gaussen, has numerous publications on the morphology of gymnosperms and, among them, on pines. The most thorough work in this area is that by Ferré (1941, 1952, 1953), Campo-Duplan (1950), Flous (1936, 1937), and, of course, by Gaussen himself.

In 1960 Gaussen published Chapter XI of the voluminous and not yet completed *Les Gymnospermes Actuelles et Fossiles.* This chapter is devoted entirely to the classification and description of pine species and their phylogeny. The chapter also includes descriptions of fossil pines, and brief accounts of the enemies of pines and the geography of the genus; also a great many interesting remarks about pines such as *"Au Nouveau Mexique les graines* [of *P. edulis*] *ont été utilisées pour l'alimentation des chevaux."* Unfortunately, no bibliography is included; apparently it will appear at the end of the whole treatise.

In constructing his phylogenetic classification of pines Gaussen used many characters, chief among which were:

1. The juvenile forms, based on de Ferré's researches. Here great importance is attached to the vascular strands in cotyledons, first proposed by Boureau (1938) and elaborated by Flous (1936).
2. Position of resin ducts in the needles, and
3. Size of pollen grains.

Two phylogenetic charts were constructed in which, on the abscissae, groups of pine species are arranged by the position of resin ducts in the needles. On the ordinate, the species in each group are arranged by the size of pollen grains. Gaussen's system is shown in an abbreviated form in Table 9–4.

Arrangement of the sections and classification of pines to fit these sections are drastically different from classifications of pines used by previous investigators. It appears that too much emphasis was placed by Gaussen on the size of pollen grains. Unfortunately, all schemes of identification of pine species by pollen grains, based on one or at most two variables (major and minor axes of the pollen grain) as used by Campo-Duplan (1950) and adopted by Gaussen (1960), are not accurate enough. In the opinion of Ting, who has been actively engaged in using pollen grains of pines for taxonomic purposes (see reference to Axelrod and Ting in Literature Citations in Chapter 2), identification of pine

**Table 9–4.** Classification of Pines According to Gaussen (1960)

*Pinus*

| *Ducampopinus* | *Eupinus* | *Cembrapinus* |
|---|---|---|
| Sec. I, *Kremphioides* (only one species, *P. krempfii* Lecomte) | Sec. II, *Taedoponderosoides*<br>Sec. III, *Merkusioides*<br>Sec. IV, *Halepensoides*<br>Sec. V. *Khasyosilvestroides*<br>Sec. VI, *Parryanoides*<br>(this section contains Shaw's subsections *Cembroides, Balfourianae,* and *Pineae*) | Sec. VII, *Armandioides*<br>Sec. VIII, *Parvifloroides*<br>Sec. IX, *Stroboides*<br>Sec. X, *Flexilioides* |

species based on the measurements of pollen grains is not as simple as it appears to be.[*] Within the sample representing the pollen of a pine species, the difference between the largest and the smallest grain may reach $20\mu$. Individual samples of the same species differ, usually to the extent of $10\mu$ of mean value. While the two subgenera of the genus *Pinus, Haploxylon* and *Diploxylon* (with *P. krempfii* probably grouped with the former), can be distinguished on morphology of their pollen, it is not always so with the species. According to Ting, only three or four pine species can be recognized by this character.

For positive identification of pines by their pollen grains, Ting recommends statistical methods in the following order: size, coefficient of variation, number of class in frequency distribution, mode location, and a "Cos A Index" to express three means of measurements (both axes of the grain and the size of the air sacs).

Gaussen's (1960) work on pines is not a revision of the genus *Pinus,* although it contributed to that end; moreover, apparently it was not intended as a finished product; it is merely a chapter of his general, not yet completed, treatise on gymnosperms. The contribution of Gaussen and his co-workers to our knowledge of the genus *Pinus* is very valuable. His ideas, often revolutionary, should be carefully considered by all interested in the taxonomy of the genus *Pinus*. Of especial interest are de Ferré's researches on juvenile characters of pines (Ferré, 1952).

## CLASSICAL AND EXPERIMENTAL TAXONOMY

Pines discussed in the preceding chapters were presented as Linnean species (linneons), each having a generic and specific name. Only a few

[*] William S. Ting, University of California, Los Angeles, personal communications, 1964.

varieties were described and some unnamed pines mentioned. Linnean binary nomenclature is indispensable; all researches dealing with pines have to be referred to the generally accepted binomials. When this rule is not observed, confusion results (for examples see Mirov, 1963). When a new pine is not described in accordance with the principles and rules of nomenclature (for these see Benson, 1962, or Lawrence, 1955), it cannot be placed in the proper place and it cannot be readily identified. When one encounters, for instance, a pine described as *"le pin du moyen Annam"* (see page 545), one feels that one is again in the age of herbalists of pre-Linnean times (see Chapter 1).

It is also evident that without having the category of "species," it would not have been possible to discuss different aspects of the genus *Pinus*. "The purpose of giving a name to a plant . . . is solely to supply a means of referring to it and not to indicate its character or history" (Lawrence, 1955), and it is a perfectly good reason to use binary nomenclature for pines. This type of taxonomy is called "classical, conventional, descriptive taxonomy"; "alpha taxonomy of Turrill"; and "orthodox taxonomy" (Heslop-Harrison, 1953). At the same time, however, there are many examples in the preceding chapters where the classical concept of species could not be applied to pines. There are "good" species and there are also "bad" species. These terms are frequently used both in quotation marks and without them by many botanists. (Cf., for instance, Heslop-Harrison [1963] and definition of "good" species by this writer [Mirov, 1963].) "Good" pine species such as *P. lambertiana* No. 3 or *P. pinea* No. 73, and many others, are clearly delimited. They can be identified without difficulty. On the other hand, "bad" pine species are elusive, difficult to identify in the field and more so in the herbarium. They intercross freely with other species. Within the genus *Pinus* the "bad" species are those that cannot be easily separated from other species on morphological characters alone and that have no clearly delimited specific borders. There often exists a maze of intermediate forms between one species and another. A good example is *P. pseudostrobus* No. 54 of Mexico, which has many varieties and varieties of varieties. These varieties intercross and the intermediate forms are difficult to describe. Moreover, *P. pseudostrobus* hybridizes with *P. montezumae* No. 47 and perhaps with some other species, and all this complicates the classification of pines. Even "good" species of pines, whose rank is indisputable, may cross naturally and produce fertile hybrids that, if they are of a recent origin, may form hybrid swarms, as in the case of *P. contorta* No. 16 × *P. banksiana* No. 32 (see reference to Mirov [1956] in Literature Citations, Chapter 7), or if they are old, they result in a new species, which possibly is the case of *P. densata*, a product of (Tertiary ?) hybridization between *P. tabulaeformis* No. 102 and *P. yunnanensis* No. 103.

The "goodness" of some species in the genus *Pinus* (i.e., their "inability" to cross with other species) may depend merely on their geographical isolation. *Pinus griffithii* No. 91 of the Himalaya does not cross with *P. gerardiana* No. 92, although they may occur in the same general area, presumably because of genetic barriers; on the other hand, when *P. griffithii* was brought in contact with *P. ayacahuite* No. 33 of Mexico in an arboretum in England, they intercrossed naturally and produced a fertile hybrid pine known as *P. holfordiana* (Dallimore and Jackson, 1948). *Pinus griffithii* also has been crossed with *P. monticola* No. 4, as well as with *P. strobus* and *P. flexilis.* There are many more examples where intercrossing between pine species is prevented only by their geographical isolation.

Thus, the concept of species in the genus *Pinus* cannot always be based on the genetic characteristics; the dictum that a species is a group of interbreeding populations that are genetically isolated from other species cannot always be applied to pines. To arrive at a workable concept of species in the genus *Pinus,* the botanist has to consider and adapt the methods of experimental taxonomy.

According to Heslop-Harrison (1953), classical taxonomy and experimental taxonomy, alpha and omega taxonomy of Turrill, are two different disciplines. Their methods are different (that is, in alpha taxonomy they are based upon individuals and the type concept while the methods of "omega taxonomy" are based upon populations using statistical methods). In alpha taxonomy "the giving of names [is] accepted as an important process," in omega taxonomy, "nomenclatural matters [are] considered of little importance." I don't agree with the Heslop-Harrison definitions. In my opinion experimental taxonomy should serve to supplement classical taxonomy. We saw how useful was the classical approach in studying different aspects of pines, but we also saw how experimental taxonomy helped to elucidate some problems of the classical taxonomy (references to Duffield [1952], Critchfield [1957], in Literature Citations, Chapter 4). The experimental approach is especially useful when species are still in the process of formation as we find in the secondary center of evolution of the genus *Pinus* in the highlands of Mexico and Guatemala. I agree with Heslop-Harrison (1953) that the matter of nomenclature has been considered of little importance in experimental taxonomy. Perhaps that is why there is so much confusing terminology, but this situation can be easily remedied. The experimental approach is indispensable in any taxonomic study. Our present knowledge of plant taxonomy, based on experiments, is too meager. Perhaps it is too early to claim it to be represented by the last letter of the Greek alphabet, omega. It should be both "alpha and omega, beginning and end," as originally had been stated on a different occasion a long time ago.

Our concept of species in the genus *Pinus* is based both on classical and experimental taxonomy; on consideration of all its characters: morphological, genetic, geographical, physiological, ecological, and chemical. Species of the genus *Pinus* are not comparable one to another. Each has its own magnitude. Some species, judging by the number of named varieties, are stable; for instance, *P. resinosa* No. 21, or *P. roxburghii* No. 93, or *P. massoniana* No. 94 are not variable, while others are very variable (*P. pseudostrobus* No. 54, *P. tabulaeformis* No. 102). Sometimes even species of a relatively limited distribution follow the same trend: *P. attenuata* No. 17 is not variable while *P. muricata* No. 18 is strikingly variable. Some species are senescent (*P. aristata* No. 6, *P. balfouriana* No. 5); others are vigorous and expanding (*P. ponderosa* No. 14, many Mexican species, *P. sylvestris* No. 69).

## DIFFERENT APPROACHES FOR TAXONOMIC STUDIES OF PINES

### Morphological Approach

It is seen from the preceding pages of this chapter and also from the historical sketch of classification of the genus *Pinus* (Chapter 1) that, originally, pine taxonomy was based essentially on external morphology. It still is.

Engelmann (1880) inquired much more deeply than anyone before him into the external morphology of pines: their "flowers," size of their pollen grains, a more accurate description of the "female ament" and differences in cone structure; he also described serotinous cones. He was apparently the first to use internal morphology for the classification of pines; he distinguished his sections by the position of the resin canals in the needles (peripheral, parenchymatous, or internal) and he also used the presence or absence of "strengthening cells" around the resin canals. Engelmann was aware of variations in the morphology of the vascular bundles of needles—"single in the terete and mostly in the quinate leaves; it is double in the broader triangular or ternate and in the semi-terete or binate leaves." He did not think the morphology of the vascular bundles to be of diagnostic importance, for he found occasionally both single and double bundles in the same species.

Koehne (1893) used internal characters of needles to divide the whole genus into the two subgenera, *Haploxylon*, having one vascular bundle, and *Diploxylon*, which has two bundles. *Pinus krempfii* (see p. 540) also has one vascular bundle.

Position of resin canals was also used by Shaw (1914) for differentiation among species of his *The Genus Pinus*.

The two sections, or subgenera, can also always be distinguished by the scarious bracts subtending the short shoots. In haploxylon pines, the bract is non-decurrent and thus the branches are smooth. In diploxylon pines, the bract is decurrent, causing the branches to be rough. The basal sheath of the short shoot is deciduous in all haploxylon pines except *P. nelsonii* No. 38, but it is persistent in all diploxylon pines except the three species (Nos. 40, 41, 42) of the group *Leiophyllae*.

Bailey has contributed much to our understanding of the structure and evolution of tissues of trees and, among them, the pines. Even in his early articles (Bailey, 1910) he indicated the value of wood structure for taxonomic purposes. Shaw's (1914) classification of pines using ray structure is based largely on Bailey's researches.

Morphological characters always will play the most important part in the classification of pines. When morphological characters are not sufficient for the identification of pines or for placing them into appropriate groups, or for deciding if they deserve the rank of species or not, then other approaches may be useful.

## Genetic Approach

Genetic aspects of pines have been discussed in Chapter 4. Some species have very efficient genetic barriers that permit their identification without difficulty. Other pines have a capacity for hybridizing, showing a closer affinity to some species in preference to others. Earlier in this chapter, it was shown how useful hybridization experiments proved to be in a revision of certain *Diploxylon* groups of the genus (Duffield, 1952; Critchfield, 1963). In the Mexican–Central American highlands, where species are young and still evolving, the problem of applying genetics to taxonomy is extremely difficult; it calls for a well-prepared biosystematic inquiry, hybridization tests, and a thorough field study of variability within the complex species (see later discussion on taxonomic problems, p. 540). The difficulties of identifying pine species lie firstly in their variability, which is evident in all subspecific "experimental" categories (Heslop-Harrison, 1953) down to the individual trees, and secondly, in the remarkable capacity of some pine species, recognized by classical taxonomy as such, to hybridize. This capacity is found throughout the area of the genus *Pinus* but is most common in Mexico–Central America and to a lesser extent in eastern Asia—i.e., in the two regions of secondary speciation of the genus (see Chapter 4).

## Geographical Approach

Geographical isolation has been used for a long time in classification of pines and for deciding on their taxonomic standing. *Pinus monticola* and *P. strobus* are morphologically so similar that they could be lumped into one species if not for their mutual geographical remoteness. In Shaw's (1914) diagnosis of the two species, the only difference cited is in the phyllotaxy of their cones (a character that was condemned by some as not very reliable [Engelmann, 1880]). Shaw noted that "Nuttall (Sylva iii, 118) followed Hooker in considering it [*P. monticola*] to be a variety of *P. strobus*." *Pinus chiapensis* may be separated from *P. strobus* chiefly (but not entirely) on geographical grounds. It happens occasionally that when a decision is based first on geographical distribution, later experimental studies may reveal some small but consistent morphological differences. Actually this was the case with *P. chiapensis* (Andresen, unpublished). Three pines of southeastern Asia—*P. yunnanensis* Franchet No. 103, *P. khasya* No. 104, and *P. insularis* Endlicher No. 105—were described on the basis of geographical distribution alone and, although Wu (1947), who studied these pines in herbaria, came to the conclusion that they belong to the same species, there may be still a reason to consider them as belonging to distinct taxa. Their geographical distribution is disjoined.

Although *P. ayacahuite* No. 32 naturally crosses with *P. griffithii* (i.e., they display genetic affinity that has not been lost during the amazingly long period of their separation), it seems justifiable to recognize these two pines as two different species, in spite of their close genetic kinship.

## Physiological and Ecological Approach

Benson (1962), in discussing the value of physiological-ecological characters for plant taxonomy, selected *P. ponderosa* as an example. He indicated how important are considerations of differences in amount of precipitation, in temperature, and other factors for understanding reasons for past and present migrations of species and varieties and for their segregation as ecologically adapted populations. Benson's statements can be amplified to include considerations of the effects of mycorhiza, fires, animals, capacity of pines to invade denuded areas, their "flowering" not being affected by photoperiodicity, the astonishing adjustment of the same species to different soil conditions, incapacity of pines to reproduce in a uniformly humid and hot climate, and a surprising tolerance of some pine species to dry and hot conditions. All these and other factors are discussed in Chapter 6 and all of them should be considered in taxonomic studies of pines.

## Paleobotanical Approach

In the study of the evolution of the genus *Pinus*, paleobotany is one source of information. Paleobotany gives us broad hints as to the former distribution of pine species and their adjustment to and development in different paleogeographical regions—for instance, their disappearance at the end of the Tertiary period in Europe, as compared with their undisturbed development since the Cretaceous (man's influence excluded) in eastern Asia. Reports of finding a pine lacking distinct annual rings are important (cf. Chapter 2, pp. 85 and 86). Occurrence of a Miocene pine with wood parenchyma and thin-walled epithelial cells surrounding resin canals (Lilpop, 1924) or the description of a broad-leaved pine (Jeffrey, 1908) throws some light on the possible relationship of *P. krempfii* to the rest of the pines (see p. 540). Reports on the recognition of haploxylon and diploxylon pines as early as the Cretaceous period show the antiquity of these two groups.

Identification of fossil species, however, is an extremely difficult matter. This subject was discussed at the beginning of Chapter 2. Lately, with the advent of palynology, the identification of fossil pines becomes much easier. But it is emphasized that the material should be studied according to sound statistical methods. This approach has been mentioned on pages 529–30.

## Chemistry in the Taxonomy of Pines

Application of chemistry to plant taxonomy is new. Some difficulties of reconciling the two disciplines have been discussed by Mirov (1963). Three books on this subject were published in the last two years (Hegnauer, 1962; Swain, 1963; Alston and Turner, 1963). Pines are mentioned in all three of them. The number of publications on the subject of chemistry in taxonomy has been increasing steadily (Duffield, 1952; Mirov, 1956; Erdtman, 1959, 1963; Haller, 1962).

It was mentioned in Chapter 7 that the cell-wall components of all of the genus *Pinus* have a similar chemical composition; thus they are not suitable for distinguishing one pine species from another. On the other hand, the extraneous materials that can be extracted from the trees may vary considerably from one species or variety to another and accordingly can be used for taxonomic purposes.

Some of the extraneous substances of pines discussed in Chapter 7, such as fats, are yet incompletely known; waxes are almost totally unknown. Using pine needle oil as a criterion for classification of pines is still much in the experimental stage, although some plausible advances have been made in this field (see reference to Savory [1962] in Literature Citations, Chapter 7).

Cyclitols occasionally have served a useful purpose in identifying pines. Roezl's *P. bonapartea,* described as containing a sugary exudate (Roezl, 1858; see reference in Literature Citations, Chapter 2), could not have been any other species but *P. ayacahuite,* our No. 33, known in Mexico as *pino de azucar,* i.e., sugar pine. At the same time it shows that California sugar pine, *P. lambertiana* No. 3, also renowned for its sugary exudate, apparently is closely related to *P. ayacahuite.* In other haploxylon pines, cyclitols are found only in minute quantities, either in wood, bark, cones, or needles (Chapter 7).

Alkaloids are apparently found only in a limited number of pine species, but what little is known is quite useful for taxonomic purposes. The occurrence of alkaloids in all three species of the group *Macrocarpae* (see Table 10–1) and also in *P. jeffreyi* No. 13, seems to be an additional evidence of the validity of the group and of its close relationship to the above species (No. 13) (see reference to Tallent *et al.* [1955] in Literature Citations, Chapter 7).

Anthocyanins are useful for studies of pines but for purposes other than taxonomy (see reference to Romberger [1963] in Literature Citations, Chapter 5). Bark and sapwood polyphenols are as yet little explored.

**Heartwood Polyphenols.** Of all groups of chemical compounds discussed in Chapter 7, heartwood polyphenols have been studied more than any other extraneous materials of pines. Most of the original work on heartwood polyphenols was done by Erdtman and his associates (see Chapter 7) and continued by Japanese wood chemists. An outstanding result of these studies was the finding that the subgenus *Haploxylon* differs from the subgenus *Diploxylon* in the chemical composition of its polyphenols. A biochemical interpretation of these differences caused Erdtman (1959) to remark that haploxylon pines were forerunners of diploxylon pines.

When one descends below the subgeneric level of the genus *Pinus,* polyphenolic compounds are of little value for classification of pines except perhaps for the few tendencies in the subgenus *Haploxylon* such as in the group *Gerardianae* (Chapter 7, p. 471). In the subgenus *Diploxylon* most of the species have the same polyphenols in their heartwood.

Up to the present, almost all pine species have been analyzed for composition of their polyphenols. It appears highly desirable to extend the survey of the occurrence of polyphenols in the remaining species of the genus *Pinus.* Further studies may produce unexpected and useful data. For the most recent presentation of the distribution of polyphenols in pines, consult Erdtman (1963).

A serious drawback in studying the chemistry of heartwood polyphenols lies in the difficulty of obtaining heartwood samples for analysis. The trees have to be either cut or damaged; therefore it is not always possible to obtain many samples from many trees of a population unless it be from a logging operation. A single sample from a single tree to represent a species is often misleading. In the laboratory, even such a method as paper chromatography is time-consuming. The preparative analysis of polyphenols would take much more material and the separation of the components would require months. With all these difficulties taken into consideration, the use of polyphenols as an aid for the classification of pine species is suitable only for a broad segregation of the two subgenera. Heartwood polyphenols of the controversial *P. krempfii* have not yet been investigated.

**Components of Turpentines.**   Pine turpentine is composed of terpenes with occasional occurrence of alkanes, aromatic hydrocarbons, aliphatic aldehydes, a phenol ether (methyl chavicol), and, in one (or perhaps two) species, an aliphatic ester, ethyl caprylate. Of all these substances, terpenes are the most common.

Turpentine components have been studied more extensively than other pine components; we now have information on almost all pine species and also on the variability of these compounds within some species (Mirov, 1961; see also references in Literature Citations, Chapter 7). There is not much difference in the composition of turpentines of the two subgenera of the genus *Pinus*, *Haploxylon* and *Diploxylon;* perhaps in the former there are more sesquiterpene and diterpene hydrocarbons. Turpentine composition of *P. (Ducampopinus) krempfii* (see p. 540) is not known. Within the two subgenera, the components of turpentines often proved to be useful for the identification of pines. My studies of distribution of terpenes and associated compounds among the species of the genus *Pinus* have helped me to understand the difficulties of correlating taxonomy and chemistry so frequently reported for different plant species and for different groups of chemical substances (Mirov, 1961, 1963). The difficulties are encountered when sampling is inadequate; the procedure followed by many (see Chapter 7), but questioned only by few, is to analyze one sample taken from one tree to represent the whole species. Our experiments with turpentines have shown that there is a considerable individual variation in composition of turpentines; the same was mentioned by Lindstedt and Misiorny (see reference in Literature Citations, Chapter 7) for polyphenols of *P. sylvestris* No. 69. The situation is more complicated when a species is of a complex nature, occupying a large area and thus often composed of several varieties, each having common major components, but at the same time each possessing its own peculiar composition of turpentine. Such is *P. ponderosa* No. 14, which we studied more intensively, analyzing samples from different parts of its extensive area (see Chapter 3, No. 14).

A serious difficulty in correlating the chemistry of turpentines (and this is true for any chemical substance) and the taxonomic position of a species is encountered in cases in which there are no definite genetic barriers to intercrossing (see Chapter 4). Such is the situation in Mexico–Central America, or in southeastern Asia where one species merges into another imperceptibly. However, the most important cause of disagreement between chemistry and taxonomy in general, and thus in the case of turpentine components, seems to lie in the fact that the morphology and chemistry of plants follow different paths of evolution. Sometimes the two paths may approach one another or even merge into one; more often they are far apart.

In correlating the composition of turpentine with the taxonomic position of a pine, one also should remember that the genus *Pinus* of today is different from the genus *Pinus* of past geological periods. The chemical relationship of pines that existed, say, during the Jurassic period, was most likely different from what it is now. During the evolution of the genus, many ancient species became extinct and many new species appeared. At present we have merely patches of an old chemical pattern. Some of these patches are difficult to fit into the present taxonomic structure of the genus; others fit well and are useful in understanding the relationships of living pines.

When the above-noted difficulties of correlating chemistry of turpentines to taxonomy of pines are taken into consideration, this approach often may be useful. A good example is *P. jeffreyi* No. 13, which superficially looks like *P. ponderosa* No. 14 and which for a long time had been considered as a variety of that species. At present, it is generally considered as a separate species. The turpentine of *P. jeffreyi* does not contain terpenes as that of *P. ponderosa* does, but consists of an alkane, *n*-heptane, with an admixture of aldehydes. The presence of aldehydes in the oleoresin of this species (which can be determined quickly in the field) is the most consistent single indicator for differentiating it from *P. ponderosa* (Haller, 1962).

*Pinus ponderosa* is a very widely distributed species (Chapter 3, No. 14). It varies considerably both morphologically and chemically. But throughout its extensive range, composite samples of turpentine (taken from many trees of a population) always contain large amounts of $\Delta^3$-carene (Mirov, 1961, p. 89, Table 32). *Pinus engelmannii* No. 53 of northern Mexico, according to Shaw (1914), is a variety of *P. ponderosa*. Absence of $\Delta^3$-carene in its turpentine is sufficient reason to elevate *P. engelmannii* to the rank of species. On the other hand, *P. arizonica* No. 43, listed in this book as a species, perhaps should be considered as related much closer to *P. ponderosa* than *P. engelmannii* for it contains some $\Delta^3$-carene. *Pinus sibirica* No. 67, according to Shaw (1914), is a synonym of *P. cembra* No. 70, *P. pumila* No. 68 being considered merely its dwarf variety. Chemical analyses, however, show (Mirov, 1961, pp. 30–33) that *P. sibirica* and *P. pumila* turpentines both contain $\Delta^3$-carene while *P. cembra* turpentine does not. Chemical composition of these three species, in context with paleogeography (Chapter 2), throws an entirely different light on their interrelationship. Ferré (1960) thinks that *P. pumila* is closer to *P. parviflora* (i.e., *P. pentaphylla* No. 83) than to *P. cembra* (see p. 545).

Occurrence of cembrene (see Chapter 7, p. 51) in *P. albicaulis* No. 1, of western America, in *P. koraiensis* No. 82, in *P. armandi* No. 86, of eastern Asia, and in *P. peuce* No. 71 of the Balkans helps us to understand the migration route of pines from their origin in the north (see Chapter 8) both to California and to southeastern Asia and, in the latter case, via Tertiary ranges to the Mediterranean region (see Chapter 2).

The above examples indicate the usefulness of applying knowledge of turpentine composition to taxonomic studies of pines. Much has yet to be done, especially at the subspecies level. With modern methods of analysis perhaps more possibilities will be discovered. Of especial interest is an inquiry into the distribution of sesquiterpenes and diterpenes among the species of the genus *Pinus*.

It would be a futile task even to attempt to devise a biochemical classification of pines that would replace the existing botanical classification, but at the same time the biochemical characters of pines may well be used to establish or clarify relationships that are not discernible by other methods.

## TAXONOMIC PROBLEMS OF THE GENUS *PINUS*

Shaw's system for classification of the pines, greatly improved by Duffield's rearrangement of the subsection *Pinaster*, provides a framework for future studies of pines. Within this framework, information about species is unevenly distributed and a great deal is still unknown. In the following pages we shall review the whole genus and indicate where, in our opinion, uncertainties lie, what are their causes, and where most taxonomic studies should be done.

We shall begin our survey with the controversial *P. (Ducampopinus) krempfii* (Fig. 10–6), which was placed by Pilger (1926) in the subsection *Balfourianae*, section *Paracembra* of the subgenus *Haploxylon*. Gaussen (1960) created a new (the third) subgenus, *Ducampopinus*, to accommodate this pine. In Table 9–2 this species appears without number at the end with other new, unnamed, or uncertain species. In Chapter 3, it is mentioned briefly on page 299. The story of its discovery follows.

In 1921 Krempf found, in the mountains of southern Viet Nam, a pine-like conifer that was described by Lecomte (1921) as *P. krempfii*. In 1924 Lecomte published some additional information on this species, mentioning variability in the appearance of its needles (Lecomte, 1924). Later, Chevalier elevated this pine to the category of an independent monospecific genus and named the pine *Ducampopinus krempfii* (Chevalier, 1944). Ferré (1948, 1953) thought that the description of this pine as the basis for a new genus was perhaps premature because of insufficient material having been available, and mentioned a considerable variability in the size of the needles of Krempf pine. In a rather preliminary way, de Ferré suggested a subdivision of the genus *Pinus* into four subgenera: *Ducampopinus, Cembrapinus, Paracembrapinus,* and *Eupinus.* Gaussen (1960, p. 7) followed in part de Ferré's ideas when he subdivided the genus into his three subgenera: *Ducampopinus, Eupinus,* and *Cembrapinus.* (See Table 9–4 and Plate 9–1.)

A broad-leaved variety of *P. krempfii* was studied by Buchholz (1951). He was inclined to consider Krempf pine as an independent genus *Ducampopinus* Chevalier. He based his contention on the presence of wood parenchyma (which is absent in the genus *Pinus*) and on the absence of ray tracheids and horizontal resin canals. Later investigations have shown that both ray tracheids and horizontal resin canals are present in the wood of *P. krempfii.*

Budkevich (1958) found that the epithelium of the resin canals has thin walls, as is the case in all other species of the genus *Pinus.* Wood parenchyma was present. The pits on the cross-field were neither of the large (fenestriform) type nor of the simple unbordered (pinoid) type. Rather they were the bordered, narrow type (which she designated as "taxoidoid type"); this is supposedly more primitive than the cross-field pitting of all other types. Ray tracheids were present but not numerous. They had smooth walls and bordered pits. Horizontal resin canals were observed in the rays.

I. W. Bailey of Harvard University, who examined the anatomy of an eight-year-old branch of *P. krempfii* taken from an herbarium specimen procured by the present writer from Viet Nam, found both vertical and horizontal resin canals. The thin primary walls of normal epithelial cells of both vertical and horizontal canals were found to be unlignified, but they stained deeply in Sudan III, suggesting that the walls, as in some other pines, may be suberized. The ray parenchyma had relatively thick, lignified secondary walls; the pitting was of the form that occurs characteristically in *Picea, Larix, Pseudotsuga, Cedrus, Keteleeria, Pseudolarix, Tsuga,* and *Abies,* and also in several species of haploxylon pines (Nos. 5, 6, 7, 8, 9, 36, 92; see Table 1–1). The presence of a single vascular bundle in the needles and the occurrence of calcium oxalate crystals in

**Plate 9–1.** *Pinus krempfii* (Lecompte, 1921) twig and cone. Scale is in centimeters.

the phloem and cortex of the stem indicated characters of the subgenus *Haploxylon*. Ray tracheids were absent, probably because the twig was too young. Bailey is of the opinion that presence of wood parenchyma, reported by Buchholz and by Budkevich, is abnormal, being caused by injuries.*

*Pinus krempfii* is a tree from 12 to 30 m high, with brown-red, rather thin, shallowly furrowed bark; leaves in twos; flat, finely serrated, 3 to 7 cm and more long, 2 to 5 mm wide. Stomata are numerous on the upper (ventral) surface but very rare on the lower surface. Resin canals 6 to 12, commonly 8, two on the upper part and 6 or so on the lower. Cones are 7 to 9 cm long, 3 to 4 cm wide (Plate 10–1), resembling those of *P.*

* I. W. Bailey, personal communications during 1964.

*balfouriana* No. 5. Foliage occurs in tufts on the ends of branches. *Pinus krempfii* grows mixed with broadleaf trees of the upper story in dense forests in the mountains northeast of Dalat, Viet Nam (at Kong Klang, near and to the southwest of Nhatrang, in the mountains called by the French—*Massif de la mère et de l'enfant*). The Vietnamese call this pine Thông-sre (thông means pine).

Ferré (1948) suggested a close relationship of *P. krempfii* to *Pseudolarix* and *Keteleeria,* and Gaussen (1960) even thought that it was a (Tertiary ?) hybrid of either of the two with *Pinus.* The type collected by Krempf (No. 1537) at the herbarium of the Muséum d'Histoire Naturelle at Paris is from Nhatrang. The present writer saw, in the British Museum in London, a specimen of this pine originally identified as *Podocarpus* sp. with a handwritten note by Buchholz changing the name to *P. krempfii* var. *poilanei* Lecomte. In the Paris herbarium, Krempf's type had needles 4 cm long and 2 mm wide. Some varieties (*poilanei* ?), however, had much longer and broader saber-curved needles over 6 cm long and up to 4 mm wide.

In the United States, apparently, no herbarium specimens were available until 1961. Those procured by the writer from the Forest Service of Viet Nam were given to the Herbarium of the Institute of Forest Genetics, Placerville, Calif. Duplicates were sent to Gray Herbarium, Harvard University, University of Wisconsin, University of California at Berkeley, and the National Herbarium, Washington, D.C.

Jeffrey (1908) found the remains of a conifer in the Middle Cretaceous in the Raritan (Upper Potomac) deposits of Kreischerville, Staten Island, New York. Its leaves were flat, reminiscent of those of *P. krempfii.* From Tertiary lignites of Poland, Lilpop (1924) described a pinelike conifer whose wood had resin canals (thin-walled epithelium) and possessed wood parenchyma. Pitting on the crossfield of the ray tracheids was described as of a "pinoid type." Perhaps further studies of this interesting conifer would reveal some other characters indicating its phylogeny. Possibly *P. krempfii* is a connecting link between the genus *Pinus* and the other genera of the family. It is still a very little known conifer.

In Shaw's Group I, *Cembrae Koehne* (Table 9–1), hybridization experiments of *P. albicaulis* No. 1 with other haploxylon pines are desirable, especially with *P. pumila* No. 68, *P. koraiensis* No. 32, and *P. sibirica* No. 67; also with western American pines of Series 3, *Strobi,* particularly with *P. flexilis* No. 2.

In Shaw's Group II, *Flexiles* Shaw, and Group III, *Strobi* Engelm., which later he combined (Shaw, 1924) in one group, *Strobi,* there are many taxonomic problems. In eastern Asia, several pines of the group *Strobi* form a discontinuous series of vicarids usually all called *P. parviflora* (Fig. 9–1). *Pinus pentaphylla* No. 83 in the north of Japan is replaced

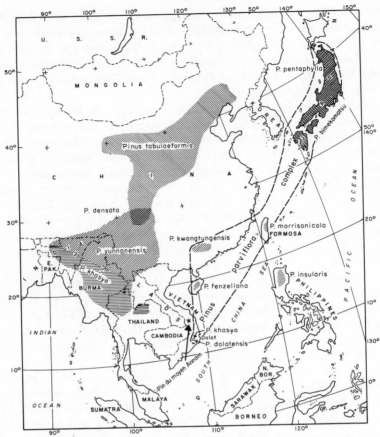

**Fig. 9–1.** Problems of pine taxonomy in eastern Asia.

with a certain overlap by *P. himekomatsu* No. 84 (see Chapter 3). In Taiwan there is found another vicarid of the *P. parviflora* complex, *P. morrisonicola* No. 85 (*P. formosana*). *Pinus uyematsui,* which is generally considered as a synonym of *P. morrisonicola,* occurs at an altitude of 2300 m, i.e., between the areas of *P. morrisonicola* (300 to 2300 m) and *P. armandi* (2300 to 3300 m) and is regarded by de Ferré as a species having characters similar to *P. griffithii* No. 91 and *P. peuce* No. 71. Ferré also mentioned *P. wangi* Hu and Cheng of Yunnan (see reference to Wang [1961, p. 136] in Literature Citations, Chapter 3). Relationship of this haploxylon pine to the other haploxylon species of this region is uncertain. Wang (1961) mentioned it in a rather ambiguous way, describing "A group of white pines (group *Strobi*) recognized as *P. kwangtungensis, P. fenzeliana, P. wangi,* and *P. morrisonicola,* scattered over the evergreen oak forest region from Yunnan to Hainan and Taiwan, a distance of 2000 km, but they rarely form a forest of any extent. These few white pines which are morphologically similar, represent perhaps a large continuous population which now persists only in the form of isolated geographical segregates" (see reference to Wang [1961], in Literature Citations in Chapter 3).

Ferré (1960) maintains that although *P. wangi* belongs to the "*P. parviflora* complex," some of its characters resemble those of *P. armandi* No. 86 or even *P. griffithii* No. 91. Perhaps here, de Ferré says, we have an ancestral type from which the three complexes—*P. armandi*, *P. parviflora* (Nos. 83 and 84), and *P. excelsa* (*P. griffithii* No. 91)—have originated. *Pinus peuce* No. 71 is included in the "*P. excelsa* complex."

Furthermore, from Hainan, Handel-Mazzetti described *P. fenzeliana* No. 89. In Kwantung, southeastern China, occurs still another species of "*P. parviflora* complex," *P. kwangtungensis* No. 90.

In Viet Nam there is one yet undescribed pine that Ferré (1960, Chapter 3, p. 115, Fig. ix–6) calls "*pin du moyen Annam.*" Apparently it also belongs to the "*P. parviflora* complex.*" It is found in middle Annam, on the "*Massif du Pou-Atouat*" between Hue and the Bolovens, at about 1500 m above sea level, at 15 degrees 30 minutes north altitude. Ferré based her report on a Chevalier herbarium specimen (only a branch; no cones) collected in 1918 at Thua-Lun, "*Forêt de Luong,*" Viet Nam (Fig. 9–6). At the first opportunity, more complete specimens of this pine should be collected and studied.

In the extreme north of the "*P. parviflora* complex" lies the area of *P. pumila* No. 68. In de Ferré's opinion, this species has many characters common to *P. parviflora* (i.e., *P. pentaphylla* No. 83). On the other hand, its affinity to *P. sibirica* is also certain (both species contain considerable percentage of $\Delta^3$-carene in their oleoresin). Through *P. pumila* the "*parviflora* complex" possibly is connected with *P. sibirica*.

*Pinus dalatensis* (Ferré, 1960) (i.e., No. 88) is a newly described haploxylon pine of southern Viet Nam (type, H. Gaussen, Trai-Mat, 6 km from Dalat, December, 1957, Herb. Lab. Forest. Toulouse). It is closely related to *P. griffithii* No. 91 and to *P. peuce* No. 71.

Another taxonomic problem in the group *Strobi* is concerned with one species, *P. armandi* (see Chapter 3, species No. 86). This pine occupies a large geographical area from Upper Burma to Japan, Formosa, and Hainan. Its distribution is discontinuous. Besides the continental occurrences, it is found on the two small islands at the southern tip of Japan where it is recognized as *P. armandi* Franch. var. *amamiana* Hatsuima or as *P. amamiana* Koidzu, Fig. 9–6. *Pinus armandi* of Taiwan, also known as *P. mastersiana* Hayata, occurs on the island of Hainan. The above brief résumé indicates that the "*P. armandi* complex" should

be investigated biosystematically. *Pinus armandi* has a common diter-
pene, cembrene, with *P. albicaulis* No. 1 of western America and with *P. peuce* No. 71 of the Balkans. Moreover, it has been crossed with *P. lam-bertiana* No. 3.

Among the New World pines of the group *Strobi* (see Table 9–1), the taxonomy of *P. flexilis* No. 2 and its relation to *P. strobiformis* No. 35 (*P. ayacahuite* var. *brachyptera*) was investigated by Steinhoff (1964). The geographical boundary between No. 2 and No. 35 runs through the canyons of the Colorado, the Arkansas, and the Rio Grande. Evidently pines No. 2 and No. 35 intercross. The relation of *P. strobiformis* to *P. ayacahuite* still remains to be investigated. Martínez (1948, p. 111) de-scribes the *P. ayacahuite* complex in the following translated words:

There are three distinct types of *P. ayacahuite:* a) A southern type (mainly in Guerrero, Oaxac? and Chiapas [and extending to Central America]), b) A Central type (chiefly in Morelos, Hidalgo and Puebla), c) A Northern type (mostly found in Sonora, Chihuahua and Durango). The southern type, origi-nally described by Ehrenberg in 1838, was considered as typical [*P. ayacahuite* Ehr. var. *ayacahuite*]. It is distinguished by its large, narrow and fragile cone scales and narrow, slender seed-wing. The central form was described by Roezl as *P. veitchii* and as *P. bonapartea* and by Gordon as *P. loudoniana*. Its characteristics are: coarse heavy and wide cone-scale, and larger seed with broader and shorter wing. The northern form was described by Engelmann (Wisliz, Mem. Tour North. Mex. 102. 1848) as *P. strobiformis;* it has heavy broad cone-scales, with large reflexed apophyses and a seed with very short or completely wanting wing.

Shaw (1909) considers *P. ayacahuite* composed of var. *typica* of the south, var. *veitchii* of the center, and var. *brachyptera* of the north. The variety *veitchii* is considered by Martínez as an intermediate form be-tween the two other varieties.

The relation of *P. lambertiana* No. 3 to *P. ayacahuite* also should be investigated. Although, as was already mentioned, this species was suc-cessfully crossed with *P. armandi* No. 86 of eastern China, all attempts to cross it with western American pines have failed. There is some resem-blance between *P. lambertiana* and *P. ayacahuite;* they both have the capacity of abundant exudation of pinitol (methyl inositol, see Chapter 7, p. 468) when wounded. Occasionally *P. lambertiana* cone scales and long peduncles have striking resemblance to those of *P. ayacahuite* (Plate 9–2).

Another uncertain haploxylon pine of Mexico is a recently discovered pine described as *P. strobus* var. *chiapensis* Martínez (1940). Its taxo-nomic status is still under investigation. Martínez (1948) mentioned some differences between this pine and *P. strobus* of the eastern United States. In the field, the two pines look rather different. Considering its geographical isolation from *P. strobus,* its subtropical habitat (this writer

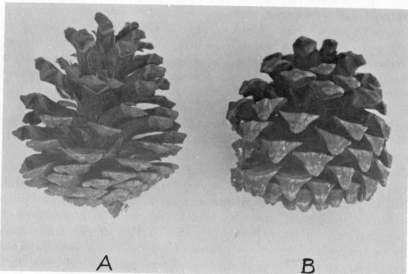

**Plate 9–2.** Cones. *Top: P. lambertiana* No. 3—*A,* normal cone; *B,* cone resembling that of *P. ayacahuite* No. 33. *Bottom:* differences of cone scales within the *P. pseudostrobus* complex—*A,* cone of typical *P. pseudostrobus* No. 54, with soft, thin scales; *B,* cone of a pine that is also considered by some (e.g., Shaw, 1914) as *P. pseudostrobus* but was described by Martínez (1948) as var. *oaxacana* and later was elevated to the rank of species as *P. oaxacana* No. 57 (Mirov, 1958). (U.S. Forest Service photos.)

saw it growing naturally in some places amidst coffee and banana plantations), and its consistent morphological differences from *P. strobus,* it
should perhaps be elevated to the rank of species.

Shaw's Group IV, *Cembroides* (piñon pines), may be separated into
two subgroups: one consisting of four species—*P. monophylla* No. 7,
*P. edulis* No. 8, *P. quadrifolia* No. 9, and *P. cembroides* No. 36—which
come in contact one with the other and which possibly intercross. Of
these, No. 36 has a very large area (southeastern U.S. and Mexico) and
No. 9 of California is rare and local. The second group consists of three
species (Nos. 37 , 38, and 39), all Mexican, all extremely rare and
isolated one from the other (although No. 36 occurs together with Nos.
37 and 38). No breeding experiments have been done with piñon pines
yet. It is desirable to study the relationship of these seven species. From
a chemical point of view this group of pines is by no means homogeneous
(Mirov, 1961; see reference to Mirov, Zavarin, and Bicho [1962], in
Literature Citations, Chapter 7).

The two species forming Shaw's Group V, *Gerardianae*—*P. gerardiana*
No. 92 and *P. bungeana* No. 87—are little known botanically, although
the latter has often been planted near temples. Both are three-needle
species, a rather unusual phenomenon in haploxylon pines. In their
heartwood polyphenol composition, they have much in common, and both
differ in this respect from the rest of the haploxylon pines. There is no
important difference in the composition of their turpentines. No breeding
work has been done with these species. This is a good project for the
biosystematists of India or Pakistan and China.

The two five-needle "foxtail pines" of western North America, which
comprise Shaw's Group VI, *Balfourianae,* are also little known. A hybrid
derivative possibly occurs in nature at least in one place in the White
Mountains of California where we once found cones on *P. aristata* trees
having characters of *P. balfouriana* cones. Pollen of the latter could
easily be transported by westerly winds from the Sierra Nevada across
Owens Valley to the White Mountains. Their geographical isolation in
other places prevents their more frequent crossing. Chemically, both in
polyphenols and in terpenes, the two are similar. It would be interesting
to analyze biosystematically these two pines.

The first three groups of the (section) subgenus *Diploxylon* in Shaw's
classification are: VII, *Leiophyllae,* VIII, *Longifoliae,* and IX, *Pineae.*
In Group VII, *P. chihuahua* No. 40 is a three-needle pine and *P. leiophylla* No. 41 is a five-needle pine. The two differ considerably in chemical composition (Mirov, 1961). This writer is in accord with Martínez
(1948), who considers these two pines independent species. Possibly
they hybridize in nature. The third pine in this group is *P. lumholtzii,*
one of the few pines whose turpentine consists largely of limonene.

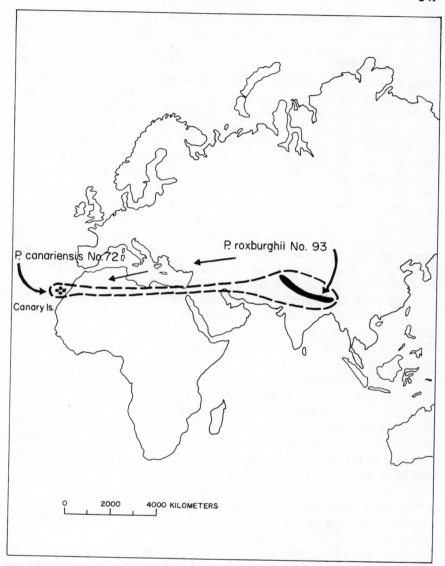

**Fig. 9–2.** Geographical isolation of the two species of the pine group *Longifoliae*.

Martínez (1948) remarked that some taxonomic research is needed in this group.

The two pines of Shaw's group *Longifoliae* became distinct species by virtue of long geographical isolation (Fig. 9–2). When brought together (see Chapter 3, Nos. 72 and 93), they hybridize naturally. They should be studied biosystematically. *Pinus pinea* No. 73 is the sole member of Shaw's group *Pineae*. It is truly an enigmatic species. Gaussen (1960) put it together with piñon pines and other pines in his Section VI, *Parryanoides*, which is composed of Shaw's Groups IV, V, VI, and IX. *Pinus pinea* is a typical Mediterranean pine, but Francini (see Chapter 3, No. 73) suggests that it is a newcomer there, migrating from a region of warm, temperate climate, different from that of the Mediterranean region. Regarding its possible origin also, see Chapter 3, No. 73. Chemically it is also unusual. Although its polyphenols (see Chapter 7) are the same as those in most of the diploxylon pines, its turpentine is unusual for it consists almost entirely of *l*-limonene. It contains sesquiterpenes caryophyllene (found also in *P. pinaster* No. 80) and humulene and also small quantities of diterpene, cembrene (which is found in haploxylon pines and reported in a diploxylon, *P. thunbergii* No. 97). There are also traces of *n*-heptane. Perhaps it is a newcomer to the Mediterranean, but it appears to be an ancient pine that lost its affinities with other pines. It never has been successfully crossed with any other pine species. A biosynthetic monograph on this pine is needed.

Most of the taxonomic work has been done in Shaw's subsection *Pinaster*, which consists of Groups X, *Lariciones;* XI, *Australes;* XII, *Insignes;* and XIII, *Macrocarpae* (see Table 9–1), i.e., in Duffield's Groups X, XI, XII, XIII, and XIV (Table 9–3). A great deal yet remains to be done in these groups.

In Duffield's Group X, two pines stand out: *P. resinosa* of northeastern America (No. 21), and *P. tropicalis* No. 66 of the Caribbean region (see Chapter 3). These two pines are the only species of Group X, *Lariciones*, found in the New World. *P. resinosa* does not hybridize with American pines, but it has been crossed with *P. nigra* (see reference to Critchfield [1963b] in Literature Citations, Chapter 4). No experimental work has yet been done with *P. tropicalis*, although its hybridization with *P. caribaea* has been suspected. It would be interesting to study these two pines, using methods of experimental taxonomy.

The remaining twenty-one species of Group X, which are Eurasian pines, will be discussed presently. (See Table 9–3.)

*Pinus nigra* No. 74 is a very variable species; new varieties are still being described. Delevoy (1949) divided *P. nigra* into two subspecies, each containing several varieties. This arrangement is shown in Table 9–5. There are many other varieties of *P. nigra;* some of them were even given the rank of species. Such is *P. monspeliensis*, discovered (but not published) by Salzmann. In 1851 Dunal published it validly under the name of *P. salzmanni* (see Debazac, 1963). *Pinus heldreichii* No. 75 is considered by some authors (Shaw, 1914) as a variety of *P. nigra*. *Pinus leucodermis* is a variety of *P. heldreichii*. Chemically, *P. heldreichii* and

**Table 9–5.** Arrangement of *P. nigra* and Its Varieties According to Delevoy (1949)

| | |
|---|---|
| *P. nigra* Arn. subspecies *occidentalis* | |
| var. *salzmanni* Asch. and Graebn. | Cevennes |
| var. *pyrenaica* Car. | Pyrenees |
| var. *hispanica* Cook | Spain |
| var. *marocana* (?) | Morocco |
| var. *poiretiana* Asch. and Graebn. | Corsica |
| var. *mauretanica* Maire and de Peyer. | Algeria |
| *P. nigra* Arn. subspecies *orientalis* | |
| var. *calabrica* Loud. | Calabria |
| | Sicily |
| | France |
| | Abruzzi |
| | Pantelleria |
| var. *austriaca* Asch. and Graebn. | Austria |
| | Hungary, Balkans |
| var. *hornotica* Beck. | So. Austria |
| var. *gocensis* Georg. | Serbia occid. (and perhaps black pine of France and Calabria) |
| var. *dalmatica* Vis. | Dalmatia |
| var. *bosniaca* Elwes | Bosnia |
| var. *banatica* Georg. and Ionescu | Rumania |
| var. *pallasiana* Asch. and Graebn. | Crimea |
| var. *caramanica* Loud. | Asia Minor |
| var. *fenzlii* Ant. and Kotsch. | Asia Minor |

its variety *leucodermis* are distinguishable from *P. nigra* and its varieties by a large percentage of limonene in its oleoresin (Mirov, 1961).

*Pinus montana* is known in three main varieties (see Chapter 3, No. 76). Preliminary studies of the turpentine of this pine indicated its complexity. It is desirable to compare chemical compositions of these varieties, using either oleoresins (Mirov, 1961) or needle oils (see reference to Zanini *et al.* [1961] in Literature Citations, Chapter 7). Reports on possible natural hybridization of *P. montana* with other species (see Chapter 3, No. 76) should be verified.

*Pinus sylvestris* No. 69 occupies an enormous area from Scotland and Scandinavia to northern Mongolia. Its Mediterranean habitat extends from Spain to Transcaucasia. This pine has been studied ecologically and silviculturally more than any other pine; many varieties and horticultural forms have been described and new ones are currently being published. A list of varieties is given by Gaussen (1960). There are also records of natural hybridization of *P. sylvestris* with *P. montana* No. 76, *P. nigra* No. 74 (see Gaussen, 1960), and *P. tabulaeformis* No. 102 (Wu, 1956). The whole *P. sylvestris* complex has been recently monographed by Pravdin (see reference to Pravdin [1964] in Literature Citations, Chapter 3).

*Pinus sylvestris* in the Mediterranean region (see Chapter 3, pp. 257, 260) presents an additional problem. *Pinus sylvestris* of the mountains of the Iberian Peninsula, of the Alps, and of the Apennines is relatively well studied, but in the eastern Mediterranean area it is little known. Some taxonomists consider the pine of the main Caucasian Range (Greater Caucasus) as an independent species, *P. hamata* or *P. sosnovskyi* Nakai. A pine belonging to the *P. sylvestris* complex and growing in Transcaucasia is taken to be the same species. Following priority rules, the whole Caucasian complex of *P. sylvestris* is known as *P. kochiana* Klotsch, *P. sosnovskyi* Nakai and *P. hamata* Sosn. being its synonyms. Others consider *P. kochiana* of Transcaucasia a species independent of *P. sosnovskyi*. Ecologically, *P. kochiana* is different from the pine of the northern Caucasus. It is extremely drought resistant and forms open groves.*

*Pinus armena* Koch also apparently is the same pine as *P. kochiana*. The Transcaucasian pines of the *P. sylvestris* complex extend to Turkey. Below are given synonym references to the Caucasian pines (see also Fig. 9–6):

*P. kochiana* Klotsch, (1949). Linnaea **22**:396.—*P. silvestris* L. var. *hamata* Steven, (1838). Bull. Soc. Nat. Moscou **I**:51.—*P. armena* C. Koch, 1849. Linnaea **22**:297.—*P. montana* Mill. var. *caucasica* Medw. (1905) Derev. i kustarn. Kavkaz. 2nd Ed. **I**:11.—*P. sylvestris* L. ssp. *hamata* var. *kochiana* Fomin, (1914) Monit. Jard. Bot. **XXXIV**:15–24, 34:15–24.—*P. hamata* D. Sosn., (1925). Fl. Tifl. (1925) **1**:11.—*P. sosnovskyi* Nakai, (1939). Tyosen Sanrin Kaiho, n.I67 (Indig. Spec. Conif. and Taxads. Korea and Manchuria. **IV**:333.

There are many indications that the Caucasian pine is different from the *P. sylvestris* of northern Eurasia. Paleographic history of the two is different (see Chapter 2). Their morphology is different. *Pinus kochiana* has a recurved prickle on the umbo of its cones while the northern *P. sylvestris* has a minute prickle or its remnant. There is an old report on the difference in rotations of turpentine of the two pines: That of the northern *P. sylvestris* is dextrorotatory, that of the Caucasian pine is levorotatory (see Chapter 2, pages 84 and 85; and Chapter 3, pages 257 and 260). A more thorough investigation into turpentine chemistry of the two pines might throw some light on their relationships. Some botanists say that *P. sylvestris* of northern Eurasia and *P. hamata* of the Caucasus come in contact in Bulgaria (Cherniavski, 1954).

The four Mediterranean pines—*P. halepensis* No. 77, *P. brutia* No. 78, *P. pityusa* No. 79, and *P. eldarica* No. 81—present a very interesting biotaxonomic study. Consult description of these pines in Chapter 3 under the indicated numbers. That Nos. 79 and 81 are mere varieties of *P. brutia* is almost certain. *Pinus brutia* and pines Nos. 79 and 81 contain

---

* I am indebted to Professor A. A. Iatsenko-Khmelevsky of Leningrad, U.S.S.R., for his comments on the *P. sylvestris* complex in the Caucasian region.

$\Delta^3$-carene, while the closely related *P. halepensis* does not. *P. sylvestris* (or *P. kochiana*) also contains $\Delta^3$-carene. Could it be possible that the *P. brutia* complex is a result of Tertiary hybridization between the ancestors of *P. halepensis* and *P. sylvestris* (see references to Papajoannou [1963] and Mirov [1955] in the Literature Citations, Chapter 3)?

*Pinus pinaster* No. 80 is a well-defined species. Fieschi and Gaussen separated from it the Corsican *"Pin de Corté"* and named it *P. mesogeensis*. It is found all the way from Greece to Morocco (Gaussen, 1960). Other suggested varieties of this pine are mentioned under No. 80 in Chapter 3 of this book.

In turning to the eastern Asiatic pines of Duffield's Group X, *P. densiflora* No. 95, *P. thunbergii* No. 97, and *P. massoniana* No. 94 are well defined. For some reported varieties of *P. massoniana,* such as var. *henryi* (which according to Shaw [1914] is a variety of *P. tabulaeformis*), see Wu (1956).

*Pinus luchuensis* No. 98, *P. hwangshanensis* No. 100, and *P. taiwanensis* No. 99 are considered by Wu (1956) as one species. Chemically, however, these three species are quite different. Apparently Nos. 99 and 100 are closer to each other than to No. 98.

In taking into consideration their geographical isolation and chemical differences (see Mirov, 1961), it seems wiser to consider these three pines as separate species, although in the herbaria they may look similar.

*Pinus merkusii* No. 101 is a relatively non-variable pine. Only in northern Viet Nam does it look sufficiently different from typical *P. merkusii* to be called var. *tonkinensis* (Chevalier, 1944) (see Chapter 3, No. 101; Fig. 9–6). *Pinus merkusii* of the Philippines, however, appears to be somewhat different chemically, for its oleoresin contains only minute amounts of $\Delta^3$-carene, while *P. merkusii* from Burma and Sumatra contains large quantities of this terpene. *P. merkusii* turpentine from Viet Nam has not been analyzed yet.*

In the northern part of China grows *P. tabulaeformis* No. 102 (previously known as *P. sinensis*). Its area is very large. This species has several named varieties that are listed in Chapter 3, No. 102. In the north it possibly crosses with *P. sylvestris* No. 69. In the northeast it comes so close to *P. funebris* No. 96 that Shaw (1914) considered this latter species to be a synonym of *P. sinensis* (i.e., of *P. tabulaeformis*). Komarov, who described *P. funebris,* and other investigators (see reference to Komarov [1934] in Literature Citations, Chapter 3) are inclined to think that perhaps *P. funebris* should be considered as a northernmost race of *P. densiflora* No. 95. In the southwestern part of its area, i.e., in Yunnan, *P. tabulaeformis* merges into *P. yunnanensis* No. 103. Supposedly, the

---

* Unpublished data, see also Mirov (1961).

two intercrossed there (apparently during the Tertiary) and the hybrid swarm developed into a new species, *P. densata* Masters (Fig. 9–6; see also Chapter 3, p. 300). *Pinus tabulaeformis*, with its numerous varieties, offers extremely interesting research possibilities, especially if its variety *pseudosylvestris* could be shown (see Chapter 3) experimentally to be a hybrid between this species and *P. sylvestris*, and if *P. densata* could be proved a hybrid between *P. tabulaeformis* and *P. yunnanensis*.

In the southwestern portion of its geographical area, *P. yunnanensis* gradually merges into *P. khasya* No. 104; this latter pine extends westward to the Khasi Hills of Assam, India. In adjacent parts of Burma, it is known as *P. insularis* No. 105, for some botanists (Shaw, 1914; Wu, 1956) believe that the two are the same. In Thailand and in southern Viet Nam where this pine occurs in disjointed patches, it is known as *P. khasya* again.

*Pinus insularis* was originally described from Luzon, Philippines, and later its name was applied by some botanists to *P. khasya* and to *P. yunnanensis*. The story of the nomenclature of these three pines is vividly told by Wu (1947). In herbaria, indeed, it is difficult to tell these three pines apart, but chemically they are different. *Pinus khasya* in Assam is tapped for turpentine and rosin production; *P. insularis* is not well suited for this purpose. The reason is that the oleoresin of *P. khasya* of Assam contains but little β-phellandrene, while the oleoresin of *P. insularis* of Luzon contains large amounts of this easily polymerized terpene. It solidifies into a sugary mass and thus interferes with the flow of the oleoresin from the wound to the container. There are also some differences in the sesquiterpene fraction of turpentines of the two pines. *Pinus khasya* from Viet Nam is closer in chemical composition to *P. insularis* of Luzon than to *P. khasya* of Assam.* More experimental work should be done with these three pines of southeastern Asia, using all available approaches, before their taxonomic relationship is established (Fig. 9–1).

In Duffield's Group XI (Table 9–3), pine species of the eastern United States have been well studied and their genetic relationship has been established (Critchfield, 1963). In contrast, the Caribbean species need a great deal of taxonomic attention. These are *P. caribaea* No. 62, *P. occidentalis* No. 64, and *P. cubensis* No. 65. In this group are also included the southern Florida pine recently described by Little and Dorman (1952; see reference in Literature Citations, Chapter 3) as *P. elliottii* var. *densa*. Geographically it belongs to the Caribbean area and chemically (large amounts of phellandrene in its oleoresin; see reference to Mirov, Frank, and Zavarin [1965] in Literature Citations, Chapter 3) it is closer to *P. caribaea* than to *P. elliottii* No. 23 of the mainland. Its relationship to these two species should be thoroughly investigated. A

* Unpublished data by Dr. Eugene Zavarin of Forest Products Laboratory, University of California, Berkeley.

working hypothesis offered here is that *P. elliottii* var. *densa* is a Caribbean species of very recent arrival in Florida. In its expansion north it reached the southern limits of the area of *P. elliottii*. Hybridization between the two is feasible. One of the questions to be answered is: Whence did it get its grass stage (Chapter 6, p. 417)—directly from *P. palustris* of the north or through Mexican pines via the Caribbean islands?

Apparently *P. caribaea* No. 62 migrated to the Caribbean islands from Central America. In this latter part of its area a problem arises: *P. caribaea* forms the pine savannas (see Chapter 6, p. 449) of the coast of Honduras, British Honduras, and Nicaragua. Is the inland form that occurs in the mountains of Central America a variety of the coastal *P. caribaea*, or is it an independent species? Is it a product of hybridization of *P. caribaea* and *P. oocarpa*, as Williams (1955; see reference in Literature Citations, Chapter 3) postulated?

Loock (1950; see reference in Literature Citations, Chapter 3) separated the coastal "slash pine" of Central America from the "slash pine" of the southeastern United States (both then known as *P. caribaea*) because of considerable morphological differences between the two pines. He proposed to name the Central American "slash pine" *P. hondurensis*, but now, since the slash pine of the American Southeast is known as *P. elliottii*, there are no objections to calling the coastal Central American pine (at least tentatively) *P. caribaea*. Perhaps the name *P. hondurensis* should be retained to designate the "mountain form of *P. caribaea*" of Central America (Plate 9–3; Fig. 9–6, page 564). The main problem, of course, is whether to consider *P. caribaea* as a single species spreading from the Bahamas and Cuba to the Moskitia coast of Nicaragua (Fig. 9–3). *Pinus elliottii* var. *densa* also should be included in this study.

Recently Barrett and Golfari divided *P. caribaea* into three varieties. Variety *caribaea* Morelet is characterized by needles in fascicles of three, rarely four; cones 5 to 10 cm long, seeds with adnate wings; it is found in western Cuba, at altitudes from 50 to 350 m. Variety *hondurensis* Barr. and Golf. has needles in fascicles of 3, sometimes 4, 5 (and 6 in young trees), cones 6 to 14 cm long; seeds generally with articulate wing; it grows in Central America from sea level to about 850 m altitude. The third variety, *bahamensis* Barr. and Golf., has needles in twos and threes; cones 4 to 12 cm long; seeds generally with articulate wing; it grows in the Bahamas and Caicos, at sea level in a tropical climate, but with six or seven months' drought (Barrett and Golfari, 1962). Further studies of *P. caribaea* are desirable.

Another study should be concerned, as was already mentioned, with *P. tropicalis* No. 66, a stranger from Duffield's Group X among the pines of Group XI. Does it cross with *P. caribaea* and with *P. elliottii* var. *densa* No. 63? Where did it get its "grass stage"? The taxonomic relationship of

**Plate 9–3.** *Pinus* sp., Upper Rio Choluteca Valley of the mountains of inner Honduras. Altitude about 900 m. This pine is generally called the "mountain form of *P. caribaea.*" (Photo by Carl L. Johannessen.)

*P. occidentalis* and *P. cubensis* (Nos. 64 and 65; see Chapter 3) also should be investigated.

In Duffield's Group XII, the relationship of *P. jeffreyi* No. 13 and *P. ponderosa* No. 14 was well studied by Haller (1962; see reference in Literature Citations, Chapter 4). The taxonomic status of *P. washoensis* No. 15 is still uncertain, although some advancement has been made in this direction by Haller (1959, 1961; see reference in Literature Citations, Chapter 3).

The remaining fifteen pines belonging to Duffield's Group XII are Mexican pines, although *P. arizonica* No. 43 occurs also in New Mexico and in Arizona where it was discovered. Martínez (1948) described

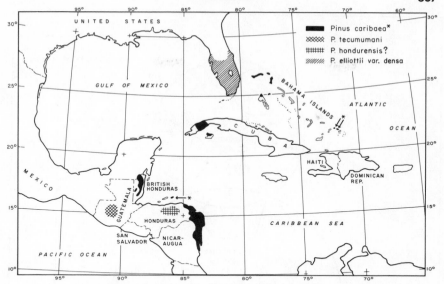

**Fig. 9–3.** Taxonomic problems in the Caribbean area.

*P. arizonica* var. *stormiae,* which grows in the states of Coahuila and Nuevo León. *Pinus arizonica* is considered by some as a variety of *P. ponderosa* No. 14 (Little, 1953). The three other pines of northern Mexico are *P. engelmannii* No. 53, *P. durangensis* No. 48, and *P. cooperi* No. 51. They do not grow south of the state of Durango. These three species do not belong either to the *P. ponderosa* complex of the north or to the *P. montezumae* complex of Mexico. They would comprise a compact group for separate biosystematic study.

*Pinus montezumae* No. 47 is a widely distributed pine growing from northeastern Mexico to Chiapas and farther to the highlands of Central America. With several other pines it forms a complex formerly considered as one species, *P. montezumae* (Shaw, 1914) (Fig. 9–4). Martínez (1948) divided it into four species: *P. montezumae* No. 47, *P. michoacana* No. 52, *P. hartwegii* No. 49, and *P. rudis* No. 50. A diagram taken from Martínez shows species of this complex and its relation to other pine groups of Mexico (Fig. 9–4).

Aguilar (1961) discovered in Guatemala a pine that he named *P. quichensis* (Fig. 9–6). Its morphological characters were intermediate between those of *P. montezumae* and *P. oocarpa* No. 59. In Guerrero, Mexico, Larsen found a pine that had both *P. montezumae* and *P. pseudostrobus* characters.* Zobel and Cech (1957; see reference in Literature

---

* Egon Larsen, New Zealand Forest Research Institute, personal communication, 1962.

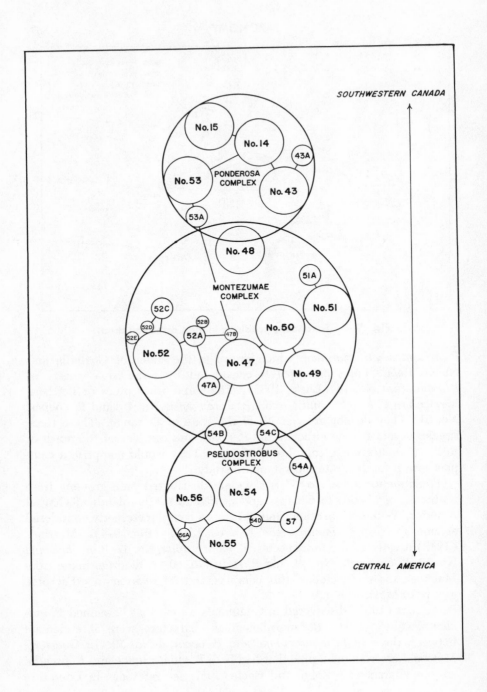

Citations, Chapter 3) collected in Nuevo León some pine material that resembled *P. montezumae.*

In the warmer parts of Mexico, there exists another complex of pines (Fig. 9–4). It consists of *Pinus pseudostrobus* No. 54, *P. tenuifolia* No. 55, *P. douglasiana* No. 56, *P. oaxacana* No. 57, and varieties of *P. pseudostrobus: apulcensis, coatepecensis, estevezi,* and a forma *protuberans* (Martínez, 1948). Nomenclatural difficulties of this complex are mentioned in the description of *P. oaxacana* (Plate 9–2; see reference to Mirov [1958] in Literature Citations for Chapter 3). By no means have all varieties of the *P. pseudostrobus* complex been discovered. Larsen, who collected in Mexico, found in Michoacán a pine belonging to the *Pseudostrobus* complex. He named it *P. martinezii* (Larsen, 1964) (Fig. 9–6).

It is certain that *P. oaxacana* crosses naturally with some varieties of *P. pseudostrobus.* On the other hand, it apparently crosses with *P. montezumae. Pinus oaxacana* turpentine contains a large percentage of *n*-heptane; *P. montezumae* does not contain this alkane. In a mixed *oaxacanamontezumae* stand in Chiapas the author found *P. montezumae* with a considerable admixture of *n*-heptane in its turpentine. Martínez (1948) believes that *P. pesudostrobus* has a close relationship (*"estrecho parentesco"*) with *P. montezumae.*

---

**Fig. 9–4.** Three great pine complexes of America:

    A. *Pinus ponderosa* complex, comprising *P. ponderosa* Laws. No. 14; *P. arizonica* Engelm. No. 43 and its variety, *stormiae* Mart. No. 43A; *P. engelmannii* Carr. No. 53 and its variety *blancoi* Mart.; and *P. washoensis* Mason & Stockwell No. 15.

    B. *Pinus montezumae* complex, which consists of *P. montezumae* Lamb. No. 47, with its variety *lindleyi* Loudon No. 47A and forma *macrocarpa* Mart. No. 47B; *P. michoacana* Mart. No. 52 including its varieties: (1) *cornuta* Mart. No. 52A, with forma *nayaritana* Mart. No. 52B, and (2) *quevedoi* Mart. No. 52C, with formae *procera* Mart. No. 52D and *tumida* Mart. No. 52E; *P. durangensis* Mart. No. 48; *P. hartwegii* Lindl. No. 49; *P. rudis* Endlich. No. 50; and *P. cooperi* Blanco No. 51, with its variety *ornelasi* Mart. No. 51A.

    C. *Pinus pseudostrobus* complex, embracing *P. pseudostrobus* Lindl. No. 54 and its varieties: *apulcensis* Shaw No. 54A, *coatepecensis* Mart. No. 54B, *estevezi* Mart. No. 54C, and forma *protuberans* Mart. No. 54D; *P. tenuifolia* Benth. No. 55; *P. douglasiana* Mart. No. 56; *P. oaxacana* Mirov No. 57; and *P. martinezii* Larsen No. 56A. (See Chapter 3, pages 217, 219.)

Numbers after species names refer to Tables 1–1 and 1–2. (After Martínez, 1948. Somewhat modified.)

Another complex species of Mexico is *P. teocote* No. 45. This pine has a broad geographical distribution. Although *P. teocote* (see Chapter 3) is not as variable as some other Mexican pines, Shaw (1914) distinguished within it a var. *macrocarpa*. Martínez (1948) remarked that in the north *P. teocote* sometimes resembles *P. arizonica* No. 43, while in the south it looks similar to *P. lawsonii* No. 44. *Pinus teocote* offers interesting material for a biosystematic monograph.

Shaw's group *Macrocarpae*, which Duffield considered a part of his Group XII, is still an intact group of three pines: *P. sabiniana* No. 10, *P. torreyana* No. 11, and *P. coulteri* No. 12. Morphological characters of these three species have much in common. Their turpentines are similar and all three contain alkaloids, a circumstance that is very unusual in pines (see reference to Tallent *et al.* [1955] in Literature Citations, Chapter 3). As regards the position of the group *Macrocarpae* among other groups, there is no doubt that it is close to Duffield's Group XII. In fact Duffield abolished the group *Macrocarpae* by moving it to his Group XII. *Pinus jeffreyi* may be considered a connecting link between Group XII and the *Macrocarpae* pines. Within the group *Macrocarpae*, *P. sabiniana* was well monographed by Griffin (1962; see reference in Literature Citations, Chapter 3). There had been suggestions of the existence of varieties of this species: var. *explicata* Jepson, forma *macrocarpa* Epling (Stockwell, 1939). Griffin, however, found no biosystematic justification for establishing such subspecific categories. This is a good example of an intensive study of a pine that has not resulted in splitting a species into several varieties. *Pinus sabiniana* has been successfully crossed with *P. torreyana* and *P. coulteri*.*

*Pinus torreyana* is a pine of more restricted distribution than any other species of the genus *Pinus*. It occupies an area of about 350 ha. on the coast of southern California and it occurs also on a small island, Santa Rosa, off the coast. Formerly it was more widely distributed (see Chapter 2, page 34).

Both *P. torreyana* and *P. pinea* No. 73 of the Mediterranean region have very large and heavy cones; chemical composition of their turpentines is similar (Mirov, 1961). *P. pinea* has not been crossed with any other pines.

*Pinus coulteri*, unlike the two other species of the group *Macrocarpae*, hybridizes naturally with *P. jeffreyi* No. 13; it was studied by Zobel (1955; see reference in Literature Citations, Chapter 4).

More work should be done with the pines of the group *Macrocarpae* before it is dispersed, as in Gaussen's (1960) system, which placed *P. torreyana* next to *P. michoacana* No. 52 (i.e., put it in the *Montezumae*

---

* Unpublished report, Institute of Forest Genetics, 1963.

complex); *P. coulteri* between *P. engelmannii* No. 53 and *P. durangensis* No. 48; and *P. sabiniana* between *P. attenuata* No. 17 and *P. banksiana* No. 32 (of Duffield's Group XIII).

Duffield's Group XIII, *P. banksiana, P. contorta* No. 16, *P. virginiana* No. 27, and *P. clausa* No. 28, has been well studied (Critchfield, 1963; Fig. 9–5). For variability of *P. contorta* see Chapter 3.

Jeffers and Black (1963) contributed recently to elucidation of intra-specific variability of *P. contorta*. They applied methods of multivariate analysis to nineteen variables of nine provenances of *P. contorta*. In the words of the authors "the analysis confirms the broad division of *P. contorta* into inland and coastal provinces [as Critchfield showed; see Chapter 3, p. 168, sp. No. 16] but suggests an independent classification which accounts for an even greater degree of botanical variation." How advisable it is to do this "splitting" depends chiefly on the purpose of the research; in Jeffers and Black's it was apparently to select provenances with desirable timber properties. It does appear, however, that taxonomy of the genus *Pinus* should be based on concepts that are somewhat broader.

As an inquiry into subspecific variability in pines, Jeffers and Black's study is a noteworthy contribution.

Intraspecific variability of *P. banksiana* as well as the extent and results of its hybridization with *P. contorta* yet remains to be investigated.

Duffield's Group XIV consists of seven species: three of western America (*P. attenuata* No. 17, *P. muricata* No. 18, and *P. radiata* No. 19) and four Mexican pines (*P. pringlei* No. 58, *P. patula* No. 61, *P. greggii* No. 60, and *P. oocarpa* No. 59). The three western American pines have been well studied paleobotanically by Mason (1932; see reference in Literature Citations, Chapter 2), and taxonomically by Duffield (1951; see reference in Literature Citations, Chapter 4), and Forde (1962; see reference in Literature Citations, Chapter 4). On the other hand, the four Mexican pines are little known. *Pinus pringlei* No. 58 possibly hybridizes with *P. patula* No. 61, for Martínez mentioned (1948) the existence of inter-mediate forms between these two species in the area of Cuicatlan, Oaxaca. *Pinus pringlei* is a pine of subtropical environment and of relatively limited distribution. Roughly, it grows in southwestern Mexico, from Michoacán to Oaxaca; *P. greggii* No. 60 is a pine of the Mexican northeast extending to the central eastern part of the country. Apparently these two pines do not come in contact. The area of *P. patula* is between the areas of the two other pines, overlapping somewhat the area of *P. greggii* and coming close to that of *P. pringlei*. *Pinus patula* var. *longepedunculata* Loock (see Chapter 3, No. 61) was described from Oaxaca. It appears that the three above described pines offer a compact group *Patula* of Martínez for a biosystematic study.

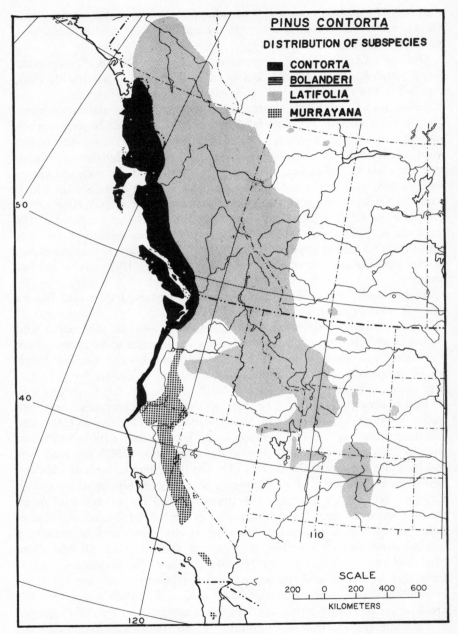

**Fig. 9–5.** Approximate geographical distribution of the four subspecies of *P. contorta* No. 16. (From Critchfield, 1963.)

The fourth Mexican pine of the Group XIV *Insignes, P. oocarpa,* is a five-needle species of wide distribution from southern Chihuahua to El Salvador and Nicaragua; it is very variable. Martínez recognizes a three-needle form of this species (forma *trifoliata,* found in Durango) and three varieties: *manzanoi* Mart., of ill-defined distribution in the state of Hidalgo; *ochoterenai* Mart., of Chiapas; and *microphylla* Shaw, of Sinaloa and Jalisco. In Central America, *P. oocarpa* presents some more taxonomic problems; for example, there is found one pine that Schwerdtfeger (see reference in Literature Citations, Chapter 3) described without Latin diagnosis as *P. tecumumani.* In some characters, it resembles *P. oocarpa,* while in others it looks like *P. pseudostrobus.*

Standley and Steyermark (1958) disagreed with Schwerdtfeger as to the validity of specific rank for this pine; they identified his herbarium specimens of *P. tecumumani* as *P. oocarpa.* But in the concluding paragraph of their discussion of the status of this pine, the authors of the *Flora of Guatemala* remarked that after all, the herbarium type material of *P. tecumumani* seems best interpreted as representing a somewhat variant form of *P. oocarpa,* although it is also possible that it may be considered as of hybrid ancestry between *P. oocarpa* and *P. pseudostrobus.* Thus it appears that the taxonomic status of *P. tecumumani* still awaits clarification (Fig. 9–6).

As a whole, *P. oocarpa* is a big complex, requiring a special biosystematical study that, because of the extensive area of this pine, should be considered as a major research project.

## SUMMARY

The new era in classification of pines was started in 1914 when Shaw published his *The Genus* Pinus. He was the first to use an evolutionary approach and to apply microscopic morphology of the wood for the purposes of pine taxonomy. Shaw was more familiar with Mexican pines than his predecessors; therefore his treatment of this part of the genus was better than theirs. He commented, however, on the great variability of Mexican pines that sometimes made their identification difficult.

As American haploxylon species are well delimited and thus easy to recognize, Shaw's treatment of this subgenus was satisfactory; some taxonomic uncertainty was encountered only with the northern variety of *P. ayacahuite.* The chief weakness in Shaw's classification of pines was in the diploxylon subsection *Pinaster.*

Publication of *Los Pinos Mexicanos* by Martínez in 1948 was another important contribution to our knowledge of the genus *Pinus,* especially because it further explored the complexity of Mexican pines. *Los Pinos*

WORLD, MERCATOR

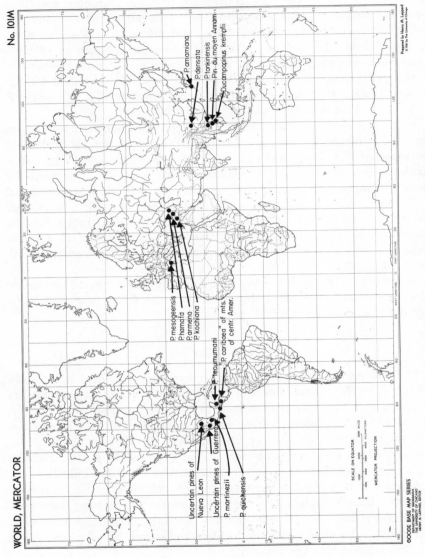

**Fig. 9–6.** Locations of some new or uncertain pine species.

*Mexicanos* became a starting point for all subsequent studies of the genus *Pinus* in Mexico and Central America.

Duffield (1952) based his rearrangement of Shaw's subsection *Pinaster* on hybridization experiments performed at the Institute of Forest Genetics, U.S. Forest Service. Certainly *Pinaster* has a different meaning to us now from what it had to Brunfels (reference in Literature Citations, Chapter 1), who, after Pliny, dismissed it with one brief sentence: "Pinaster *nihil aliud est quam* Pinus sylvestris." (*Pinaster* is nothing but another *P. sylvestris*.) Duffield's proposed changes were contested by Gaussen (1955), who, in 1960, himself published on the classification of pines; the size of pollen grains played an important part in this classification. Studies of different aspects of pines in Gaussen's laboratory at Toulouse, especially researches of de Ferré, are very important and these should be studied carefully.

For construction of a reliable classification of pines a concept of species should be clearly formulated. Difficulties in applying a conventional definition of species to pines are encountered because genetic barriers to crossing do not always exist with the genus *Pinus* even in the indisputable species.

While some pine species do not cross with others, many intercross freely, and when they do the hybrids are fertile. Moreover, in the southern parts of the area of the genus *Pinus* in Mexico–Central America and, to a lesser extent, in eastern Asia, one pine species may imperceptibly merge into another, resulting in a maze of intermediate forms. This was unintentionally shown by Roezl (1857, 1858; see reference in Literature Citations, Chapter 2), who collected and named over one hundred "species" in central Mexico alone.

The classical concept of species is indispensable in work with pines; but an experimental biological approach is also needed to understand the real nature of species in the genus *Pinus*. A species should not be established on the basis of a single character, be it genetic incompatibility or the size of pollen grains. All feasible approaches should be used: morphological, genetic, geographical, physiological, ecological, paleobotanical, and chemical.

Application of chemistry to the taxonomy of pines has been discussed in this chapter at some length because the approach is new. It is useful when its complexity is understood. Chemical characters of pines are not used in any existing classification, although there is a suggestion of their usefulness in Duffield's rearrangement of diploxylon pines (see also Hegnauer [1962, pp. 399–402 and 410]). In special cases, the application of chemical methods proved to be useful.

The most important consideration is that a species is composed of individuals and there exists variability in all characters: morphological, genetic, and chemical. In some species variability in a population is small; in others it is very large. When two pine species cross, the variability in the intermediate populations is extremely complicated.

A genetic approach in the reconstruction of the system of the genus *Pinus* may be considered the most important achievement in the taxonomy of pines since Shaw's *The Genus* Pinus was published in 1914 and the work at the Institute of Forest Genetics, U.S. Forest Service, has contributed much to this end.

Shaw-Duffield classification provides a framework for future taxonomic studies of pines. Most of the work with the subgenus *Haploxylon* is to be done in eastern Asia, where there are many vicarid species of haploxylon pines, some not accurately identified and where there occurs (in Viet Nam) the enigmatic *P. krempfii*, which is possibly a link between the genus *Pinus* and other genera such as *Pseudolarix* and *Keteeleria*. If left in the genus *Pinus*, *P. krempfii* will probably form a third subgenus, *Ducampopinus*. There are also some unsettled taxonomic problems with the diploxylons of eastern Asia.

Most of the taxonomic work on the subgenus *Diploxylon*, however, is needed in the species of the Mexican–Central American highlands. Lesser but equally important studies are needed in many species throughout the area occupied by the genus. Some are suggested in this chapter; many more are left for others to explore.

## LITERATURE CITATIONS

AGUILAR G, JOSÉ IGNACIO. 1961. Pinos de Guatemala (3d ed.). Min. de Agr. Dir. Gen. Forest., Guatemala City.

ALSTON, R. E., and B. L. TURNER. 1963. Biochemical systematics. Prentice-Hall, Inc., Englewood Cliffs, N.J.

BAILEY, I. W. 1910. Anatomical characters in the evolution of *Pinus*. Amer. Nat., 44:284–93.

BARRETT, WILFREDO H. G. Y LAMBERTO GOLFARI. 1962. Descripción de dos nuevas variedades del "Pino del Caribe" *Pinus caribaea* Morelet. Caribbean Forester, 23: 59–71.

BENSON, LYMAN. 1962. Plant taxonomy: Methods and principles. The Ronald Press Co., New York.

BOUREAU, E. 1939. Recherches anatomiques et expérimentales sur l'ontogénie des plantules de Pinacées et ses rapports avec la phylogénie. Thesis, Fac. Sci., Poitiers. Ann. des Sci. Nat. Bot. Biolo. végétale. 11th series, 1:1–219.

BUCHHOLZ, J. T. 1951. A flat-leaved pine from Annam, Indo-China. Amer. Jour. Bot., 38:245–52.

BUDKEVICH, E. B. 1958. Anatomicheskoe stroenie drevesiny (Anatomical structure of wood of) *Ducampopinus krempfii* (Lecomte) A. Chevalier. Bot. Zhur. S.S.S.R., 43:1156–60.

CAMPO-DUPLAN, M. VAN. 1950. Recherches sur la phylogénie des Abiétinées d'après leurs graines de pollen. Trav. lab. forest. de Toulouse. Tome II, Sect. I, Vol. IV, Art. 1.

CHERNIAVSKI, P. 1954. Beliiat bor v Bulgariia (*Pinus hamata* in Bulgaria). Gorsko Stopanstvo, 10:257–62.

CHEVALIER, A. 1944. Notes sur les conifères de l'Indochine. Rev. de Bot. Appl. et d'Agr. Trop., 24:7–34.

CRITCHFIELD, W. B. 1963. Hybridization of the southern pines in California. (South Forest Tree Improvement Com. Pub. 22.) Forest Genet. Workshop Proc. Macon, Ga., 1962. Pp. 40–48.

DALLIMORE, W., and A. B. JACKSON. 1948. A handbook of Coniferae (3d ed.). Edward Arnold, Ltd., London.

DEBAZAC, E. F. 1963. L'aire spontanée du pin de Salzmann en France. Rev. Forestière Franç. No. 10. Pp. 768–84.

DELEVOY, G. 1949. A propos de la systématique de Pinus nigra Arnold. Sta. de Rech. de Groenendaal Trav. Ser. B, No. 12. Pp. 1–37.

DUFFIELD, J. W. 1952. Relationships and species hybridization in the genus Pinus. Ztschr. f. Forstgenetik u. Forstpflanzenzüchtung, 1:93–97.

ENGELMANN, GEORGE. 1880. Revision of the genus Pinus, and description of Pinus elliottii. Acad. Sci. St. Louis, Trans., 4:161–90.

ERDTMAN, H. 1959. Conifer chemistry and taxonomy of conifers. (4th Internatl. Cong. Biochem.) Vol. II. Biochemistry of wood. Pergamon Press, Ltd., Oxford, England. Pp. 1–28.

————. 1963. Some aspects of chemotaxonomy. In Chemical plant taxonomy, ed. by T. SWAIN. Academic Press, Inc., New York. Pp. 89–125.

FERRÉ, Y. DE. 1941. La place des canaux résinifères dans les feuilles des Abiétinées. Soc. His. Nat. de Toulouse Bul., 76:199–204; et Trav. Lab. For. de Toulouse Univ. Tome 1, Vol. III, Art. 12.

————. 1948. Quelques particularités anatomiques d'un pin indochinois: Pinus krempfii. Soc. Hist. Nat. de Toulouse Bul., 83:51–56.

————. 1952. Les formes de jeunesse des abiétacées. Ontogénie-Phylogénie. Trav. du Lab. Forest. de Toulouse Univ. Tome II, Sect. 1, Vol. III, Art. 1. Pp. 1–284.

————. 1953. Division du genre Pinus en quatre sous-genres. Acad. des Sci. Compt. Rend., 236:226–28.

————. 1960. Une nouvelle espèce de pin au Viet Nam, Pinus dalatensis. Soc. d'Hist. Nat. de Toulouse Bul., 95:171–80.

FLOUS, F. 1936. Classification et évolution d'un groupe d'Abiétinées. Trav. Lab. For. de Toulouse Univ. Tome I, Vol. II, Art. 17.

————. 1937. Caractères évolutifs du cône des Abiétinées. Compt. Rend. Acad. des Sci., 204:511–13.

GAUSSEN, HENRI. 1955. Classification des pins diplostélés. Compt. Rend. Acad. des Sci., 251:1366–69.

————. 1960. Les gymnospermes actuelles et fossiles. Fasc. VI. Les coniférales. Chap. 11. Généralités, Genre Pinus. (Toulouse [City] Univ. Lab. Forestier. Trav. Tome 2, Vol. 1, Fasc. 6, Chap. XI.)

HALLER, JOHN R. 1962. Variation and hybridization in ponderosa and Jeffrey pines. Calif. Univ., Pubs., Bot., 34:123–66.

HEGNAUER, R. 1962. Chemotaxonomie der Pflanzen. Vol. I. Birkhaüser, Basel and Stuttgart.

HESLOP-HARRISON, J. 1953. New concepts in flowering-plant taxonomy. William Heinemann, Ltd., London.

————. 1963. Species concepts: Theoretical and practical aspects. In Chemical plant taxonomy, ed. by T. SWAIN. Academic Press, Inc., New York. Pp. 17–40.

JEFFERS, J. N. R., and T. M. BLACK. 1963. An analysis of variability of Pinus contorta. Forestry, 36:199–218.

JEFFREY, EDWARD C. 1908. On the structure of the leaf in Cretaceous pines. Ann. Bot., 22:207–20.

KOEHNE, E. 1893. Deutsche Dendrologie. F. Enke, Stuttgart.

LARSEN, EGON. 1964. A new species of pine from Mexico. Madroño, 17:217–18.

LAWRENCE, GEORGE H. M. 1951. Taxonomy of vascular plants. The Macmillan Co., New York.

LECOMTE, H. 1921. Un pin remarquable de l'Annam. Bull. Mus. Natl. d'Hist. Nat., Paris, 27:191–92.

——. 1924. Additions au sujet de *Pinus krempfii*, H. Lec. Mus. Natl. d'Hist. Nat., Paris, Bul., 30:321–25.

LILPOP, T. 1924. Materiały do flory drzew lignitowych Polska (Materials contributing to knowledge of the lignites in Poland). Serv. Geol. Pologne Bul., 2:387–401.

LITTLE, ELBERT L., JR. 1953. Check list of native and naturalized trees of the United States (including Alaska). (U.S. Dept. Agr., Agr. Handbook No. 41.) Government Printing Office, Washington, D.C.

MARTÍNEZ, MAXIMINO. 1948. Los Pinos Mexicanos (2d ed.). Ediciones Botas, Mexico [City].

MIROV, N. T. 1956. Composition of turpentine of lodgepole × jack pine hybrids. Canad. Jour. Bot., 34:443–57.

——. 1961. Composition of gum turpentines of pines. (U.S. Dept. Agr. Tech. Bul. No. 1239.) Government Printing Office, Washington, D.C.

——. 1963. Chemistry and plant taxonomy. Lloydia, 26:117–24.

PILGER, R. 1926. Genus *Pinus*. In Die natürlichen Pflanzenfamilien. Vol. XIII. Gymnospermae. Ed. by A. ENGLER and K. PRANTL. Wilhelm Engelmann, Leipzig.

SHAW, GEORGE RUSSELL. 1909. The pines of Mexico. (Arnold Arboretum Pub. No. 1.) J. R. Ruiter & Co., Boston.

——. 1914. The genus *Pinus*. (Arnold Arboretum Pub. No. 5.) Houghton Mifflin Co., Boston.

——. 1924. Notes on the genus *Pinus*. Arnold Arboretum Jour., 5:225–27.

STANDLEY, PAUL C., and JULIAN A. STEYERMARK. 1958. Flora of Guatemala. Chicago Nat. Hist. Mus., Fieldiana. Bot. 24, Part 1.

STEINHOFF, RAPHAEL JOHN. 1964. Taxonomy, nomenclature, and variation within the *Pinus flexilis* complex. Unpublished Ph.D. dissertation, Michigan State University of Agriculture and Applied Science, East Lansing.

STOCKWELL, W. P. 1939. Cone variation in Digger pine. Madroño, 5:72–73.

SWAIN, T. (ed.). 1963. Chemical plant taxonomy. Academic Press, Inc., New York.

WANG, CHI-WU. 1961. The forests of China. (Maria Moors Cabot Found. Pub. No. 5.) Harvard University, Cambridge, Mass.

WILLIAMS, L. 1955. *Pinus caribaea*. Ceiba, 4:299–300.

WU, CHUNG-LWEN. 1947. The phytogeographic distribution of pines in China. Unpublished Master's thesis, Yale University School of Forestry, New Haven.

——. 1956. The taxonomic revision and phytogeographical study of Chinese pines. Acta Phytotaxonom. Sinica, 5:131–64.

# 10

# Concluding Remarks

Pines as we see them around us belong to an old genus—the oldest in the whole family Pinaceae—whose development goes back to the Mesozoic era. But *Pinus* is not a senescent, disappearing genus. On the contrary, it is vigorous and developing. Although since the end of the Tertiary period they have retreated somewhat in the north, pines have advanced in the south to reach Sumatra in southeastern Asia, and Nicaragua in Central America.

Notwithstanding considerable destruction of pine forests by man, their area in many places is larger now than it was before glaciation (see Chapter 2, page 41). And pines are still advancing. The present area occupied by pines should not be considered as being the surviving remains of a once more widely distributed genus.

In the preceding chapters, an attempt has been made to analyze the factors that might have been responsible for survival, evolution, and post-Tertiary rejuvenation of the genus. In the present chapter, the salient points will be briefly recapitulated.

In Chapter 4, we saw that the genus *Pinus* possesses certain genetic characteristics that have played an important part in its development. All pine species so far examined have the same number of chromosomes of generally similar morphology; aberrations are rare. No natural polyploid species have been reported.

The subgenera, *Haploxylon* and *Diploxylon*, have definite genetic barriers that prevent intercrossing of the two. Within the two subgenera, some groups have been shown to possess strong barriers to hybridization while others do not. Piñon pines, i.e., the group *Cembroides*, apparently possess adequate barriers to prevent intercrossing of their species with any other haploxylon pines.

Intercrossing of pines belonging to different groups has been done chiefly within the subgenus *Diploxylon*, and the information obtained served to develop a better rearrangement of pine classification within the subgenus (see Chapter 9).

An outstanding property of pines is their genetic stability; species separated one from the other by oceans for many million years intercross freely when brought together. This seems to indicate that, throughout the ages, although pine species might have become separated by water or desert for a considerable length of time, when the contact between them was restored, exchange of genes between these possibly inbred populations was resumed.

In many species, genetic affinity has been lost, and some developed barriers to hybridization with others. We have examples of such species still existing. On the other hand, we have now many pine species that intercross freely with other species, and this tendency is observed in all parts of the area occupied by the genus *Pinus*. Especially conspicuous is the free hybridization among the diploxylon pines of the Mexican–Central American highlands, where a secondary center of evolution is formed. Environmental conditions are exceptionally favorable there for evolution of pines. A wet season alternates with a dry season; a great diversity of ecological niches is formed; the whole area is under a certain ecological strain; a sudden change from wet to dry weather creates exceptionally favorable conditions for hybridization.

In the Mexican highlands, the vertical distribution of pines has a wide amplitude in a small area. Because the gradient is steep, and because the distance from tropical lowlands to the line of permanent snow is often very short, changes in environment are many and sudden. At the same time, the temperature of the air is generally sufficiently high, and hence the growing season is long. The purer atmosphere of the highlands is rich in ultraviolet radiation, which may affect the physiology and genetics of reproduction.

Since strictly in the highlands of Mexico–Central America there are only two haploxylon pines and since these do not come into contact (or perhaps because they have sufficient barriers to prevent intercrossing), there is no comparable upsurge of hybridization in the subgenus *Haploxylon* there.

In eastern Asia, the situation is somewhat different. A minor secondary center of speciation is located there, but there is no such abundance of pine species as in Mexico. There is only a gradual replacement of one diploxylon species by another: *P. tabulaeformis*—(*P. densata*, a hybrid?)—*P. yunnanensis*—*P. khasya*—*P. insularis*. The relationship of other diploxylon pines in other parts of eastern Asia does not suggest a major surge of evolution. Hybridization among haploxylon pines, which are more numerous in eastern Asia than in Mexico, is complicated by the disjunct distribution of closely related species.

As a whole, the present development and speciation of pines take place predominantly in the New World, or, more exactly, in the Mexican highlands.

Paleobotanists tell us that pines developed in the uplands (see Chapter 2). Present altitudinal distribution (see Chapter 3) also indicates that the most suitable environment comprises the mountain slopes and plateaus of moderate altitude, from about 1000 m to 2500 m.

Camp (1956) wrote that the upland forest (presumably gymnosperm, for he mentioned pinopsid trunks) came into being in the Carboniferous period. He stated that "the forests were not necessarily characterized by heavy precipitation, but dry periods must have been prevalent at times." These early gymnosperms, many of which were xeromorphs, possibly were the ancestors of *Pinus*.

The end of the Paleozoic era and the beginning of the Mesozoic constituted the driest period in the history of our planet. The arid climate was surprisingly widespread in the earliest Permian, extending into much of the Lower Triassic (Krishtofovich, 1959). Evidence of this exists in many parts of the Northern Hemisphere (Seward, 1941). Mesic plants of the Upper Carboniferous period disappeared, and plants better suited to the drier climate took their place (Clements and Chaney, 1936).

Both morphology and physiology of pines, discussed in Chapters 5 and 6, indicate that *Pinus* developed not in a uniformly hot and humid climate but in a climate characterized by a cool season alternating with a warm and dry season, where there was already an abundance of sunshine and where soil was poor in nutrients, porous, and thus well drained. Such an environment would have been conducive to development of mycorhiza (see Chapter 6, page 400), which has played an important part in the history of the genus *Pinus*.

At present, pines grow in surprisingly diversified places: on the arid plateaus of western America and in the tropical lowlands of the Caribbean area (where there is, however, a prolonged dry season). They do not occur naturally in ever wet, uniformly hot and humid tropics. When planted there, they grow but do not reproduce. For their normal development, they require alternation of seasons: either dry and wet or warm and cold, often a combination of both types.

No matter where pines grow, they retain their ancestral xeromorphism; it is evident in pine fossils of all ages. Their physiology is that of xerophytes; pines can withstand considerable drought, and they show great tolerance to sunlight.

The xeromorphism of pines may suggest to some that the genus underwent its primary development in semiarid parts of low latitudes, such as southwestern North America. The fossil record, however, indicates that the oldest, i.e., Mesozoic, pines were located not in the southwestern but rather in the more northerly parts of the hemisphere. Moreover, during the Permian-Triassic, aridity was not restricted to southwestern America; it was surprisingly widespread (Seward, 1941).

## ORIGIN OF PINES IN TIME

The oldest known pine fossils come from deposits of the Jurassic period of the Mesozoic era. At that time, the genus was already differentiated into two groups (now known as the two subgenera) so distinct that some botanists considered them as different genera (see Chapter 1), possibly the subgenus *Haploxylon* preceding the *Diploxylon* (Erdtman, 1959). Such a degree of differentiation indicates that pines were already well established prior to the Jurassic (Mason, 1927).

In view of the above consideration, reports on occurrence of pine pollen in the Triassic strata (see Chapter 2) should not be disregarded. The incipient development of the genus *Pinus*, of course, goes back even to older times, as witnessed by the finding of fossils described as *Pinoxylon, Pinites,* or *Prepinus*, from the Permian deposits (Knowlton, 1919; Krishtofovich, 1941).

Krishtofovich (1959; reference in Literature Citations, Chapter 2) is of the opinion that pines played a subordinate part in the Mesozoic and even in the Tertiary floras; only during the Quaternary did they acquire significance as a major component of forests. According to Krishtofovich:

. . . any kind of absence of pines in the Mesozoic floras, or any reference to "missing links" reported in literature are [sic] usually caused by the fact that the new elements in any Flora, being rare and sporadic during the first stages of their evolution, are also rarely presented in fossil floras. A botanical entity, such as a genus, is usually discovered in a fossil state only when it becomes dominant and thus more conspicuous.

There always exists an extreme paucity of species in all floras of the past. As a rule, in any fossil flora only one or two, rarely several, species comprise 70 to 90 percent of the total material and only the remaining 10 to 30 percent are represented by other species. This has been demonstrated by careful tabulations of Chaney [1924] in America and also by findings of Krishtofovich and Baikovskaia in a Sarmatian flora of Ukraine (Krynka) and in the Cretaceous floras of Tasgaian in the Amur region.

Lack of pines observed in many fossil floras might have been caused by their occurrence on slopes so far above the sites of deposition that their foliage and seeds could not readily enter the sedimentary record (Chaney and Hu, 1940).

Having taken into consideration all of the available evidence, it is not unreasonable to conclude that the genus *Pinus* originated from some ancestral stock during Permian-Triassic times, differentiated during the

Upper Triassic from the closely related genera *Cedrus* and *Larix*, and began its long development, which still continues at present.

## LOCUS OF PRIMARY DEVELOPMENT OF PINES

The family Pinaceae developed in the Northern Hemisphere (Florin, 1940). The genus *Pinus* is also believed to be of northern origin. The fossil record supports this contention. Convincing geomorphological evidence and absence of pine fossils from Indochina and Central America indicate that pines are of recent origin there. Were they there during the Mesozoic era, they surely would be growing now in many places of the Southern Hemisphere, but there are none there. Florin considers absence of fossils of the family Pinaceae south of the Equator to be of great significance in study of the evolution of conifers.

To determine in what part of the north *Pinus* originated is difficult. The fossil record does not give us very many clues in that respect. The broad area of northern Eurasia, which is considered as the area of origin of many plants, might have been the initial place of development of the genus *Pinus*. It is, roughly, the area designated by Axelrod (1960) as that of the Arcto-Tertiary flora.

The genus *Pinus* might have developed anywhere in northern Eurasia or northern America. The past and present distribution of pines (see Fig. 1–1, and Chapters 2 and 3) only tells us that they came from the north. Perhaps assembly of pines on both sides of the Pacific indicates that they came from the northwest in America and from the northeast in Asia. It should be remembered that throughout the history of the earth these parts of the two continents were often one broad land mass that came to be known as Beringia. Numerous boreal plants radiated from the Bering Sea area (Hulten, 1937). Geographical distribution of certain chemical compounds found in pines is considered in Chapter 8 as support of the possibility that pines developed in the Bering Sea area.

## MIGRATION

From their area of primary development in the north of Asia and America, pines spread all over the Northern Hemisphere and even crossed the Equator in one place (see Chapter 3, under species No. 101). To indicate the routes of migration of the genus *Pinus*, especially during the Mesozoic era, is as difficult and speculative as to decide on the area of its origin. Throughout the long history of the genus, land masses submerged, rose again, and united to form migration bridges; climates changed, and deserts or ice fields were formed where pines had lived before. Pines themselves have changed; many species have disappeared and new ones have developed. Migration and evolution are concomitant in all plants (Mason, 1954), and pines are no exception. Possible routes of migration were discussed in Chapter 2. Mesozoic migration brought pines to all of the northern parts of the Northern Hemisphere. The Tertiary migrations brought pines to Mexico and Central America, whence they spread in a reverse (northward) migration to the Caribbean area and possibly to the southern part of Florida. In Asia, pines migrated during the Tertiary to the southeastern part of the continent, and from there via latitudinal mountain ranges to the Mediterranean area. Pines migrated to the Philippines later, possibly at the time of general cooling during the Pleistocene glaciation in the north. It is possible that pines migrated to northeastern Europe from America via Greenland and other Arctic islands and then spread southward. How much contact there was in the Tertiary between the western European pine region and the Mediterranean area is difficult to say. Possibly Mediterranean pines were developing independently from those of western Europe; their contact might have been with southeastern Asia.

As to the relation of the Tertiary pine forests of western Europe and the northern part of Asia, it might have been that some elements of the genus *Pinus* migrated westward across the continent; there was also a migration of pines from western Europe eastward. A careful analysis of Tertiary fossils throughout the width of Eurasia is required to form a definite opinion on this subject. Some creditable work already has been done along these lines (Chapter 2).

The pattern of postglacial migration of pines was different for different species, as shown in the re-occupation of northern Eurasia by *P. sylvestris* and by *P. sibirica* (Chapter 2). Postglacial invasion by pines of areas available after retreat of the ice shield was to provide good evidence of the pioneer-invader capacity of *Pinus*, which probably has been in force throughout its history. Many of the characteristics of pines helped them to migrate and spread over a large area of the earth. How much specific value each characteristic has had (for example, photoperiodicity; see Chapter 6), we can only surmise.

The genus *Pinus* as it exists now is still little known to us. The genus is divided at present into over 100 species. Some of these species are senescent and on their way out; others are well developed and vigorous; both groups are relatively easy to classify, to name, and to identify. These are "good" species (see Chapter 9). But there are also many pines that do not obey classification rules. They are not "bad" species, as some taxonomists call them; they merely do not yield to conventional taxonomic treatment and, consequently, should be studied via different approaches, some of which are suggested in this book. This multiple approach also helps one to better understand the origin, migration, survival, and evolution of the genus *Pinus*.

## LITERATURE CITATIONS

Axelrod, Daniel I. 1960. The evolution of flowering plants. In Evolution after Darwin, Vol. I: The evolution of life: Its origin, history and future, ed. by Sol Tax. The University of Chicago Press. Pp. 227–305.

Camp, Wendell H. 1956. The forests of the past and present. In A world geography of forest resources, ed. by Stephen Haden-Guest, John K. Wright, and Eileen M. Teclaff. The Ronald Press Co., New York. Pp. 13–47.

Chaney, Ralph W. 1924. Quantitative studies of the Bridge Creek Flora. Amer. Jour. Sci., 208:127–44. (Also called ser. 5, Vol. VIII.)

—— and Hu, Hsien Hsu. 1940. A Miocene flora from Shantung Province, China. Part II. Physical conditions and correlation. Geol. Survey China, Peiping. (China Geol. Survey. Paleontologica Sinica. New series A. No. 1. Whole series No. 112.) (Reprinted in Carnegie Inst. Wash. Pub., 507:85–140.)

Clements, F. E., and R. W. Chaney. 1936. Environment and life in the great plains. (Carnegie Inst. Wash. Sup. Pub. 24.) Pp. 1–54.

Erdtman, Holger. 1959. Conifer chemistry and taxonomy of conifers. In Symposium II: Biochemistry of wood. 4th Internatl. Cong. Biochem., Vienna, 1958, Proc., 2:1–28.

Florin, Rudolf. 1940. The Tertiary fossil conifers of south Chile and their phytogeographical significance. (Svenska Vetensk. Akad. Handl. Tredje Serien Band 19, No. 2.)

Hultén, Eric. 1937. Outline of the history of arctic and boreal biota during the Quaternary period. Aktiebolaget Thule, Stockholm.

Knowlton, F. H. 1919. A catalogue of the Mesozoic and Cenozoic plants of North America. (U.S. Geol. Survey Bul. 696.)

Krishtofovich, A. N. 1941. Katalog rastenii iskopaemoi flory SSSR (Paleontology of U.S.S.R.). Vol. XII Supplement. Akad. Nauk. S.S.S.R. Paleontological Inst., Moscow.

Mason, Herbert L. 1927. Fossil records of some west American conifers. (Carnegie Inst. Wash. Pub. 346.) Pp. 139–58.

——. 1954. Migration and evolution in plants. Madroño, 12:161–68.

Seward, A. C. 1941. Plant life through the ages (2d ed.). Cambridge University Press, London.

# Index

*Note:* Numbers following names of pine species refer to Tables 1–1 and 1–2, pages 18–20 and 20–22.

577